VICTOR BOULLET
TOXTETH ERROR LAD
PAINTING
LIVERPOOL
2014 – 2021

ba Radin, 2019 – 2020
on linen canvas
:m x 46cm

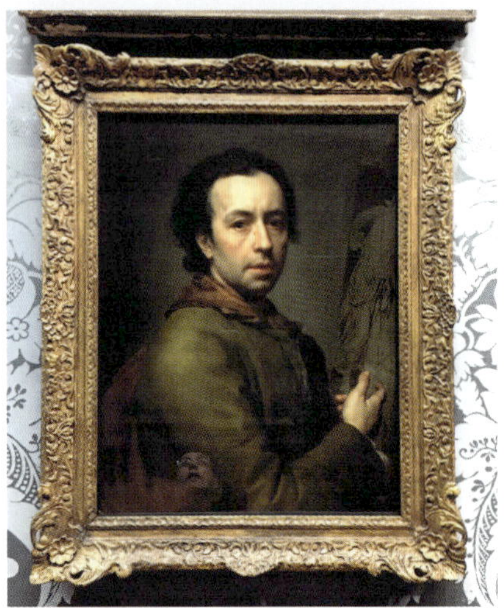

Self Portrait, 1774
By Anton Raphael Mengs
Oil on mahogany panel
Walker Art Museum, Liverpool
29 September, 2017

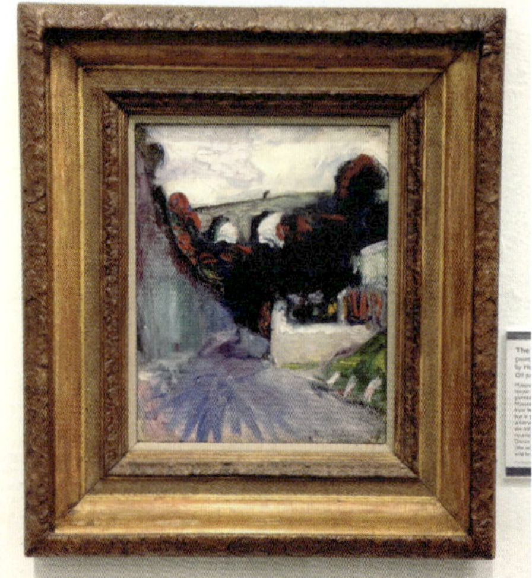

The Viaduct at Arcueil, 1998 - 1900
By Henri Matisse
Oil on canvas
Walker Art Museum, Liverpool
13 March, 2015

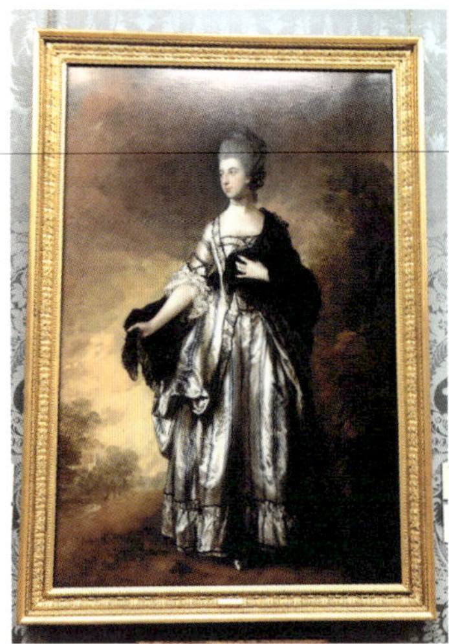

Isabella, Viscountess Molyneux, later Countess of Sefton, 1769
By Thomas Gainsborough
Oil on canvas
Walker Art Museum, Liverpool
25 February, 2018

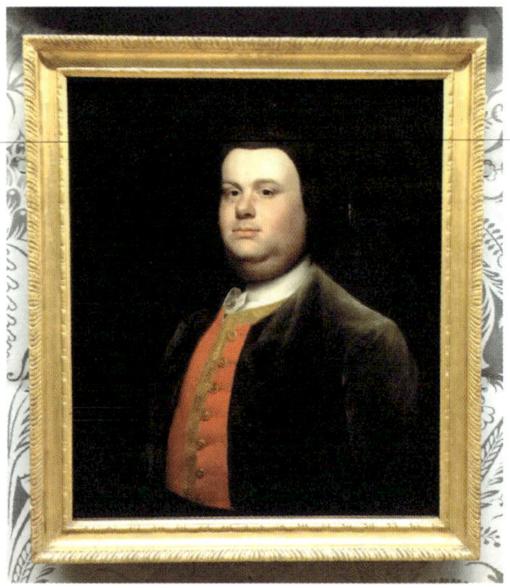

James Stanley, 1755
George Stubbs
Oil on canvas
Walker Art Museum, Liverpool
2 September, 2017

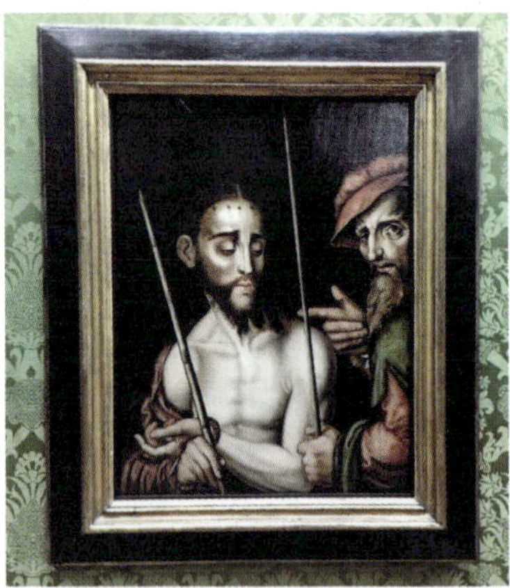

Ecce Homo, ca 1560 - 1570
By Luis de Morales
Oil on board
Walker Art Museum, Liverpool
29 September, 2017

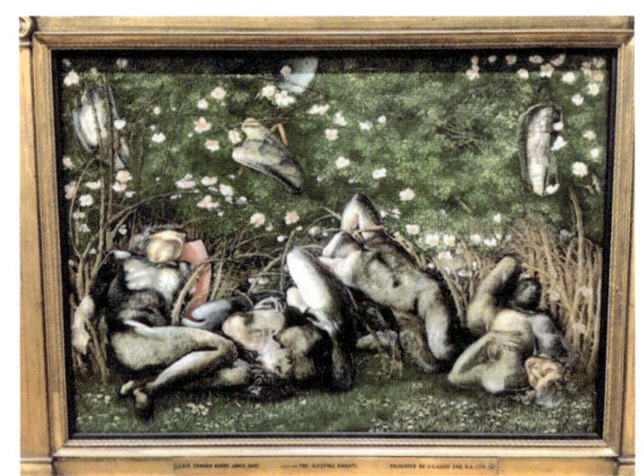

Study for the Sleeping Knights in 'The Briar Rose', 1870
By Edward Coley Burne-Jones
Oil on canvas
Walker Art Museum, Liverpool
2 April, 2017

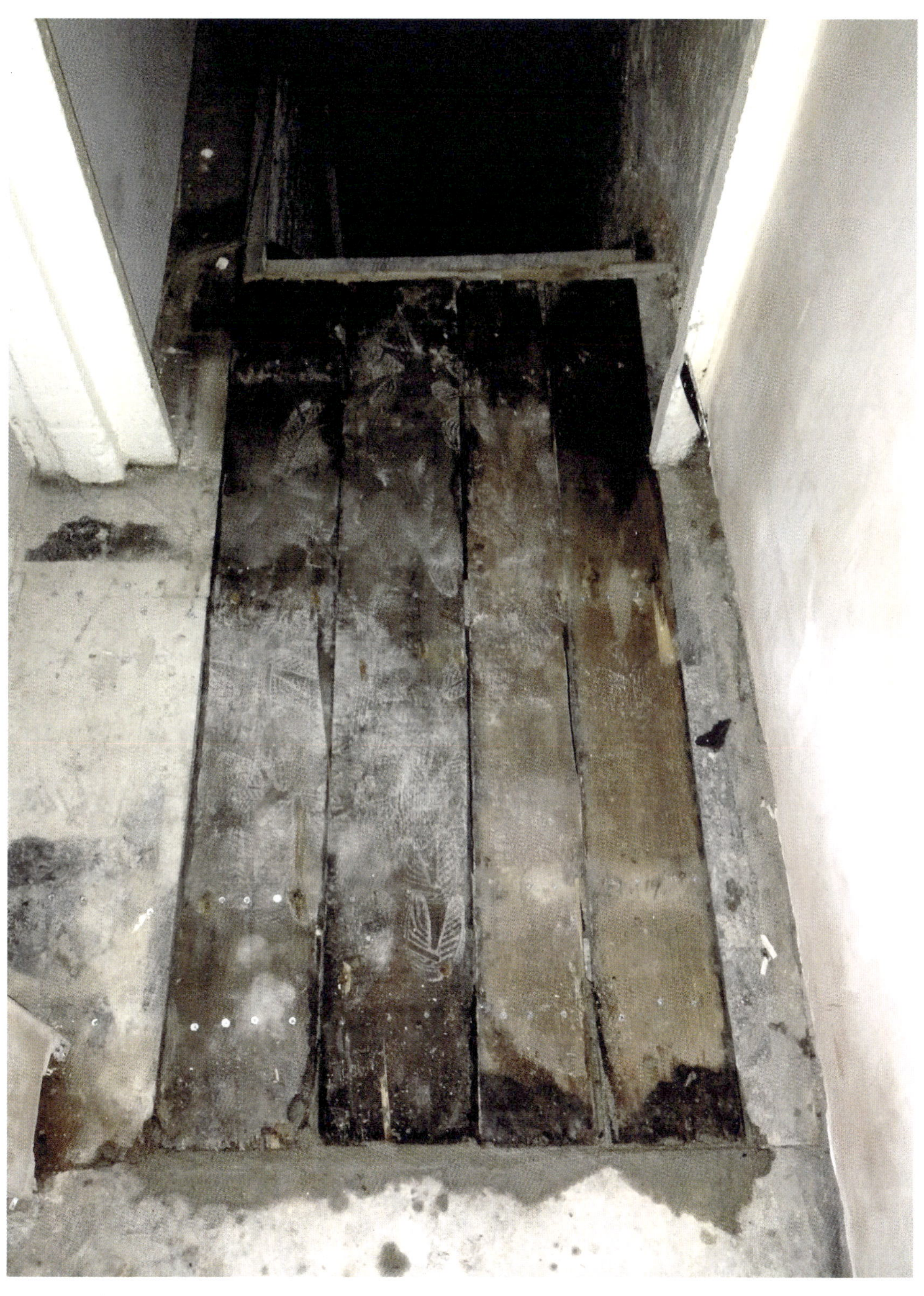

L8, Suicide, 2014
Reclaimed wood, screws and cement
iPhone image

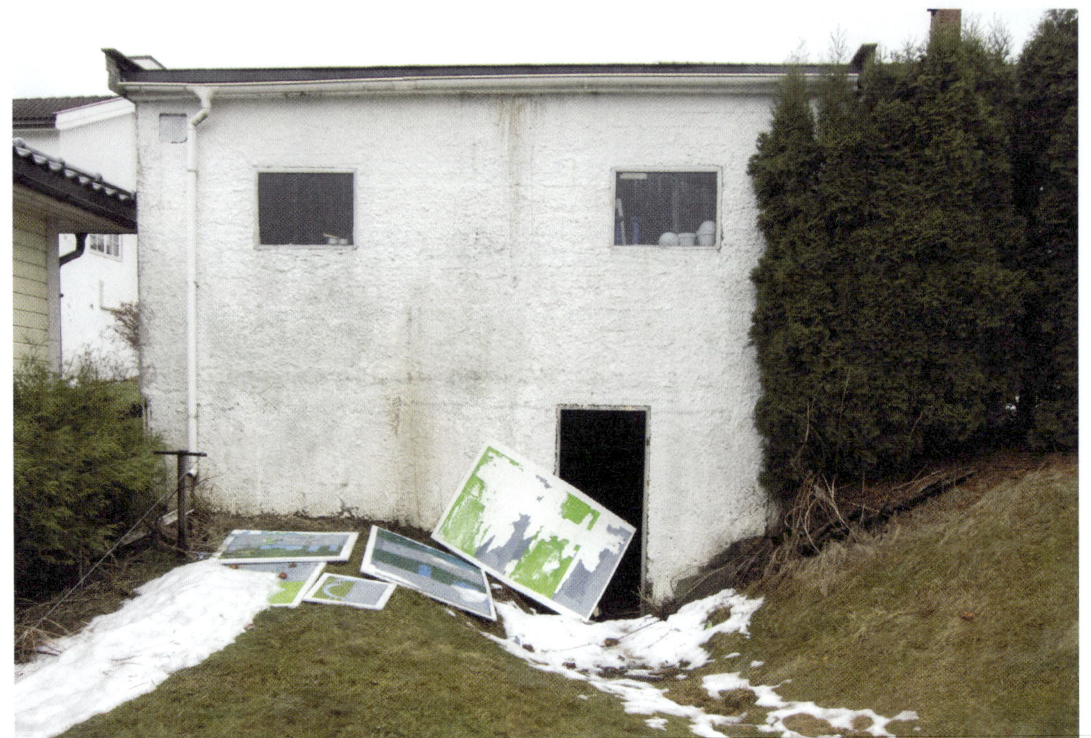

Plough Head (Green / Grey) 2014
Chez Rufus, Kjelsås, Oslo

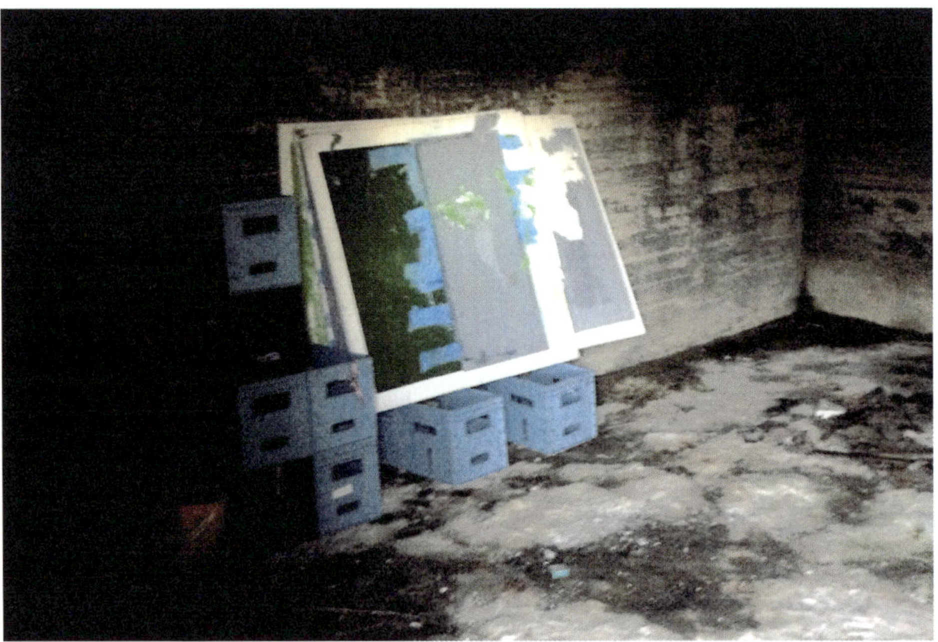

Plough Head (Green / Grey) 2014
Chez Rufus, Kjelsås, Oslo

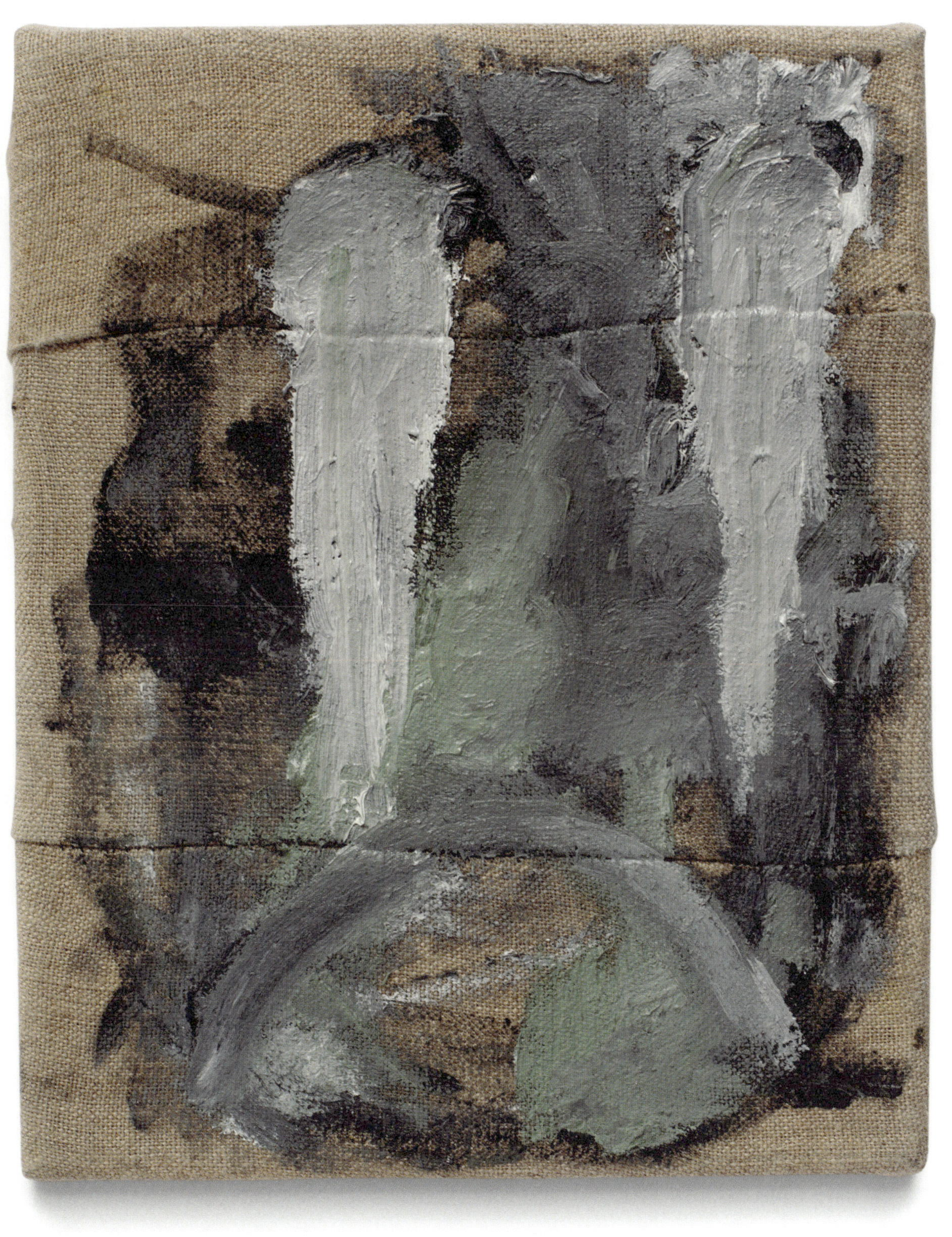

Sorrow Monger, 2015
Oil on hand stitched raw linen
20cm x 25cm

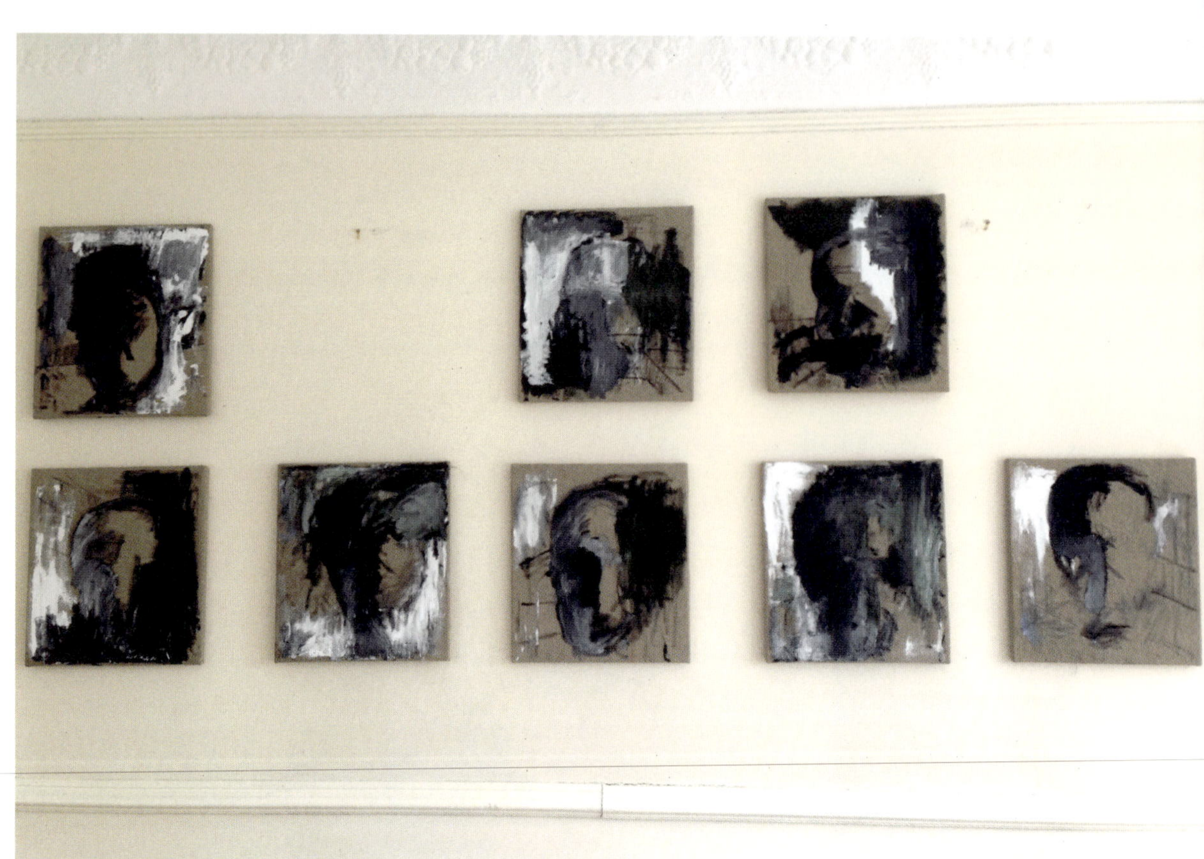

Untitled (Work overpainted) 2015
Oil on raw linen
40cm x 46cm
iPhone image

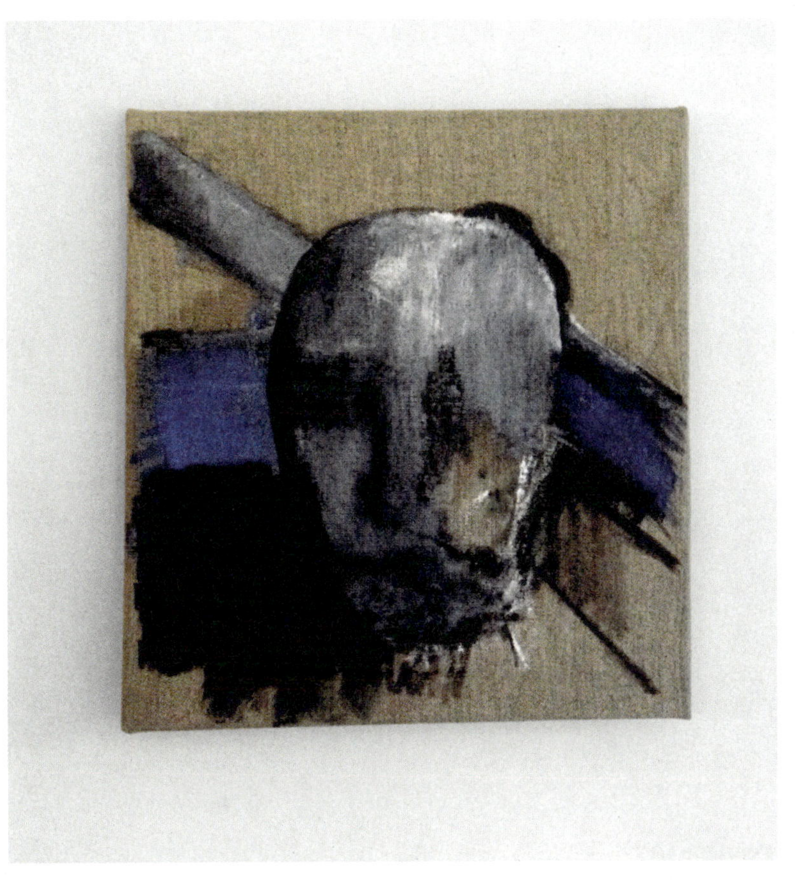

Untitled (Work overpainted) 2015
Oil on raw linen
40cm x 46cm
iPhone image

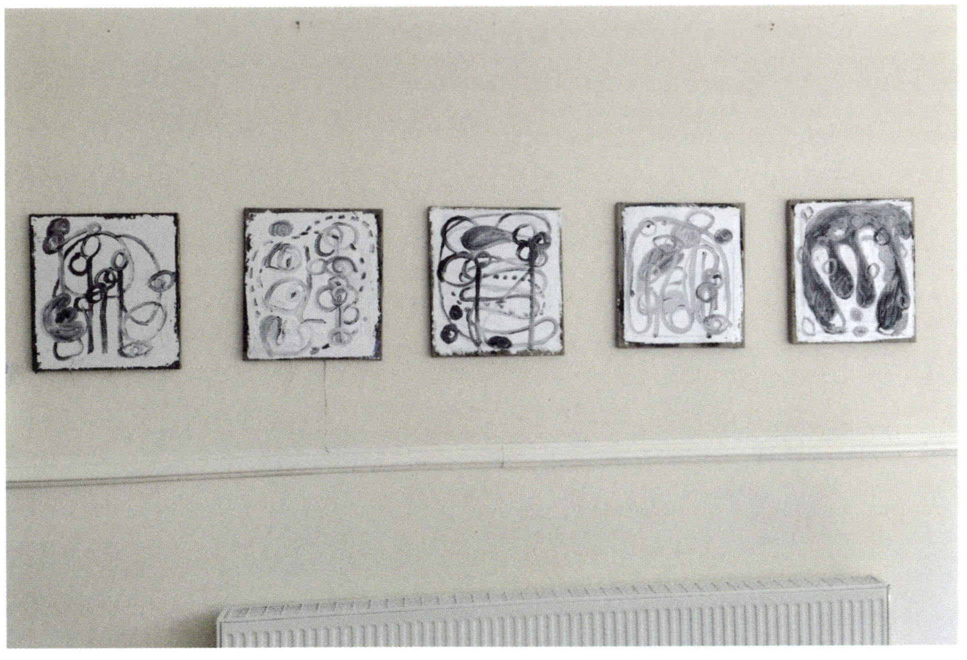

Untitled (Work overpainted) 2015
Oil on raw linen
40cm x 46cm
iPhone image

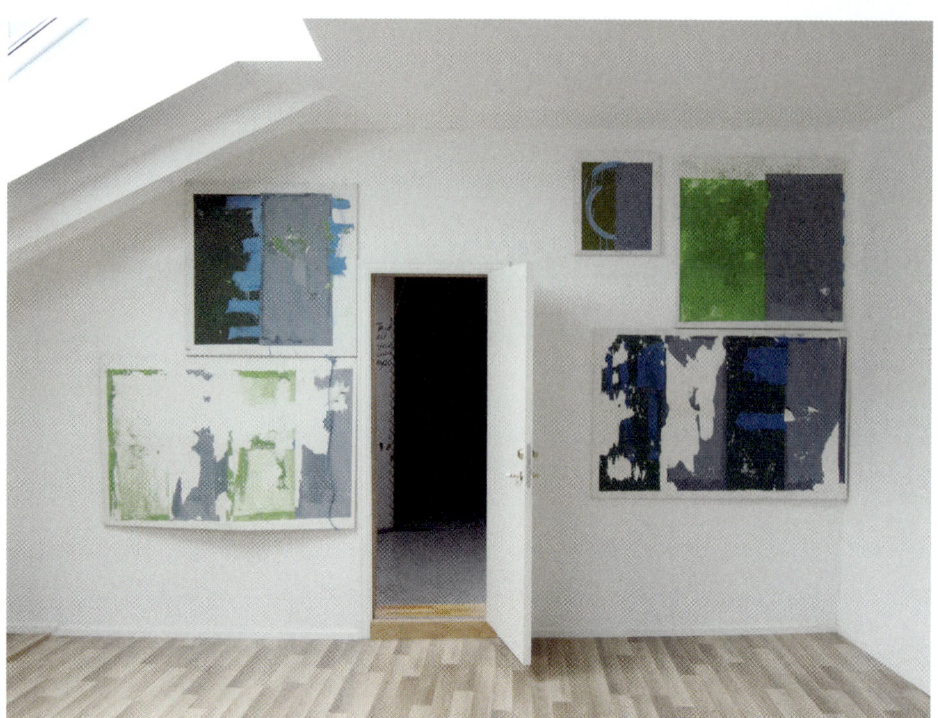

I am the Flesh Colour I Did Not Apply, 2015
Plough Head (Green / Grey) Some work destroyed
Acrylic on canvas, nylon rope
Various sizes
La Collection Moderne, Oslo

I am the Flesh Colour I Did Not Apply

My practice uncovers hypocrisy and hidden facts. This is all subjective, of course. I'm not trying to achieve some aesthetically pleasing utopia. I don't make art for pleasure or survival. I have no rules regarding material used for my expression. I am on a constant search for information. Gossip, a wonderful material that I force into my aesthetics, so work like "I am the flesh colour I did not apply" (paintings) becomes activated for social viewing.

In Oslo, These paintings are stored in a room under earth level. The Norwegian soil was dug out by my family in the early 50's so they could create a concrete storage room with a garage over. When young the entrance to this room was very dramatic and at times scary. Non of which matters, not for me, you or the paintings that comes from this place. The content of these images comes from another place.

And exactly that, I am forcing this foreign content into action, I am activating their superficial surfaces, colour and form, by giving them, these painless panels, a provenance of existential value. I am trying to justify their existence by becoming their redundant master.

At LCM the work is outside of my control and comfort zone. The work survives with excellence, but will I survive, because I will now be defined as a painter? This social definition plain is part of my work, but the pieces are separated from this contextual way of thinking. My work and I are two different entities. This separation of representation is what I have to accept as my future practice.

The art that is traded among artists is the most interesting art collections of today. The work can only be seen in artist's homes, hanging, leaning or hidden. The work is often naked, raw and without content. The work represents acceptance, a gesture of appreciation or friendship. The work is rarely rooted in capitalism or art production.

I want to be represented in homes where I have forced myself in.

The work has a dual purpose. They will be used as capital for trading. Where they become part of someones life. i.e. I am then represented in a domestic environment like a social oil parasite.

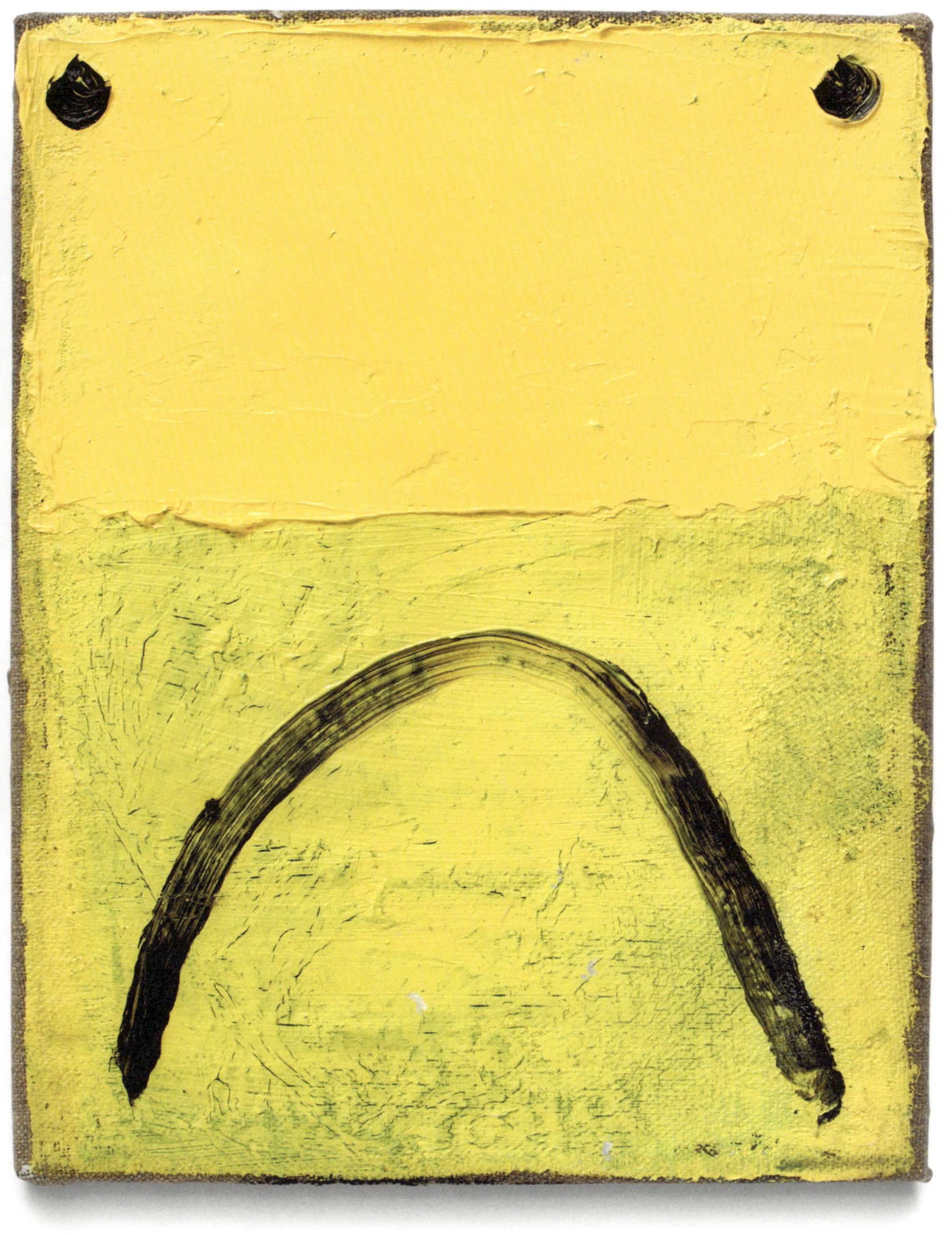

Ullet Road (Idiot) 2015
Oil on raw linen
20cm x 25cm

Ullet Road (Idiot) 2015
Oil on raw linen
20cm x 25cm

Ullet Road (Idiot) 2015
Oil on raw linen
20cm x 25cm
35mm film

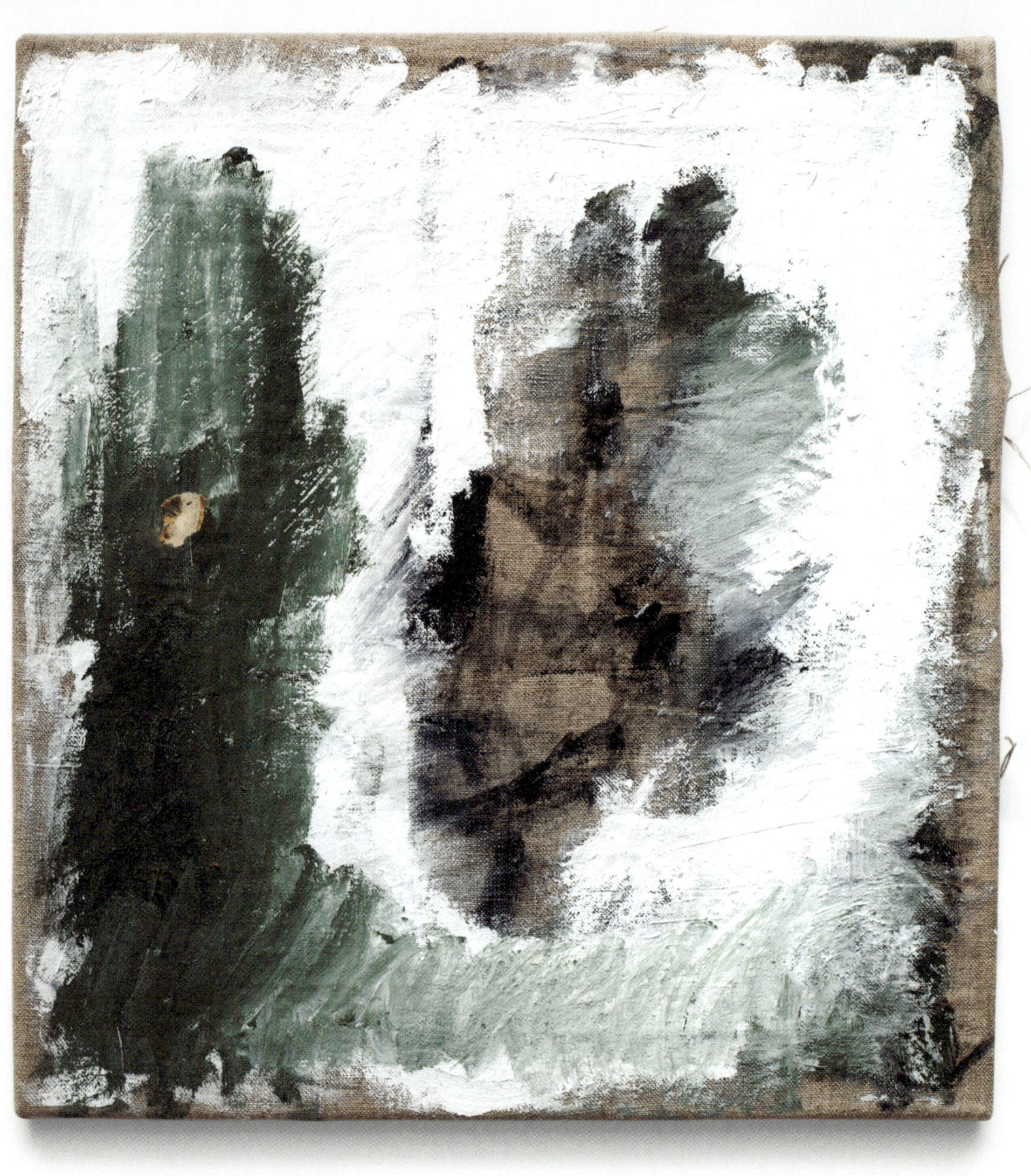

Ullet Road Looking West, 2015
Oil on raw linen
40cm x 46cm

Ullet Road Looking East, 2015
Oil on raw linen
40cm x 46cm

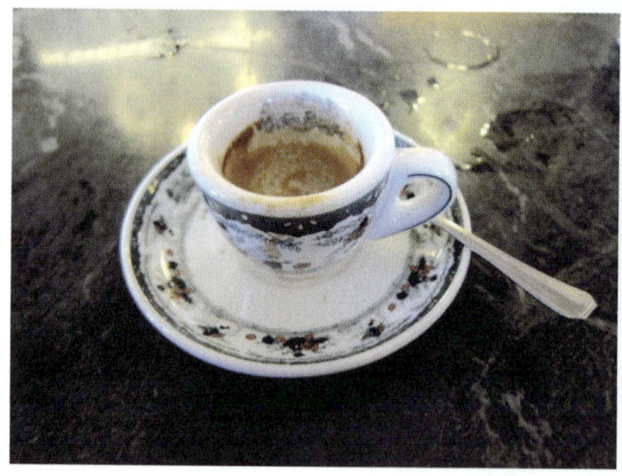

Gran Caffè Gambrinus, 2015
Napoli, Italy

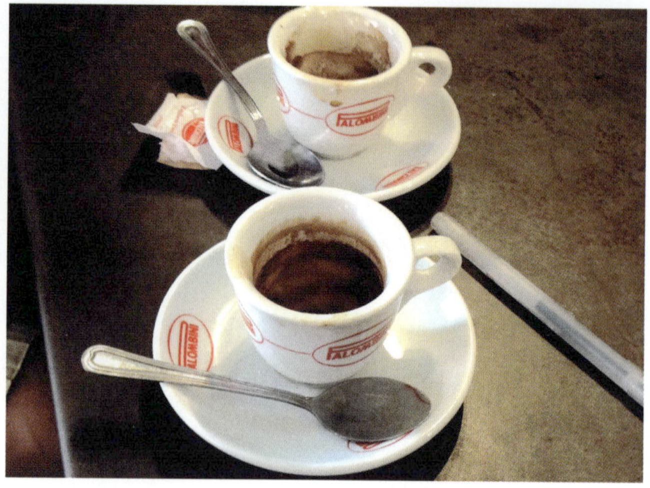

Piazza del Fico, 2015
Roma, Italy

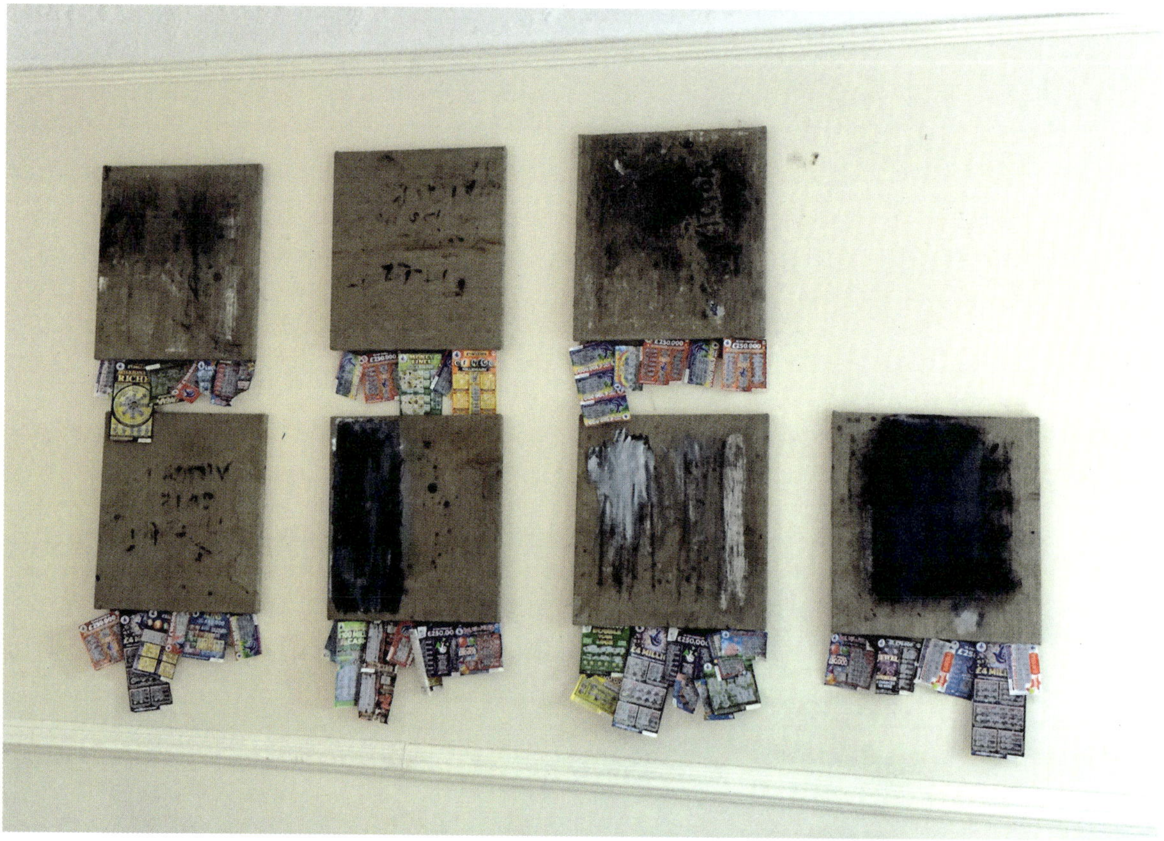

Untitled, 2015 (Work destroyed)
Oil on raw linen, scratch cards, staples
40cm x 46cm
iPhone image

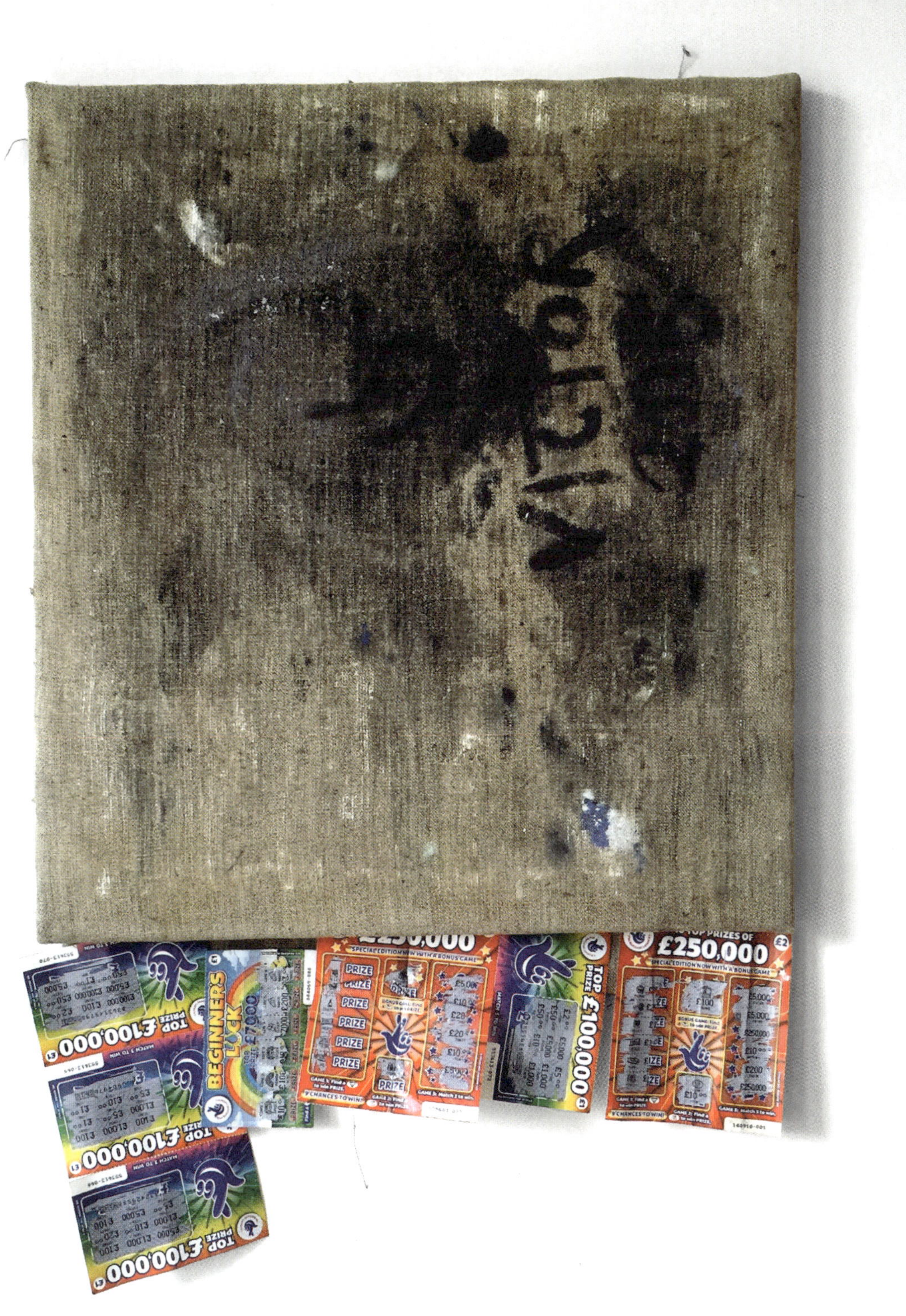

Untitled, 2015 (Work destroyed)
Oil on raw linen, scratch cards, staples
40cm x 46cm
iPhone image

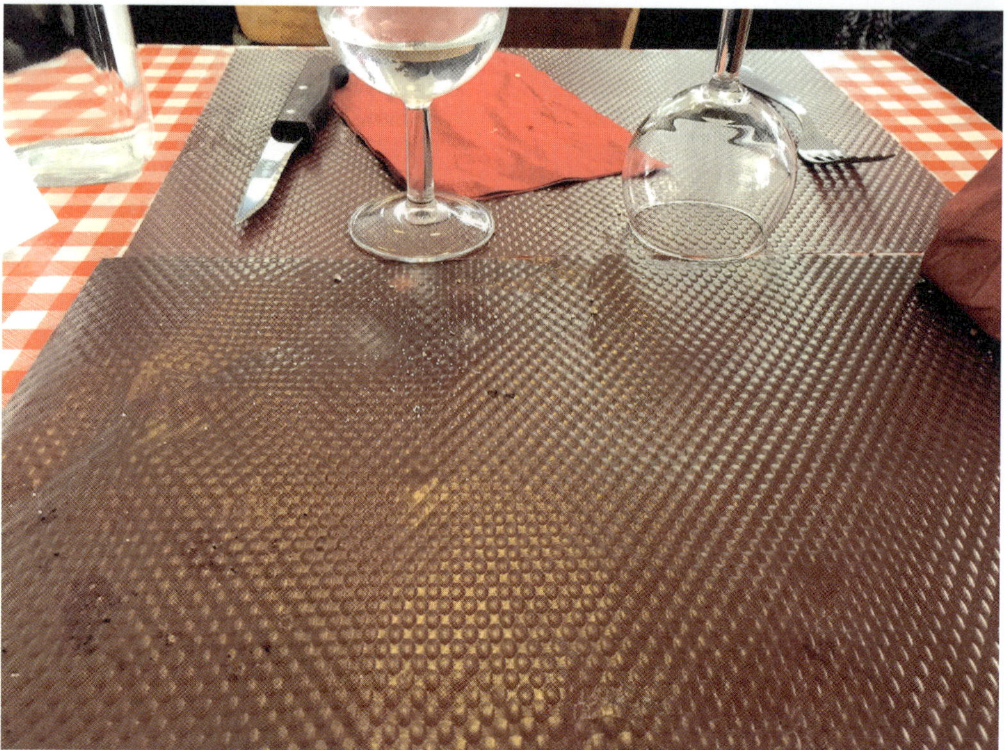

Chez Nenesse, 2015
75003 Paris

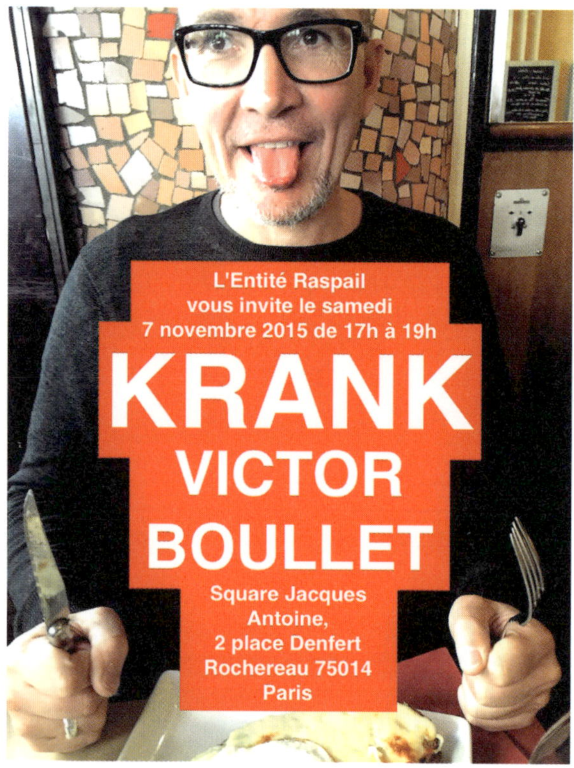

Krank Invitation, 2015
L'Entité Raspail, Paris

KRANK

I lived in Paris for nearly 9 years. I came back for a few days after a year and half away.
(Oct 2015) – I was there to feel it out and reflect on whether I wanted to die an old man in Paris.

I needed two stamps after I had visited the new Picasso museum, I had to send a postcard to a dear friend in Oslo. First I had to have a coffee at La Perle. Didier and Eric smiled when they saw me. After a quick chat they returned to work. I looked at the two men that have made my morning coffee for over eight years. John Galliano inadvertently supported La Perle with his anti-semitic rant; I sat there the morning after, news crews and Japanese bloggers snapping, talking and pointing. La Perle's annual income increased so radically that the owner, a hairy man from Marseilles had to invest the money back into the cafe. I have seen its idiotic 007-like underground ham and wine bar.

I walk to Rue Rambuteau to buy the stamps. I have lived at no. 15. I entered Rambuteau by crossing Rue des Archives. I looked down the street towards Beaubourg (Pompidou), the street had completely changed. The chaos and grit had disappeared and been replaced by tourist friendly comfort. I stopped for my stamps, but the cafe where I have bought them for over 8 years was not there. Where was it? To my astonishment it had been replaced by a large, wide, new type of concept cafe. These cafes are pre-made with all the trimmings and delivered in a container.

I walked on the left-hand side of the road, down to rue du Renard, crossed the street and took Rue Rambuteau back up to rue du Temple, so I could suck up what a capitalist plough can do to our historic soil in an extremely short time. I made a left up rue du Temple. After the Jewish museum, on the other side of the street is one of the two entrances to rue de Braque; the name has nothing to do with the painter. A German friend said something like, that is a GOODY GOODY TWO SHOES gallery. This commercial French / Italian gallery located on rue de Braque, like so many others, operates and survives from their suspect, self-made secondary market platform. The gallery owner has explained with hand gestures what makes a good artist. At that same time, on rue Vieille du Temple, he insulted my friends and me. His ethics are common. Should I battle them to stand my ground?

I didn't pop by the goody goody gallery. Instead I stopped at the all impressive Marian Goodman Gallery. The entrance door to la cour makes you feel like a peasant. Dan Graham is not an artist that I like, but I do like to look at or hear him speak, online of course. All the wall work is redundant, unnecessary and solely produced for sale. I turned my focus to the gallery space. Finally Dan Graham entered my heart. Two curved pieces of glass, some steel and a bridge like passage. I walked through it and back into it. I stopped in the middle. I connected.

A few days later or even the next day, I can't remember, I forget most things these days, I walked down the commercial road, rue de Bretagne. This street used to have a horse butcher. Now it has an all organic, trendy, blueberry muffin blog shop with bearded, tattooed diners instead. I passed the boucherie Frédéric Simonneau, 41 rue du Bretagne, and like the cafe on Rue Rambuteau, it was gone. And where they have butchered several hundred tons of meat, stood a camp man, selling overpriced chocolate bars on sticks. The racist, fat, little butcher had sold up. Over one hundred years of clients and meat was gone, sold to the neo-wave of gentrification. A problem that sneaks up on us and installs its parasitic eggs.

Early 2008, I asked Frédéric Simonneau if I could help in his boucherie. He gave me an apron and a knife right there and then. I had a problem eating red meat. Living in France not eating meat is trouble. (Meat racists).

Employees at Frédéric Simonneau's boucherie taught me a lot and I will be ever grateful, but I left after a few mornings working there. The owner brutally rubbed chicken feathers in the face of his Chinese worker, he had forgotten to flame burn the bird before showing me how tie it into shape. Bastard. He lost my friendship and business. For several years afterwards I only walked by the boucherie Frédéric Simonneau nodding a polite bonjour. Later his fat little son was part of the operation. The son would have been the 3rd generation working that boucherie.

Coffee at Le Progrès during fashion week is all fucked up. I spotted a vacant table and desperately tried to seize it, but I had vicious competition. The waiter, who I know, did not help me through the row of tables. He said: relax Victor. Sod, I lost the table. I had to back out and bumped into waiter Kevin with bad teeth, he was raised in Beaubourg, I like that.

A message to the Belleville art scene; please stop the use of mdf and plywood all together. It was like walking back in time visiting these galleries, like art-time had stood still. Why am I even seeking out and looking at this - Wood, rubbish, metal, sound, research into something, it's bleeding groundhog day. One gallery owner even tried to explain that the artist needs talent. I was told what my talents were. What can I say? Thank you? And, If I were to come back to Paris, they would support me, who are they? and why do I need support? Do I limp?

I had a coffee at Aux Folies. Some graffiti artists were working on a wall piece around the corner, the wind carried the odour from the graffiti spray cans, it was wonderful. That whiff of paint combined with coffee drinking was an all new sensation, it was probably the only real art experience I had in Paris during my visit. Besides the commercial art galleries my biggest Belleville disappointment came later that day as I walked past where an old building that came down in 2012. The lot had been filled by a neo-corrupt atrocity—a sign of the times. The changes are radical. History and traditions are evaporating, bulldozed to the ground as we speak. My problem has always been that I am caged by my beliefs.

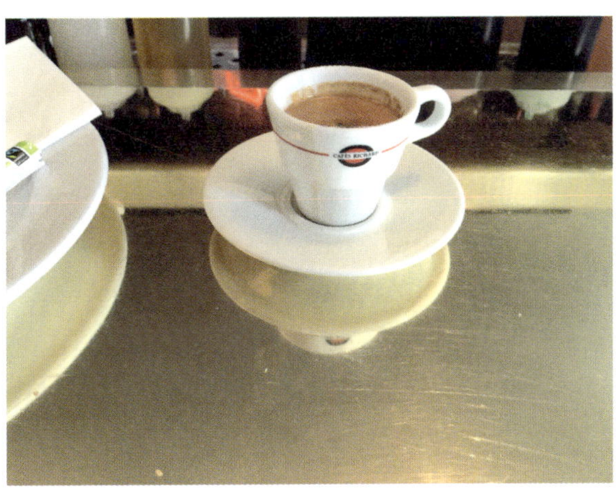

Aux Folies, 2015
75020 Paris

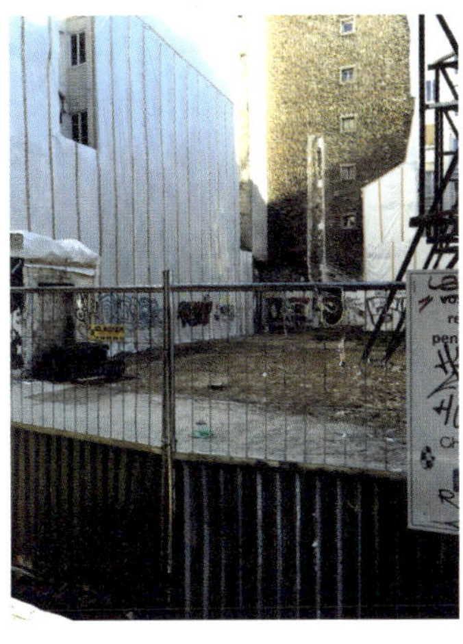

Rue de Belleville, 2015
75020 Paris

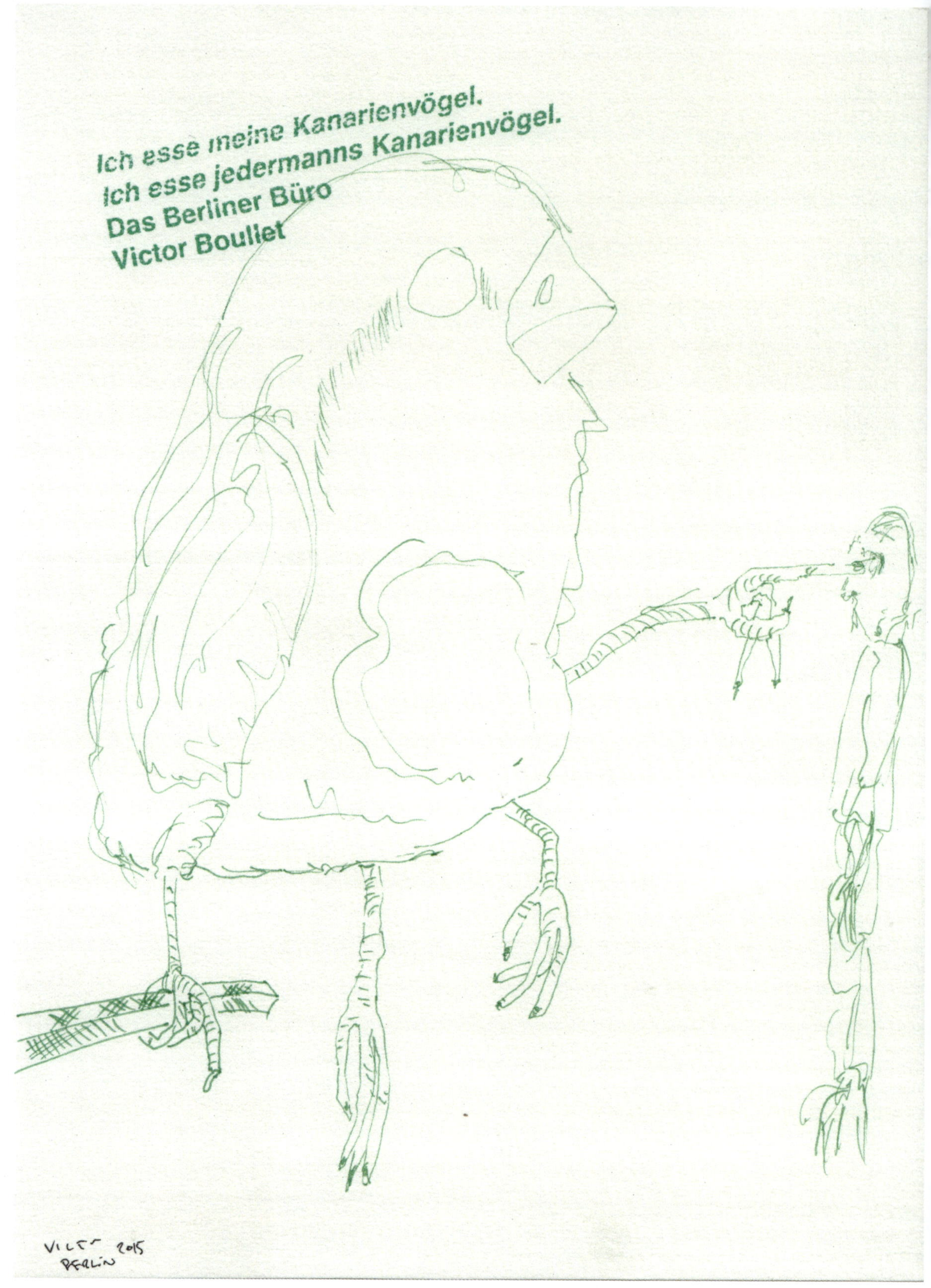

Poke the Eye Out of the Lousy Man, 2015
Muji pen and green ink stamped on paper
21cm x 29cm

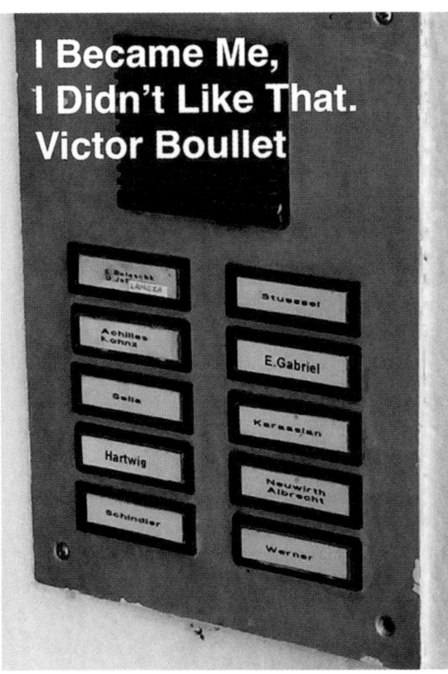

I Became Me, I Didn't Like That

"These canvases don't critique, complain and they don't lean left nor right. They have unintentionally healed me."

"Today's radical artists are tainted with their own hypocrisy, they are the sole workers of the nepotism exploited in the arts. They are the bourgeois snobs with cowardly needs for sectarian control. The radical has become today's SALON."

The two quotes above are mine, plucked away from this writing. I have pasted them back in, and on the top, to manifest my self-importance and how damaging that is to me.

For Copenhagen. (the show got cancelled)

Ullet Road in Liverpool and the negativity that I derive from it, is a personal problem. Ullet Road has pushed my narcissistic behaviour, and it's resulting material, to an all time high. Losing control over it, and the material in Copenhagen, was never part of any plan. I respect my paintings, but I don't respect what they may ultimately represent.

Whether my paintings will have any historical relevance in the future is, to me, completely irrelevant. I question much of the art being produced - most art produced today is surplus to requirements. I read a book on the 10 Irish hunger strikers that died in 1981. I can make a sculpture inspired by that book. Why should I do that? If I did do that, the title would be "There are No Problems Other Than Your Own Problem". Why mention this? Simply because I want to distance myself from producing such surplus art.

I will insist that this work, the canvases, is not surplus work created for sale or for the white cube and its many hypocritical shows. My two-faced attitude of sending the work to Copenhagen is questionable. Am I desperate for another mail-out to the many people that I don't know? I have, over the phone with Copenhagen, uttered a few vague wishes regarding the hanging, you know, how, what and where. It's all out of my control. Other than that, I want the work back, as I always do. Where I then store the work is what I drastically need to change within my practice. Art being stored for the future is questionable indeed! – I will come back to that at some later stage, this is not the time, but it has to do with surplus and self important behaviour, and it needs to stop.

When a young inexperienced animal chases a bird and it actually catches the prey, the game is over. The bird is dead and will be eaten. But, the game is truly over for the hunter, who now masters the hunt. And that is what we all crave, becoming and being seen as the master.

(Second week into residency of self / d.o.m.e. Berlin)

I feel numb, but I might get out of bed today. I have trapped myself in a luxury cage, a prize winner's crib. 3rd floor. 130sqm, Schøneberg, Berlin. Renting. Price? Non of your business.

19:07, 17 oct. 2015, I had just got off the Ubahn and was standing on the corner Potsdamerstraße / Kurfürstenstraße. I was on the phone with a friend, and out of the corner of my eye I saw a man with a walking stool, with wheels, pushing it and himself into the road, the traffic was intense, I thought, 'bloody oafish drunk'. I hung up as the man looked over and started talking to me in German. I thought, why me, why do they always have to talk to me? I answered, I don't speak German, yet. He quickly switched to English, and good English. This was a schooled drunk, is what I thought. He asked, can you help me cross the road. I uttered a superficial, yes I can. I was on my way to an art opening, and the friend I had spoken to on the phone had mentioned a second opening, so I was on my way to two separate art openings. i.e. very busy.

He, the drunk, was a tall man in his late 50s, curly dark hair. He was wearing jeans, a knitted pullover and a dark stained duvet jacket. His face was slightly misshapen and he was in need of a shave. He looked at me with quiet, small, dark eyes, desperate eyes, and said, thank you. The penny dropped, I asked, do you have MS? Yes, YES, I've got MS, he answered.

The light turned green, I took his arm and started to walk. To my amazement he was not able to walk, only drag his feet along the ground. His walking chair, on wheels, was in a poor condition. We reached the middle of road and the light turned red. We had to walk back to where we had started. As I tried to turn around, he pushed the walking chair in the other direction by accident. His feet were cemented to the ground. The next thing I knew he was starting to fallover in the middle of Potsdamerstraße. I was losing him, his arm was slipping out of my grip, the cars were coming from all directions. He was heavy and becoming heavier. Holding onto both him and his chair at the same time was a hopeless endeavour. As a matter of fact we were now both falling over. I looked around, panicking; I was in need of urgent help. A man of Indian descent, a man that sells roses on the street to people in love, saw what was going on. He rushed out into the busy road and assisted us.

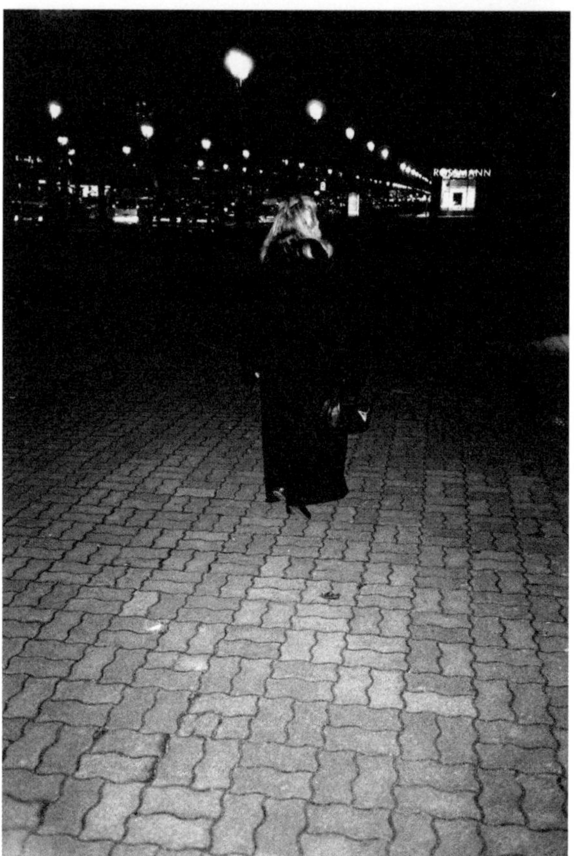

Stalking Hanna Schygulla, Berlin 2015
35mm film

Finally we found our way back to the corner where it all started. The cars were rushing by. With help from the rose salesman, I got the MS-passenger onto his homemade seat; this was not a wheelchair, but a wobbly walking chair. The light turned green, I started rolling him over Potsdamerstraße. He explained how it should be done. One wheel onto the pavement at a time and come in from an angle. As we approached the other side of the street. He lifted one hand and placed it behind his head, like he was protecting his skull. I had to be gentle to avoid tipping him over and crushing his skull on Potsdamerstraße, that simply could not happen.

We made it safely onto the pavement of Potsdamerstraße. I asked him in what direction he was heading, hoping he just wanted to buy an apple at the turkish market on the corner. I want to go two streets up, he answered. Two streets up Kurfürstenstraße. meant that I had to wheel him and his cobbled walking chair by one of the art openings, at a trendy Berlin gallery. Or, more precisely, I had to wheel him through the actual crowd on the pavement outside. Crap, was the first word that came to mind. I looked down, at the asphalt, looked at my feet, well placed on mother earth. This is it Mr Boullet, wheel him with pride through the beer drinking art crowd. Who cares, just help him.

So I started to pushed him along Kurfürstenstraße. The seat was mounted inside the walking chair, so he was facing me like a toddler as I was pushing him. His feet were resting on a homemade bar and they occasionally fell to the ground and was dragged along Kurfürstenstraße. I walked with both arms outstretched to avoid tripping over his feet, legs or knees. I felt extremely uncomfortable with the situation, especially about the way I looked, leaning over this sick man. Why me?

We approached Gallery Tanya Leighton. There they stood, the artists, on the pavement, free beer. I passed them with my art piece, Untitled (MAN WITH MS / FOUND CHAIR, WHEELS) 2015. Not one single person looked or paid attention to me, him, my jacket, his shoes, my glasses, the chair, the walk, his hair, my belt, his jumper or my Lee jeans.

My passenger and I arrived at the second street corner, Kurfürstenstraße. and Blumenthastraße. Here we are, he said. He grabbed his right leg, just above the knee, and lifted it onto the street, and then did the same with his left leg. I took his arm and helped him out of his wobbly chair, he stood up and thanked me for helping him. I nodded and said It was a pleasure.

I quickly turned around and walked back the way I had come. I entered the gallery, the newer space, which is on the other side of the original gallery. An art film was being screened. I had a quick peak round, saw a familiar face, exchanged some superficial words, and crossed the road into Tanya Leighton's original space. This all took less then five minutes.

I walked back up Kurfürstenstraße, turned right into Blumenthastraße, crossed the street, thinking about what I was going to eat tonight. I passed one of many building entrances on that street, and there he was again, the man with MS. This time he was desperately hanging onto the door and his bloody chair. I stopped, and helped him back into his chair. I asked, can I do something for you, his answered, no, not really, I'm just not sure if I have come to the right address? His project was so impossible and idiotic in my eyes. I looked at the names next to the doorbells, and read them out loud. No, it's not here, maybe the next door down, he said.

I poked my head out and looked down the road, thinking, ok, that is not too far. I wheeled him to the next entrance door. He was facing towards the street, so again I read the names of the residents out loud. I started from the top left and read them row by row, until, finally, he said JA. Thank god we found the right place. Neuwirth / Albrecht. I rang the doorbell. Waited for the German voice, but no flipping answer? I rang it again, this time with a slight panic, please answer, if not what will I do?

Then the man with MS turned his head towards me and said, I think they might be waiting for me at my place. What, really? I said. Yes, you see, they wanted to come and see me, but I wanted to walk up and see them, I wanted to visit them. Bloody stubborn bugger, is what I thought. He said, I will wait here till they come. Ok, I said. He thanked me for all the help. I smiled, nodded and left.
I walked down to Eden Eden, Bortolozzi's second space or rather her project space. I visited Eden Eden when she had her first show there, the space was truly different then, I remember. I strongly disagree with the changes she has

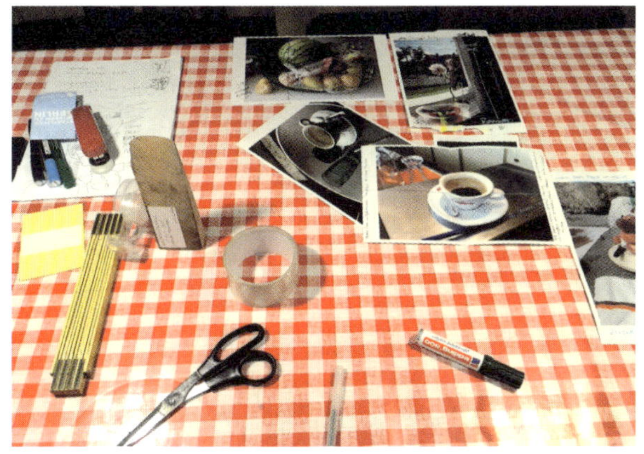

D.O.M.E Berlin Büro – Dirt Filth Man Dank
Performance / Theft / Stalking / Residence of Self
Death of Mother Earth (D.O.M.E)
4th October – 29th December, Berlin 2015

made, but there is still a little of the old space left intact. That corner, Blumenthalstraße and Bülowstraße reminds me of Oslo for some reason. And that it used to be a pharmacy, I like that.

At Eden Eden I recognised two men that came with the same Ubahne as I did, from Kotterbusser Tor. The show was noisy and smelly, I liked that part. I bumped into an acquaintance, a nice person, we exchanged hellos, small talk, I asked if she wanted to meet up for coffee, since I was in Berlin. The answer, or how I understood the answer, was that we could maybe have a coffee in December. In other words, we could have a coffee in two months. Someone else grabs the artist's attention, I nodded and went on with my business. Forget the coffee, doesn't really matter, and I understand. What I saw as a good art piece at that show, was in fact not part of the show. I even took a picture of those bunkbeds.

Half hour before I helped my MS passenger on the corner Potsdamerstraße / Kurfürstenstraße. I was climbing the stairs at Kottbusser Tor to get the U-Bahn to Kurfürstenstraße. I had two men on my right, and I crossed in front of them just as I got to the platform floor. I recognised an English accent, a London accent to be specific, the other fellow was German. I didn't turn my head, but I slowed down, to see if I could catch a few phrases. I picked up that the German was offering something from his rucksack and that the Londoner was bothered, but at the same time wanted what was offered. I understood that they didn't know each other that well, and that was why I got curious. I walked on and decided to spy some more from distance.

The U-Bahn arrived, we got on. The doors slid shut and I walked two carriages down, towards where the same two were sitting. I decided to stand opposite them and listen in on their conversation. The Londoner looked up at me twice, he reminded me of Chiwetelu Ejiofor. They were dressed rather similarly, both had a cap and a rucksack. I don't like caps. They had that familiar cool urban uniform. It struck me, of course, they must be heading to the same opening as me, they looked the part. 8 stops to go, what could I do? I noticed that the Londoner used the word *like* too often when he spoke. I decided to count how many times he actually used the word *like*.

The Londoner got a bottle of Coke Zero out, he drank some, or almost all, and then handed the bottle to the German, who wiped the top and then drank what was left. Not sure I would have done that. They talked about DJ-ing, and that some friend of the Londoner in London had been ripped off. He had DJ'ed for three hours and was paid £75. The German reacted by turning his head and uttering, really, was is das 75 pounss, whass number is das? They laughed, because what I think is that they thought they had a similar moral standard regarding what one would accept or not as payment. However, I would put money on the fact that both of these men would have played that same gig for less than £75.

The train approached Kurfürstenstraße station, The Londoner had used the word *like* 57 times.

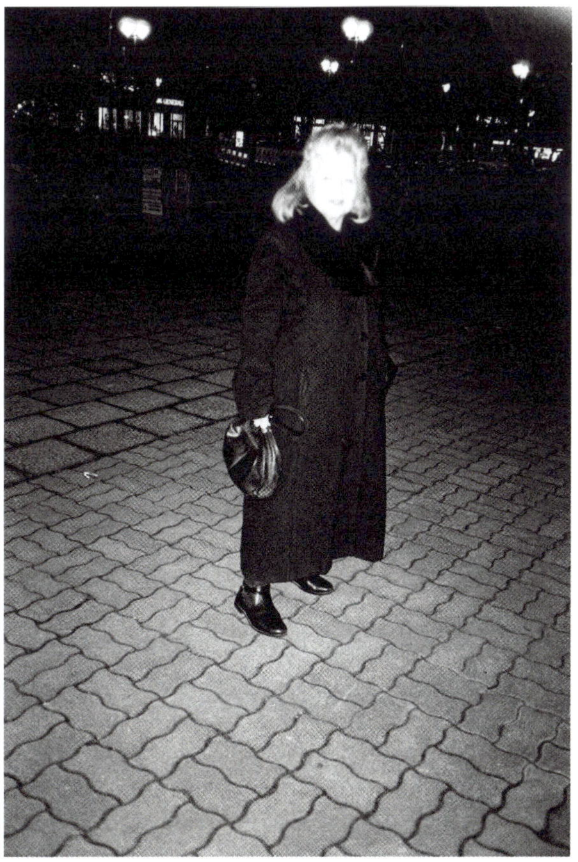

Stalking Hanna Schygulla, Berlin 2015
35mm film

ICH, 2015
Green ink stamped on paper
21cm x 29cm

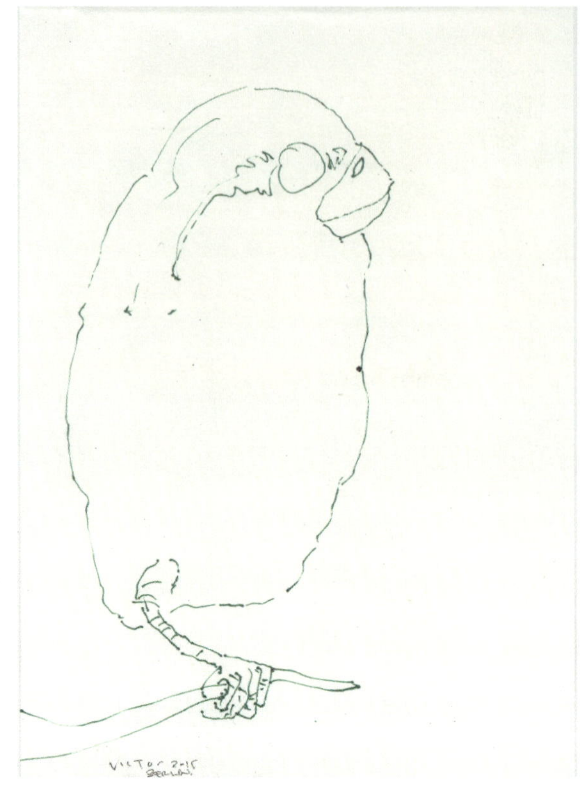

ohne Titel, 2015
Muji pen on paper
21cm x 29cm

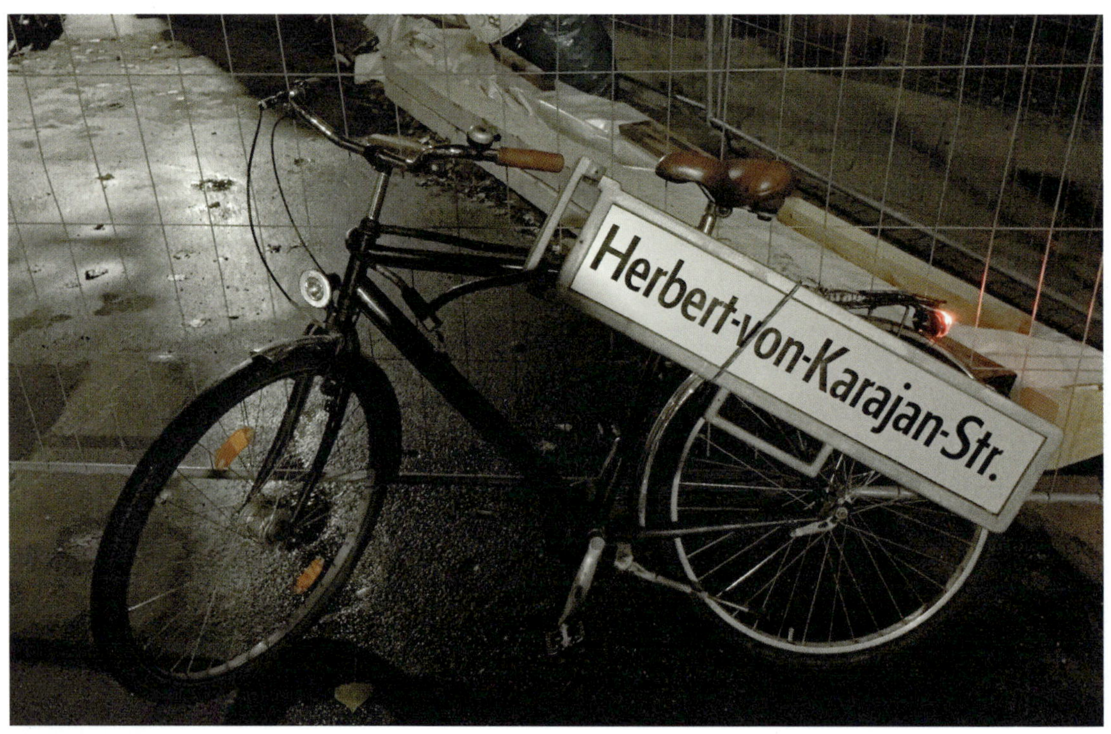

HVK – Dirt Filth Man Dank, 2015
Performance / Theft / Stalking / Residence of Self
Death of Mother Earth (D.O.M.E)
4th October – 29th December, Berlin 2015

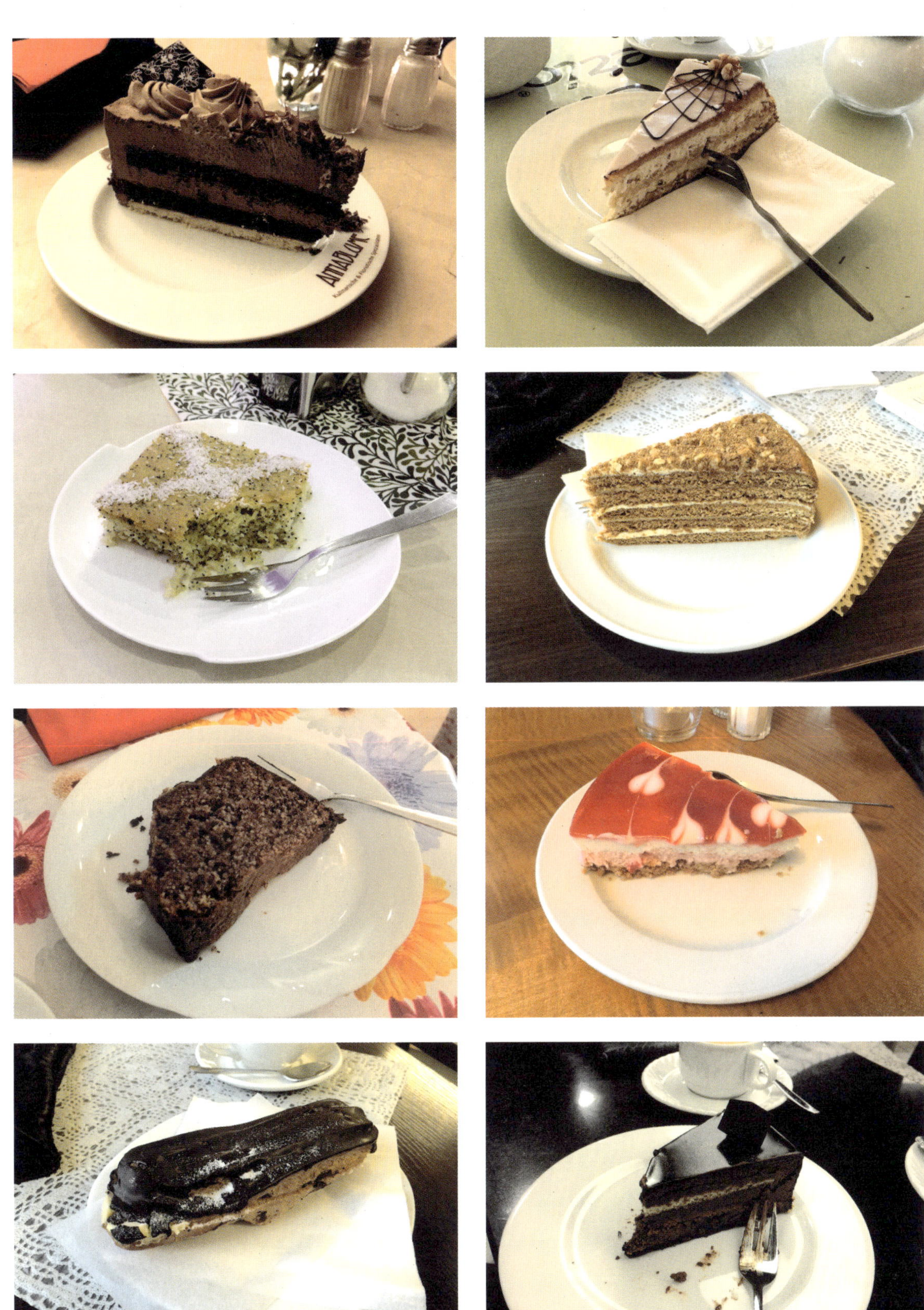

Cake Monger (Bonus) – Dirt Filth Man Dank, 2015
Performance / Theft / Stalking / Residence of Self
Death of Mother Earth (D.O.M.E)
4th October – 29th December, Berlin 2015

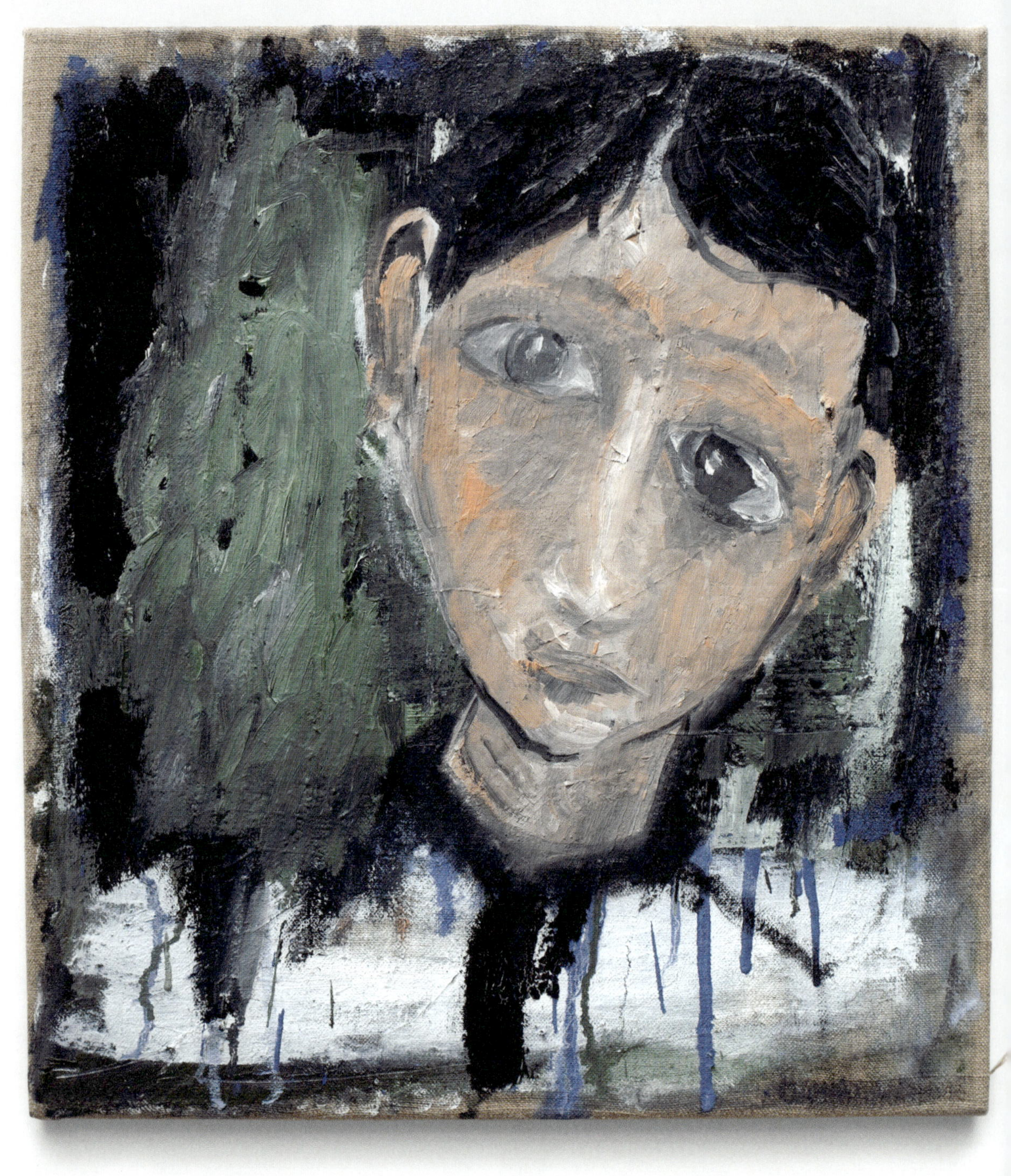

Ullet Road, my Chaïm, 2016
Oil on raw linen
40cm x 46cm

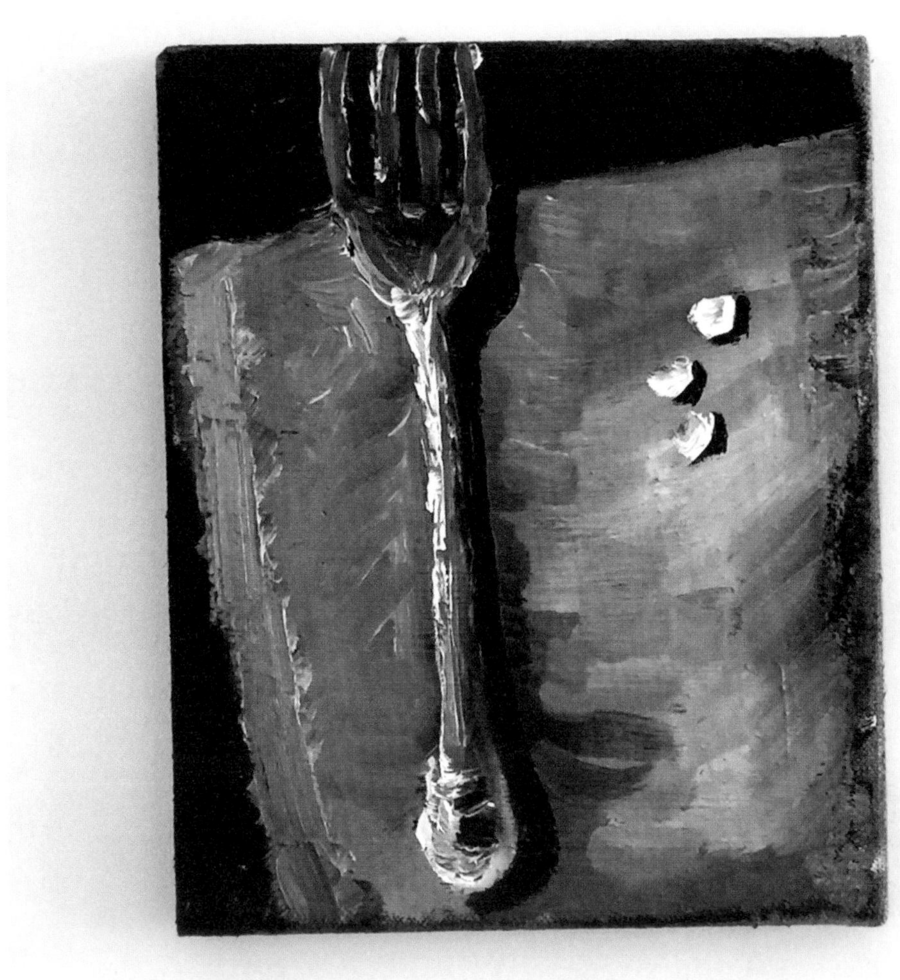

Fork and Paracetamol (Work overpainted) 2016
Oil on raw linen
20cm x 25cm
iPhone image

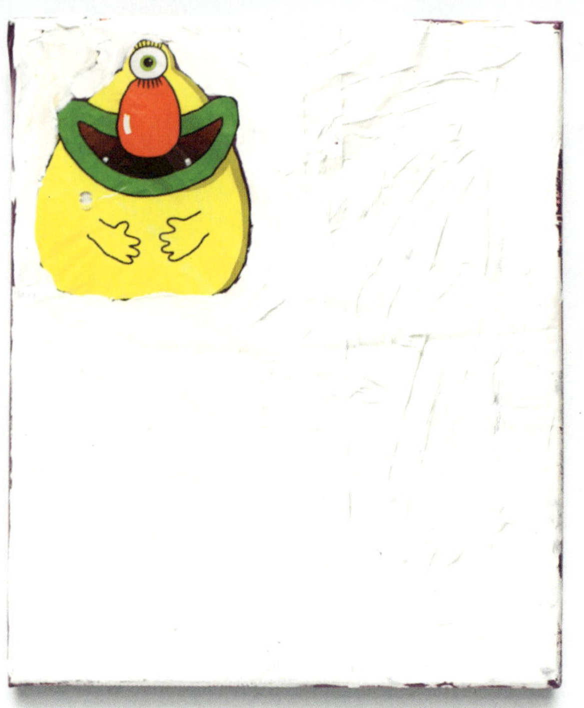

Monster (Ullet Road) 2016
Oil on crisp packet
20cm x 25cm

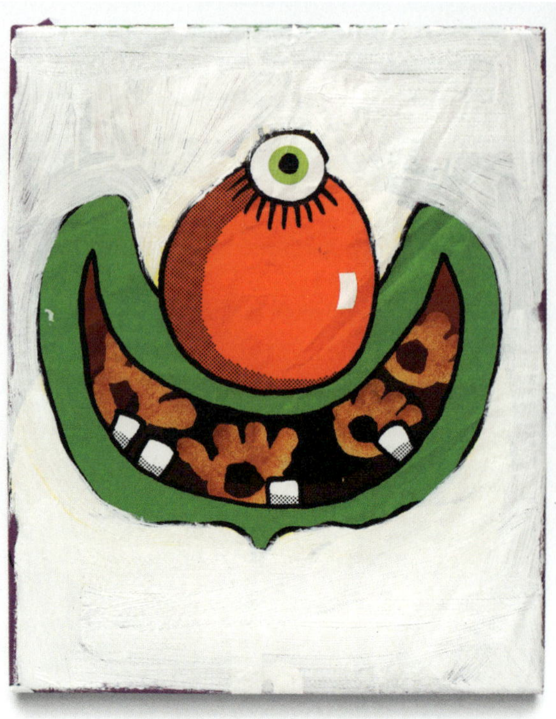

Monster (Ullet Road) 2016
Oil on crisp packet
20cm x 25cm

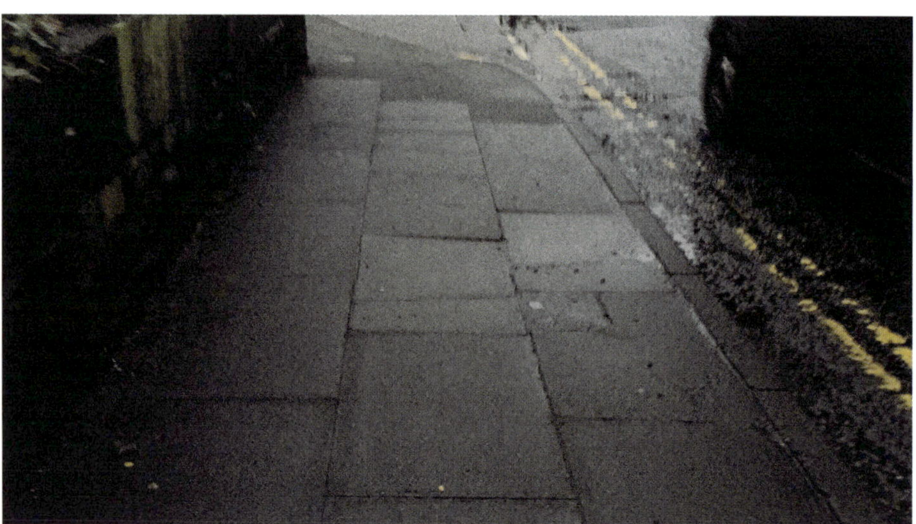

Ullet Road (08:37 – 22 January) L8, Liverpool, 2016
iPhone video 1:50min

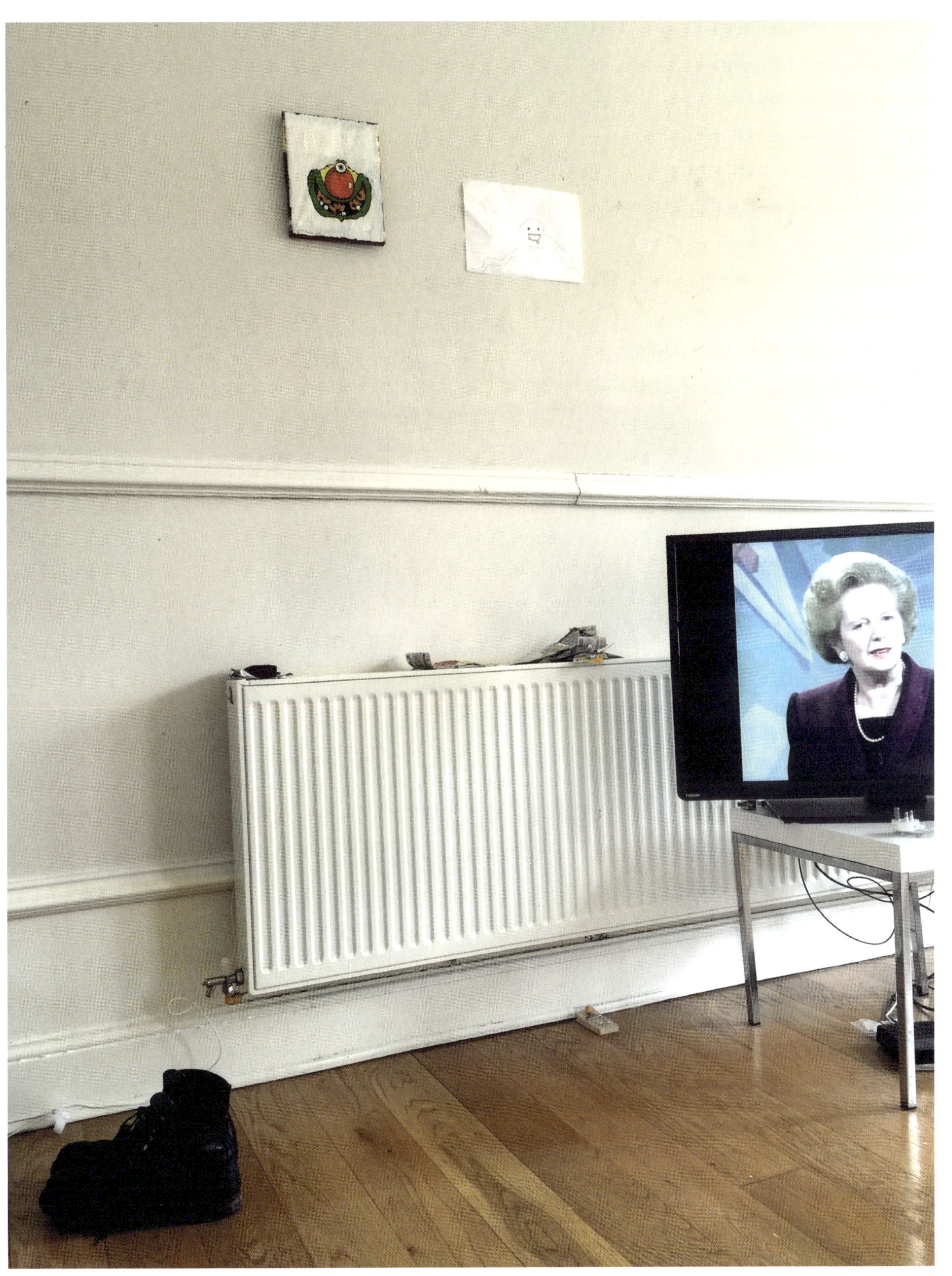

Monster (Ullet Road) 2016
Oil on crisp packet
20cm x 25cm

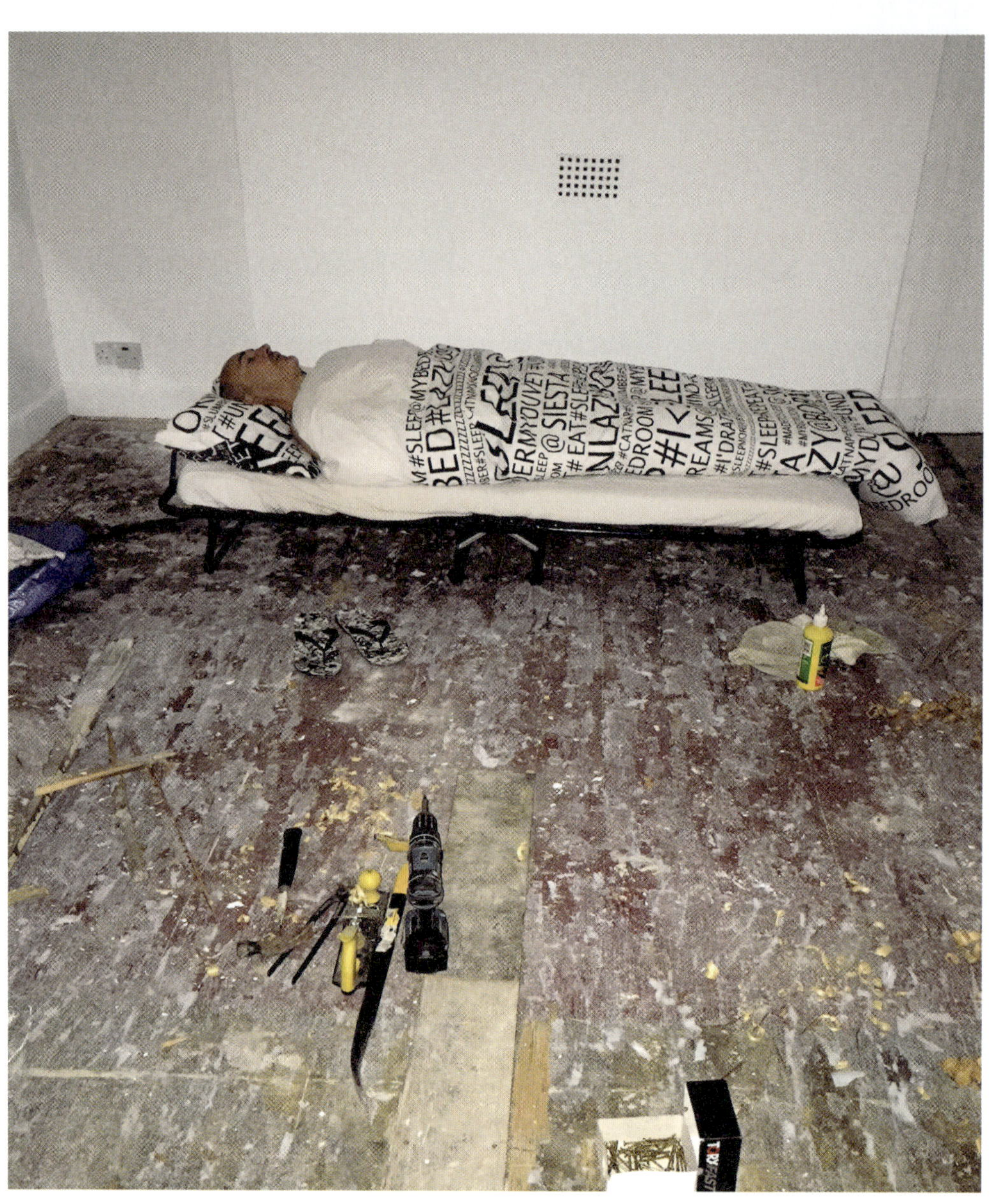

Sleeping on an IKEA foldout bed, 24 July, 2016

HUS 2016 – 2021
7 Mount Street
Liverpool L1 9HD

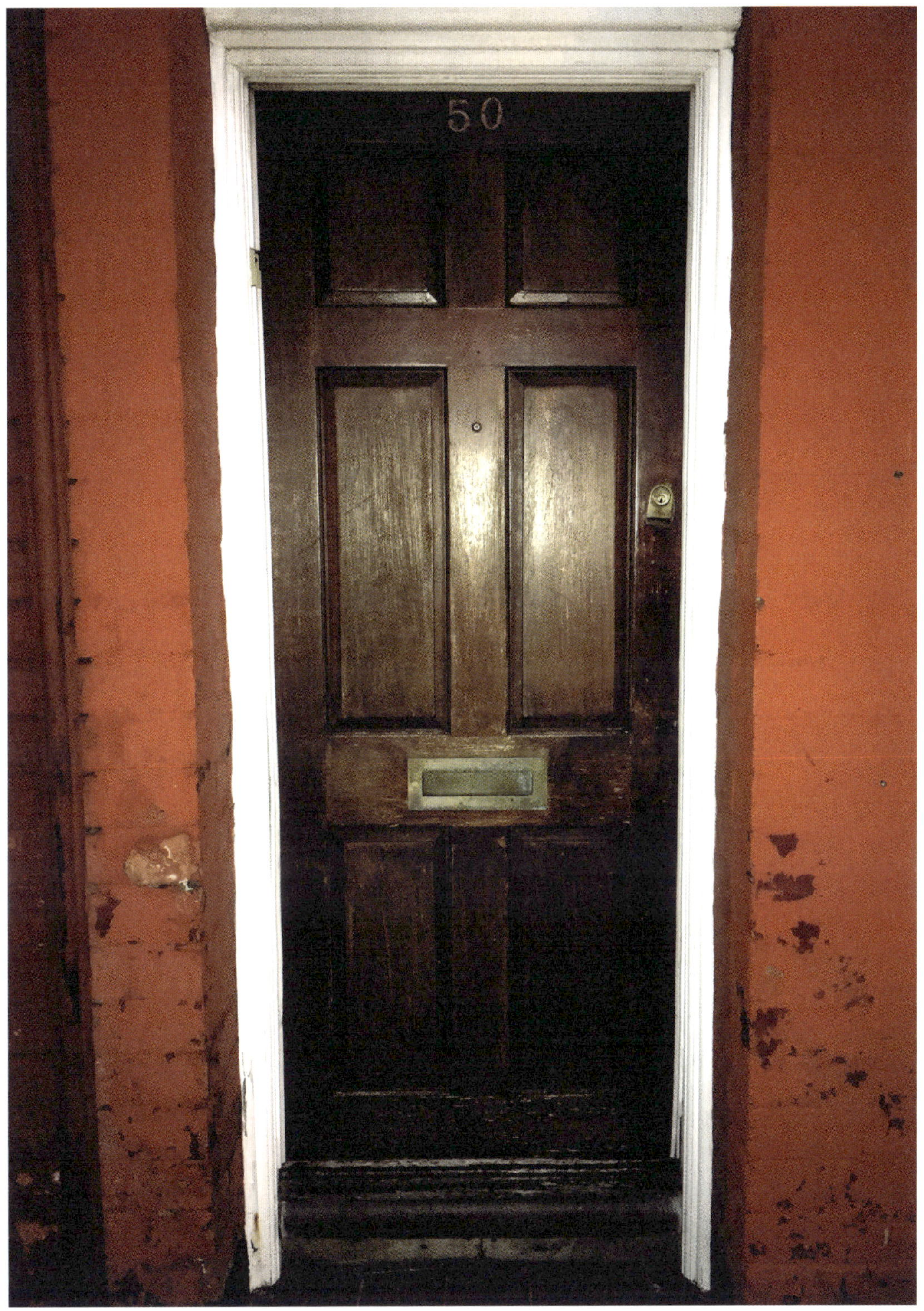

Death Of Mother Earth
Artist Residence 2016 – 2021
50 Enid Street
Liverpool L8 8HW

Death of Mother Earth demands no ideas other than your silence
Death of Mother Earth you arrive, you stay, exist, you leave
Death of Mother Earth provides basic amenities – bed, bathroom, chair, table, cooking equipment. No internet
Death of Mother Earth does not collaborate with anything commercial

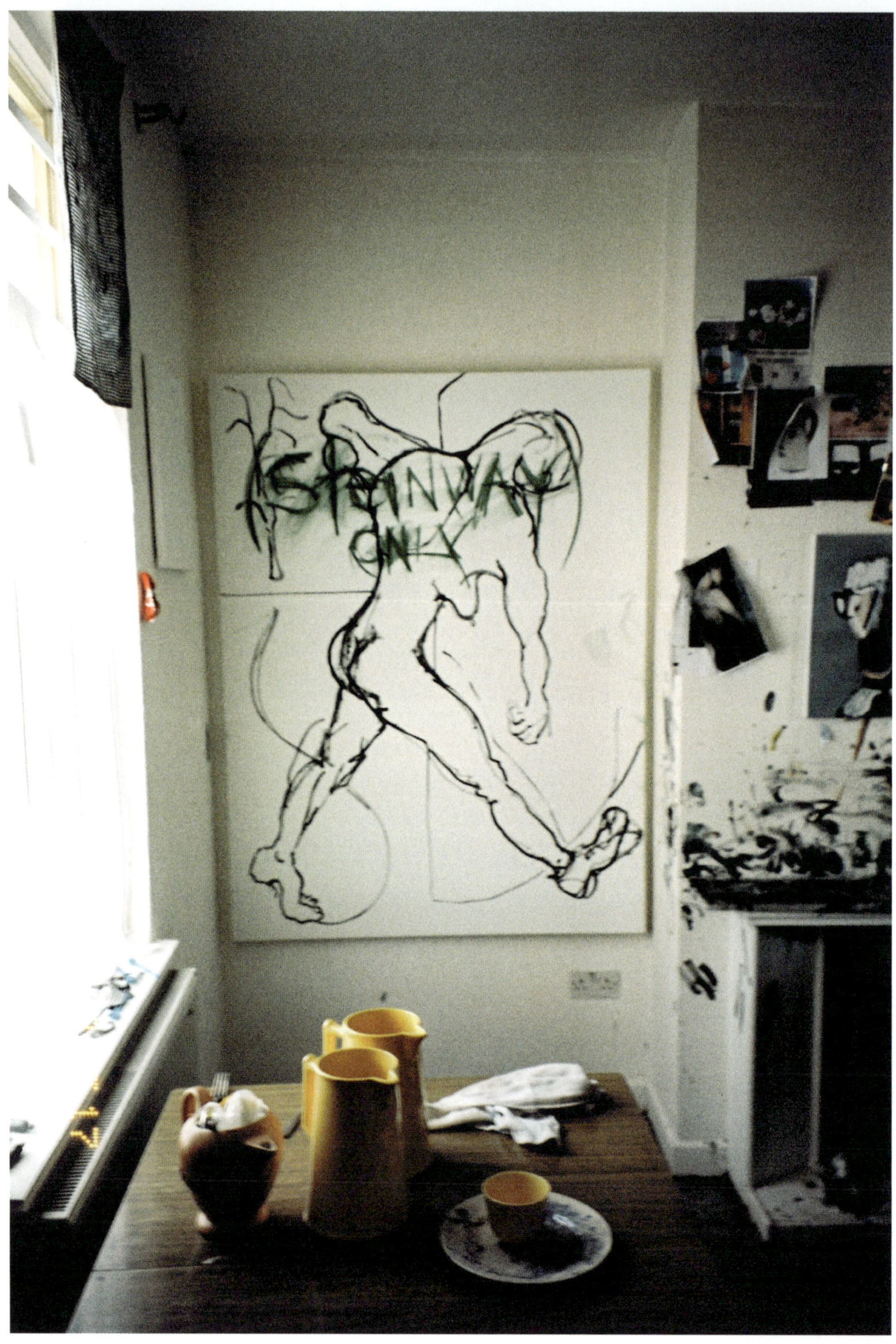

Studio documentation, 2017
(above, work destroyed)
35mm film

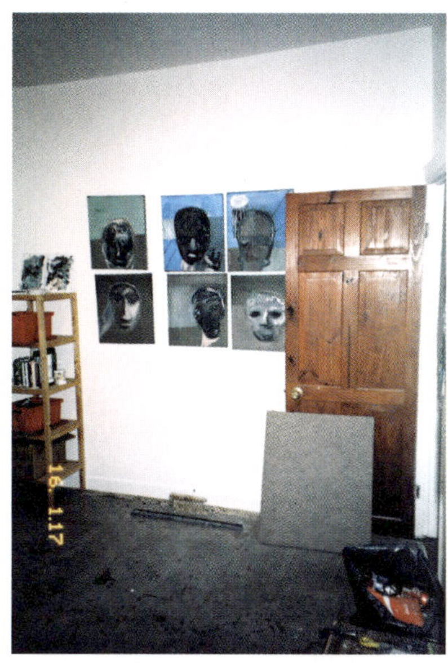
16. 1.17

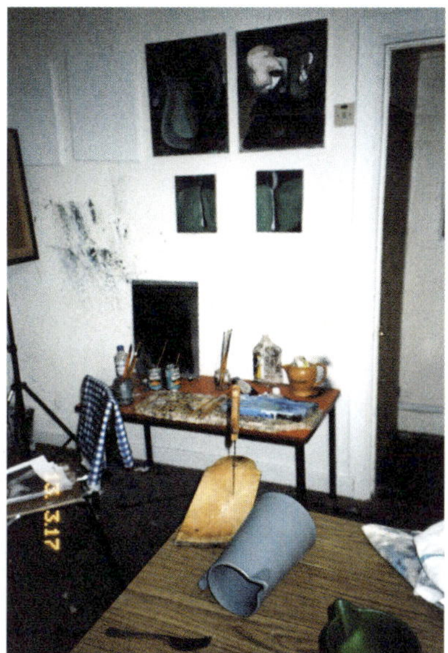

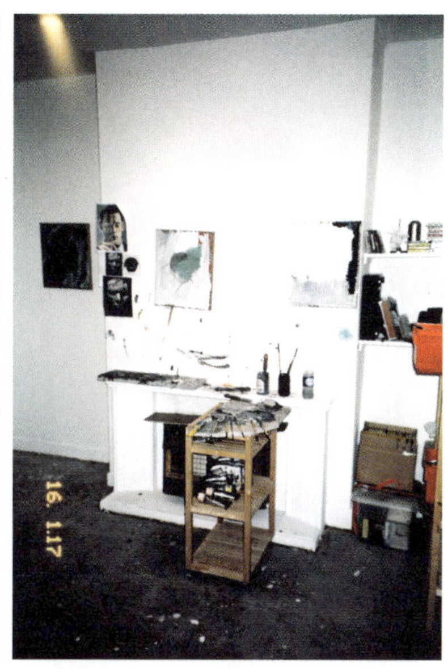
16. 1.17

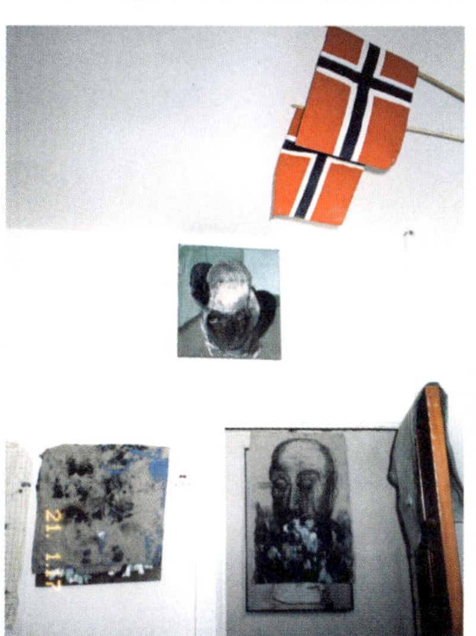
21. 1.17

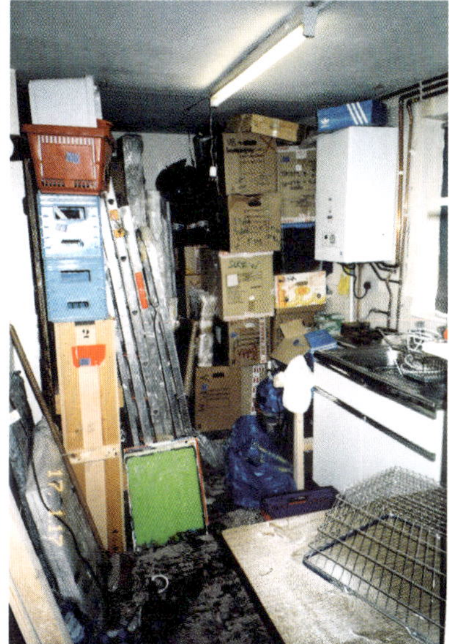

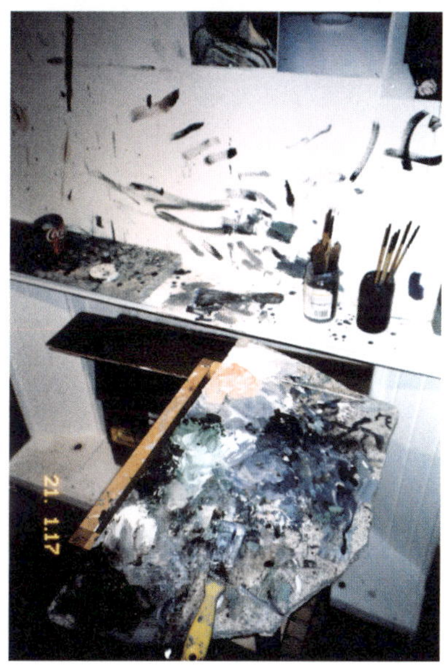
21. 1.17

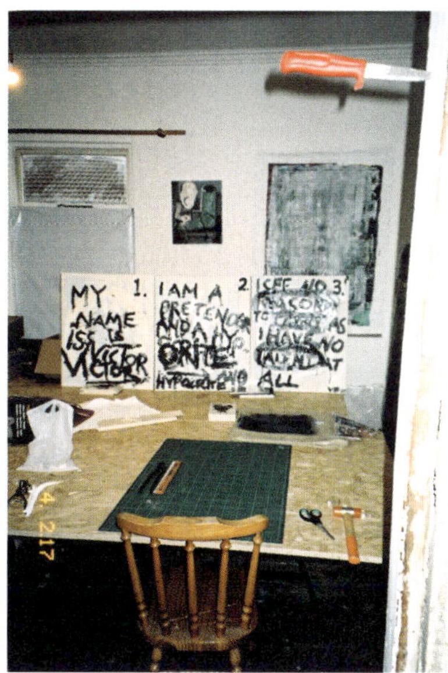
4. 2.17

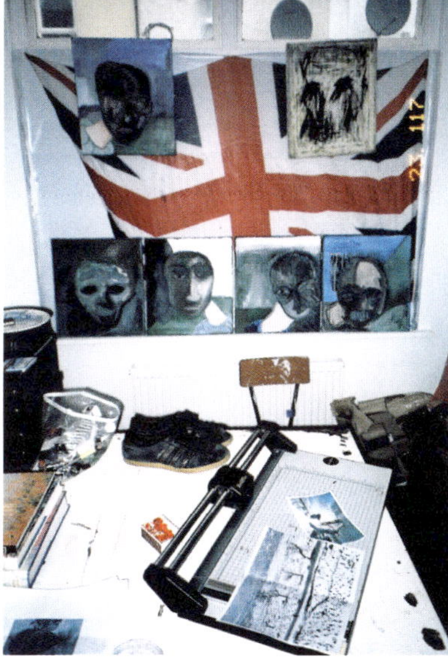

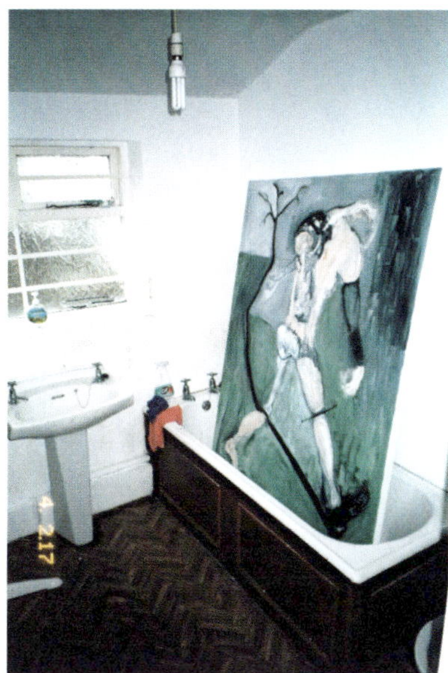
4. 2.17

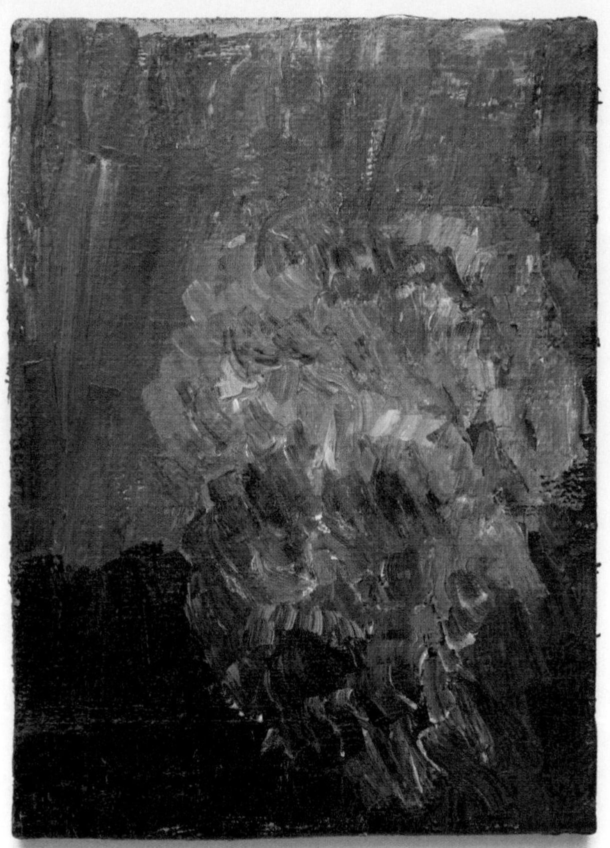

Untitled, 2016
Oil overpainted onto existing painting on linen
24cm x 35cm

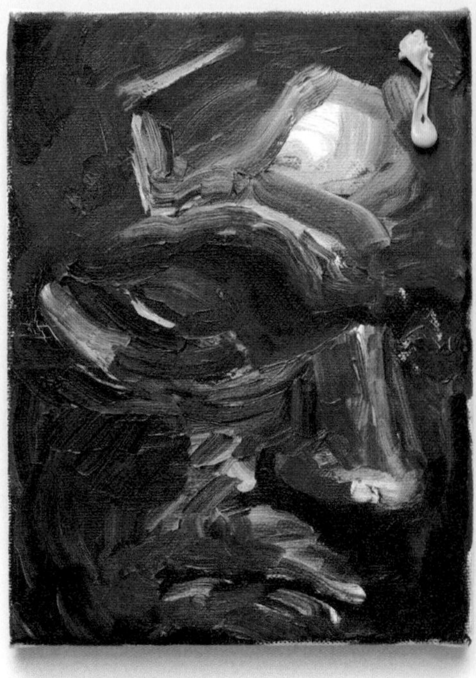

Beethoven, 2016 – 2017
Oil on canvas with chewing gum
16.5cm x 21.5cm

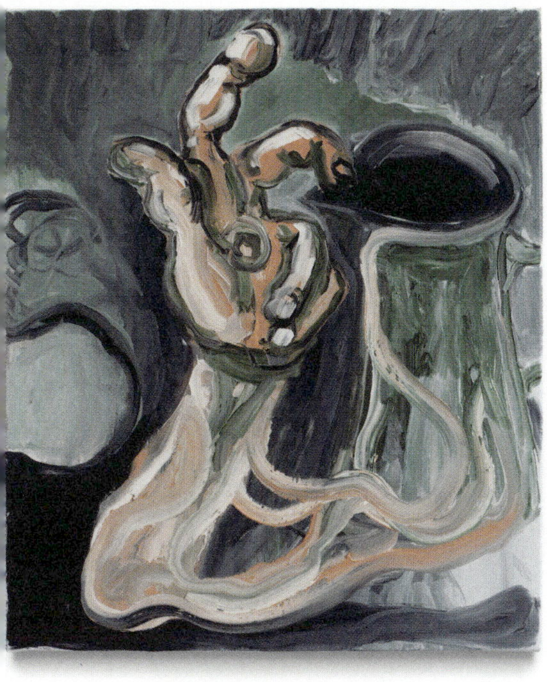

Untitled (Work destroyed) 2017
Oil on canvas
38cm x 46cm

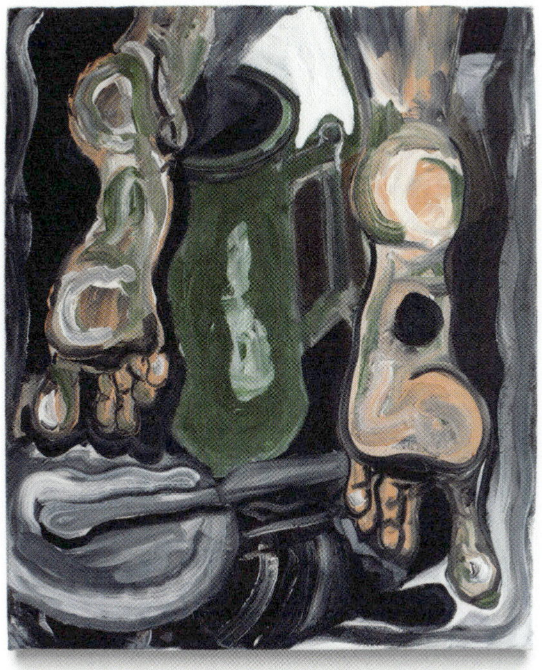

Untitled, 2017
Oil on canvas
38cm x 46cm

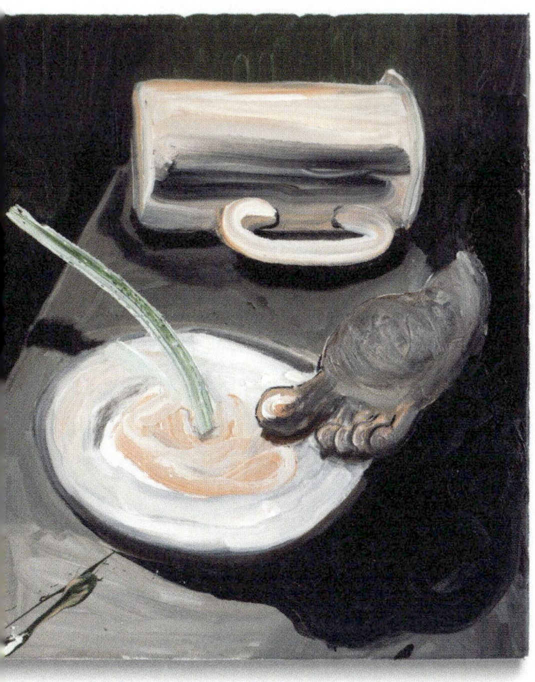

Untitled (Work destroyed) 2017
Oil on canvas
38cm x 46cm

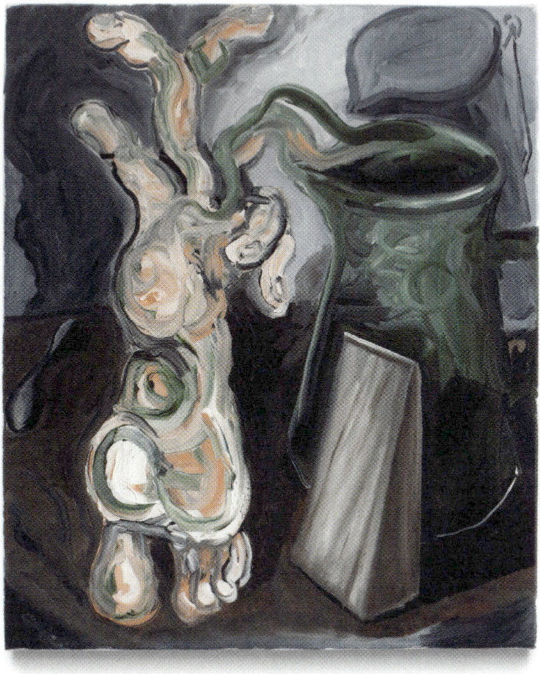

Untitled (Work destroyed) 2017
Oil on canvas
38cm x 46cm

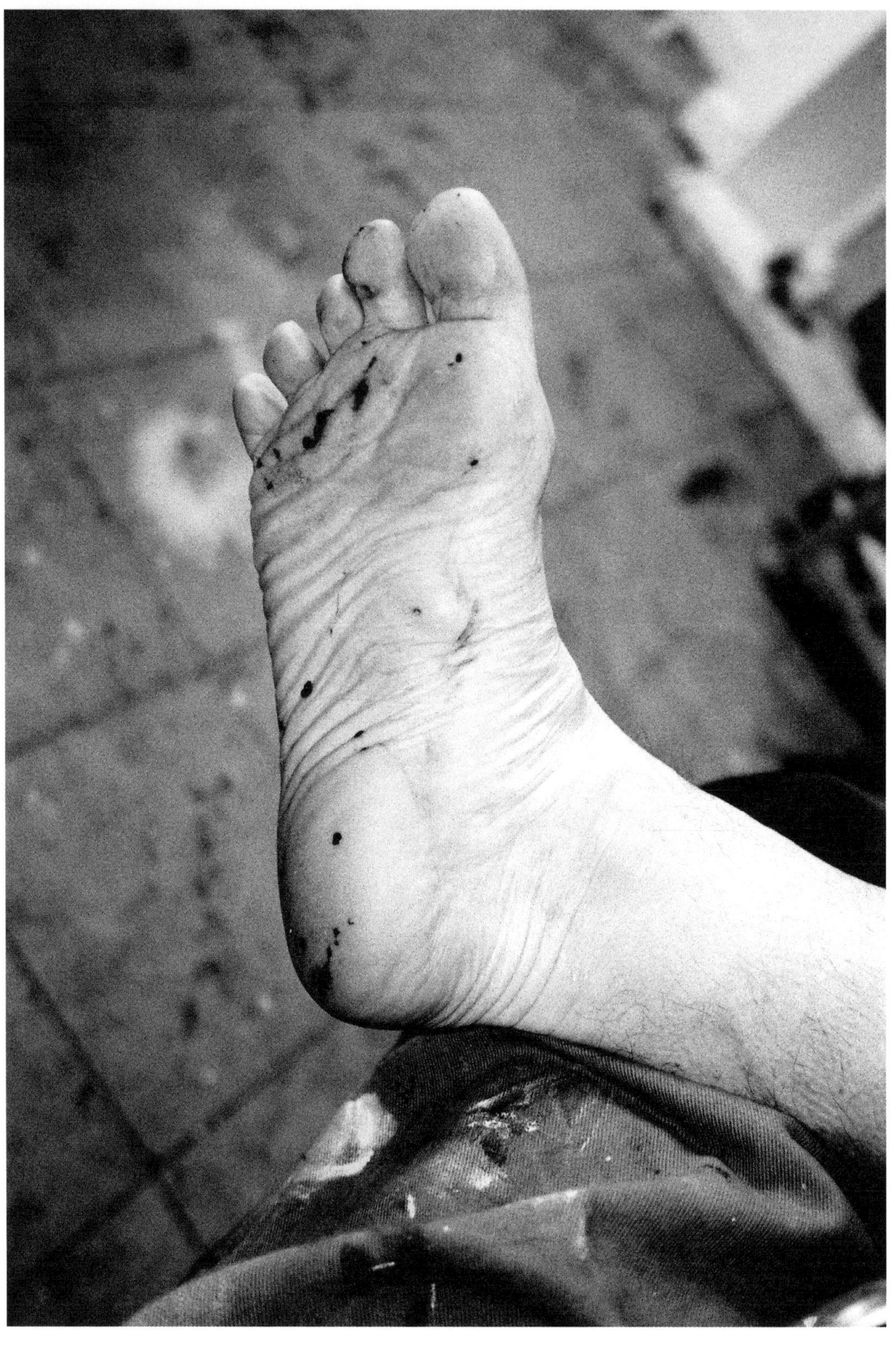

My right foot, 2017
35mm film

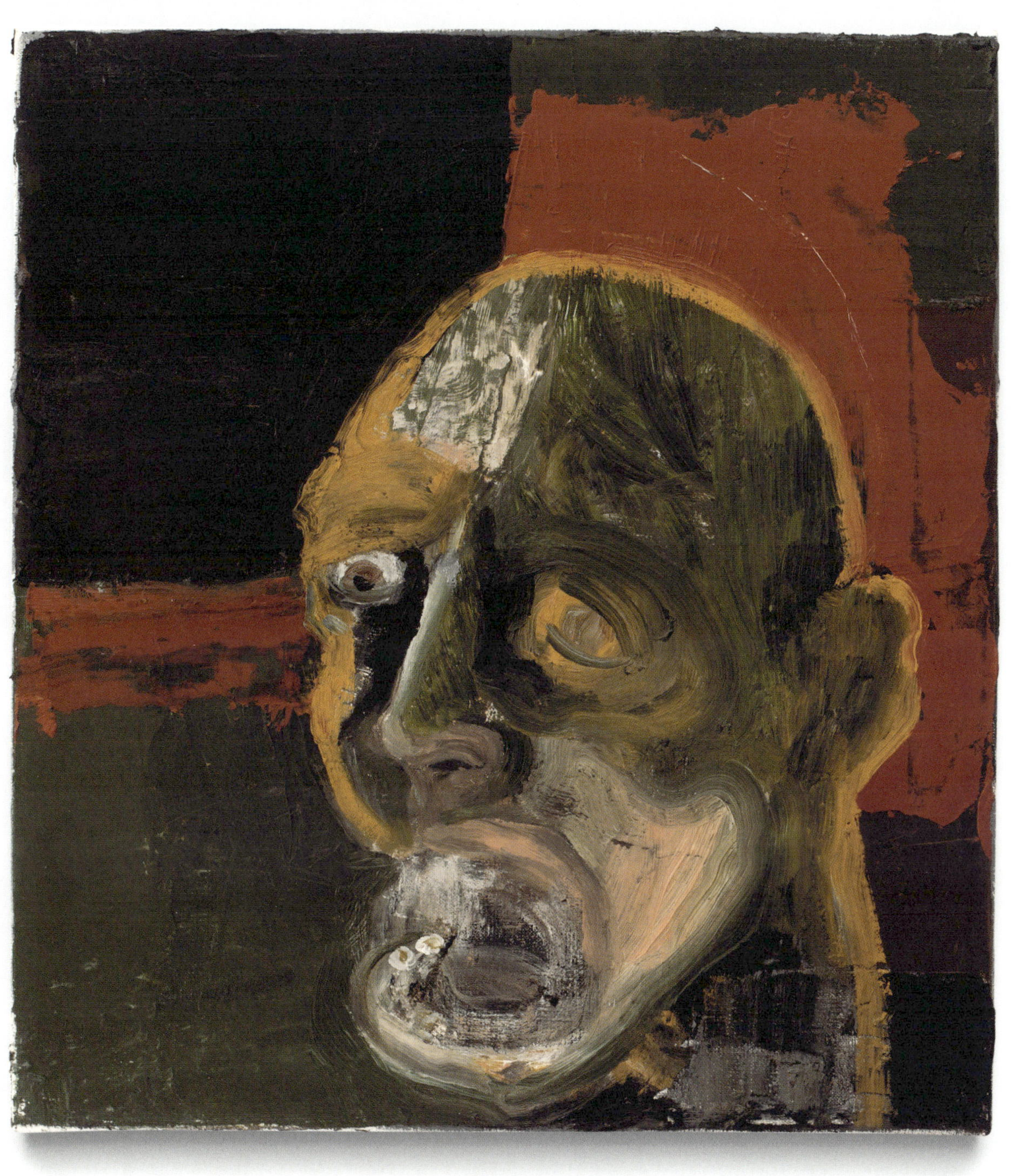

Untitled, 2017
Oil on linen canvas
40cm x 46cm

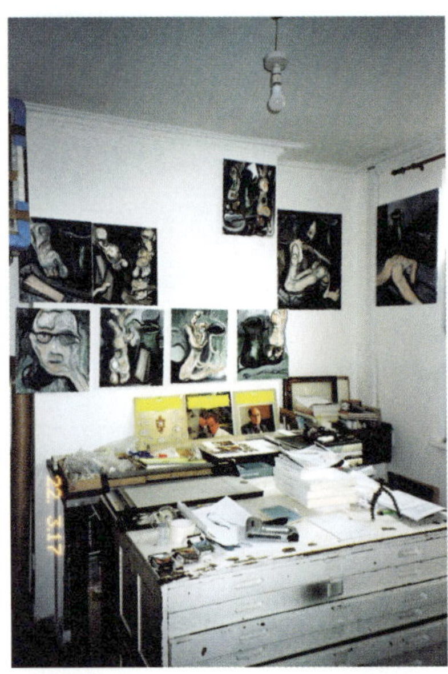
22. 3.17
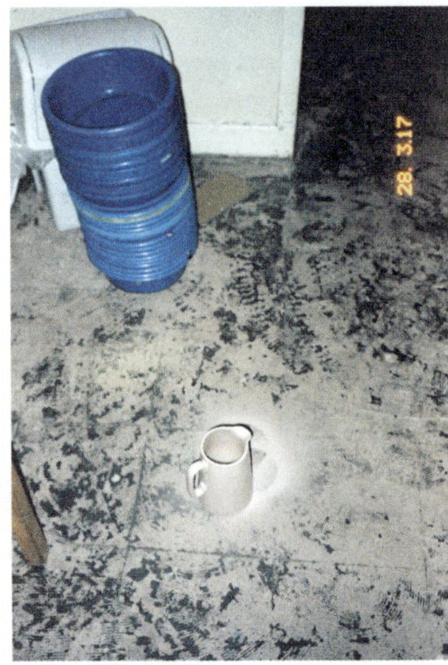
28. 3.17
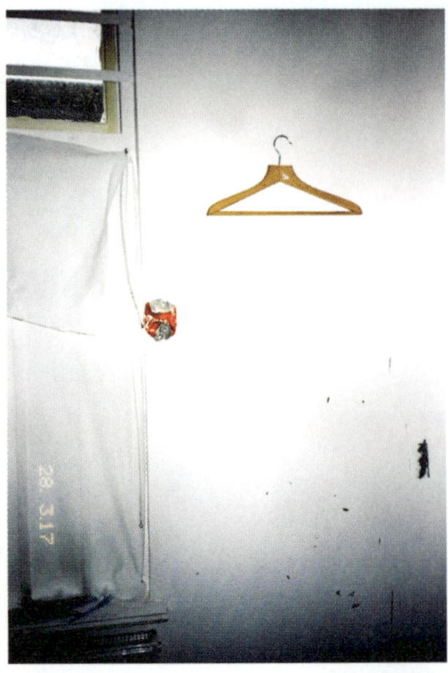
28. 3.17
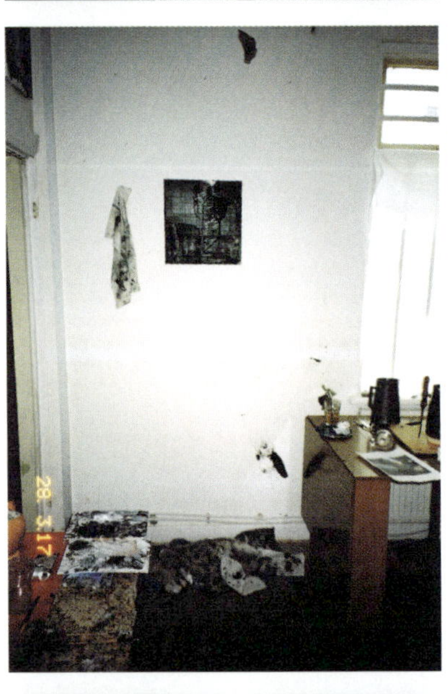
28. 3.17
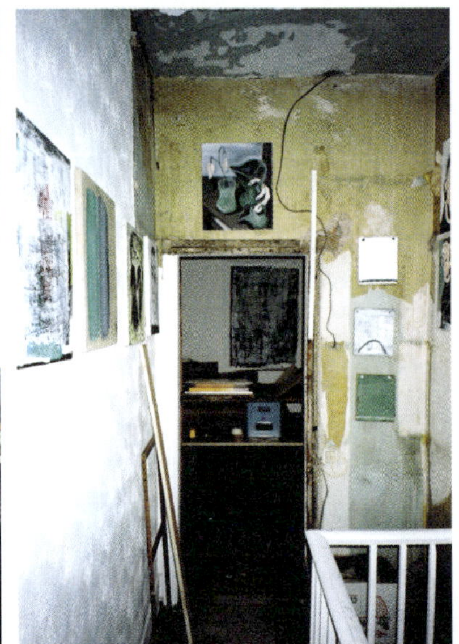
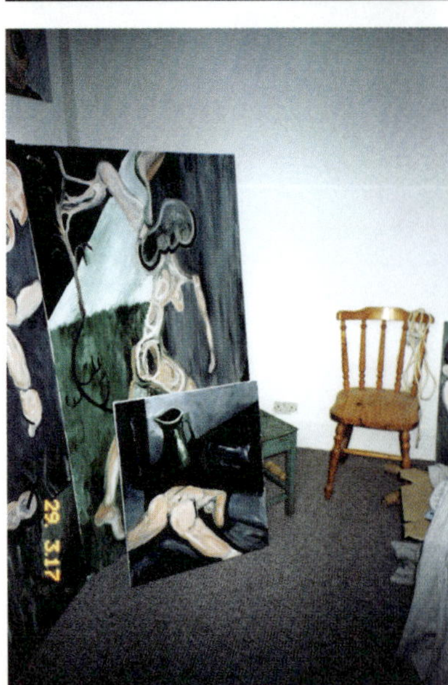
29. 3.17
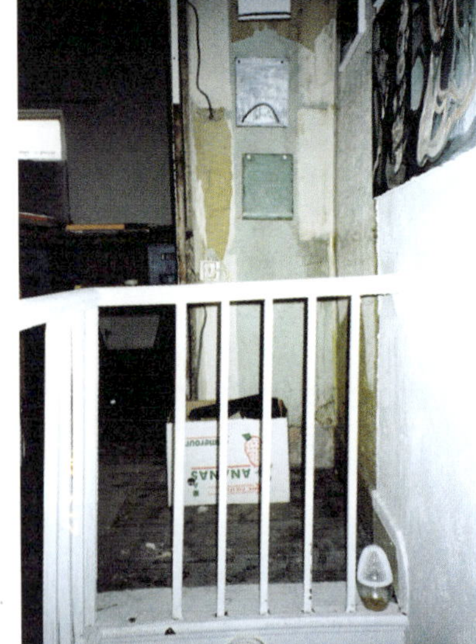
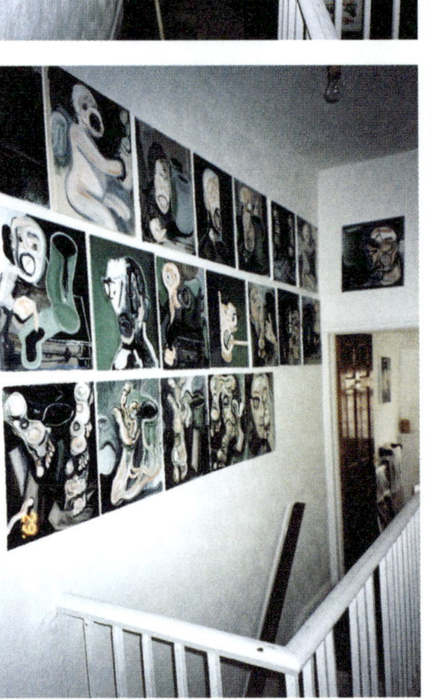
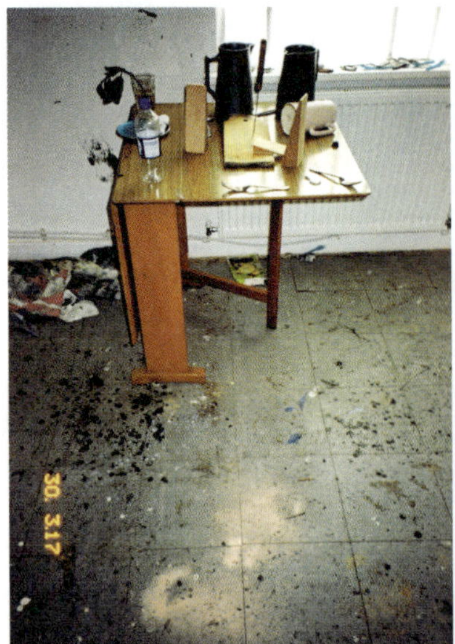
30. 3.17

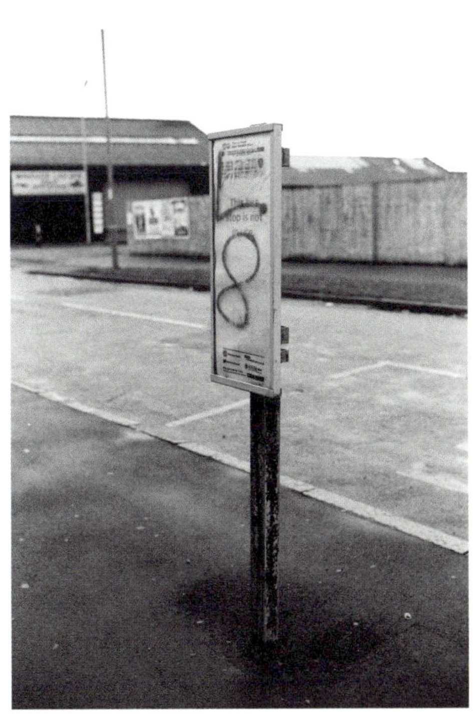

L8, Windsor Street, facing south west, 2017
35mm film

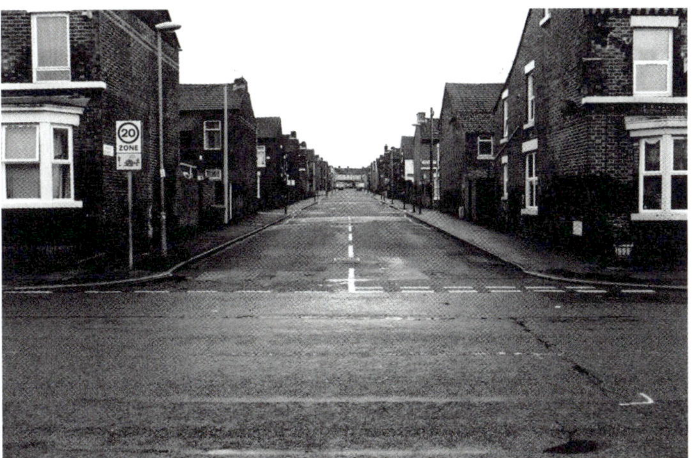

L8, Vining Street, facing south, 2017
35mm film

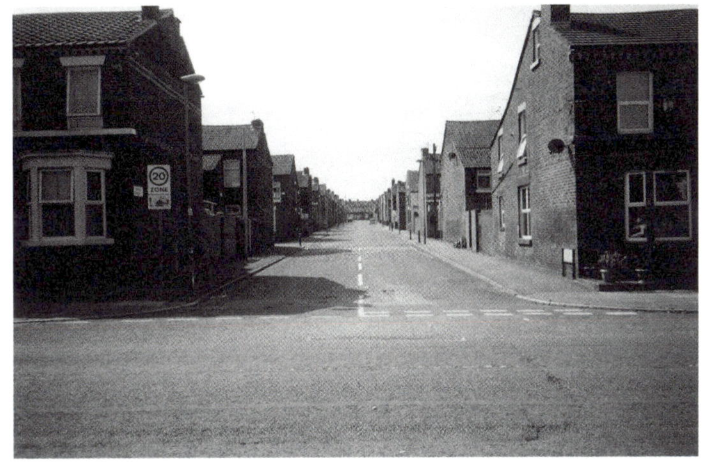

L8, Vining Street, facing south, 2017
35mm film

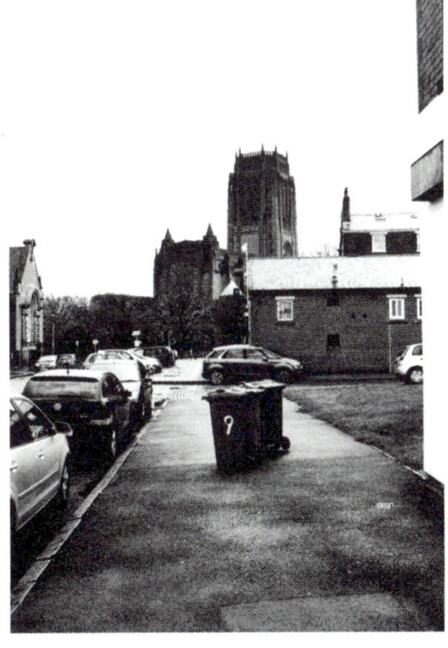

L8, Windsor Street, facing north, 2017
35mm film

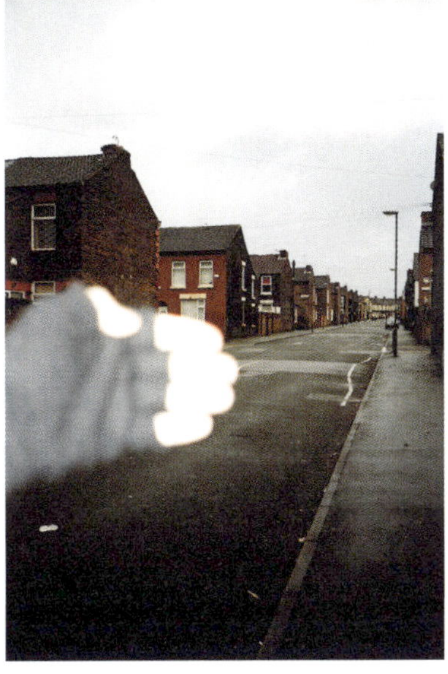

L8, Vining Street, facing south, 2017
35mm film

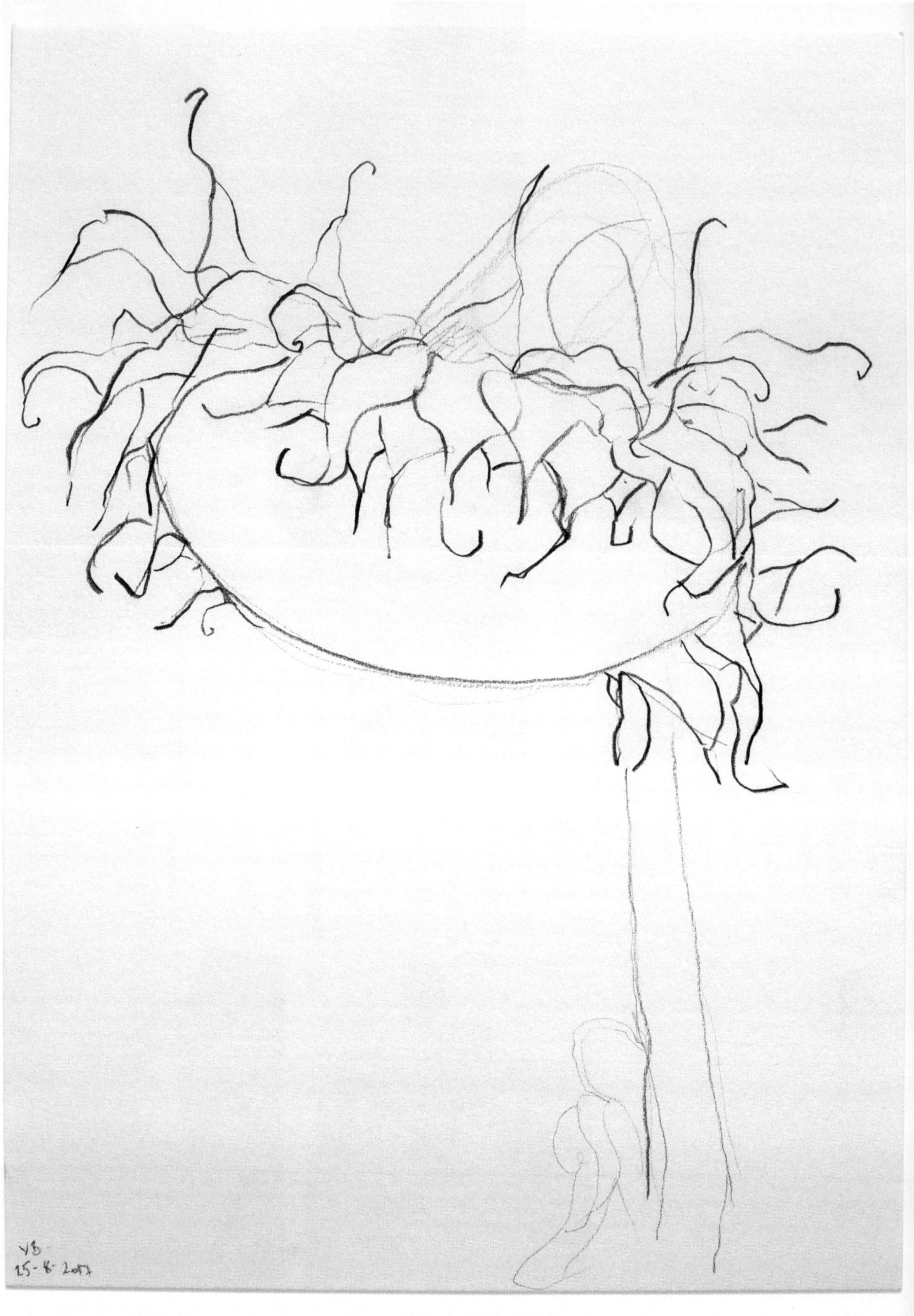
VB
25-8-2017

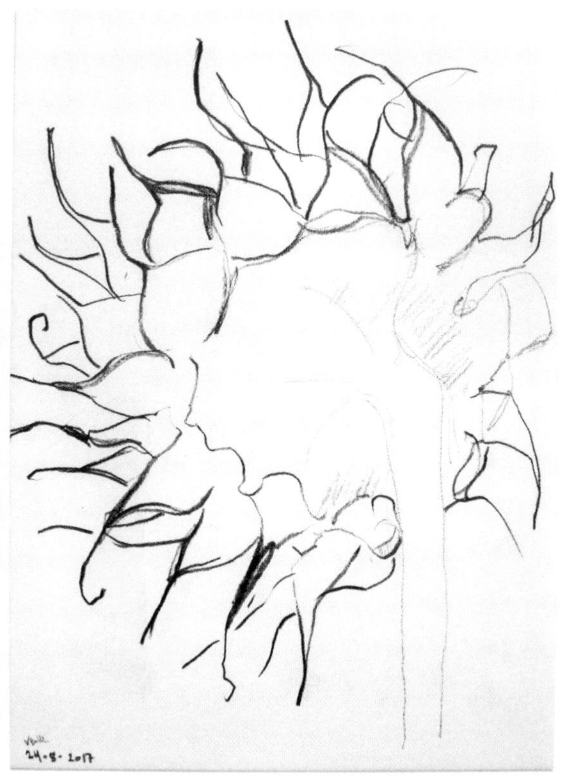

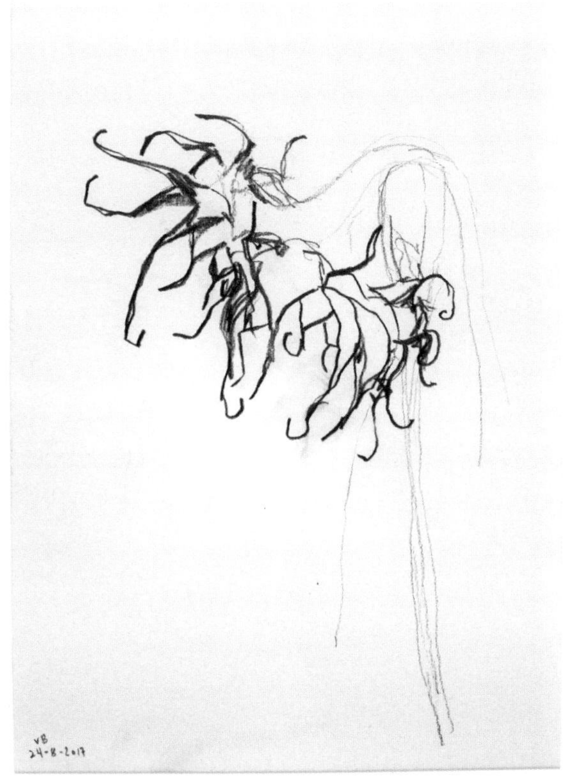

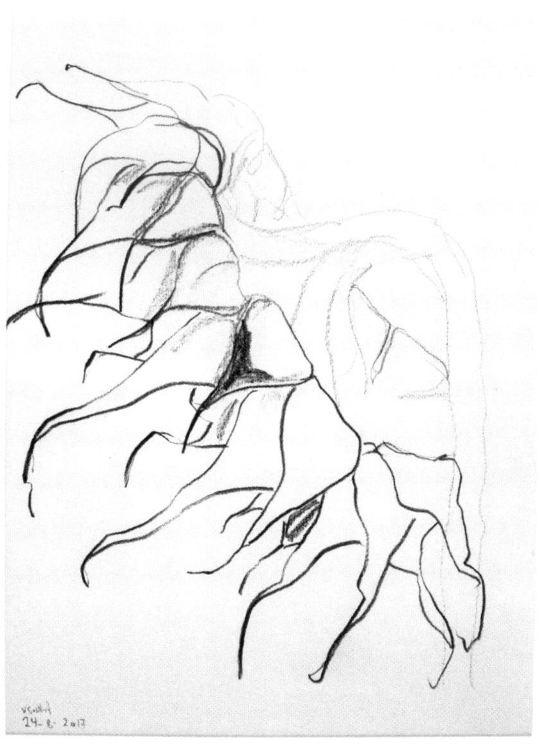

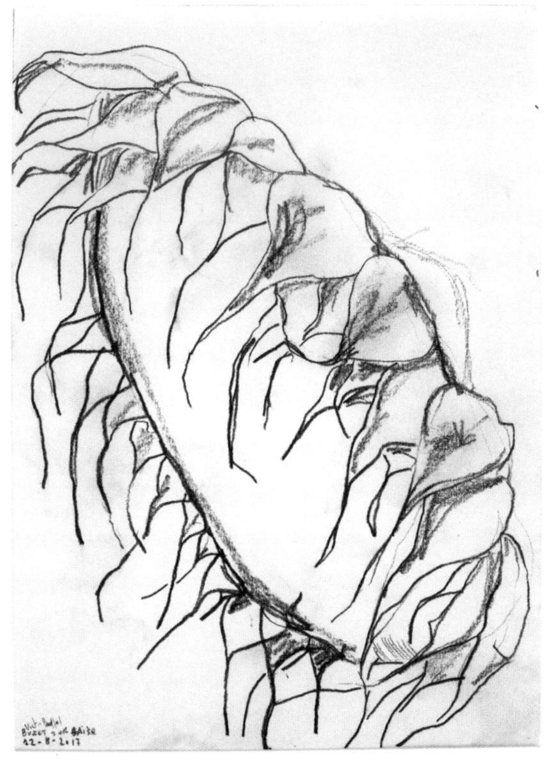

Sunflower, 2017
Pencil on paper
24cm x 32cm

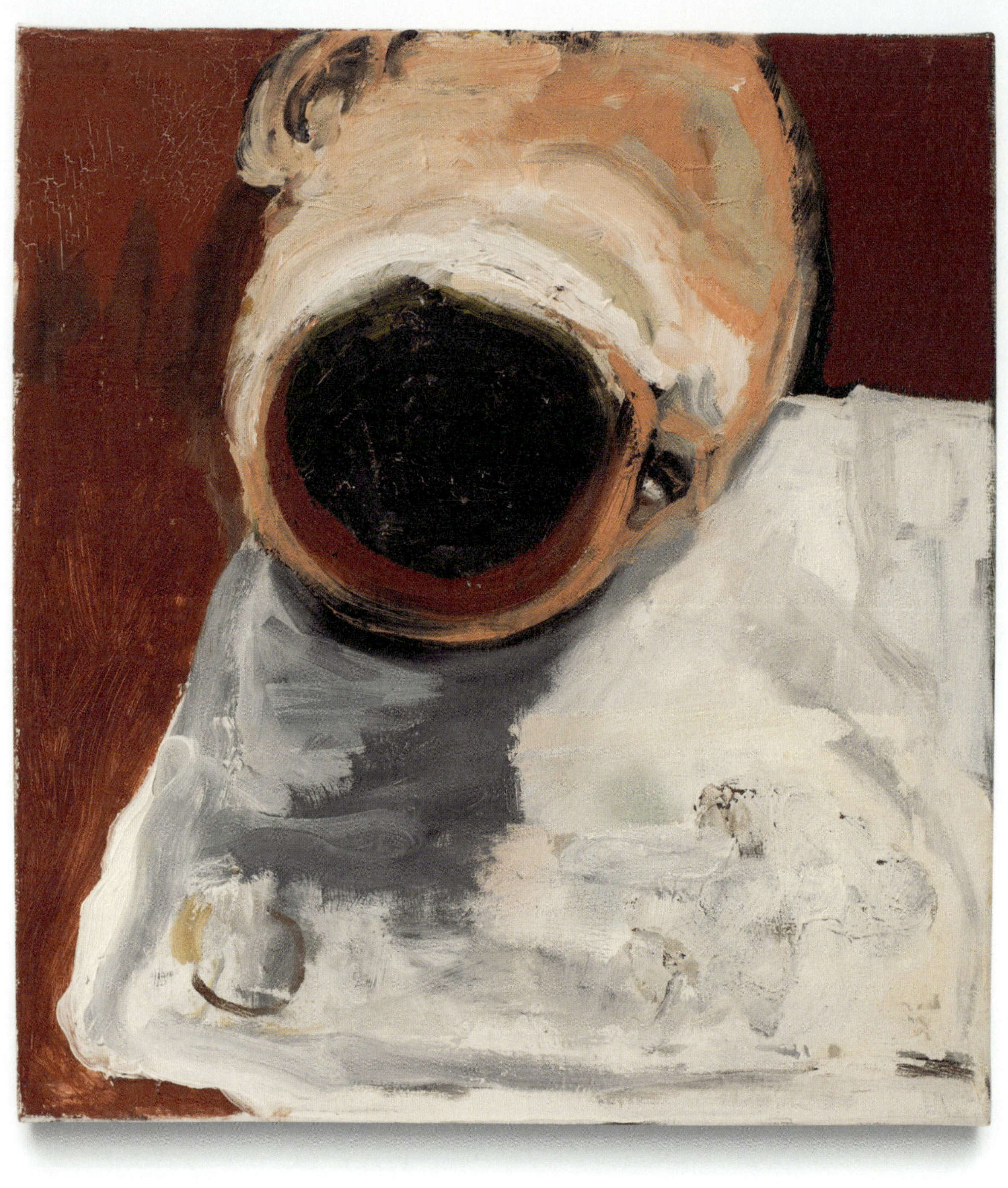

Croissant, 2017
Oil on linen canvas
40cm x 46cm

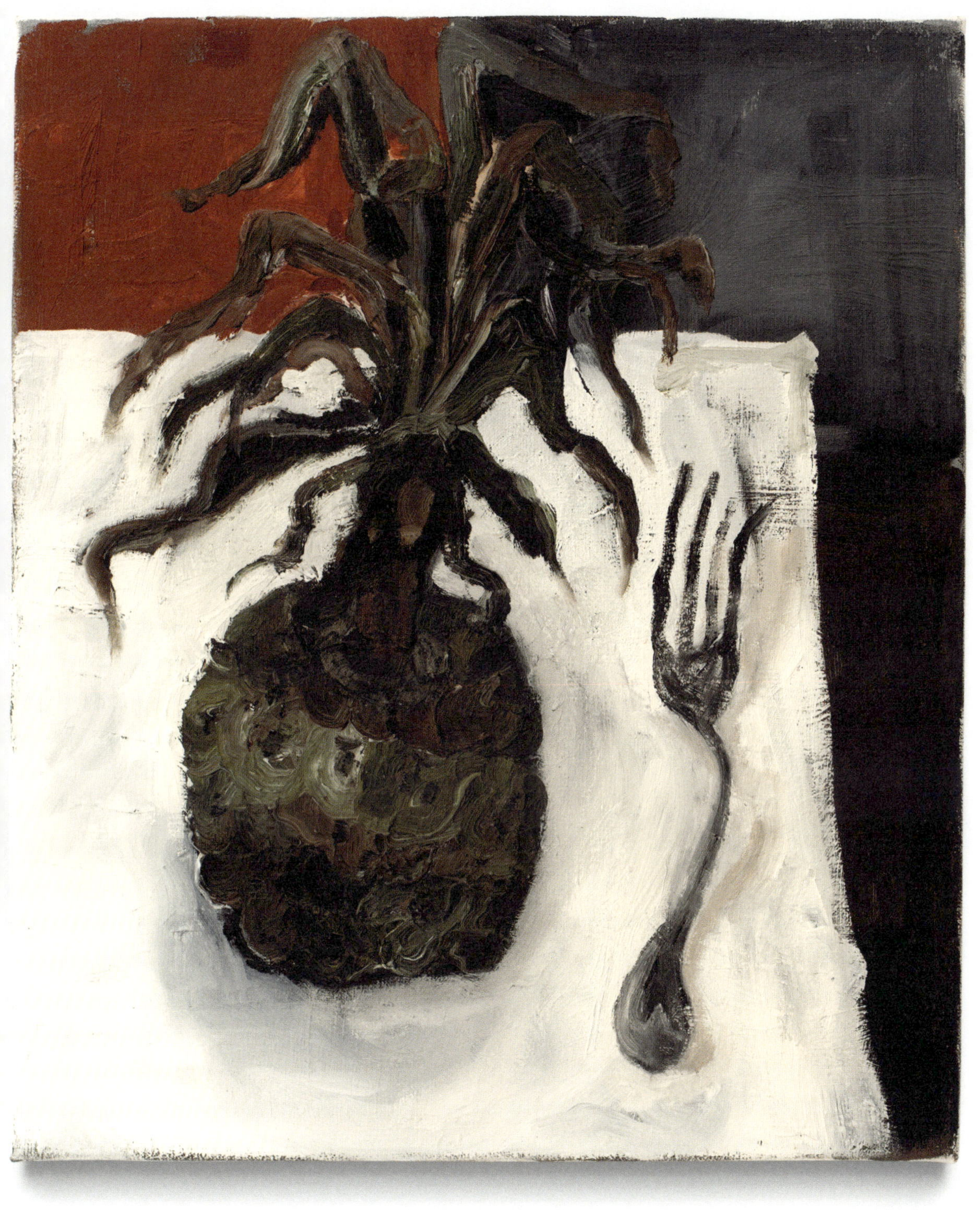

Untitled, 2017
Oil on linen canvas
38cm x 46cm

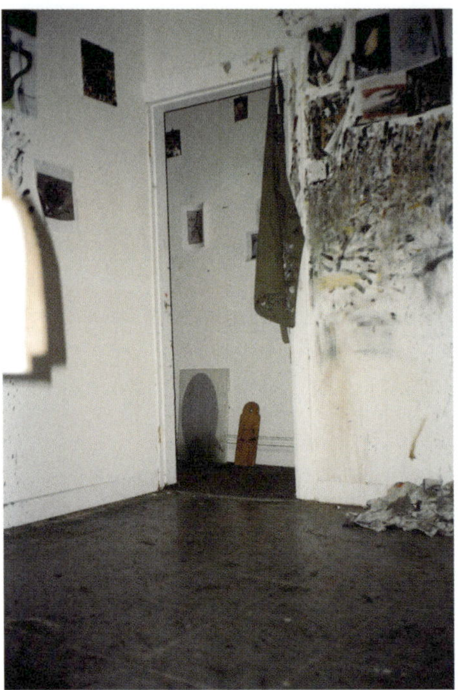

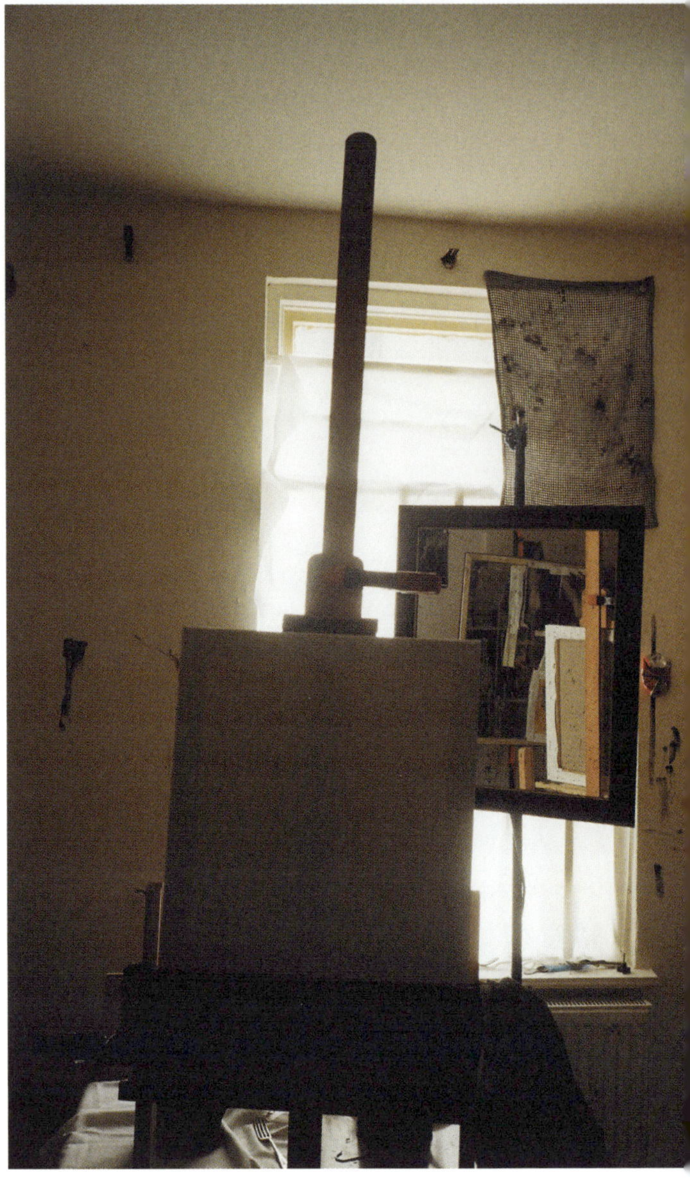

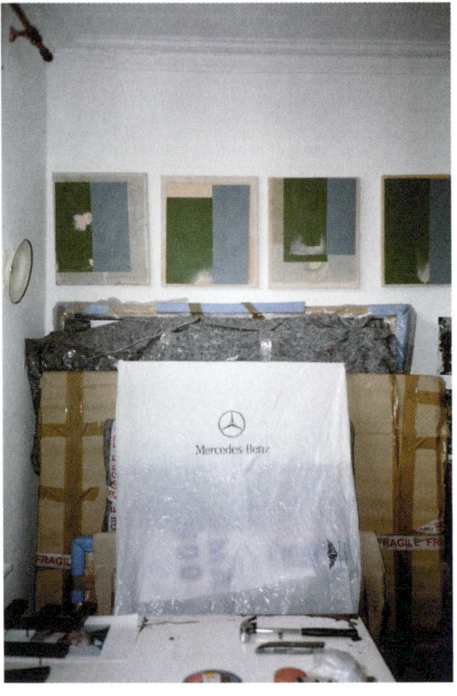

Studio documentation, 2017
35mm film

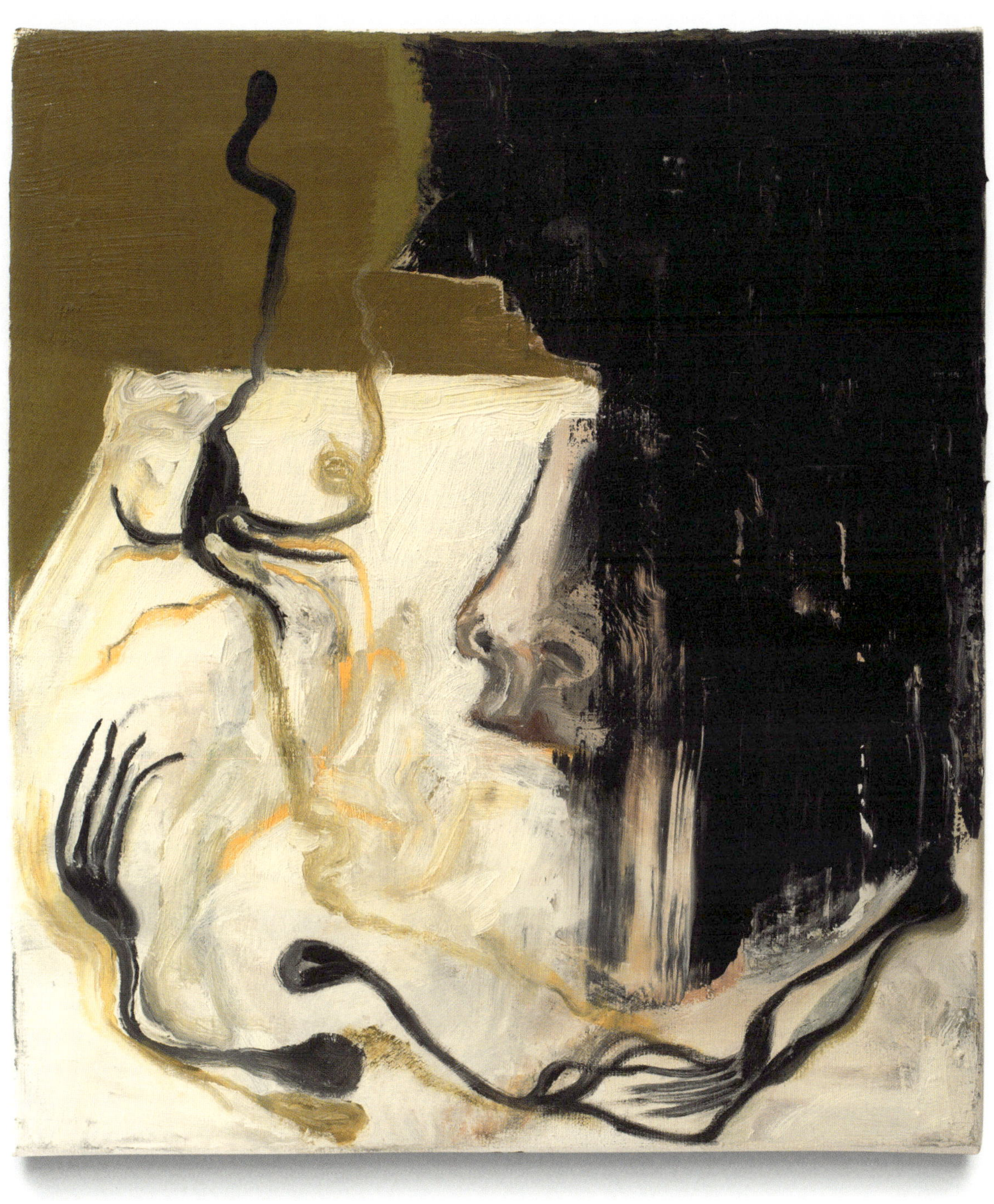

Untitled, 2017
Oil on linen canvas
40cm x 46cm

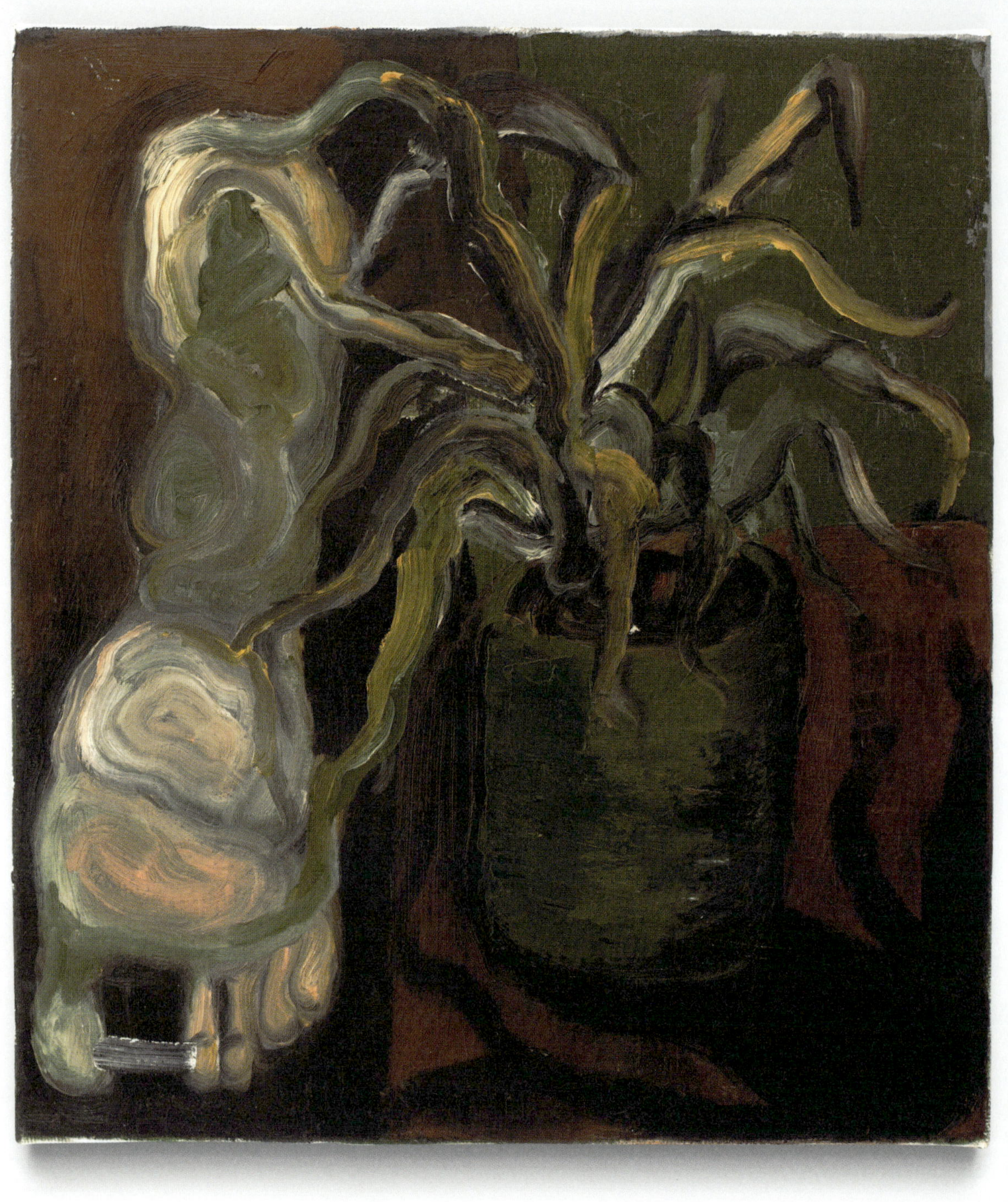

Born from Seed, 2017
Oil on linen canvas
38cm x 46cm

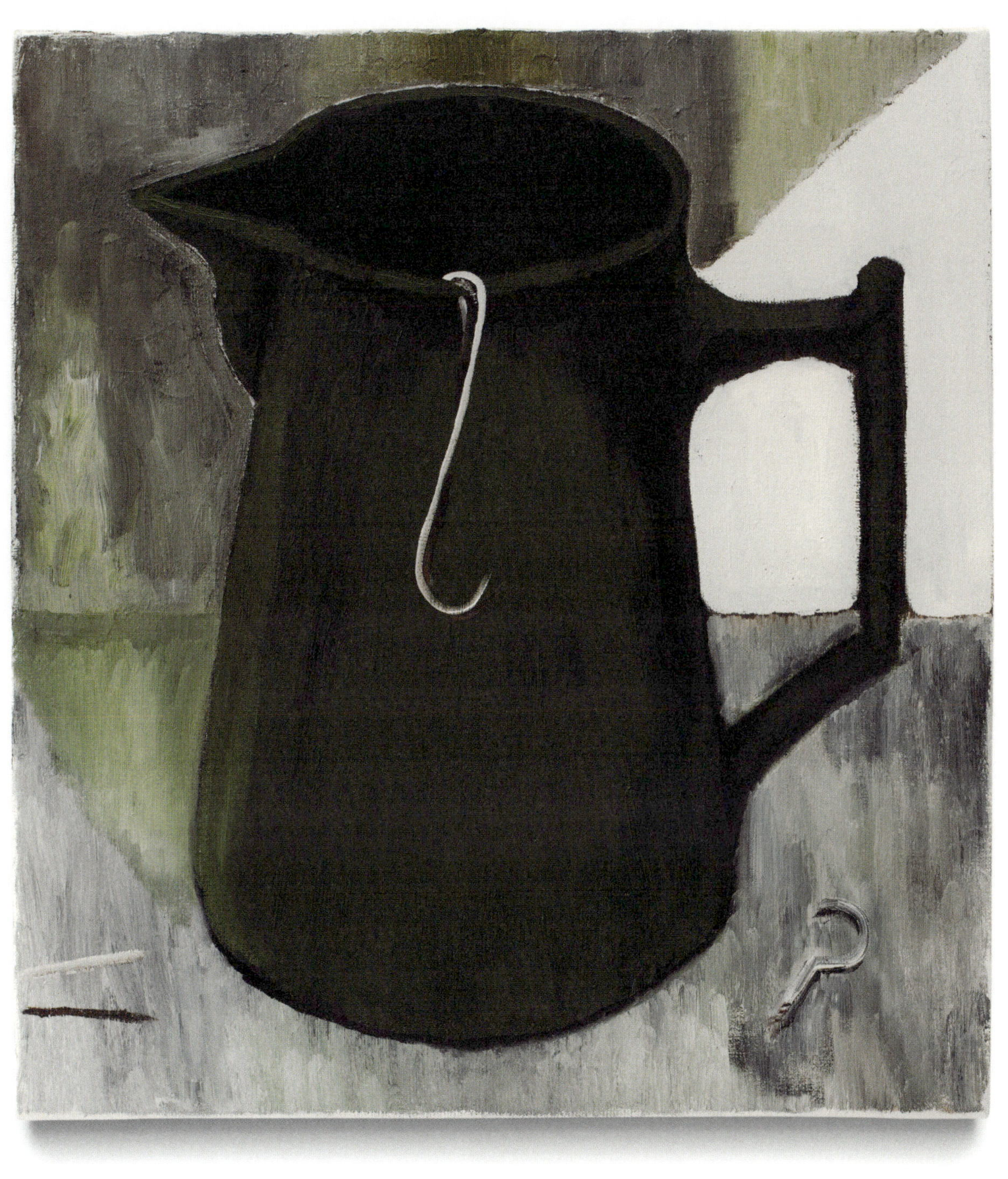

Untitled, 2017
Oil on linen canvas
40cm x 46cm

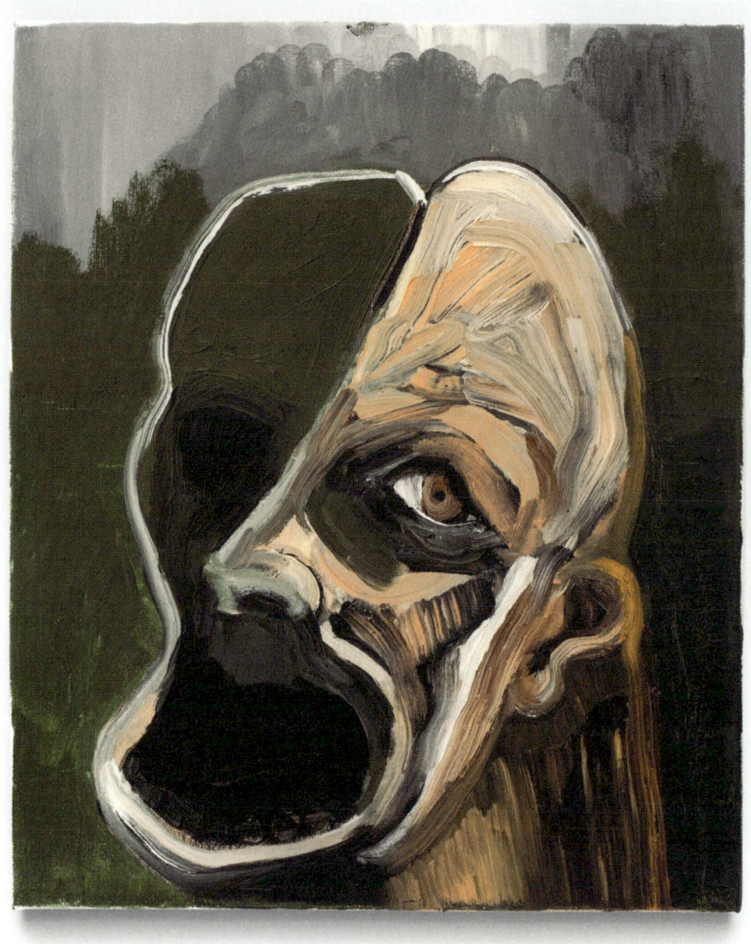

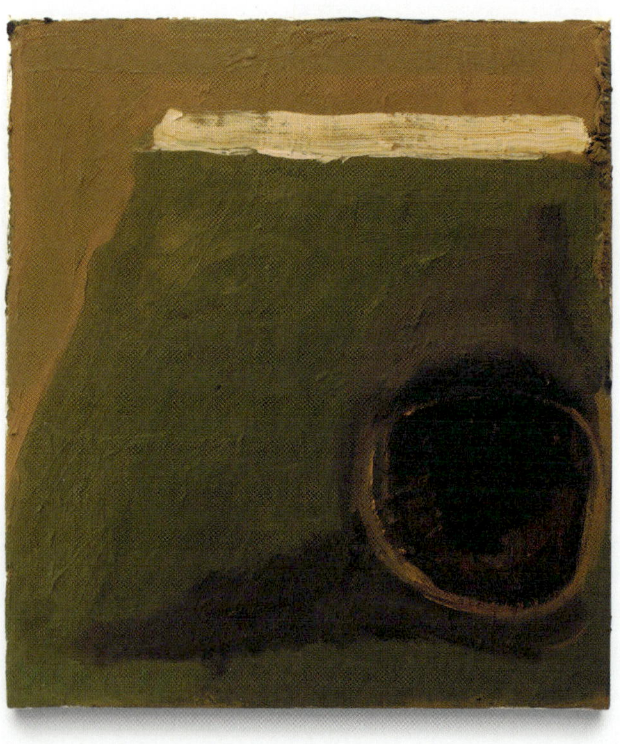

Self, 2017
Oil on linen canvas
38cm x 46cm

Hole, Table, Stuck, 2017 – 20
Oil on linen canvas
40cm x 46cm

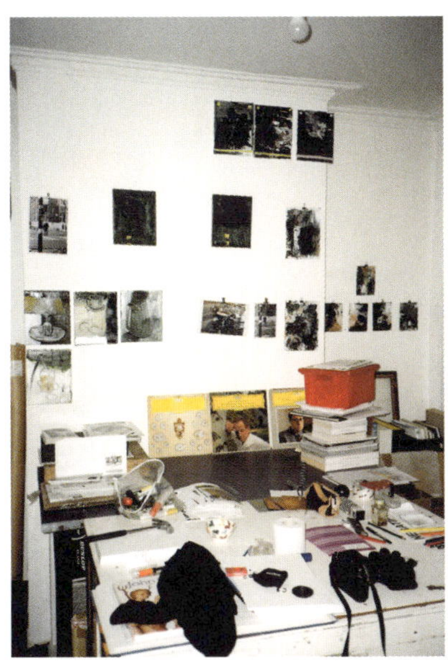
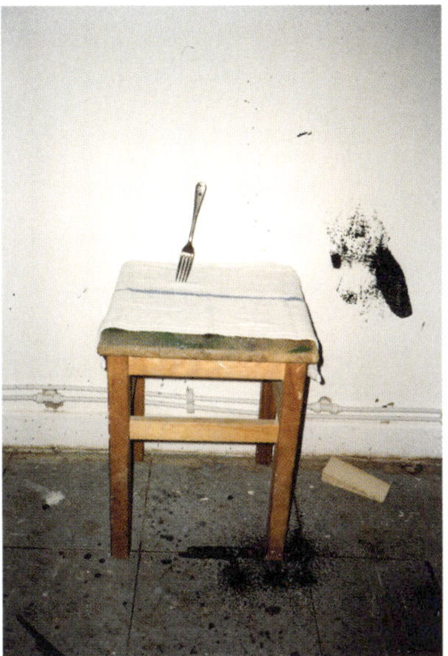
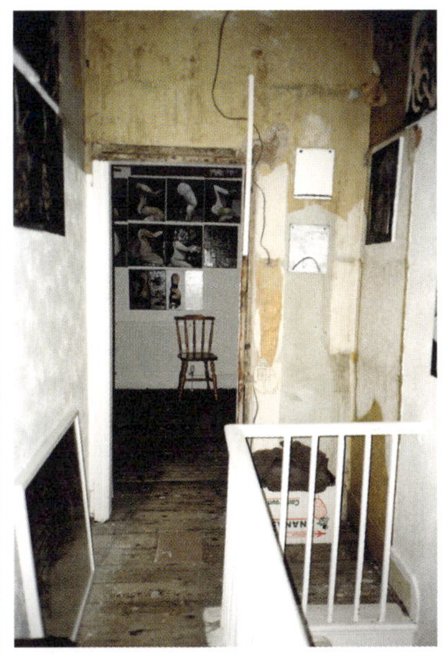
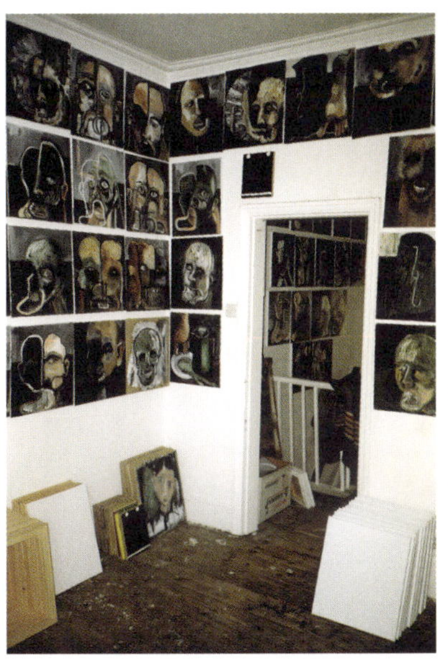
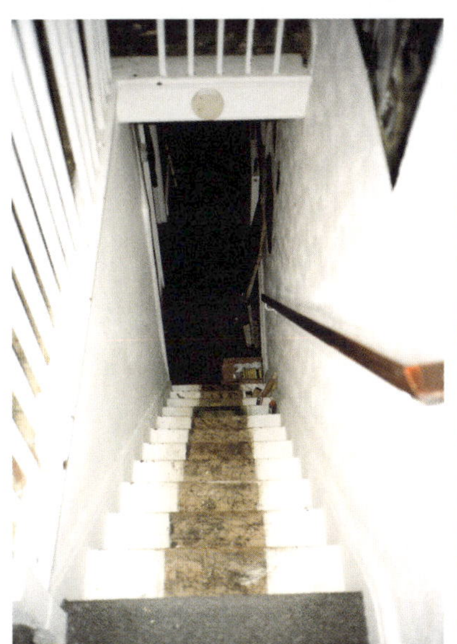
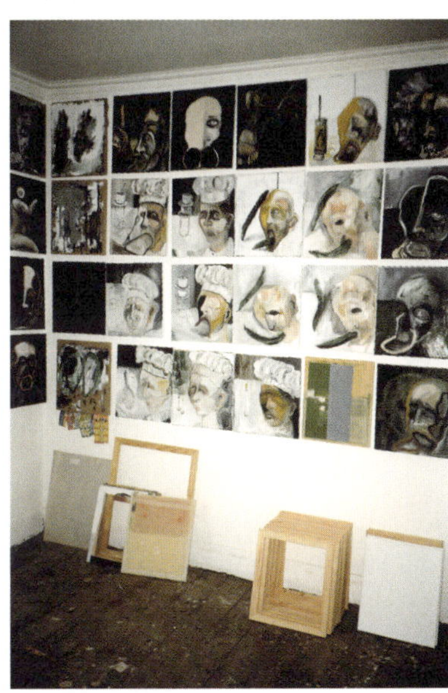
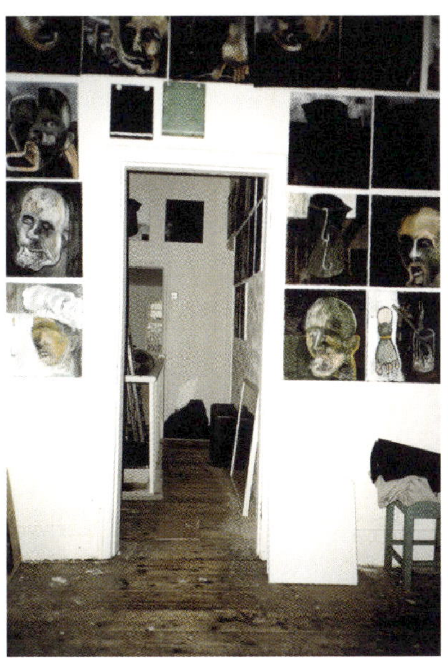
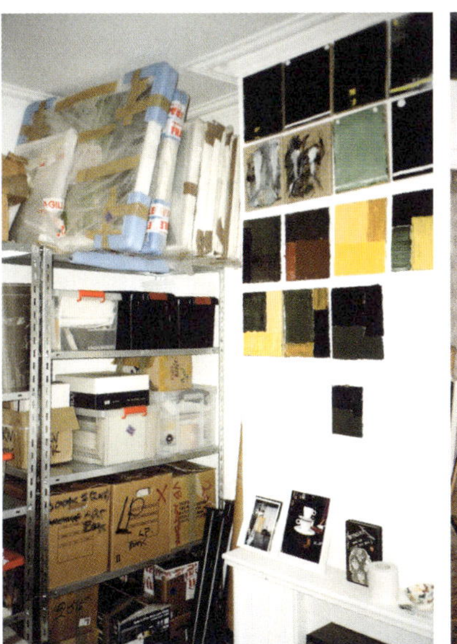
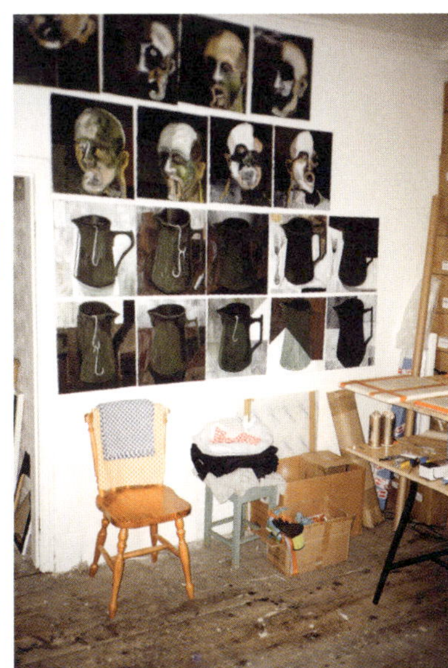

Mother, 2017
Oil on linen canvas
38cm x 46cm

Mother, 2017
Oil on linen canvas
38cm x 46cm

Mother, 2017
Oil on linen canvas
40cm x 46cm

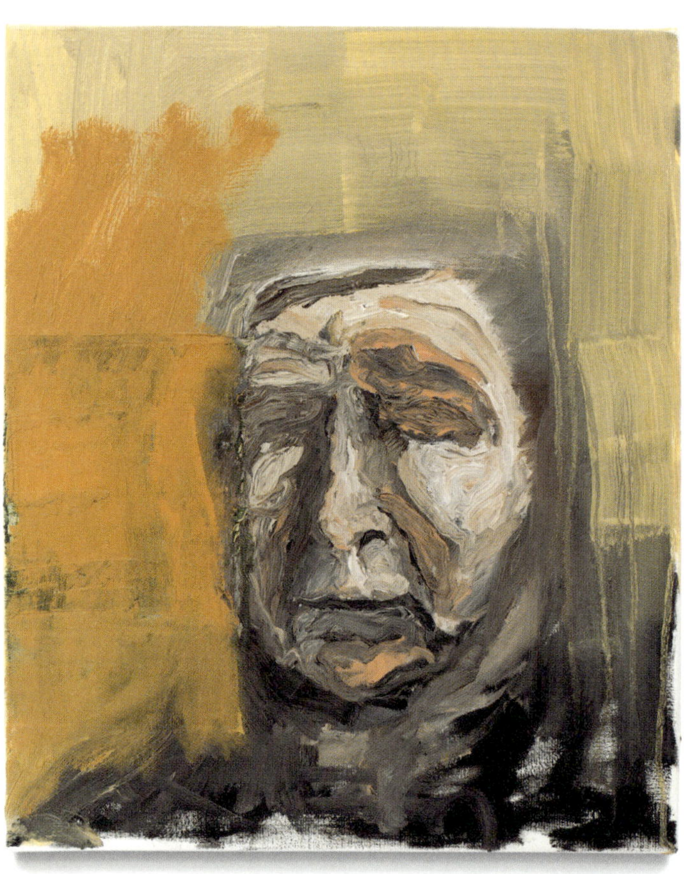

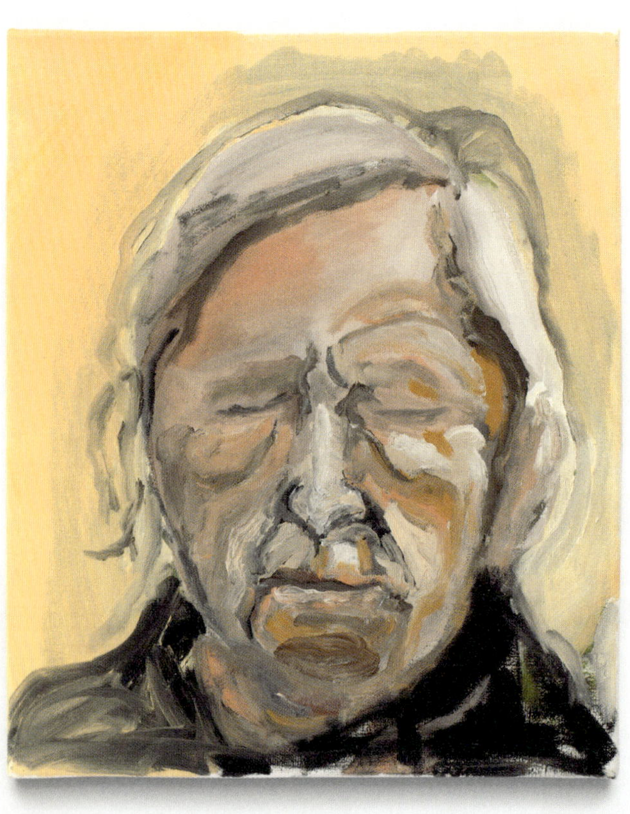

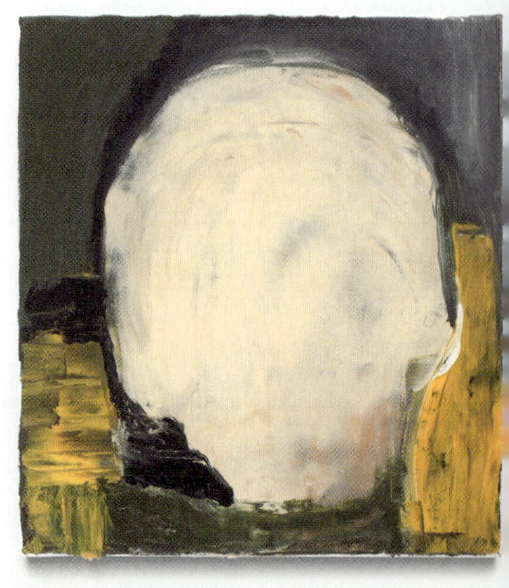

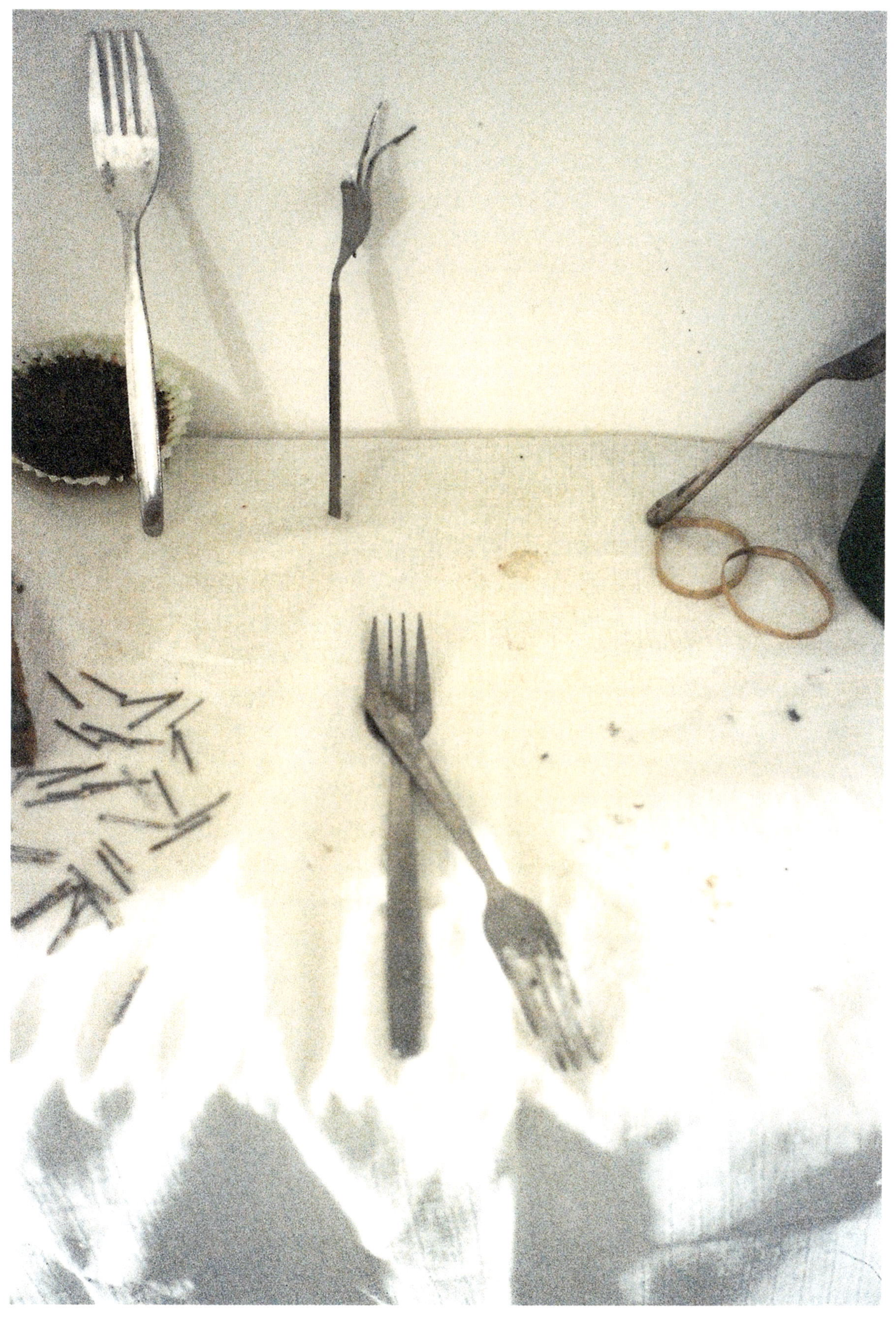

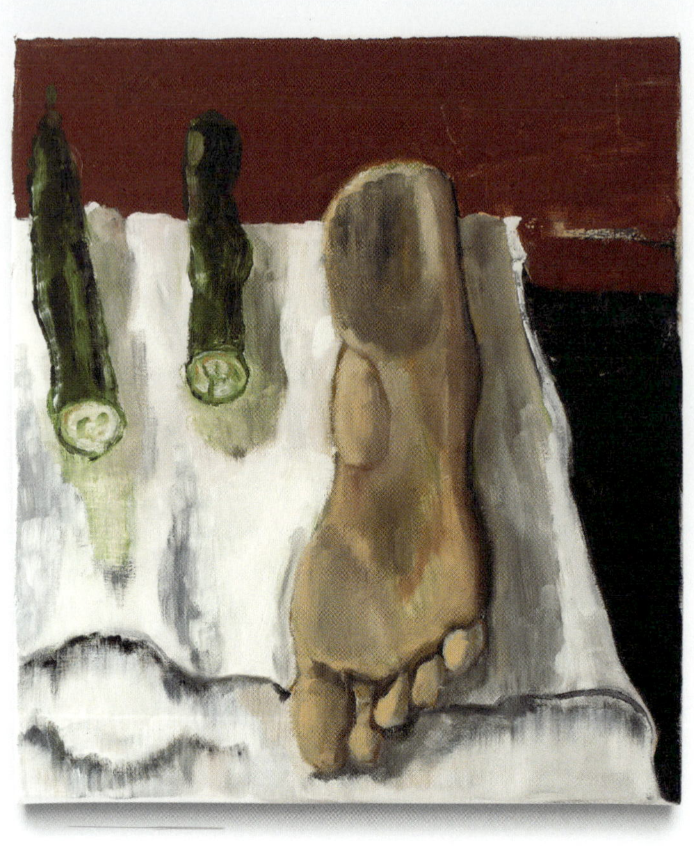

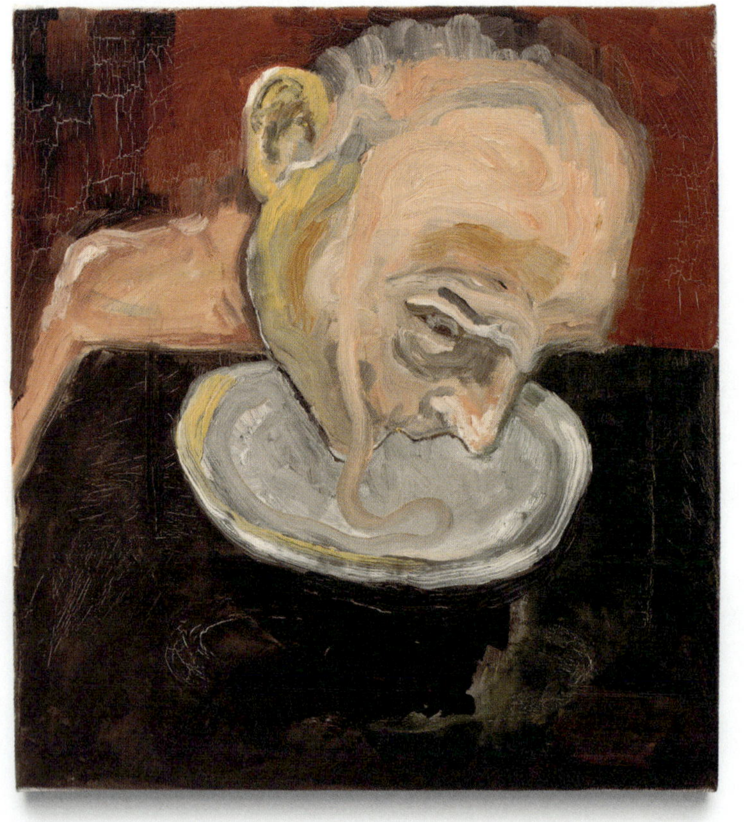

Born Radin, 2017 – 2
Oil on linen canvas
40cm x 46cm

Untitled, 2017 – 201
Oil on linen canvas
40cm x 46cm

Drunk, 2017 – 2018
Oil on linen canvas
50cm x 60cm

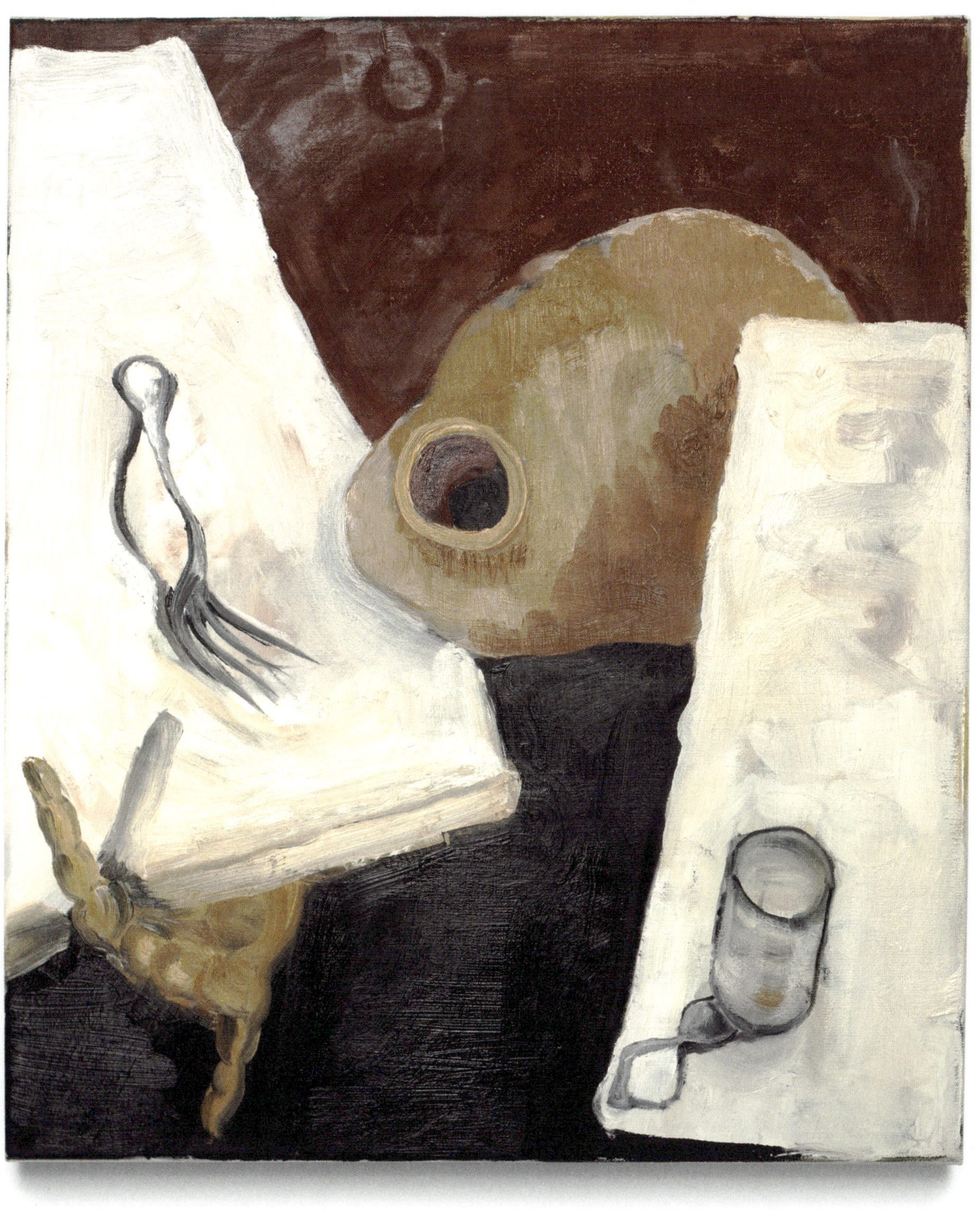

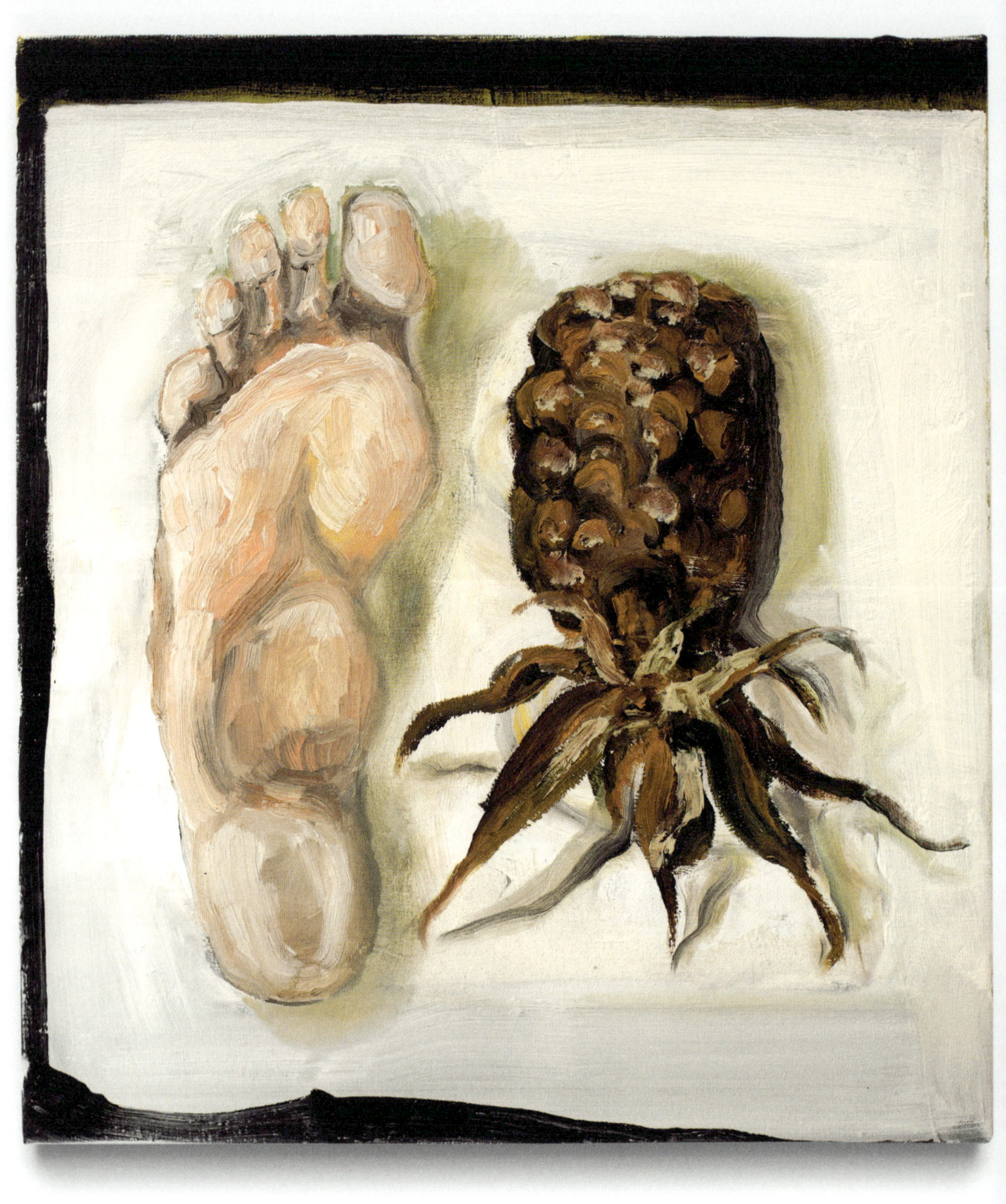

Unable to Move, 2017 – 2018
Oil on linen canvas
40cm x 46cm

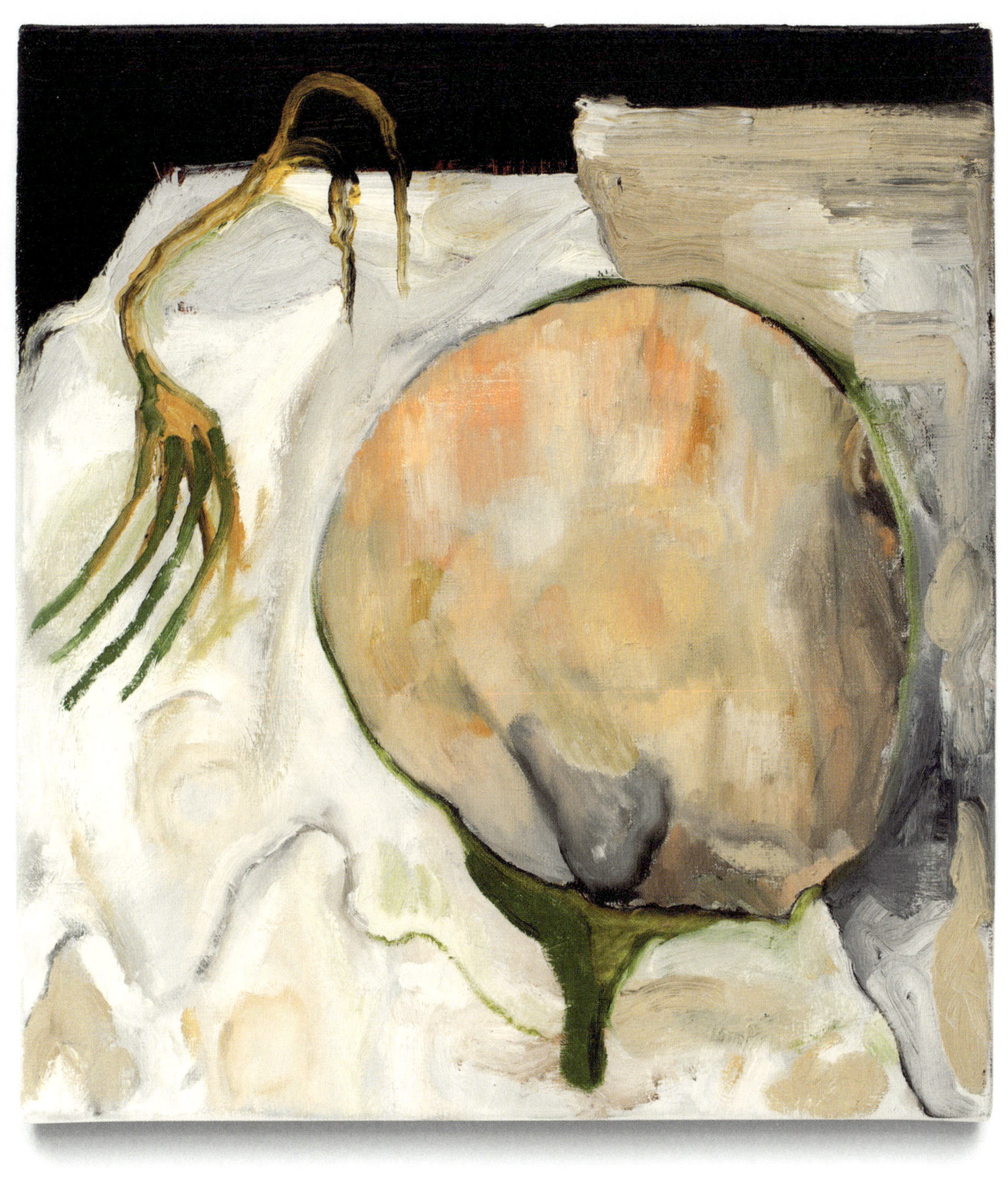

Corroded and Unable to Move, 2017 – 2018
Oil on linen canvas
40cm x 46cm

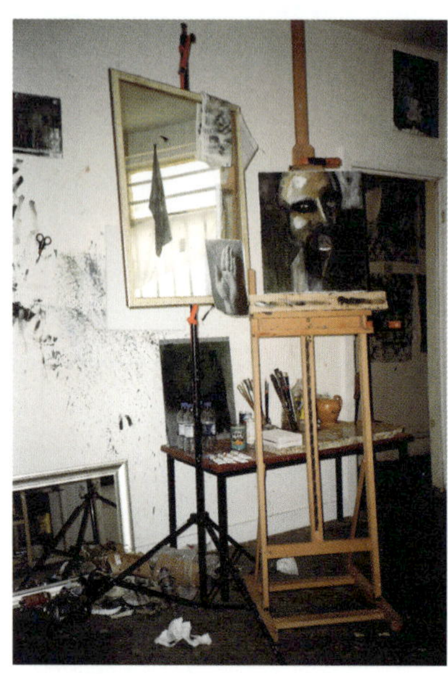
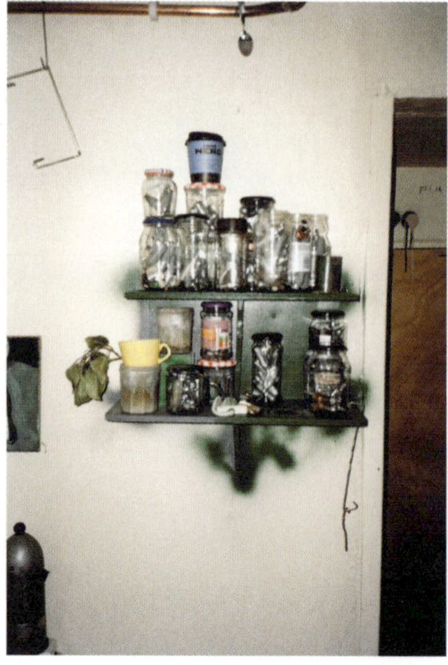
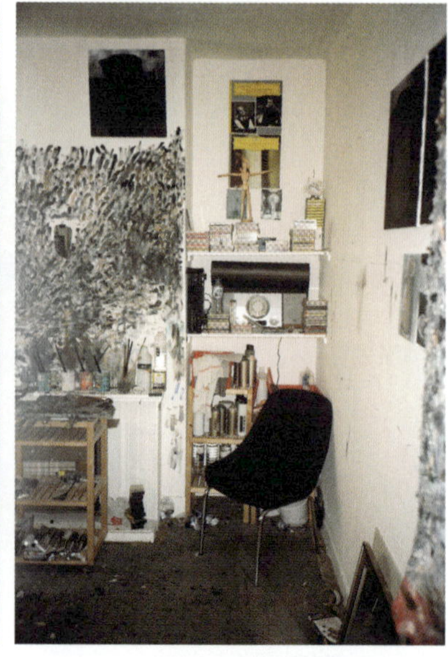
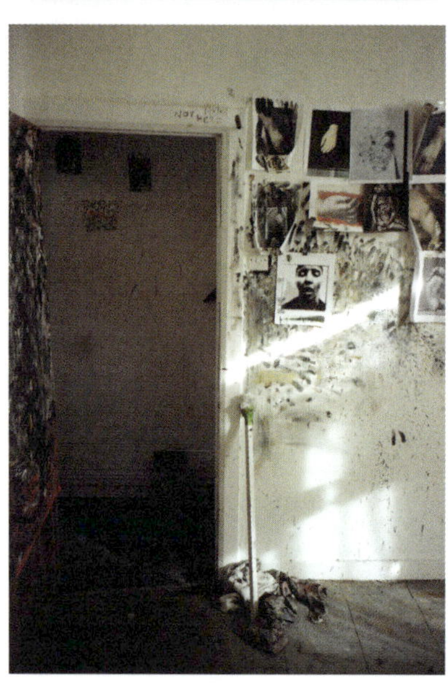
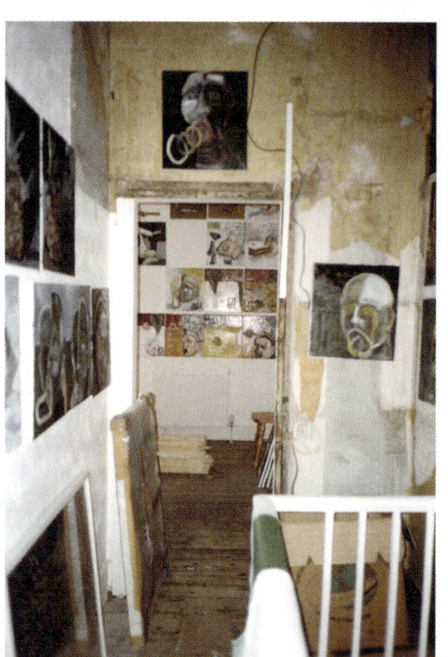
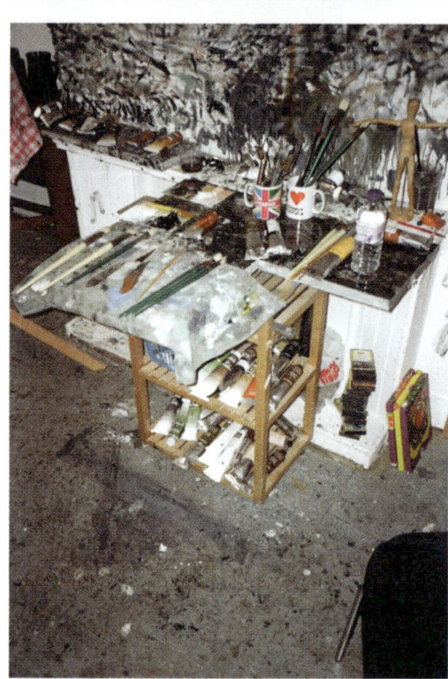
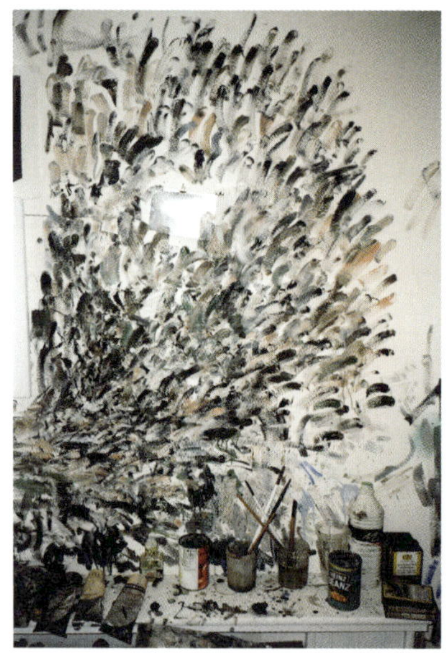
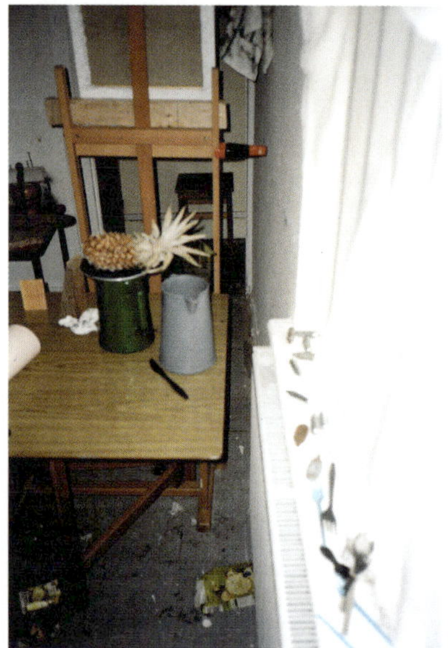
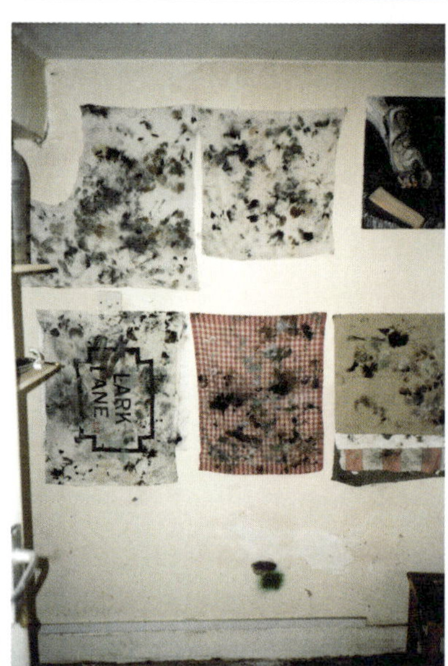
LARK
LANE

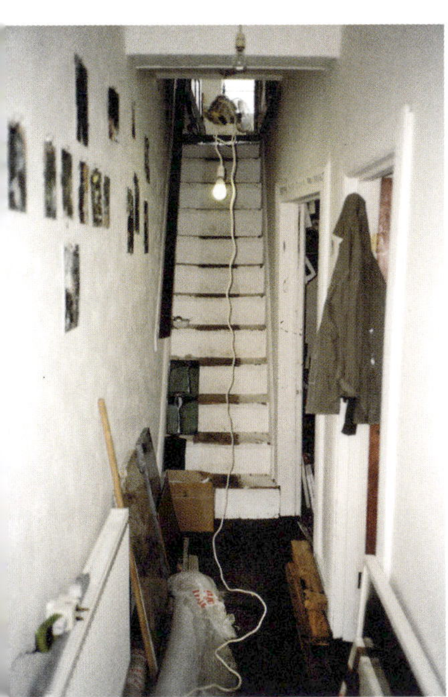

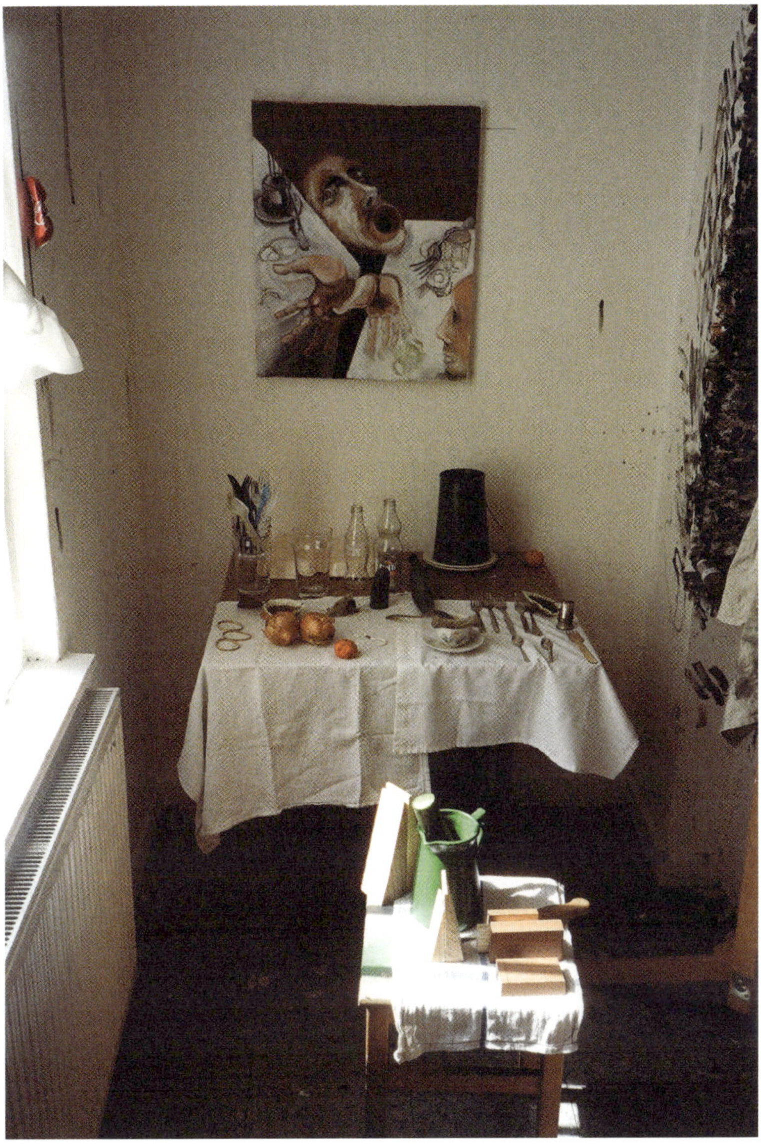

Studio documentation, 2018
35mm film

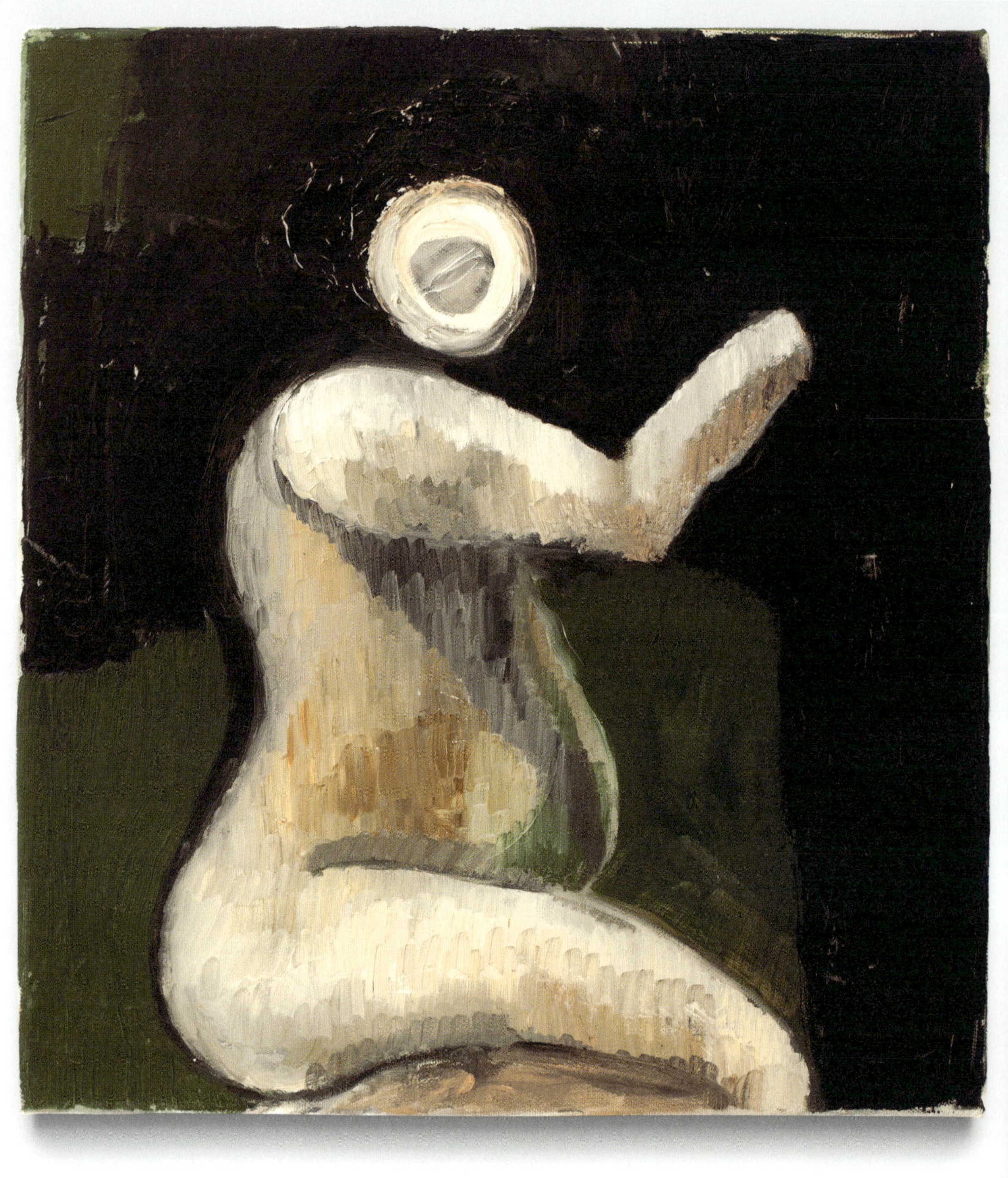

Rokeby Cherub, 2017 – 2018
Oil on linen canvas
40cm x 46cm

Untitled, 2018
Pencil, polychromos on pap
21cm x 29.7cm

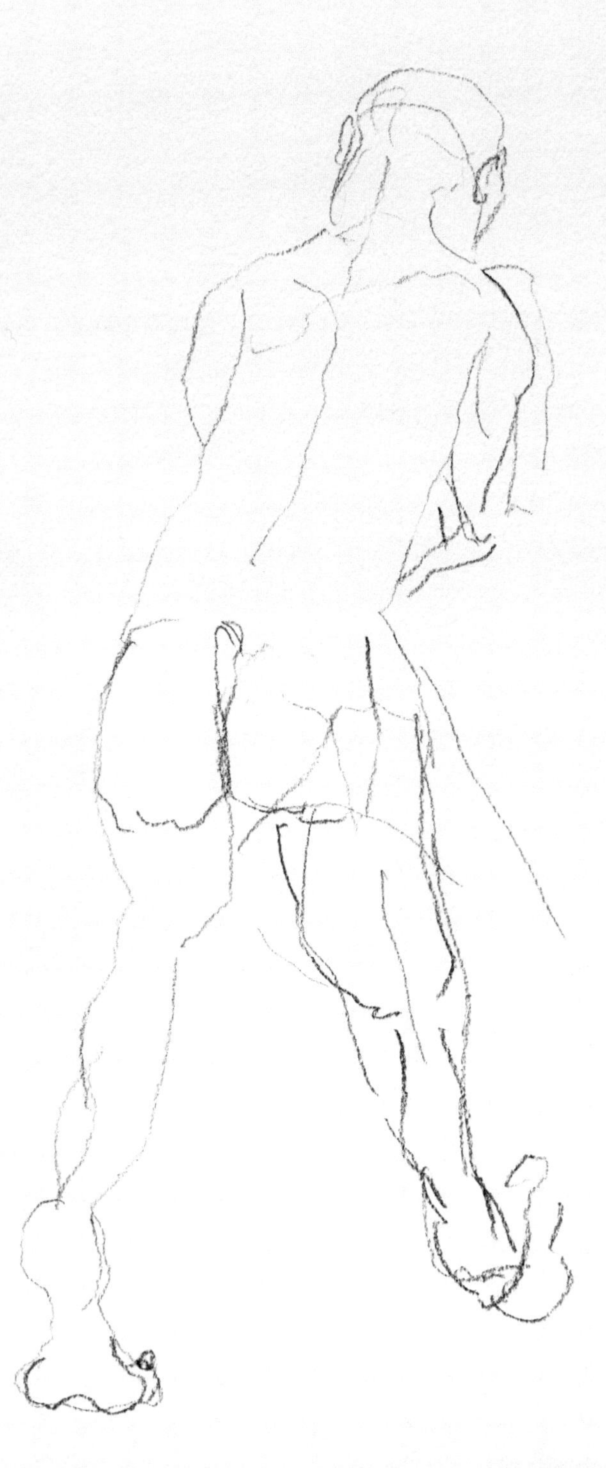
15.3.2018

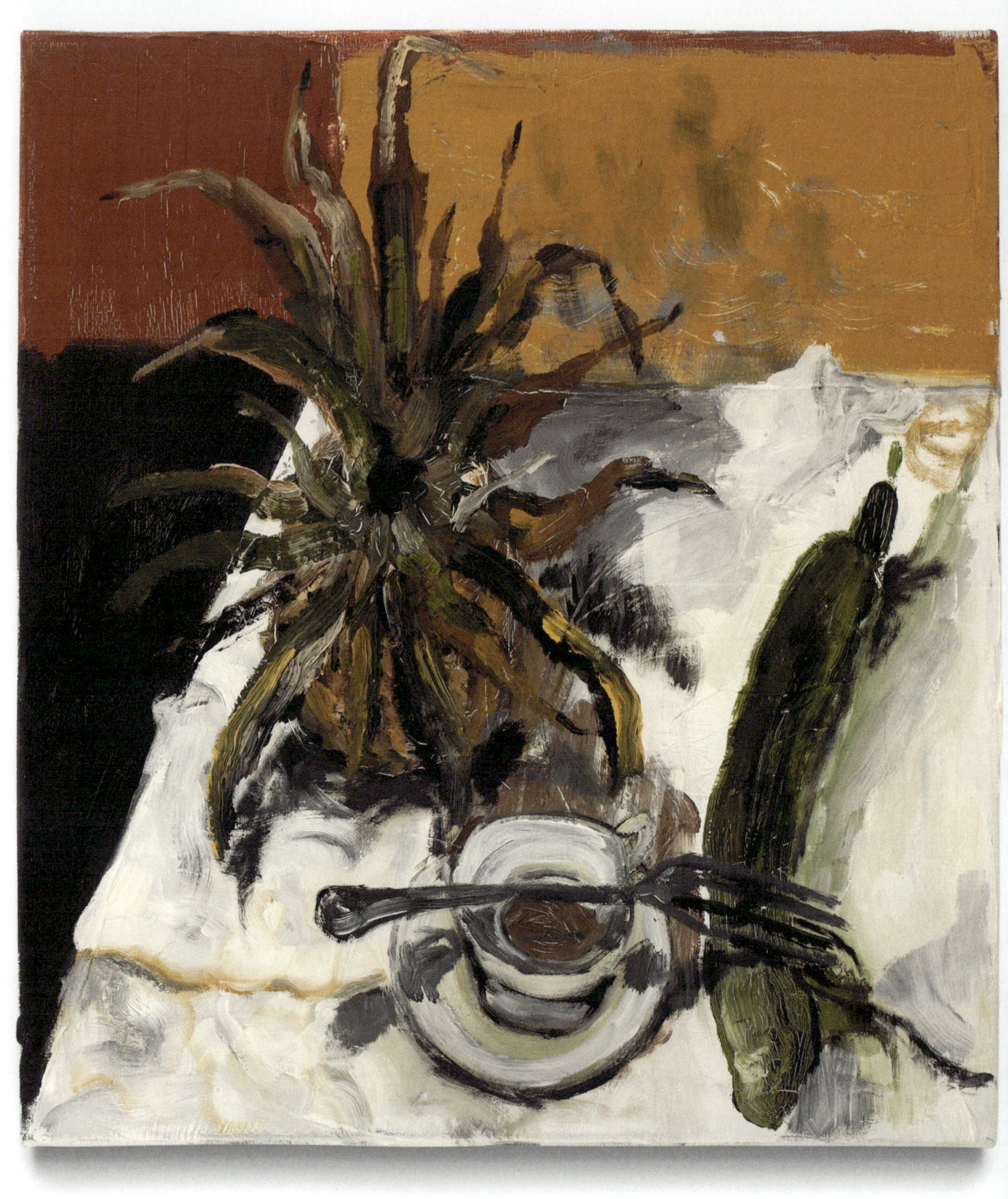

Issues with a Pineapple I, 2018
Oil on linen canvas
40cm x 46cm

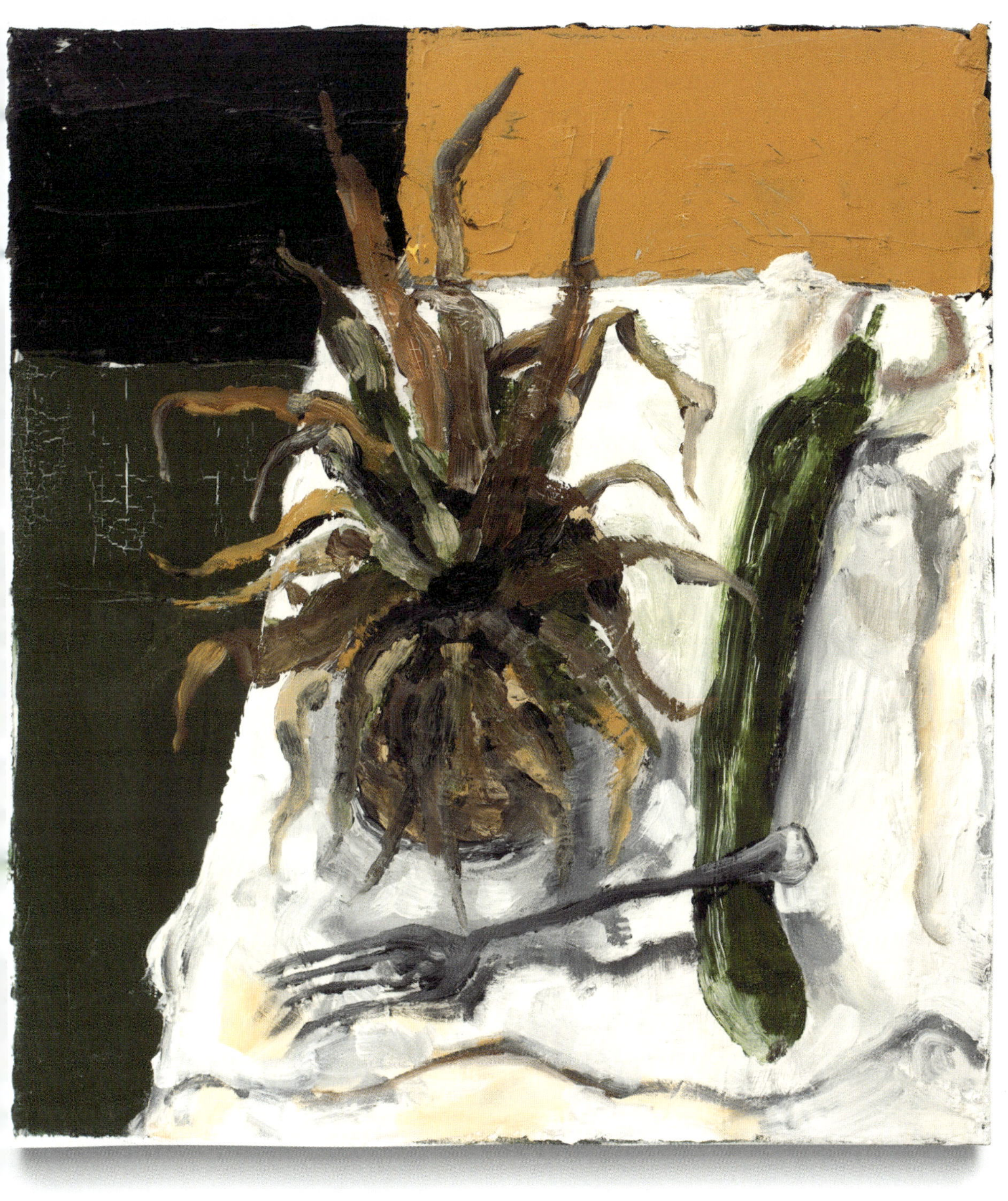

Issues with a Pineapple III, 2018
Oil on linen canvas
40cm x 46cm

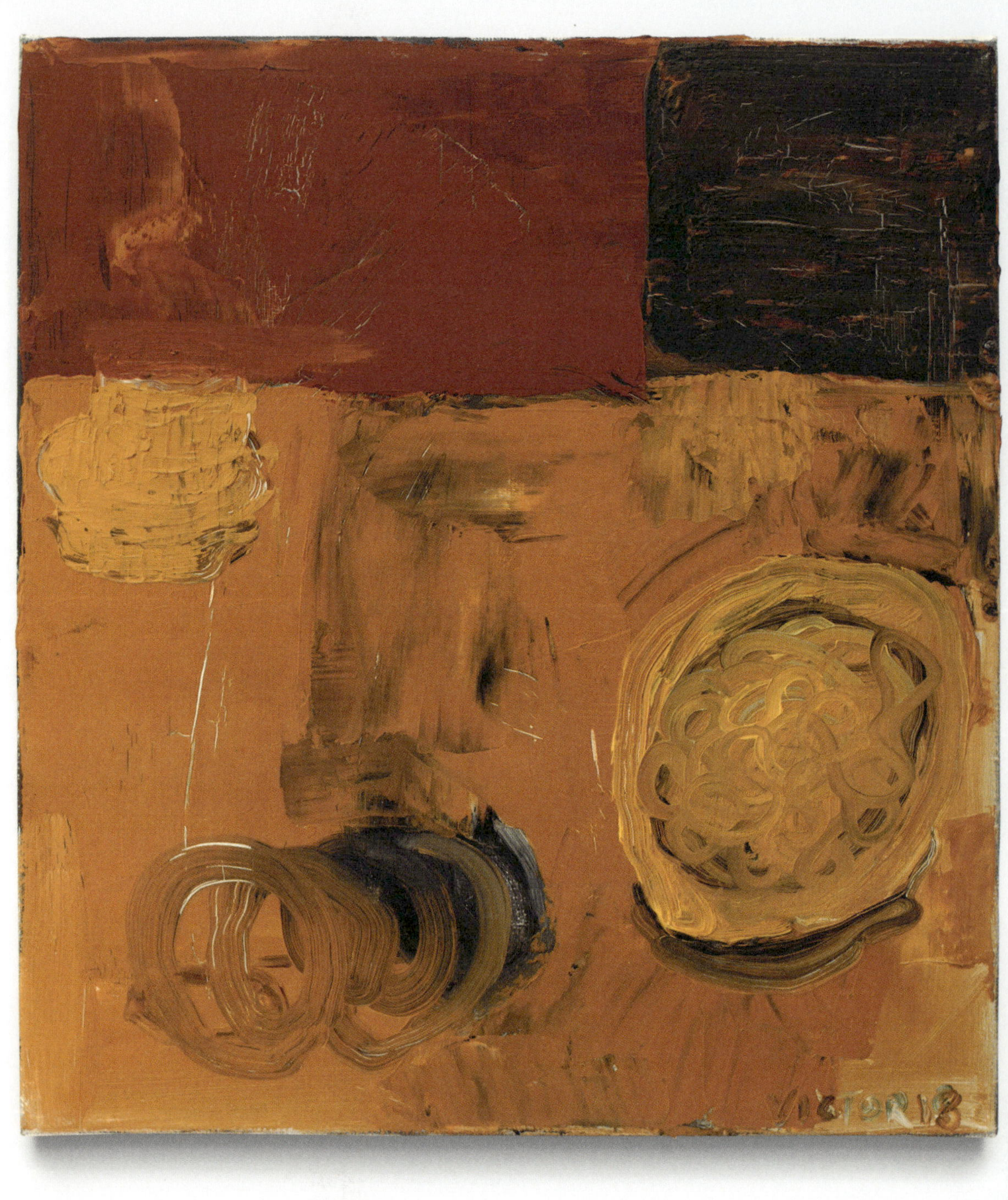

No Solution, but Spaghetti.Smoke.Coffee., 2017 – 2018 – 2019
Oil on linen canvas
40cm x 46cm

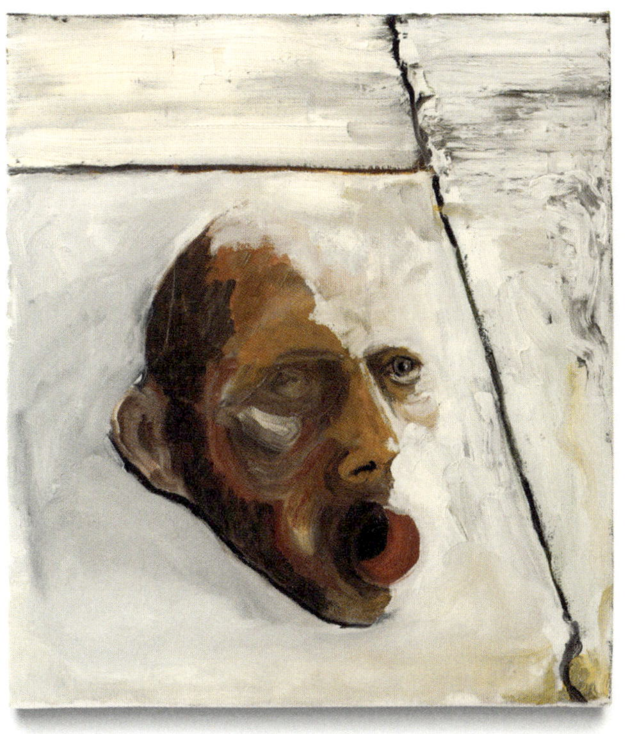

Untitled, 2017 – 2018
Oil on linen canvas
40cm x 46cm

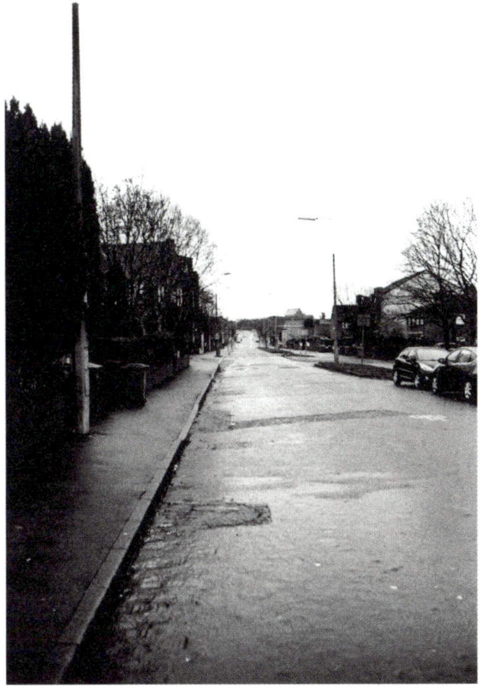

L8, Windsor Street, facing south, 2018
35mm film

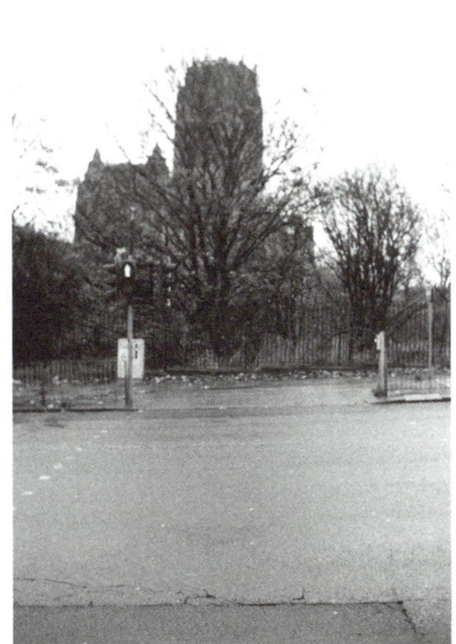

L8, Upper Parliament Street crossing, facing north, 2018
35mm film

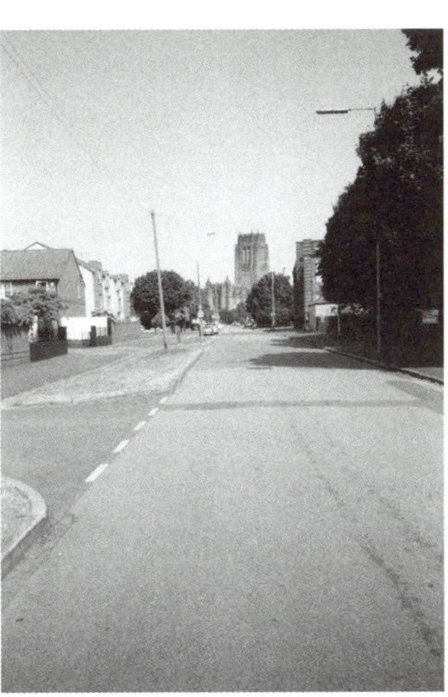

L8, Windsor Street, facing north, 2017
35mm film

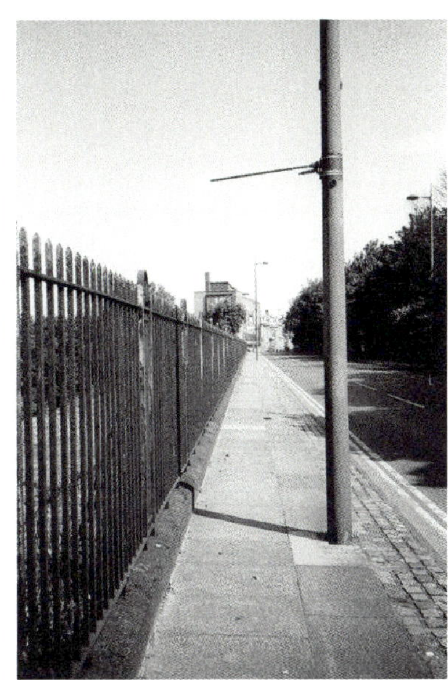

L8, Hope Street, facing north, 2017
35mm film

La Perle 2017 – 2
Oil on linen canva
40cm x 46cm

Untitled, 2017 – 2
Oil on linen canva
40cm x 46cm

Untitled, 2018
Oil on linen canva
40cm x 46cm

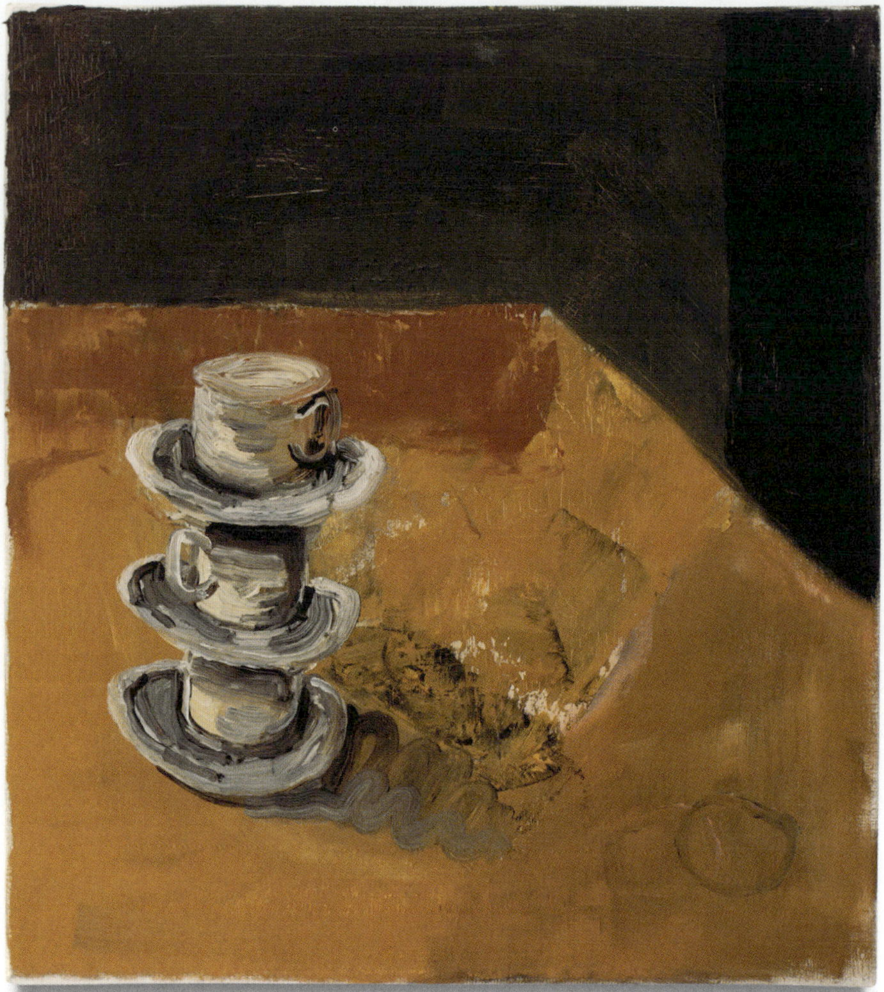

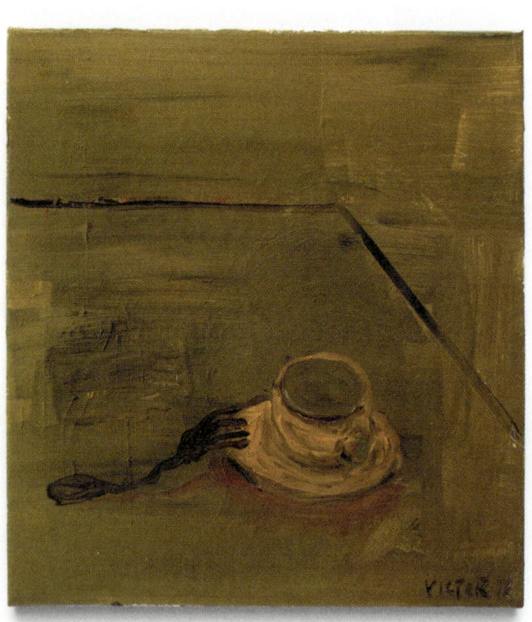

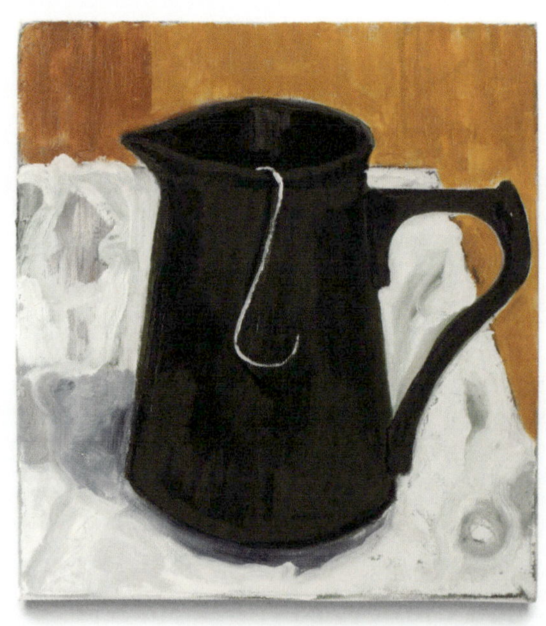

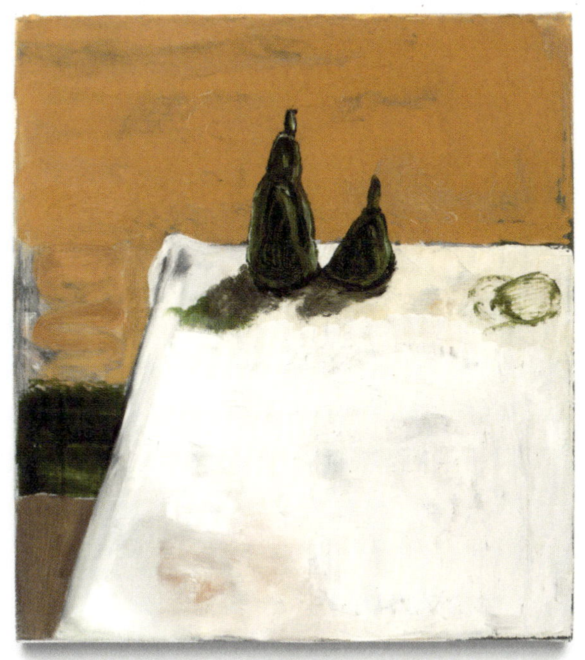

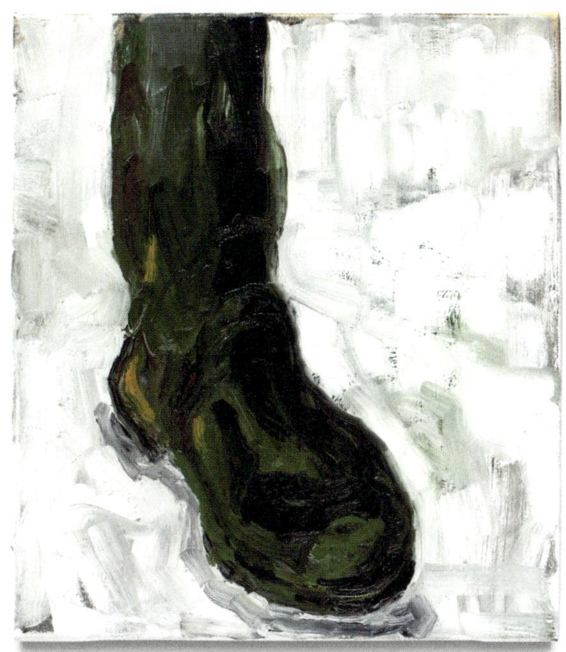

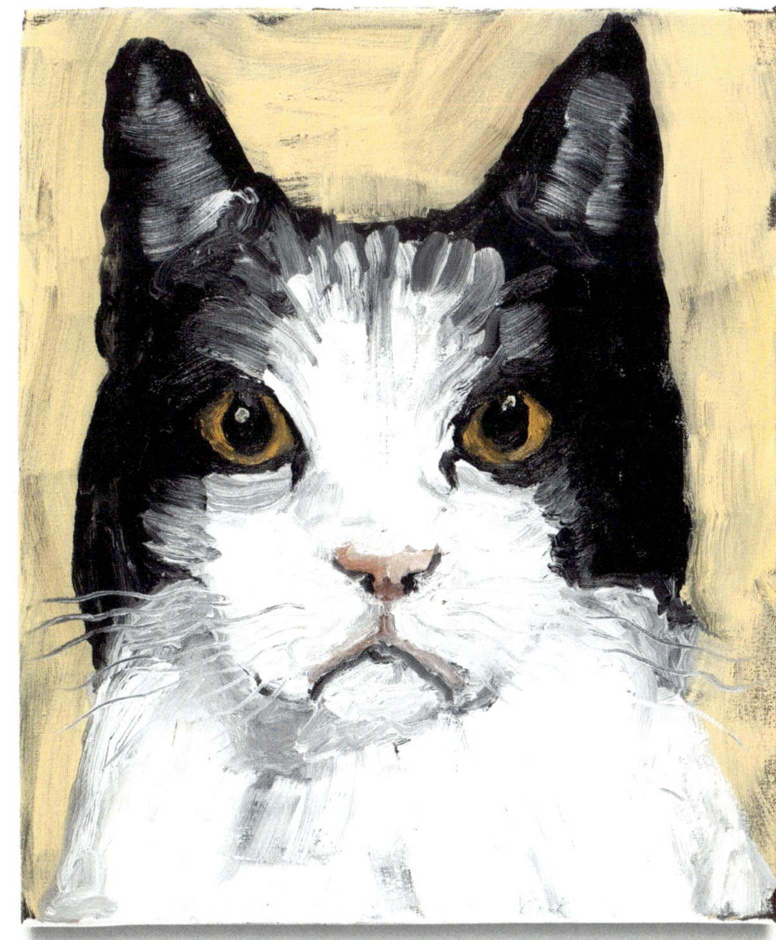

Uten tittel, 2017 – 2018
Oil on linen canvas
40cm x 46cm

Hunter, 2018
Oil on linen canvas
40cm x 46cm

George, 2018
Oil on linen canvas
40cm x 46cm

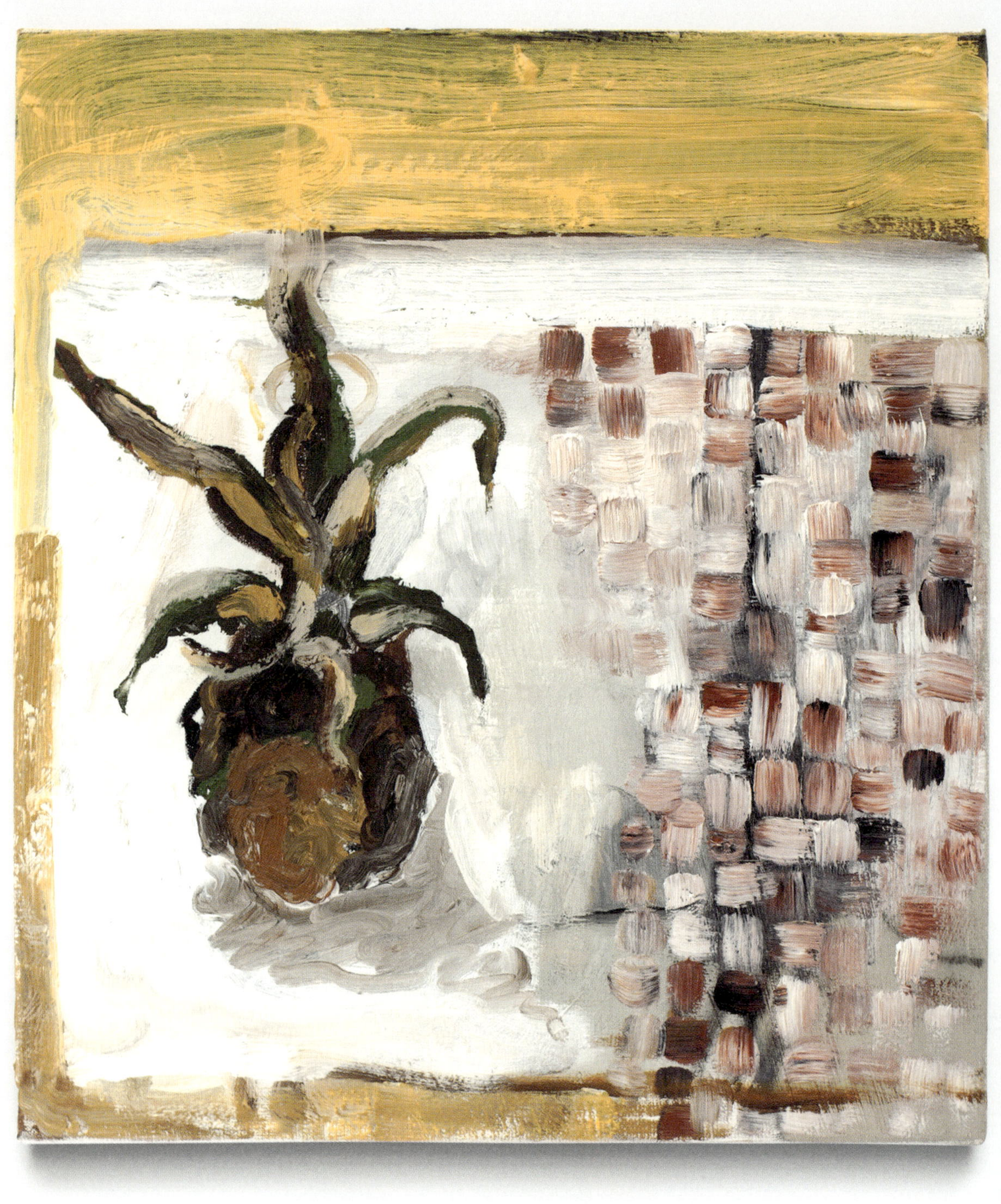

Untitled, 2017 – 2018 – 2019
Oil on linen canvas
40cm x 46cm

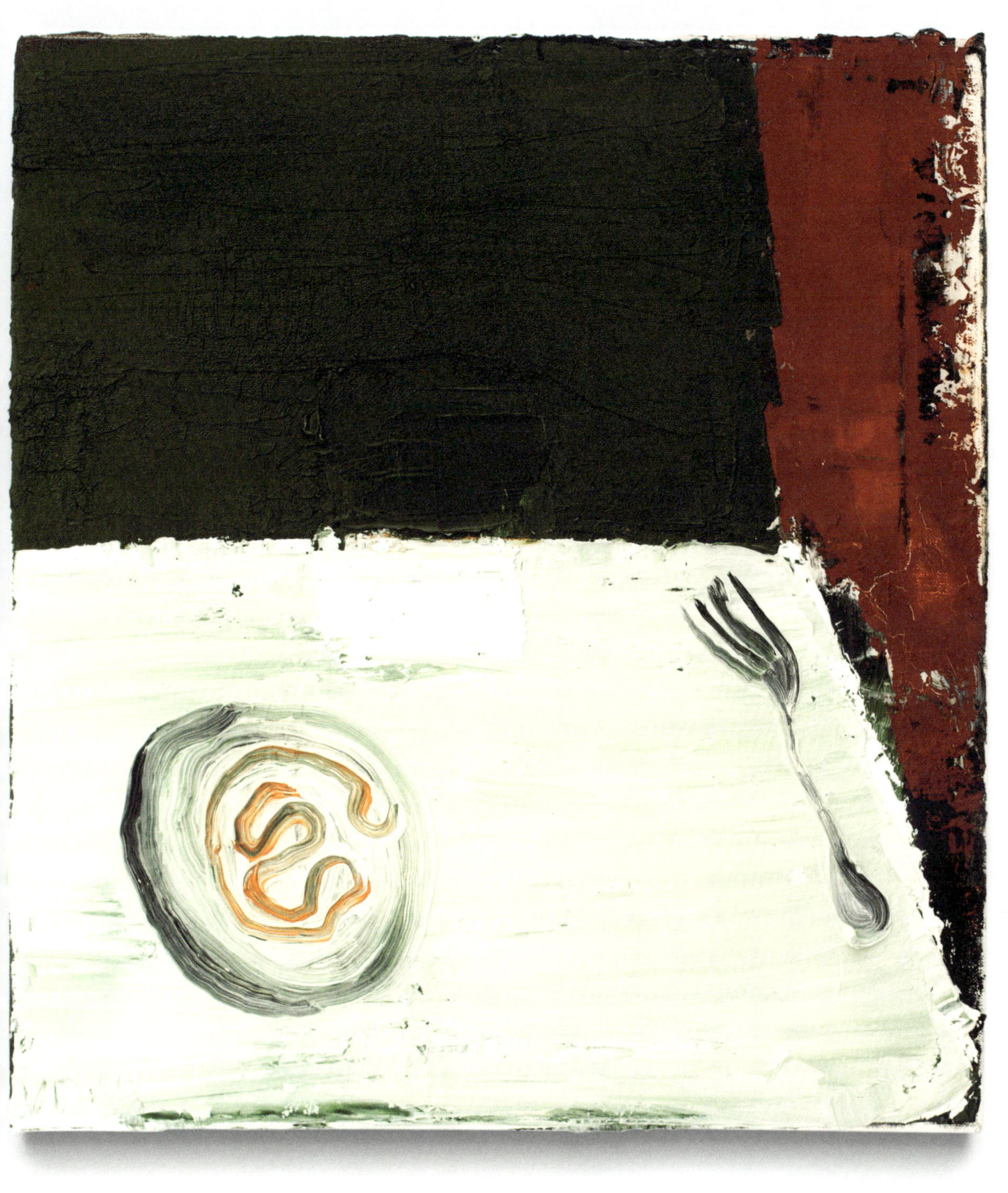

Untitled, 2017 – 2018
Oil on linen canvas
40cm x 46cm

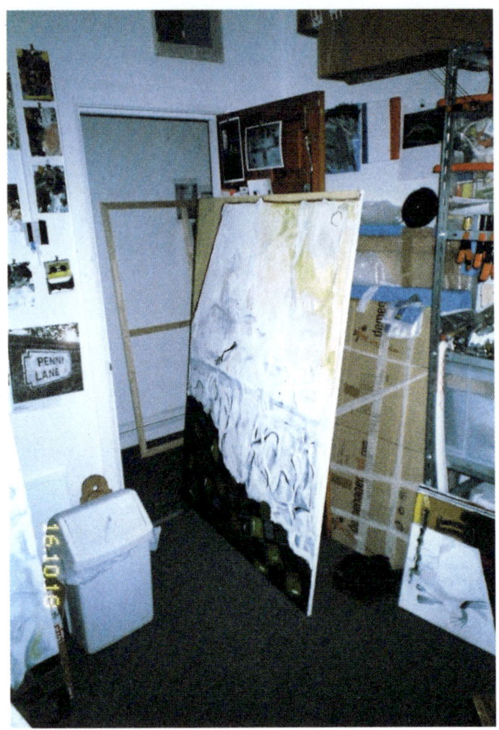

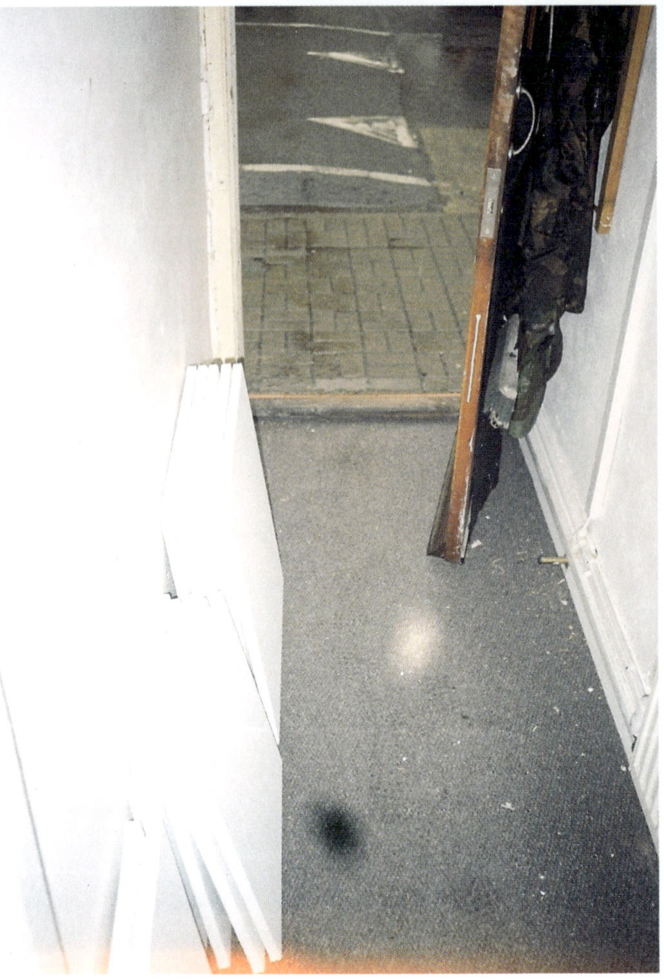

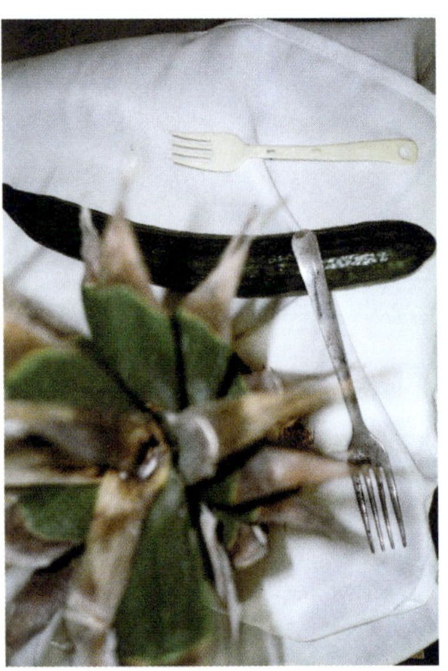

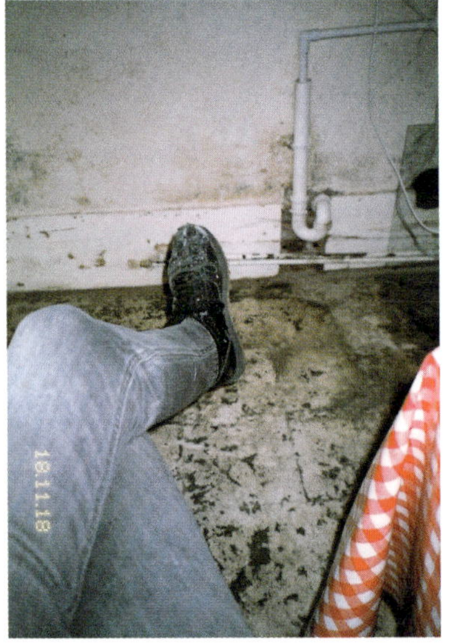

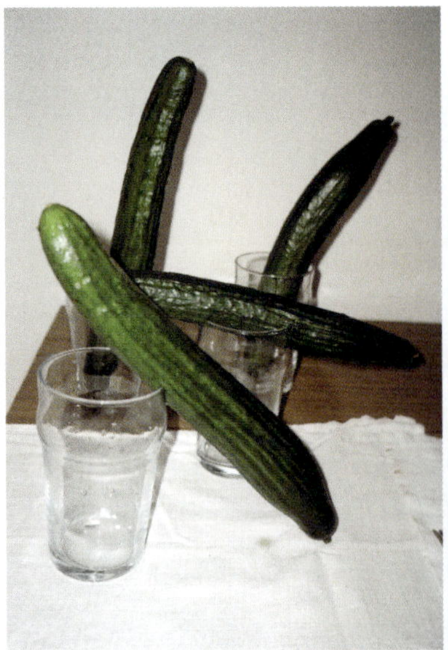

Studio documentation, 2018
35mm film

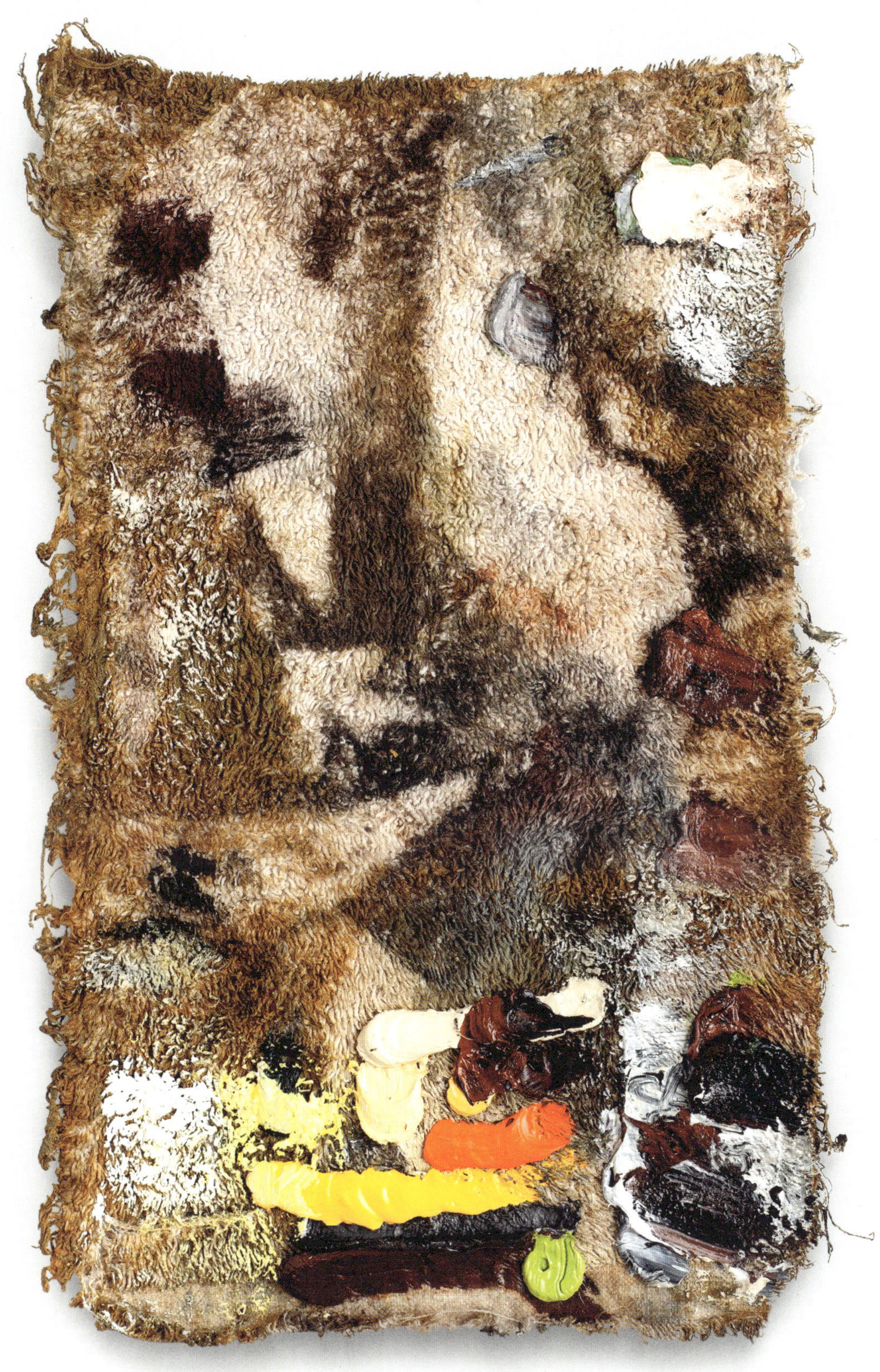

Cathedral, my Corot, 2018
Oil on found cloth (Windsor Street)
20cm x 34cm

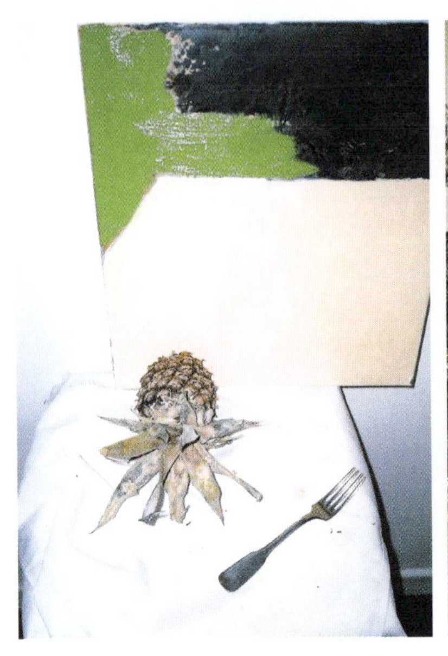
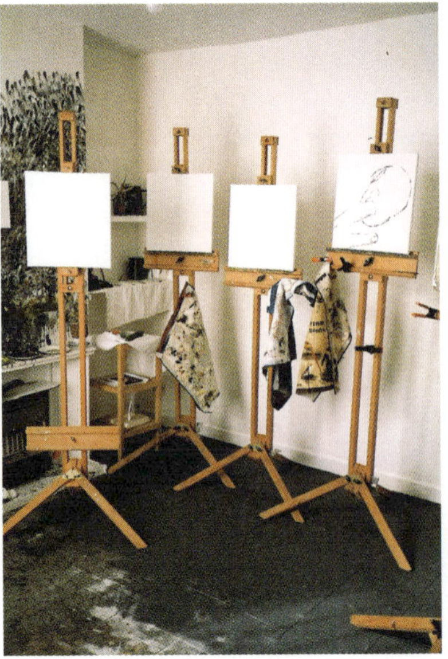
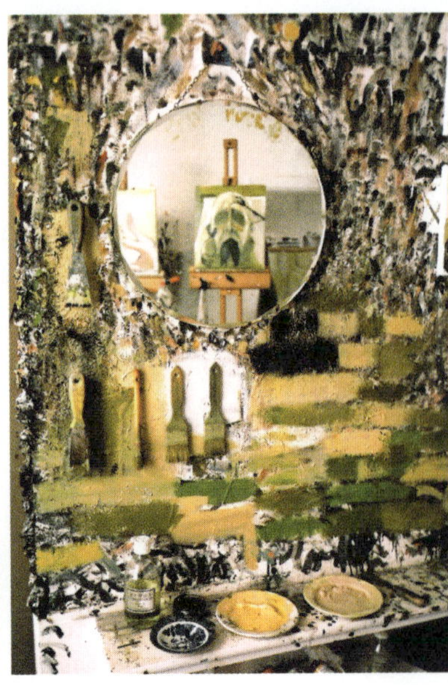
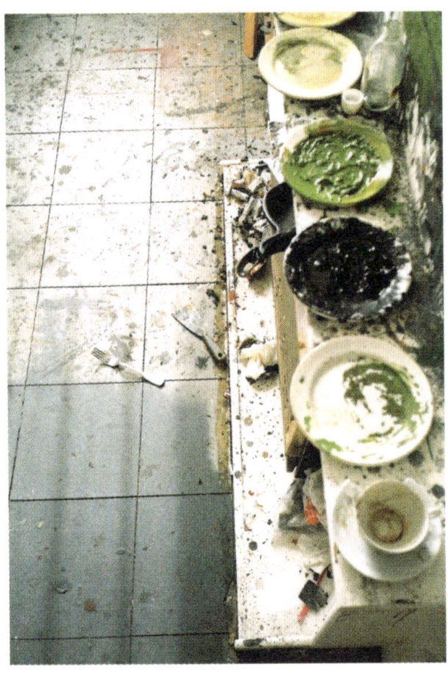
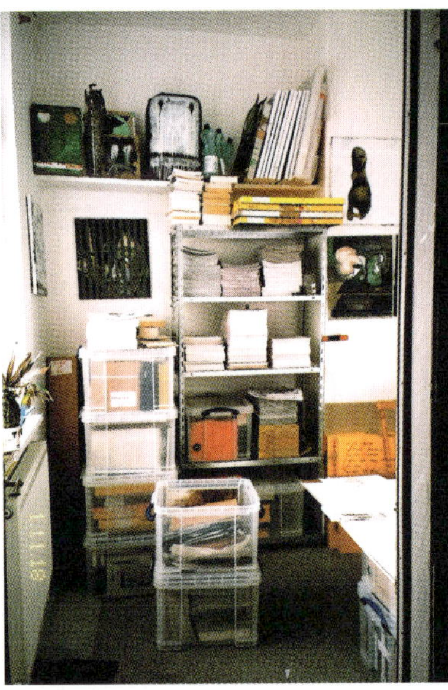
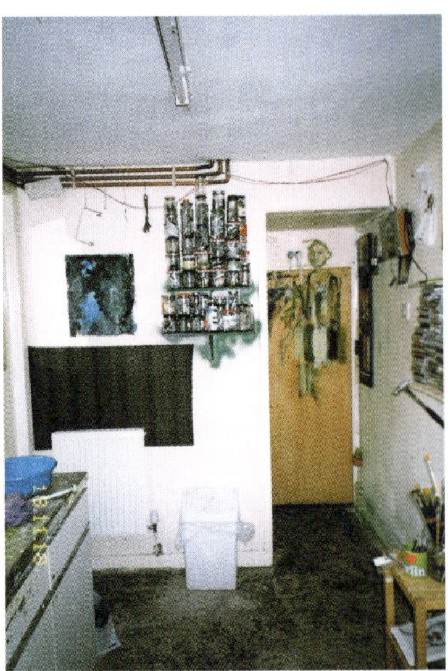
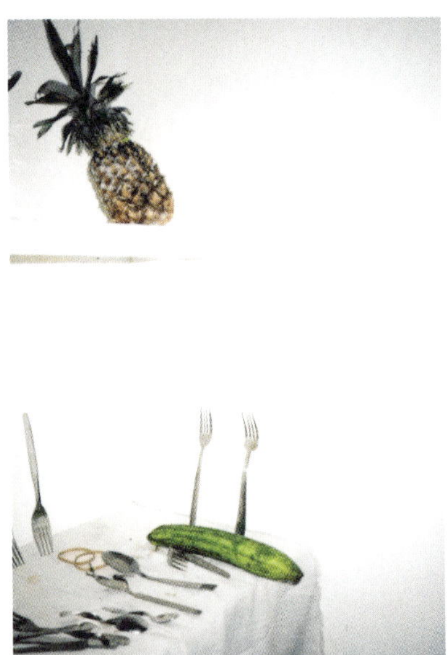
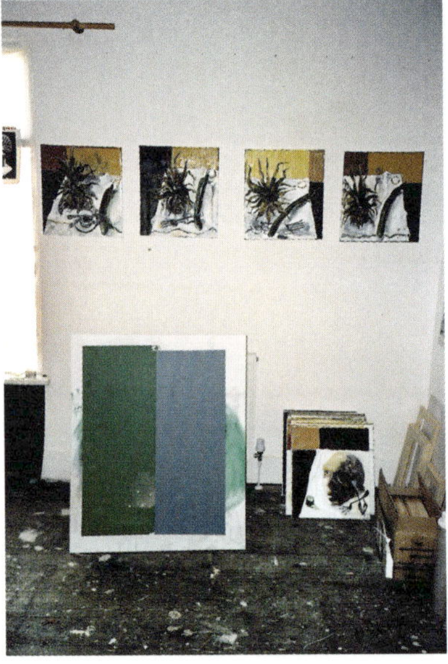
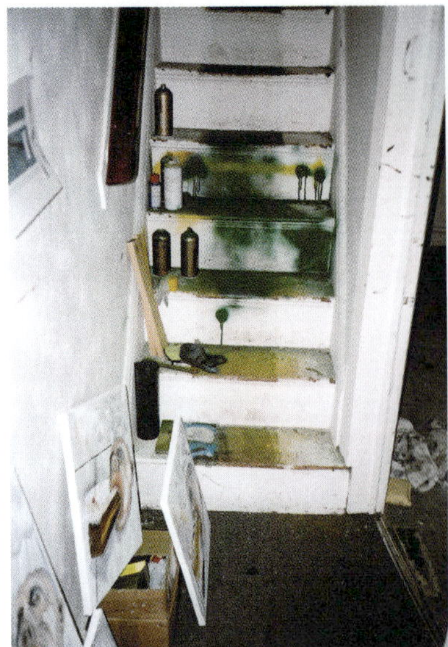

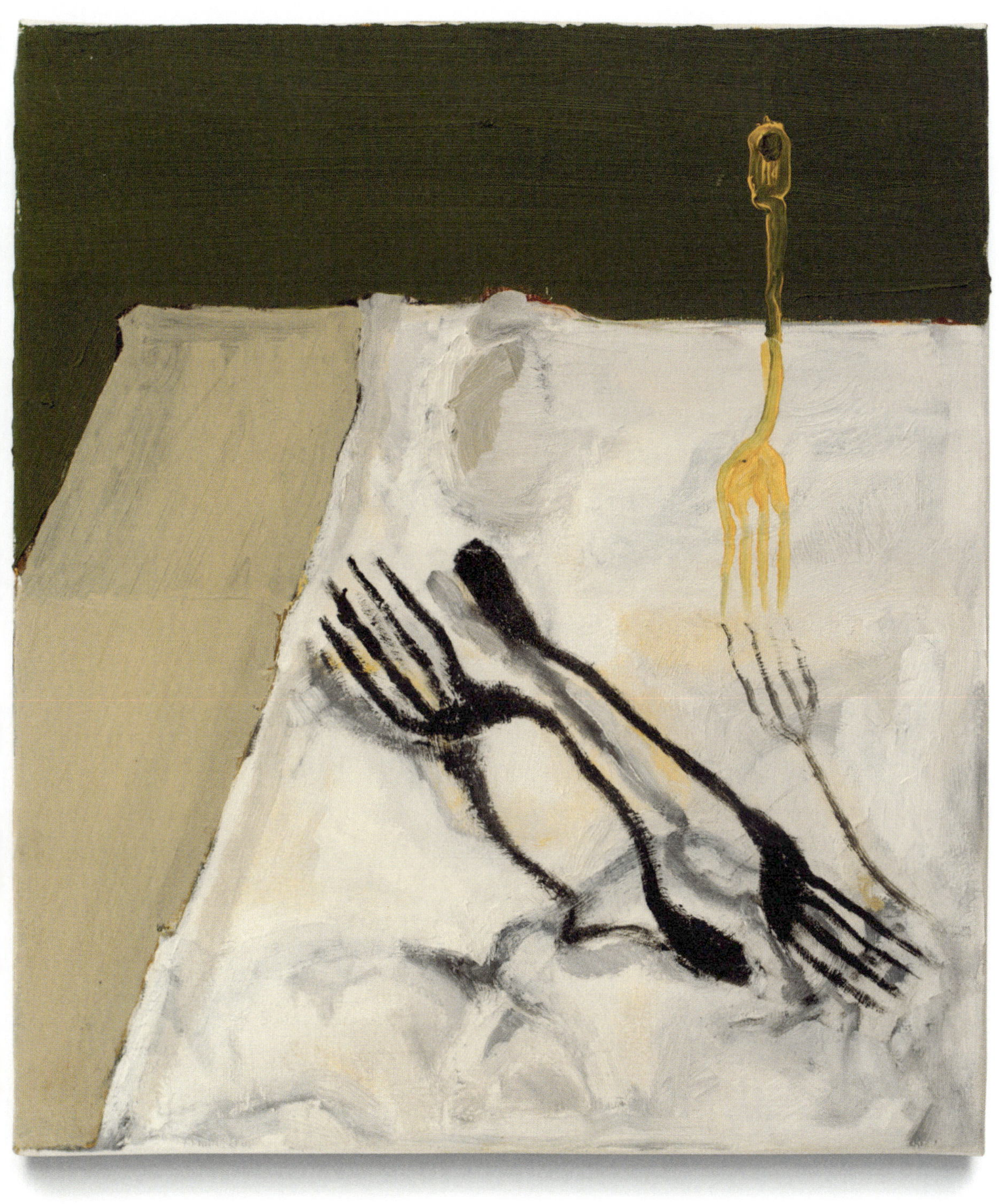

Untitled, 2017 – 2018
Oil on linen canvas
40cm x 46cm

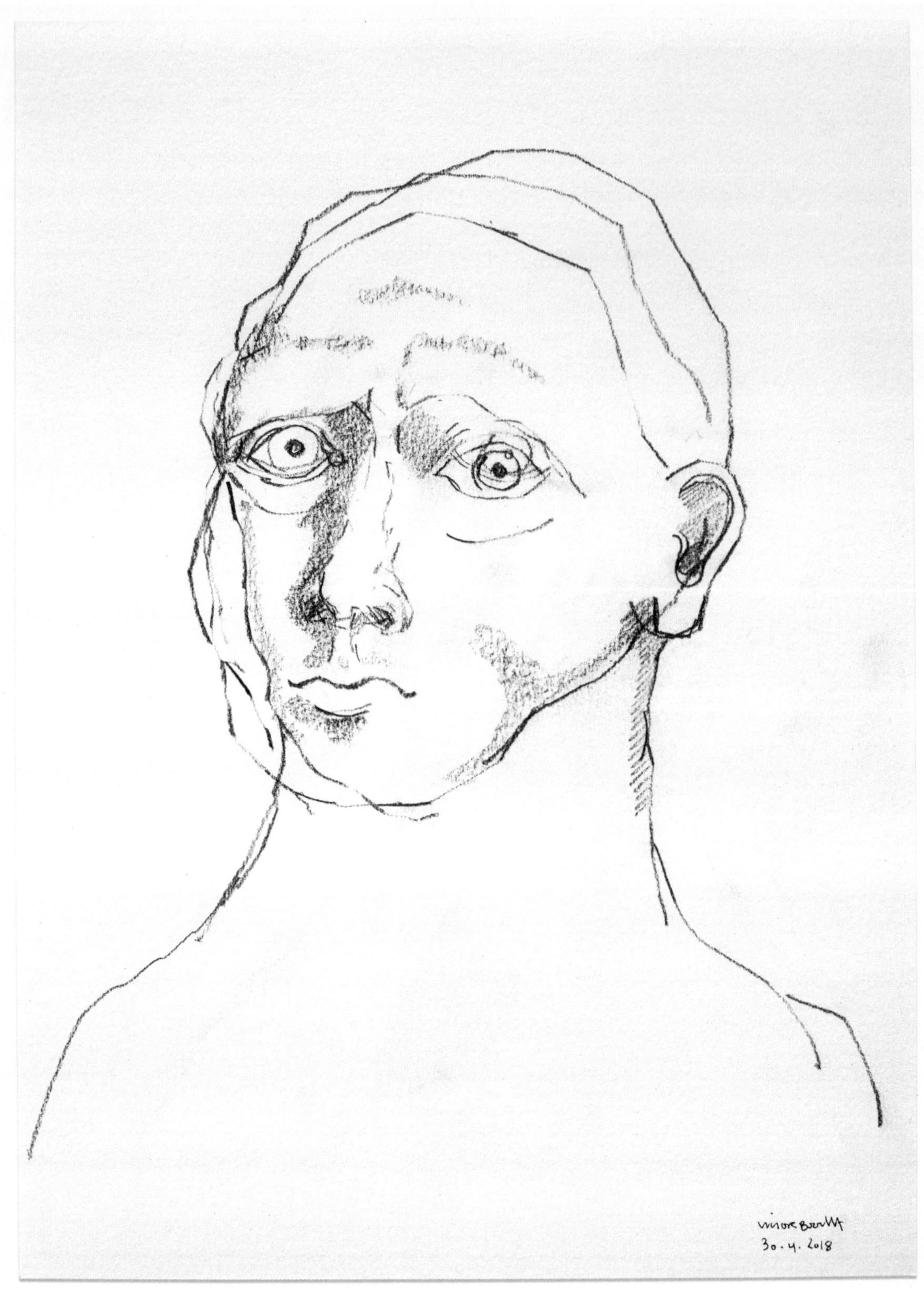

Untitled, 2018
Pencil, polychromos on paper
21cm x 29.7cm

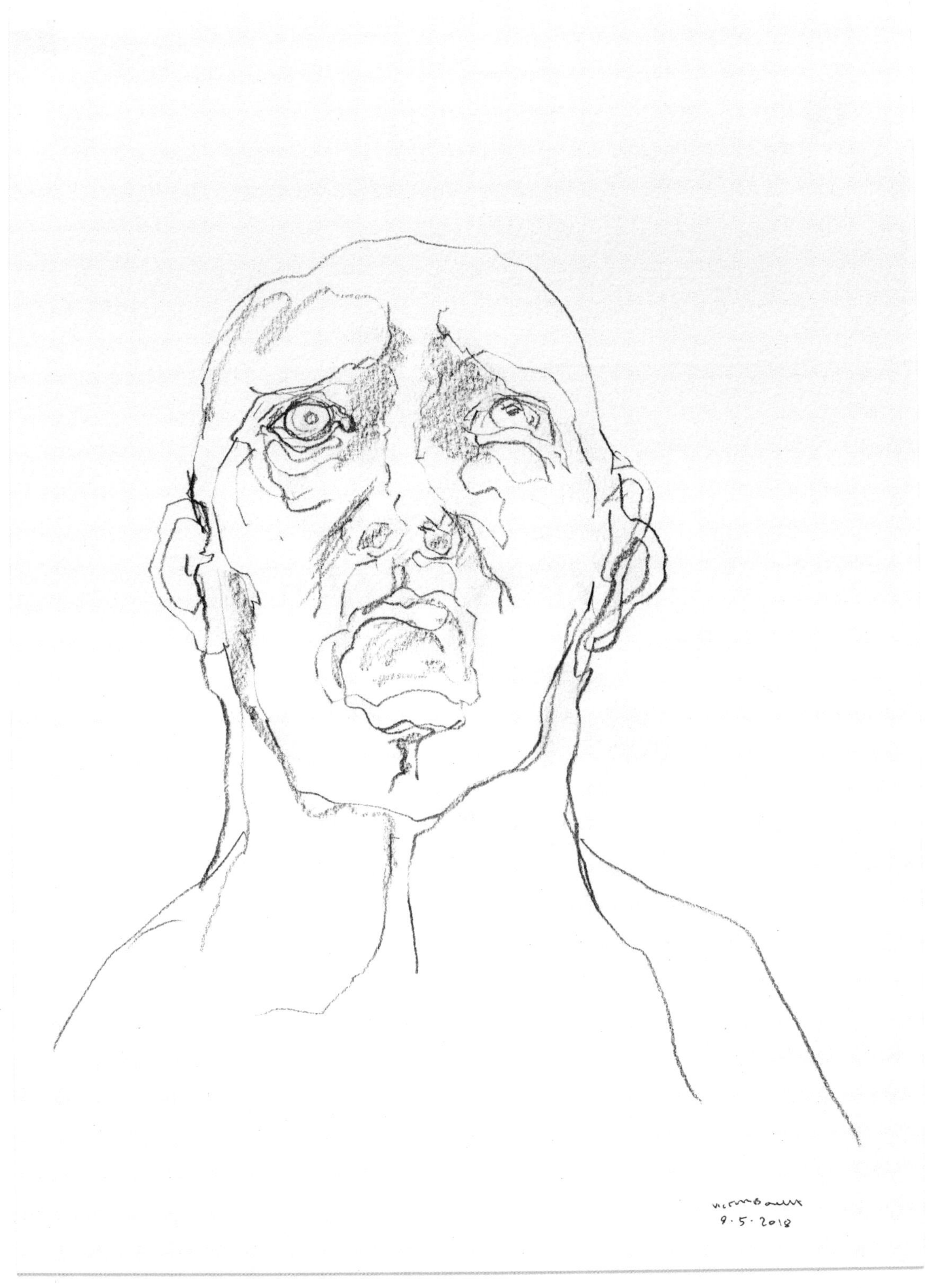

Untitled, 2018
Pencil, polychromos on paper
21cm x 29.7cm

Oliver, 2017 – 2018
Acrylic spray paint, oil on linen canvas
40cm x 46cm

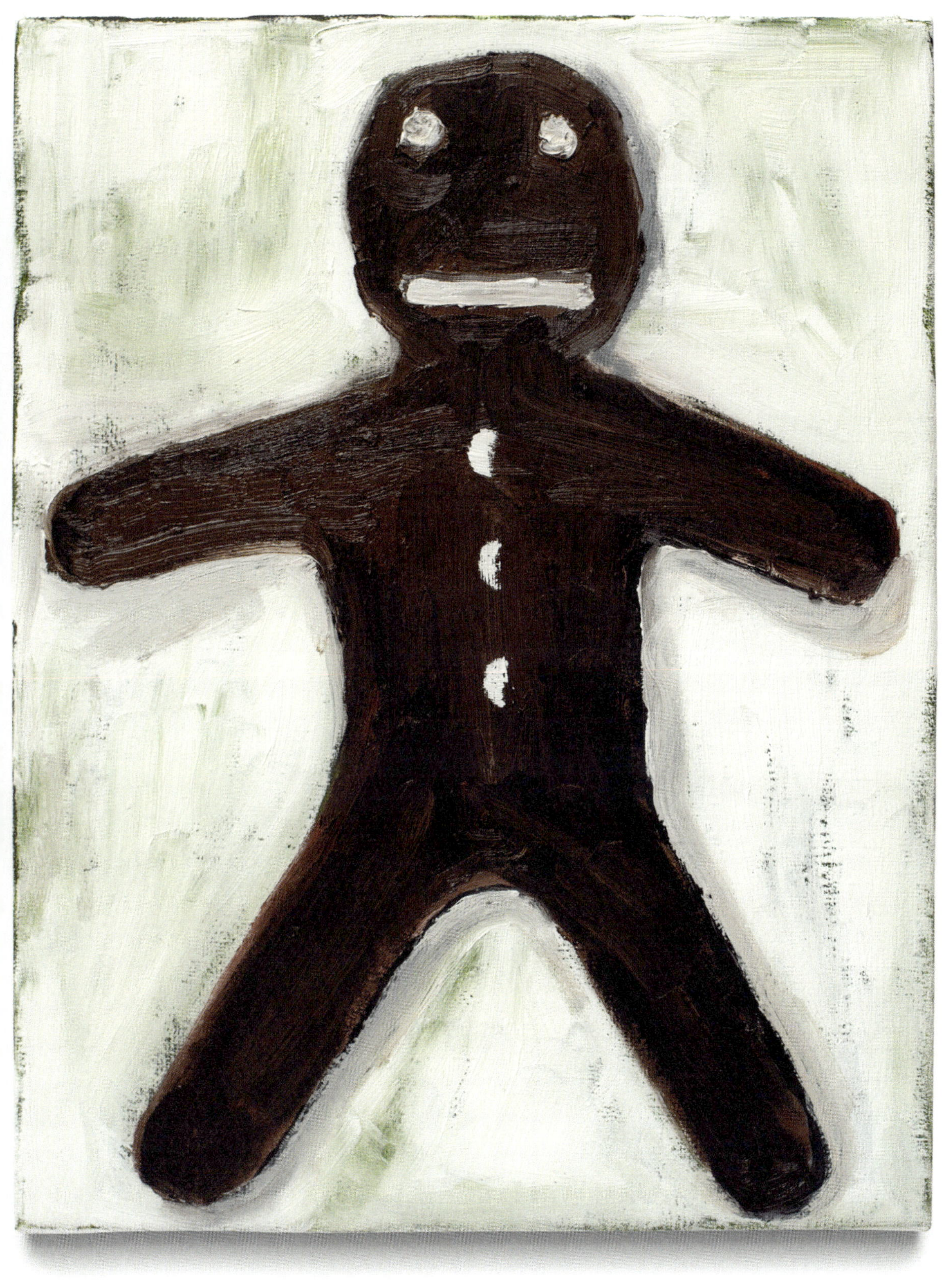

Pepperkakemann, 2018
Oil on linen canvas
30cm x 40cm

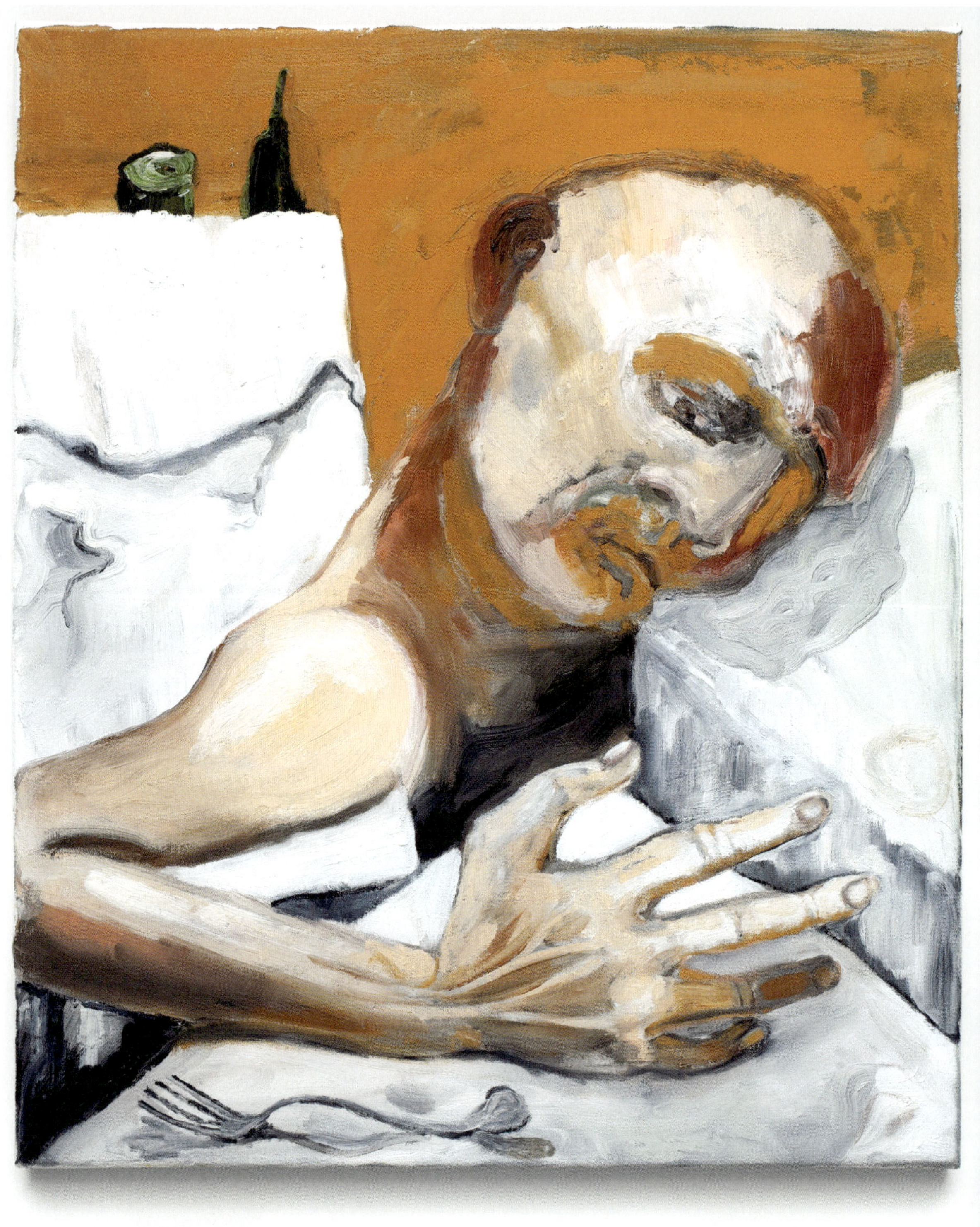

Untitled, 2018
Oil on linen canvas
50cm x 60cm

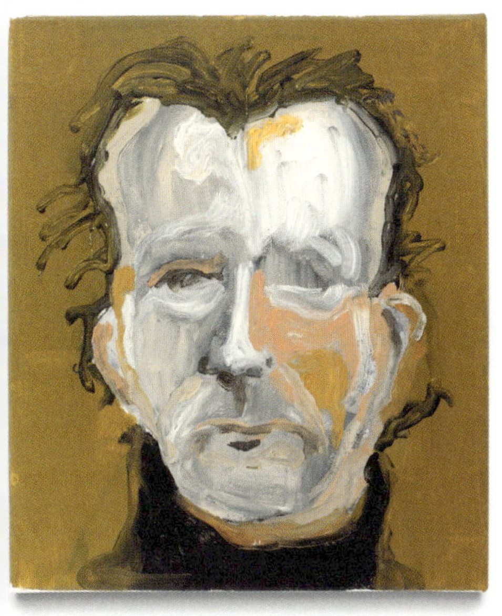

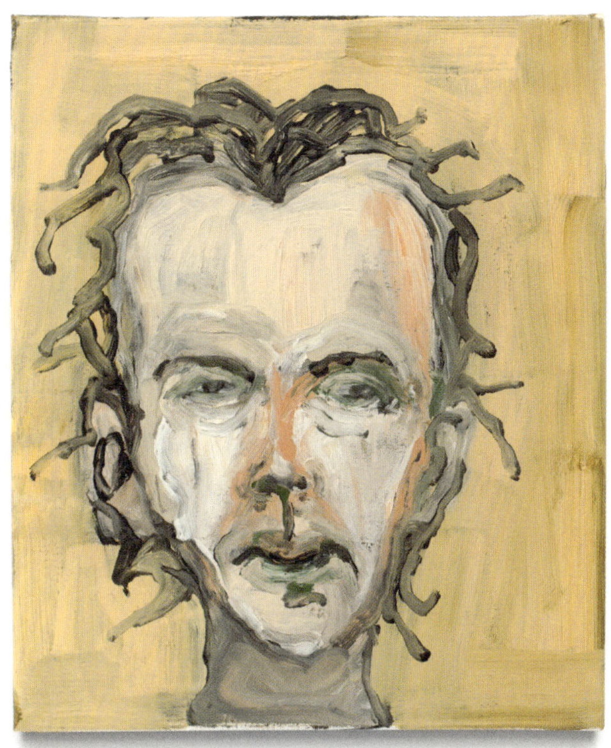

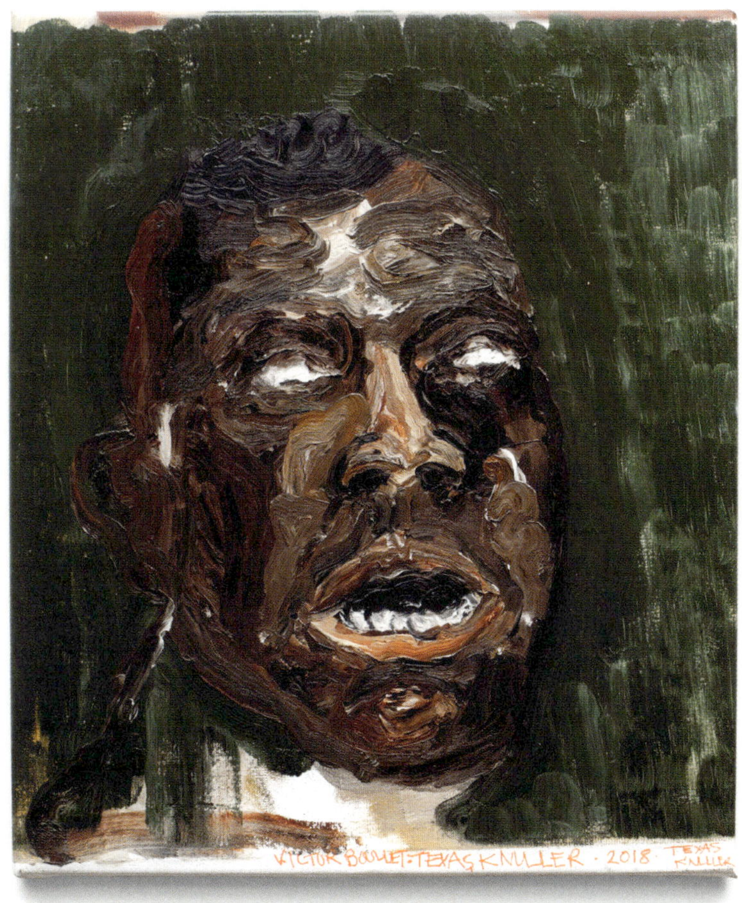

Dag Erik Elgin I, II, 2018
Oil on linen canvas
38cm x 46cm

Shaun Mayers aka Texas Knuller, 2018
Oil on linen canvas
40cm x 46cm

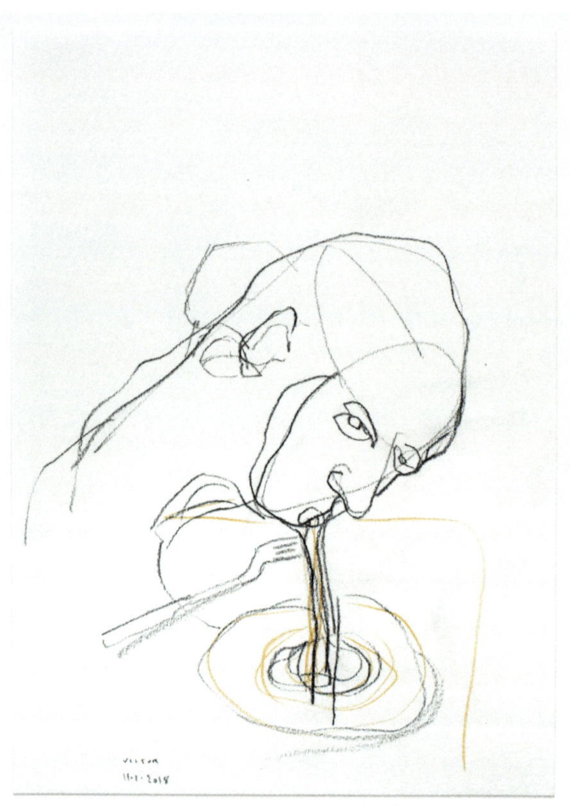

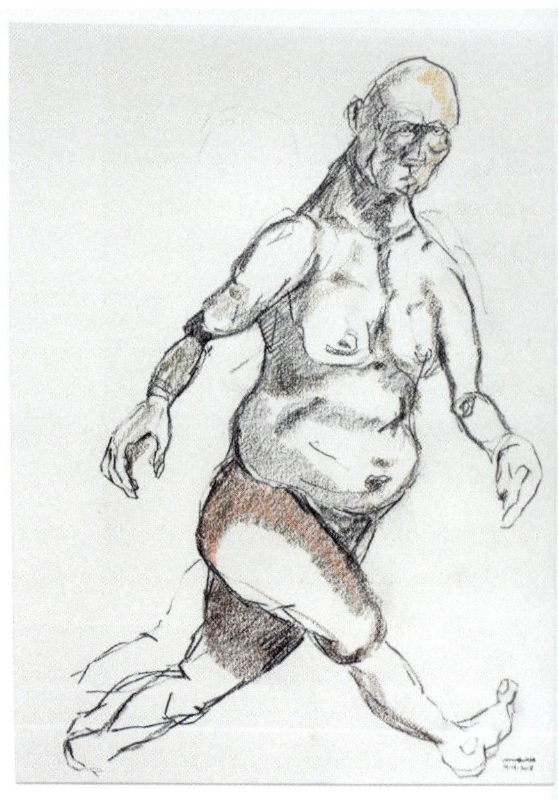

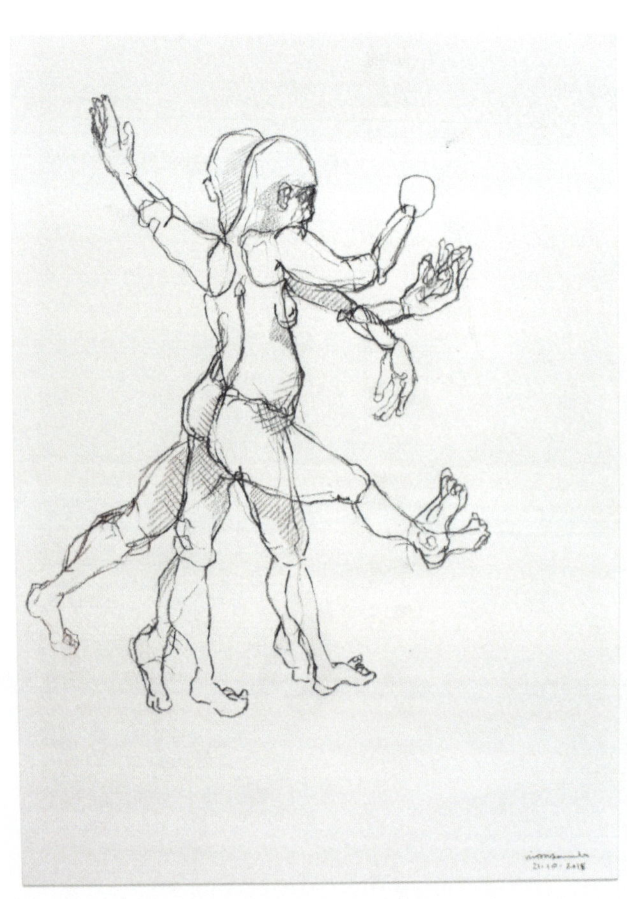

Untitled, I, II, III, 2018
Pencil, polychromos on paper
21cm x 29.7cm

Albert, 2018
Pencil, polychromos on paper
21cm x 29.7cm

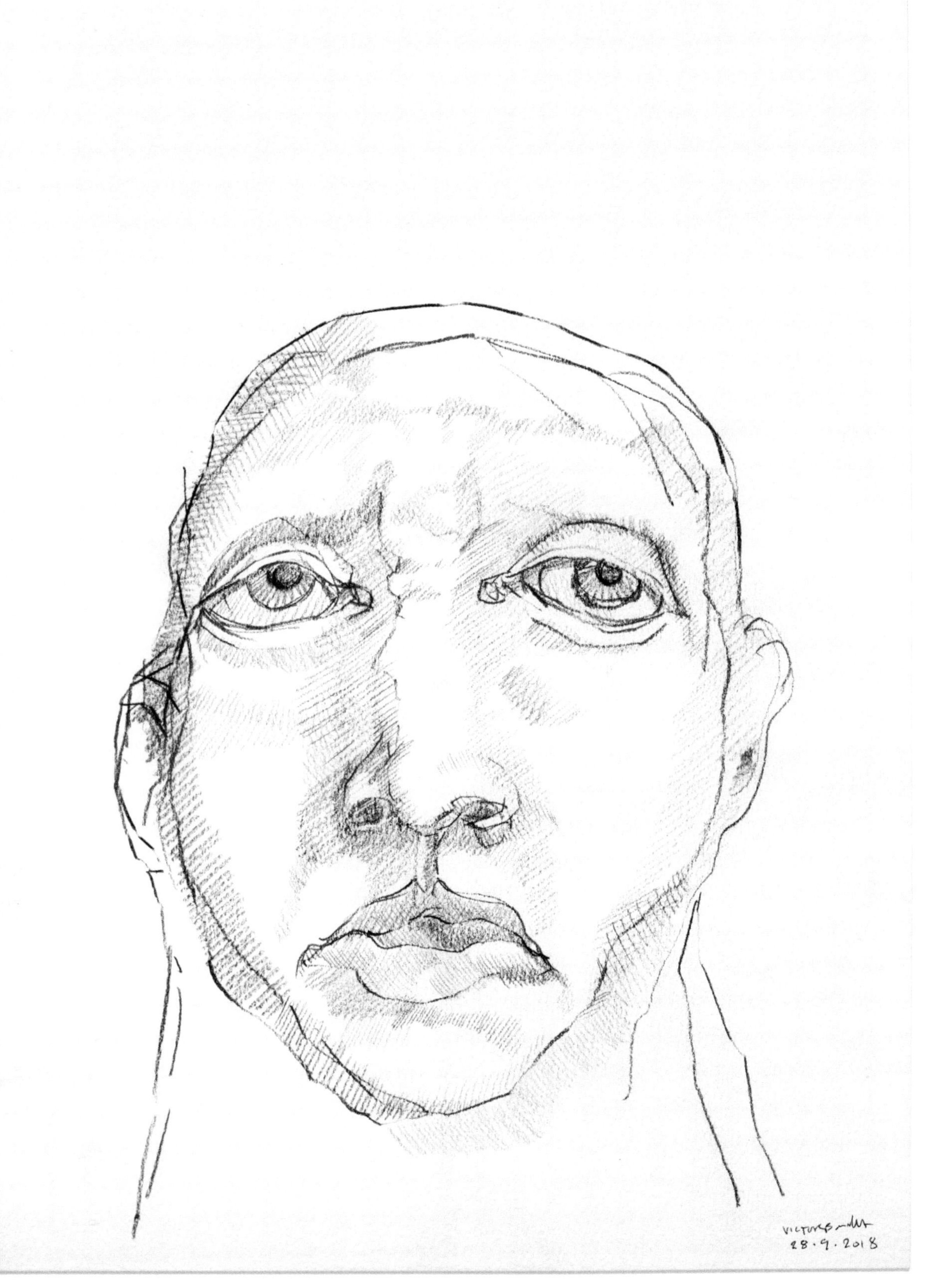
28 · 9 · 2018

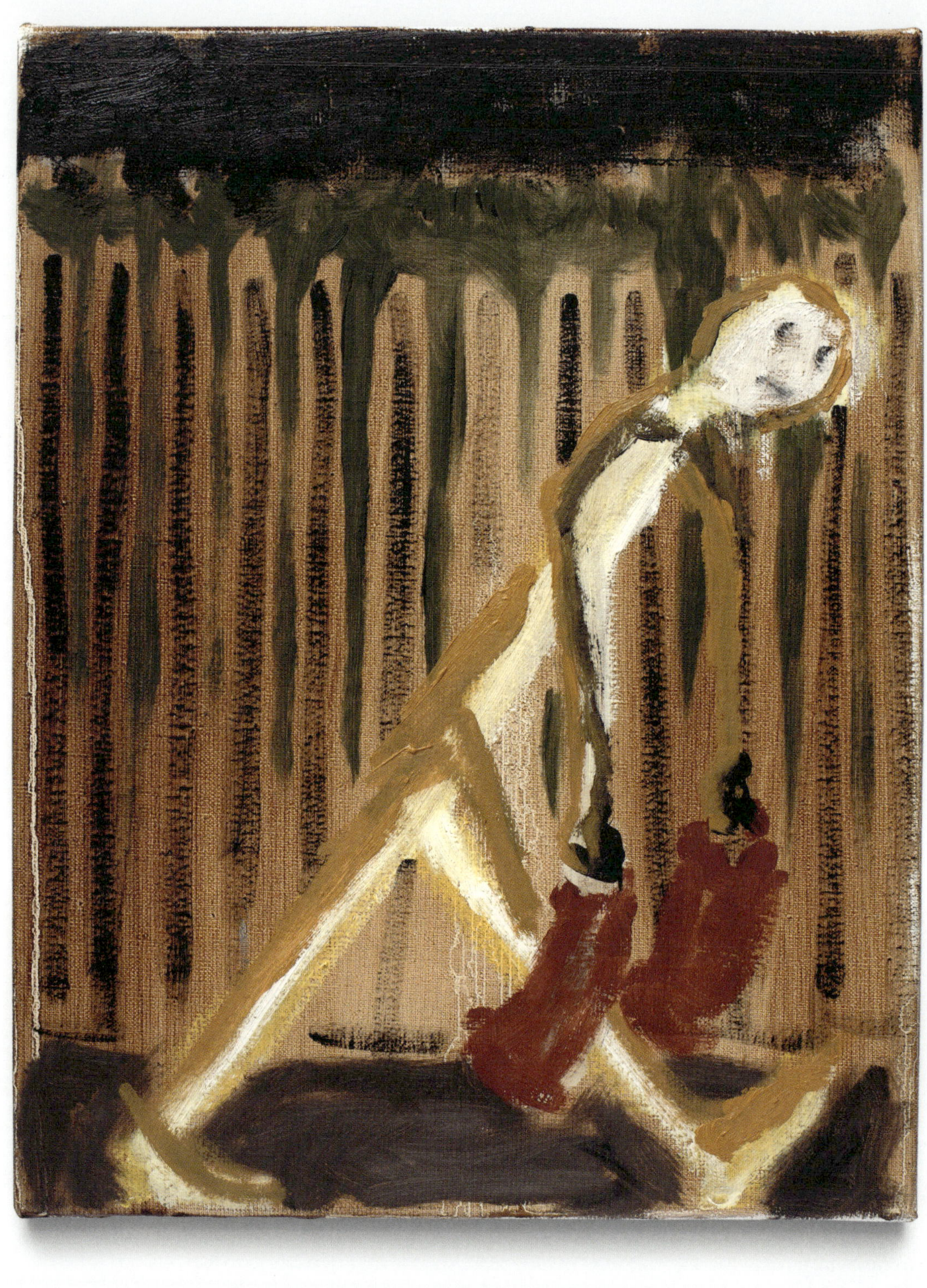

Hope street. Cathedral. Fence. From Studio, Facing L1, 2018
Oil on linen canvas
30cm x 40cm

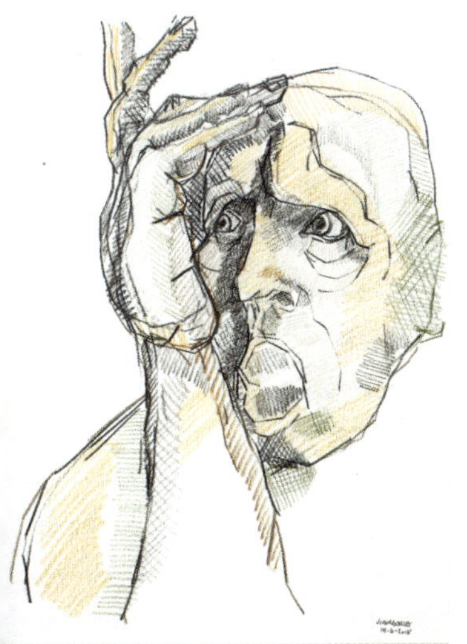

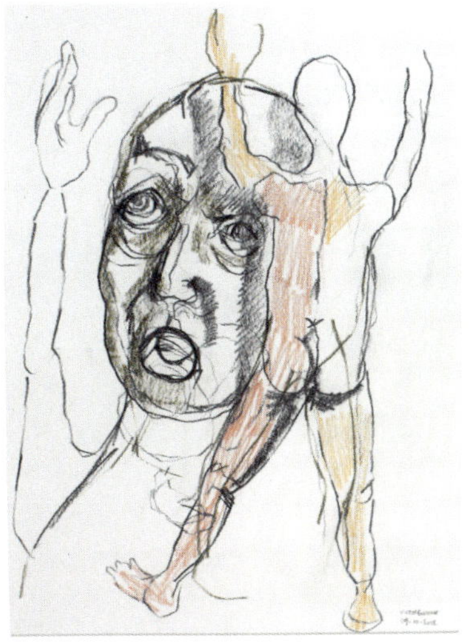

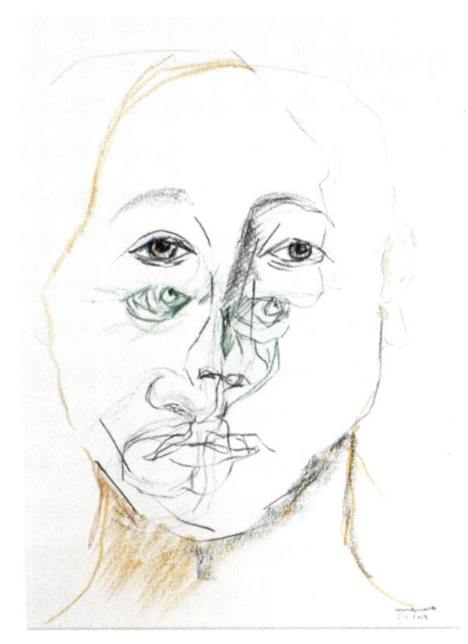

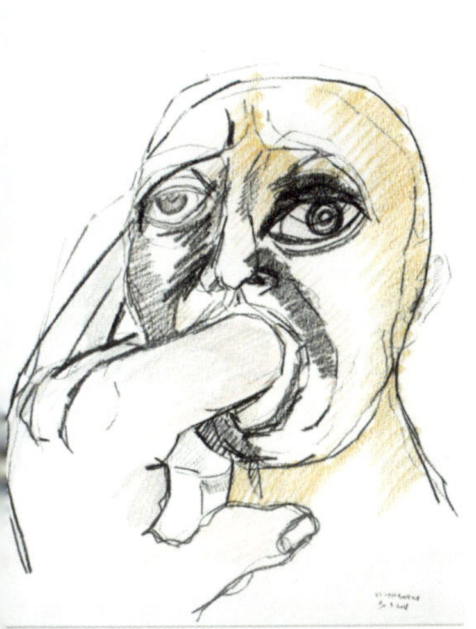

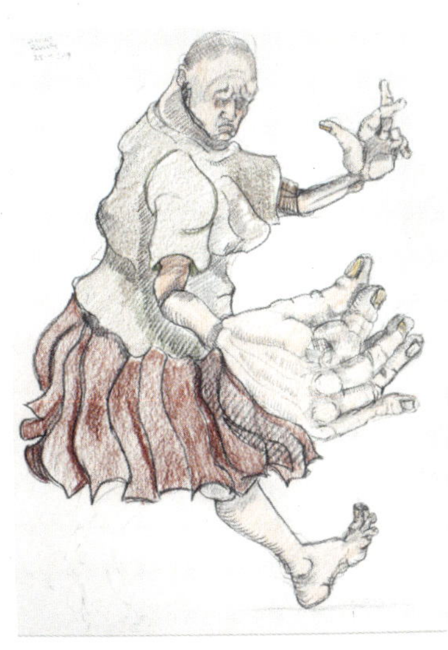

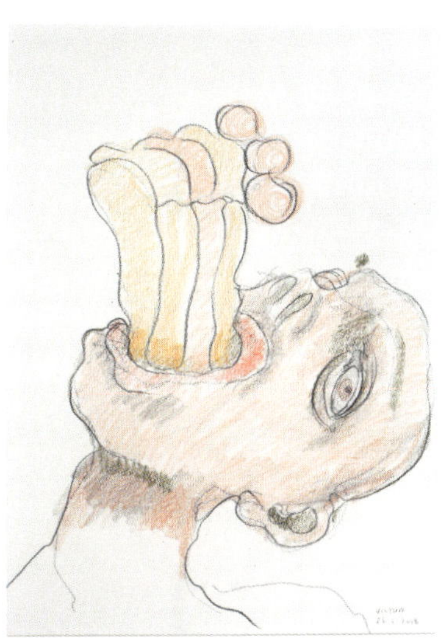

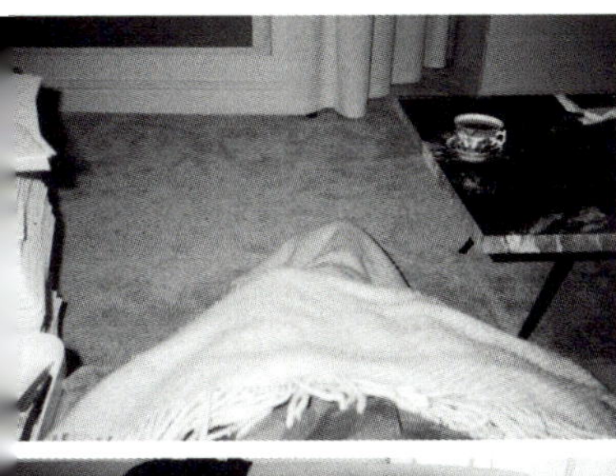

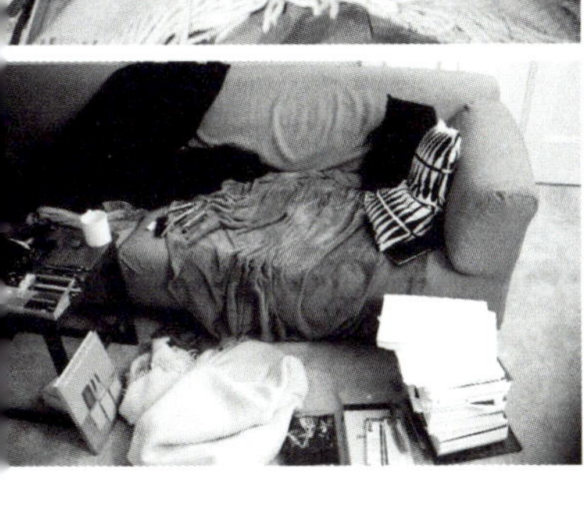

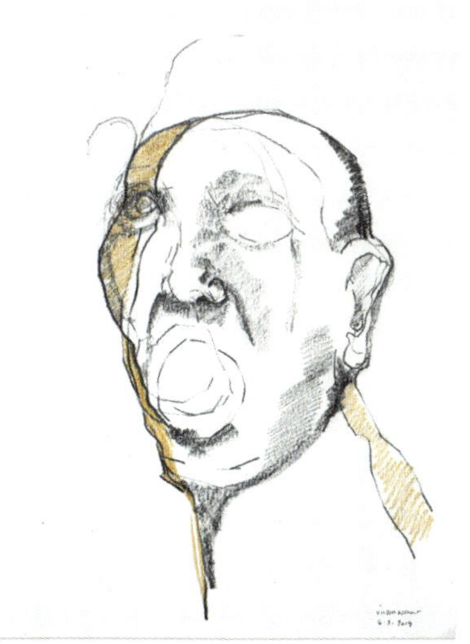

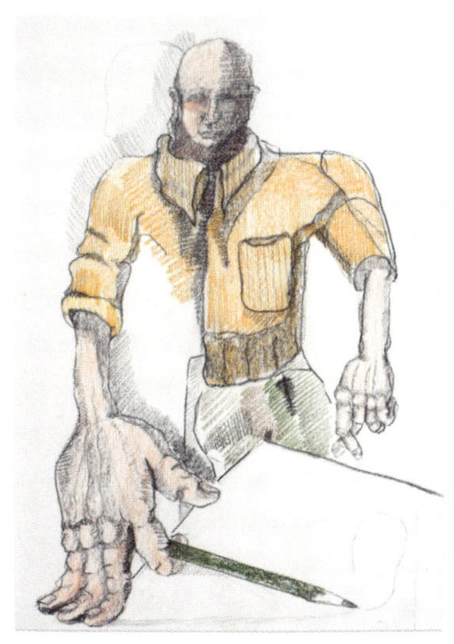

ntitled, 2018
encil, polychromos on paper
 cm X 29.7 cm

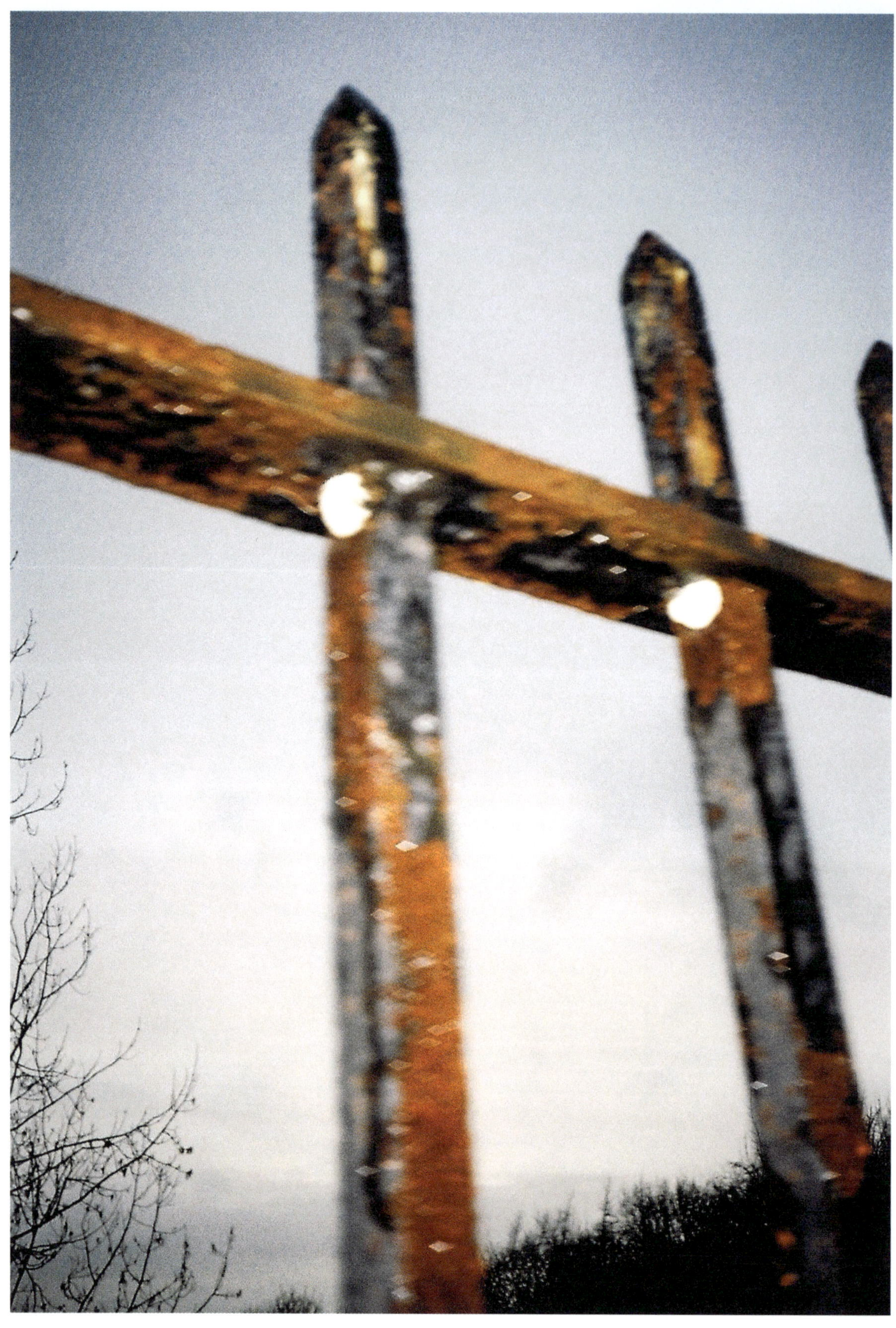

To the People of Liverpool. The Cycle of Poverty Continues, 2017 – 2019
35mm film

The Fieldwork of Painting
– Measuring the Exact Distance Between Studio and Home
by Dag Erik Elgin

In the heyday of postmodern theory it was concluded that the paintings of farmers by the French artist Jean-François Millet are all about the *exact weight* of the sacks the peasants carry on their backs. This observation has stayed with me since I read it, and I have an inkling that it might be relevant in this context. There is a specific temperature as to how the word *exact* is used here that strikingly differs from the vocabulary in the discourse of painting's so-called *extended field*. According to its authorised biography, early modernist painting allegedly freed itself from being evaluated by exact standards one and a half centuries ago. Ever since, the story of the medium's heroic struggle has itself become an indispensable part of painting's toolbox, constantly urging the medium to prove its relevance through a re-staging *outside of itself.*

By necessity this immanent gesture is performed beyond the physical borders of the pictorial field, once regarded a holy surface onto which meaning was projected.
In the post-medium era, social fantasies are directed towards another canvas generically named «space», accompanied by a discourse of «intersections», «voids», «involutions», «displacements», «ruptures», «platforms», «abysses» and «sites». This permanent displacement and ritualised challenge of the medium equals painting's new academism, which constantly demands identification of new territories of *Painting Beside Itself.* As the occurrence of potentially new homelands has increasingly diminished, the frequency of mannerist territories have grown respectively. One of which prominently concludes that the pasta served at a gallery dinner after an opening is equally significant to the exhibited works of art.

In the light of Millet and an attempt to lead the gaze back from pasta to the pictorial surface, one is tempted to ask if the exact degree of the pasta's *al dente* and the exact weight of the sacks carried on the farmers' backs are compatible standards. The pasta comment is limited to the insight that at any dinner party, painting was probably never to be trusted as a stable conversation piece. Taking the last one and a half centuries into consideration, the difference between the strategies of for example Manet's *Le Peintre de la vie moderne* and that of a post-conceptual artist at a gallery dinner becomes obvious. If the journalistic approach of early modernism directed the gaze *outside of painting* for social analysis, painting's post-conceptual strategy, allegedly focusing on *Painting Beside Itself,* has forced painting's gaze *towards itself* to monitor and identify every artist's exact position within a defined network.

Painting was probably always self-preoccupied and circulated among a limited and privileged group of people. Yet, through its shift from a material based surface to space, the medium became inscribed in defined network

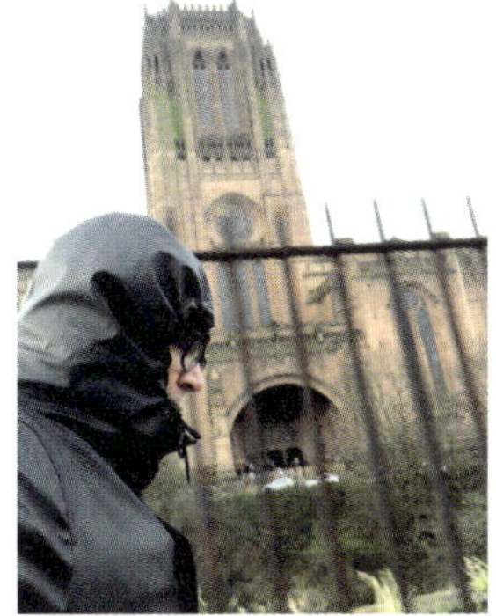

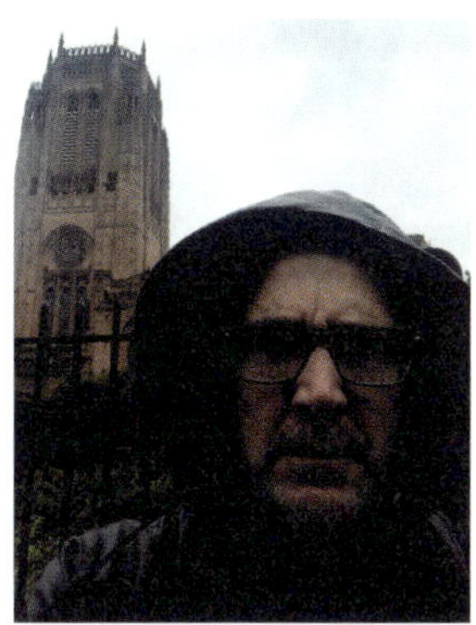

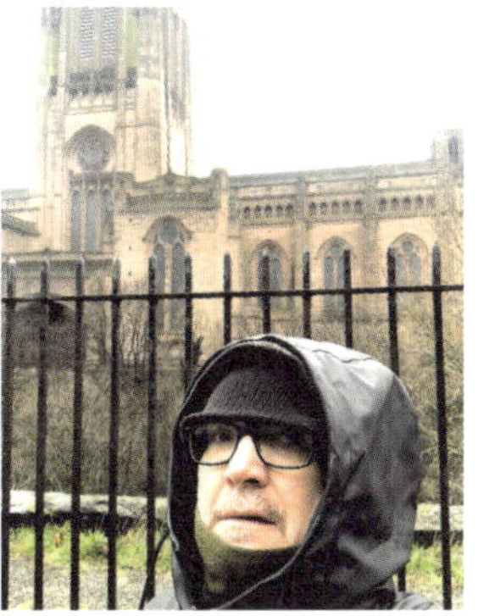

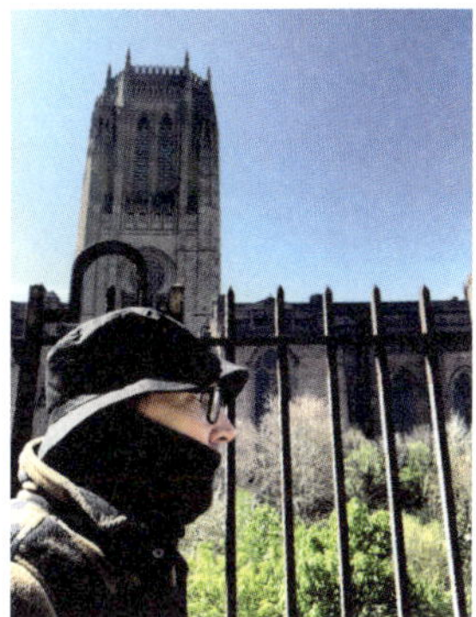

Cathedral self portraits, 2017 – 2021
iPhone images

theories compatible with the systems of evaluation favoured by the 16th century French Académie Royale. On a political level, the globalisation of the world market has undoubtedly resulted in equally globalising the art market. Whether an artist is situated in Paris, New York, Berlin, London, Oslo or Liverpool is increasingly of minor importance. Artists react to the same trends everywhere, adopting similar or identical artistic strategies. The sole standard of evaluation equals the exact position any artist occupies within a globalised network at a given time. Consequently, the once liberating leap into the void has made space generic as a medium and insignificant as a means of distinction.

First Walk

Hope Street in Liverpool is situated at the east side of the city's impressive cathedral, the glorious Cathedral Church of the Risen Christ. Victor Boullet has resided in Liverpool with his partner Lauren and his two daughters Summer and Billie from 2014, and for the past six years he has walked every morning along the Victorian wrought-iron fence that runs parallel to Hope Street on his way to the studio. The walk went from the artist's home at 7 Mount Street in Liverpool's residential Georgian Quarter to the studio at 50 Enid Street in the working-class district of Toxteth. Every single day, he attached a piece of chewed chewing gum at regular intervals onto the individual railings. In passing the cathedral on November 28, 2018 for a studio visit, Boullet directed my attention to these demarcations. I gathered that this moment, being in company with someone else, was probably the right time for its maker to cast a glance from the outside at traces of an internalised action performed as a daily routine. The moment I was made aware of the first chewing gum demarcation, my gaze wandered further to check the next fence post and the next and the next one after that again. As we were walking along, I continued to register pieces of gum in passing, realising that the entire distance was covered at regular intervals with light pink and white rubbery pieces of chewing gum. Each piece was placed with exact precision at the intersections between the horizontal fence and the vertical fence posts. The amount of chewing gum was identical on each post, reflecting the standardised portion sizes, yet the delicacy of the placement of each piece of gum communicated individual, insisting precision akin to the way brushstrokes of oil paint are placed on a canvas.

Once made aware of the scope of these material congestions, there was no way they could be mistaken as coincidental. These traces of activity in the blind-zone of the visual field communicated a monumental sensation that lingered between repetitious boredom and mania. These traces of an action of necessity by a painter on his way to the studio were obviously not intended to address the extended field of painting, nor to be an expression of *Painting Beside Itself*. Yet, they were definitely «strokes» performed in space beyond the conventional pictorial field. Perhaps this immanent integrity gave them their particular beauty; they were not made to be lifted into a pictorial field, or into the circulation of a network. They belonged to a group of non-instrumental actions executed with existential necessity. They were made with a degree of attention one would expect from any work of art, with one difference; it was not certain that anyone would even take notice of them. A specific attention to the edge zone was expressed, comparable to that of the anonymous artists behind the stained glass windows high up in the towers of the cathedrals where no human can see them.

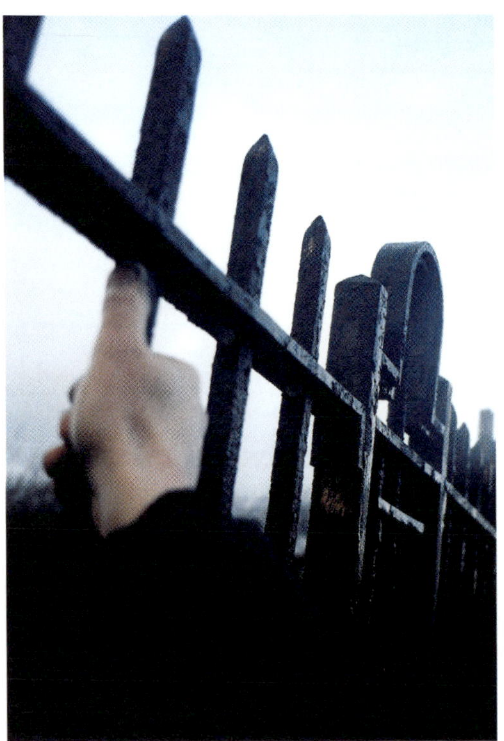

To the People of Liverpool. The Cycle of Poverty Continues, 2017 – 2019
35mm film

Second Walk

In the third arrondissement of Paris in the district of Le Marais, Victor Boullet lived with his family at the intersection of the rue des Archives and the rue des Haudriettes from 2007 to 2012. In 2009 he founded and ran the performative artwork The Institute of Social Hypocrisy which lasted until 2011. The family apartment was situated on the fourth floor of 59 rue des Archives, while The Institute of Social Hypocrisy was localised further up the street at 1 rue Charles-François Dupuis. The distance equaled a comfortable morning walk between home and institute. The straight vertical axis of the rue des Archives runs north-south along the windowless sandstone facade of the National Archive of France. At the doorsteps of the apartment at number 59, the axis of the rue des Archives is crossed by the horizontal east-west axis of the rue des Haudriettes. Café La Perle is situated at 78 rue Vieille du Temple close to the corner of the rue des Archives. Taking one's morning coffee in La Perle introduces a break with the immediate straight walking course of the rue des Archives. This habit not only breaks with the direct axis between home and work, but also connects to a significant axis of modernism and historical avant-garde as the rue des Haudriettes runs between the Musée Picasso and Centre Pompidou.

Parallel to circulating in the 19th century early modernist art market, in their inner structure, the paintings of Millet refused to be part of it. Millet was generally considered a marginal figure by the avant-garde, infamous for boasting that he only read the Bible. Still, significantly, this radically unheard of position was identified as a relevant artistic approach. Despite being immediately recognisable as a genre, it was as if the paintings of Millet possessed a residue that refused to be inscribed and controlled by the emerging art market. In psychoanalytic theory, this immanent contradiction characterises the sublime object. At first glance, a sublime object is recognised as seemingly familiar, yet its alleged normality generates an uneasy feeling lurking beneath the surface. The moment one tries to penetrate its surface and get close to the object, it dissolves. Although it is part of its DNA is to circulate in society, the reason for its attraction is based on an inaccessibility that constantly generates desire. The sublime object can only be observed from a distance, only half seen. What can be formulated, however, is that it refuses to be described. If this process of inscribing the sublime object could rely on standards of measurement, it would not have been inexplicable. The precision of weight in

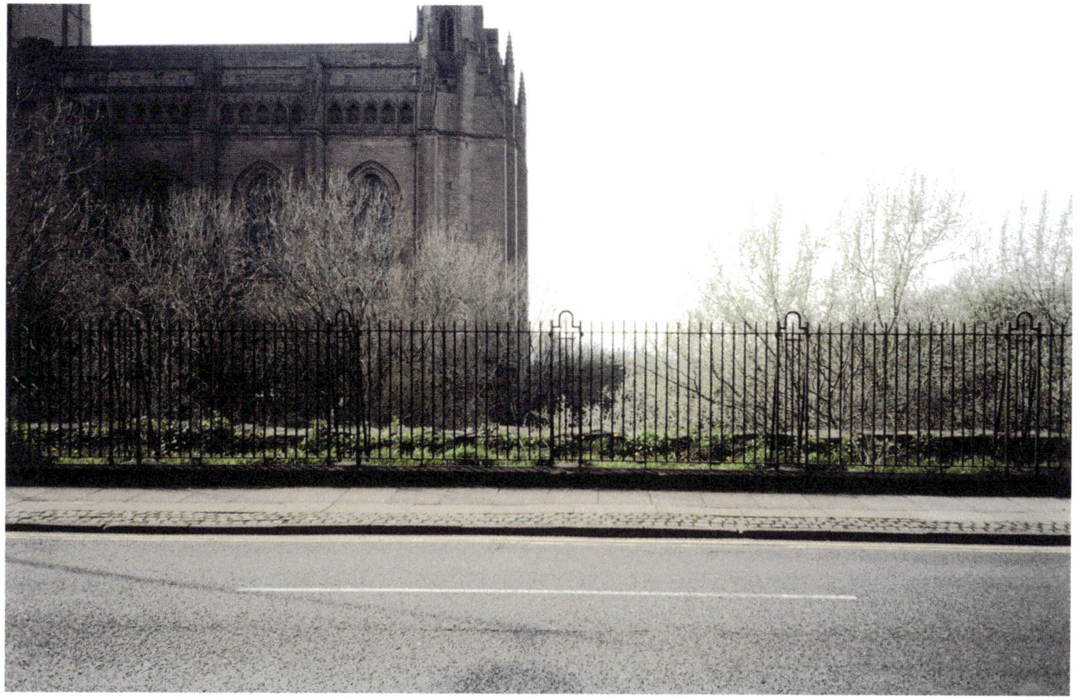

To the People of Liverpool. The Cycle of Poverty Continues, 2017 – 2019
Facing west
35mm film

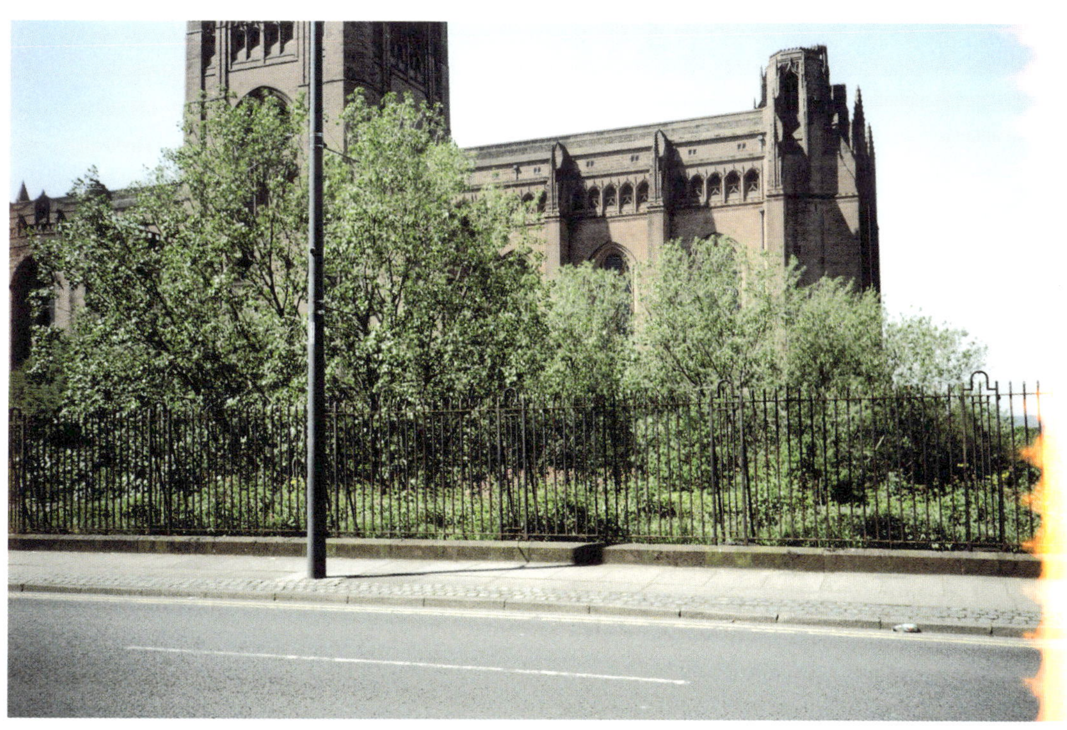

To the People of Liverpool. The Cycle of Poverty Continues, 2017 – 2019
Facing south / west
35mm film

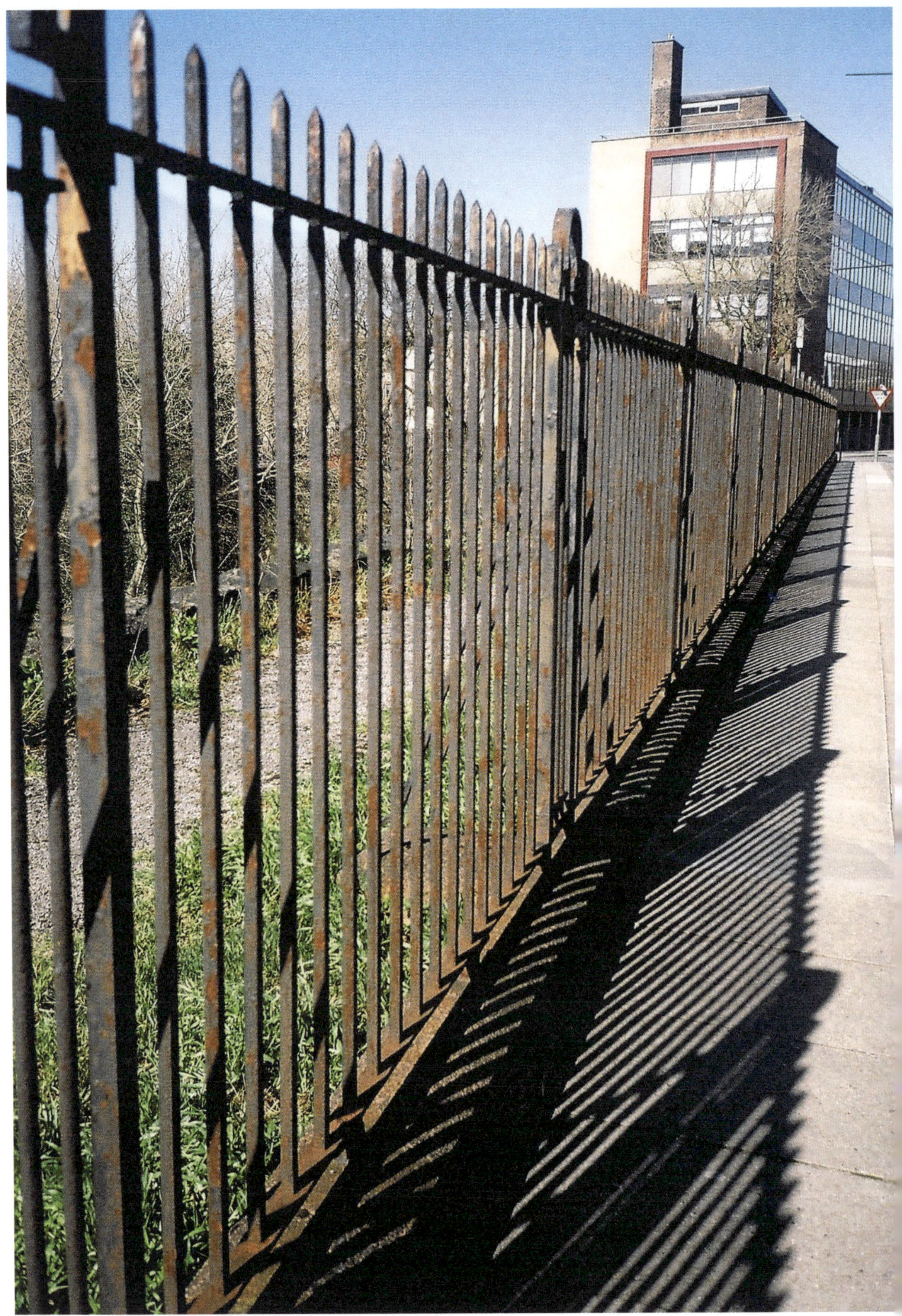

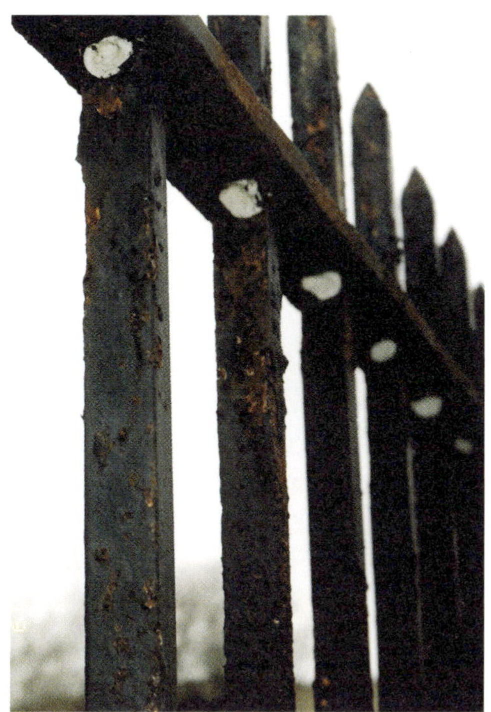

To the People of Liverpool. The Cycle of Poverty
Continues, 2017 – 2019
35mm film

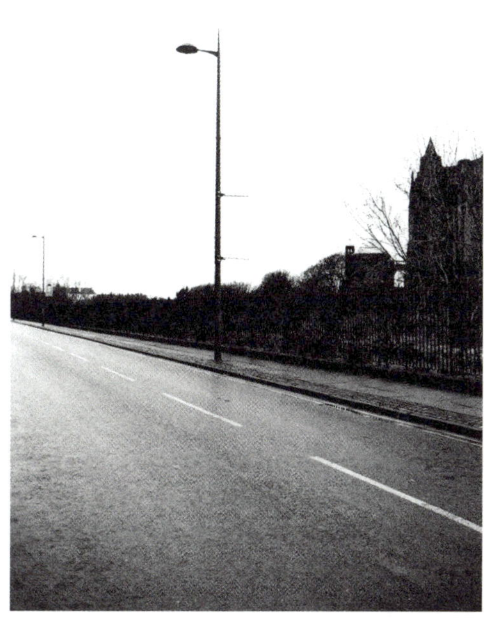

To the People of Liverpool. The Cycle of Poverty
Continues, 2017 – 2019
35mm film

the paintings of Millet is probably as close as we get in measuring the structuring unit at work here.

The Institute of Social Hypocrisy has been described as «a collaborative art program providing a fictitious level of authority behind which the artist's activities could reign free». The fictitious level of authority is of essence here: on a bureaucratic level, fictitious means non-existent. However, it is exactly this fictitious level that generates the inner core of a project that refuses to be inscribed in *the real*. If not anchored in institutional authority, where does it exist? It exists in the moment its activity takes *place*. In other words, space, and not surface is crucial here. Yet it is meaningless to define *place* as something *outside of* or *beyond* this specific site of action. The exact weight in Millet's paintings first comes into being the moment they are painted. The exact distance between home and studio is measured within the every day action of placing pieces of chewed chewing gum on the wrought iron fence that runs along Liverpool Cathedral.

If one was to ask for a measuring standard to be applied outside of these strata, it would lead the Millet painting and The Institute of Social Hypocrisy to dissolve. The hypocritical element is hypocritical only from the perspective of instrumentalisation and usefulness, and it is exactly this strategy that earned the project its position as a relevant platform. The Institute of Social Hypocrisy went directly to the core of the contemporary art world - there are few examples of projects that so openly demonstrates its urge for acknowledgement. Yet in its structure, it refused to accept the rules of recognition and positively lingered between a straightforward, overly ambitious, possible naive, and ethically transparent approach.

Again, the consequence of this activity generated and defined measuring units *relevant only within their own context*. A tenor that embraced and potentially critiqued contemporary art world standards refusing to play by its rules and measuring units. Like the bottles of uranium in Hitchcock's film *Notorious* (1946) that scarcely evaporate to the surface of the white canvas, yet are fundamental for the intrigue, The Institute of Social Hypocrisy worked as an intense undercurrent. The wave of chewing gum attached to the wrought-iron fence at intervals of exact distance, and the exact weight of the sacks in the Millet paintings are equivalents to the uranium bottles, defining exact standards of measurement beyond the neoliberal success criteria of the contemporary art world. They are examples of artistic activity that provide a sensitive optics for an alternative iconology of intervals.

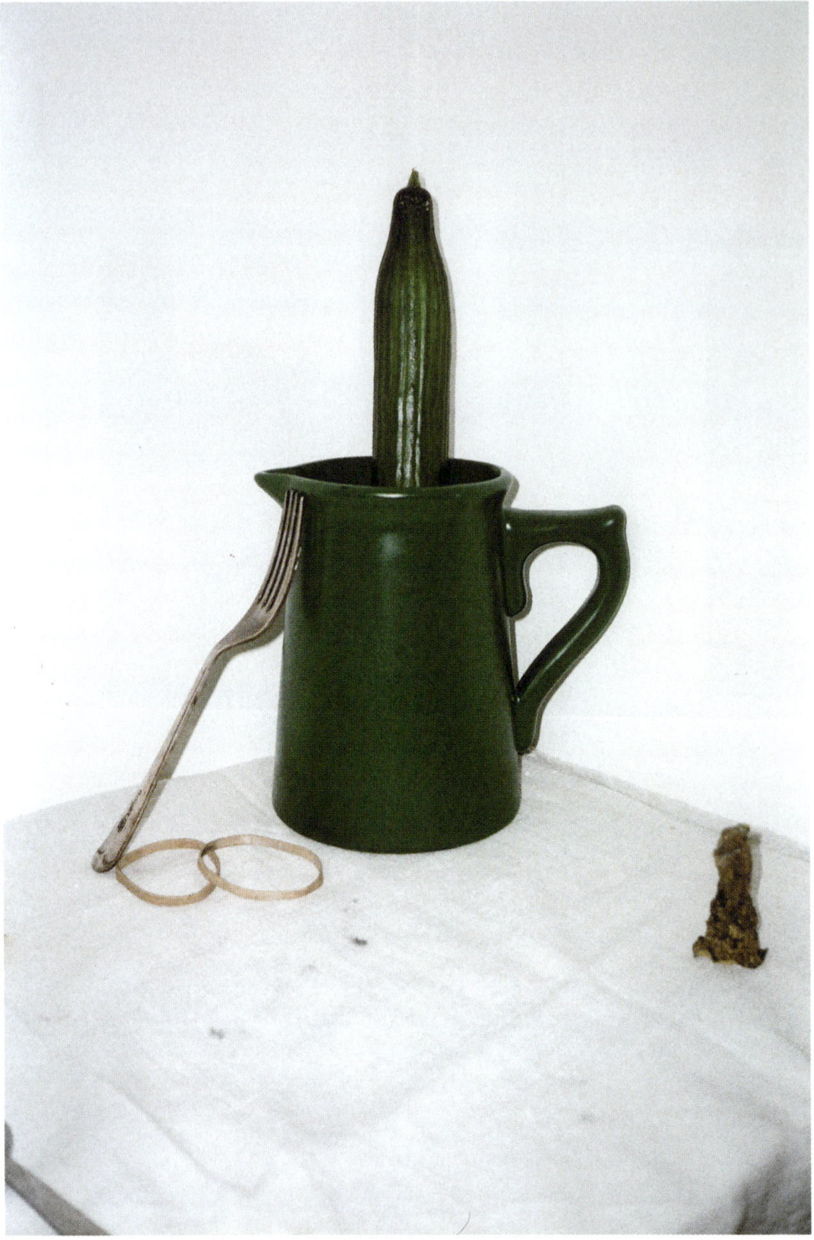

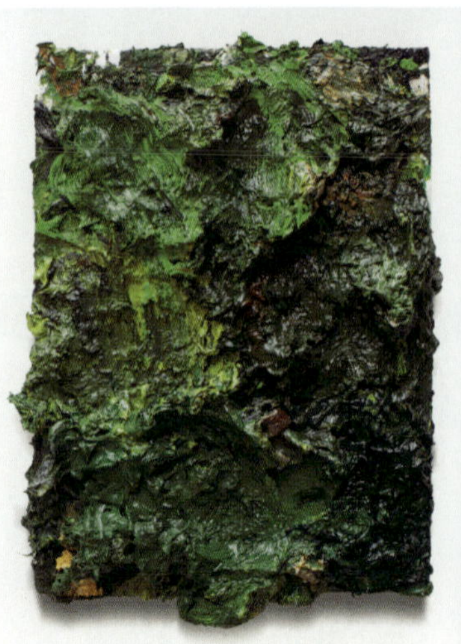

Studio Interior, 2019
Oil on canvas board
14.8cm x 21cm

Studio documentation, 2019
35mm film

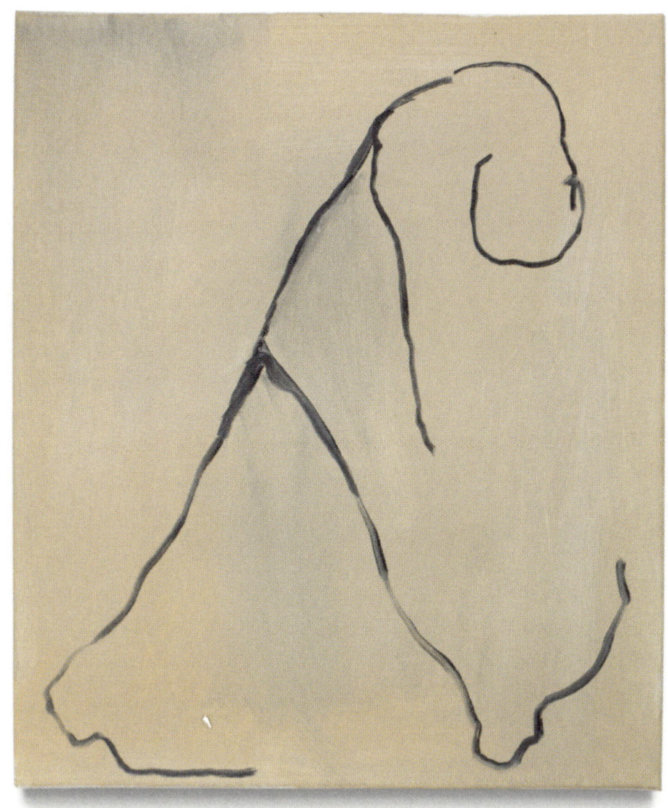

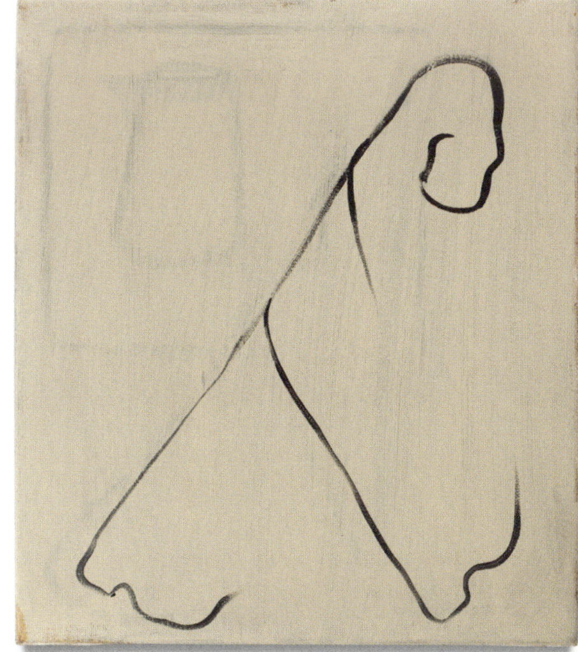

To the Studio, 2019
Oil on linen canvas
20cm x 25cm

Fail.Walk.Fail.Walk.Fail.Walk, 2019
Oil on linen canvas
50cm x 60cm

Fail.Walk.Fail.Walk.Fail.Walk.Fail.Walk, 2019
Oil on linen canvas
40cm x 46cm

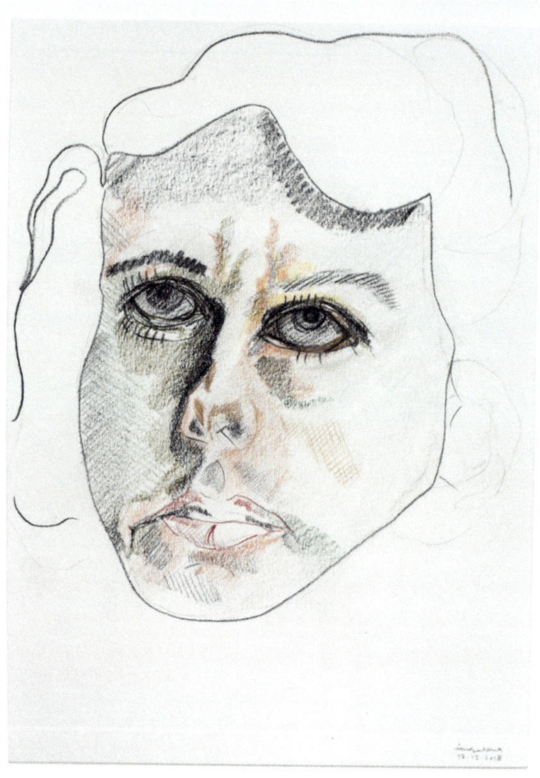

After Lucian Freud, 2019
Pencil, polychromos on paper
21cm x 29.7cm

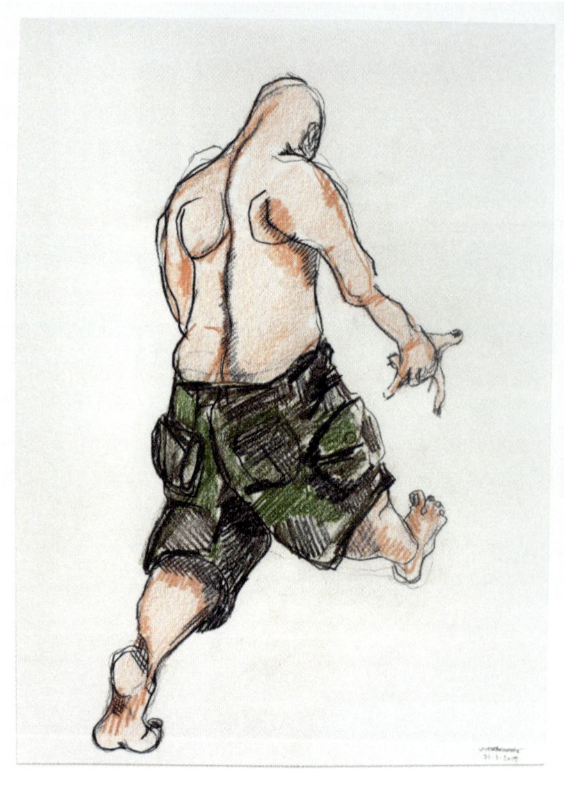

Moving Alone, 2019
Pencil, polychromos on paper
21cm x 29.7cm

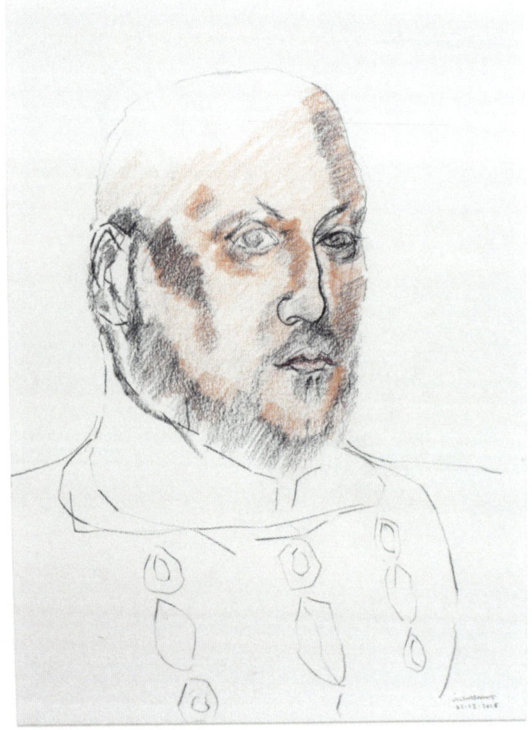

After Hans Holbein the Younger, 2019
Pencil, polychromos on paper
21cm x 29.7cm

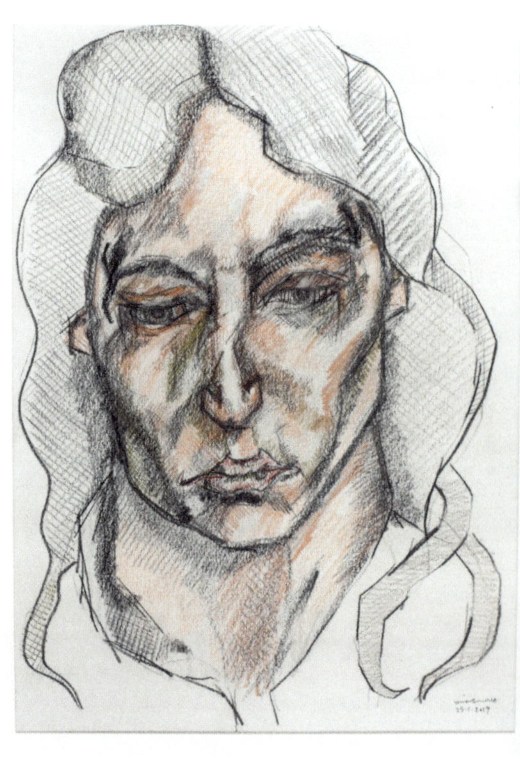

After Lucian Freud, 2019 (p.89)
Pencil, polychromos on paper
21cm x 29.7cm

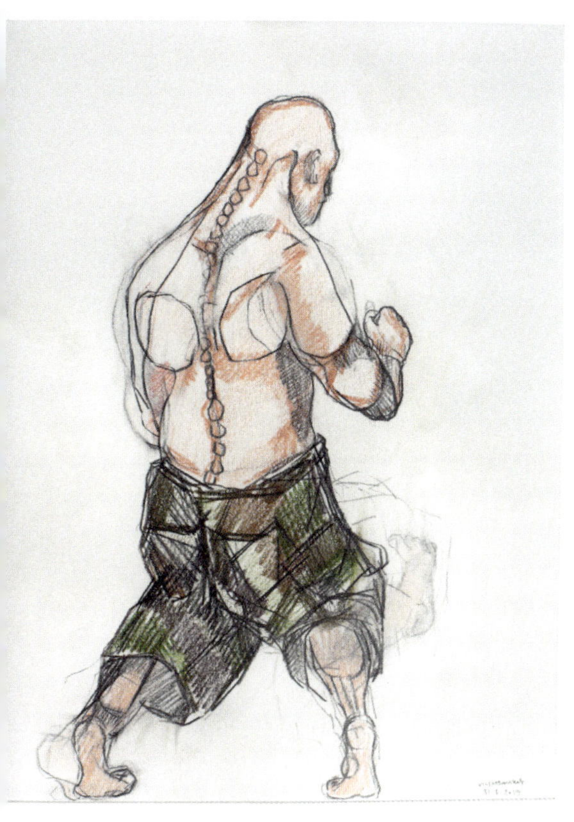

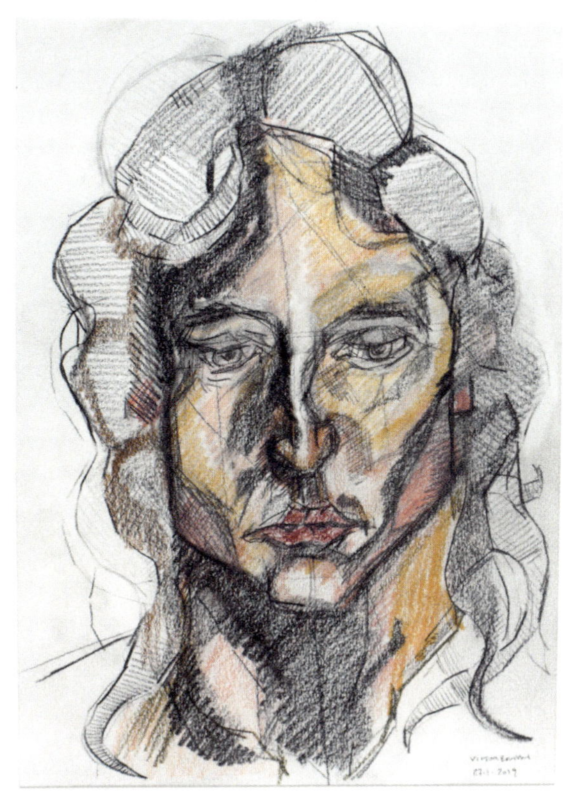

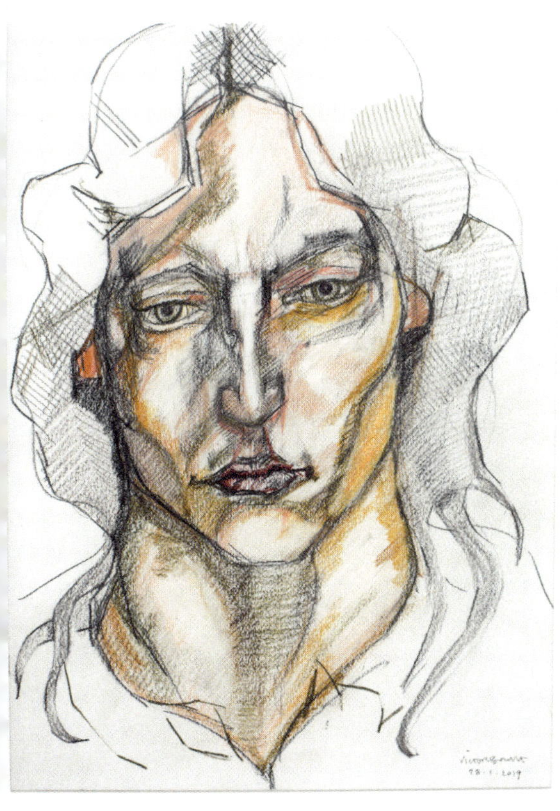

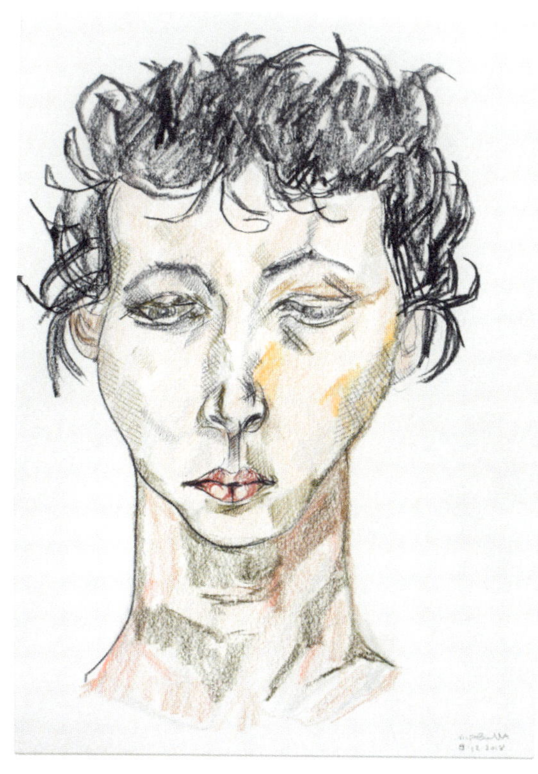

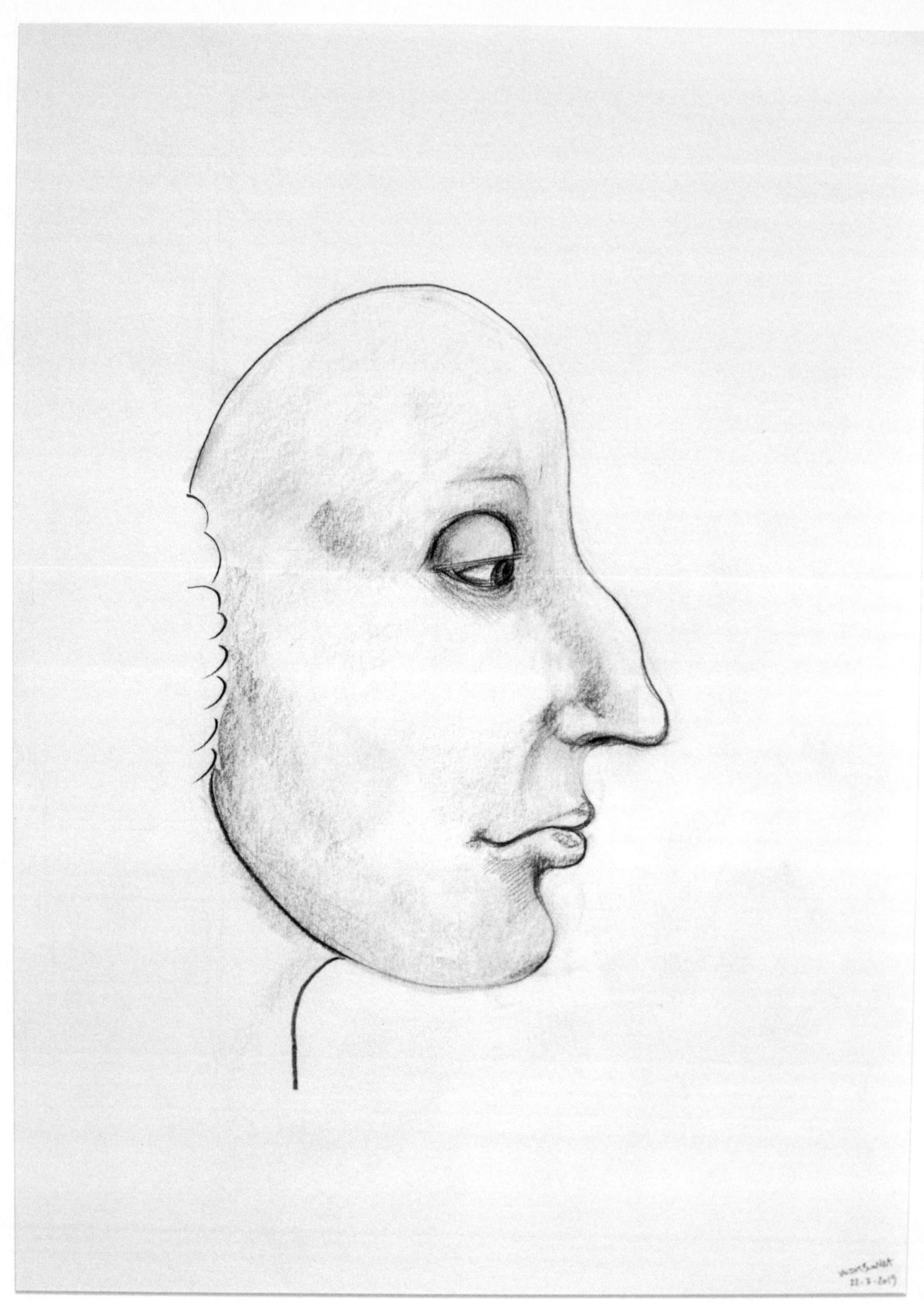

After Piero della Francesca, 2019
Pencil, polychromos on paper
21cm x 29.7cm

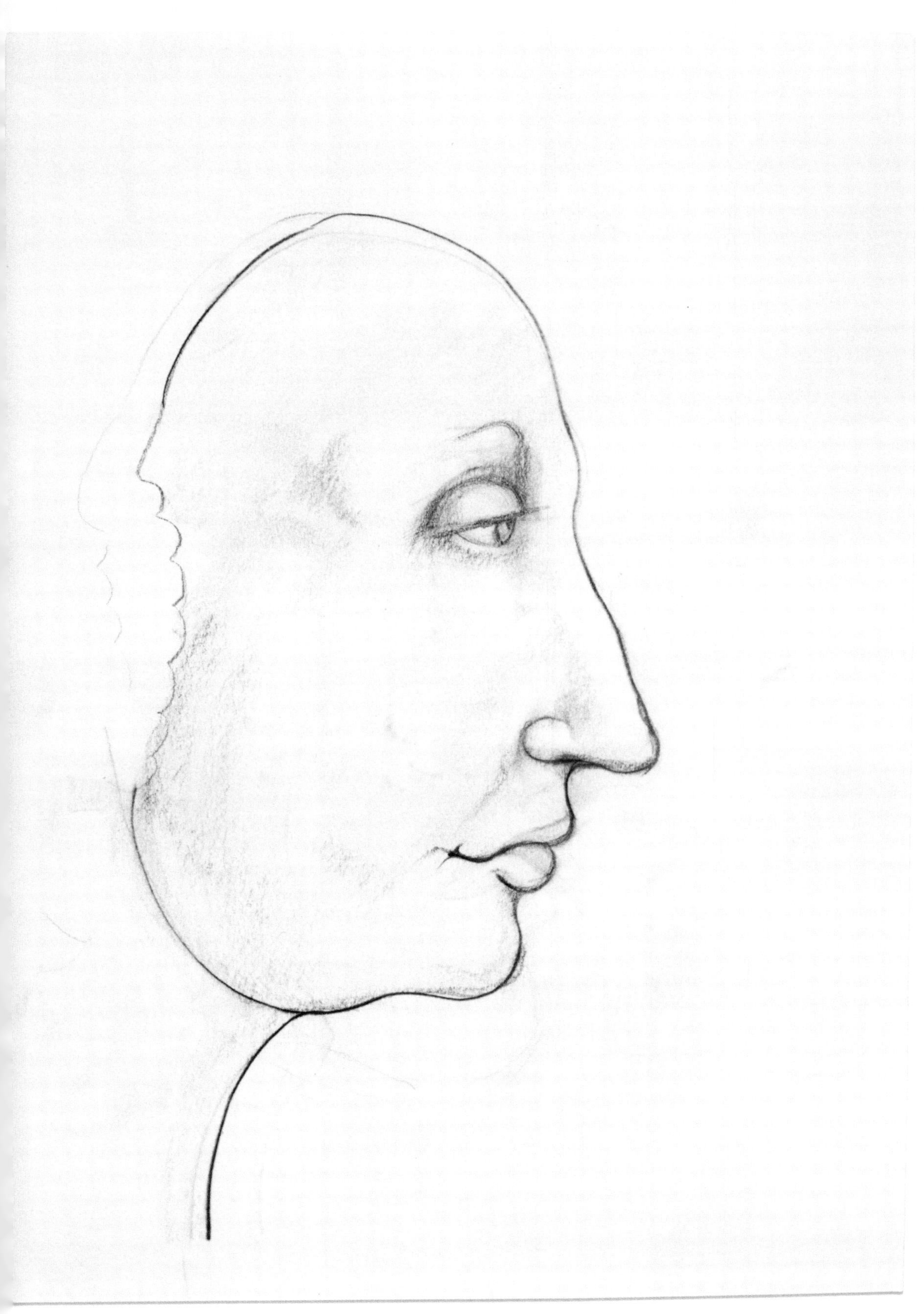

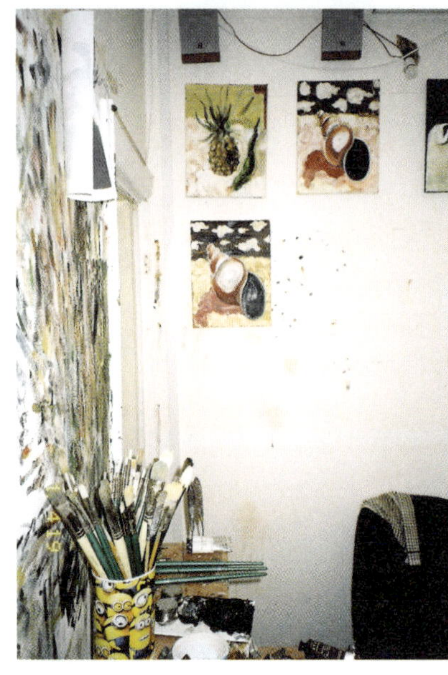
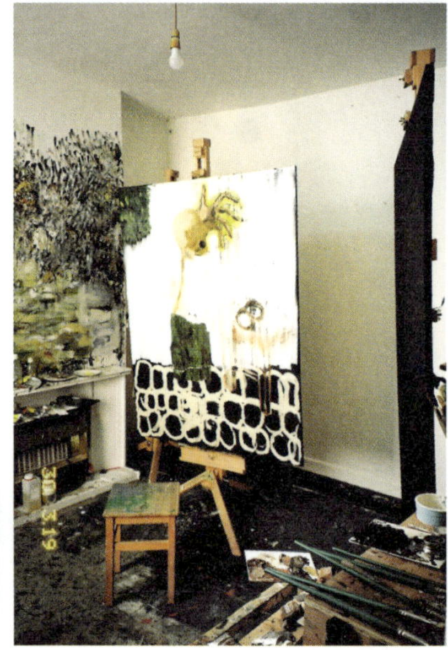
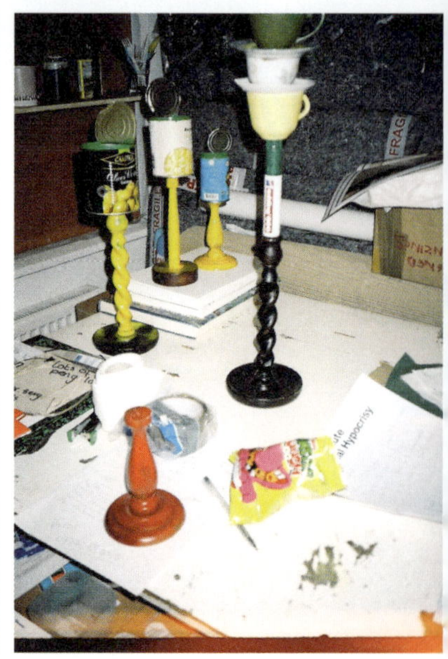
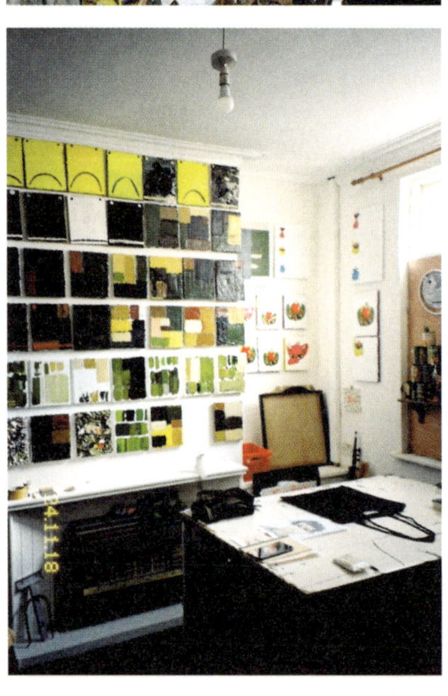
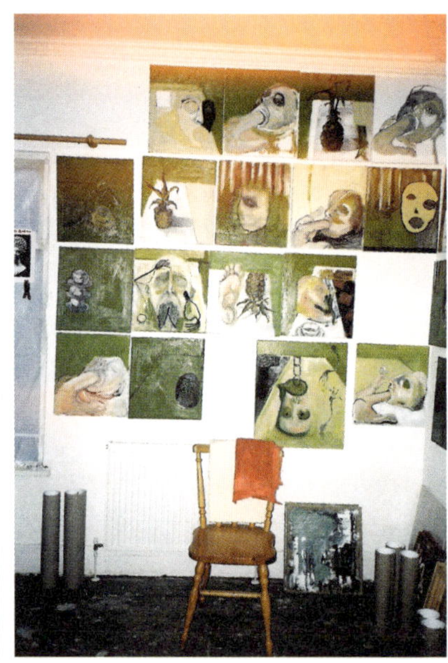
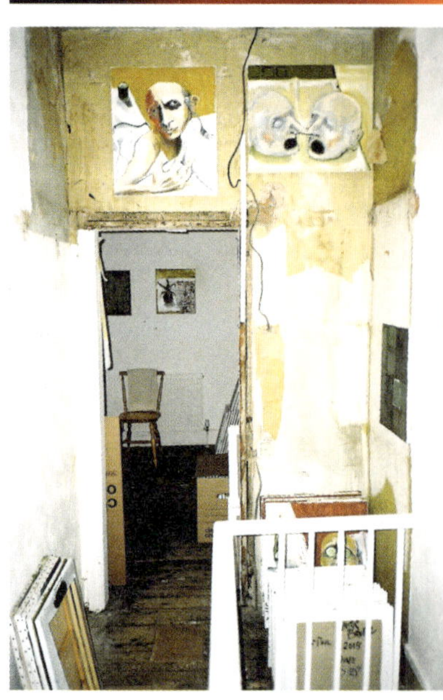
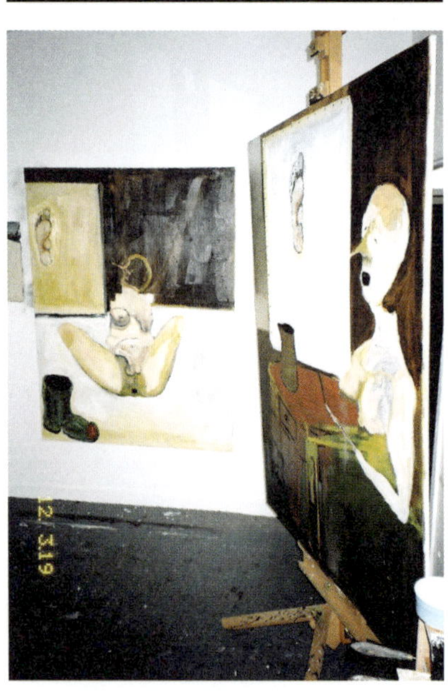
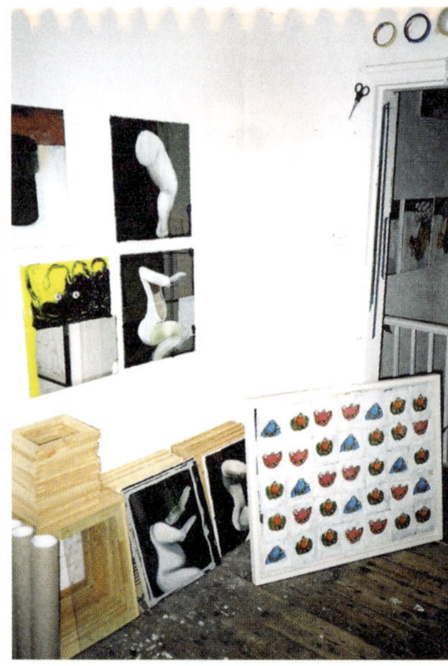
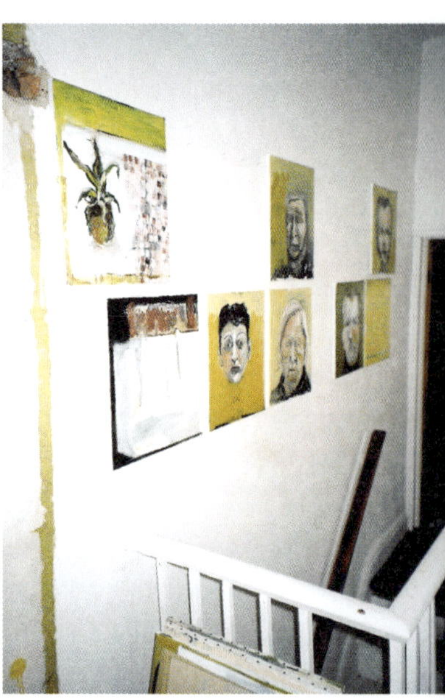

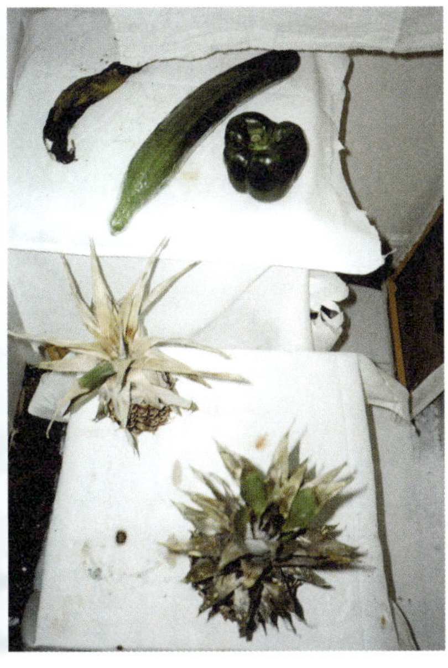

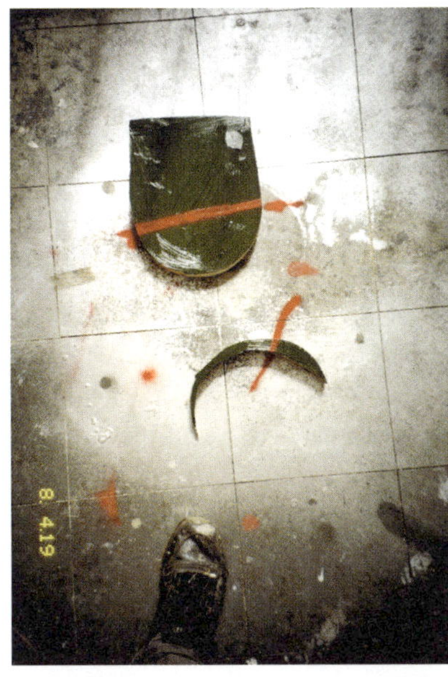
8. 4.19

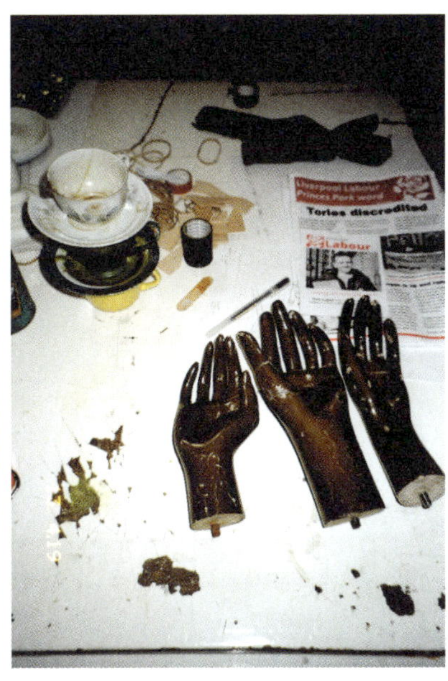
Liverpool Labour
Princes Park ward
Tories discredited
Labour

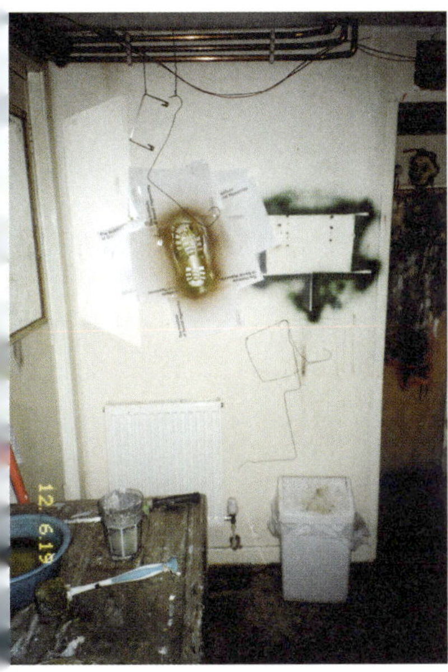
12. 6.19

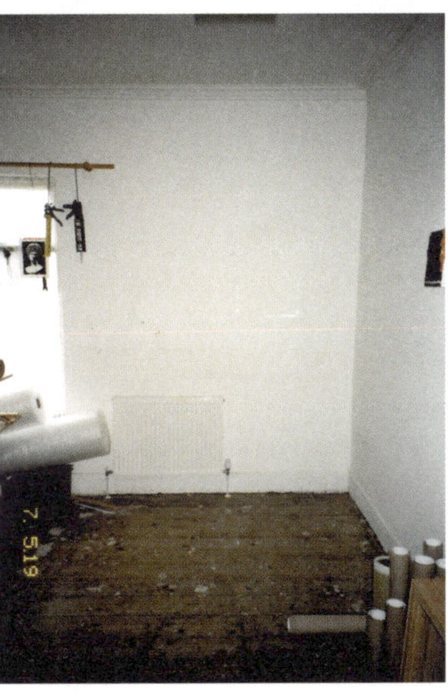
7. 5.19

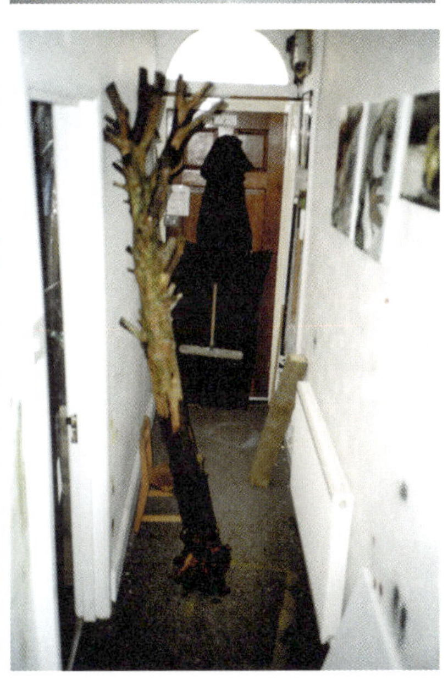

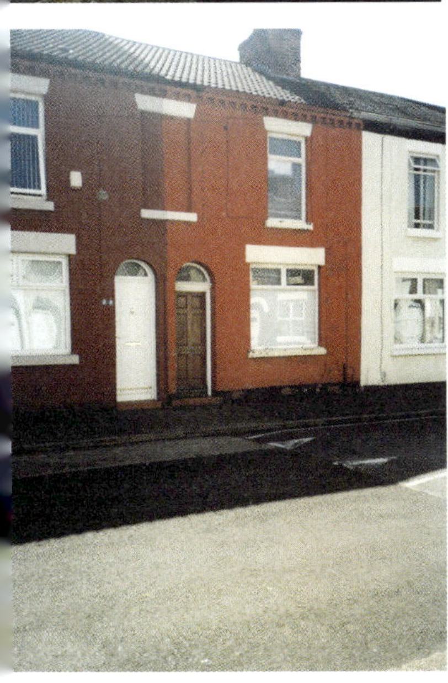

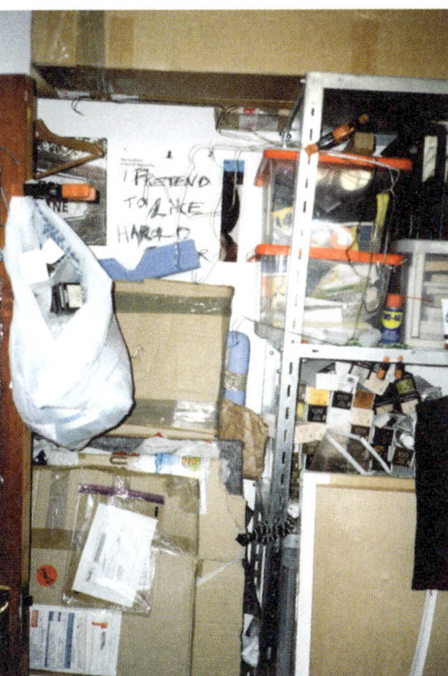
I PRETEND
TO LIKE
HAROLD

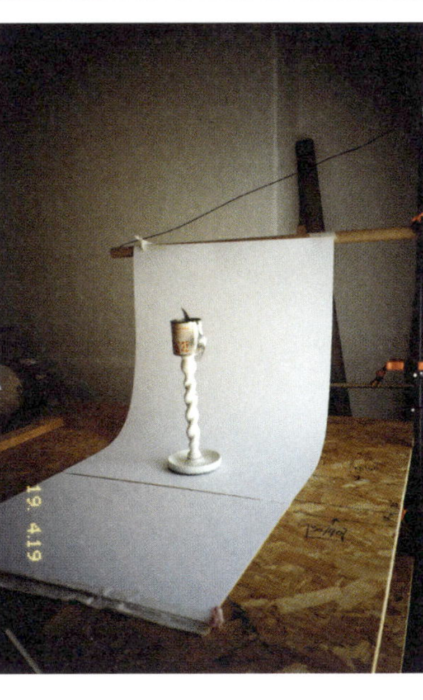
19. 4.19

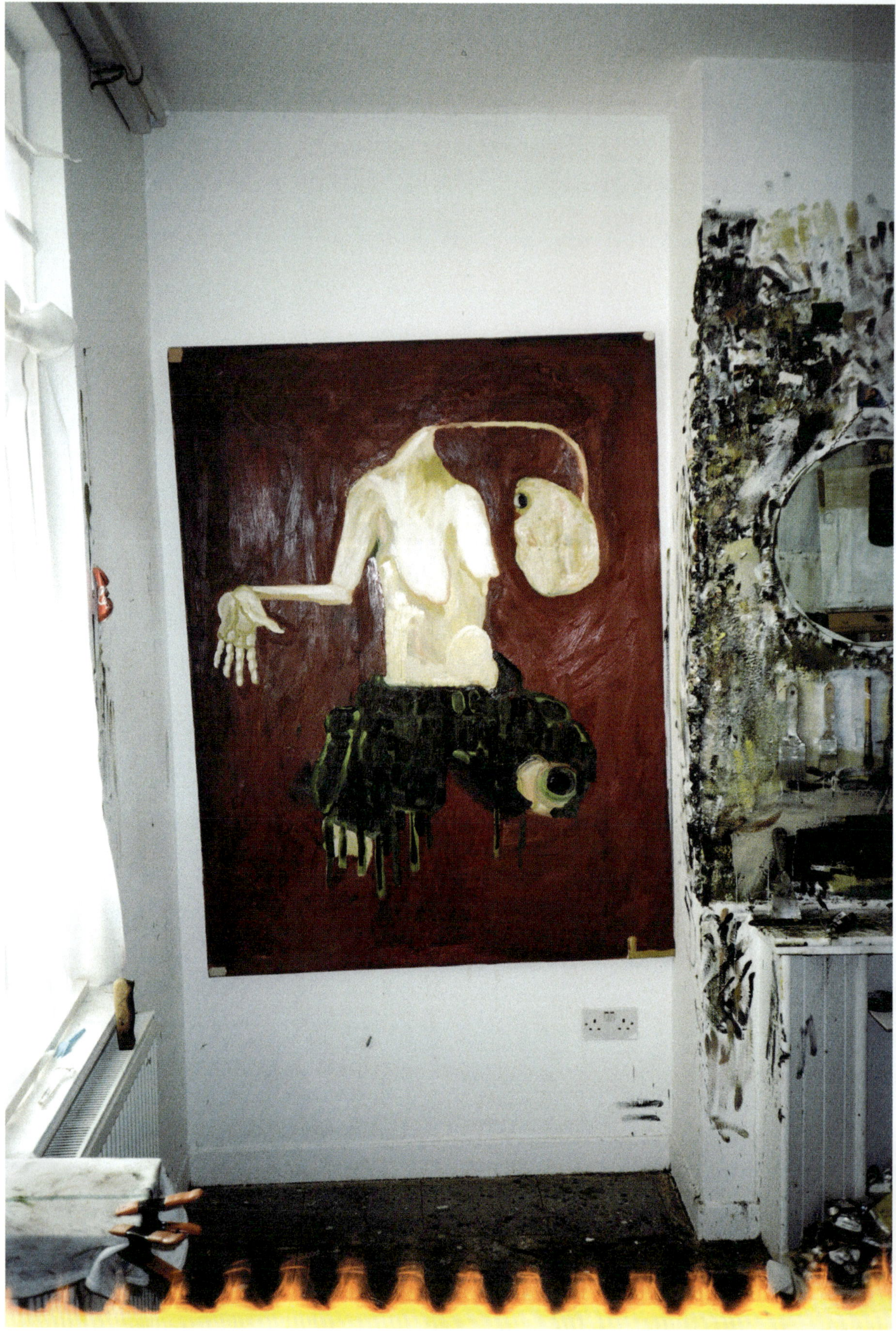

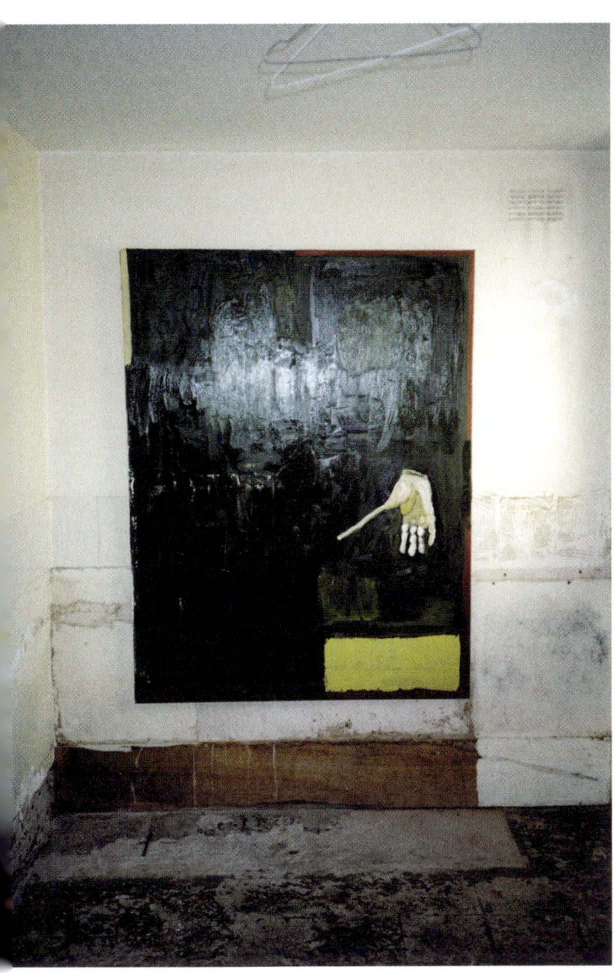

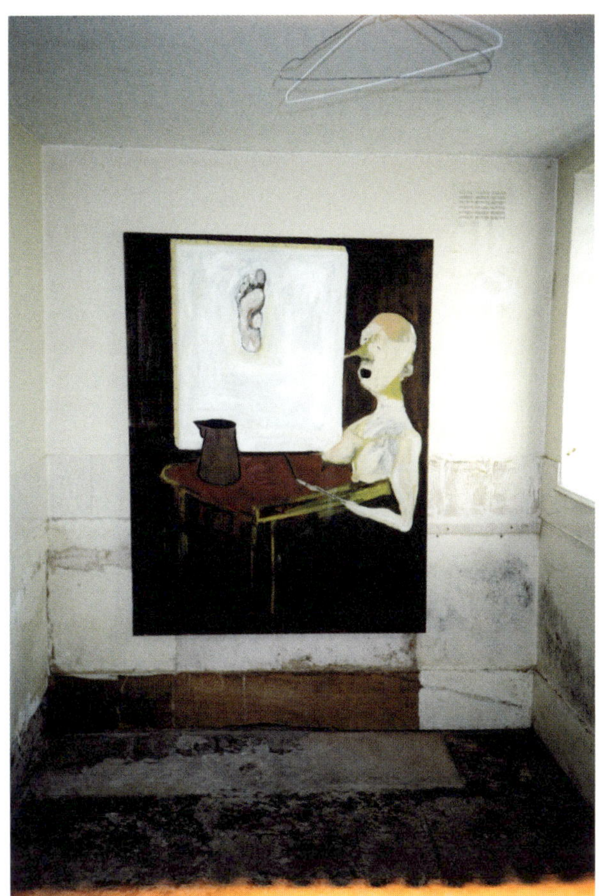

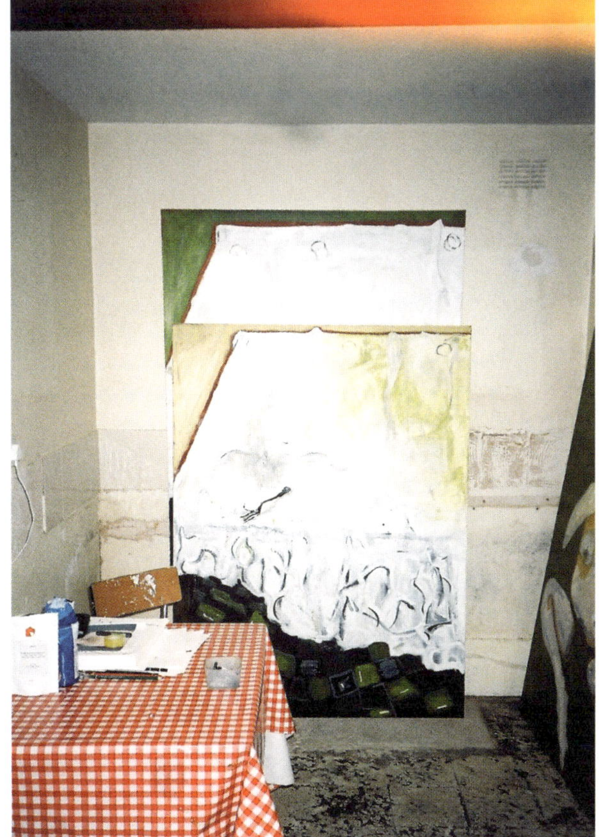

Untitled, I, II, III, 2019
Table, Stuck, 2018 – 2019
Oil on canvas
120cm x 160cm
Studio documentation, 2019
35mm film

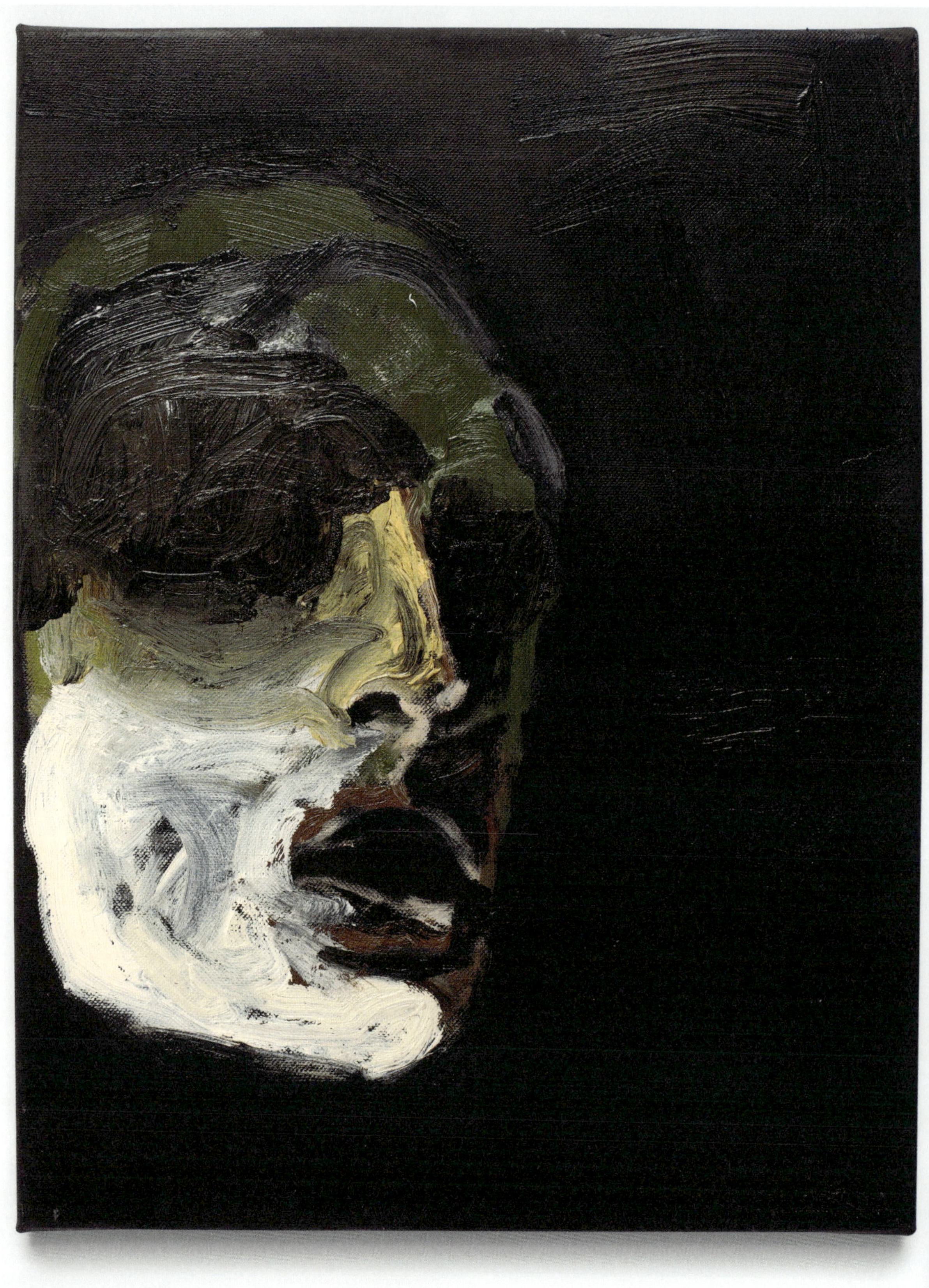

Self-portrait Without Glasses, 2019
Oil on black canvas
30cm x 40cm

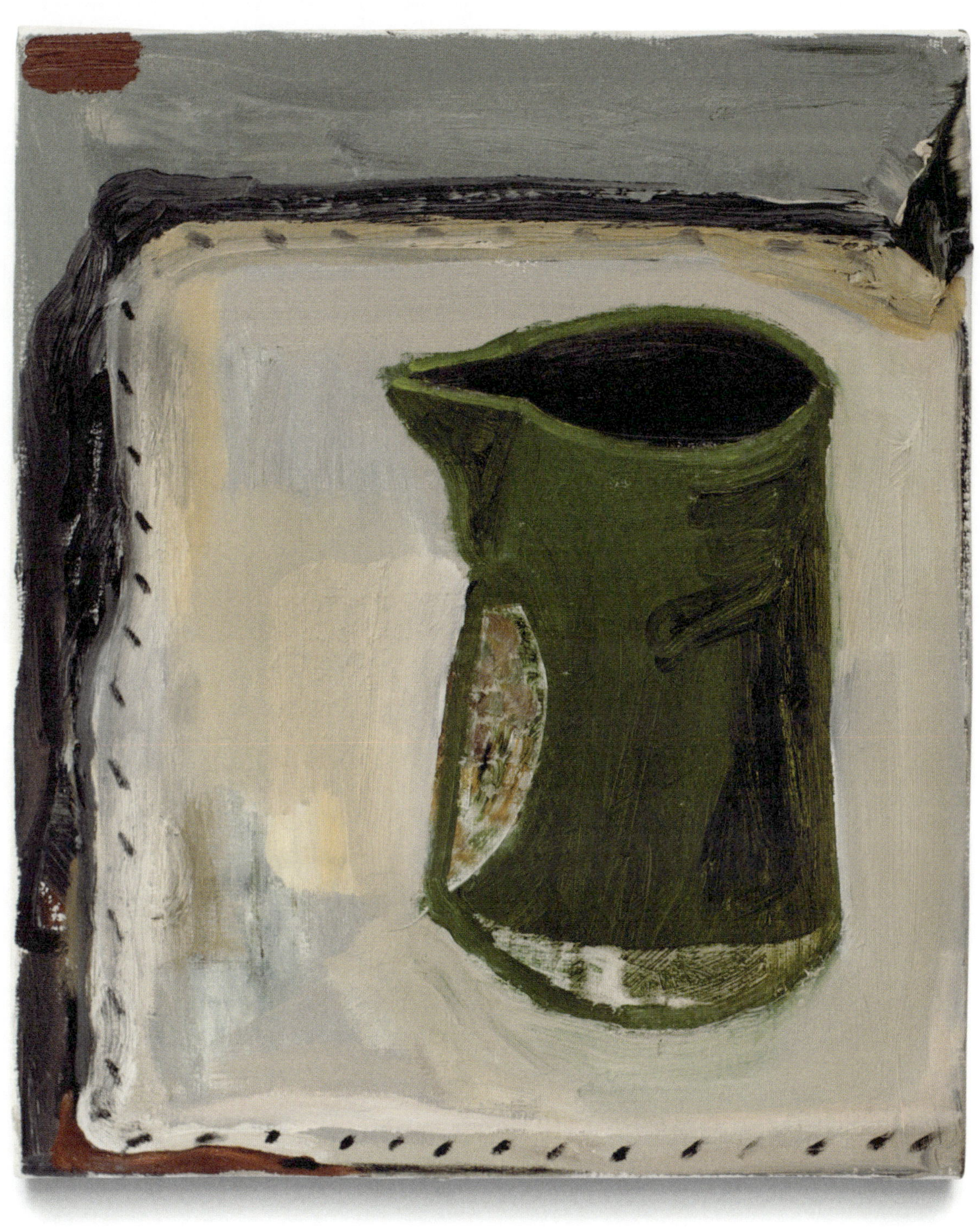

Untitled, 2019
Oil on linen canvas
38cm x 46cm

Raining Stones Everyday

23 March 2015, I crossed Ullet Road and entered Prince's park. Crossing the road you leave L17 and walk into L8. At the time I took no notice of the postcode border other than that one can see certain changes. (I truly dislike Ullet Road)

I was heading for the massive Tesco in Toxteth that day. A building that looks like it has landed onto L8 and crushed everything around it. I walked into the park and came to the middle where the 4 paths crosses, North, East, South and West. This park junction leads to 4 different park exits all funnelling out into L8. I keep walking straight on. To the right I passed a tennis court. To the left I passed some apparatus for exercising, both hopeless offers for a park in L8. It's rather the L17 young professionals that sneak in and use the facilities.

I got to know the park well, because for the first year living in Liverpool after moving from Paris, we rented an apartment in L17 across from the park. In L17 there are a great number of big, old houses from the Victorian era that belonged to families within shipping, slave trading and the power elite of old booming Liverpool. The grand houses today are bought by what I call slaughterers, they divid them up into apartments, and rent them out to young professionals.

Through family we managed to rent an apartment from a likeable landlord called Jim. Jim owns 60+ apartments in Liverpool. 2008 brought Jim the landlord to his knees, which made him understand that greed eats all. He lost his Audi TT and he still can't get an other mortgage. He did vote us out of Europe, a big mistake if you ask me. I truly hate L17 with all its brick and ivy. The street we lived on, the apartment, and my life at that moment in time had never been worse. Jim the landlord says: I prefer young professionals, doctors, teachers, couples preferably. And that was it, those people do not care about anything other than themselves, we had to move asap.

That first time I crossed Prince's Park aiming for Toxteth I exited the west side. The exit has a small gate where one can pass on each side of the columns, but this is not the main gate. The main gate is on the North side of the park, where the gates have a gold flower painted onto them. The main gate opens onto Princes Ave and Princes road that leads straight up to the Old Georgian quarter where we live today.

The park was inaugurated in 1842. And today the north side exit leads to crack dealers on the right and derelict housing on the left and roundabout straight ahead, where one can buy advertising space. Time changes everything, I find that interesting, but Liverpool heritage is suffering and paying the price. Liverpool has been raped too many times by different eras and will Brexit chisel more of its block?

I exited the park on the west side and I had one of my typical early Liverpool reactions, I stood idle, looking up and down the road, in shock, thinking why am I living here? Across the street was a yuppie converted church and the purple bins everywhere. Always desolate. And

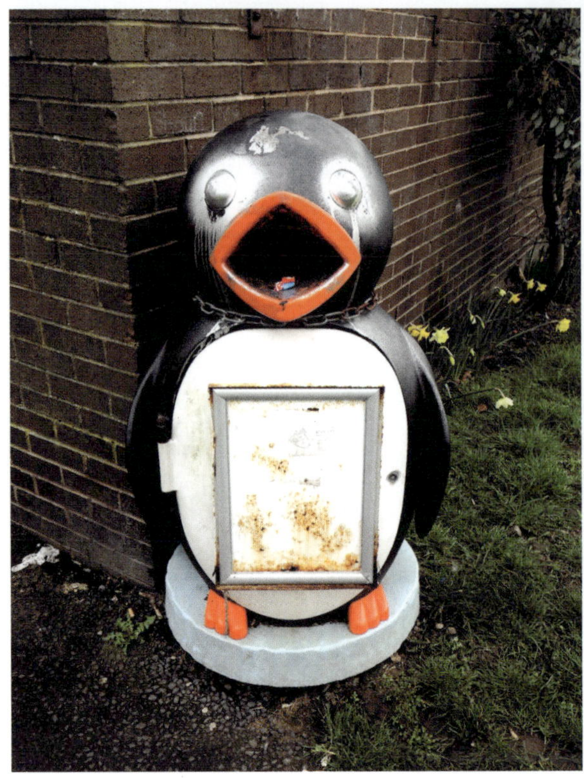

23 March, 2015
Admiral Street, L8, Toxteth
Liverpool

always ugly. That is the one thing I can't get used to, ugly emptiness. The contrast to Paris is still not an easy human adjustment for me.

I finally crossed the road and I could see that the horrible Tesco was lurking behind some trees up ahead. I came up to a pub, I crossed a tiny parking lot and followed a path that lead towards a small green park with Tesco dominating on the other side of it. I stopped, the grim architecture and the loneliness was hard on me that day, and it was too real to handle. I lifted my head from my self pity and I saw something orange pocking out out a corner up ahead.

I laughed, because to my great surprise it was a litter bin shaped like a big penguin. The beak was the hole that swallowed the garbage. It was chained to the wall, and I felt sorry for it, standing there forever eating trash. That penguin, was that me, had I become that garbage eating chained penguin?

In Oslo, 1993 I saw a film by Ken Loach, Raining Stones, hence the title of this essay. The opening scene with Ricky Tomlinson and Bruce Jones stealing a sheep made a profound impression on me. Not in my wildest imagination would I have thought that I would actually live in Liverpool, the film was set in Greater Manchester, but still. In 1993 the film was hard and real entertainment, and it's not until now that I understand that it was and is a reality that I had no connection with at all. It's Raining Stones 7 days a week when I walk the streets in Toxteth.

Shortly after I had discovered that penguin, I saw to my disappointment on my then Instagram account The Lord of Ding Dong that a young artist, who had been invited for the Liverpool Biennial, had done a so-called art reconnoitre. And that the Liverpool Biennial Crew had posted the penguin images and written something very shallow next to it. It made me so angry that I deleted my account that day and have never since bothered with Insta.

What makes me furious is that the Liverpool Biennial Crew invite people to Liverpool and then send them into areas like Toxteth or Dingle like it's a day at the zoo. They come back tail wagging with an image of a penguin bin and tag it Toxteth and Liverpool for the general art world to enjoy.

Curating a provincial Biennial should be an easy affair and a surprise for the art world. Why invite curator friendly Ryan Gander? or show dance move painting by Silke Otto Knapp? Or the art-safari popups in strange Liverpudlian places with banalities from artists like Jason Dogde, who scattered litter on a church floor in Liverpool, a place that is already littered. How can the curators insult Liverpool with such a shallow trick? It seems like the Liverpool Biennial it's only a quick career step for some of these curators. So when that Biennial Crew posted the snap of the penguin bin I knew what I had to do, and they made me do it.

The people that are born and raised on the streets of Toxteth are all proud. This is where they come from. This is what they know. This is who they are. I respect that. I drink tea, every other day with a jack of all trades, a very special character by the name of Tommy. Tommy comes from a family of nine children. They all grew up in a small terrace house in L8. His mother died when he was 13 years old. "Your Mum is the most important thing you can have" he says once or twice a week. His father was a strict Muslim, who slapped the back of their heads if they walked faster than him. The father kept chickens in their basement, he sold around 20 a day. Tommy pays for my tea as often as he can, he is a very generous man.

In this essay I will leave out the following, Julie. Susie. Jackie. Patsy. Lee. Dave. Geoff. Nigel. Egg Head Stev. Yvonne. Sean. Jack Potato. Keith. Bill.

My family and I moved to Liverpool so I could work undisturbed and in silence. We were trying to buy a house and studio in one. Never found that. So we ended up buying a Georgian town house in L1. The day we viewed the house we also learned that the couple renting it were involved with the Liverpool Biennial, one was a curator. We mentioned that they could have our apartment when we took over the house, like an easy swap for them. The couple cycled over to L17 to have a look. The curator entered our flat and loudly grabbed a book I had just received as a present. The curator is not stupid, but the curator has no social antennas, the curator is self obsessed and self centred. Jim, our then landlord, rang me a few days later and uttered his worry about this curator, he did not want to rent out his flat to them because of the curator. I laughed.

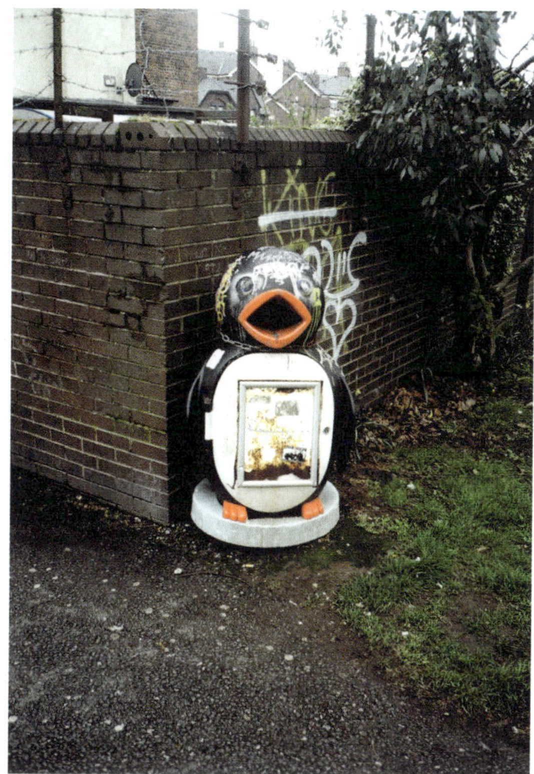

31 March, 2019
Admiral Street, L8, Toxteth
Liverpool

I was later invited to a few happenings that the other member of the couple was involved with. I was introduced to the Liverpool art crowd, but I was not interested. These happenings were very good, except the curator always managed to plough over the conversation that the other member of the couple was trying to give, and it was awkward every time. Each time I met this curator I was stunned how out of sync the person was. That was it, I had now met someone from the Liverpool Biennial Crew, and maybe that someone was capable of posting junk onto their instagram and tagging it Toxteth and Liverpool. It really irritated me.

The other day someone knocked on my studio door, in L8, it's rare, so I jumped out of my skin. The people that knock are often travellers trying to sell you a mattress or kitchen knives. But this day it was a true Liverpudlian man wanting to clear the front of my house of weeds. It's only a little strip where the foundation of the house meets the tarmac that creates the pavement.

He wanted £3 for the job "it's that time of year" he said. I am not sure what went through my tiny head, but I turned him down, and shut the door. I went back to my painting, but I was so bothered with my decision, so I stopped painting. £3 I could have paid him, it might have made a difference for him. There is another scene from the film where Bruce Jones knocks on doors, asking if he can clean their sewage. He needed the cash to pay for his daughter new dress. I should have paid him the £3. I daily think about this and feel shame. What I'm trying to understand and explain is that I learn something new everyday in L8.

Each time I open the door to my studio I don't know what to expect. I have made weapons so I can defend myself if they come knocking and attacking. I carry different types of weapons for my walks incase I'm attacked. I have respect for the streets in L8, they are friendly, but they are also very violent. And this is why the penguin image has caused such anger with me. L8 is not a safari, it's not a place you walk through in a day and snap art-superficial-research images to share your trophy via social media with the rest of the art world. The Liverpool Biennial crew should have simply explained to the artist that this is not anything they could use for their instagram. Let's not forget the American Dr and his trophy images that caused such anger on social media. And it makes me think of Robert Frank crossing America, spending 5 years sucking out his sad poem. He remained in America and he will most probably die in America, but the The Liverpool Biennial Crew have already been replaced. I like Robert Frank.

09:30, 1st April 2019. I met Tommy for a cup of tea and I asked if he is still driving Dave's van.
He asked why? I need you to help me do a job. He said no problem, what is the job. I looked at him and asked: do you have bolt cutters? He turned and looked: Why? I answered: I want to steal a penguin. He laughed. I explained why and where, not the whole story, but he said: Ok I'll do it.

09:30, 2nd April 2019. It was raining and I entered the cafe with my Death Of Mother Earth rain coat, it went silent and then the banter kicked off they talked about my rain coat, I loved it. This particular morning Ian, another handyman, with lots of missing teeth was there with Tommy. There were two girls sat across the cafe aisle. Tommy and Ian were on form that morning, they were funny, rude and being true L8 lads. I lent over towards Tommy and ask: Do you have the van today? He looked at me, jumped up and told everyone: Guess what Victor want's to nick. And he walked down the cafe aisle like a penguin. They all laughed, and I was totally embarrassed.

After our tea we drove up to have a look at the penguin. I mentioned bolt cutters, but Tommy said just loosen the nuts on the bracket and it will come loose, it's easy. We drove back and he said I'll get that for you, don't worry. I felt the relief of not doing the job, and just having the penguin being delivered on the door.

09:45, 3rd April 2019. I arrived at the cafe and it was empty. I asked for Tommy, but he had not been in. I went to the studio and called Tommy, no answer. And I felt uncomfortable calling him about this job, and also with him stealing the penguin for me. I had to do the job myself. And I was in need of a van.

Jim, our old landlord owns a van, so I called him. We chatted, and I asked if he still owned the van, he replied that he just bought a new one. I continued to ask if he still drove to town every morning to dropped off his girlfriend, to which he replied yes. I asked if he would like to do a little job with me that next morning, after his drop off. He replied yes, of course. Jim is a helpful and honest man from Rochdale.

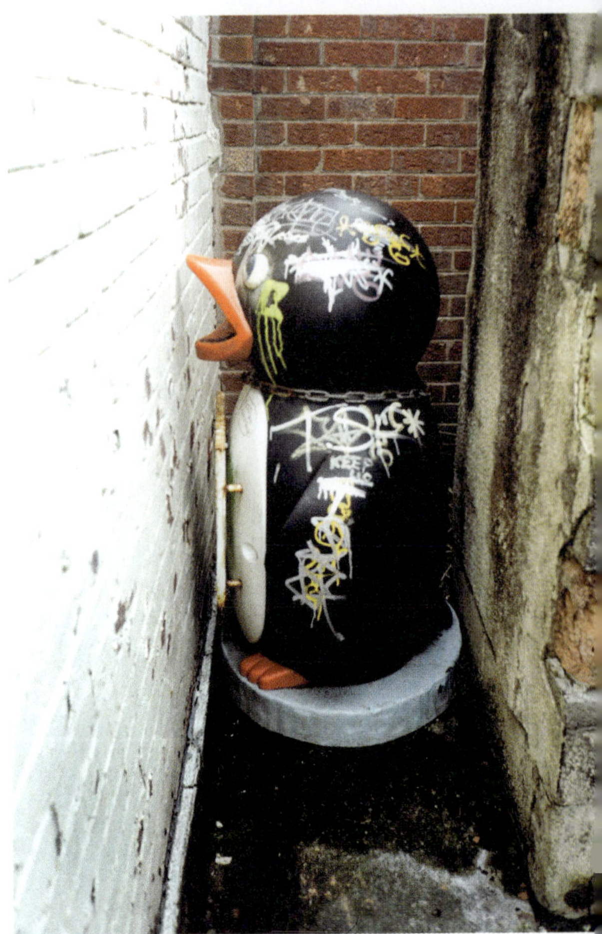

1 April, 2019
50 Enid Street, L8, Toxteth
Liverpool

07:05, 4th April 2019. Jim arrived with his new van and it was big enough for the penguin. We drove off and turned into Toxteth and I explained our job, he replied with a little nervous laugh followed by ok. We parked up at the pub. There were dog owners and the corner store chap on the other side of the street looking at us sitting in the car. Jim was nervous which made me nervous. Finally the coast was clear and we went to work. After the nuts came off I could not loosen the bracket from the wall. Fuck. Jim mentioned that a crowbar would do the job, I had a big hammer in the studio. So we drove to the studio. I quickly popped into the studio to fetch the hammer, and I stopped in the hall for a few seconds, wondering if this was necessary. Do I have to steal this penguin to prove this point? I must!

So we drove back up, but this time we parked on the south side of the pub. We had to cross the green to get to the corner where the penguins stood, it all made sense and it was Jims idea. We got out of the car and when we approached the penguin a woman came from the other side of the pub. There I was with a hammer 07:25 in the morning, she looked at me, I turned towards the penguin, I have no idea what Jim was doing. I took the claw side of the hammer and yanked the bracket loose, it was done with three goes, I turned to see if the woman had kept walking, but no, she had stopped and was now looking at us.

The penguin was free. I quickly turned it around and put my hand into the beak, told Jim to grab the other side and so he did. We were now carrying the penguin and I felt the rush of adrenaline and the scene of Ricky Tomlinson and Bruce Jones stealing the sheep popped into my head. I was now living it, I was doing it. We got to the end of the green and we stepped over a little fence and onto the parking lot. I opened the van hatch slung the hammer in and looked over to see if the woman had left, but no, she was still looking. We shoved the penguin in, feet, or base first. Got into the car and I could tell that Jim was not being himself.

My old landlord Jim had done the job with me. I liked that. He managed to turn the new van around and he made a left turn. He does not know his way around Toxteth, so he drove around up and passed the Police station and then the pub again. I said: Let's get out of here. The penguin was rolling around the in the back of the van and it stank of dog piss and poo.

The penguin fitted through my studio door by turning the beak up and the wings squeezed perfectly through the door opening. It's now in the back yard waiting for it's transport. I am nervous, because I can be killed or seriously beaten up over something like this.

I will return the penguin, it belongs to Toxteth.

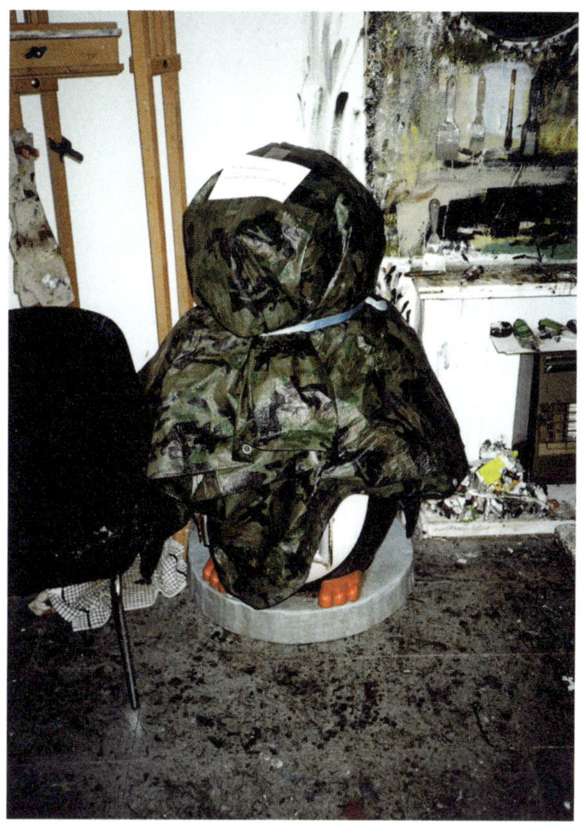

2 May, 2019
50 Enid Street, L8, Toxteth
Liverpool

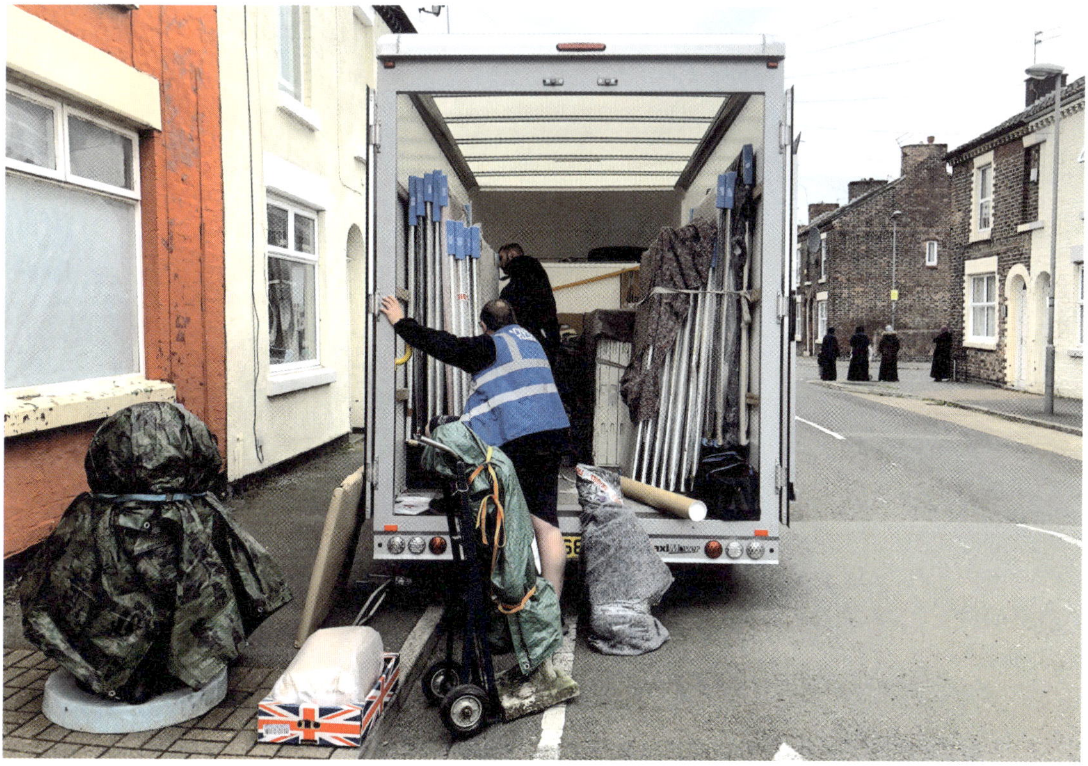

7 May, 2019
50 Enid Street, L8, Toxteth
Liverpool

Toxteth Error Lad

Victor Boullet

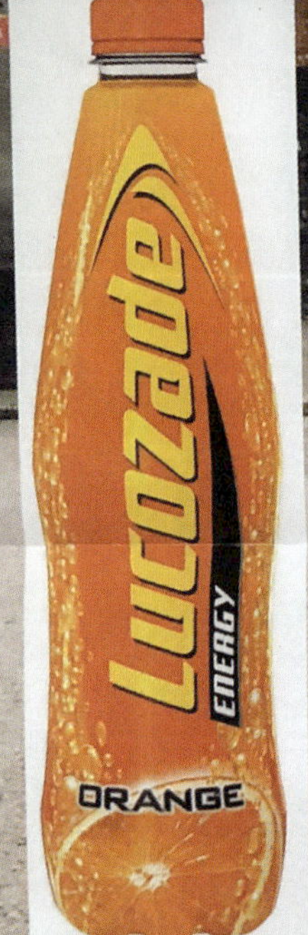

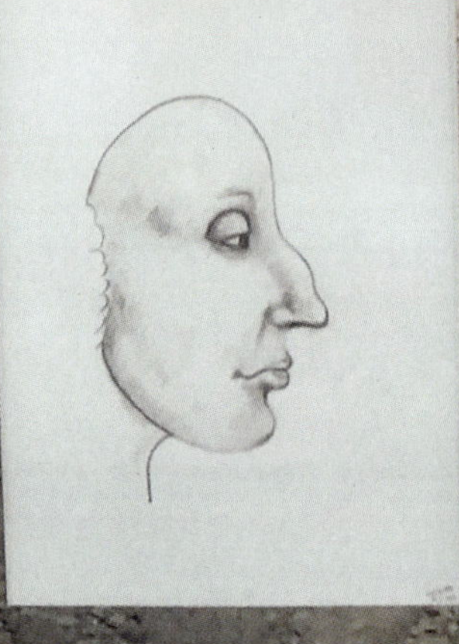

ANNA BOHMAN GALLERY
STOCKHOLM 2019

Toxteth Error Lad

I'm not entirely sure where I left off, but I'm not back to entertain. I'm still the same Victor Boullet, but I'm not that man that was running The Institute of Social Hypocrisy, things change.

I live in Liverpool, I paint. I'm white. I'm heterosexual. I vote Labour. I'm turning 50 this summer, not very comfortable with that.

Liverpool is not a place I like.

I've just had another episode with insomnia. It's not nice. I woke up last night at 01:04, twisting and turning with a very active brain. 04:07 I got up. The house was pitch black. Trying to find the door is a challenge while the floor offers all the correct noises an old Georgian house is capable of delivering.

Descending the stairs in the dark naked is not something I do very often, because I usually trap my body in bed with the hope of another minute sleep. But this time I thought a sip of water could help my hectic brain to calm down.

I entered the kitchen and the floor tiles were cold. I struggled to locate our low and small IKEA fridge, 132 litre. I dropped my arm, found the handle and opened the door.

The light from the fridge hit my face and a body shaped shadow filled the room behind me. I looked down for the water, but sadly the light had lit up my white cock, belly and tits in such a cruel manner that I felt super surprised and I could not believe how unsexy I was.

Cock, tits and a fridge, mushrooms, eggs and belly.

I quickly drank my water direct from the plastic bottle and put it back onto it's shelf and again that view of my ageing body, fuck.

I shut the door, and the room went black, I closed my eyes getting ready to manoeuvre back to the stairs, but to my horror the bright light from the fridge had been imprinted onto my retina, a white silhouette agains black, that of my two tits and stupid cock.

I got out of bed at my usual time 06:30

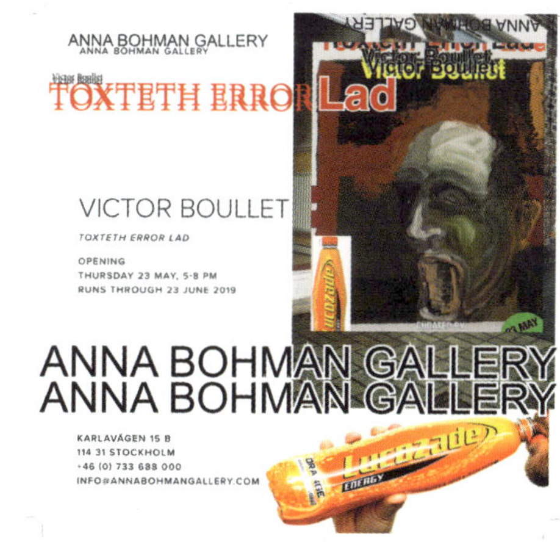

Toxteth Error Lad, 2019
Exhibition invitation
Promotional material

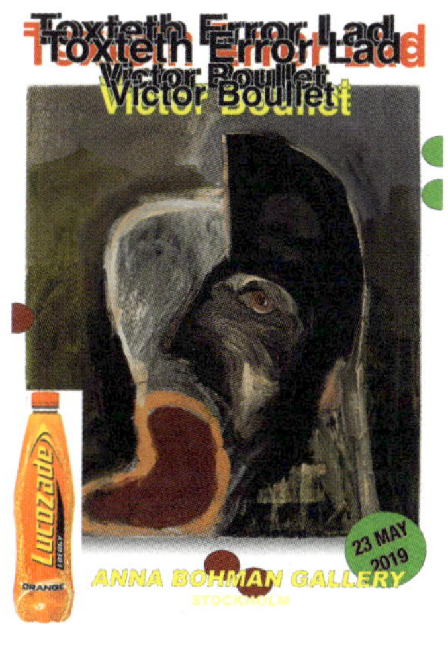

Toxteth Error Lad
Exhibition poster, 59.5cm x 42cm folded to 21cm x 30cm
Design by Texas Knuller

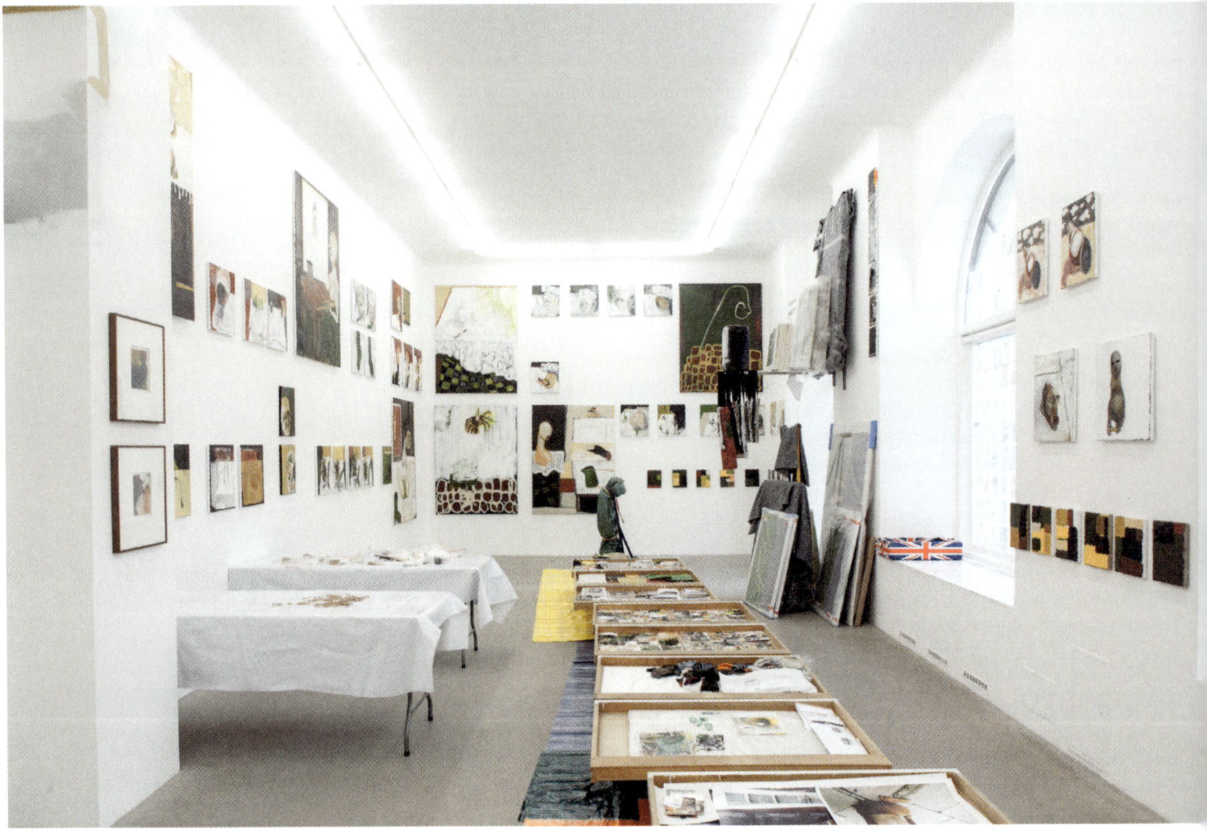

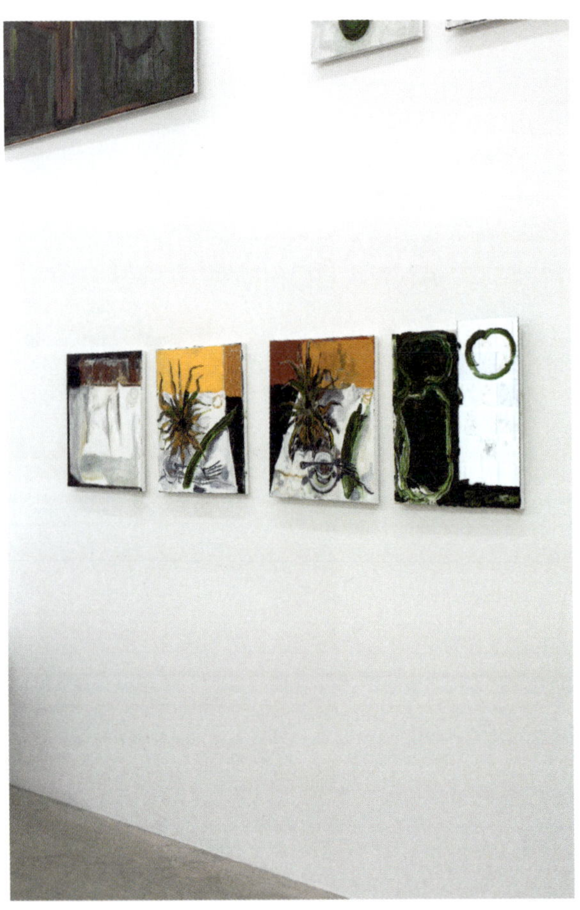

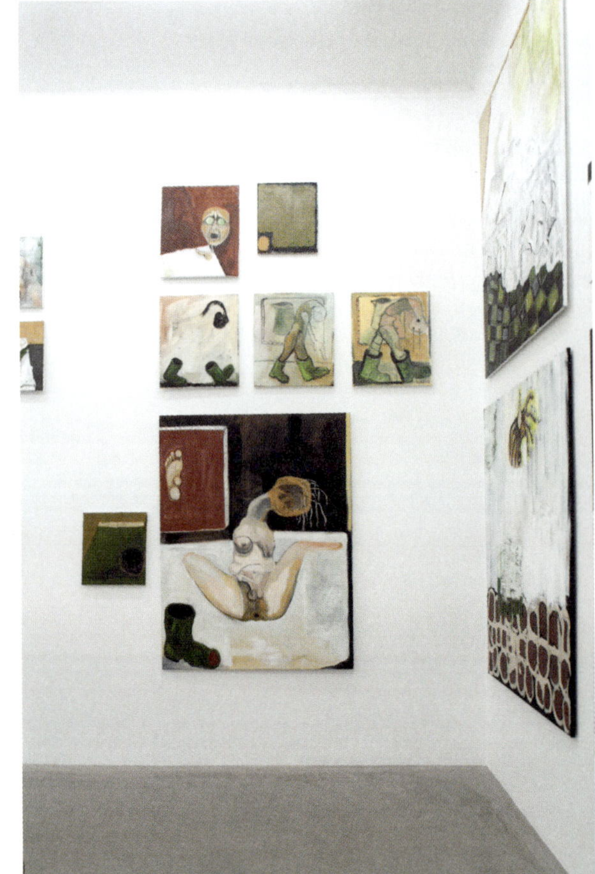

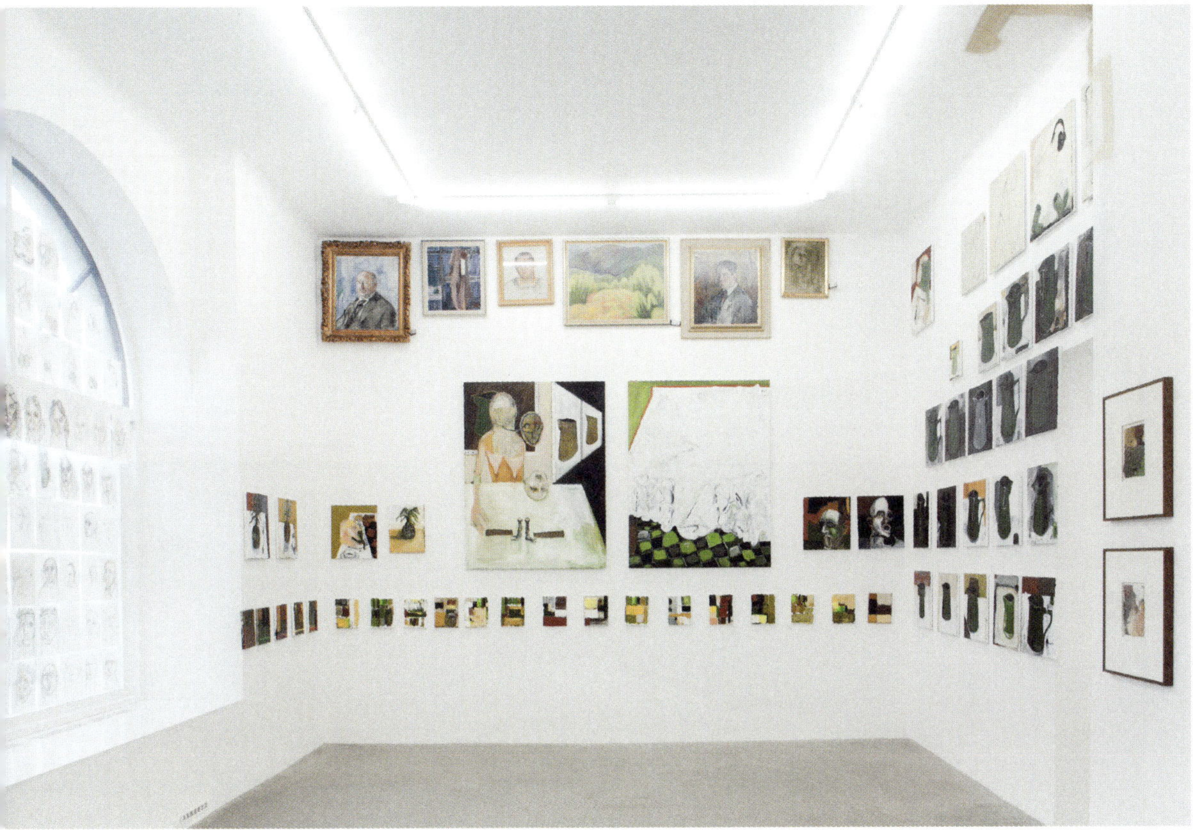

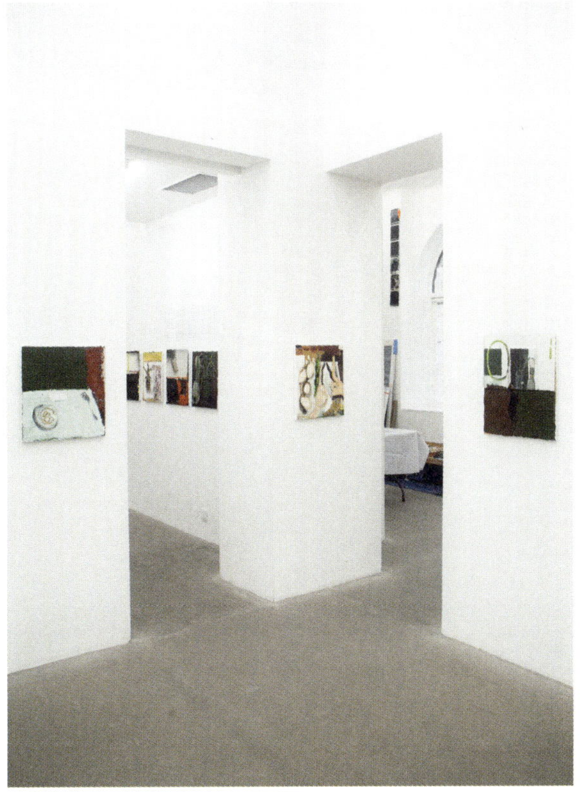

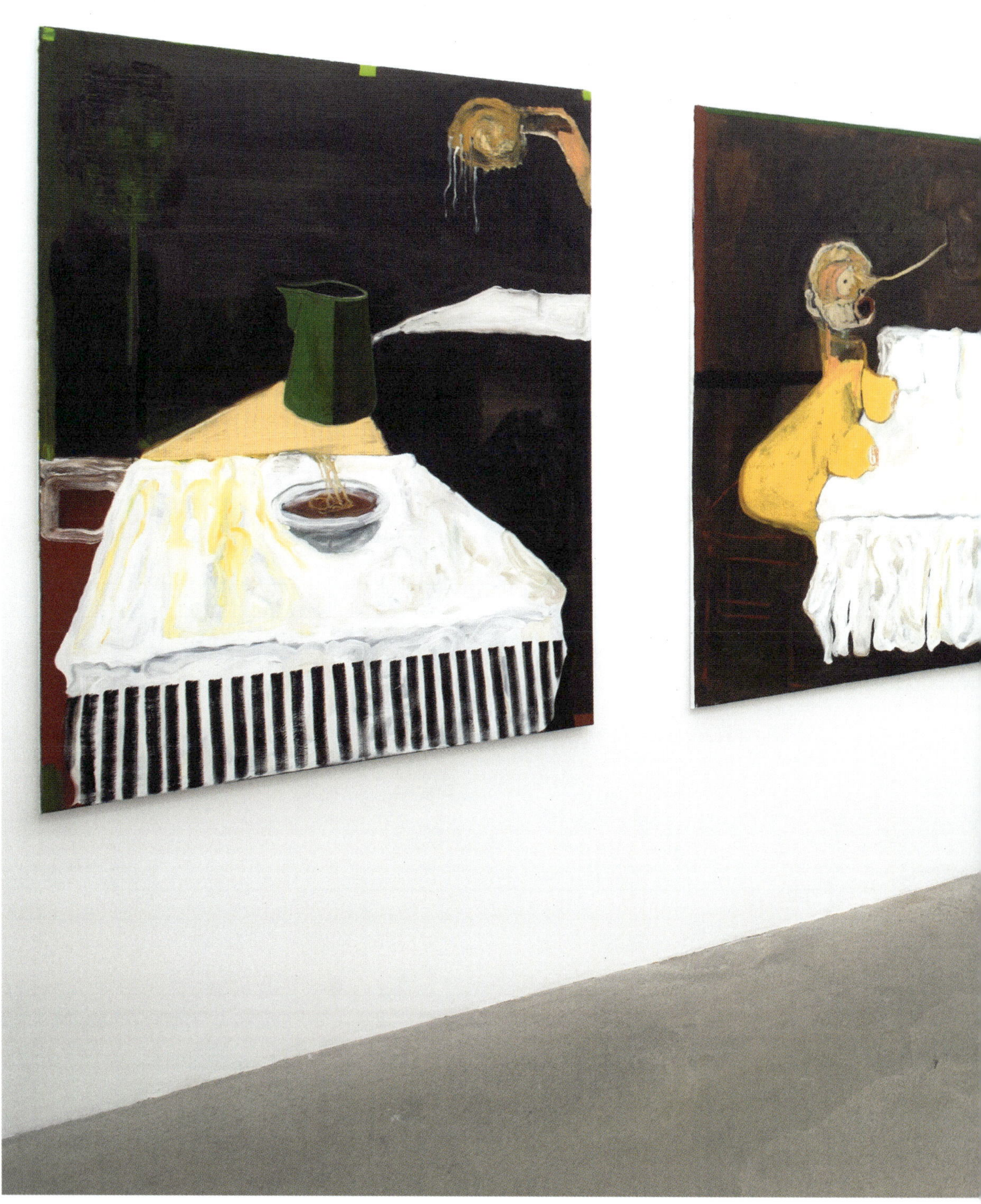

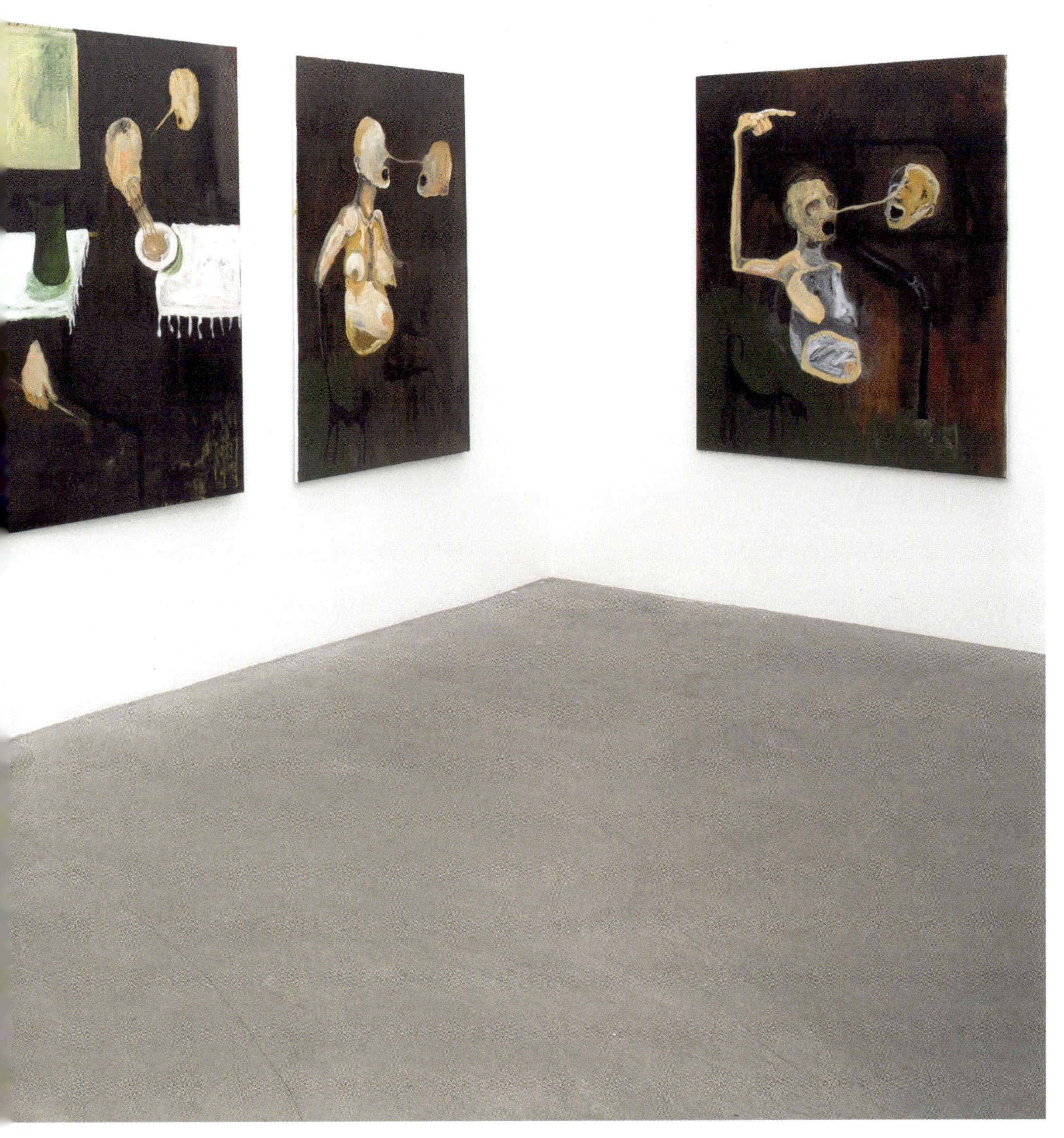

Stockholm

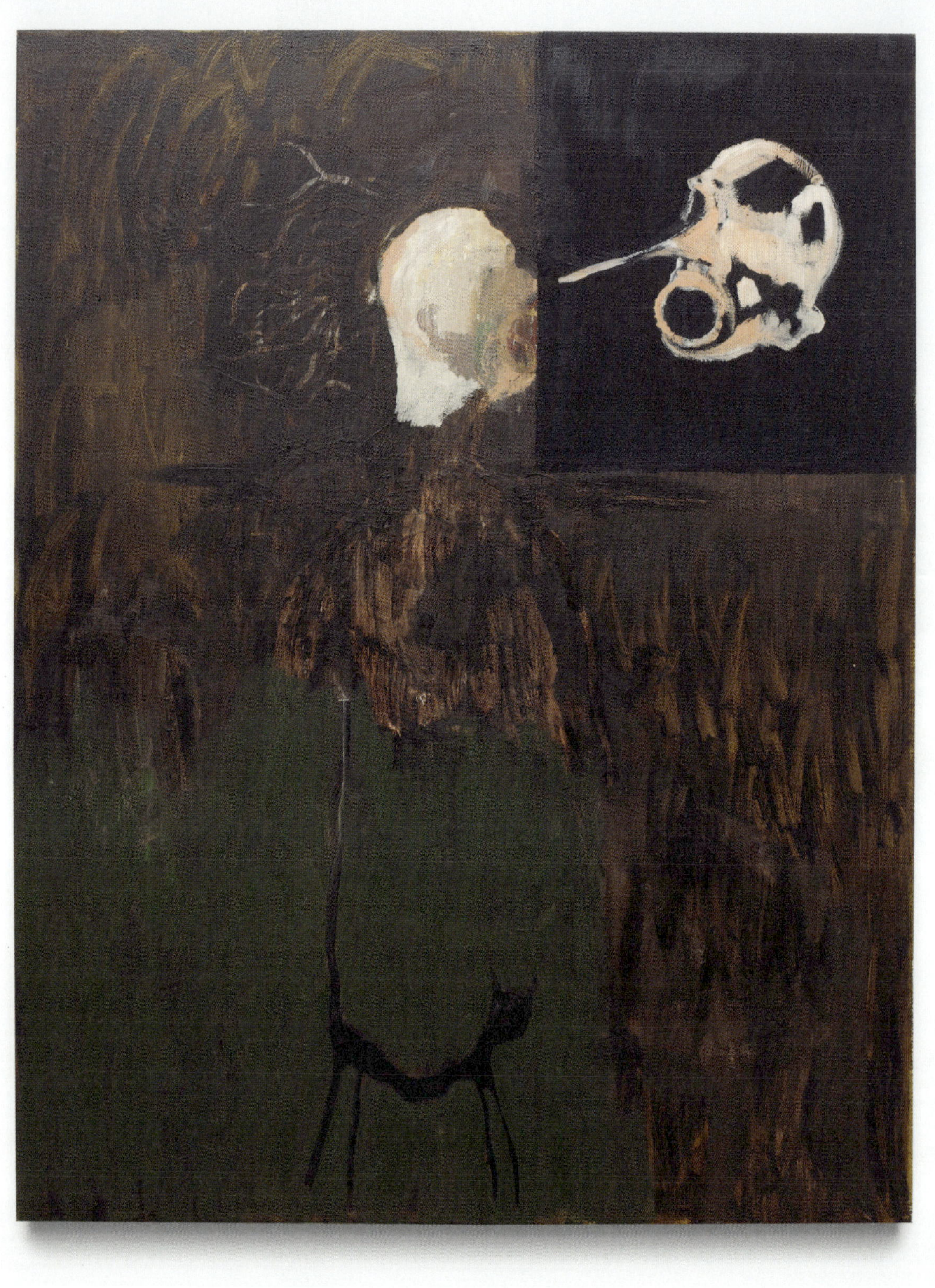

Unpleasant, Stuck, 2018 – 2019
Oil on linen canvas
120cm x 160cm

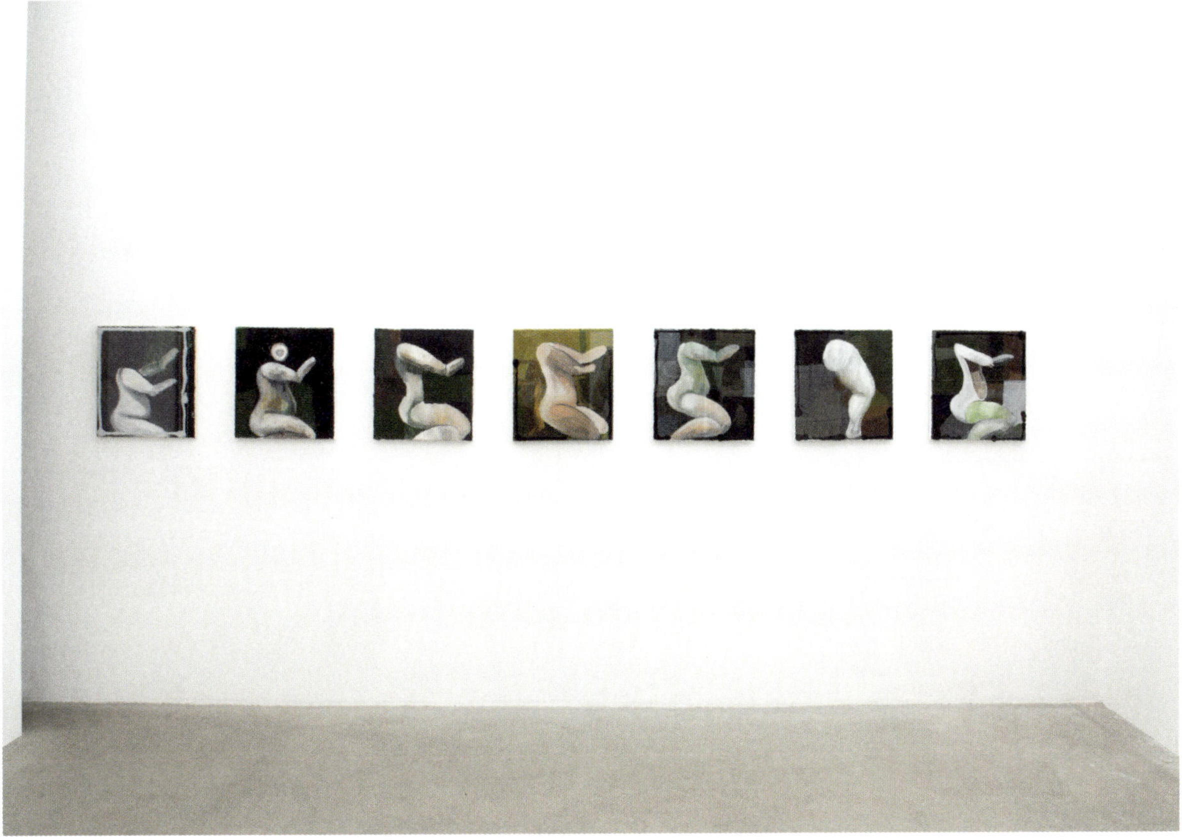

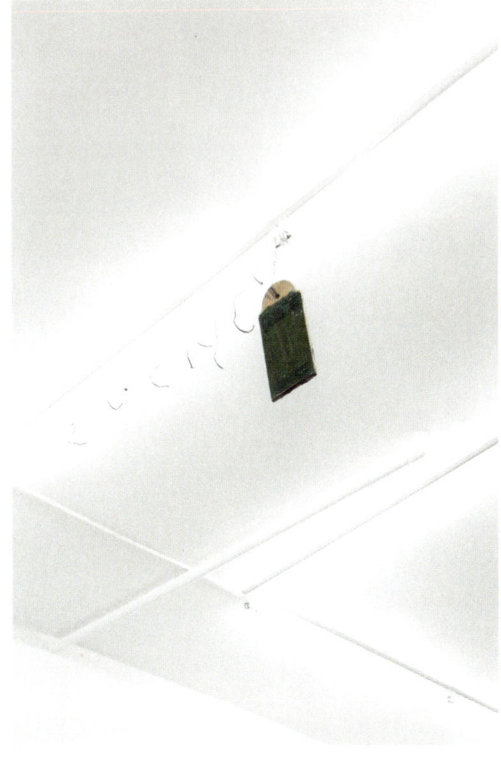

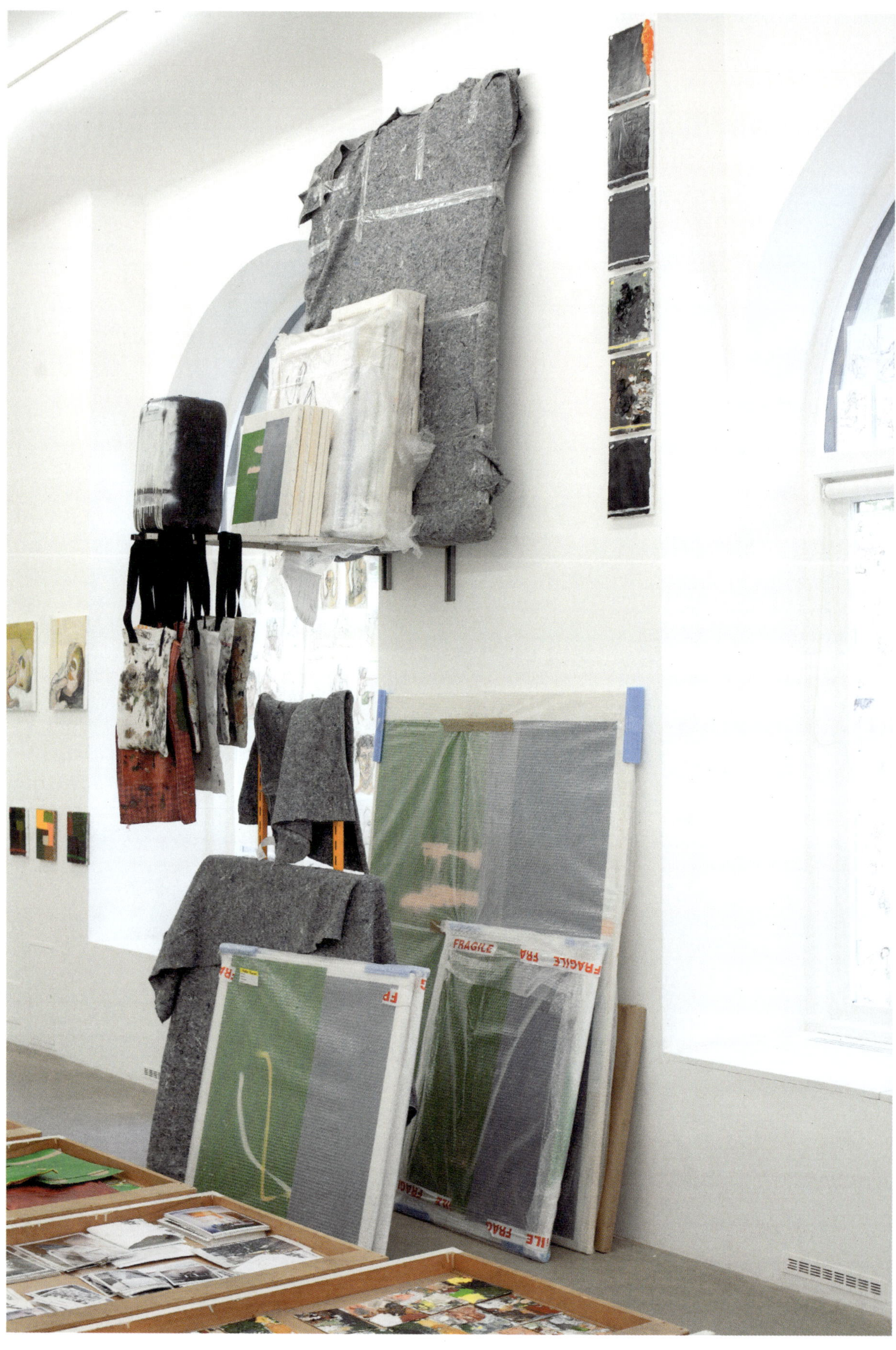
FRAGILE

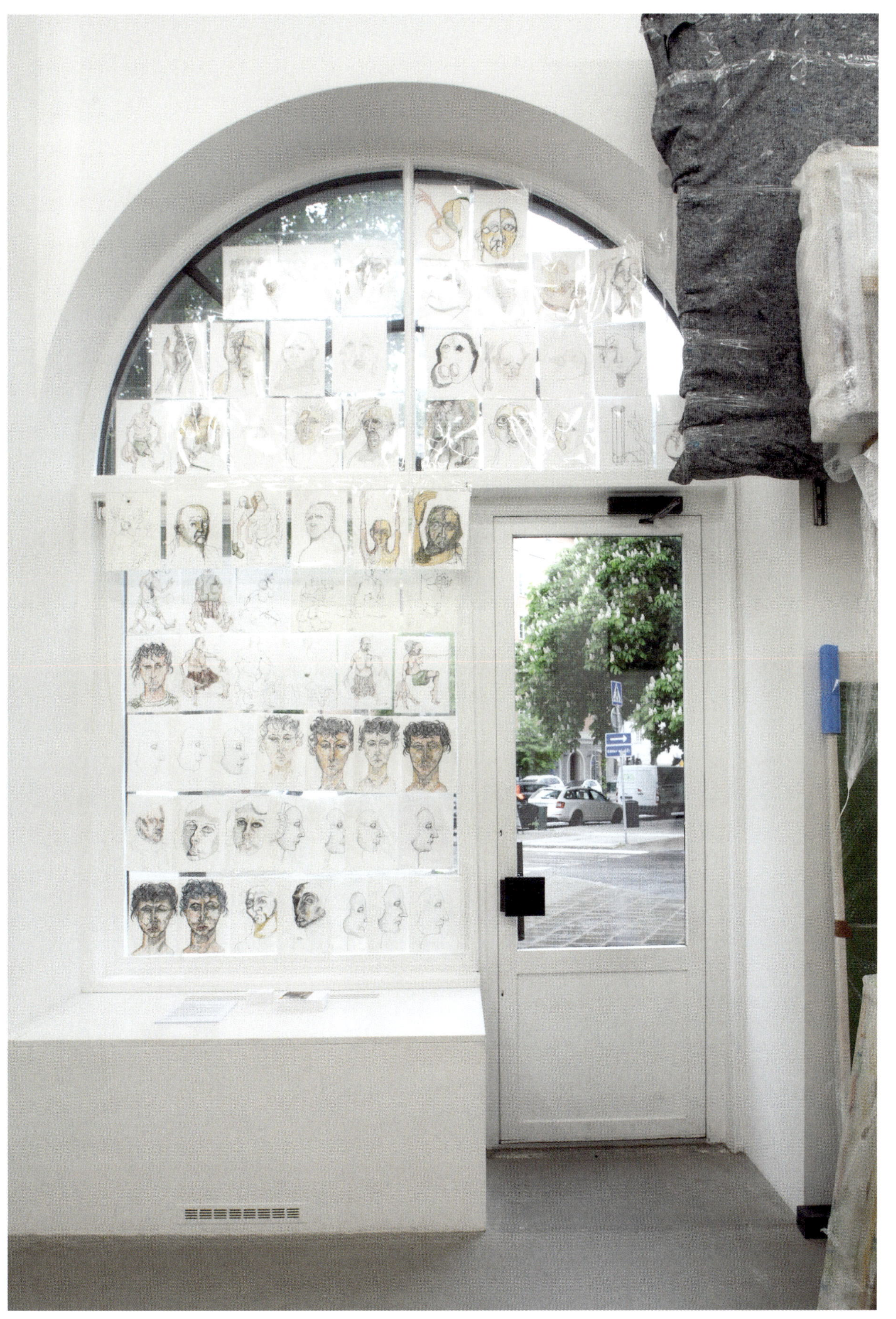

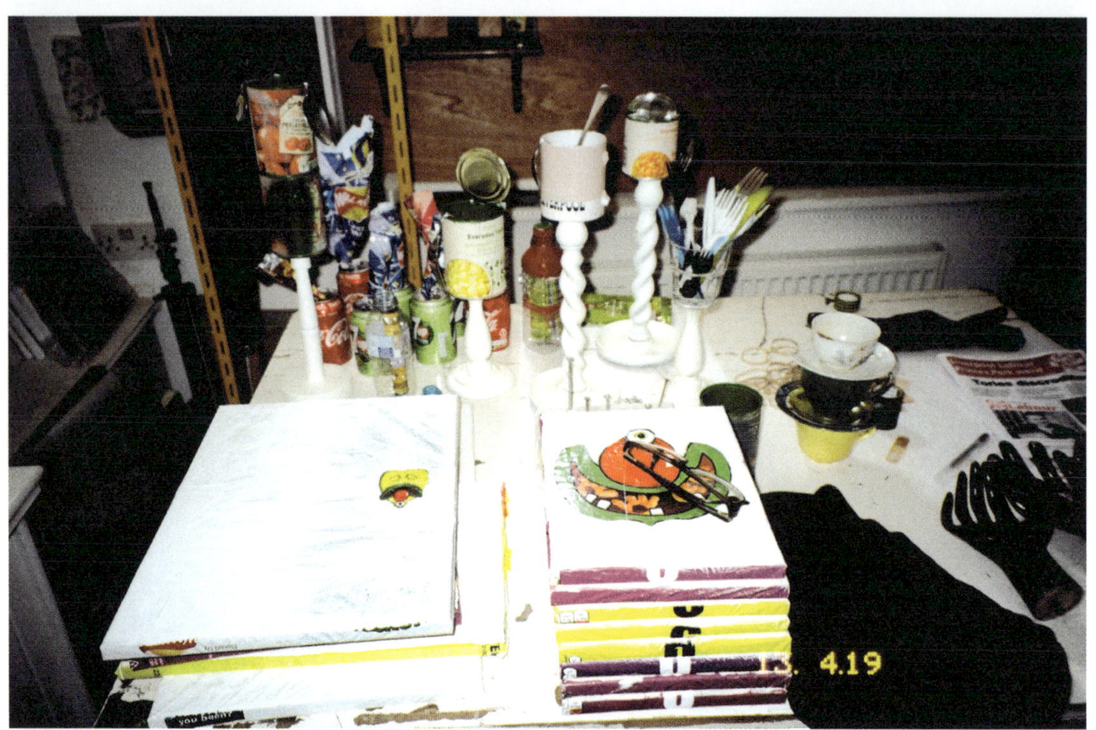

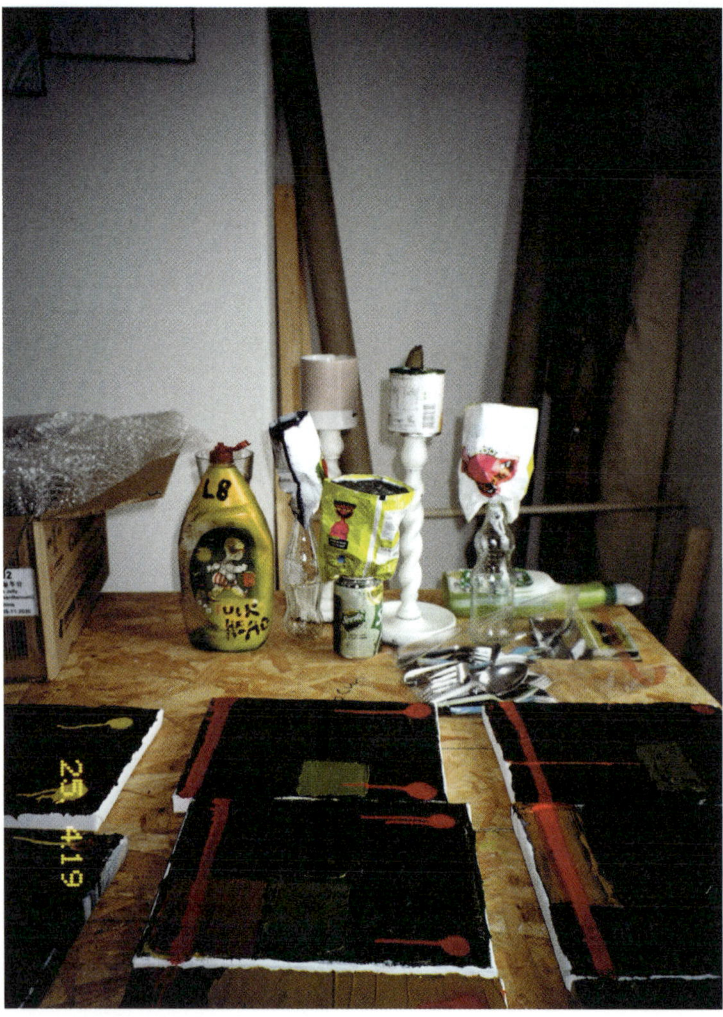

Studio documentation, 201
35mm film

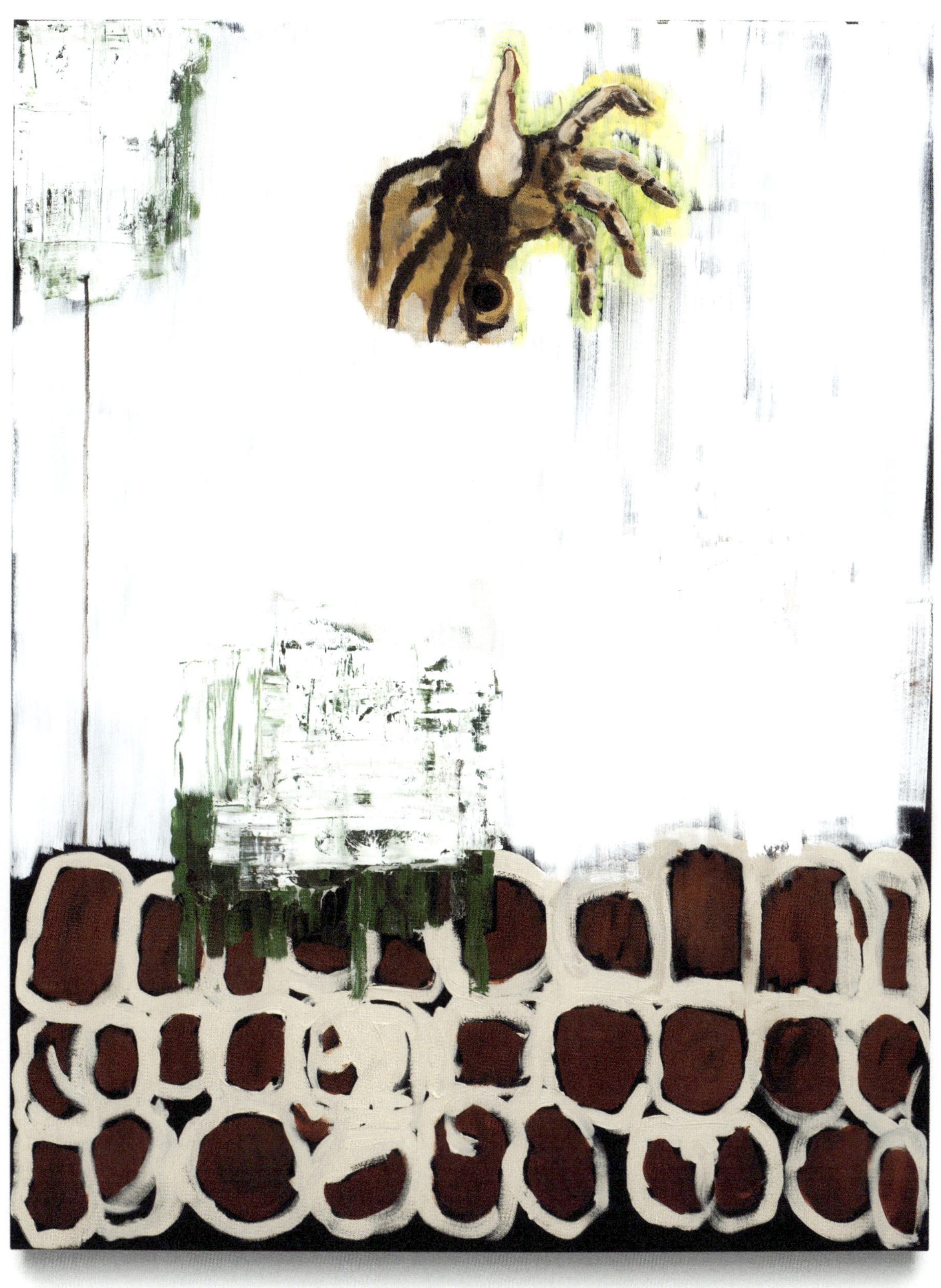

Missing the Sun II, 2019
Oil on black canvas
120cm x 160cm

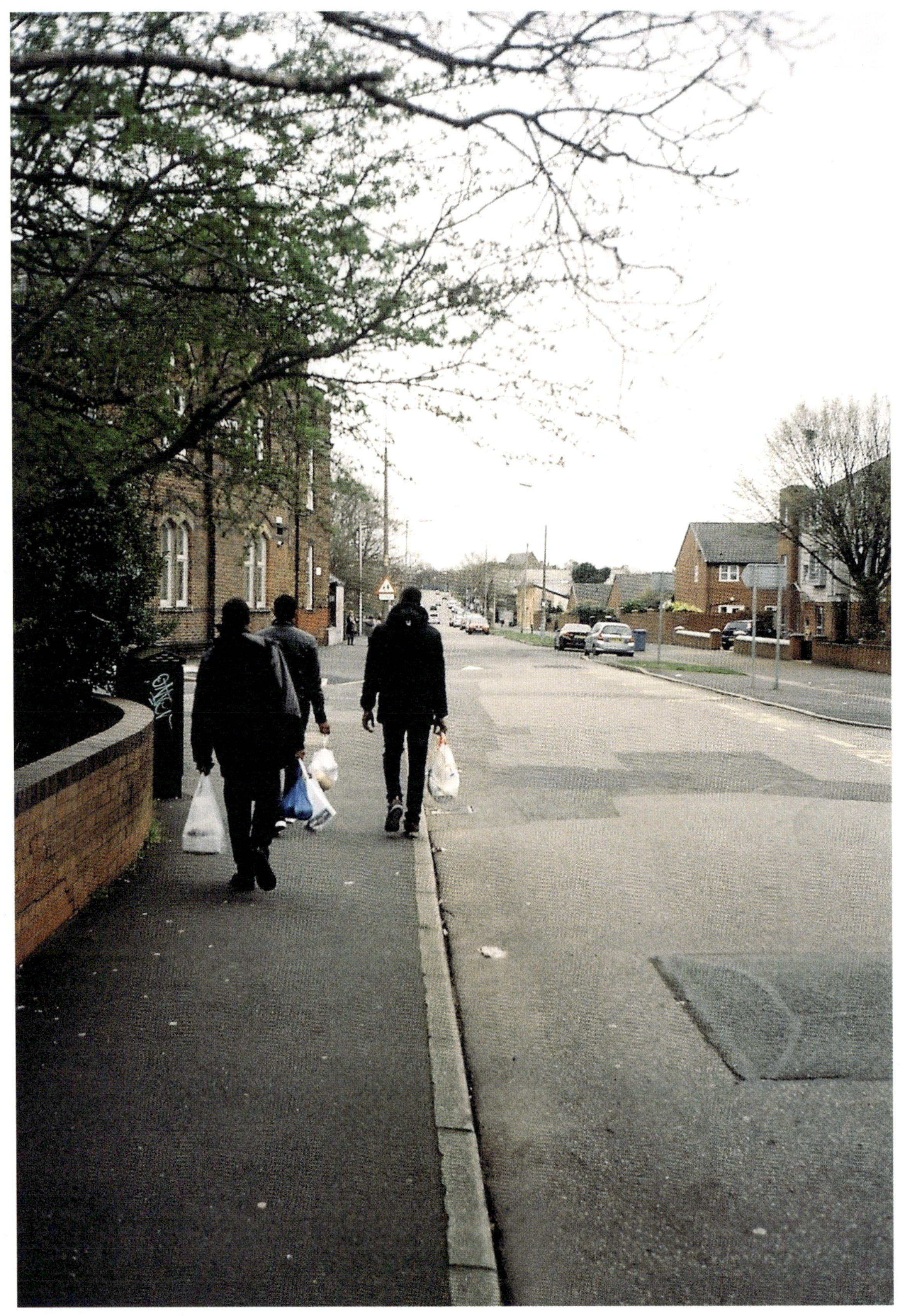

L8, Windsor Street, facing south, 2019
35mm film

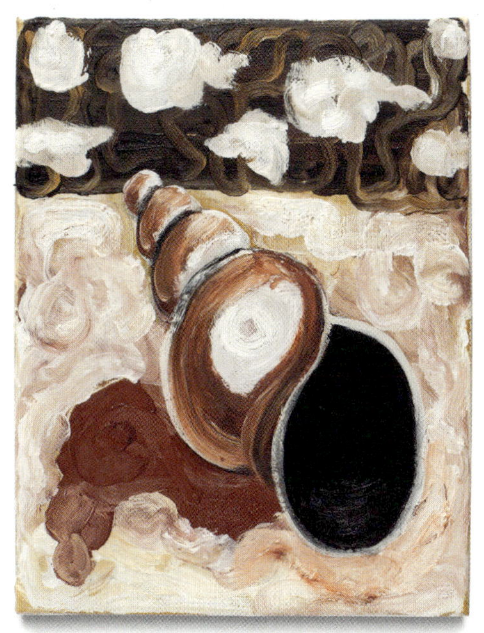

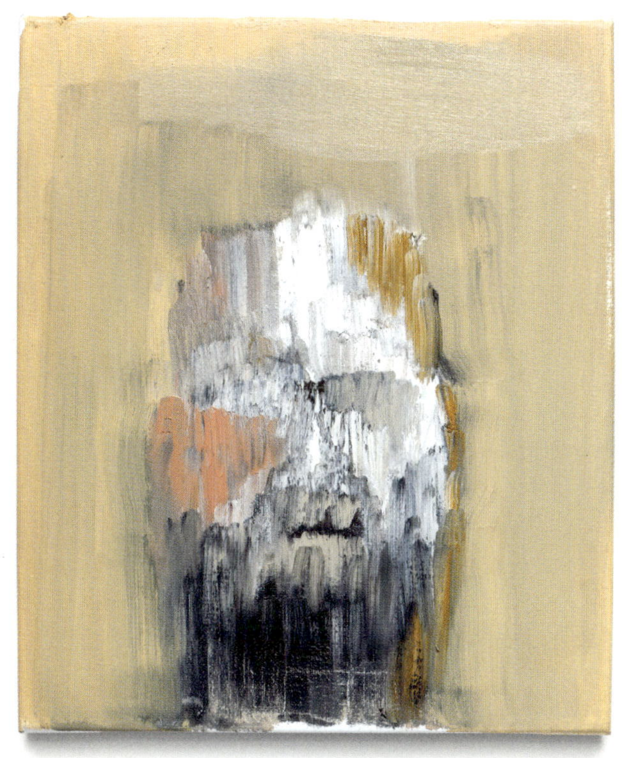

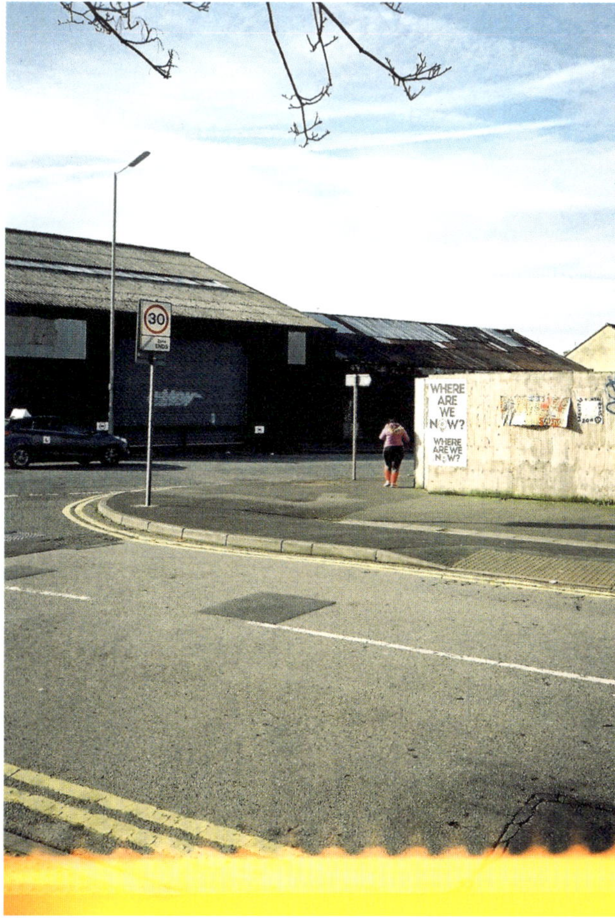

Emoji, 2019
Oil on linen canvas
30cm x 40cm

Jeremy Glogan, 2019
Oil on linen canvas
38cm x 46cm

L8, corner of Windsor Street and Upper Warwick Street, facing south west, 2019
35mm film

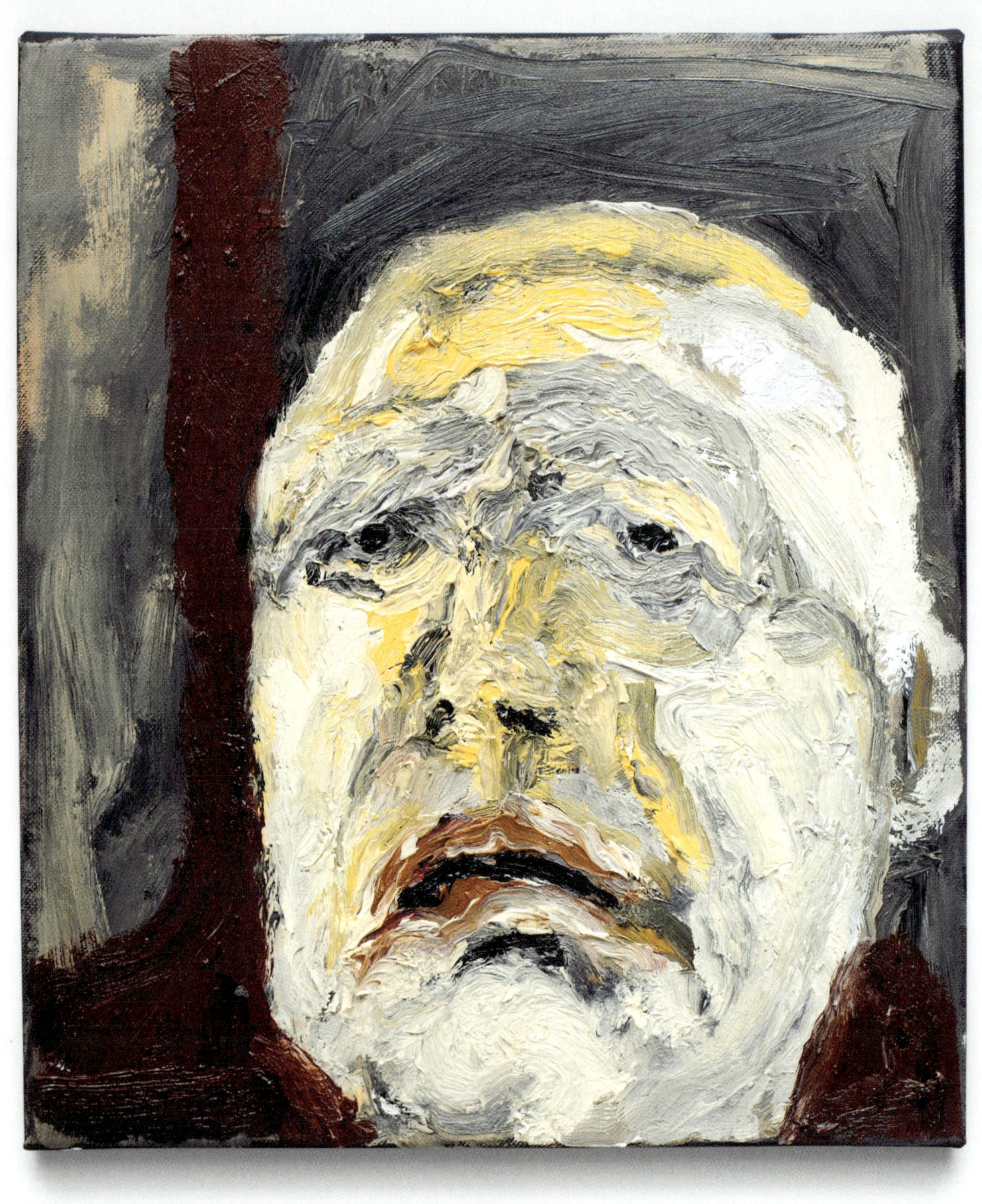

Self-portrait Without Glasses, 2019
Oil on black canvas
30cm x 35cm

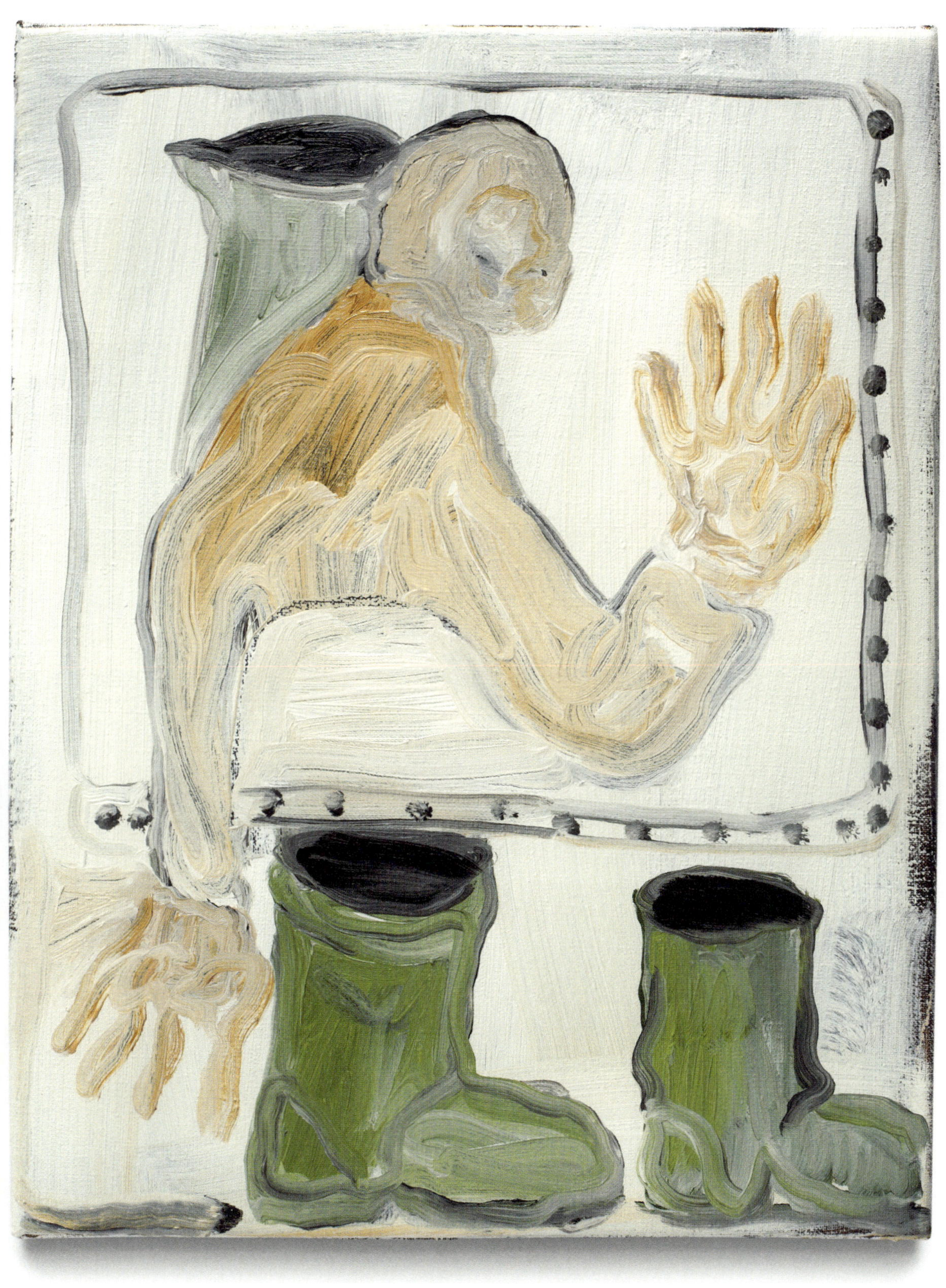

Bartolomé Esteban Murillo and Me, 2019
Oil on linen canvas
30cm x 40cm

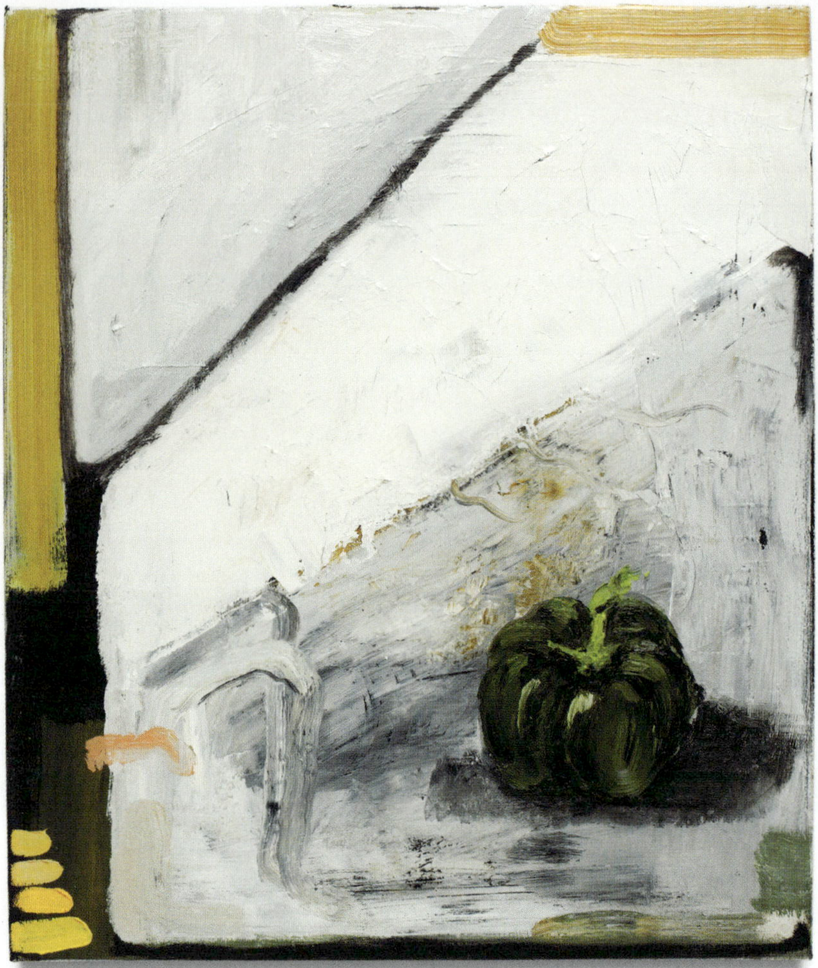

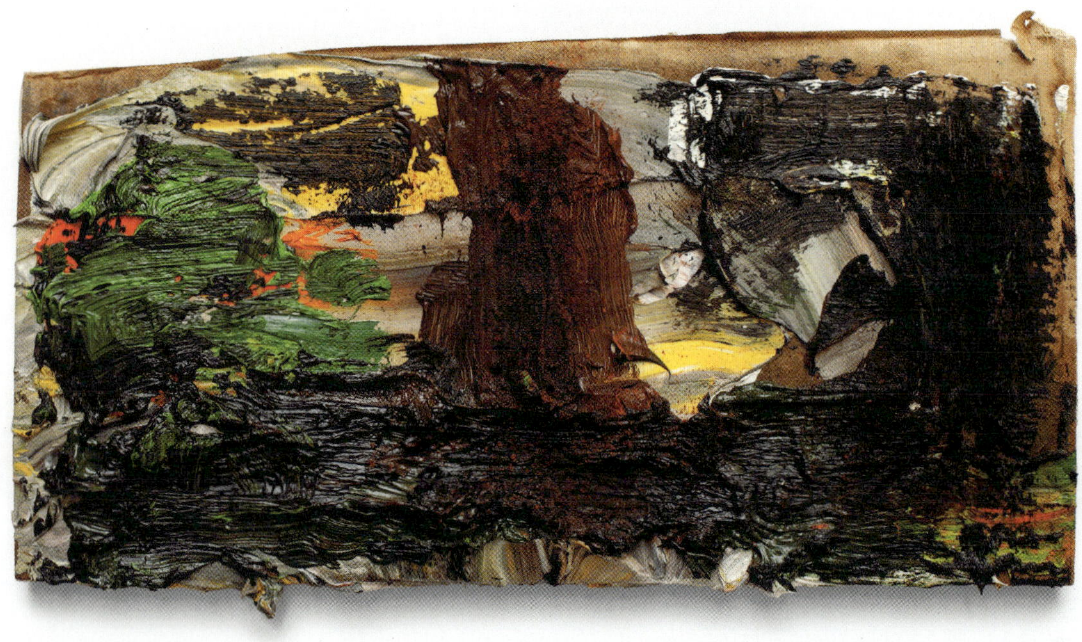

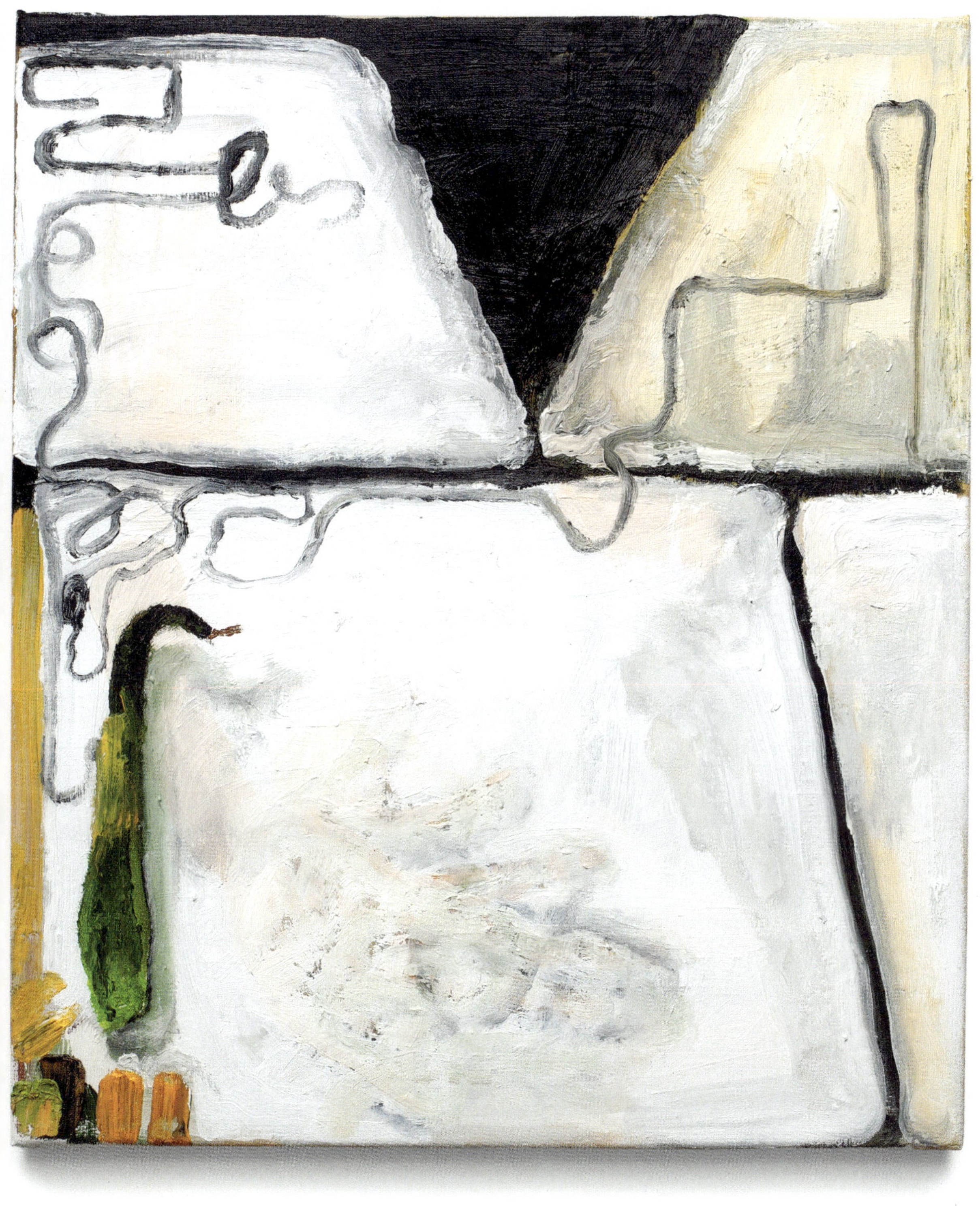

uck I, II, 2019
l on linen canvas
cm x 60cm

thedral seen from L8, Windsor Street, 2019 – 2020
l on cardboard
cm x 22.5cm

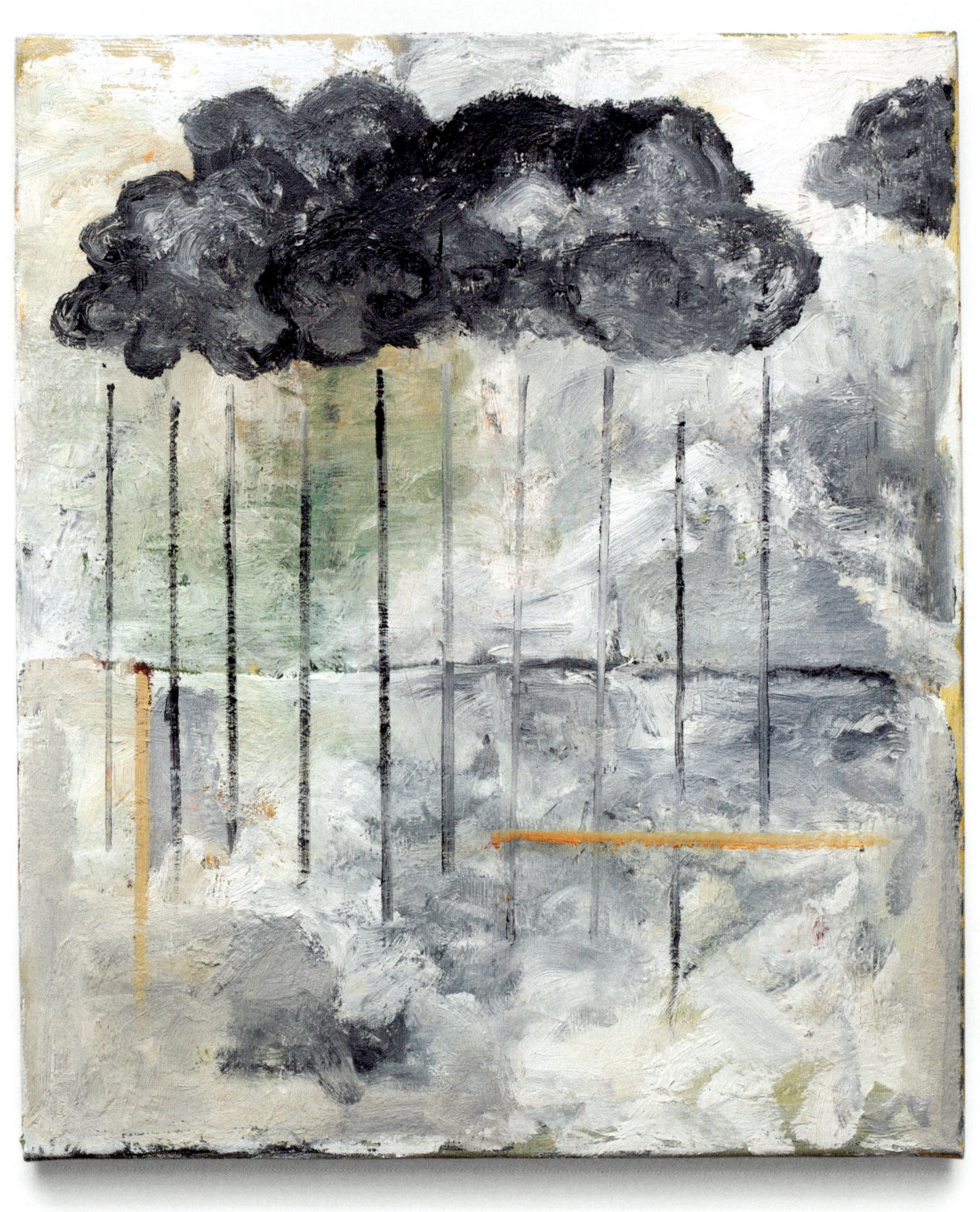

L8.Rain.Rain.Rain, 2019
Diptych
Oil on linen canvas
50cm x 60cm

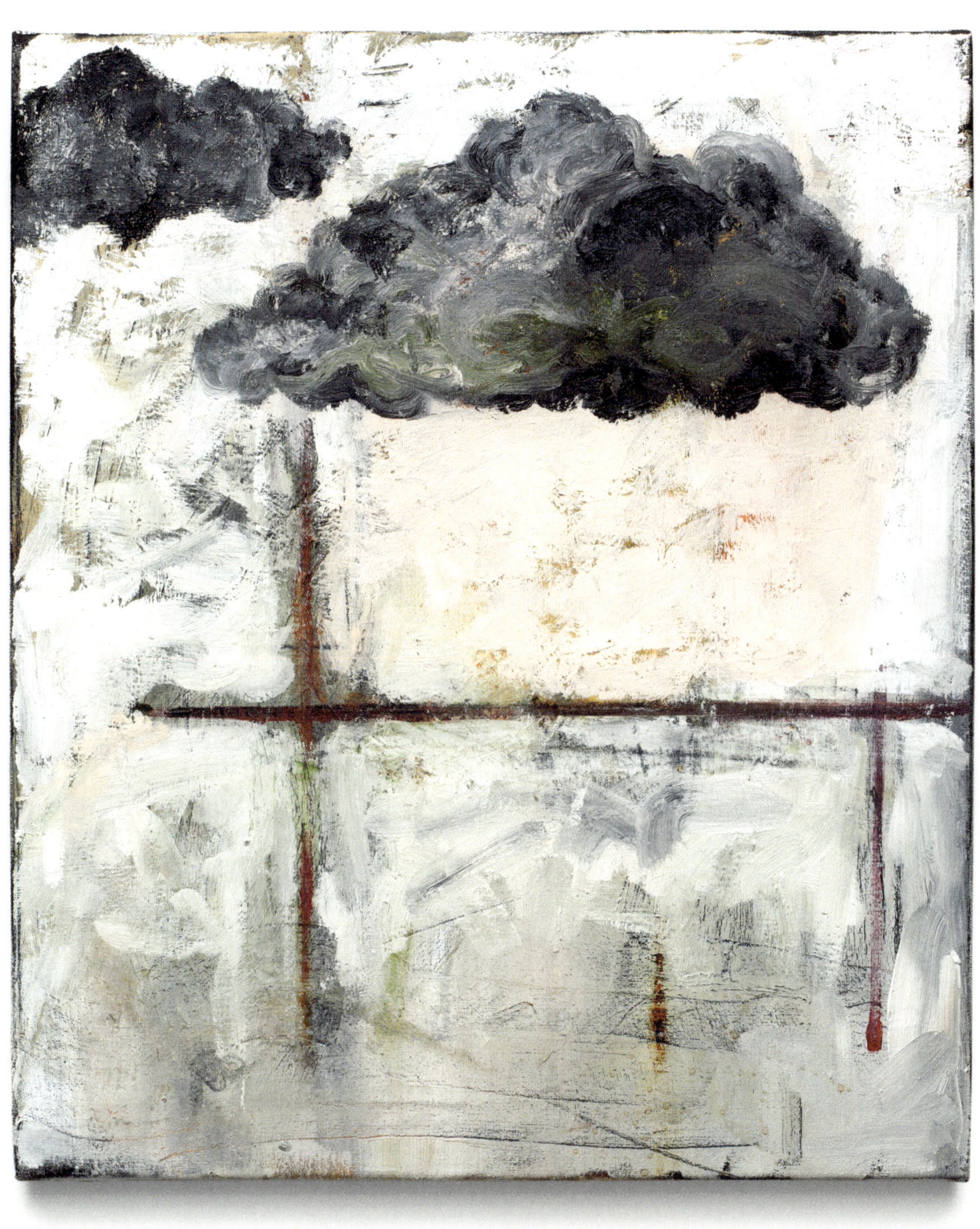

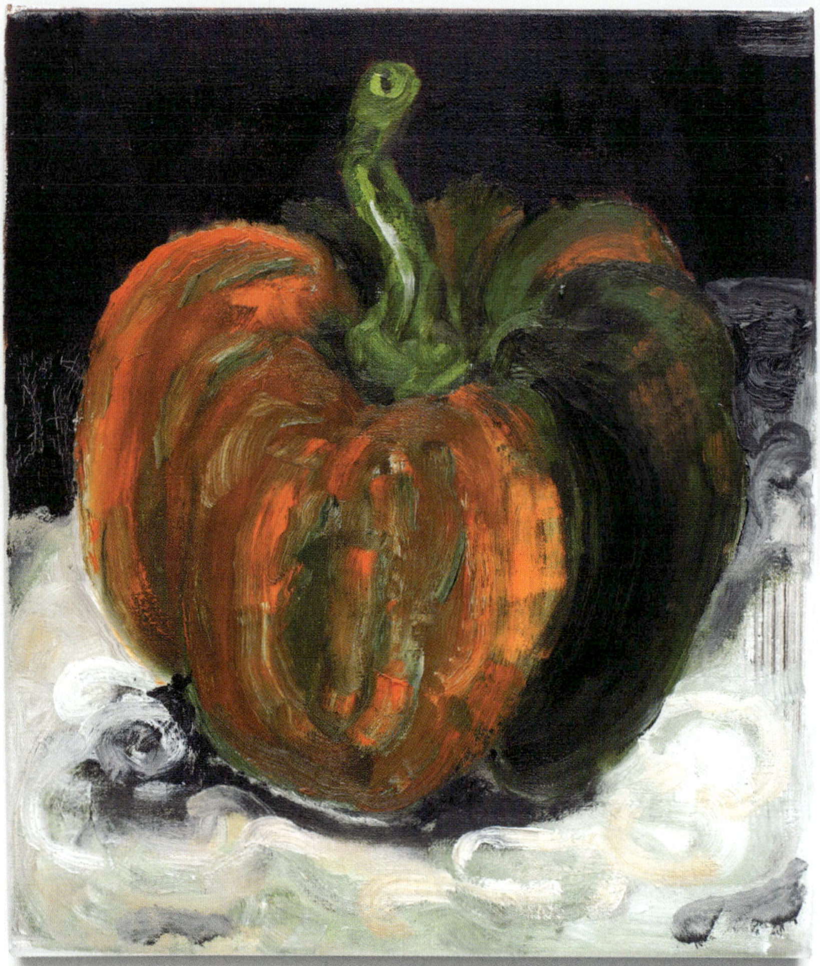

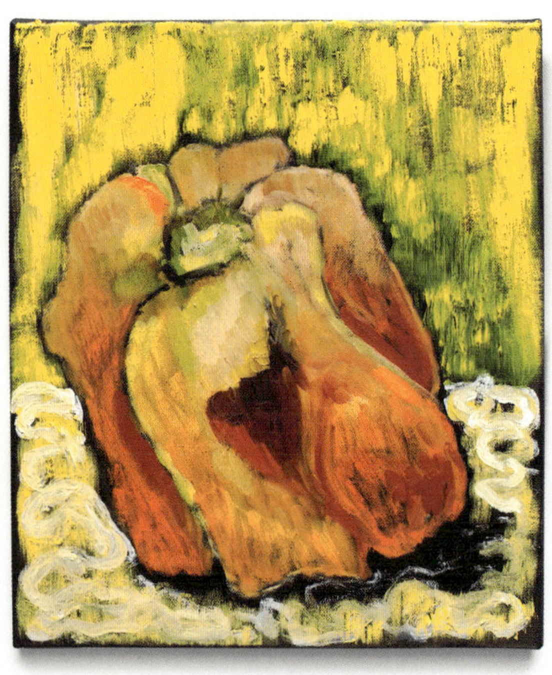

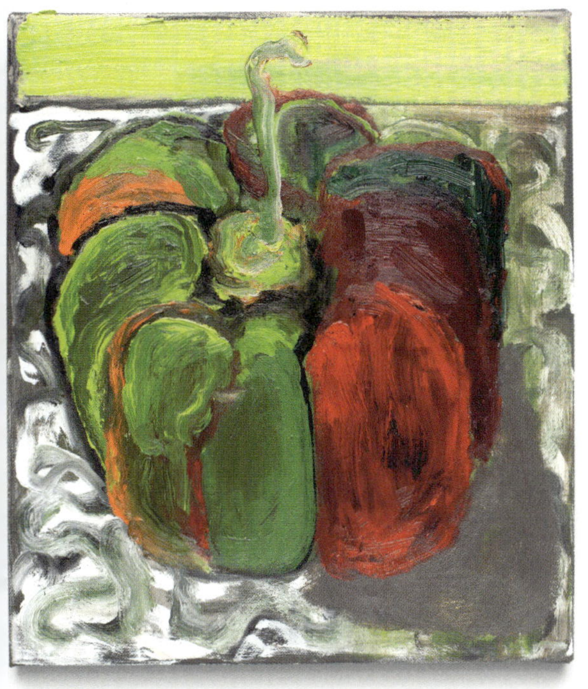

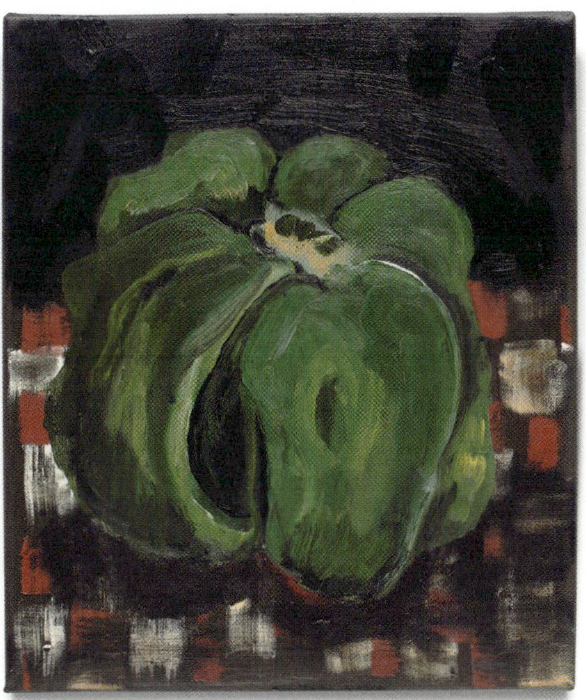

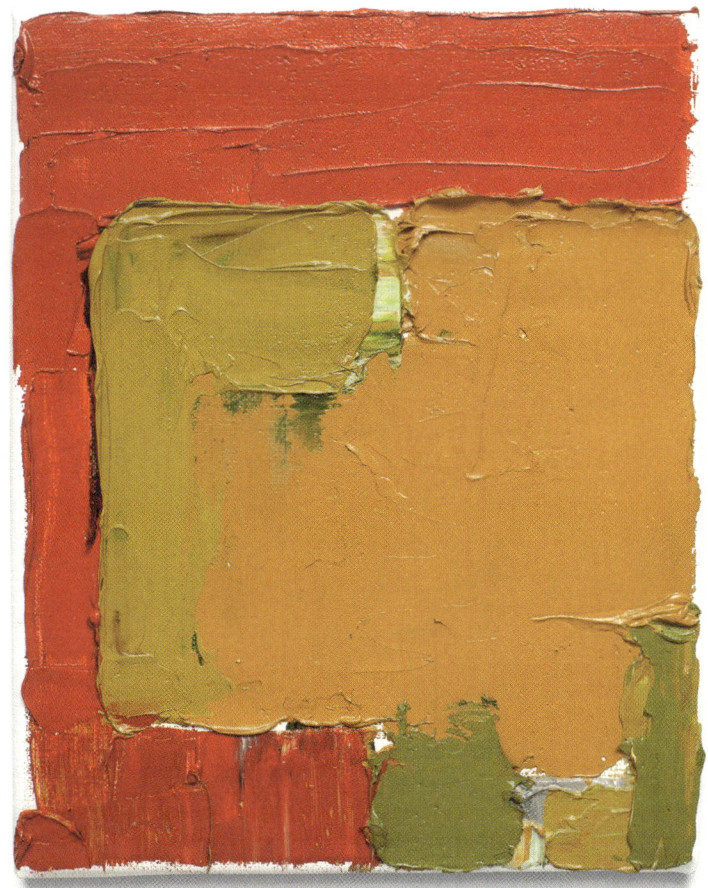

per Stolen from Jack Potato, 2019
on linen canvas
m x 35cm

the Studio, 2019
on linen canvas
m x 25cm

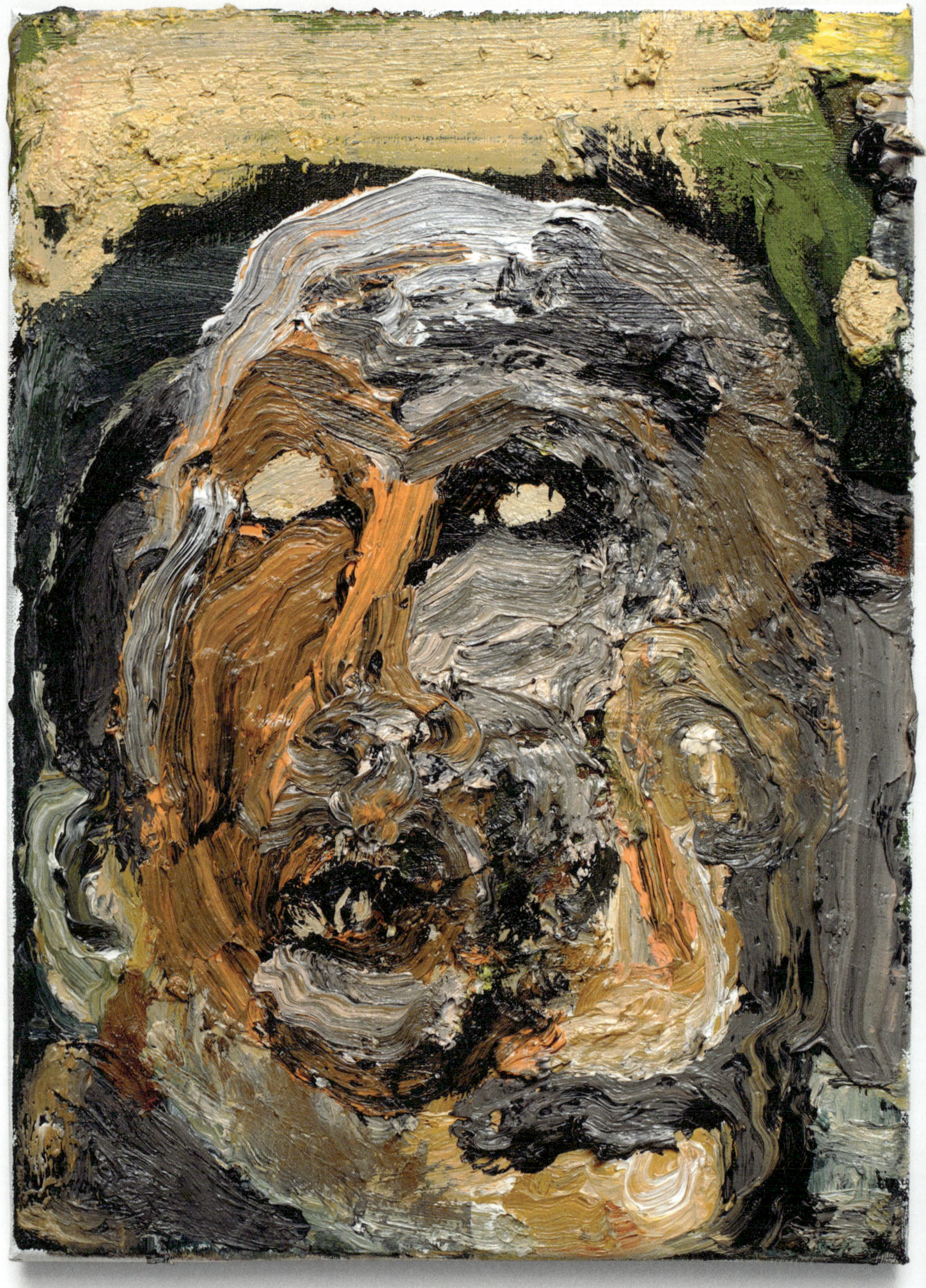

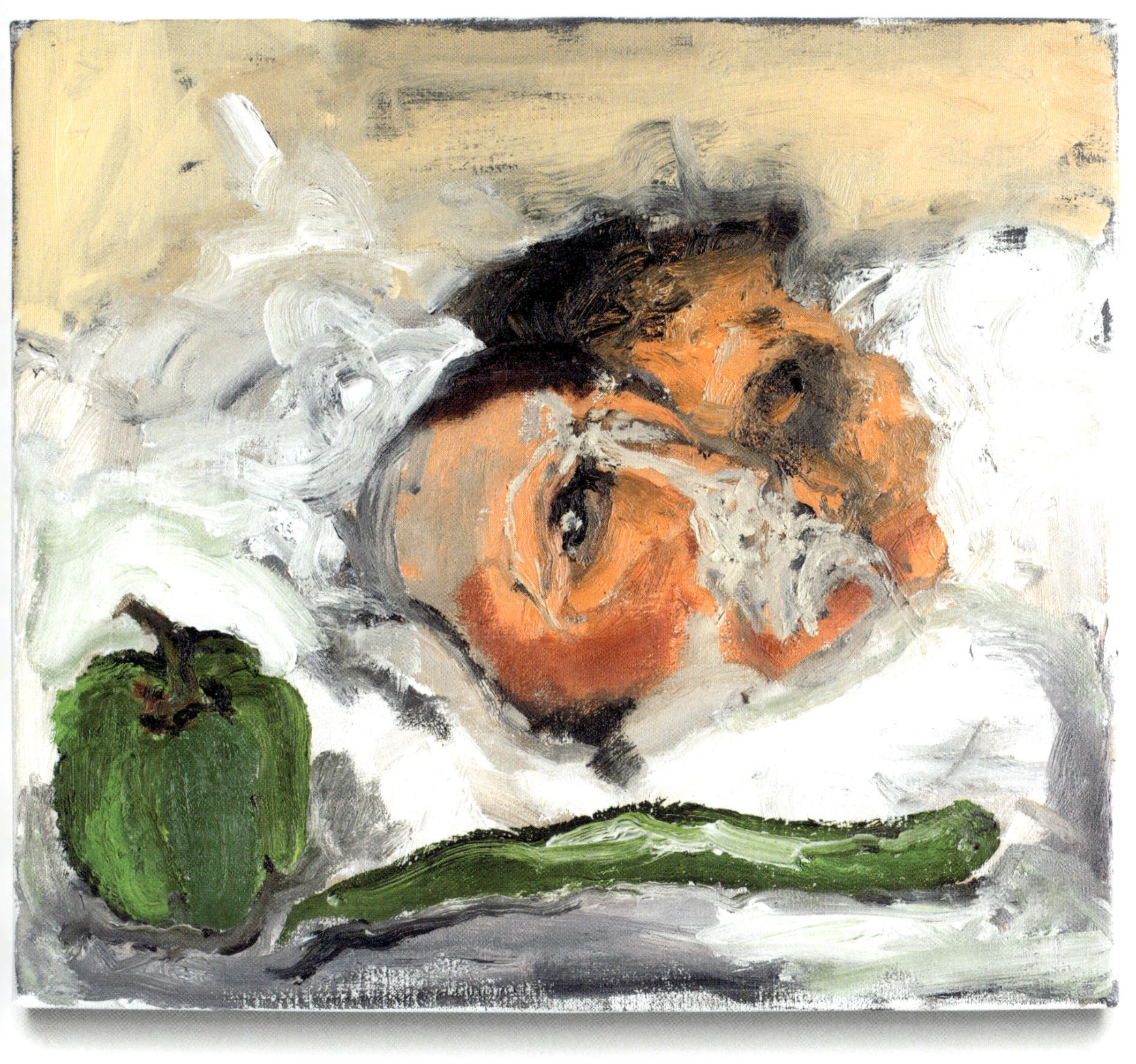

In Bed with Lauren, 2019
Oil on linen canvas
40cm x 46cm

Untitled, 2019
Oil on linen canvas
25cm x 35cm

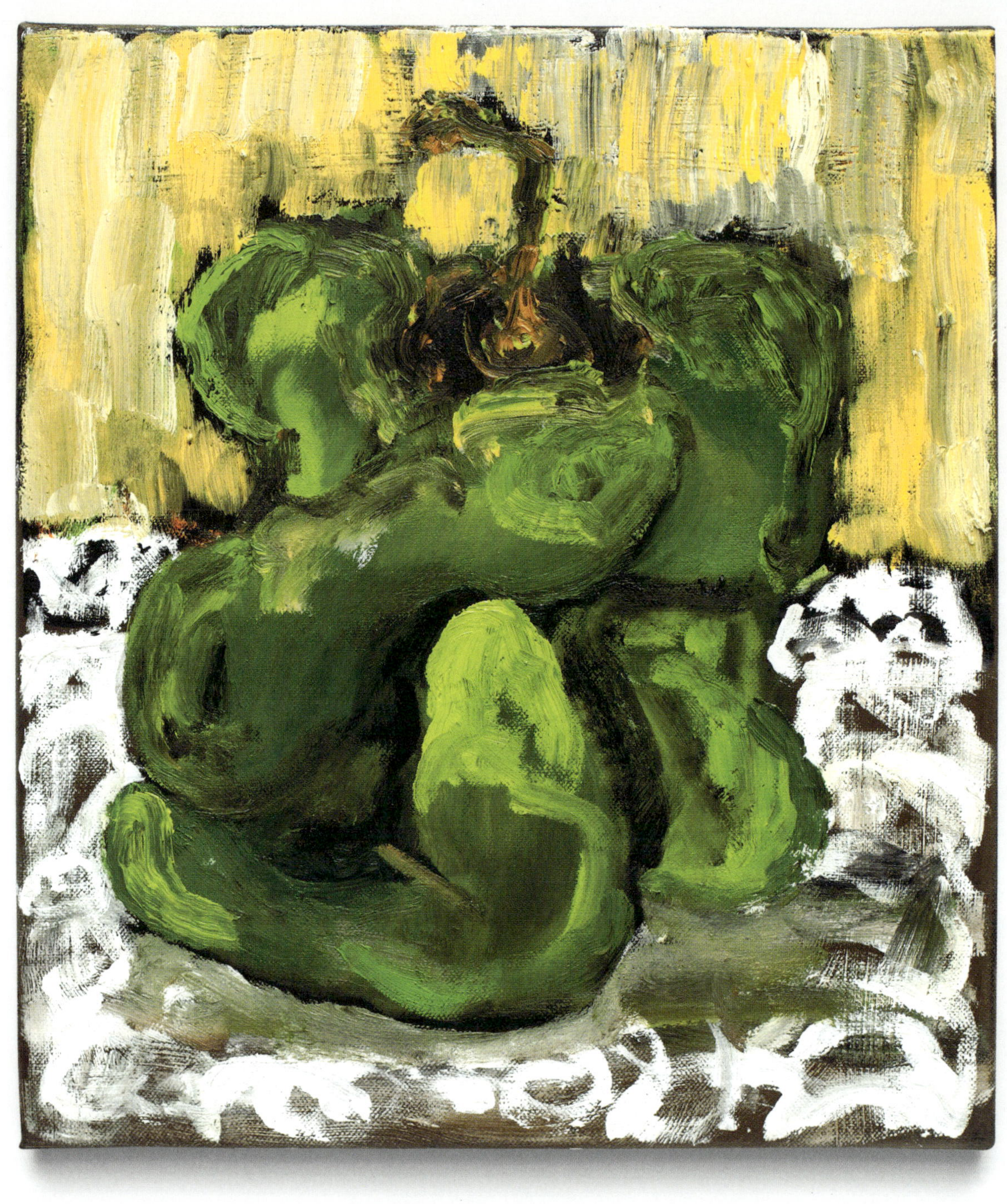

Pepper Stolen from Jack Potato, 2019
Oil on black canvas
30cm x 35cm

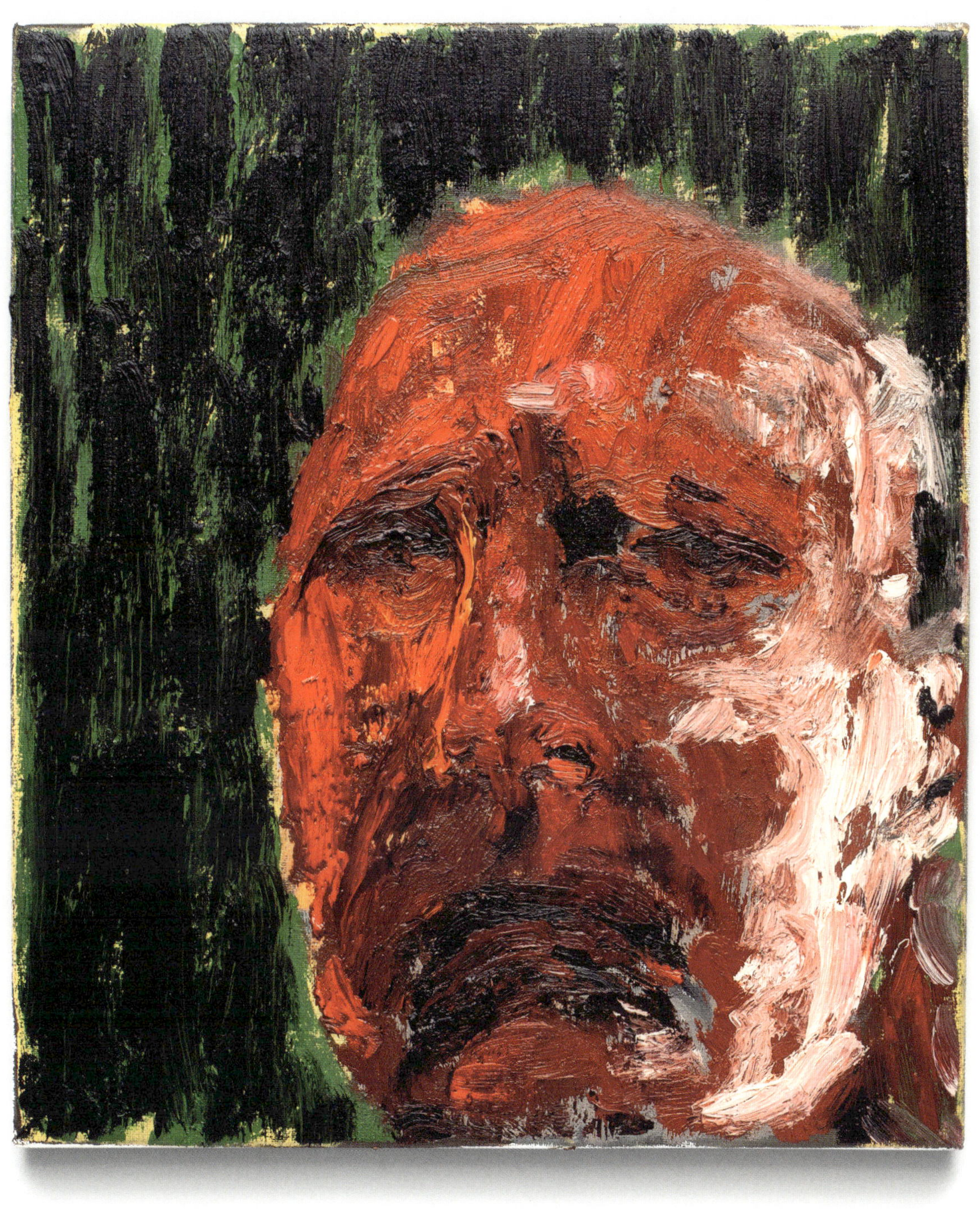

Missing the Sun and the River, 2019
Oil on black canvas
30cm x 35cm

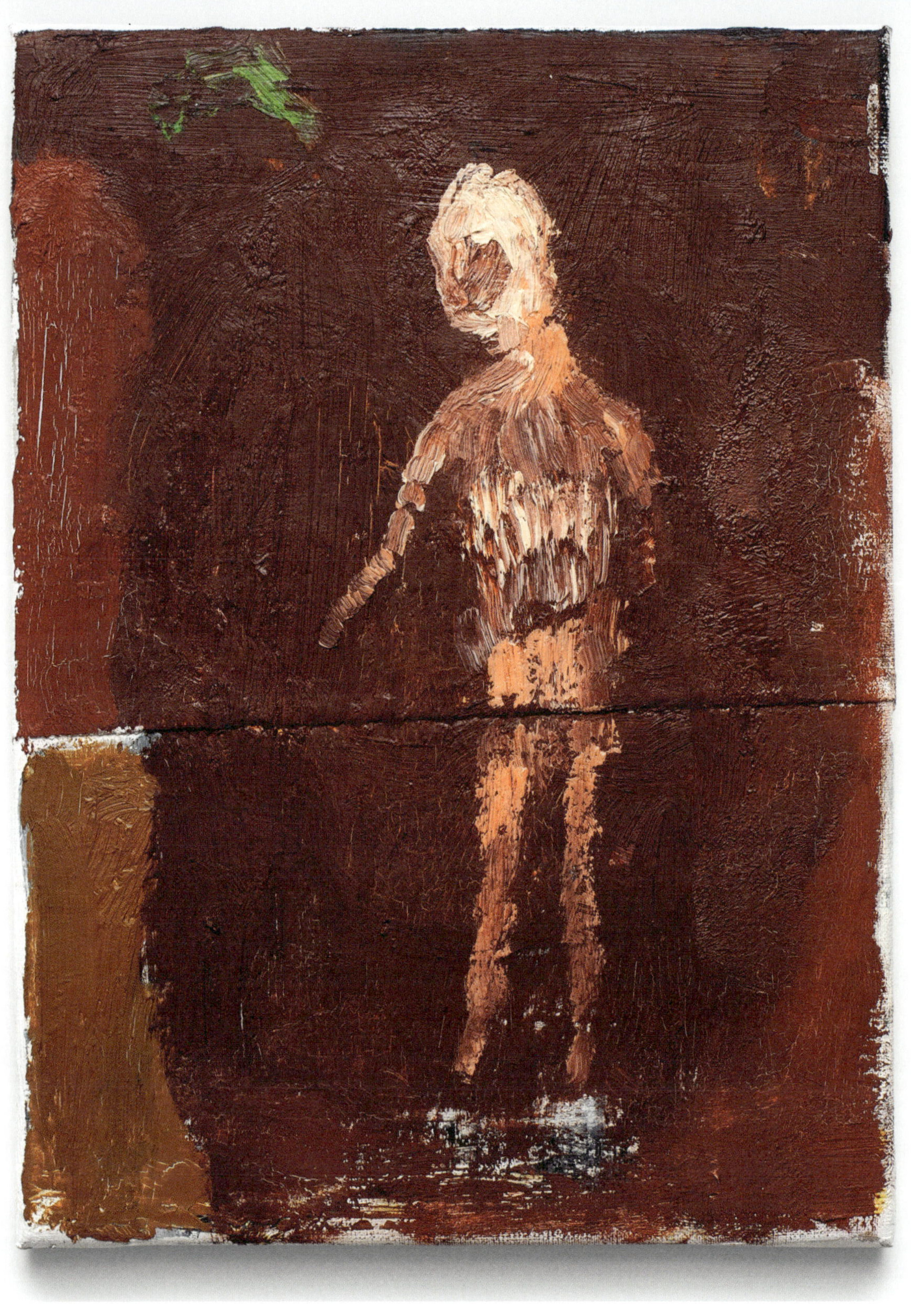

Before the Dive, 2019
Oil on stitched linen canvas
25cm x 35cm

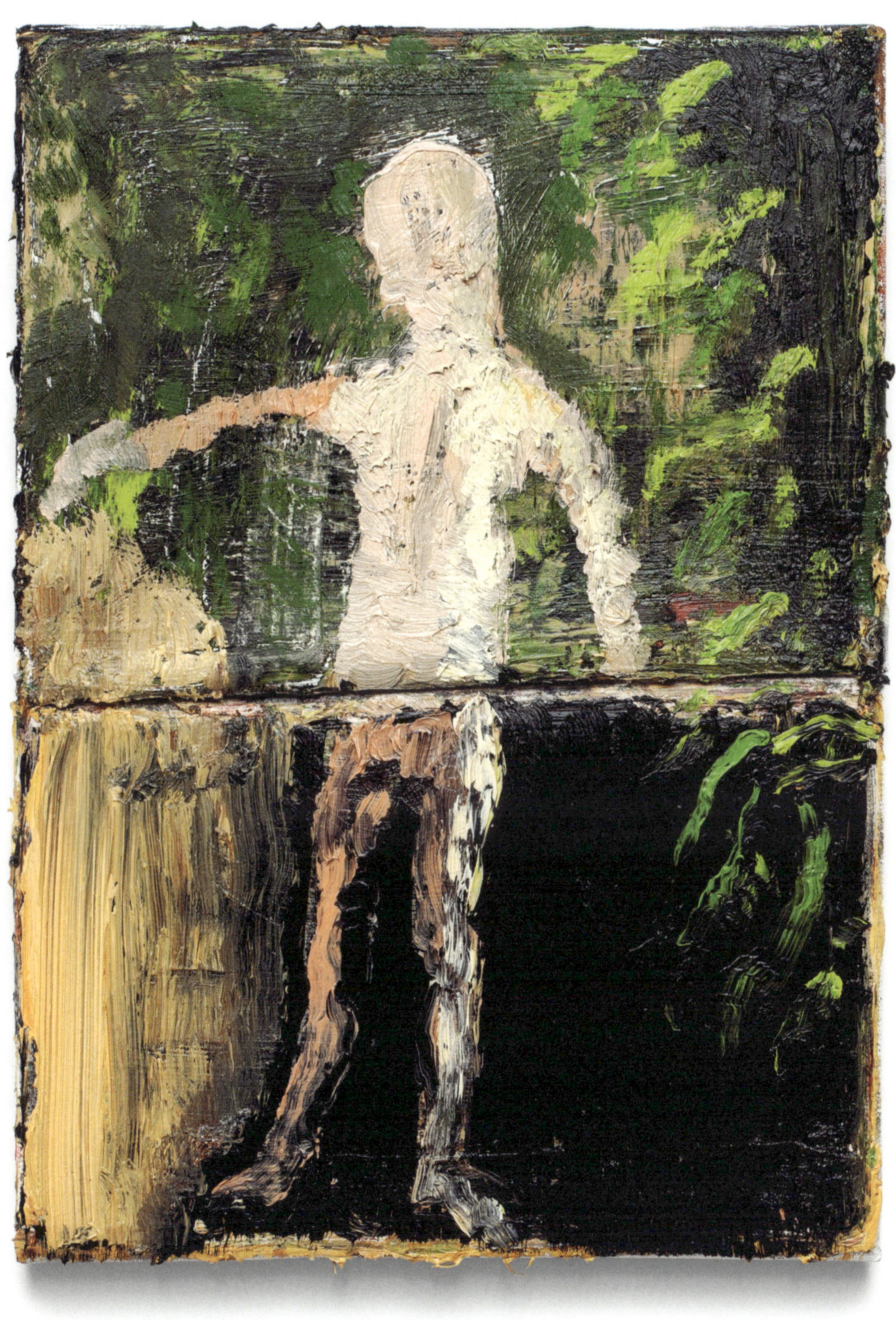

After the Swim, 2019
Oil on stitched linen canvas
25cm x 35cm

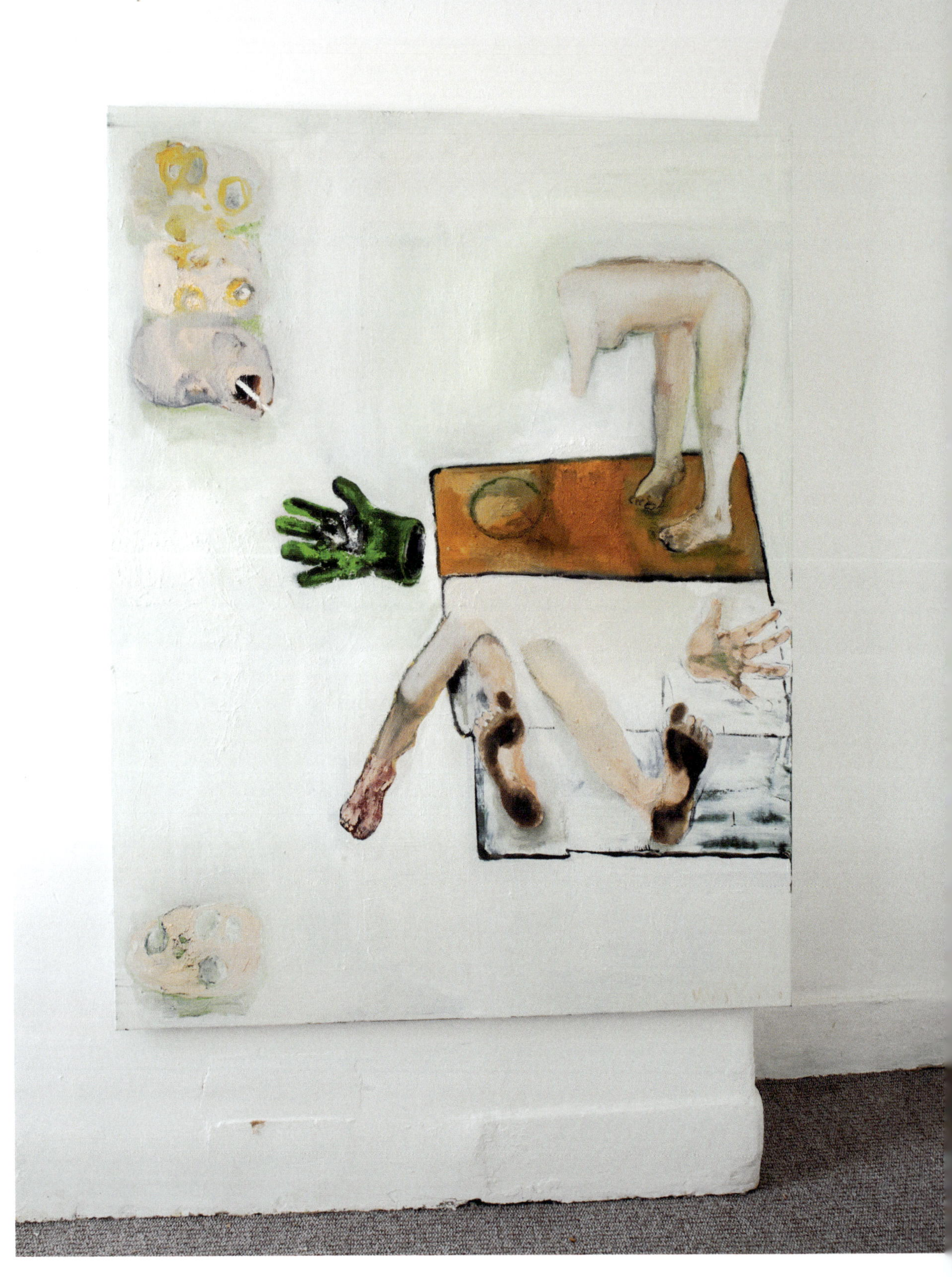

Missing the River, 2019 – 2020
Oil on linen canvas
120cm x 160cm

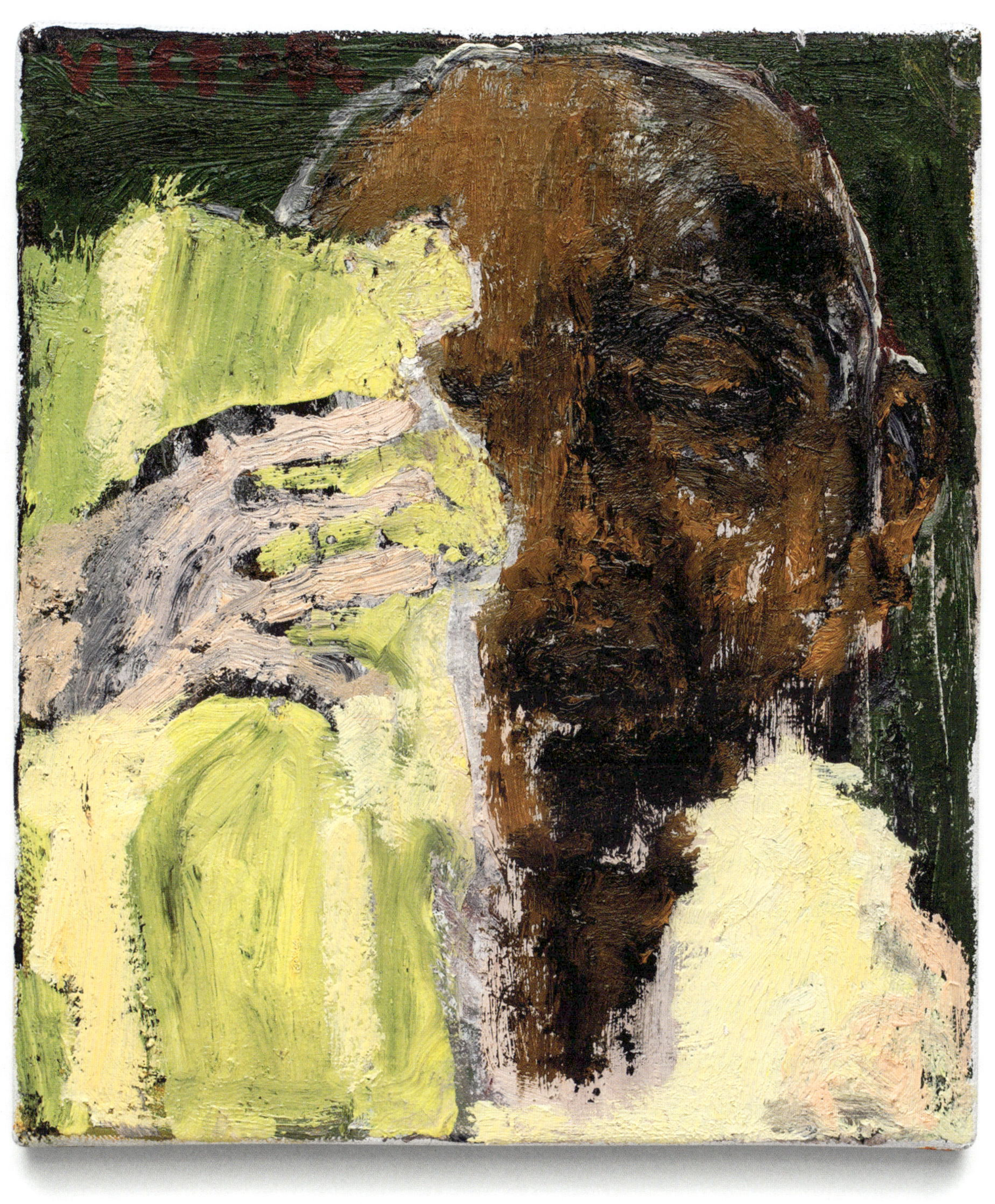

After the Swim, 2019 – 2021
Oil on linen canvas
30cm x 35cm

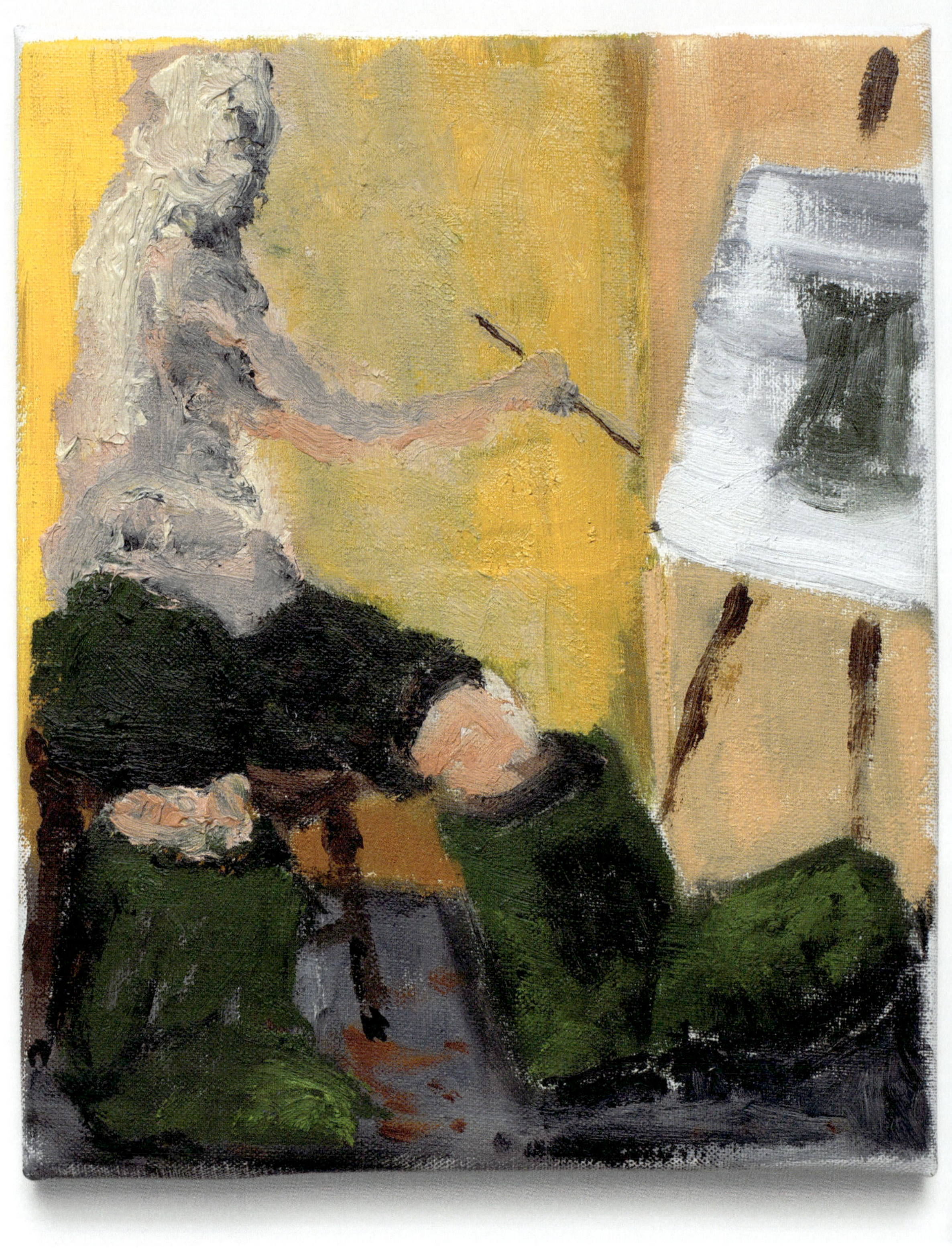

Future Self-Portrait in the Sun, 2019 – 2020
Oil on linen canvas
20cm x 25cm

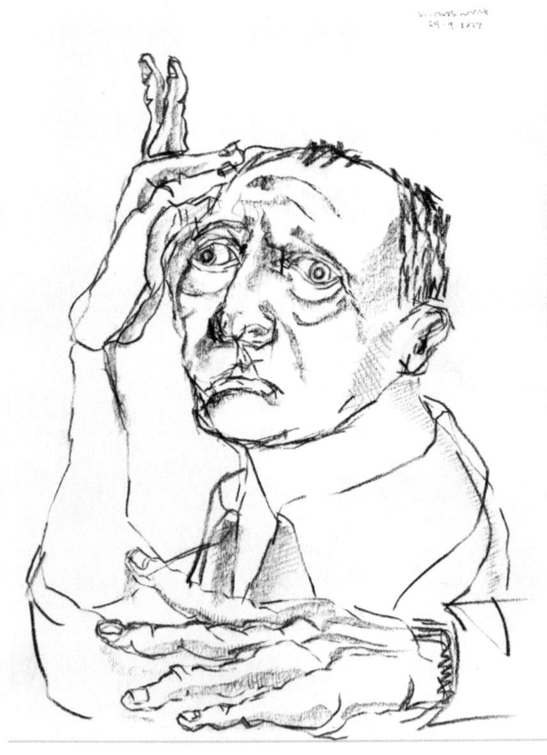

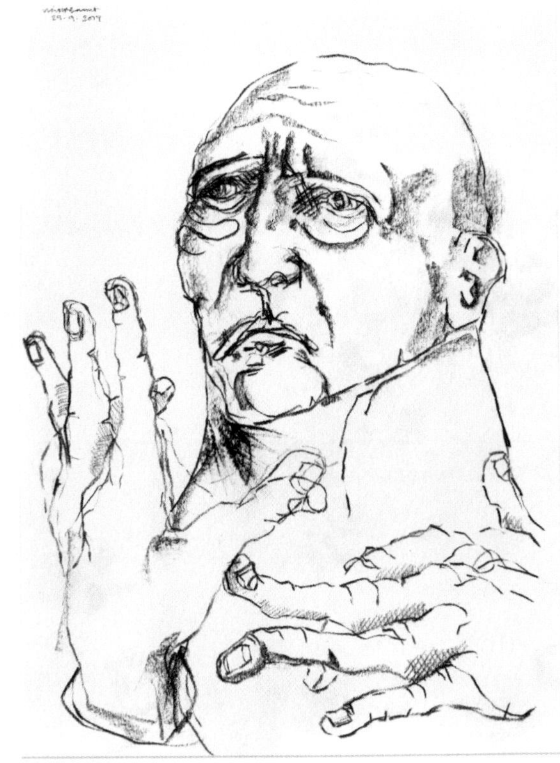

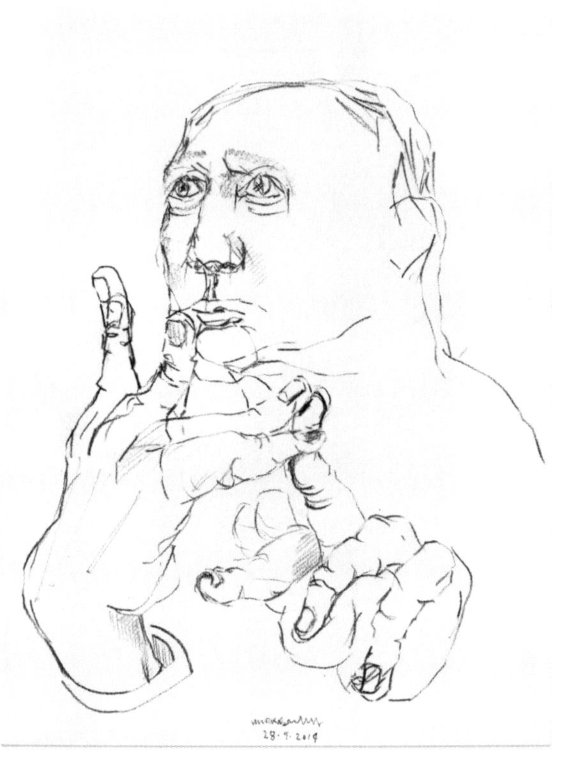

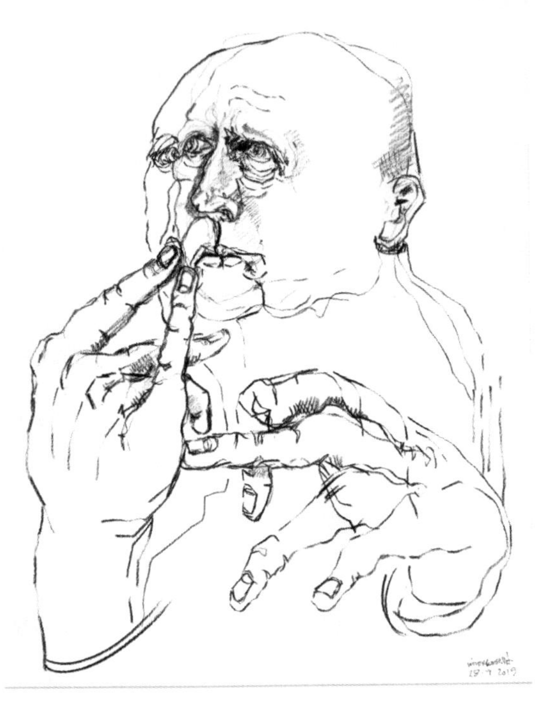

Untitled, 2019
Pencil, polychromos on paper
21cm x 29.7cm

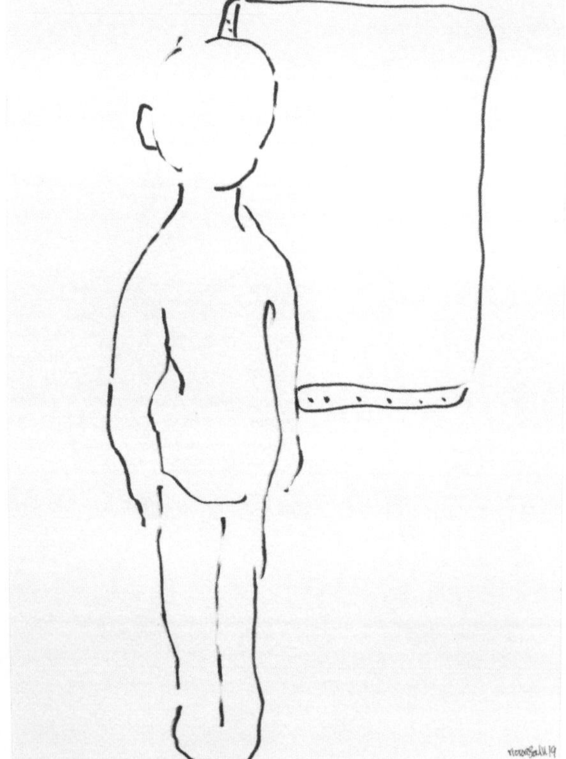

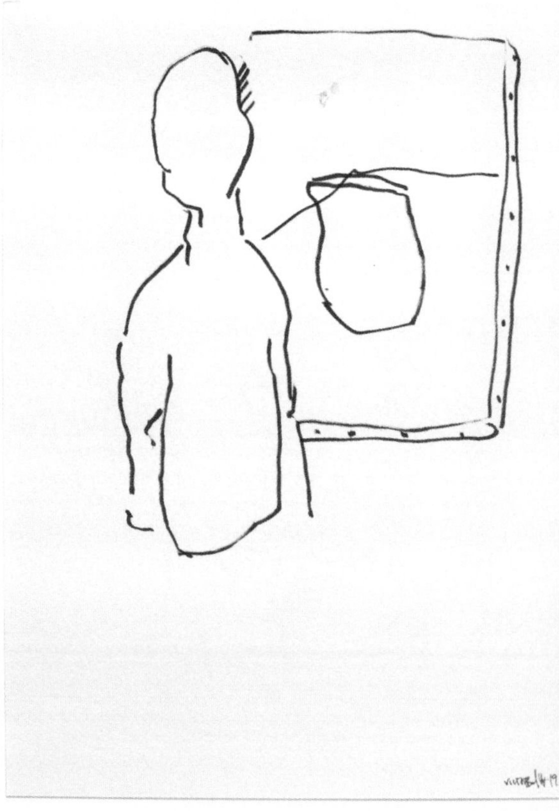

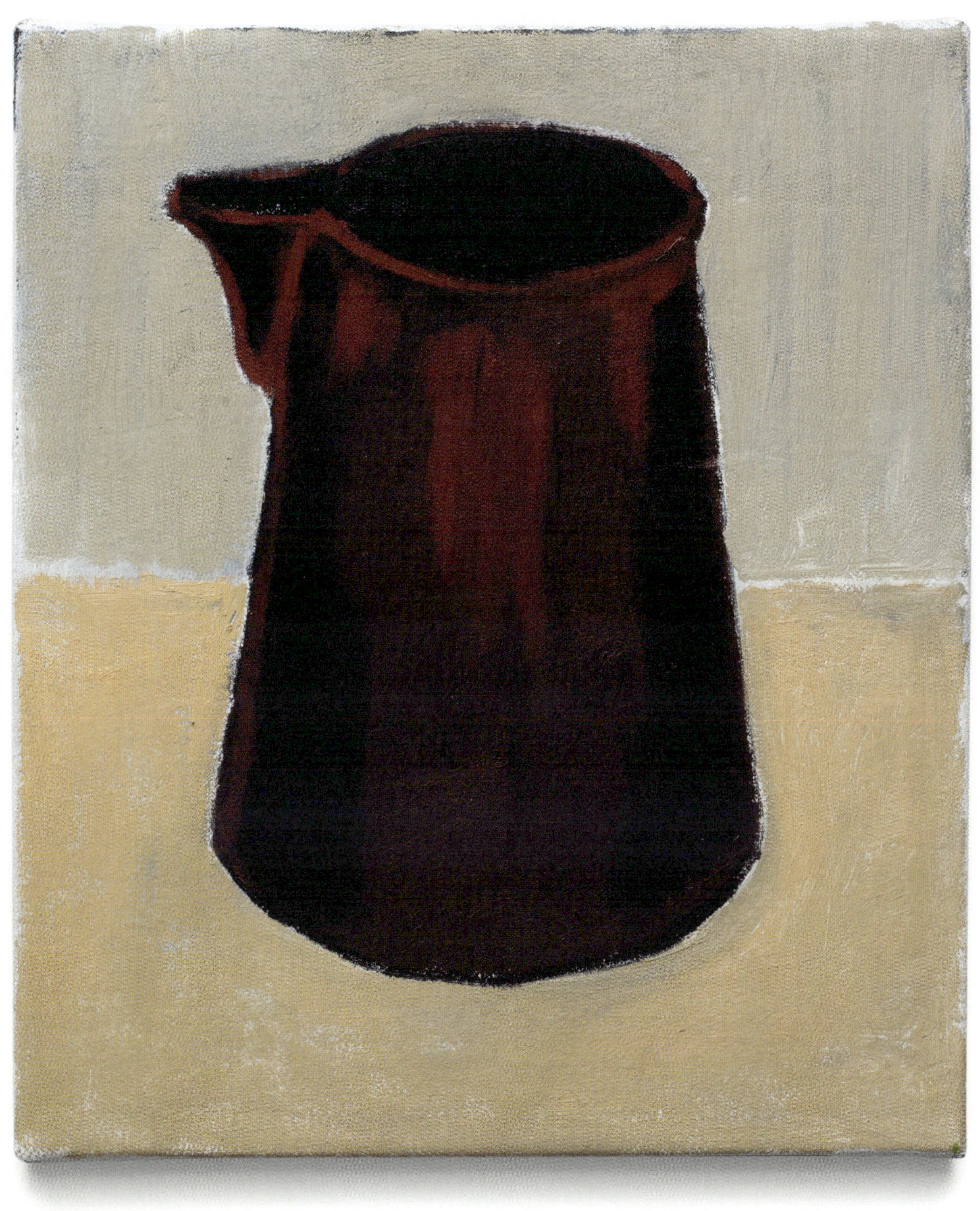

Untitled, 2019
Oil on (stitched) linen canvas
40cm x 46cm

Reperesenting I, II, 2019
Pen on paper
14,8cm x 21cm

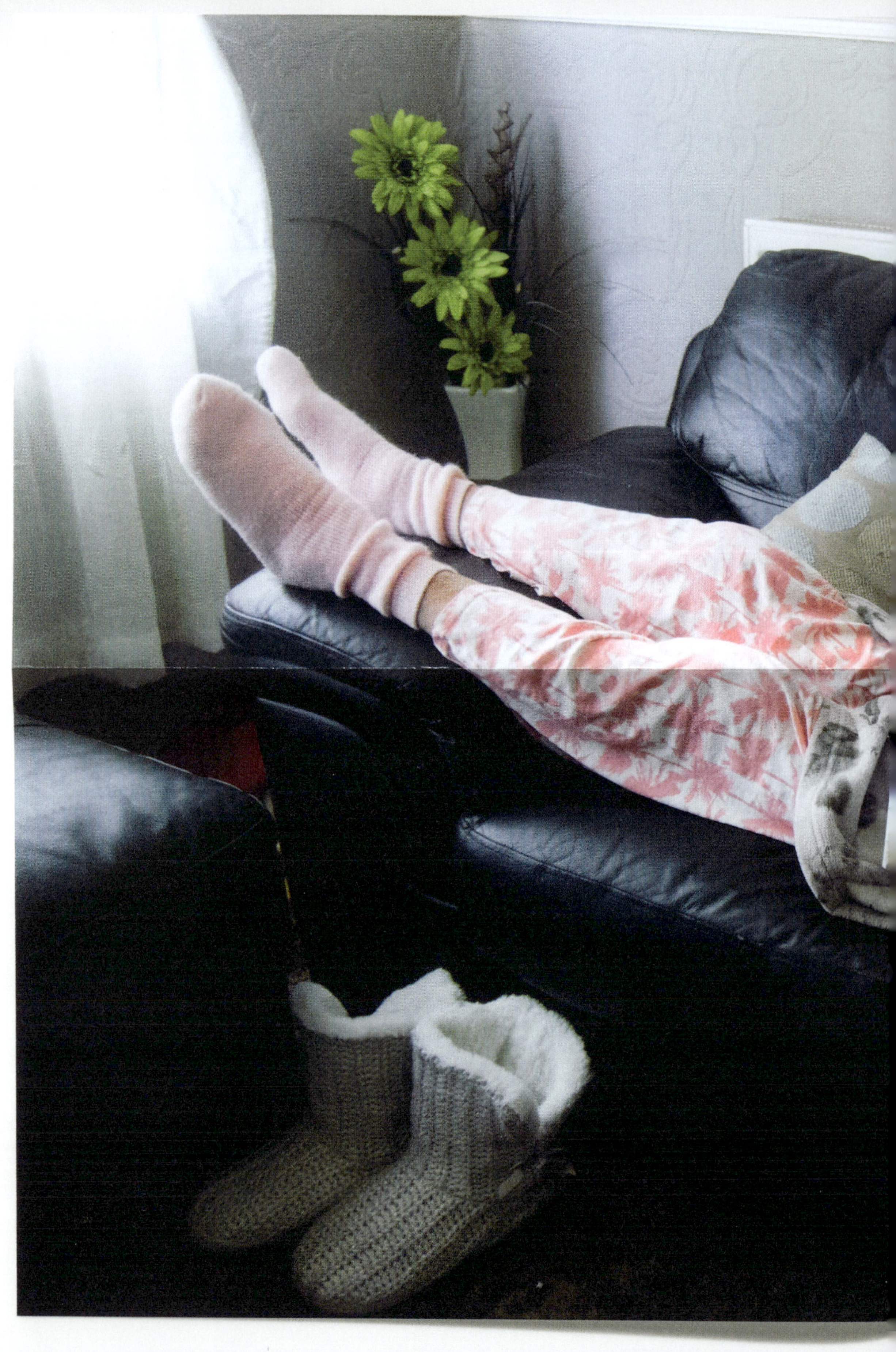

Tired of being a son
Victor Boullet

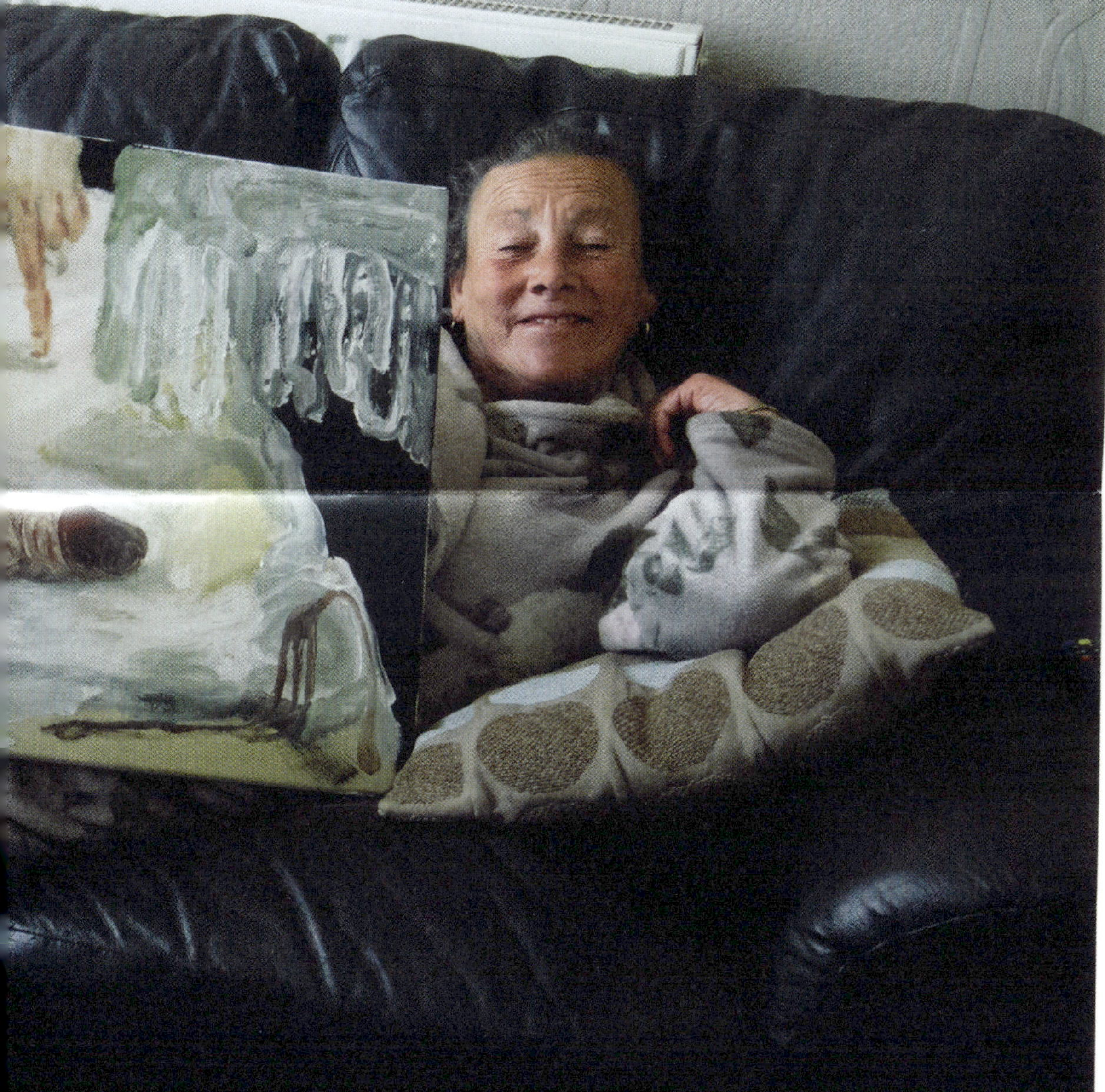

Victor Boullet
Cairo Show 2020
Oil on Canvas
L8 News
@texasknuller

Tired of Being a Son

There is a family story about two cucumbers that my father arrived with at a family weekend gathering around 2008. A few days later a cynical remark made by my mother made the cucumbers into a story and a manner of being, and finally paintings. My parents divorced in 1994. (I will share the full story at a later stage)

That beautiful and warm summer's day I didn't notice the arrival of the cucumbers or why and for what reason they were brought to the party. The complication with these two cucumbers and the remark made by my mum is that they have come to represent traits, or let's say DNA, from both my parents, that make my life at times miserable.

My cock has nothing to do with the cucumbers story, that's just me struggling with still life painting. I was born in 1969 and I own and control my cock today, without my parents comments or their lack of social skills, traits that I have inherited and am somewhat fed up with.

The woman in the fanzine photos is Patsie or Patricia. When the pensioners in the neighbourhood are paid, Patsie knocks on doors to help, but in fact she robs them of their pension. She once stole £300 out of a pocket of man that I would not want to cross. Two men went around to her house. It all got very nasty, but he got his money back and she was not seen for some time.

A few years ago she grabbed me by the arm and dragged me into her house. For some bizarre reason I let myself be dragged, curiosity I guess. I thought, now I'm being robbed, stabbed or she will offer a sexual favour for money. Instead her hand came out, shaped as a leaf, begging for money. I rejected her, but returned with a £1 crap loaf because she mentioned hunger. I handed her the bread and I received a quiet thank you and she shut the door. I walked home and felt a brutal shame that ran through me like dirt. And every time I saw Patsie, the shame over that bread, the begging and my moralistic scrooge-control-behaviour grew within me.

Rain or snow Patsie will walk around the streets in her pyjamas and slippers all bought from Primark. She was squirming around in her bed looking at cucumbers and my penis and she uttered; I'm going to cry I have never seen anything so beautiful, I love the paintings.

The cucumber story is a doubled edge sword. I hoped that by activating the paintings together with Patsie, that she could derail my project, but instead I find myself closer to my parents, just worse.

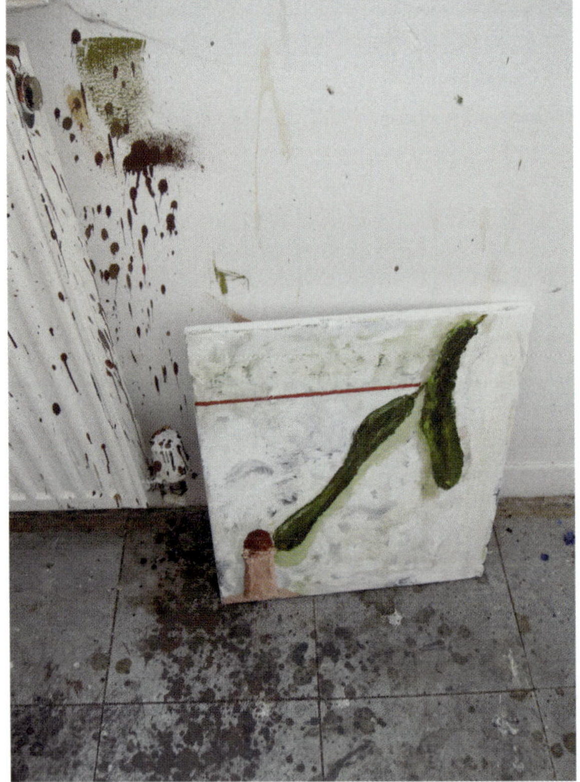

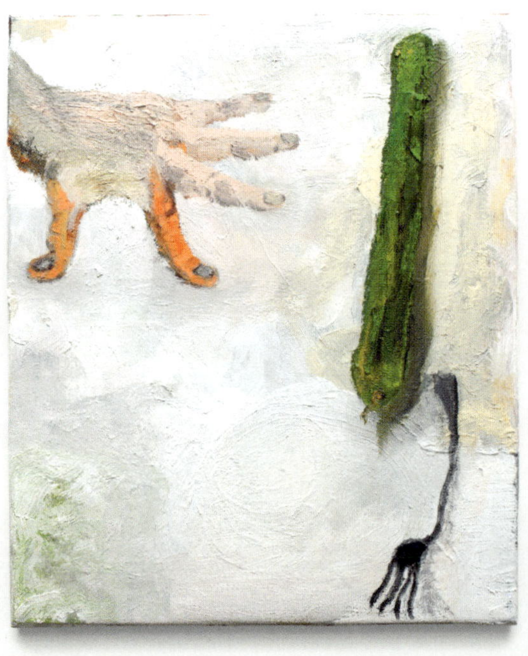

Do as I Say, 2019 – 2020
Oil on linen canvas
38cm x 46cm

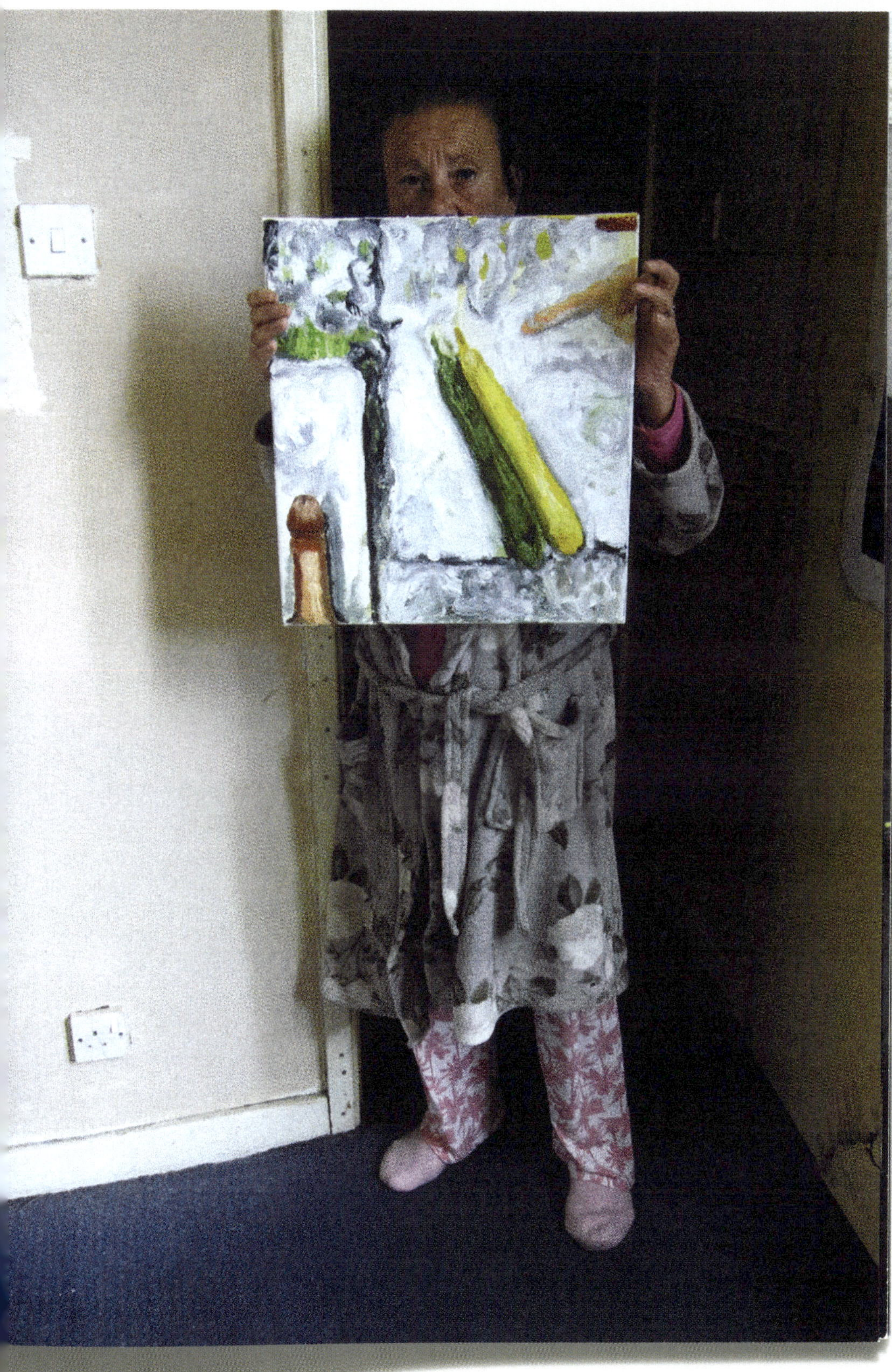

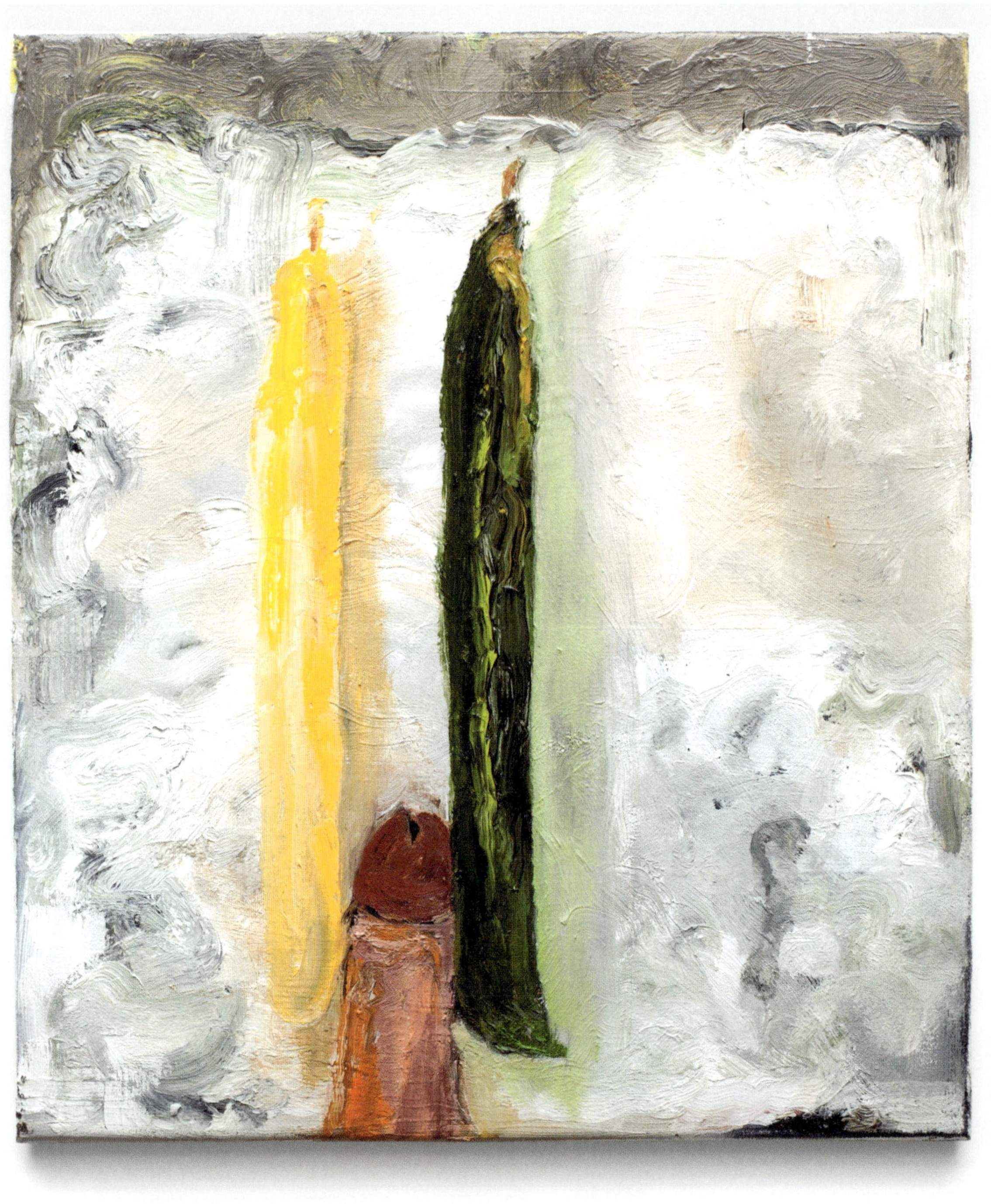

First Born, 2019 – 2020
Oil on linen canvas
40cm x 46cm

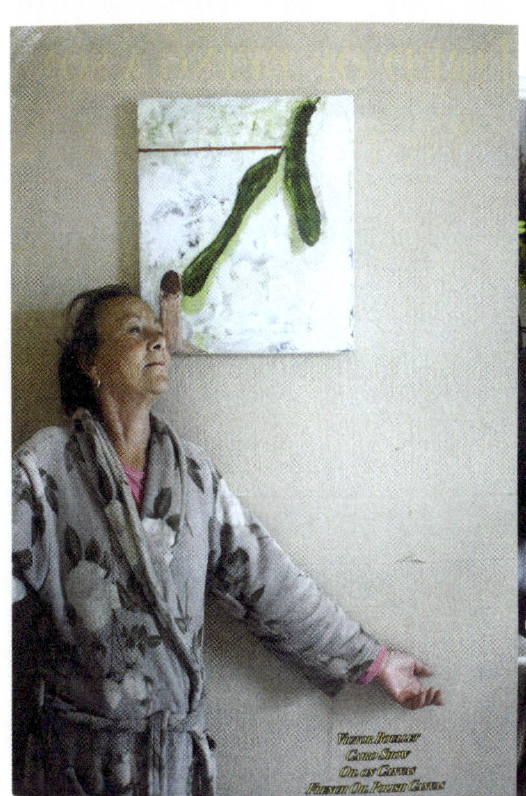
Victor Boullet
Cairo Show
Oil on Canvas
French Oil Polish Canvas

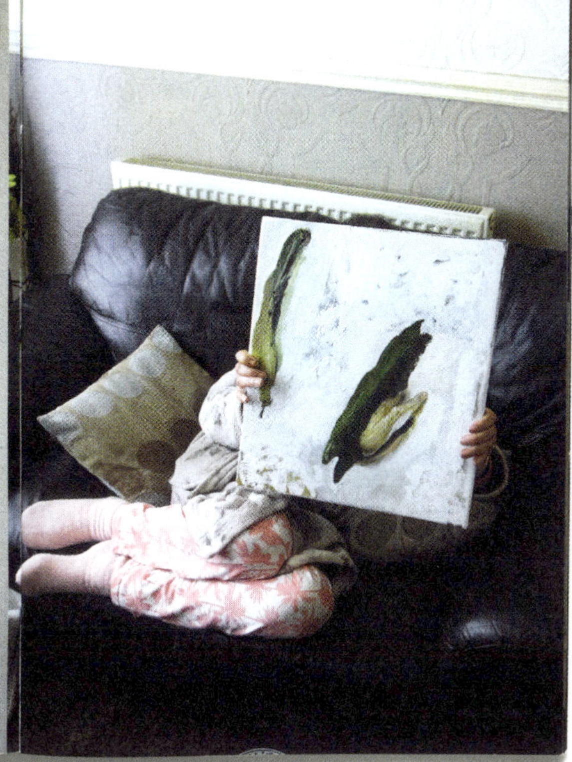

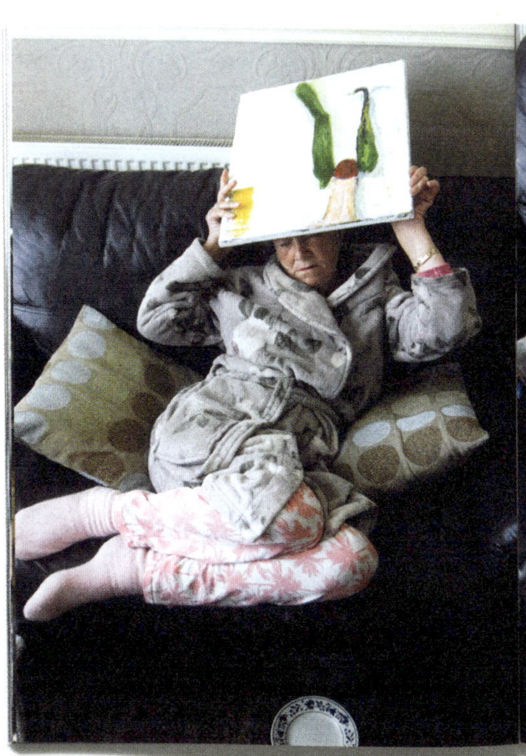

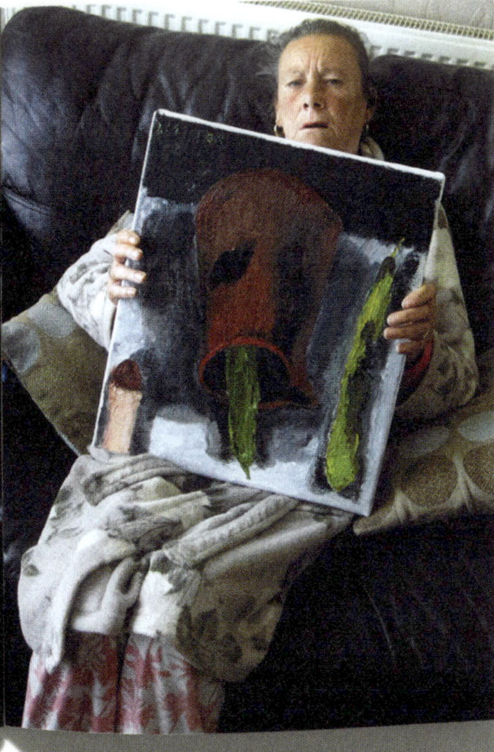

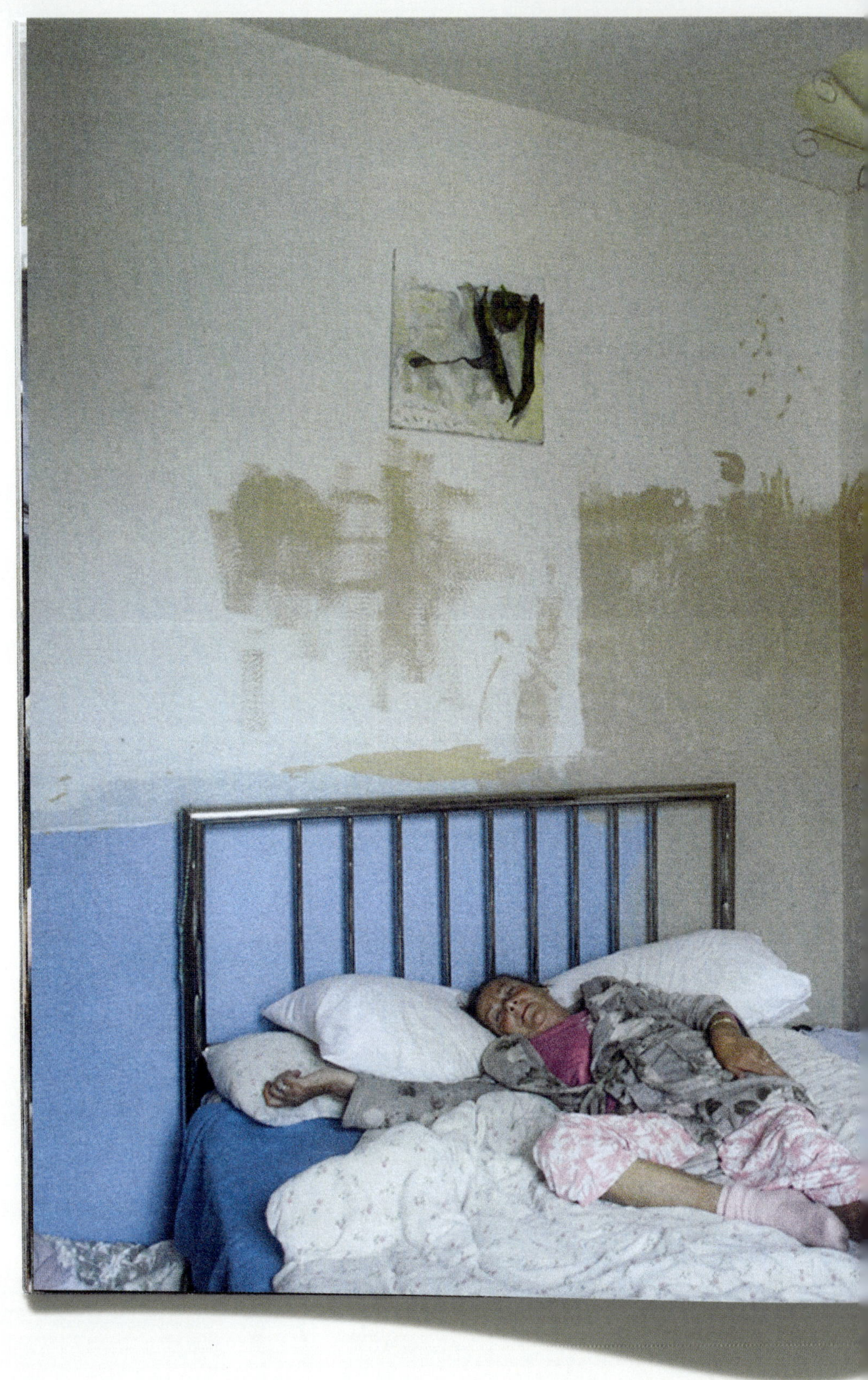

Page 136, 137
Tired of Being a Son, 2020
Poster, 30cm x 40cm folded to 15cm x 21cm
Page 139, 141, 142, 143
Tired of Being a Son, 2020
Fanzine, 15cm x 21cm. pp. 28. Ed. 50
Design by Texas Knuller

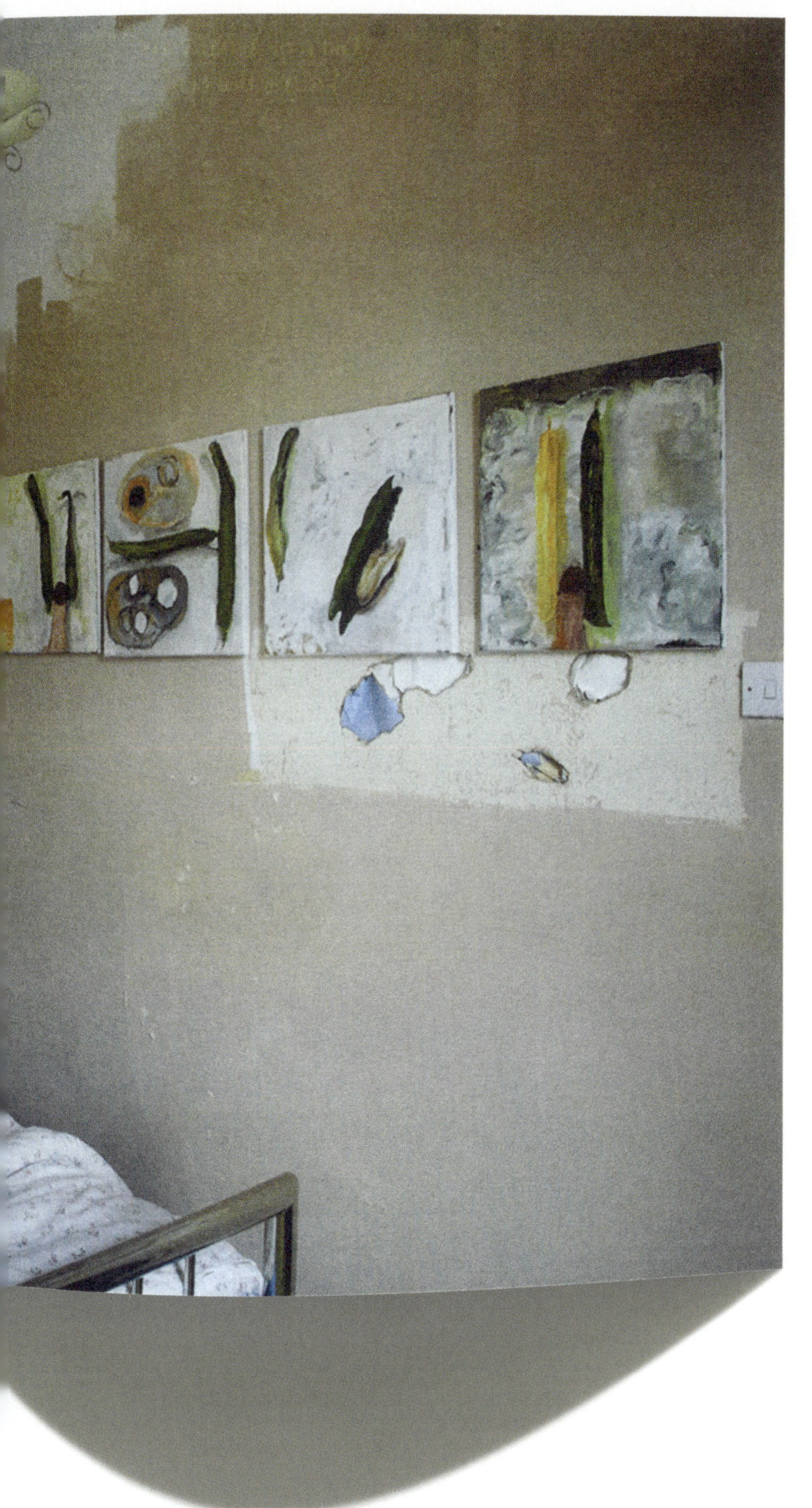

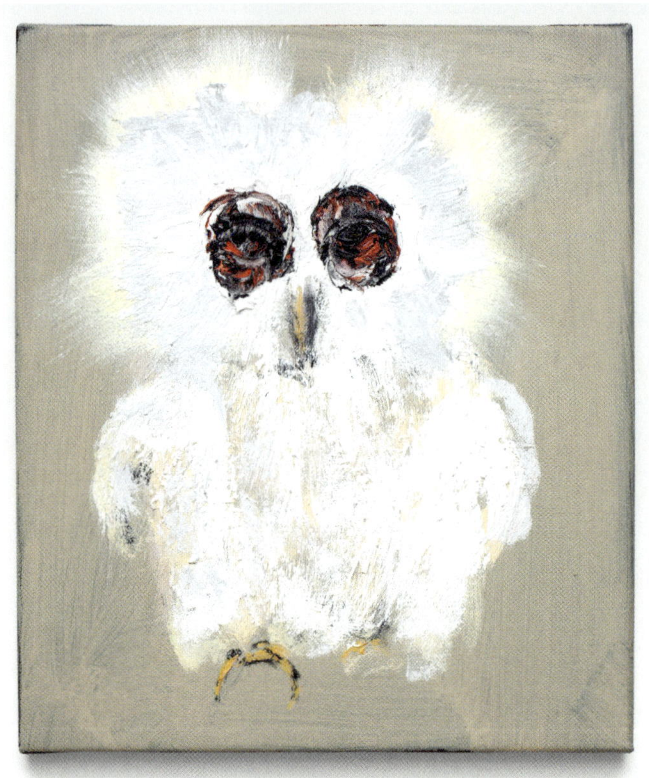

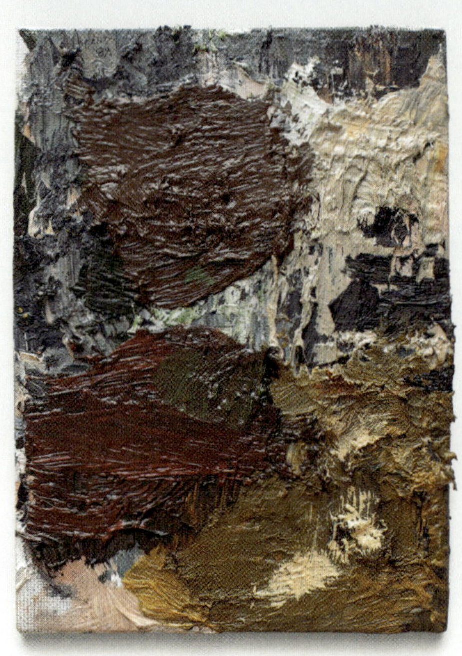

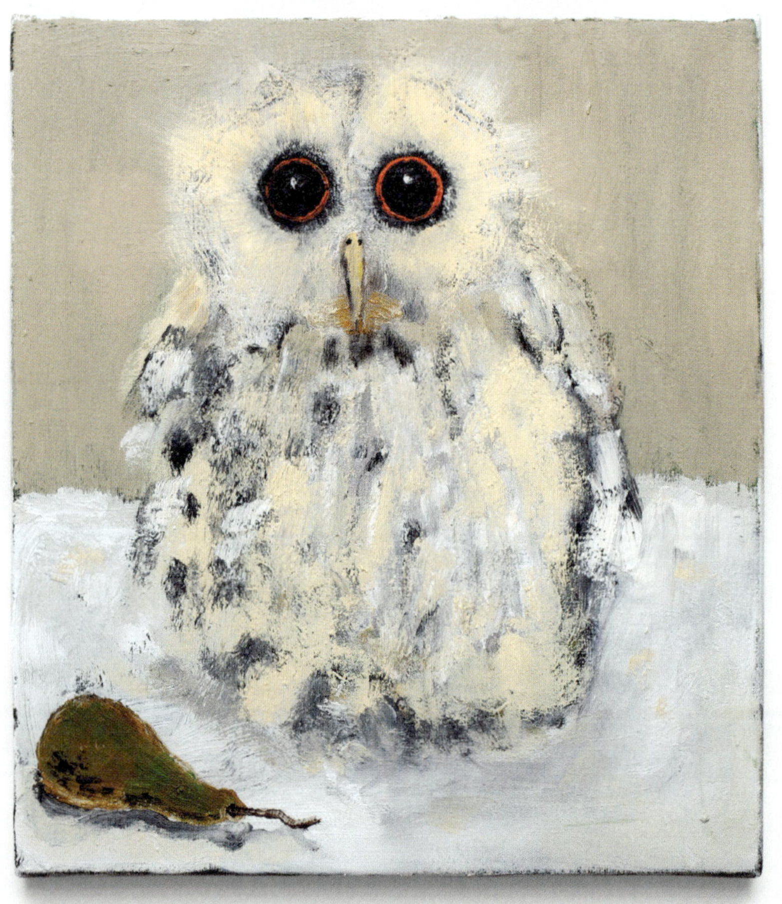

Ugle, 2019
Oil on black canvas
30cm x 35cm

Studio Interior, 2019
Oil on canvas board
14.8cm x 21cm

Ugle with pear, 2019
Oil on linen canvas
40cm x 46cm

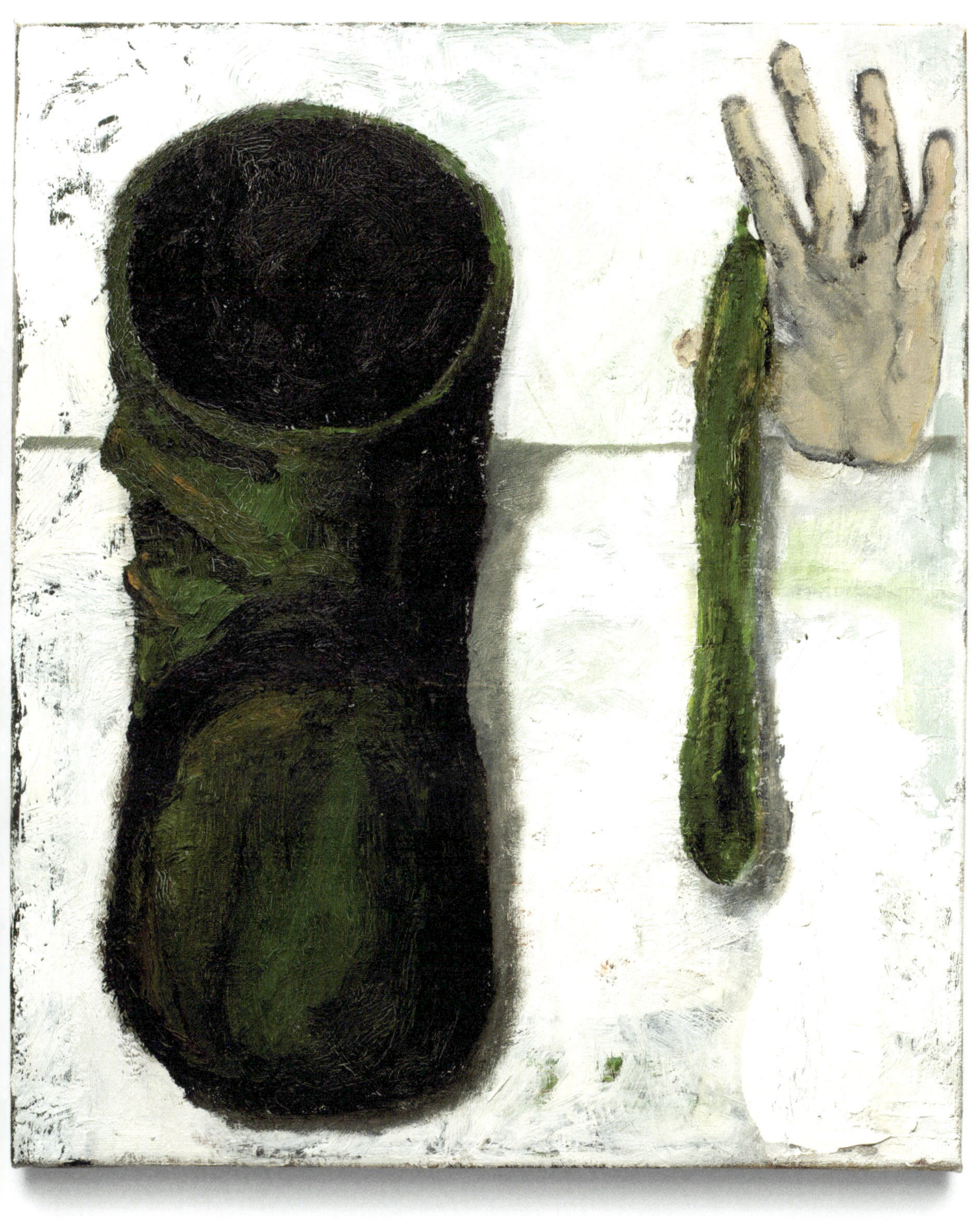

Pushed Through Her Arsehole, 2019
Oil on linen canvas
50cm x 60cm

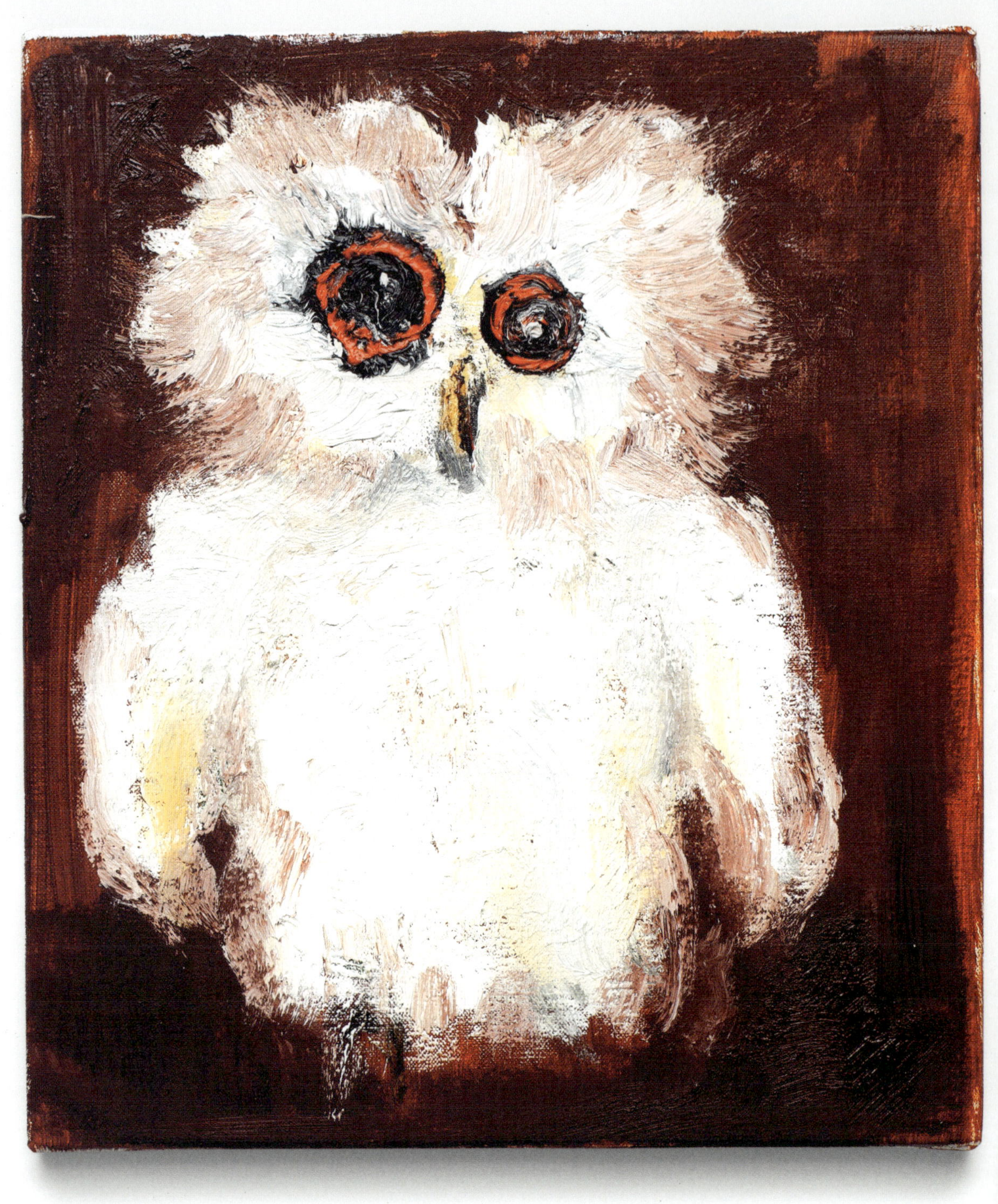

Ugle, 2019
Oil on linen canvas
30cm x 35cm

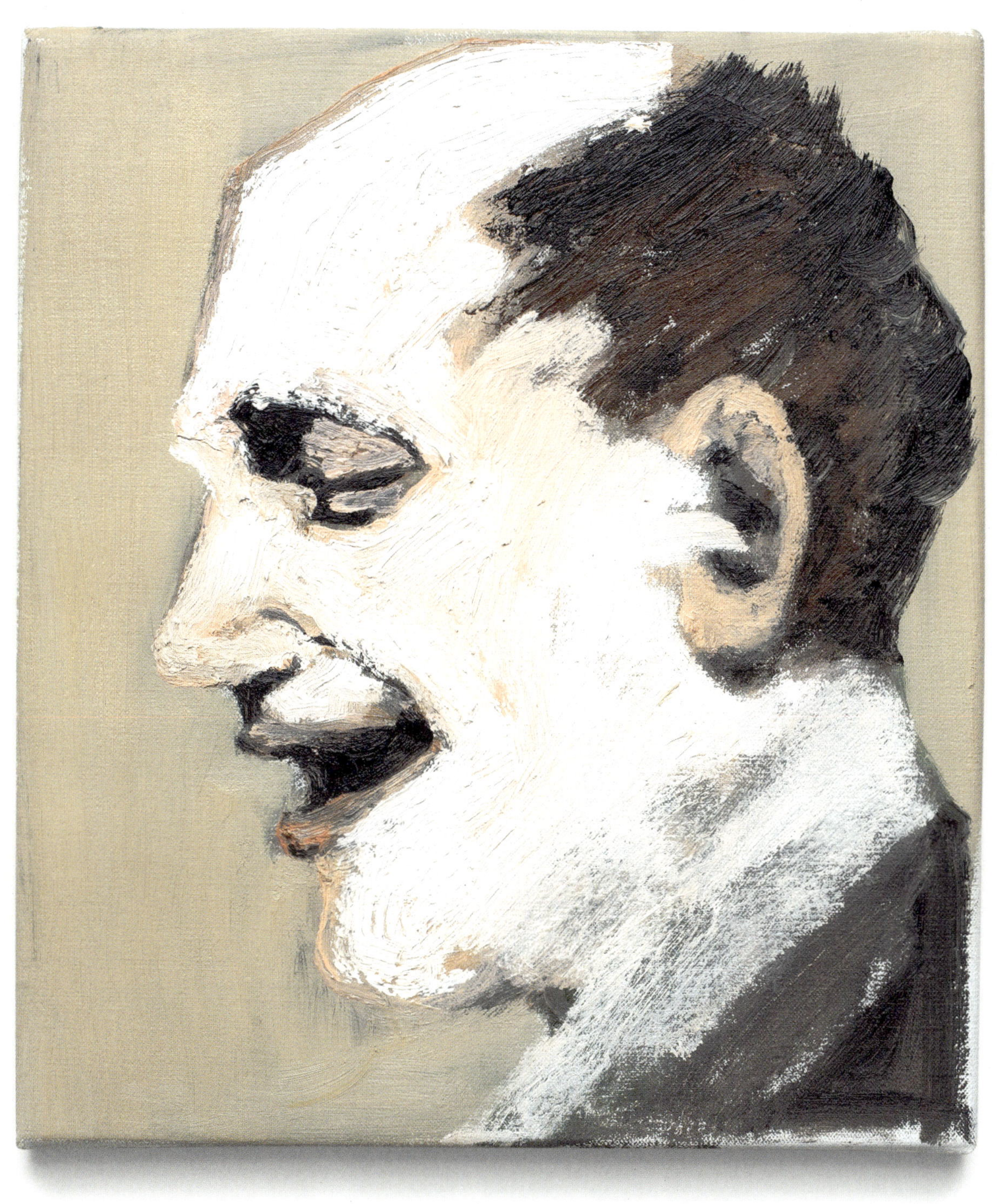

Sviatoslav Teofilovich Richter, 2019
Oil on linen canvas
30cm x 35cm

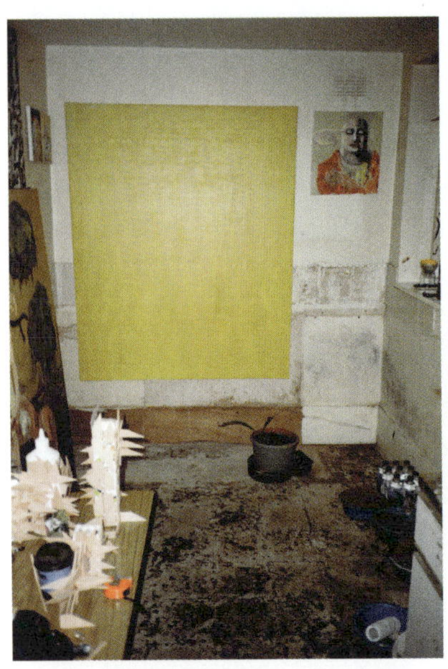
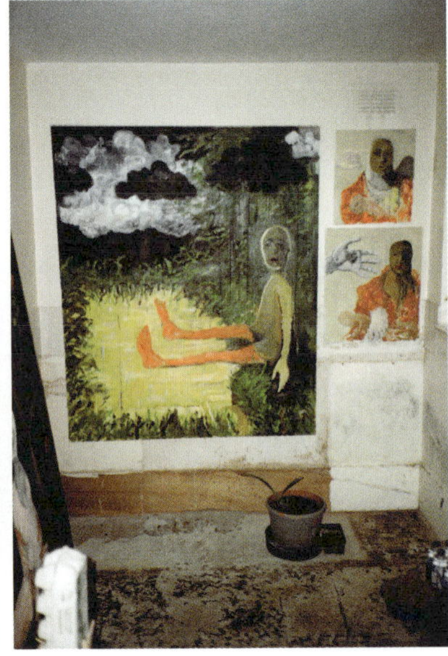
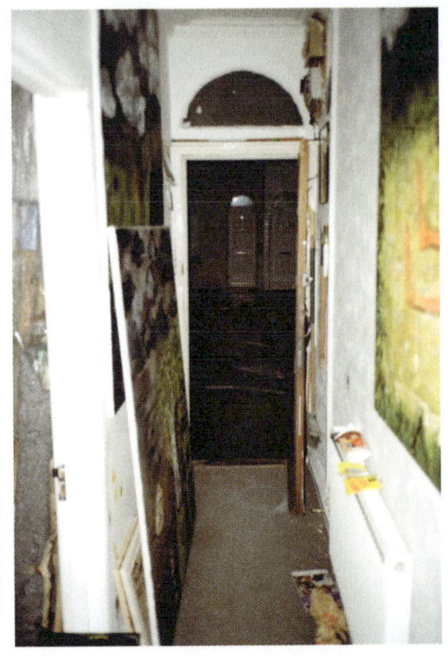
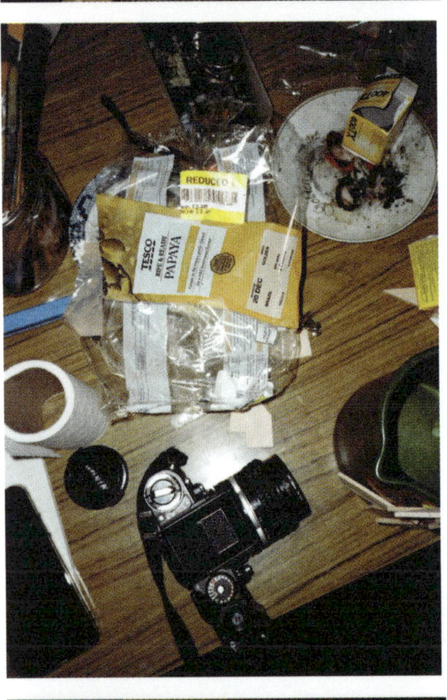
TESCO
PAPAYA
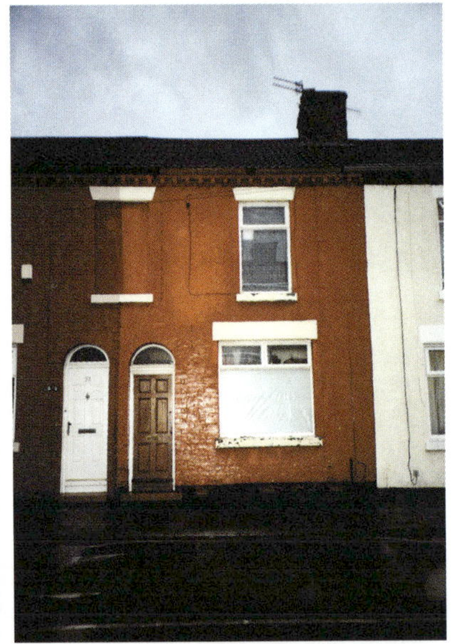
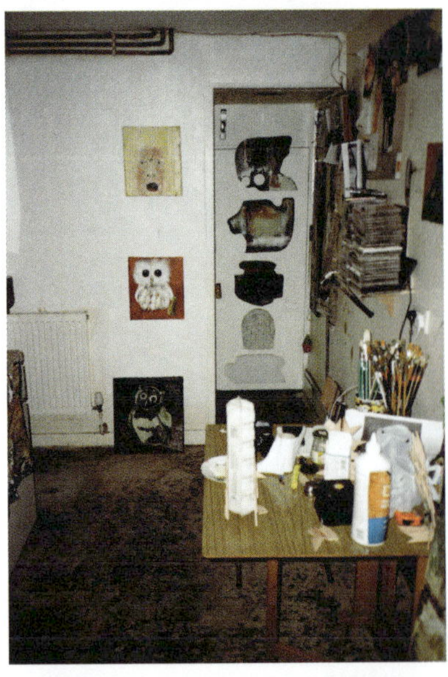
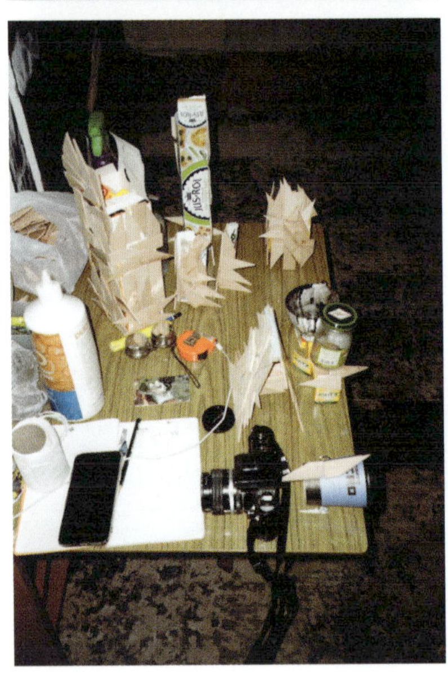
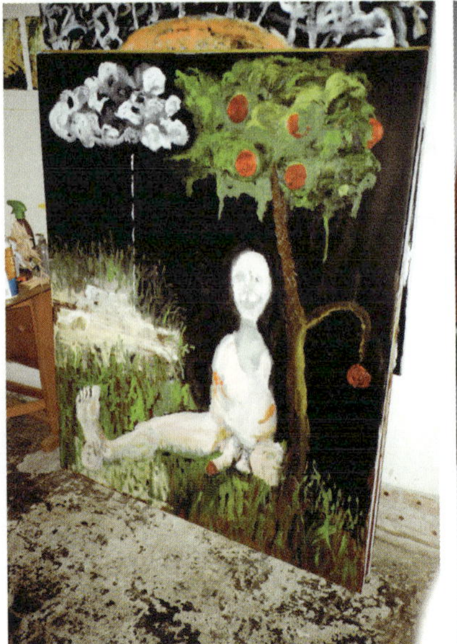
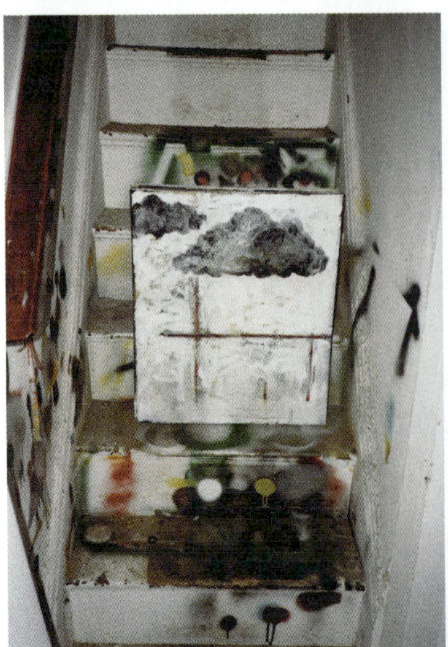

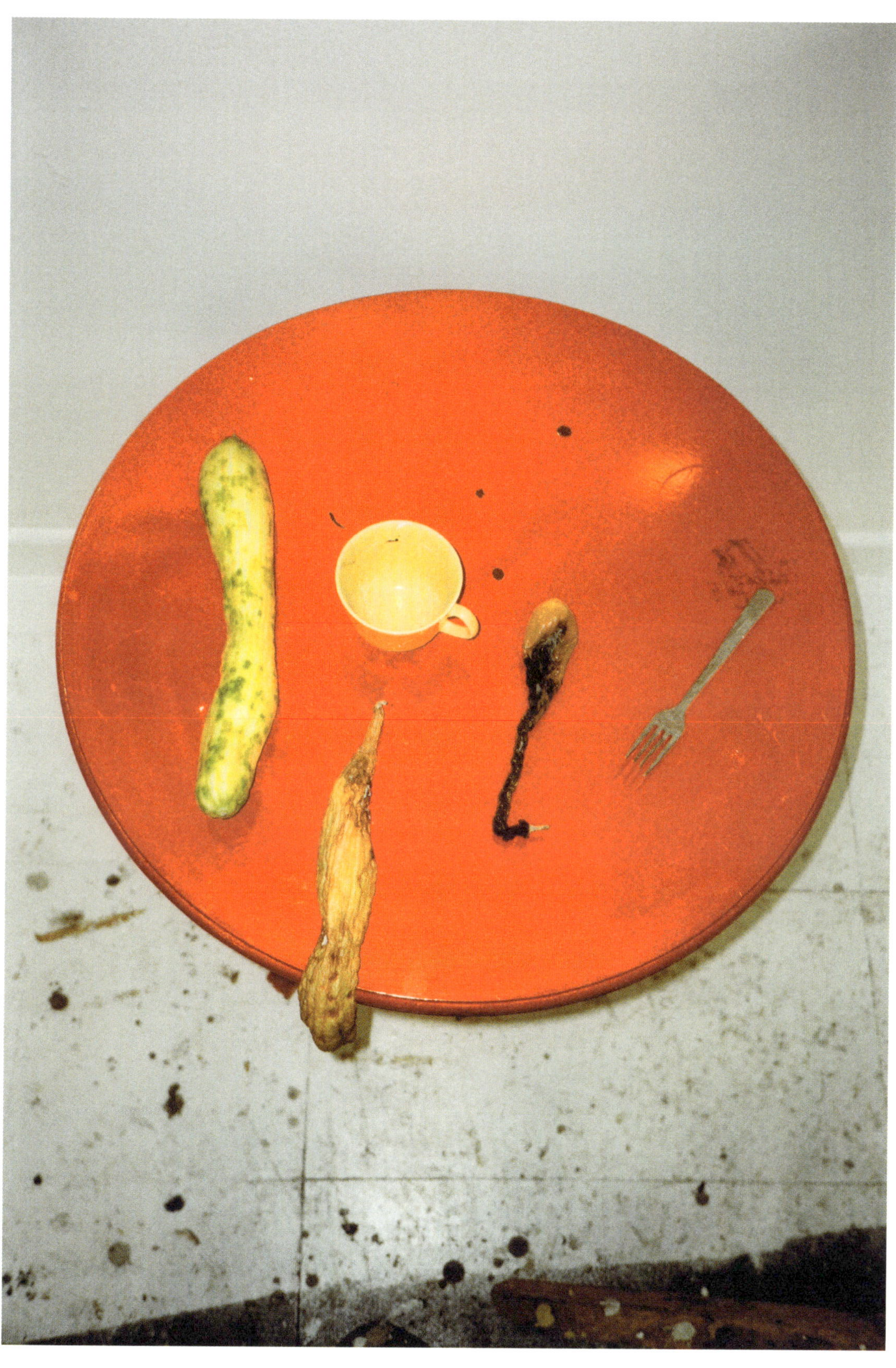

Studio documentation, 2019
35mm film

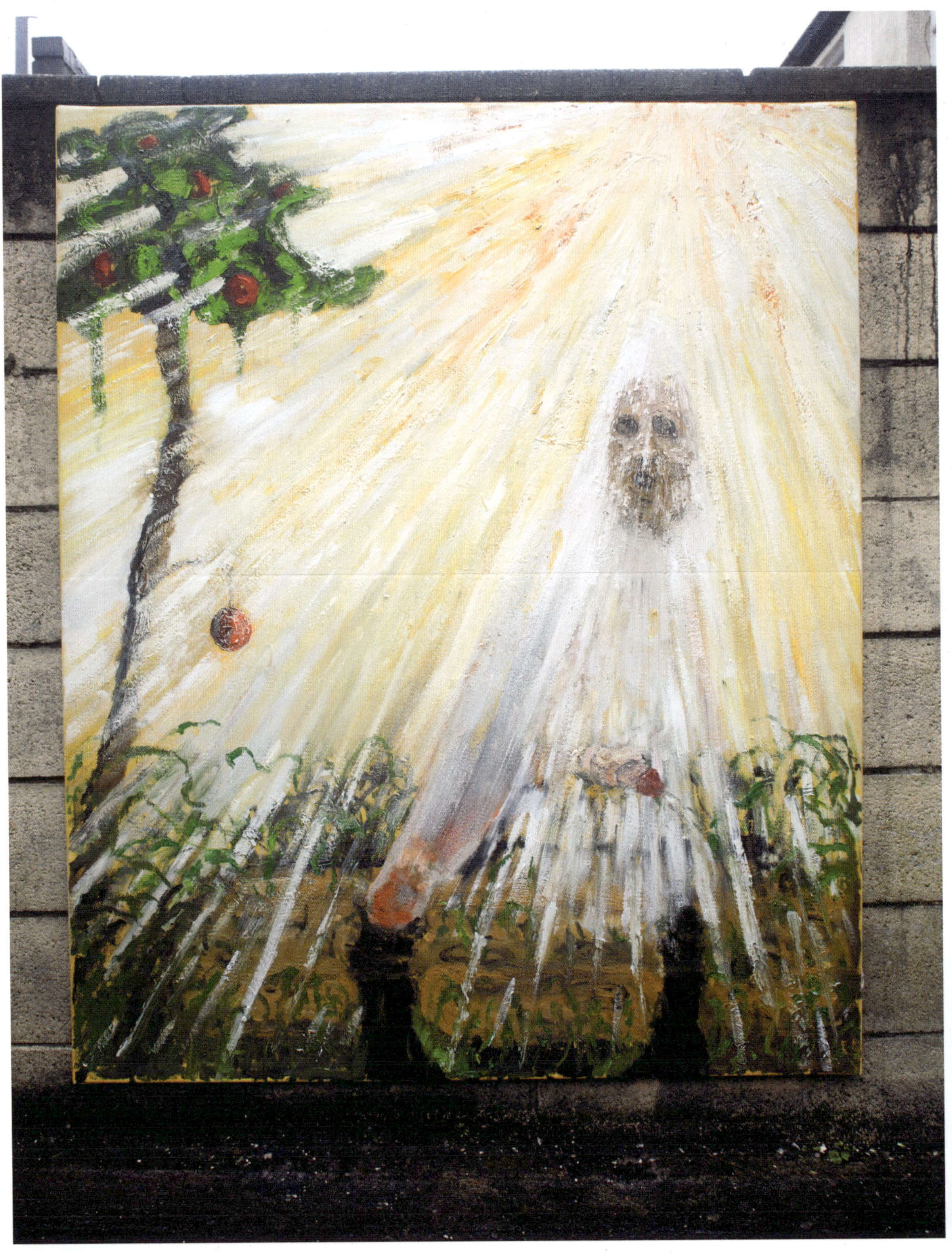

Untitled, 2019
Oil on jute
130cm x 160cm

You Kurt Me Mongrel

This show was cancelled in November 2019, but I decided to continue the work on the 10 canvases, I only managed 8 before the process stopped in March 2020.

I had been toying with the idea of hanging 10 paintings in and around the Kurt Schwitters Merzbarn, Ambleside, North West of England. There is a shabby exhibition space located in the grounds just before Kurt's dilapidated shed where his mural was removed in 1965 to the Hatton Gallery in Newcastle.

The content of the work: Kurt Schwitters exile and commitment to going back and forth from Ambleside where he lived to the barn where he made his mural. Mix that with my own walk to and from my studio, 4 times a day in Liverpool, then add the myth of the wounded man / painter. I know nothing about his walk, but my walk has become an unfriendly challenge with no gain or joy other than the sound of my feet hitting the ground.

20.8.2019 I arrived at the barn wanting to ask for a show. I met a woman, told her what I wanted, she looked up and said: You'd better speak with Ian.

Ian Hunter was obviously the boss. A quick introduction and he started cracking unfunny jokes. I told him why I was there, a snap reply: YES you can have a show, but first I have a job for you! The woman looked at me with a tired smile, she seemed trapped. He pointed: If you paint these 7 chipboards (120X240cm) you'll have your show. I looked at the chipboards thinking: what an embarrassment!

Ian Hunter insisted that we have a cup of tea first. After some time he arrived with tea, biscuits and scones. He quickly fingered the better morsels. After more than half an hour of hearing him talk, mostly about himself and a rather capitalistic plan for the barn, I looked over at my partner making an unhappy face. During his monologue he made snide remarks like: you could be a professor and endlessly name-dropped celebrity artists and architects who have donated money. It was all so discouraging.

I said: Hey, let's get this job done.

But then he started slagging off the Norwegian curator Karin Hellansjø who initiated the move of another entire shed of Kurt Schwitters in Norway. Jealousy is ugly, and he seems not to understand that when the content was removed from the barn he is left simply guarding a nostalgic cavity covered with a tarpaulin with a picture of the mural?

Again I uttered: Hey, let's get these boards painted.

I'm not going into detail about Ian Hunter's practical ability, but there I was, the court jester, painting the chipboard so I could get my show.

I mentioned my admiration of Kurt Schwitters enormous walk from Ambleside to the barn, Ian didn't listen, he was not interested, he just talked about how grand this place was going to become with his Kurt Museum. My thoughts are; Kurt Schwitters would not want a shop or a cafe or Ian Hunter for that matter, in and around that barn.

YOU KURT ME MONGREL
YOU KURT ME MONGREL
by Victor Boullet
MERZ BARN
Ambleside

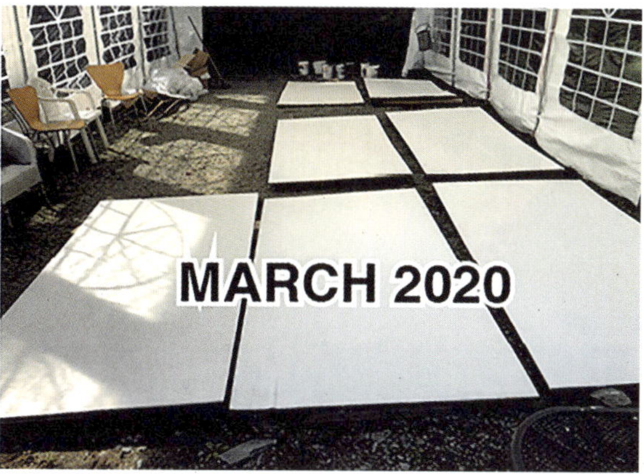

Exhibition invitation for You Kurt Me Mongrel, 2020

We agreed that my show would take place winter 2020.

Back in Liverpool I emailed him twice and received vague, sarcastic replies. I continued my work, but in November 2019 I needed some practical answers in regards to the show. This time Ian Hunter replied with a short, rude email saying: There will be no show and he offers me £40 for the work that I did. Who does he think he is, this Ian Hunter?

I decided to call him. That same quiet woman picked up the phone and passed it on to him. I said hello, and asked If he could explain, he didn't really manage to explain himself other than that I probably should not visit again? He hung up, and at this point he became my project, the fool.

Kurt Schwitters' commitment, his way of surviving in exile by using his craft as a painter and the paintings from the period in Ambleside is really what matters to me.

The Kurt Schwitters barn is a sentimental ruin and a disappointment and that is Kurt's possible vengeance against those who try to profit from artist's legacies. An eye for an eye and a tooth for a tooth.

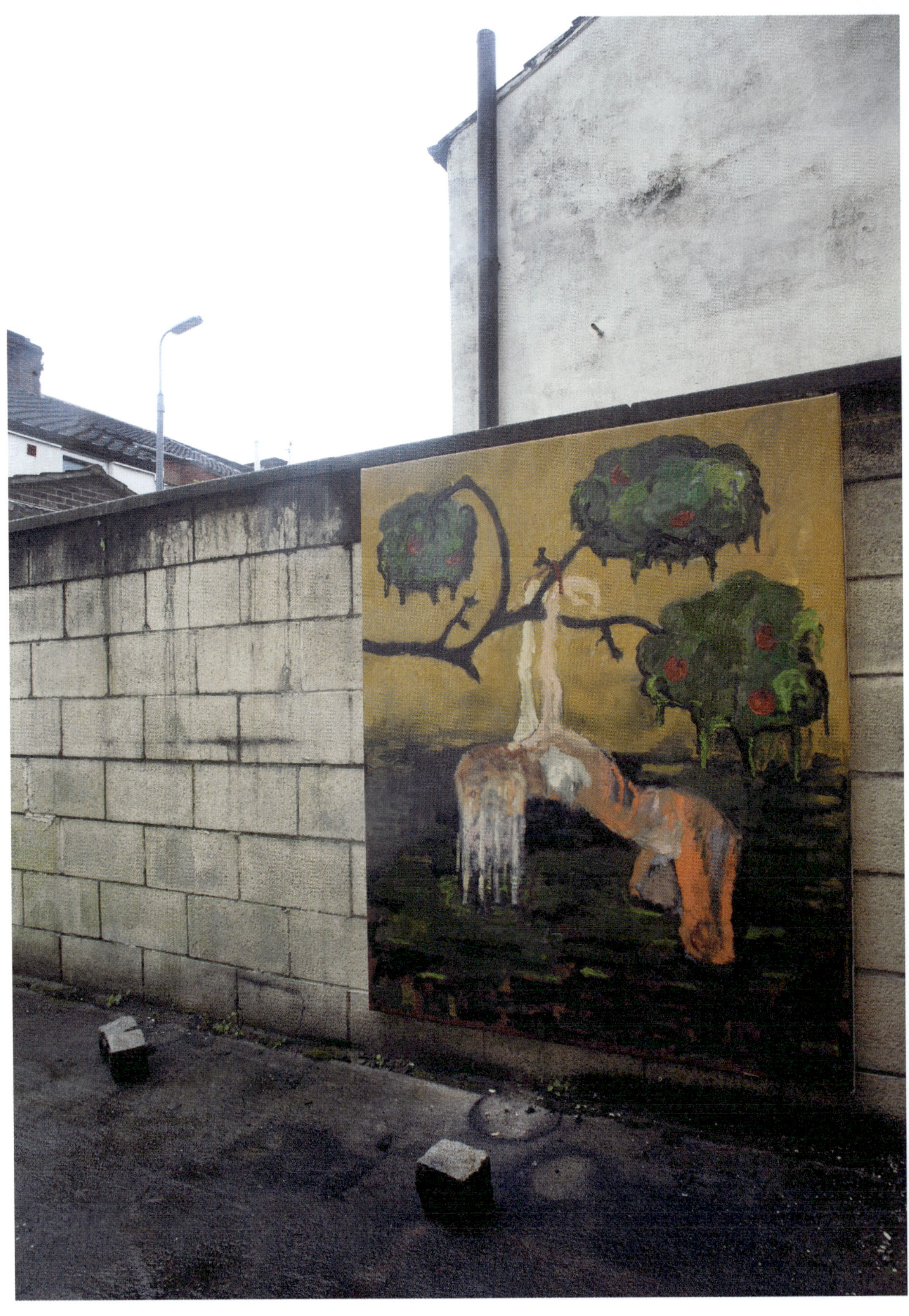

Untitled, 2019
Oil on jute
130cm x 160cm

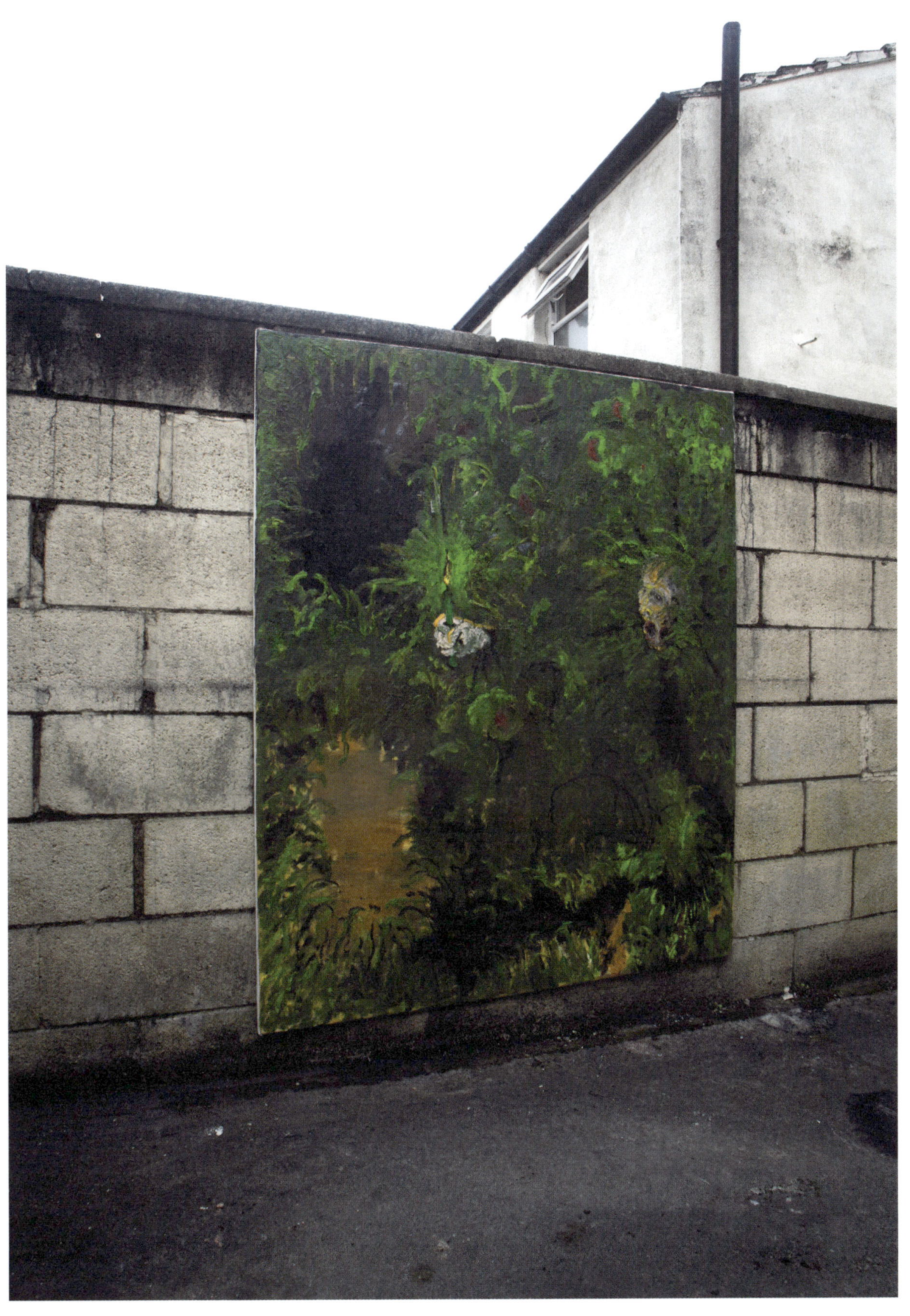

Untitled, 2019
Oil on jute
130cm x 160cm

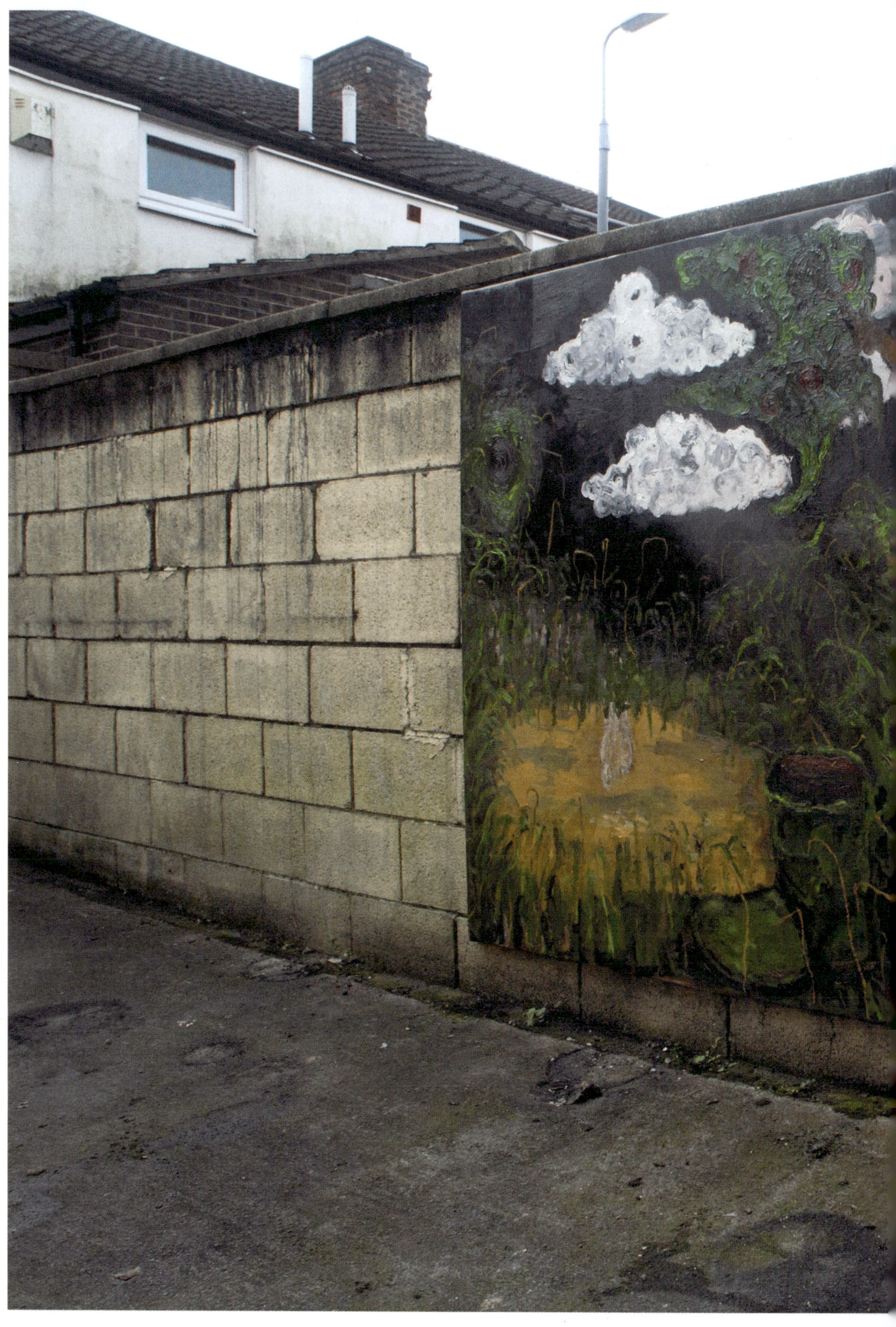

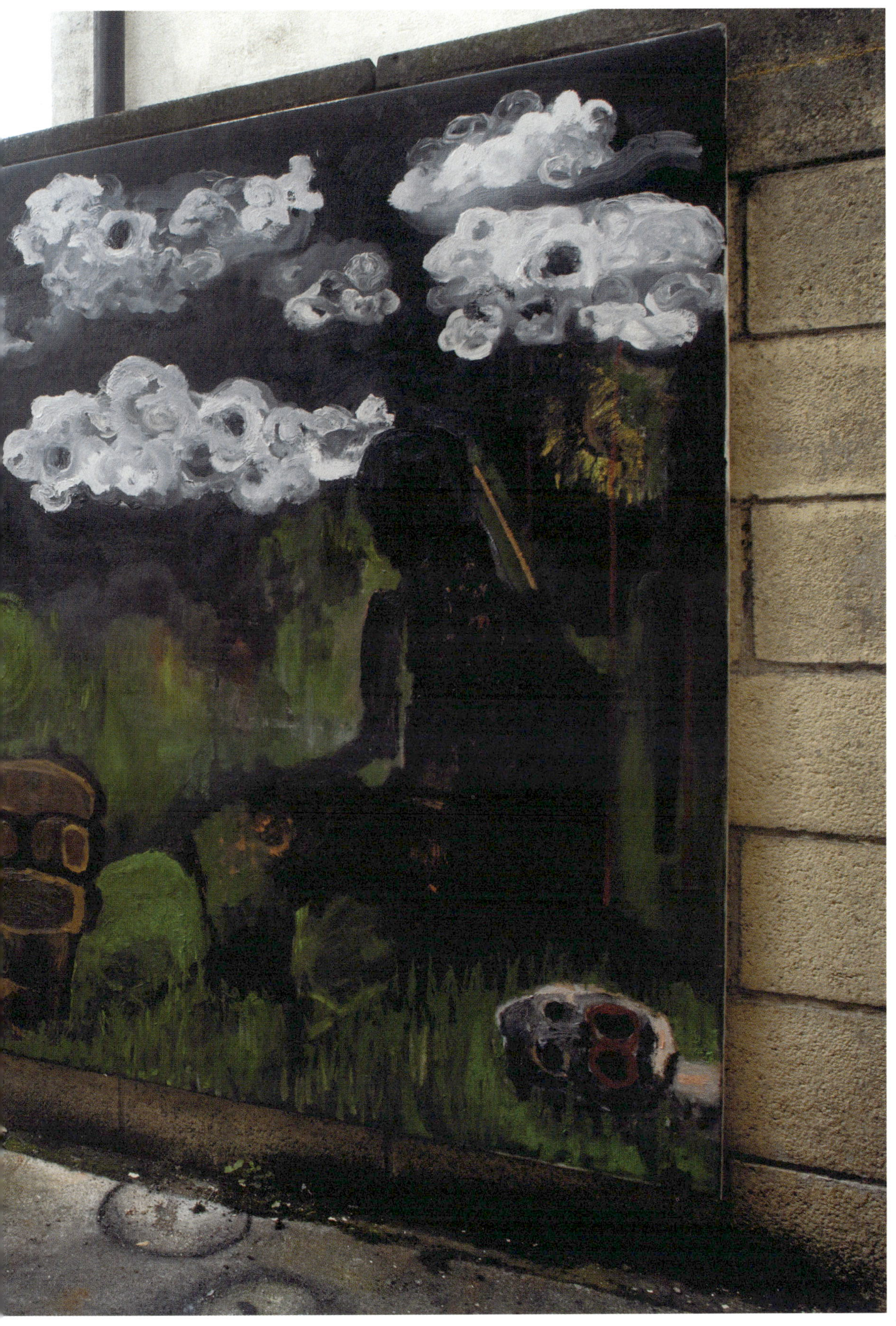

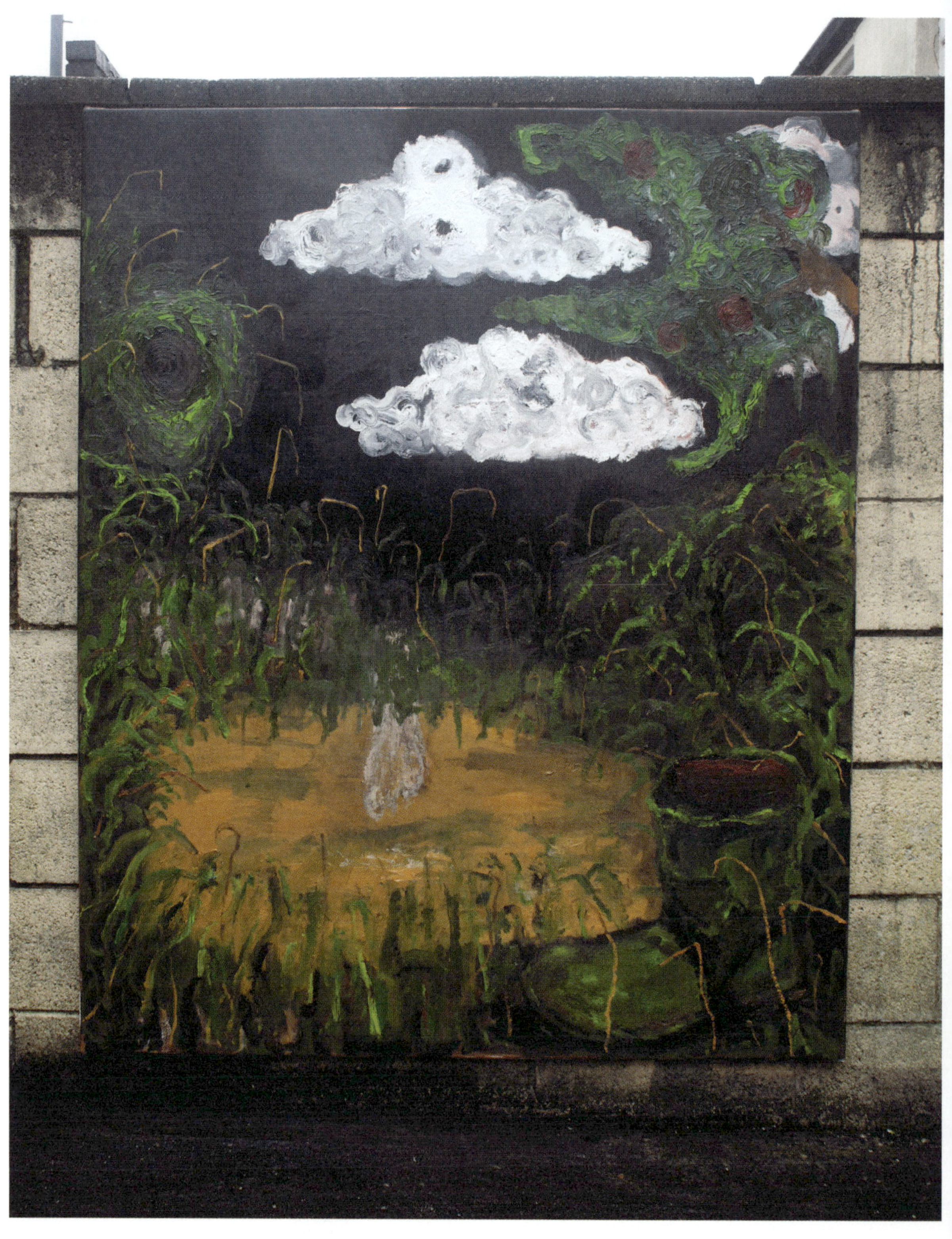

Untitled, 2019
Oil on jute
130cm x 160cm

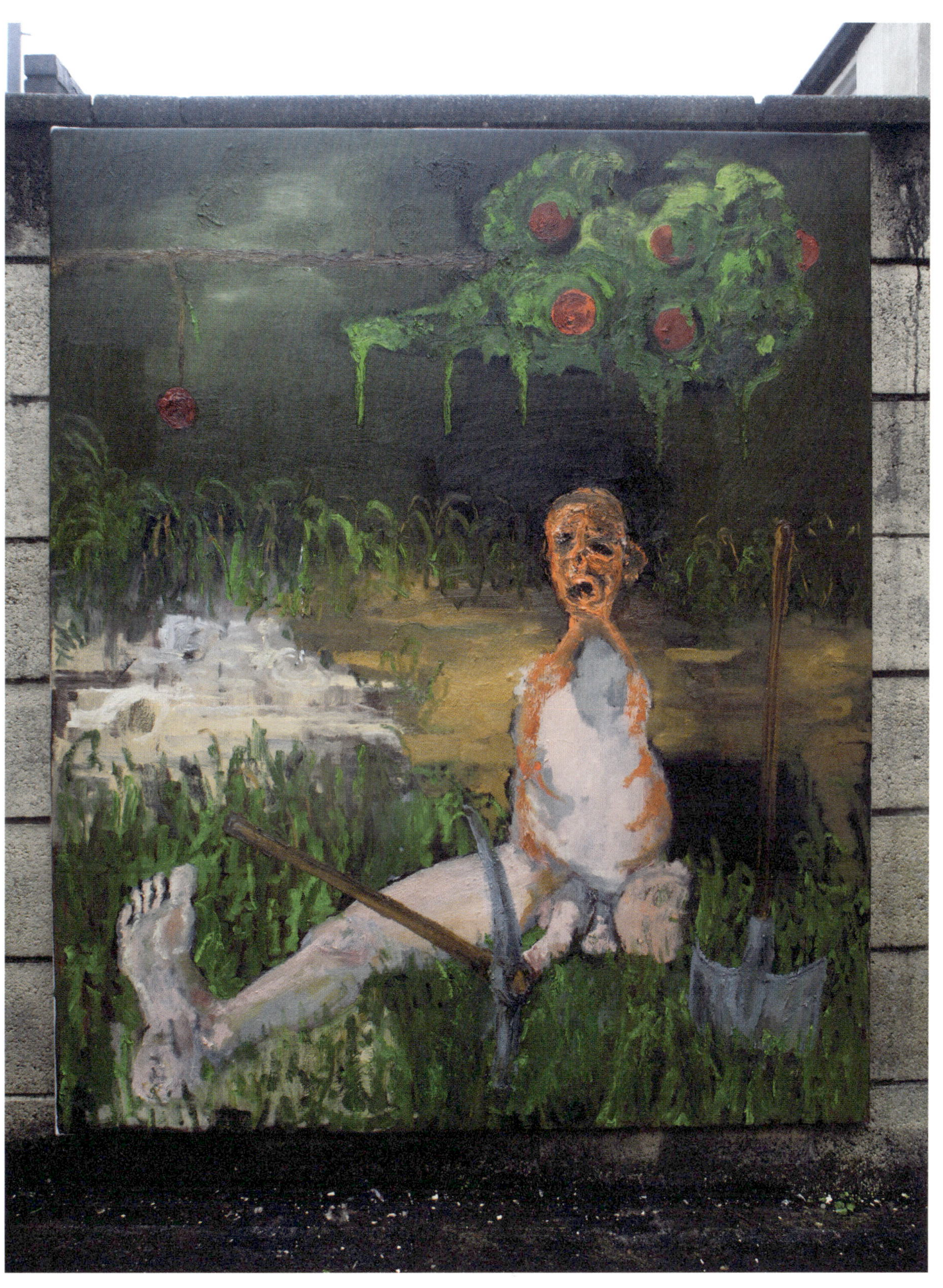

Untitled, 2019
Oil on jute
130cm x 160cm

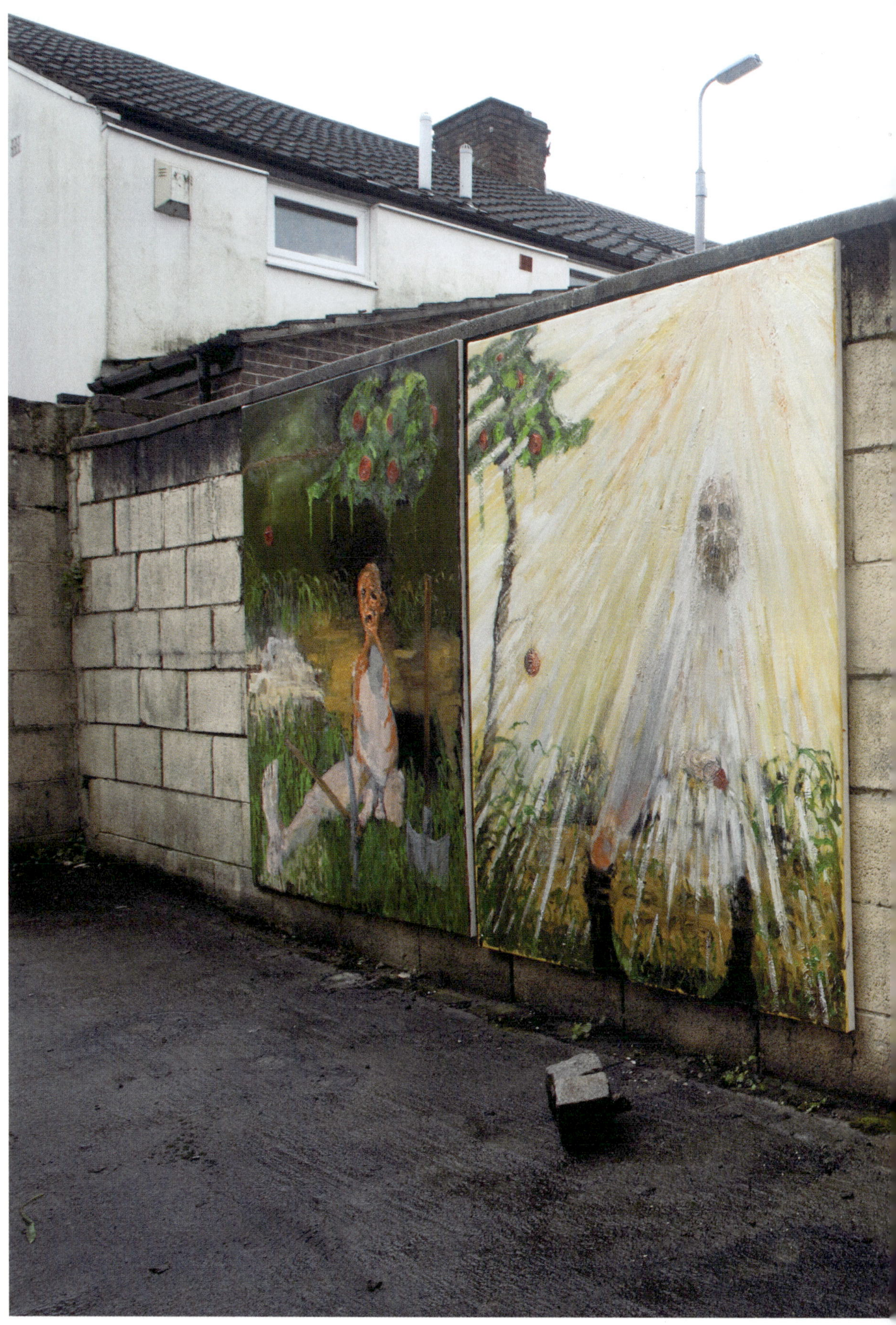

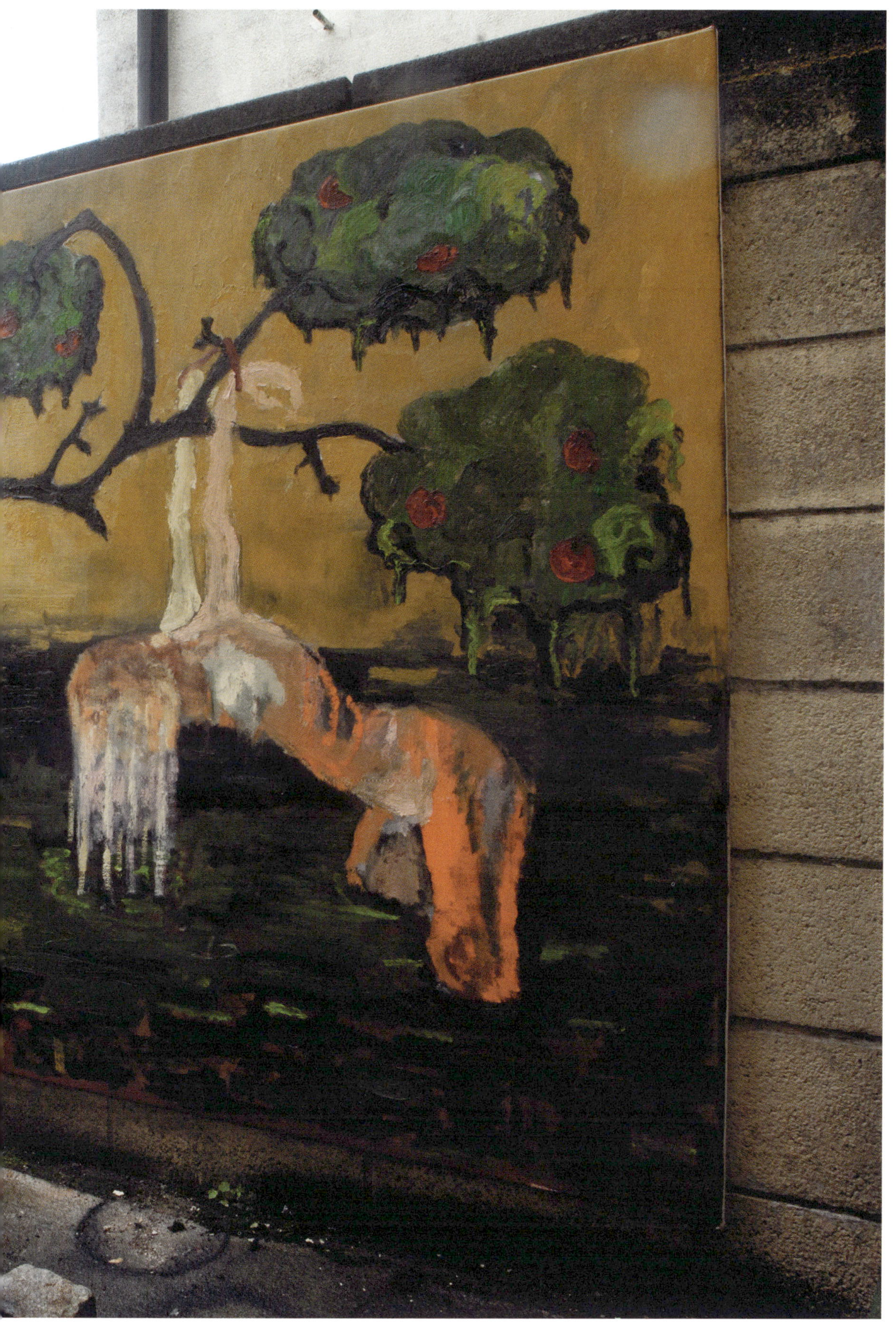

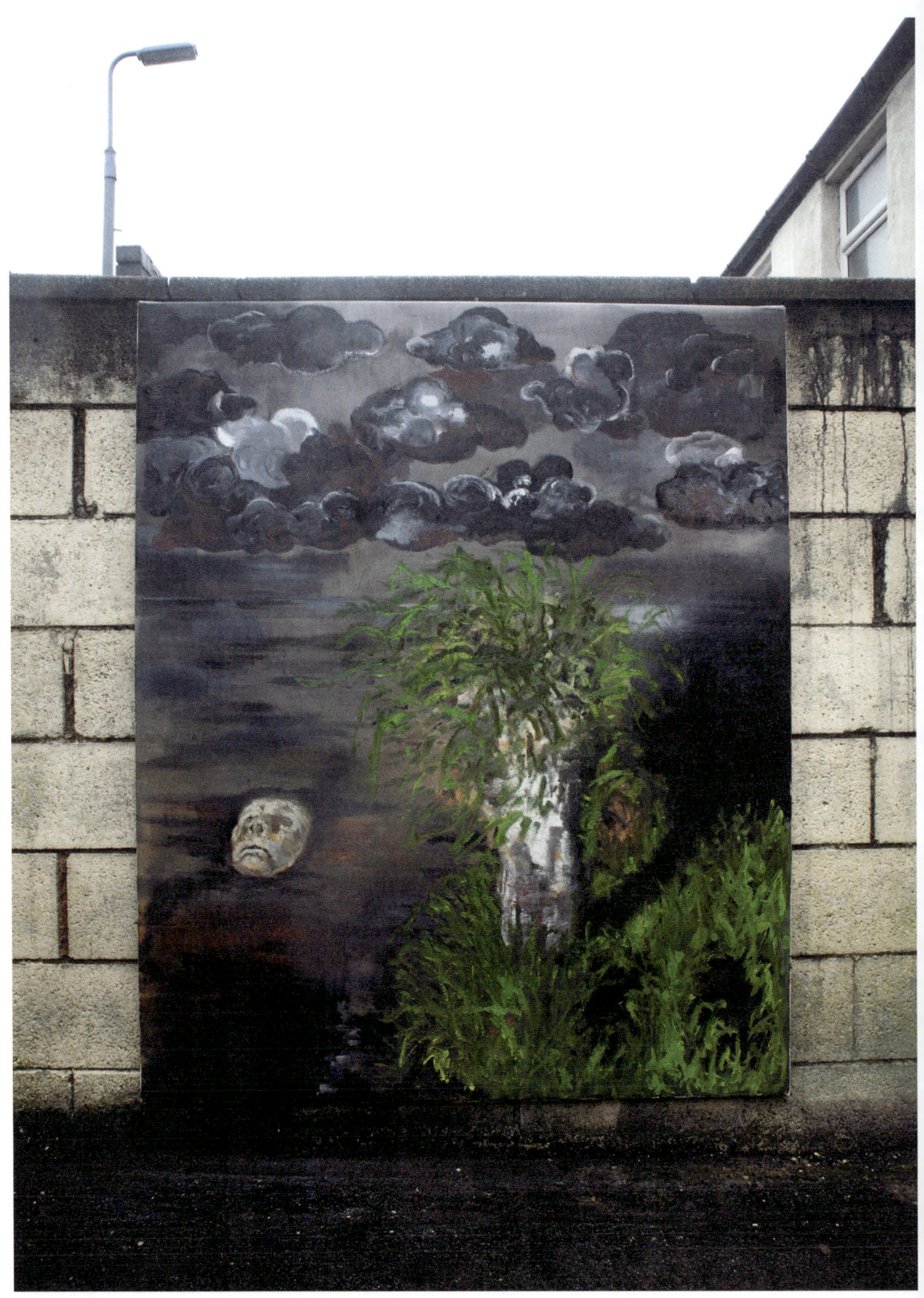

Untitled, 2019
Oil on jute
130cm x 160cm

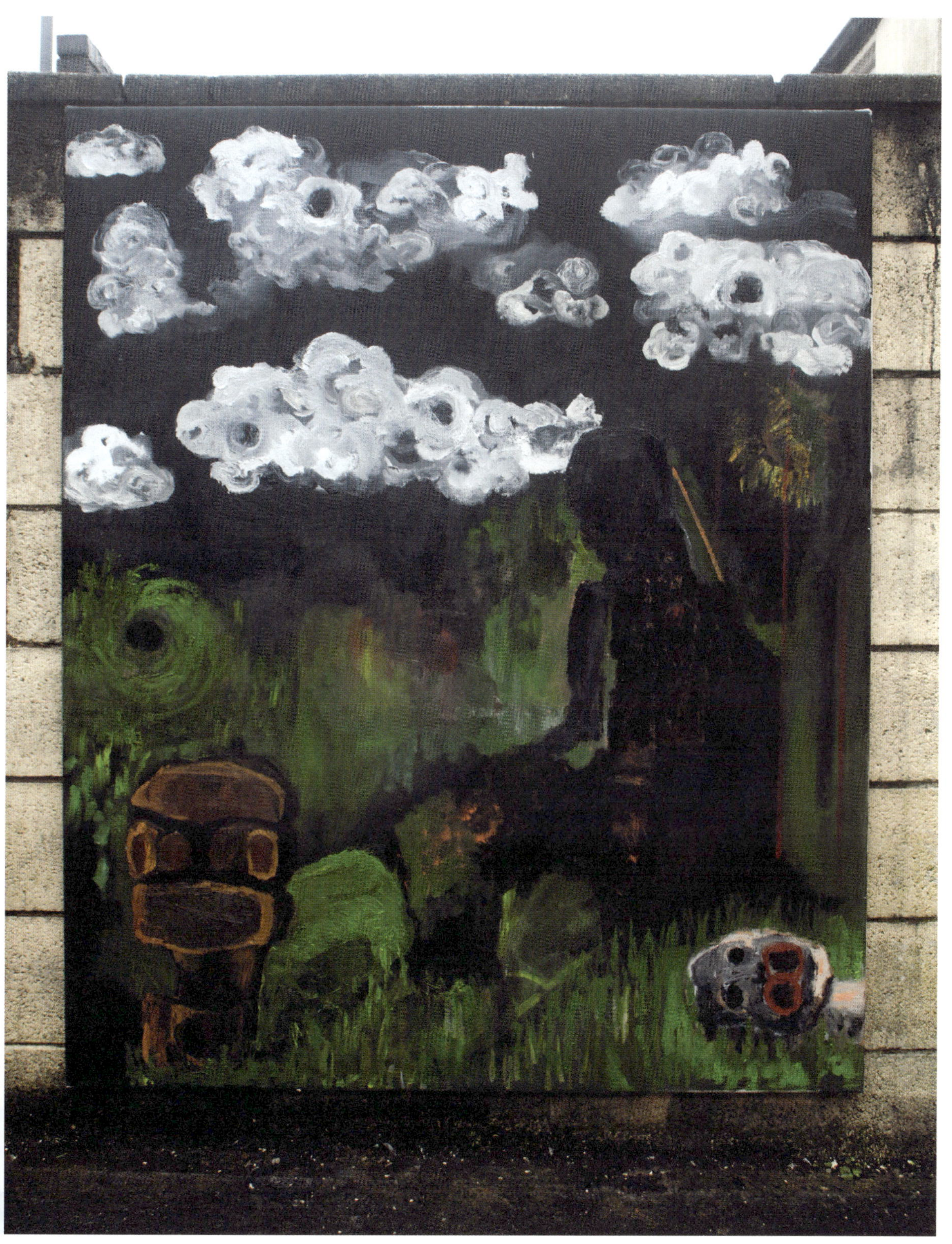

Untitled, 2019
Oil on jute
130cm x 160cm

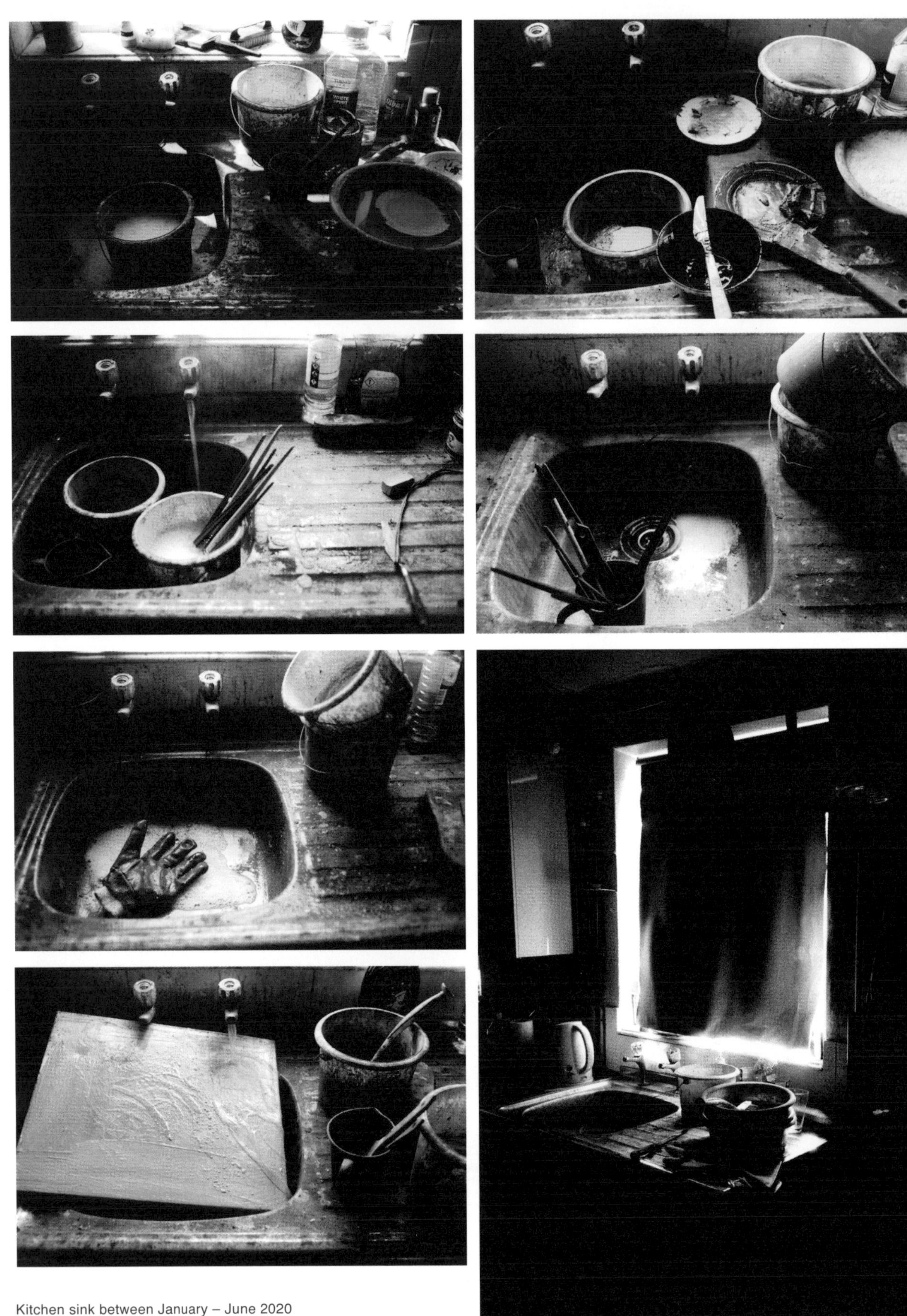

Kitchen sink between January – June 2020
35mm film

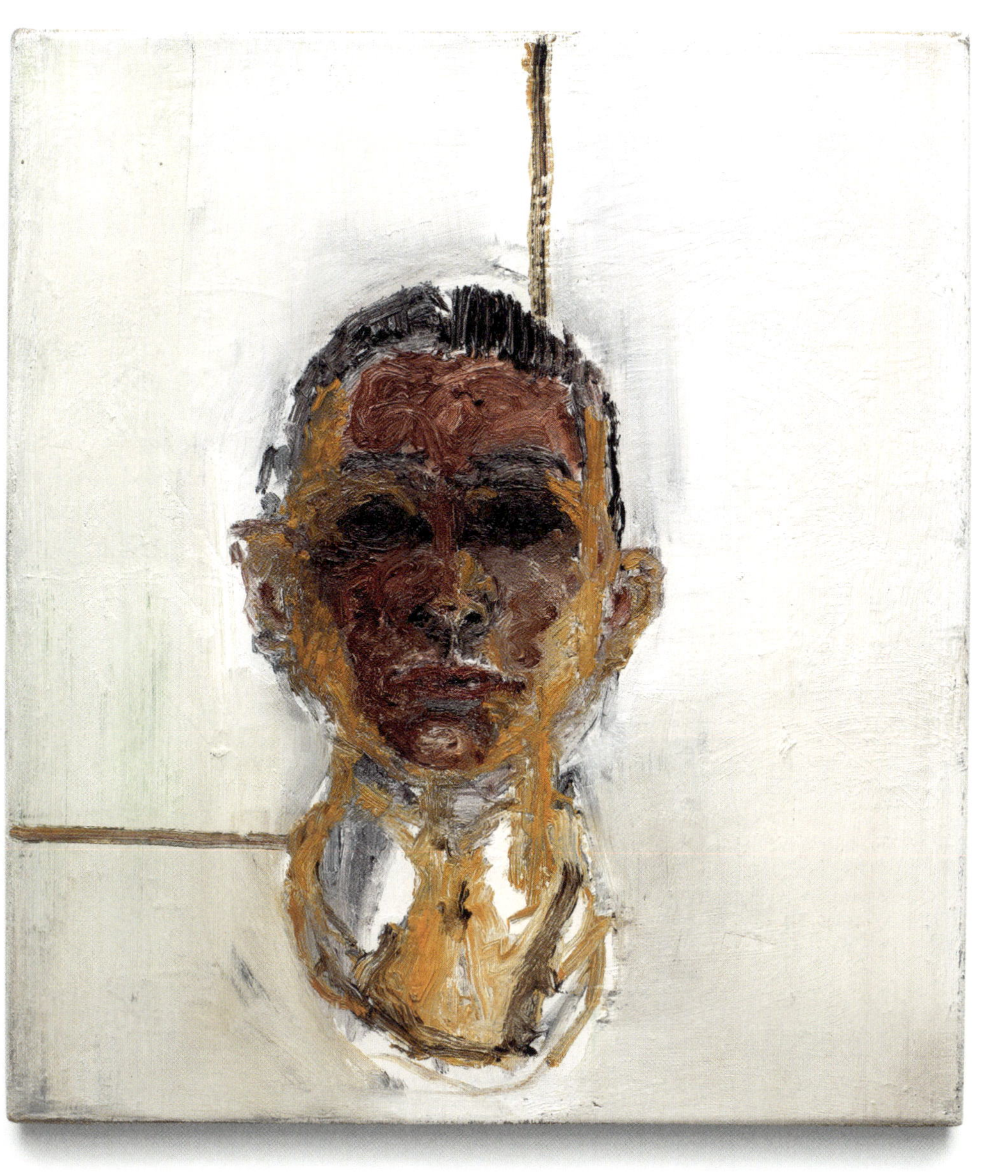

Summer, 2020
Oil on linen canvas
40cm x 46cm

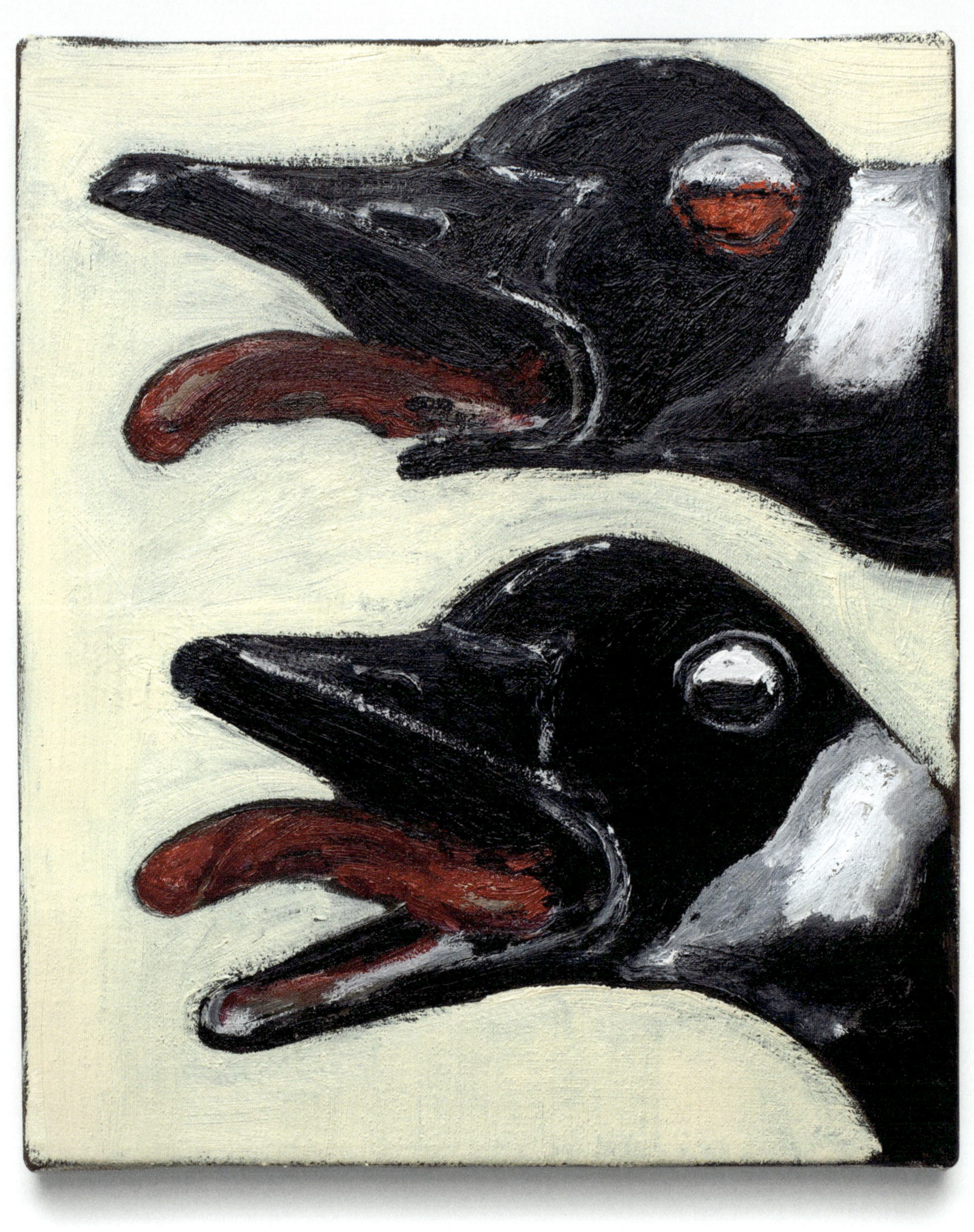

Beak Problem, 2020
Oil on jute
40cm x 46cm

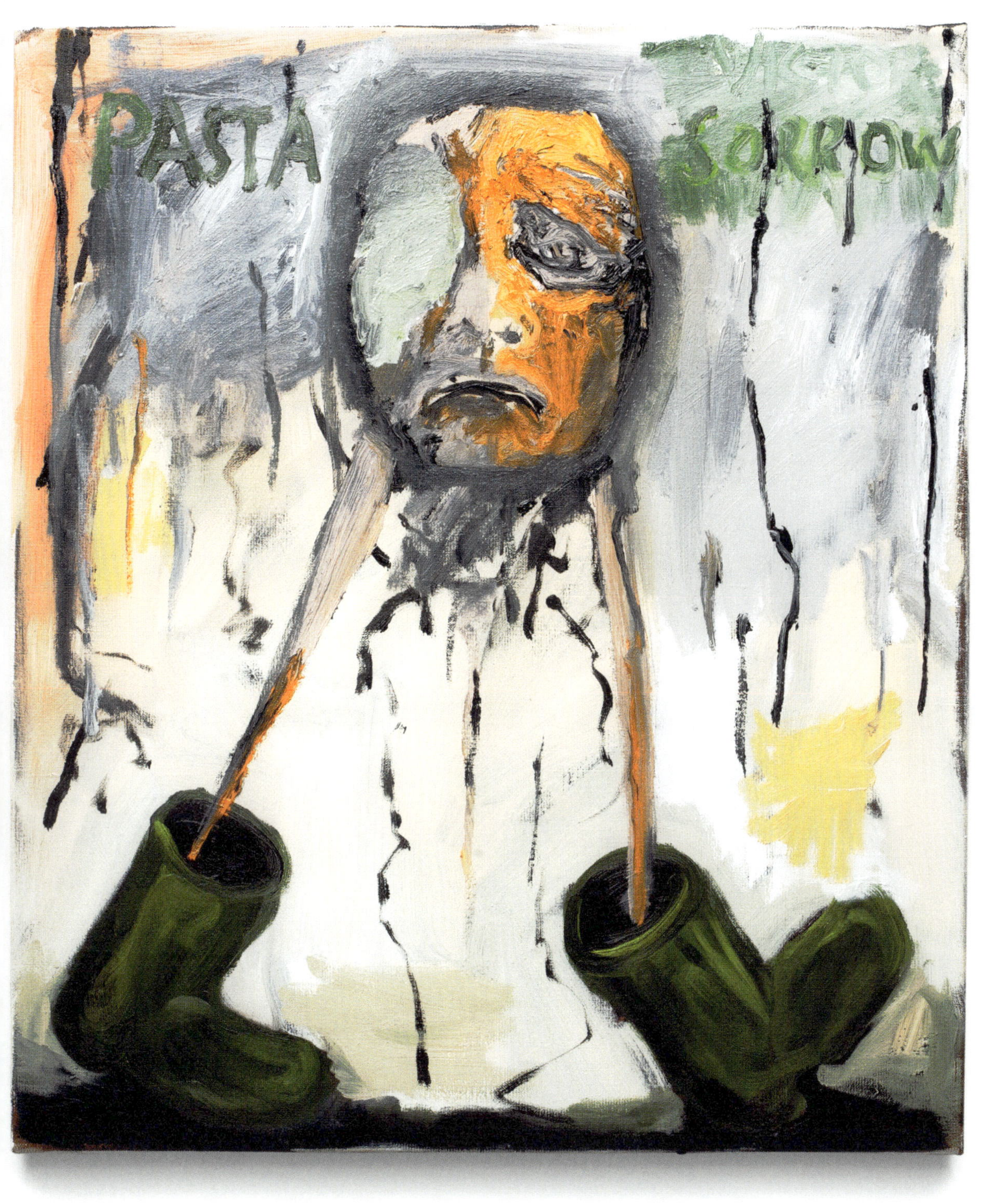

Pasta Sorrow, 2019 – 2020
Oil on linen canvas
50cm x 60cm

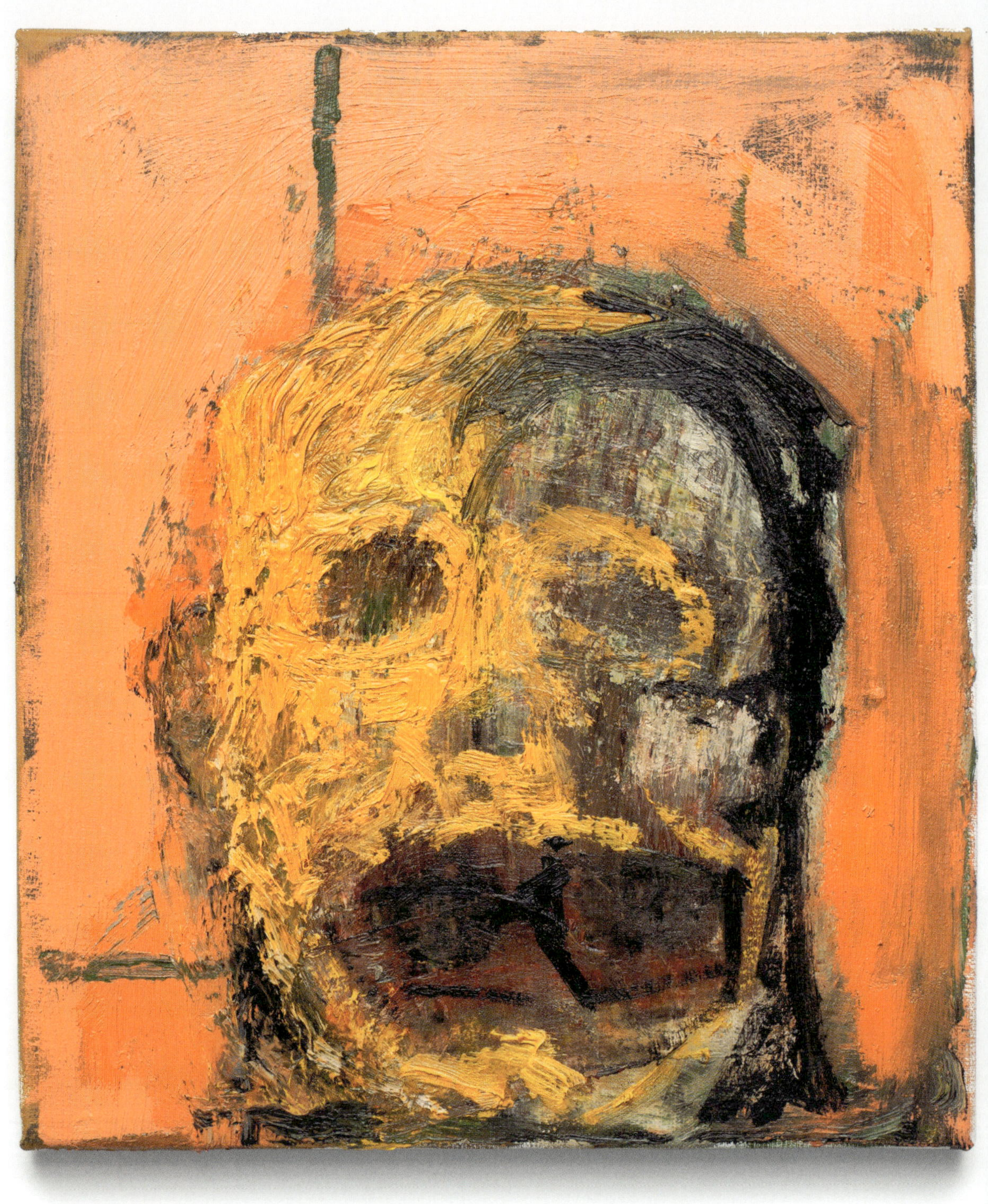

Desperate for Sun, 2020
Oil on linen canvas
30cm x 35cm

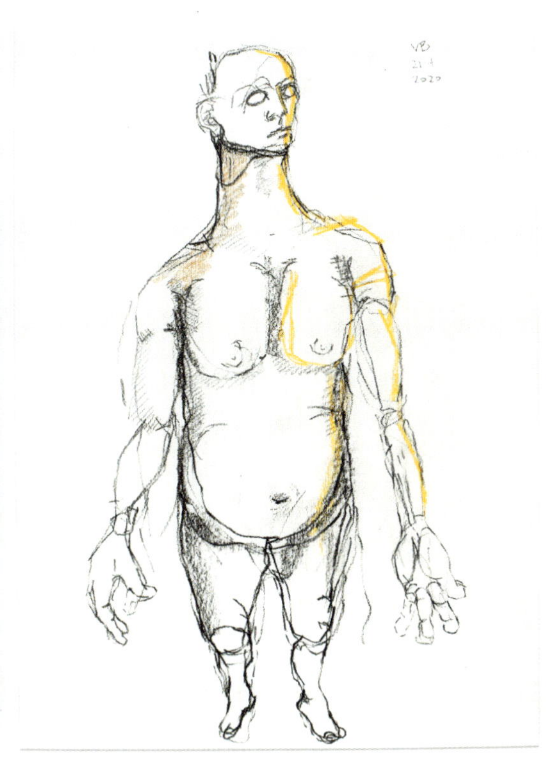

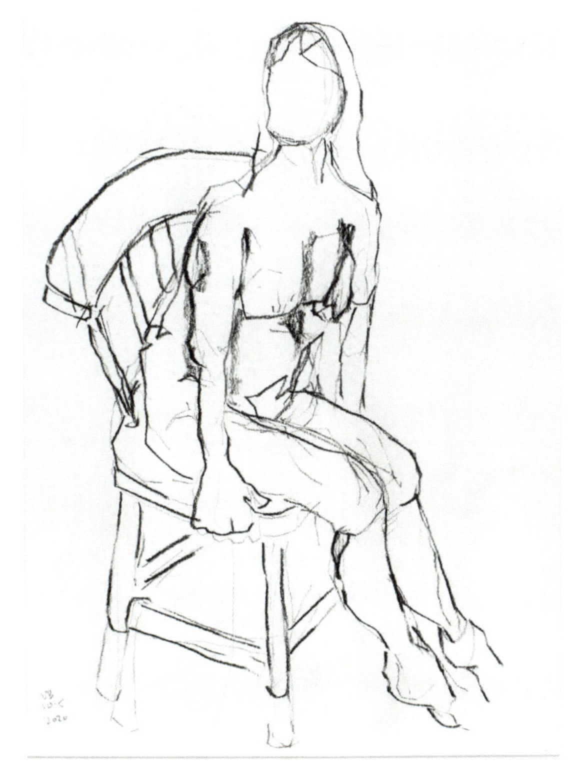

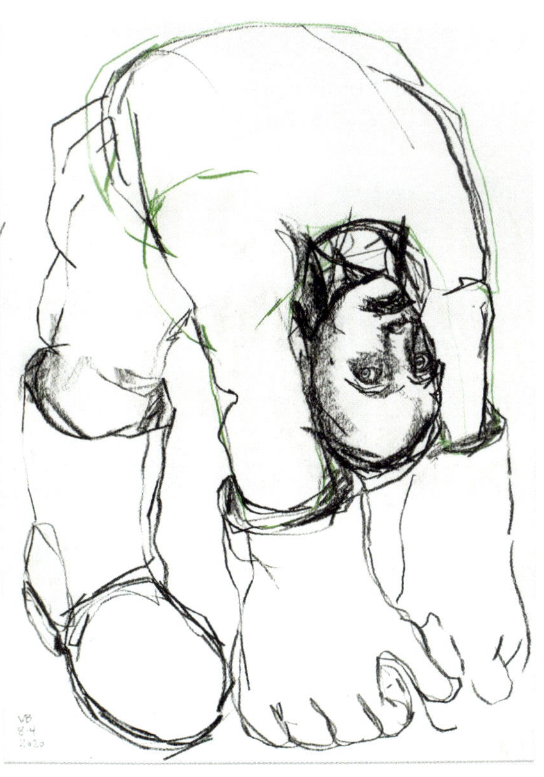

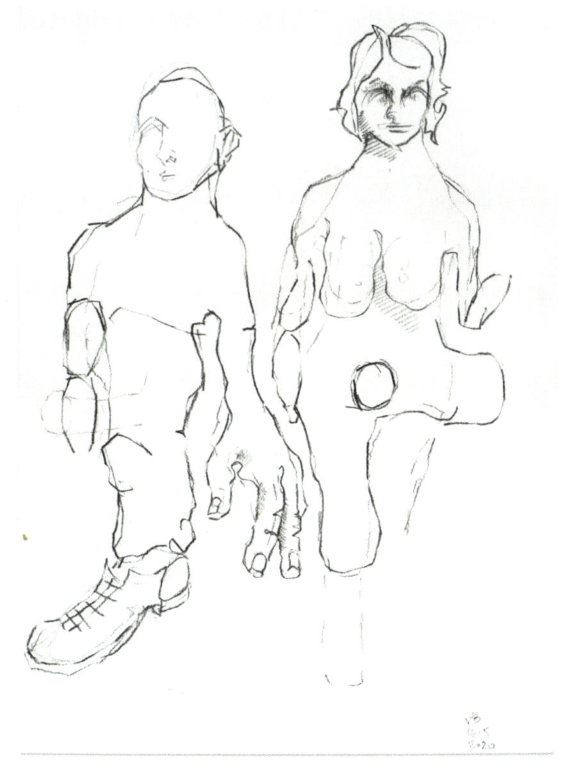

titled, 2020
ncil, polychromos on paper
cm x 29.7cm

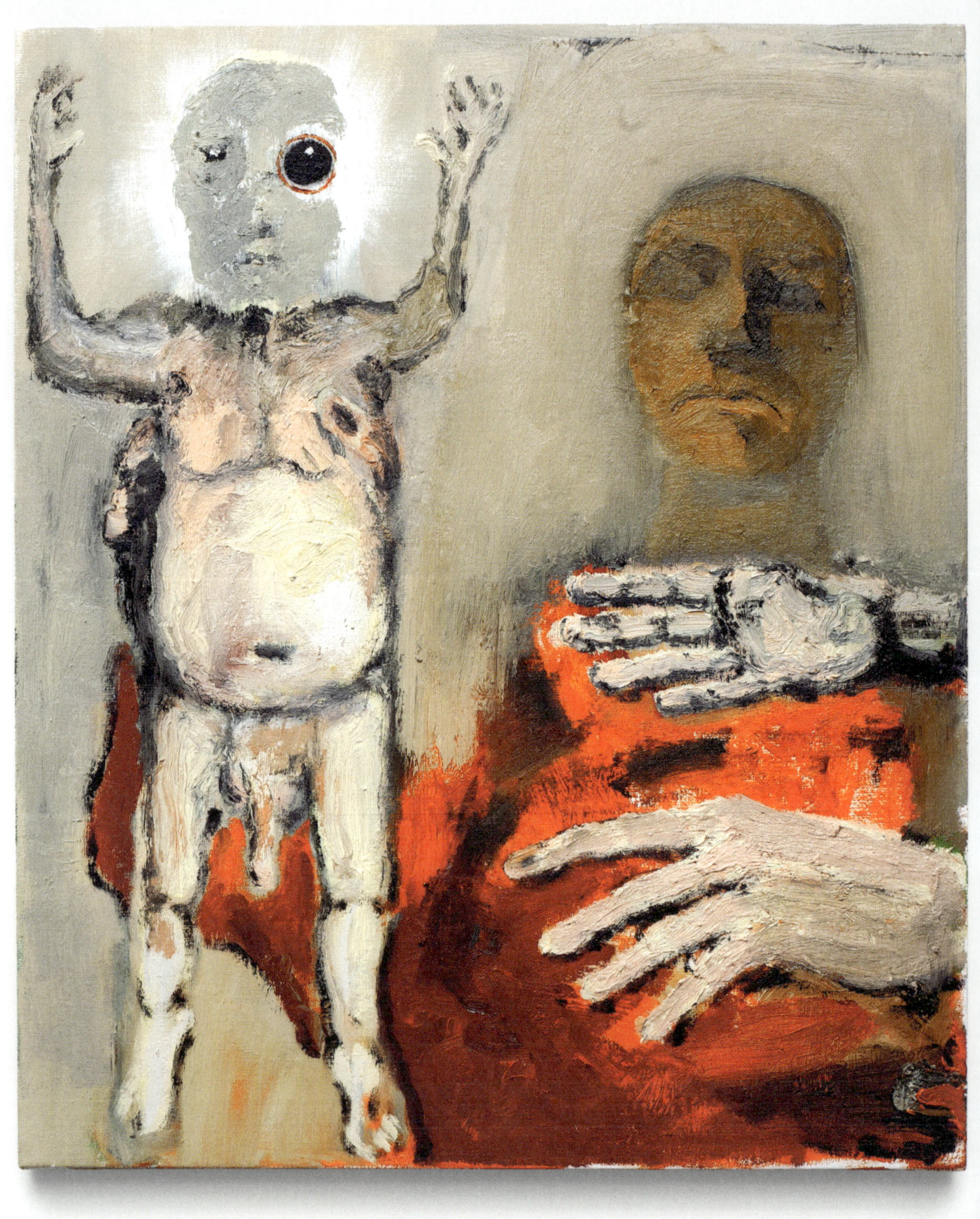

Uglylamb, 2019 – 2020
Oil on linen canvas
54cm x 65cm

glylamb

orn, then they gave me the name Victor Andreas Uglum oullet. My mother insisted on me having these Norwe-an family names stuck in between my fathers French / cottish names. Their disputes must have started early.

nese two Norwegian names annoyed me as a child. I ever used either of them. When my teacher shouted out y full name in the classroom, I remember blaming my um each and every time for those ridiculous names.

ndreas Uglum is my great-grandfather. He came from e west coast of Norway. Sogn to be precise. I know othing about this man except that he was a tailor and ad an alcohol problem.

y Father is named Victor Boullet, his father was also ctor Boullet, all bakers. So, I also worked as a baker. the late 80's I worked at my father's bakery and there orked a Pakistani man, Kushdilh Kahn. According to m he was Pakistani No. 33 arriving into Norway.

ushdilh Kahn saw my payslip at the bakery and he oked at me and uttered with a smile

our name is Uglylamb?"

ictor Uglylamb?"

glylamb?"

2019 curator Elise By Olsen invited me to take part in e Norwegian west coast exhibition (Vestlands utstill-gen) I suggested using my name Uglum and how I came Uglylamb as possible content for my project and intings.

ven though I had been curated into the show all of a dden the jury rejected me, apparently I was not enough a "West coast Norwegian". Despite the cancelation d humiliation I continued the project.

hen Kushdilh Kahn came to Norway in 1970 after a dif-ult trip via Kabul, Tehran, Istanbul, Munich, Hamburg, el to finally arrive in Oslo he was then a very popular an in the capital city of Norway, but since those days he s tasted the change of society.

m born, raised and educated in Norway, but with a me like Victor Boullet I have been excluded many nes. I remember in the 90's I was told that I could not included into a show due to my name, it was not fficiently Norwegian, she told me. In today's Norwegian ciety, this form of discrimination is still ongoing and a ily problem for some.

ese paintings are dedicated to Kushdilh Kahn.

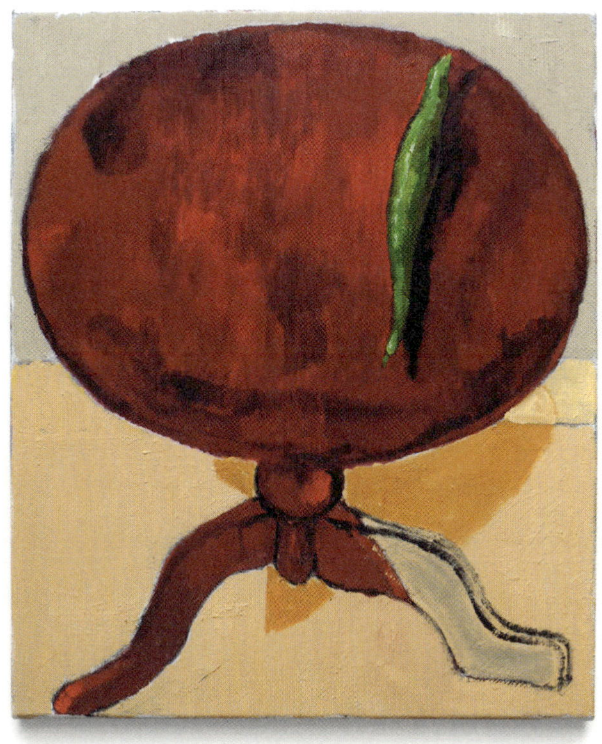

Forgot Most, 2020
Oil on linen canvas
50cm x 60cm

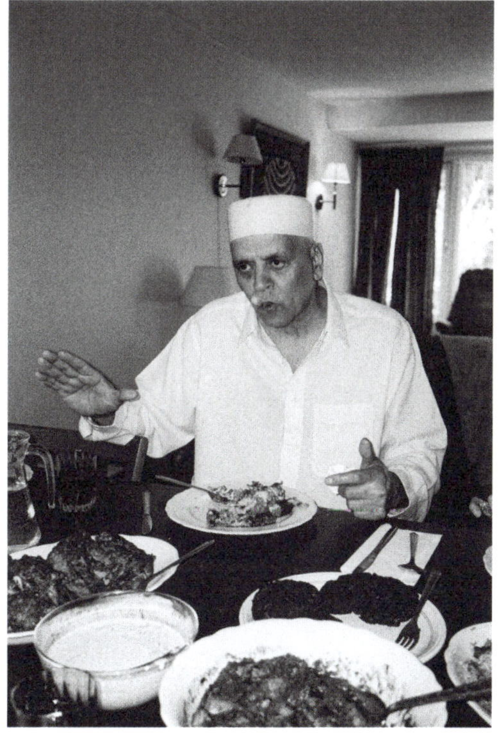

Kushdilh Kahn, Oslo, 2014
35mm film

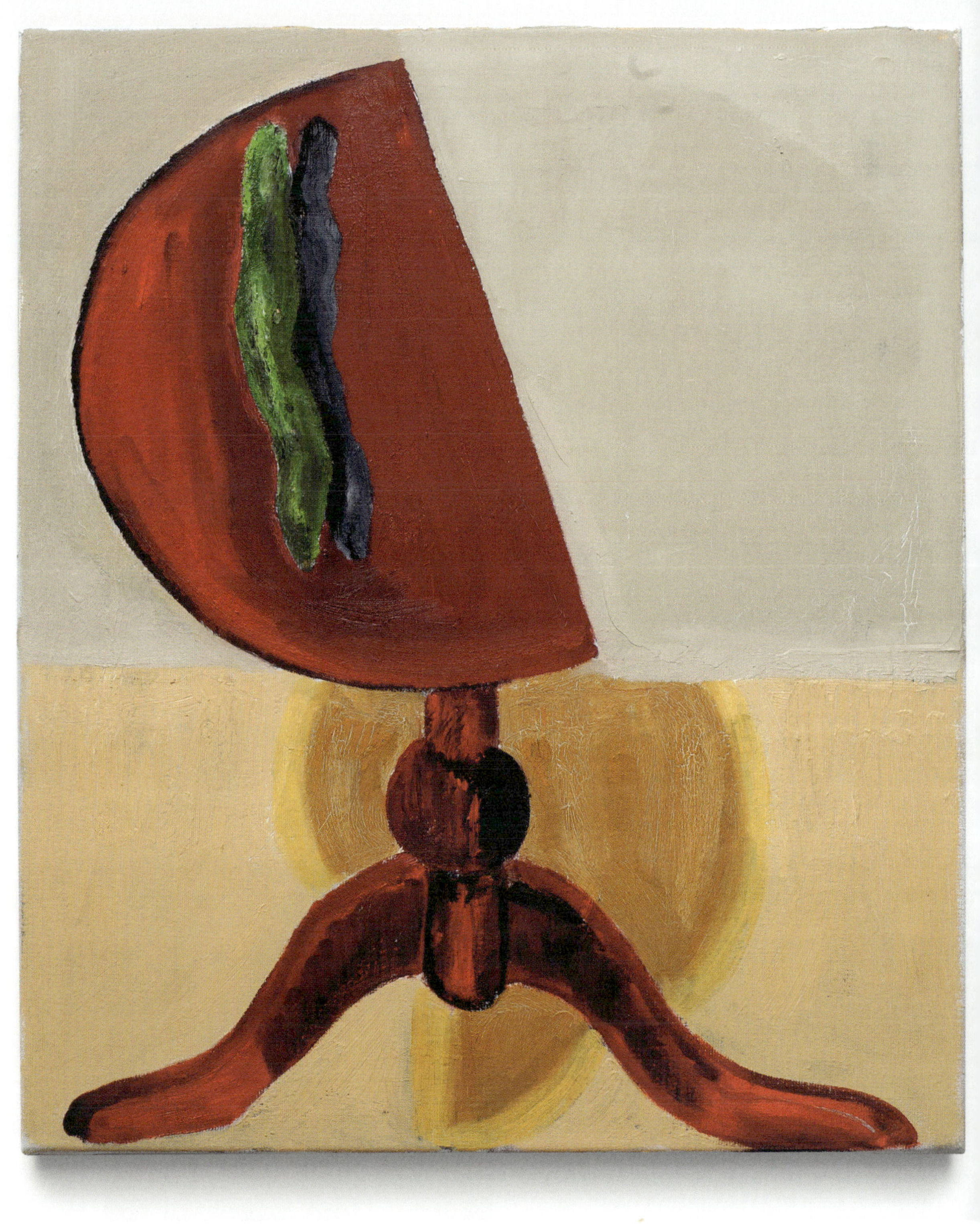

Left Us, 2020
Oil on linen canvas
50cm x 60cm

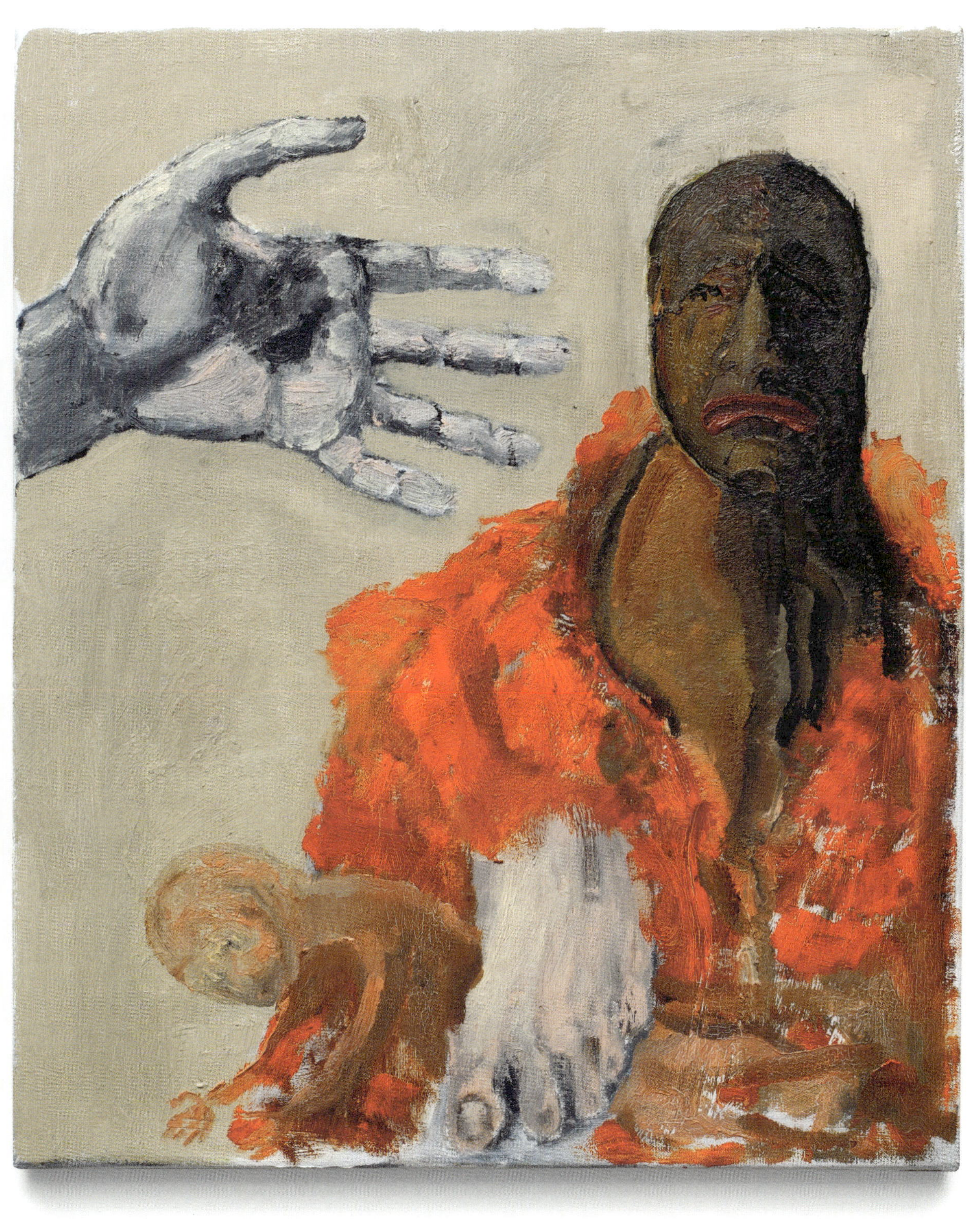

Uglylamb, 2020
Oil on linen canvas
50cm x 60cm

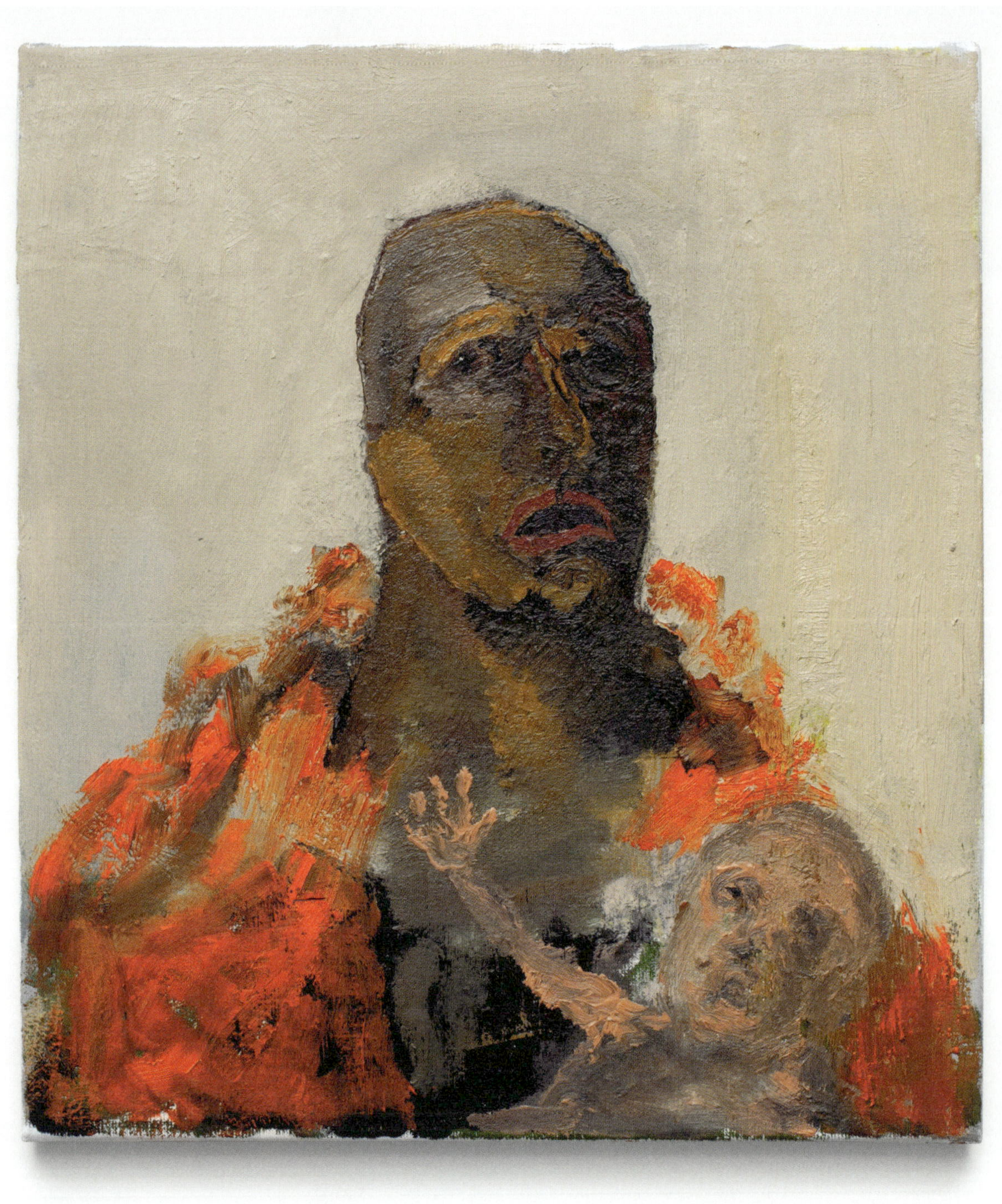

Uglylamb, 2020
Oil on linen canvas
40cm x 46cm

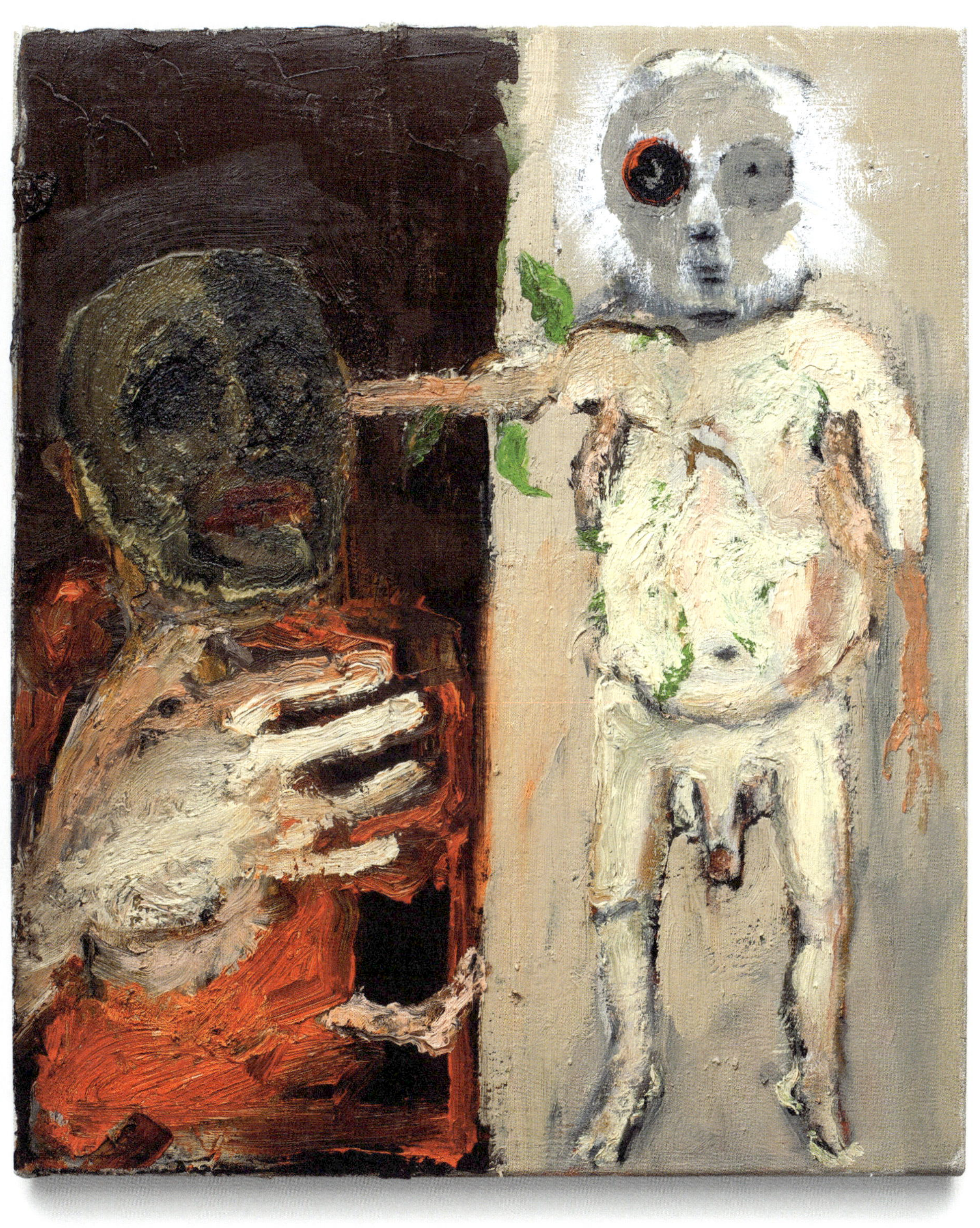

Uglylamb, 2020
Oil on linen canvas
50cm x 60cm

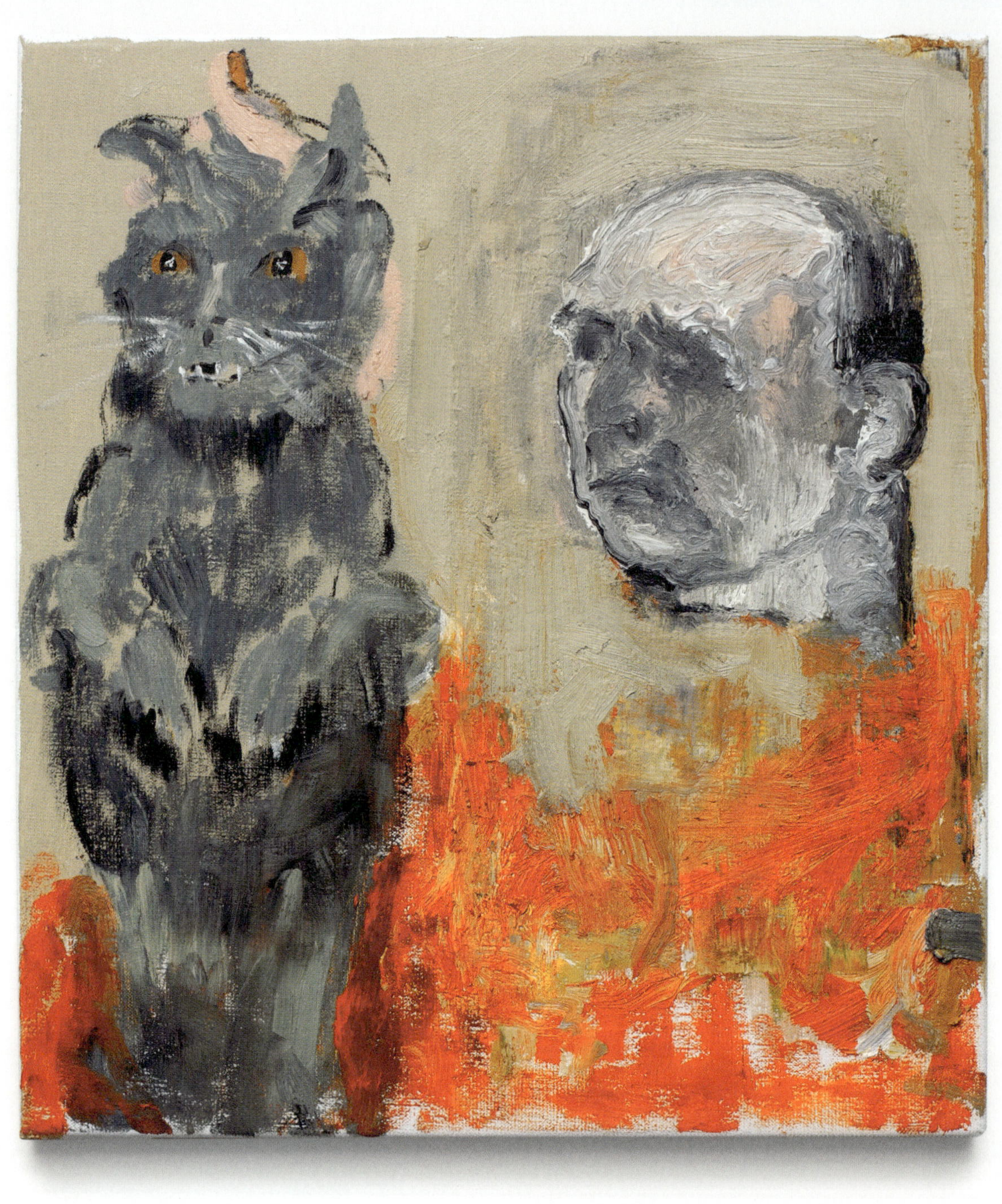

Untitled, 2020
Oil on linen canvas
40cm x 46cm

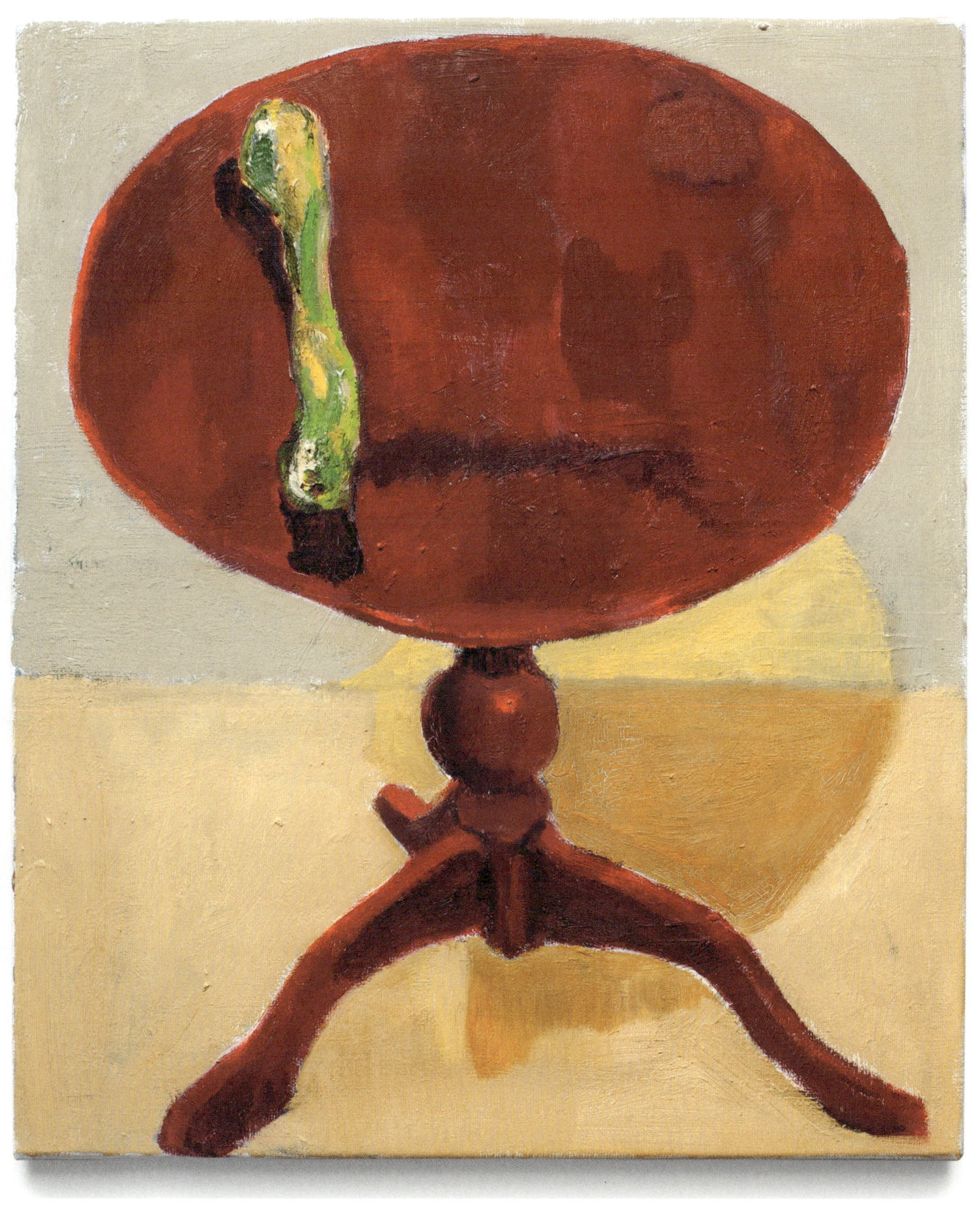

Remember Very Little, 2020
Oil on linen canvas
50cm x 60cm

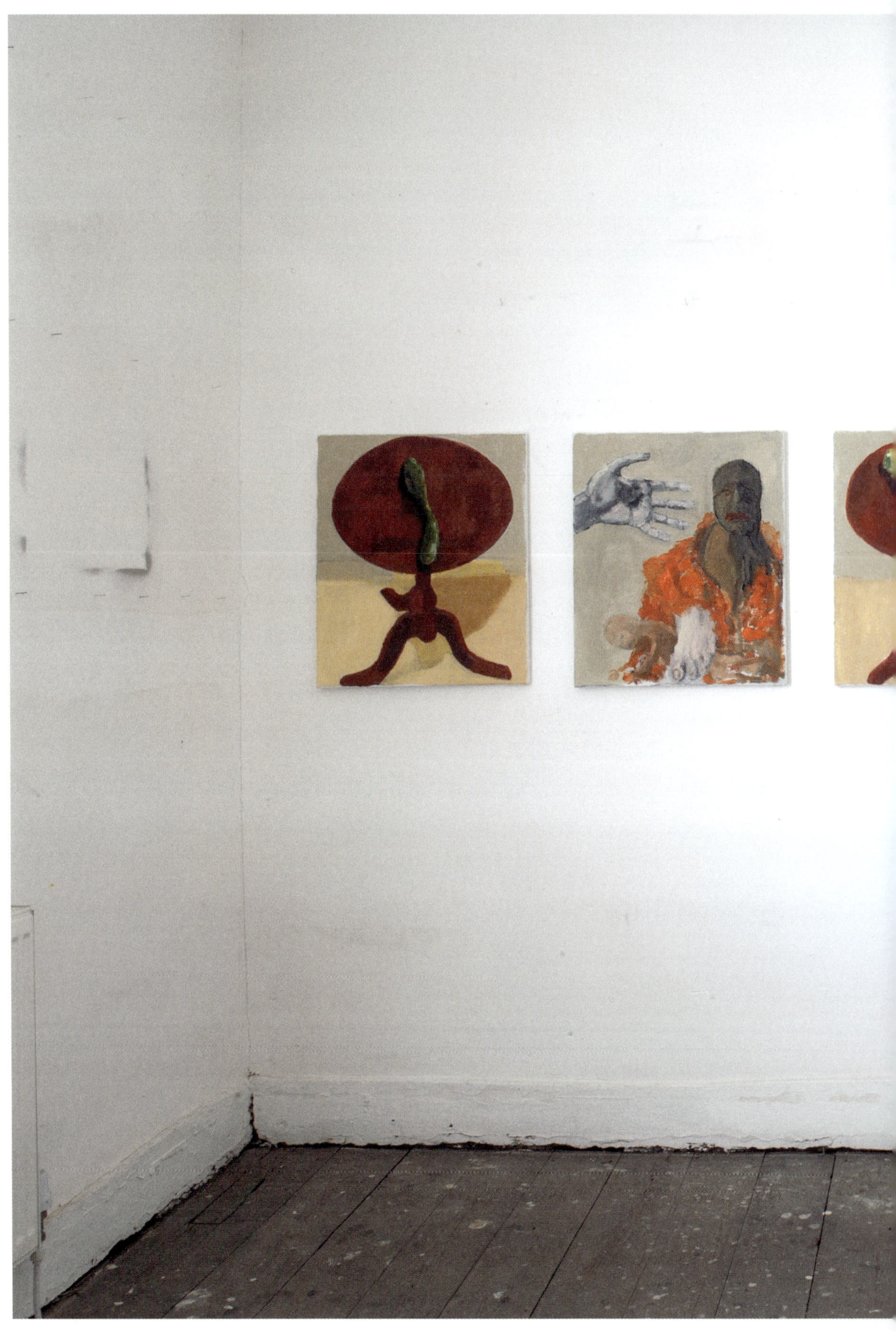

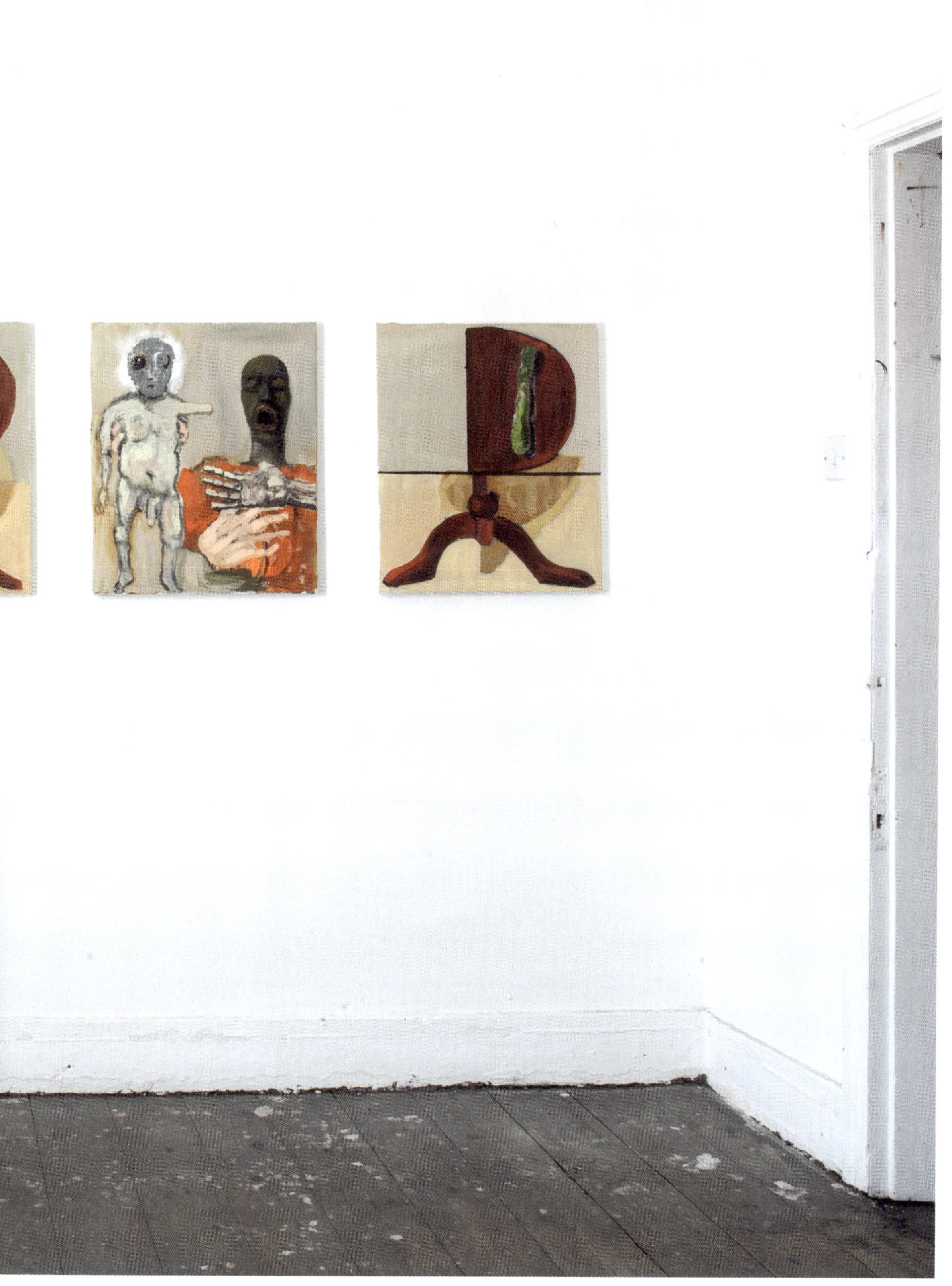

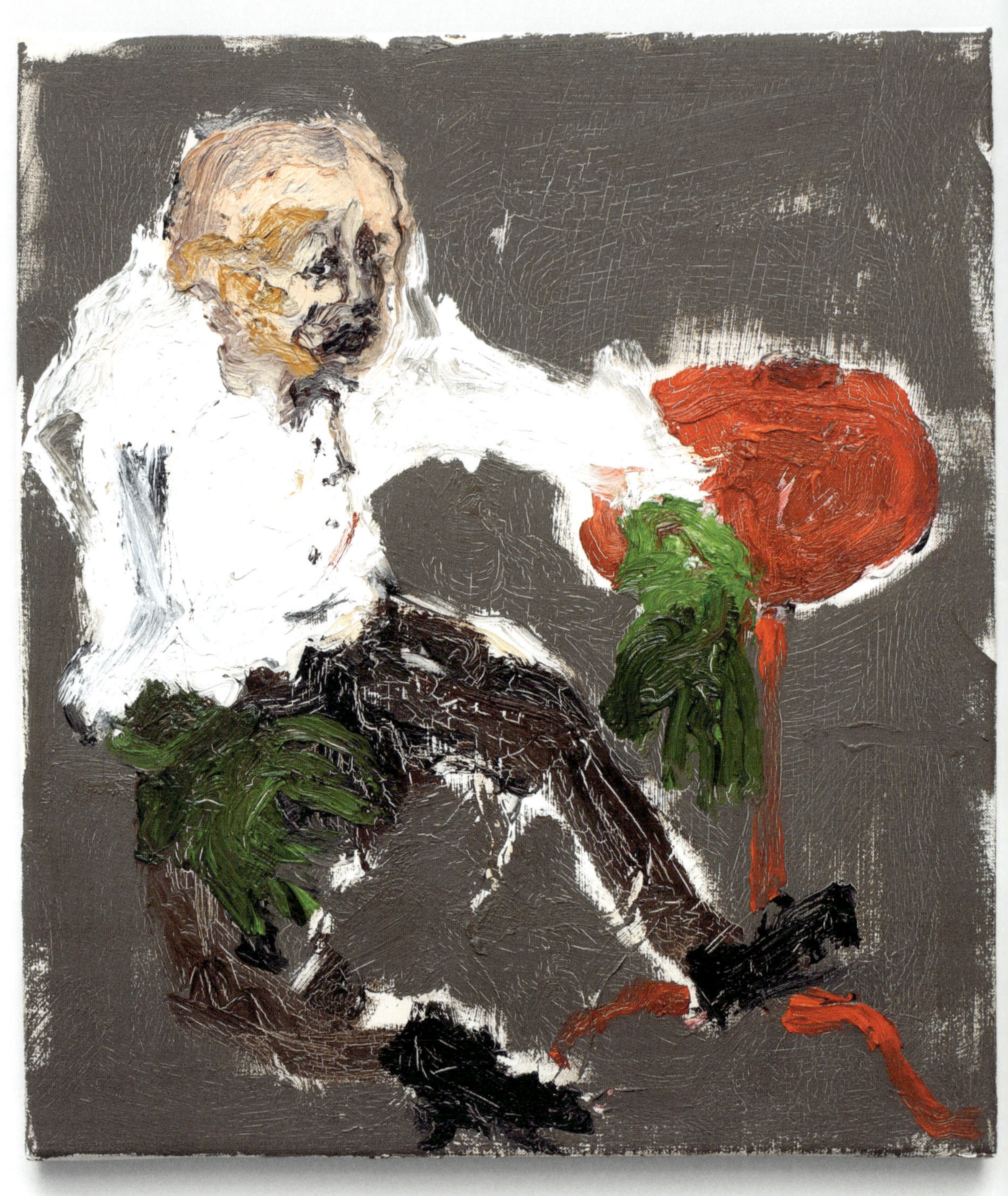

Sadman Boullet, 2020
Oil on linen canvas
40cm x 46cm

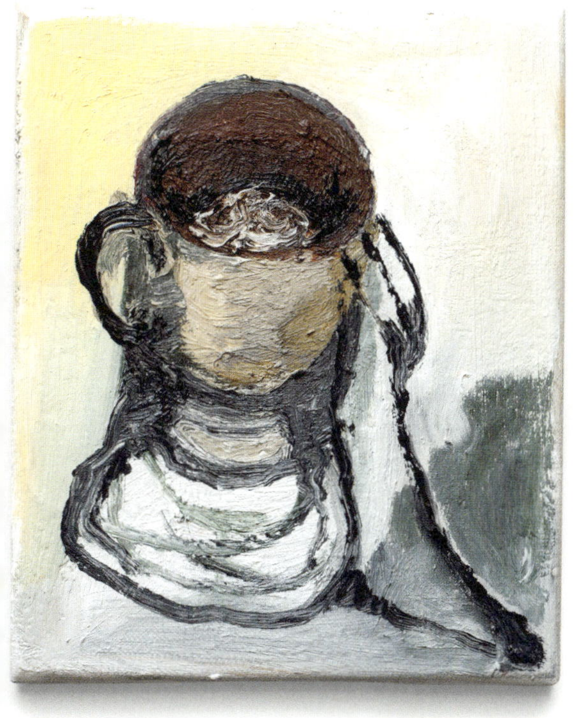

I Want Coffee II, 2020
Oil on linen canvas
20cm x 25cm

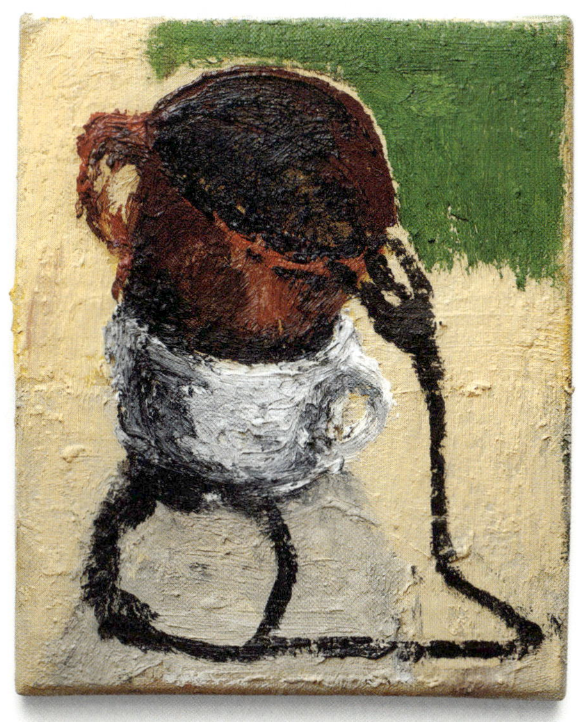

I Want Coffee IV, 2020
Oil on linen canvas
20cm x 25cm

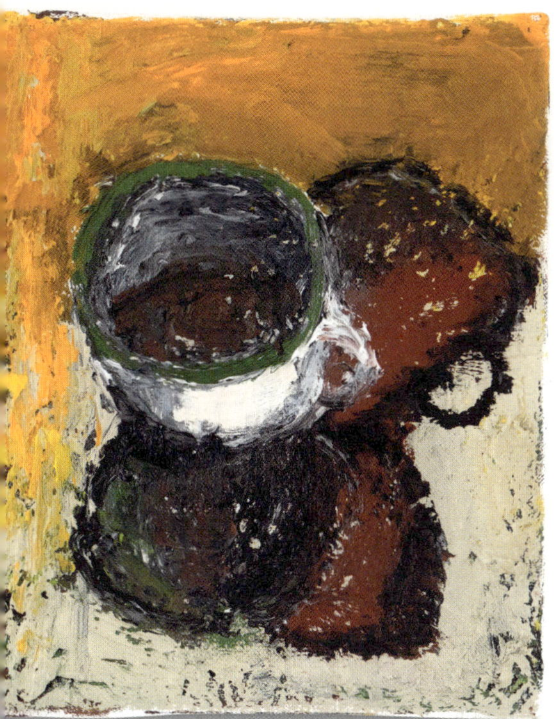

Want Coffee III, 2020
l on linen canvas
cm x 25cm

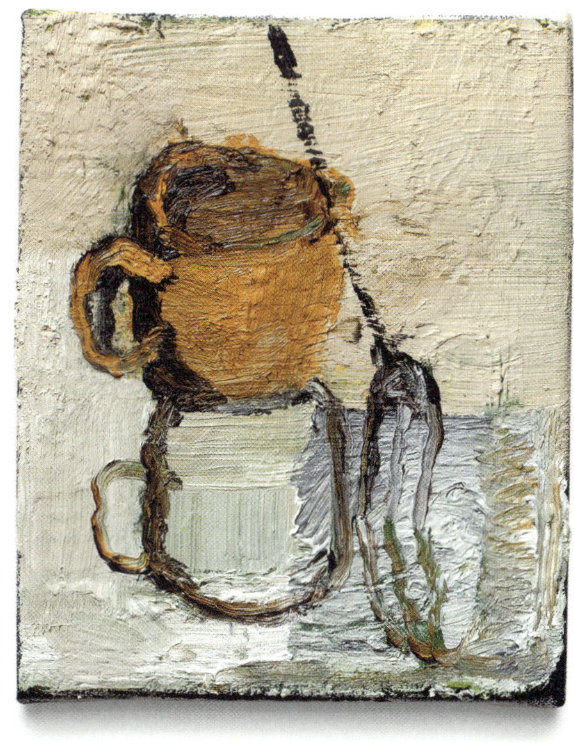

I Want Coffee I, 2020
Oil on linen canvas
20cm x 25cm

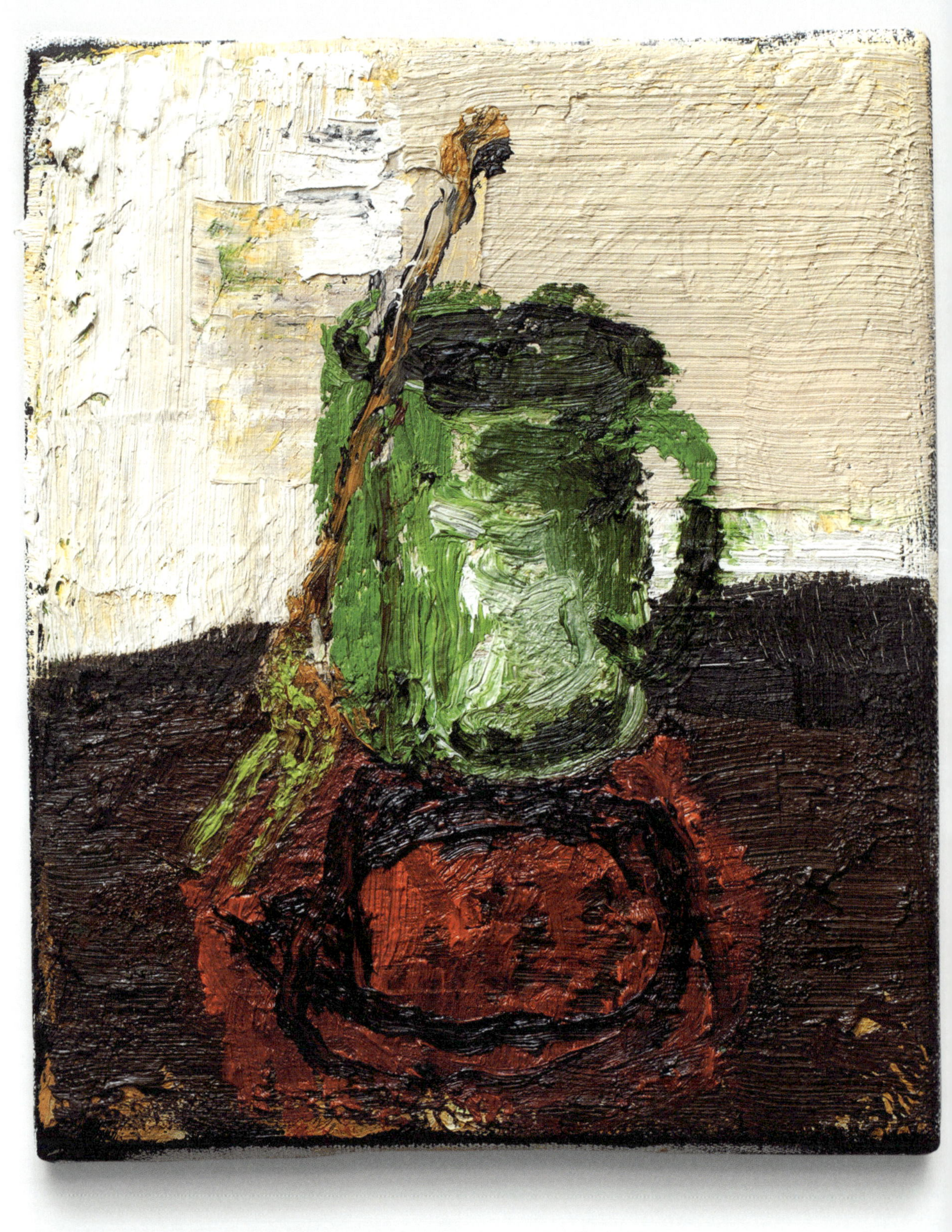

I Want Coffee V, 2020
Oil on linen canvas
20cm x 25cm

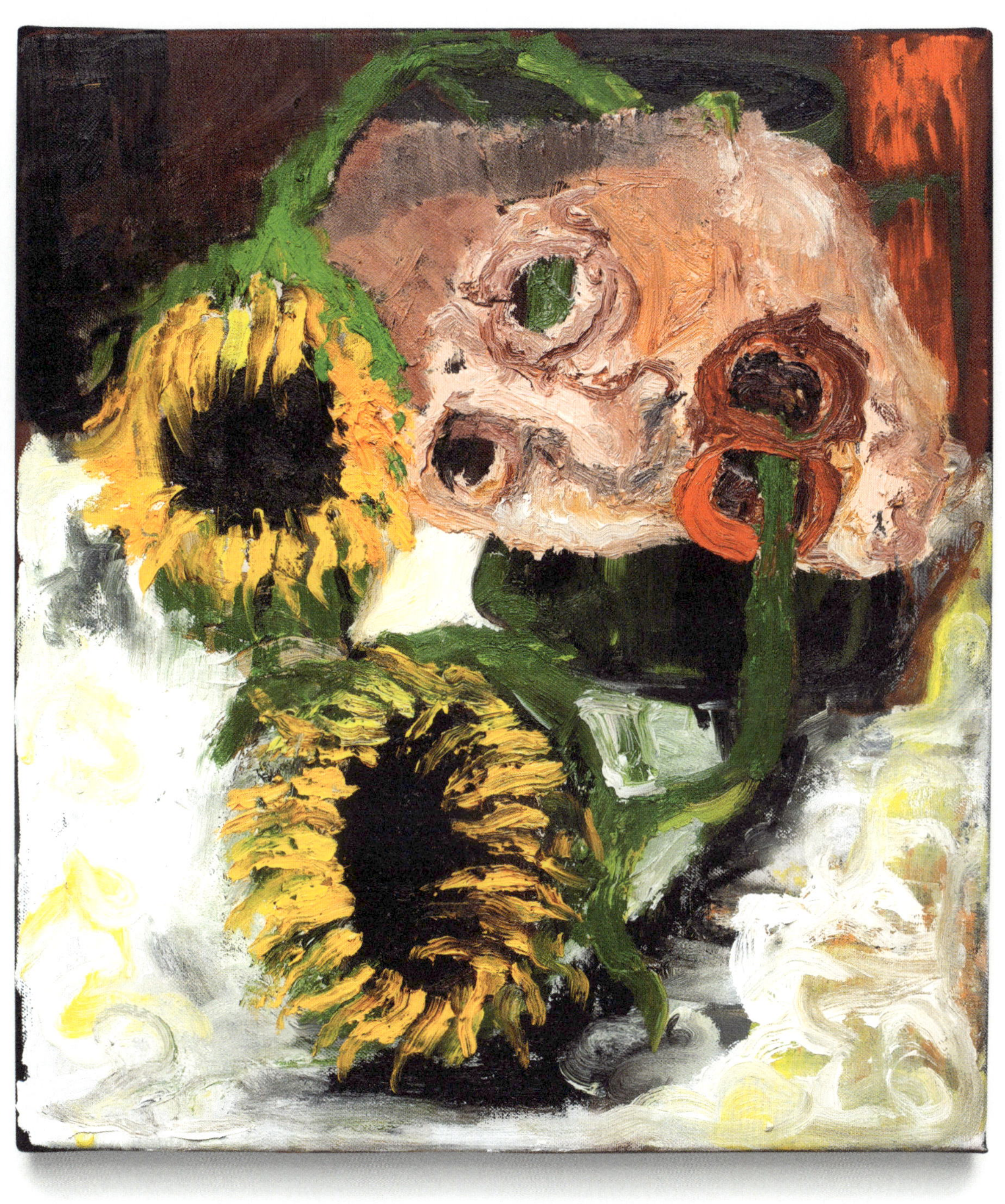

Untitled, 2019 – 2020
Oil on linen canvas
40cm x 46cm

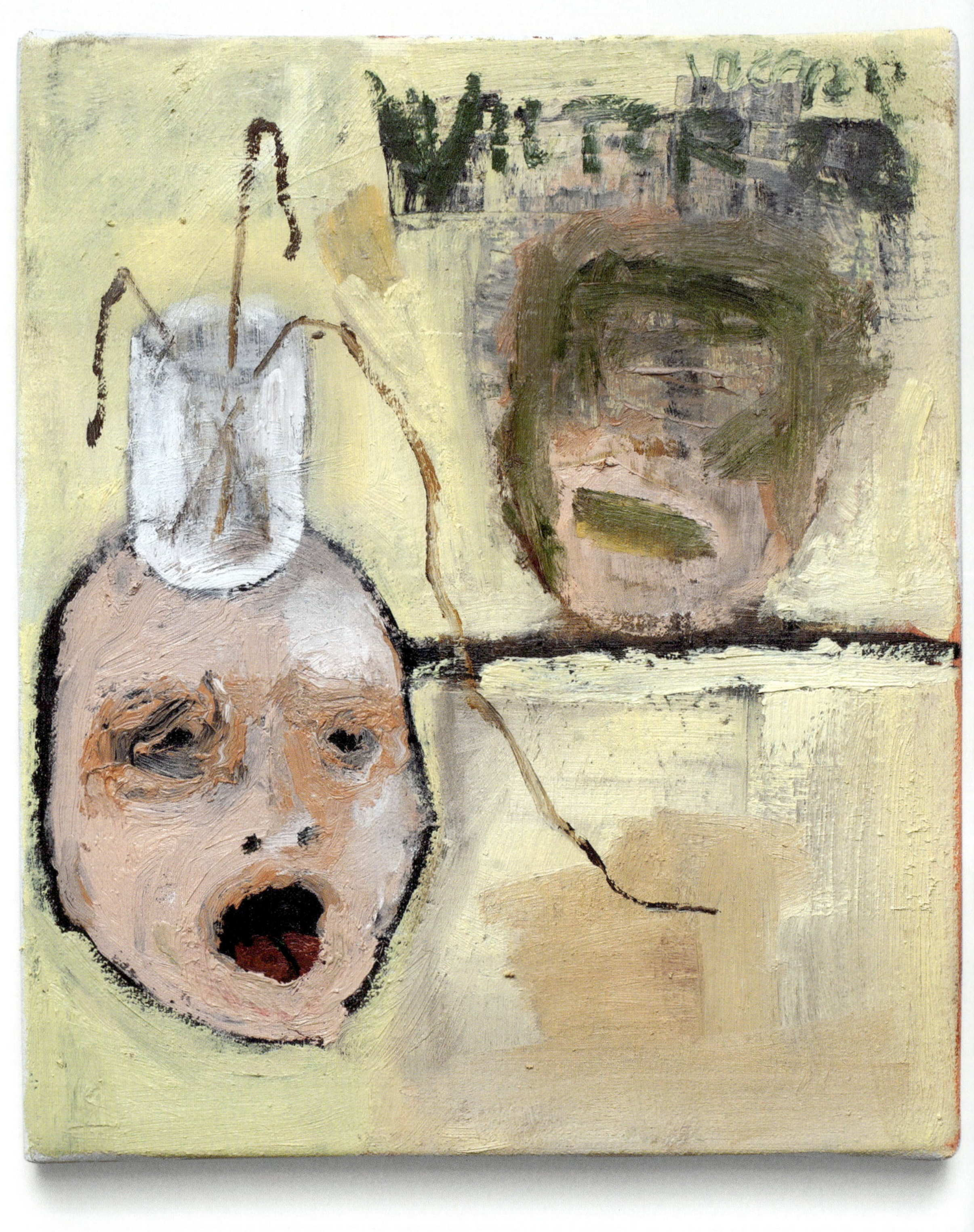

Thirsty, 2020
Oil on linen canvas
40cm x 46cm

Paintsploitation
By Stian Gabrielsen

After hoofing around Paris doing social and performative art pieces for a decade or so Victor decided to opt out of that business and the Parisian art scene and reimagined himself as a reclusive painter based in Liverpool – of all places. This increased attention to what could be called proper painting had been preceded by an intermezzo where his public installations and exhibitions began containing actual paintings: mostly small canvases with smears on them, sometimes larger monochromes, but nothing fancy. These works invoked painting as gesture but offered little in pictorial terms. Examples are the canvases he hung at a Paris butcher as part of his art safari in 2013 and the plaster boards painted to resemble a common grey and green French street hoardings – if memory serves me right – shown at Kurant in Tromsø in 2013 (incidentally, these pictures carried my name). Victor's paintings have evolved in pictorial ambition during his years in isolation. The invocation of painting through arbitrary gestures has given way to a more elaborate figurative content that aspire to conjure the presence of a haunted authorial subject via an array of tried expressionist devices. Tellingly, ghostly renditions of his own face with mouth gaping recurs, now and then accompanied by other disjoined body parts, arranged alongside cucumbers, cutlery and tableware into comical still lifes executed with impasto strokes.

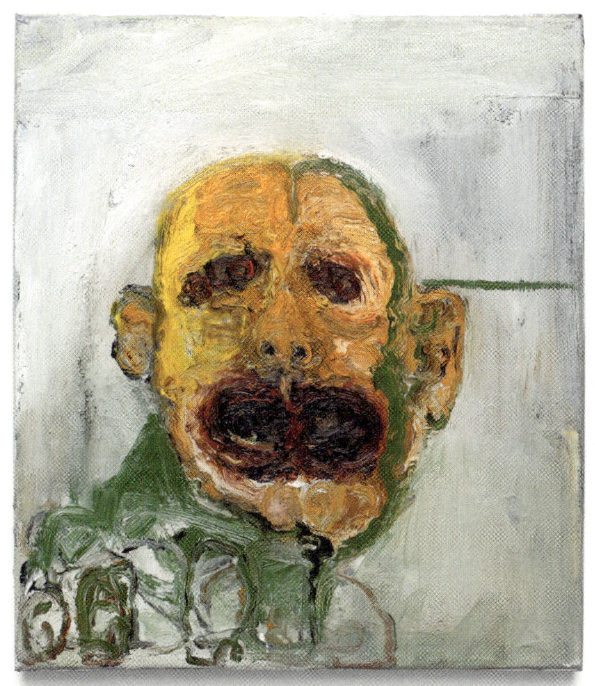

Talking to Myself, 2020
Oil on linen canvas
40cm x 46cm

Another decade has (almost) passed and Victor has decided to round off his Liverpool exile and move to London. This book, then, could be seen as a wrap party for Victor's life as a disconnected painter. I doubt he sees it that way. The maintenance of his reclusive painter identity has cost too dearly for him to accept it as just a passing act. On some level he will still admit to its performativeness, I think, how every day he has had to consciously *become* a painter by performing little rituals and sacrifices, routines that enact a certain attitude towards the world that typifies the painter. For anyone who has had the privilege of corresponding with him over the last seven years it is hard to ignore the obsessive self-observation that accompany his artworks, where he charts the biographical minutia that make up the behavioural scaffolding of this painter persona: interactions with art professionals and ordinary folks, foods he consume, acts of theft, rectal exams, family troubles etc. This diaristic newsletter sometimes takes the form of press releases for exhibitions or pamphlet launches, or stand-alone literary narratives meant to be included in some up-coming publication, but mostly it arrives as personal e-mails or phone calls to a group of friends who serve as audience to Victor-as-painter.

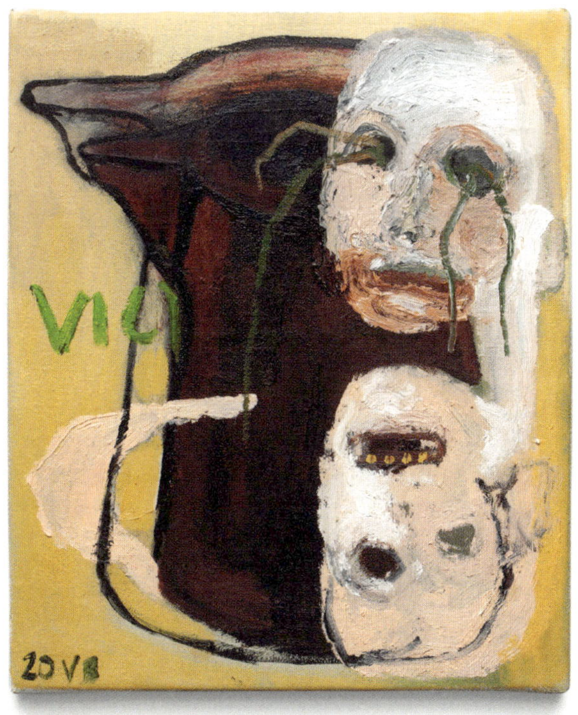

Confused Crying Twat, 2020
Oil on linen canvas
40cm x 46cm

Victor's paintings, although they are sincere things, products of real effort at solving challenges internal to the medium, also serve as a backdrop for this chronicling of non-painting activities. They are not just backdrops either; maybe it is more correct to describe them as props, or even currency. Although obviously not the social circuit-board-type pieces that his more relational and public performance works are, they definitely still actively serve

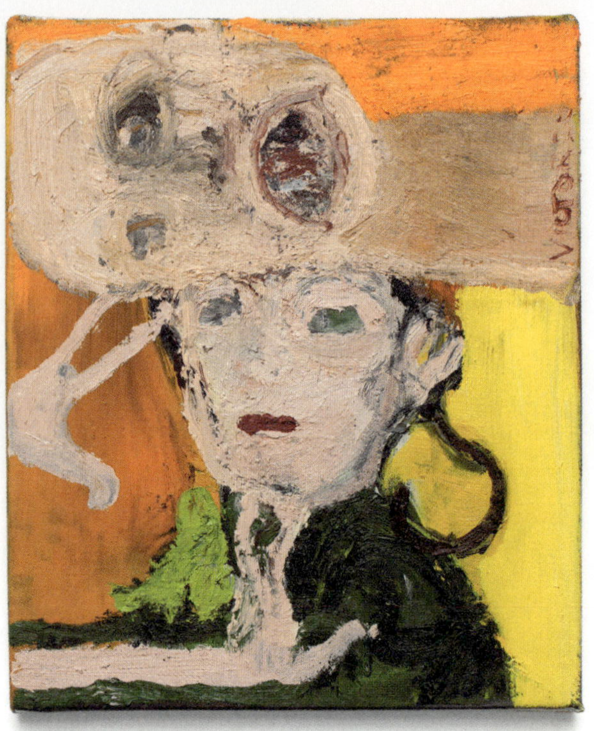

Billie and Pappa, 2020
Oil on linen canvas
40cm x 46cm

to connect Victor to others and to open up professional and social opportunities. Even as they perform the earnestness of a painting unconcerned with its use value, they refuse to be extricated from their 'networking' function. It's as if they were compelled to perform it despite themselves. This function is typically served by how his paintings are installed and put to work after they are completed. Victor's paintings are imposing, but in a literal sense; they (also) impress in a manner that has nothing to do with what they accomplish *qua* painting.

Here are a few examples of how: A couple of years back Victor brought me two impractically large canvases that had been lying around under and outside his mother's garage for a long time wrapped in plastic, which he said would look nice on my living room wall. Unwrapping them they gave off a stench of mould so intense I winced. Just air them out, Victor prescribed. Predictably that didn't help much. Recently Victor contacted a man who owns the barn that used to house Kurt Schwitter's studio and made an agreement with him to arrange an exhibition there of his paintings in return for painting a couple of barn doors for him. Their dialogue broke down, a turn of events that Victor felt warranted a public flagellation of this incorporative host, who he proceeded to abuse in an e-mail press release announcing the cancellation of his exhibition. Victor's impositions occasionally have a more sympathetic timbre, as when he arranged for his paintings to be displayed inside the home of one of his Liverpool neighbours, a middle aged woman who, in Victor's words, "has not had an easy life." These forays reveal a need for nourishment from sources beyond the studio-gallery-axis that a painting proper usually confines itself to.

The inability not to put art to work as social instrument runs deep in Victor's practice. Everything he churns out is shadowed by a kind of compulsive socio-professional opportunism. But whereas he before relocating to Liverpool seemingly sought to accelerate this cynicism into a kind of career suicide (almost literally murdering his former Paris gallerist by removing all the windows in the gallery in January), his Liverpool years have seen this aggressive confrontational ethos outfitted with what in a certain sense represents its dialectical opposite: the introverted demeanour of a tortured and withdrawn mid-nineteenth century painter, the historical personification of art religiosity, i.e. eternally postponed compensation. However, it would be to misunderstand this development to assume it was a simply about repackaging, about hiding a cynical manoeuvring behind a virtuous camouflage. The conflict is real; Victor's recent oeuvre is host to two contradictory, yet equally important impulses. His contorted self-portraits are not adequately understood as mere accessories to the staging of a faux painter-self. Rather, they should also be taken at face value, as formal explorations of the medium of painting that seeks to find fitting expressions for affective states. More specifically, they register precisely the physical and psychological deformations of the subject that accompany the ceaseless mining for lucrative (in one sense or another) opportunities that Victor's art performs – and which of course only reflects a general abstractive process of value creation that art hesitates to admit its complicity with, but which nevertheless inescapably entangles it.

If deformity in art for the early avant-gardes represented an emancipatory program that negated the disciplinary norms and institutions of bourgeois society, a horizontal desire let loose on an oppressive culture from within, it is less obvious what this same deformity does for freedom today, when the value of bodies is measured based on their capacity for generating and sharing information, regardless of corporeal integrity. In fact, entering into symbiotic relations that dissolve the physical boundaries of the subject seems to be a precondition for this extractive process. Victor's brush charts the turning of affects into commodities currently at work in all of us. The still life presents an apt template for describing the information economy's leveling of value differences between human bodies and the materials they consume. The digital disconnectedness of the physical medium of painting slows down the upcycling of creative identity (de)formation into the circuits where extraction takes place. Painting is where real bodies still can leave traces, because the material production time of painting approximates the lived time of bodies.

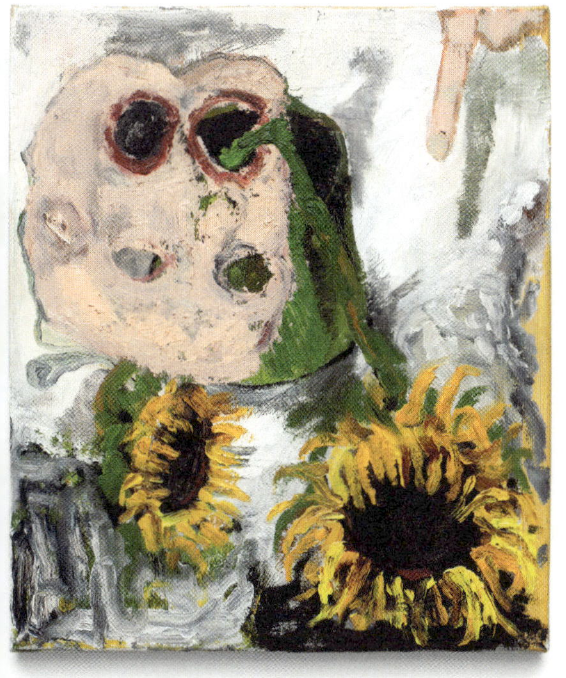

Untitled, 2020
Oil on linen canvas
40cm x 46cm

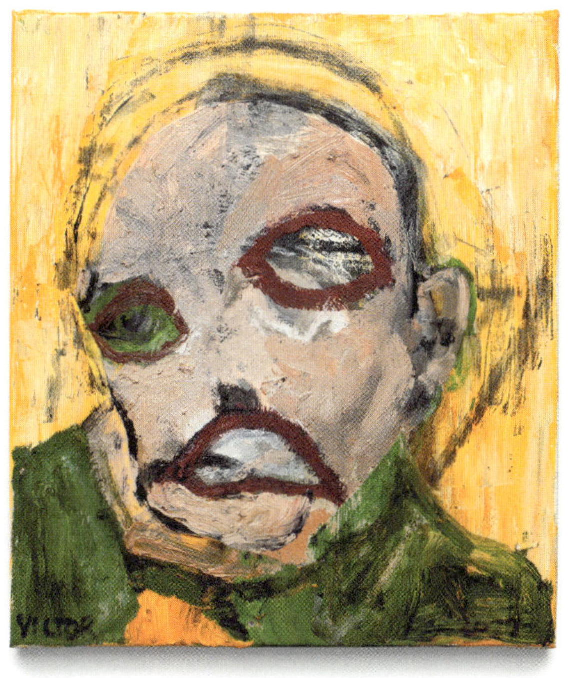

Possible Father, 2020
Oil on linen canvas
40cm x 46cm

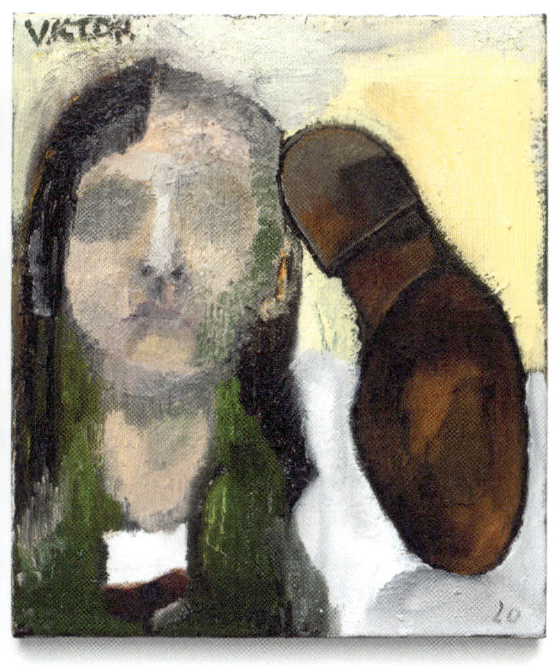

Untitled, 2020
Oil on linen canvas
40cm x 46cm

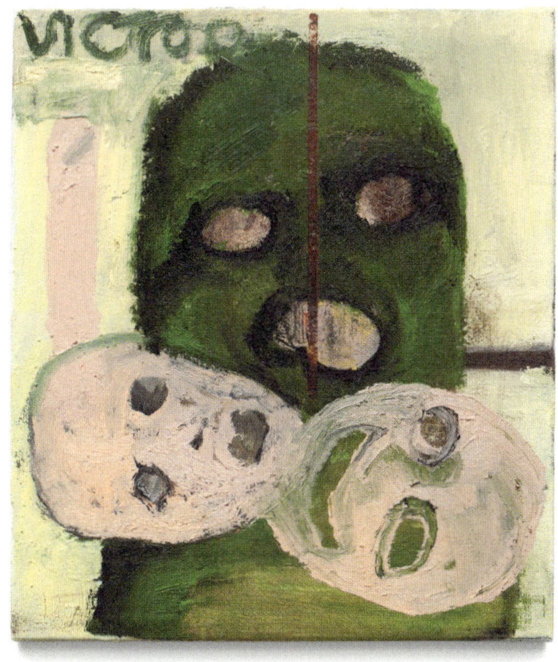

ohne Titel, 2020
Oil on linen canvas
40cm x 46cm

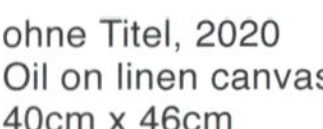

ohne Titel, 2020
Oil on linen canvas
40cm x 46cm

Waiting, 2020
Oil on linen canvas
30cm x 35cm

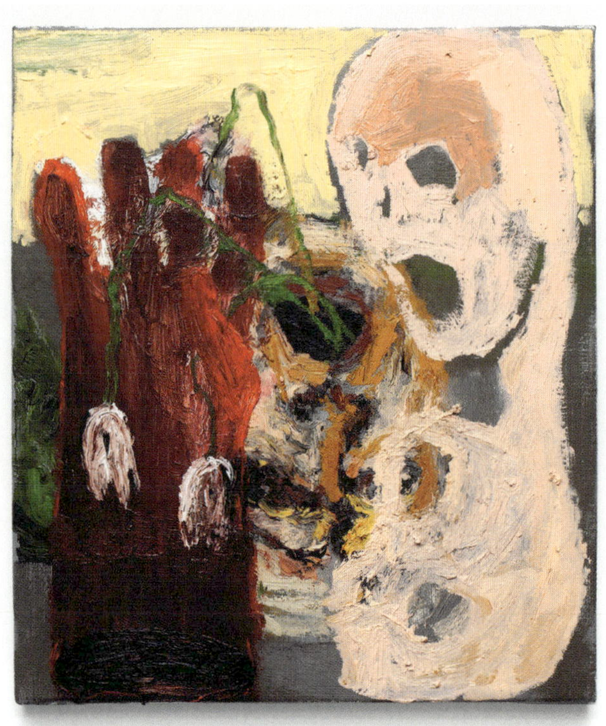

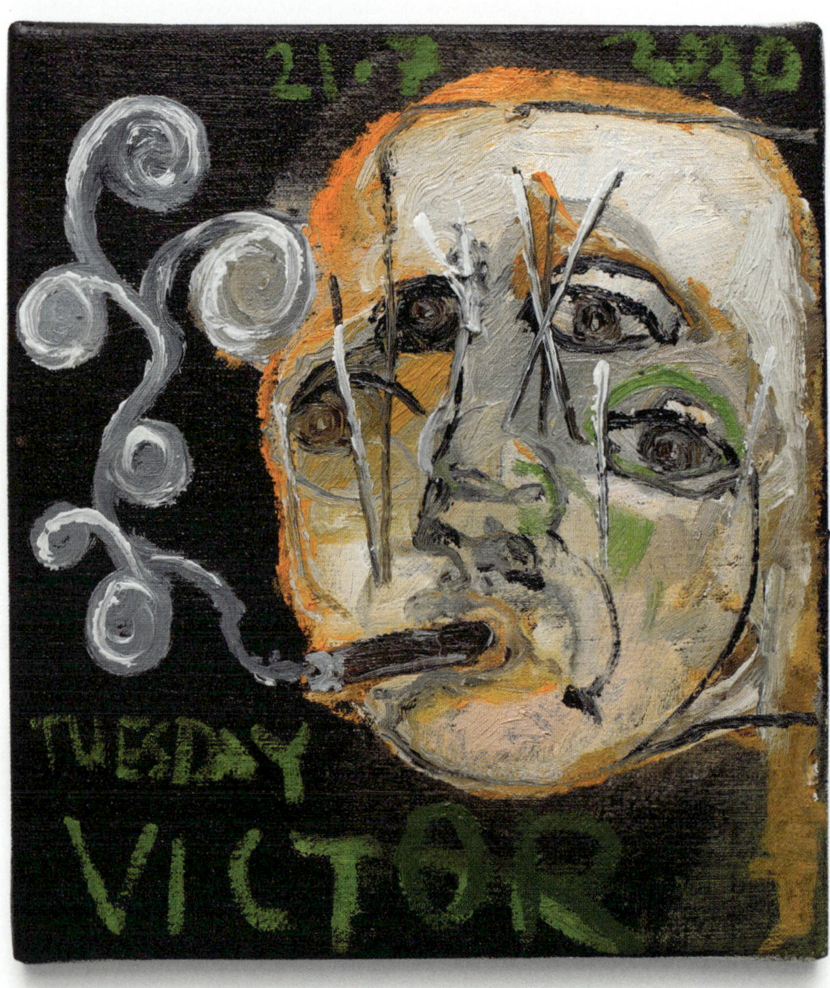

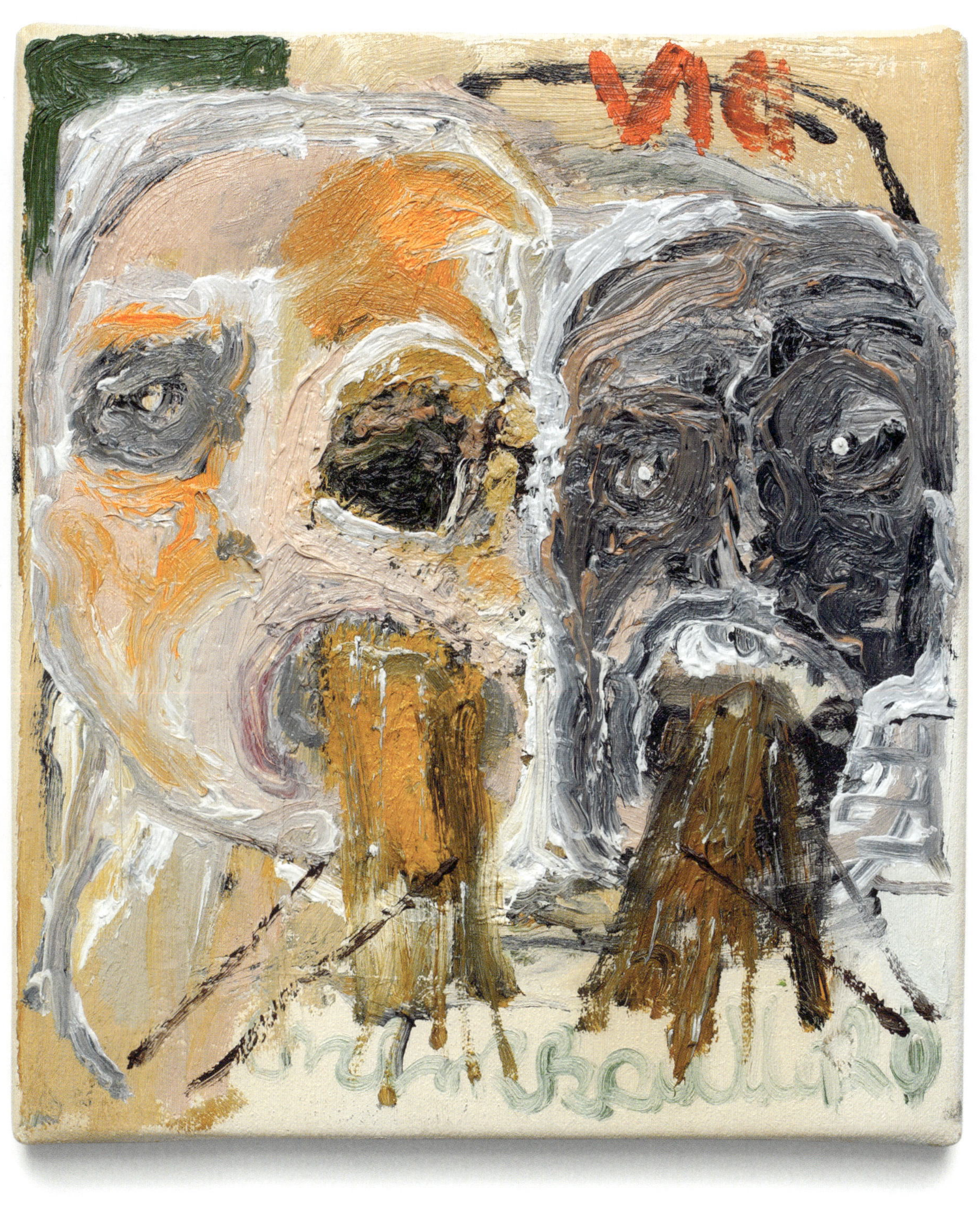

Spaghetti Aglio e Olio, 2020
Oil on linen canvas
30cm x 35cm

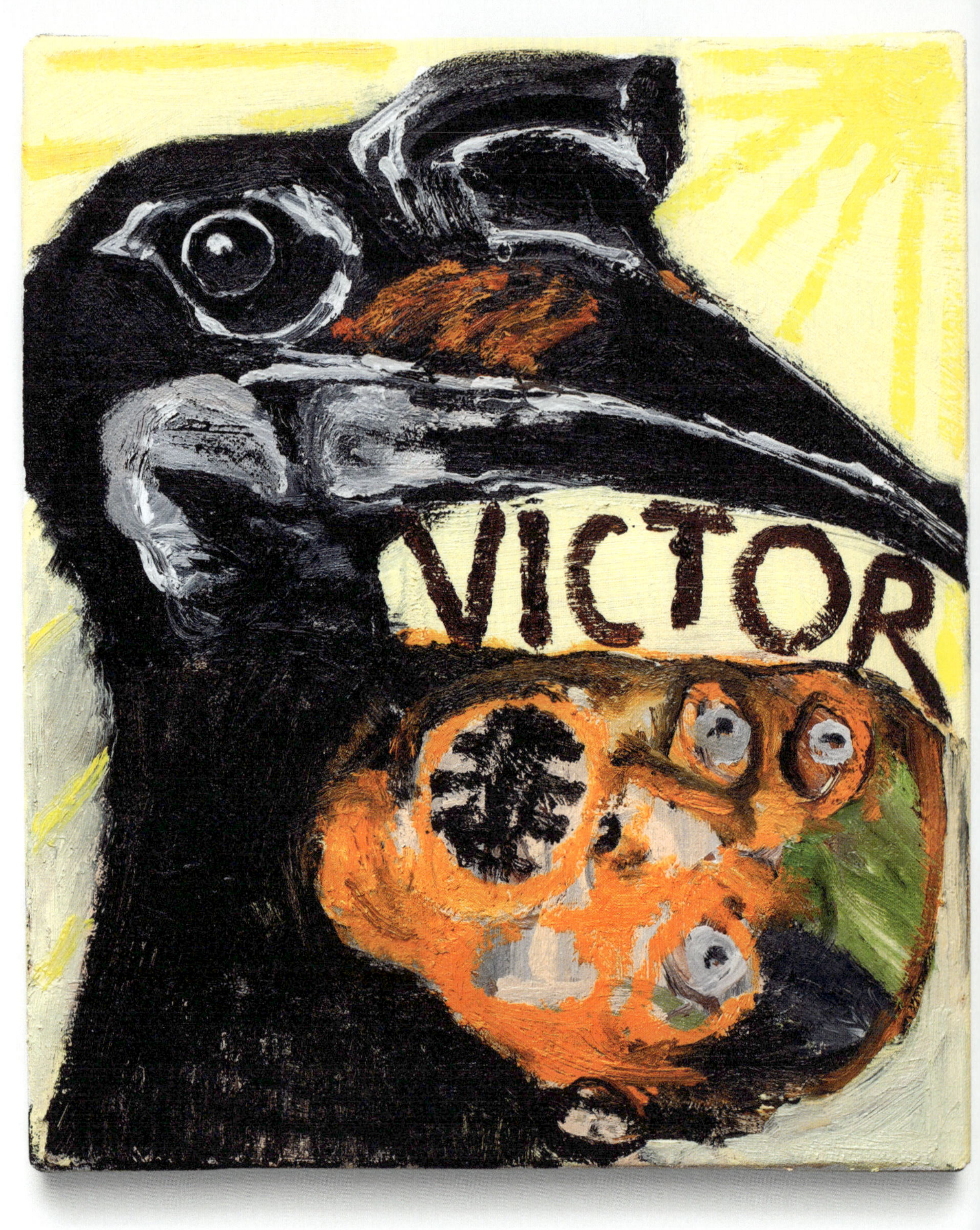

I Need Sun, 2020
Oil on linen canvas
40cm x 46cm

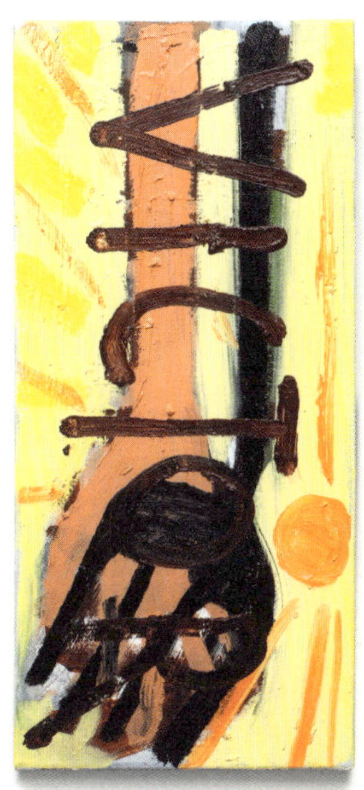

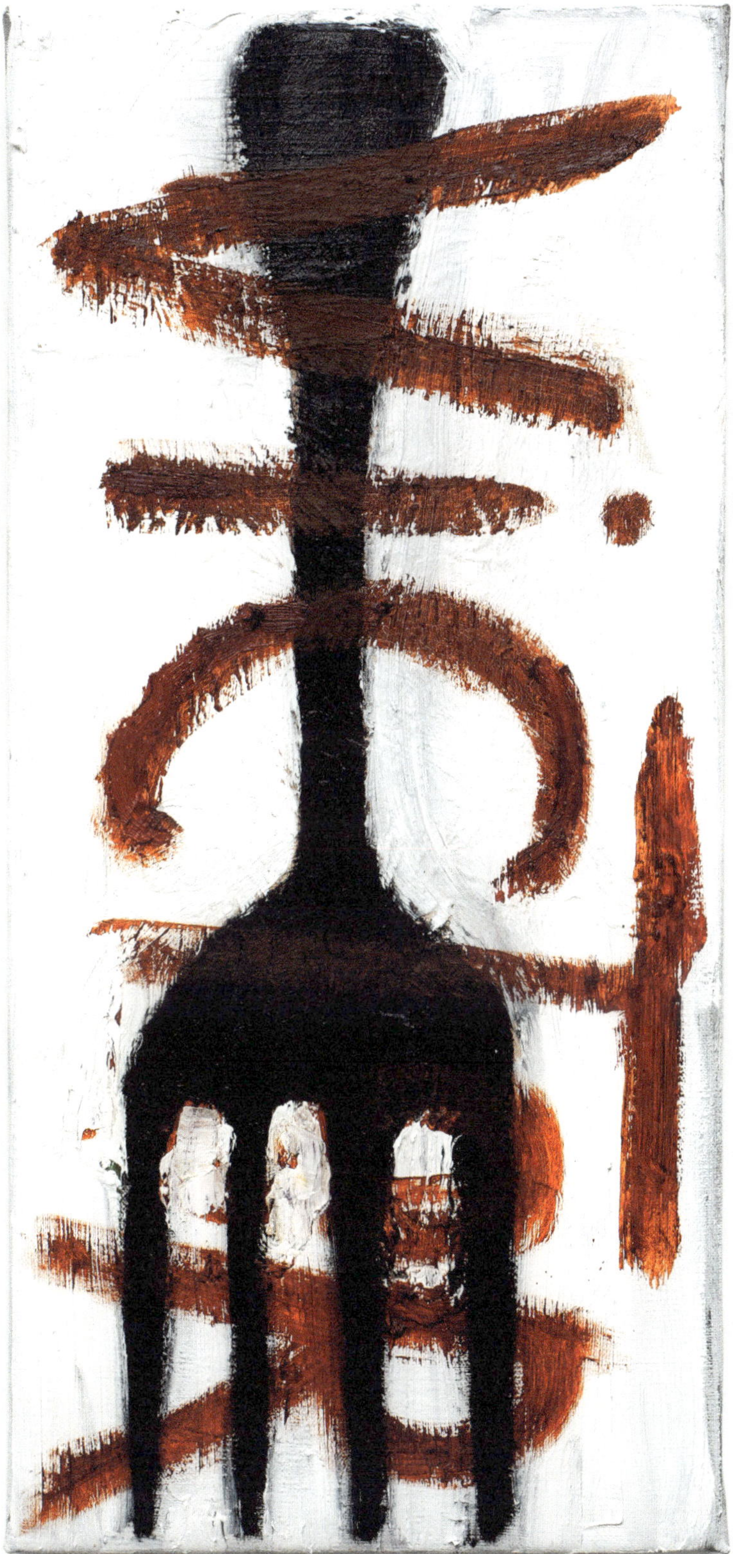

Untitled, 2020
Oil on linen canvas
25cm x 60cm

Untitled, 2020 Oil on linen canvas
25cm x 60cm

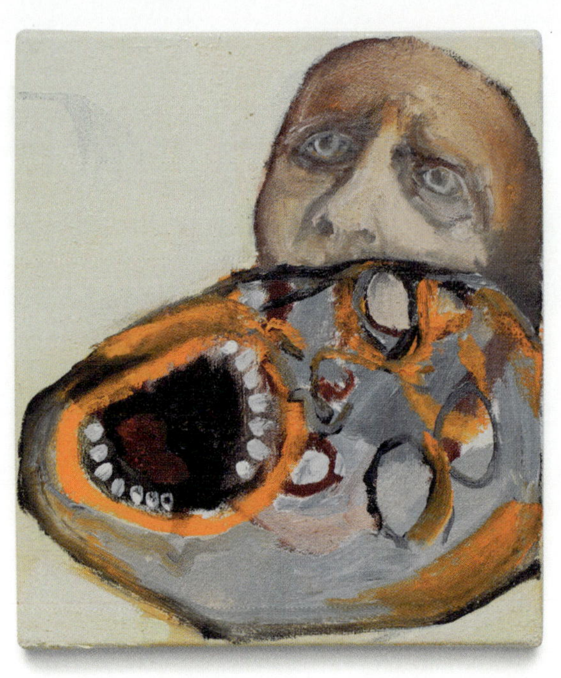

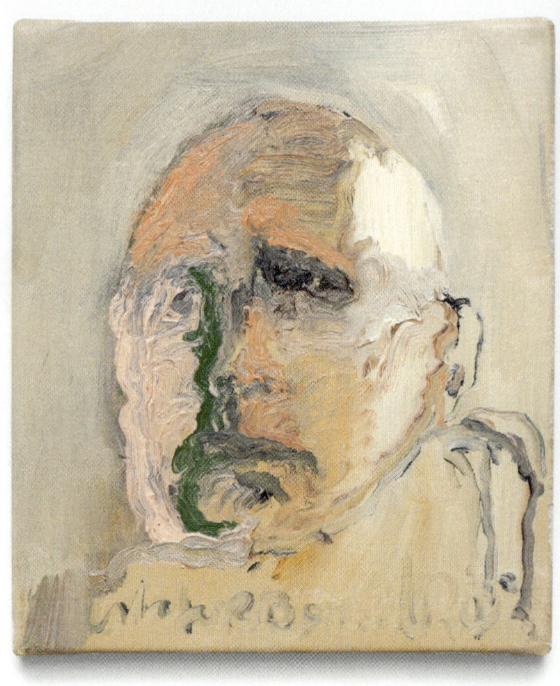

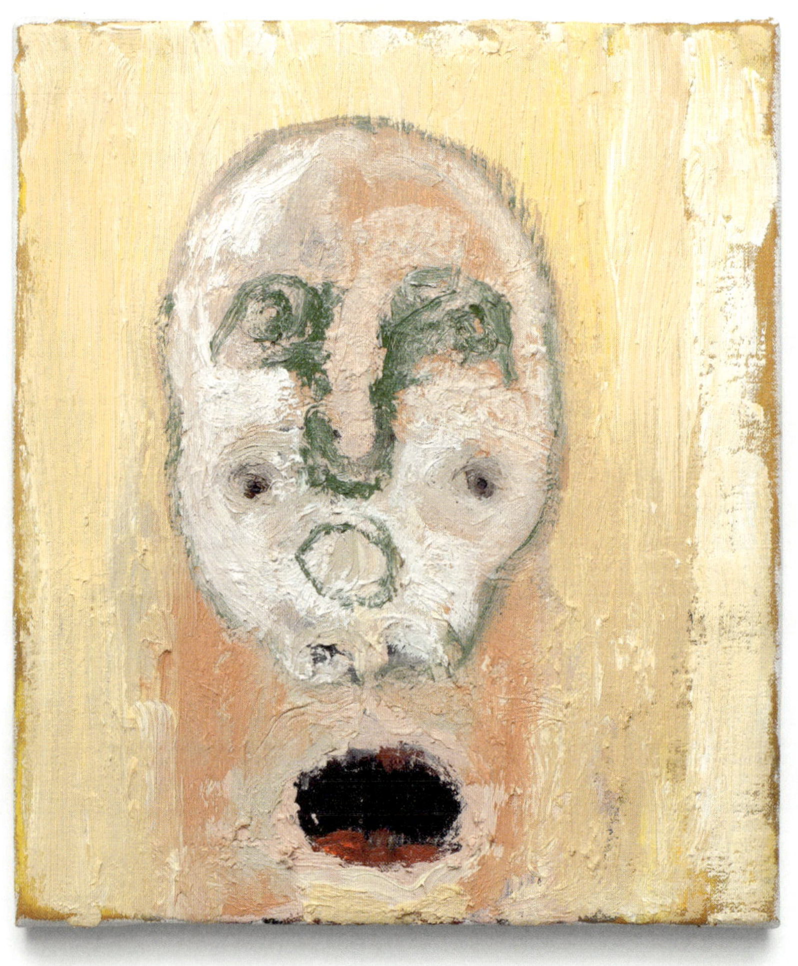

Untitled, 2020
Oil on jute
30cm x 35cm

Self-Portrait after a Stroke, 2
Oil on jute
30cm x 35cm

Untitled, 2020
Oil on linen canvas
30cm x 35cm

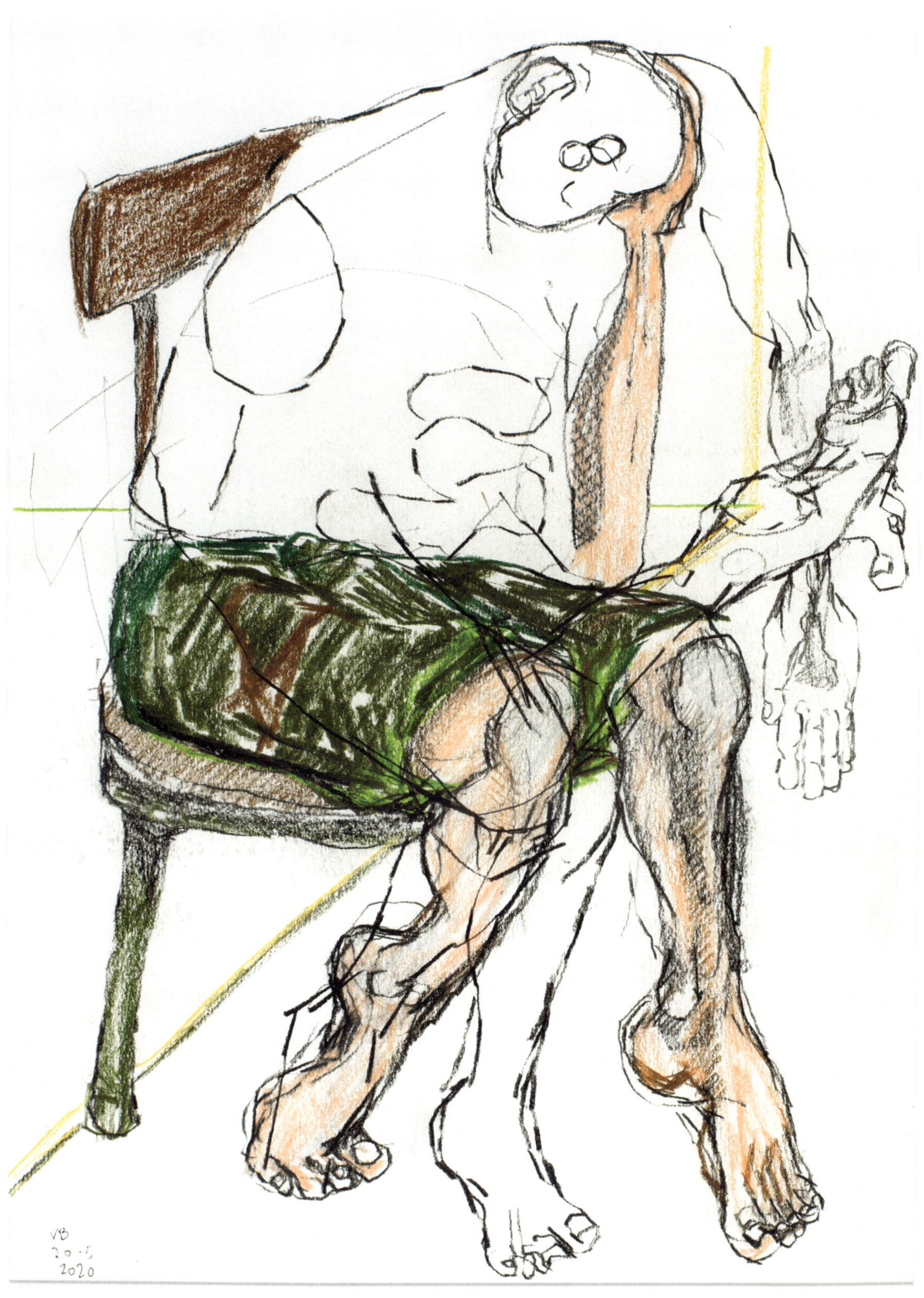

Untitled, 2020
Pencil, polychromos on paper
21cm x 29.7cm

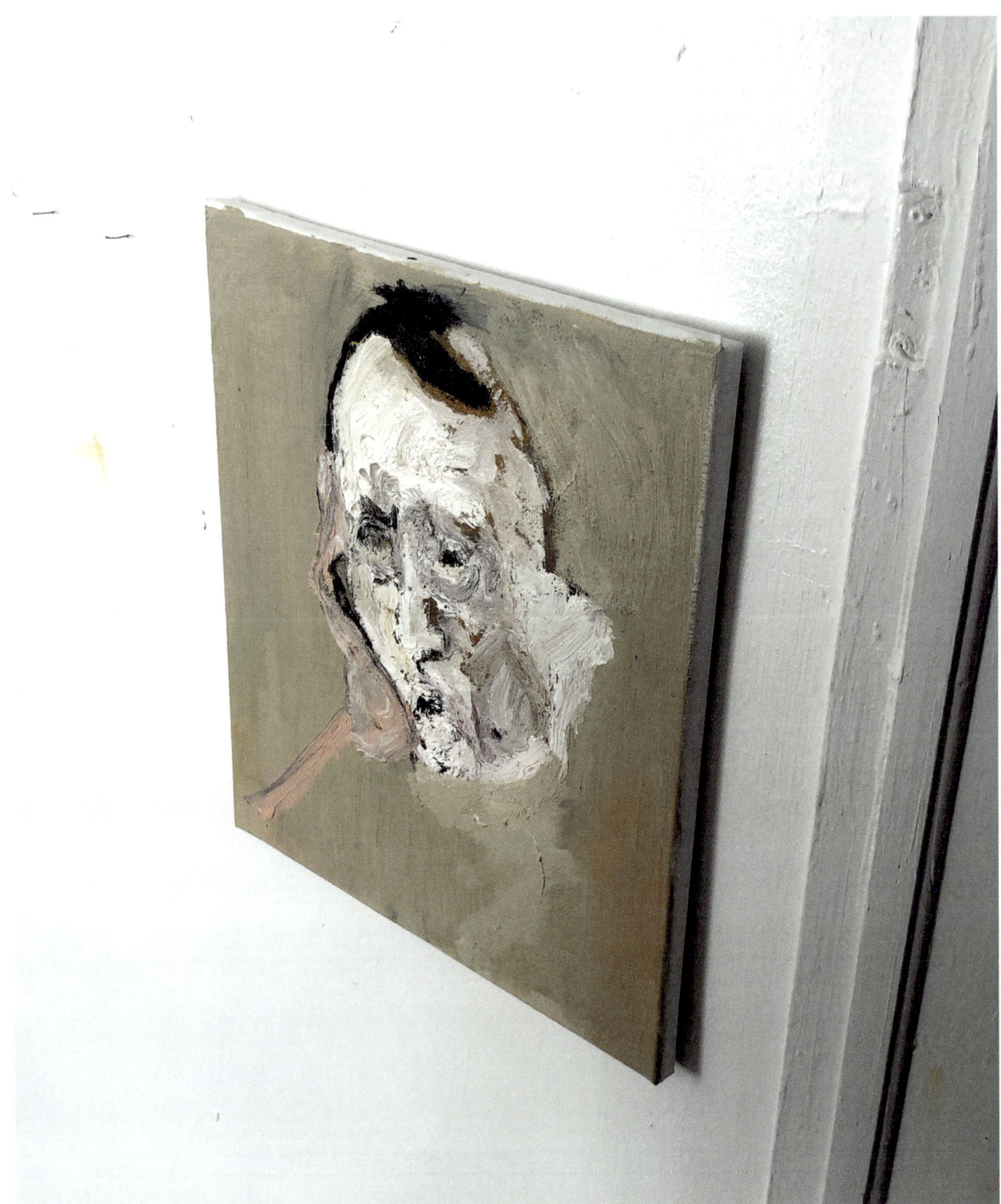

Walter Schmidinger II, 2020
Oil on linen canvas
40cm x 46cm

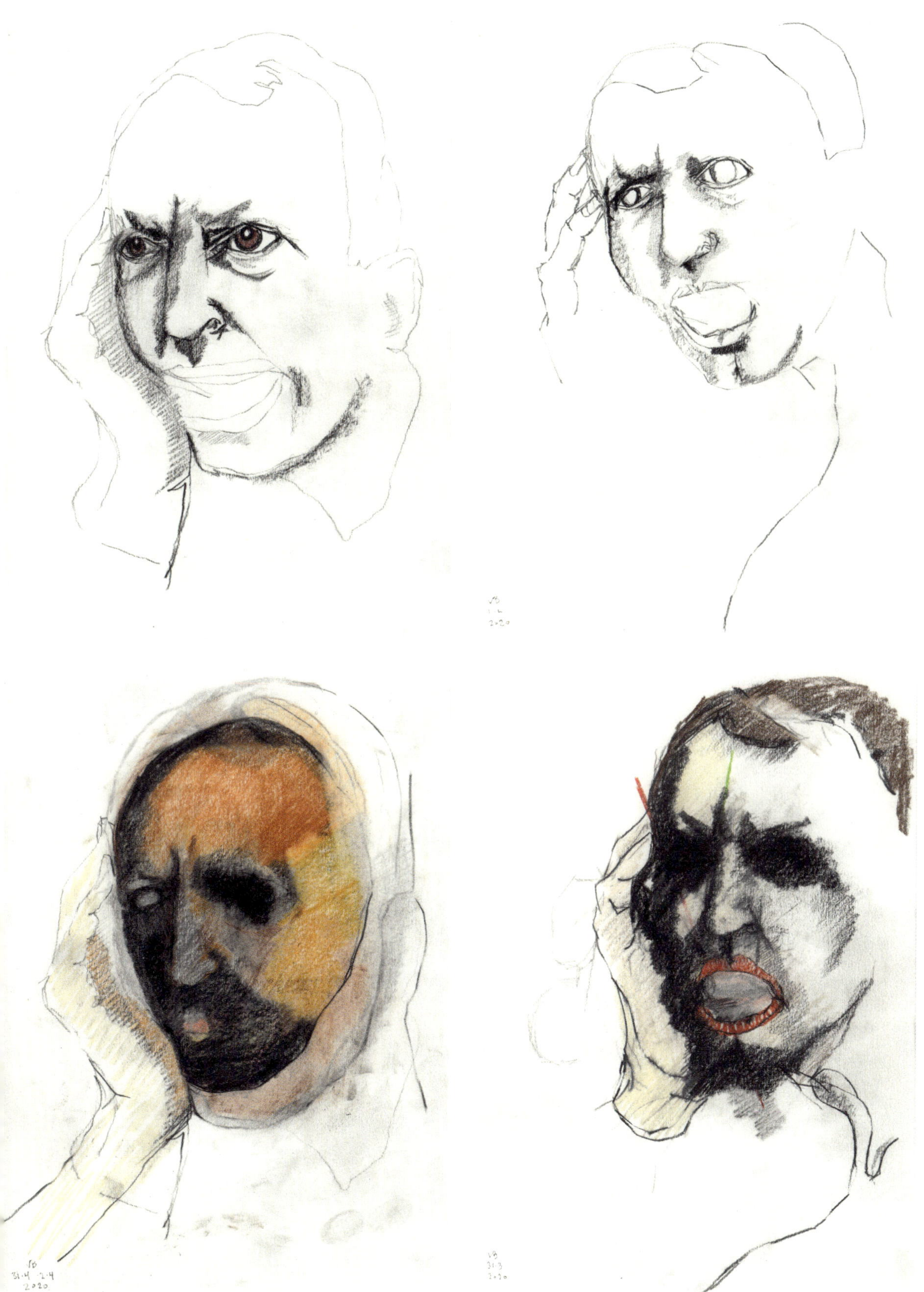

Walter Schmidinger, 2020
Pencil, polychromos on paper
21cm x 29.7cm

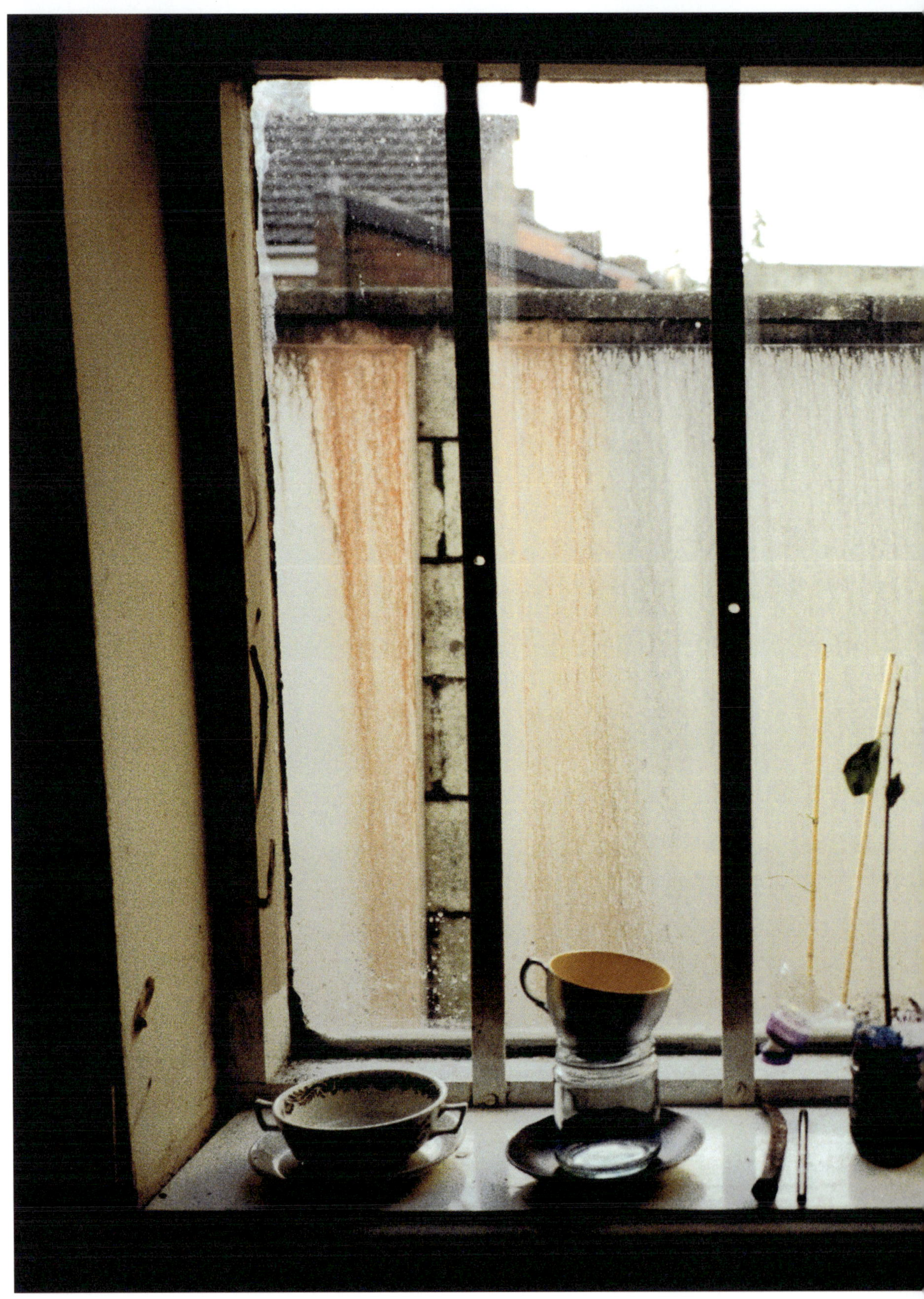

Studio documentation (facing west) 2020
35mm film

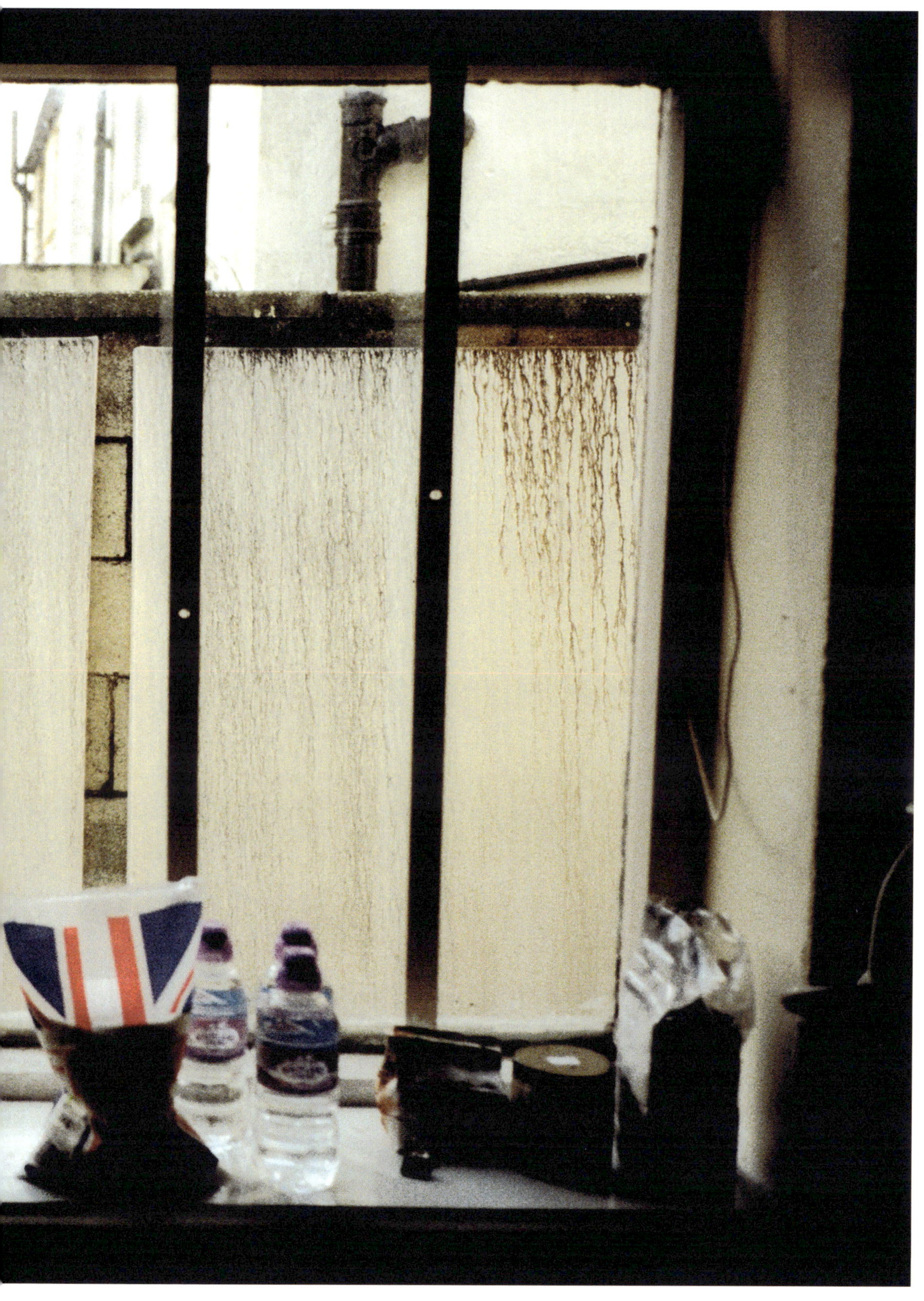

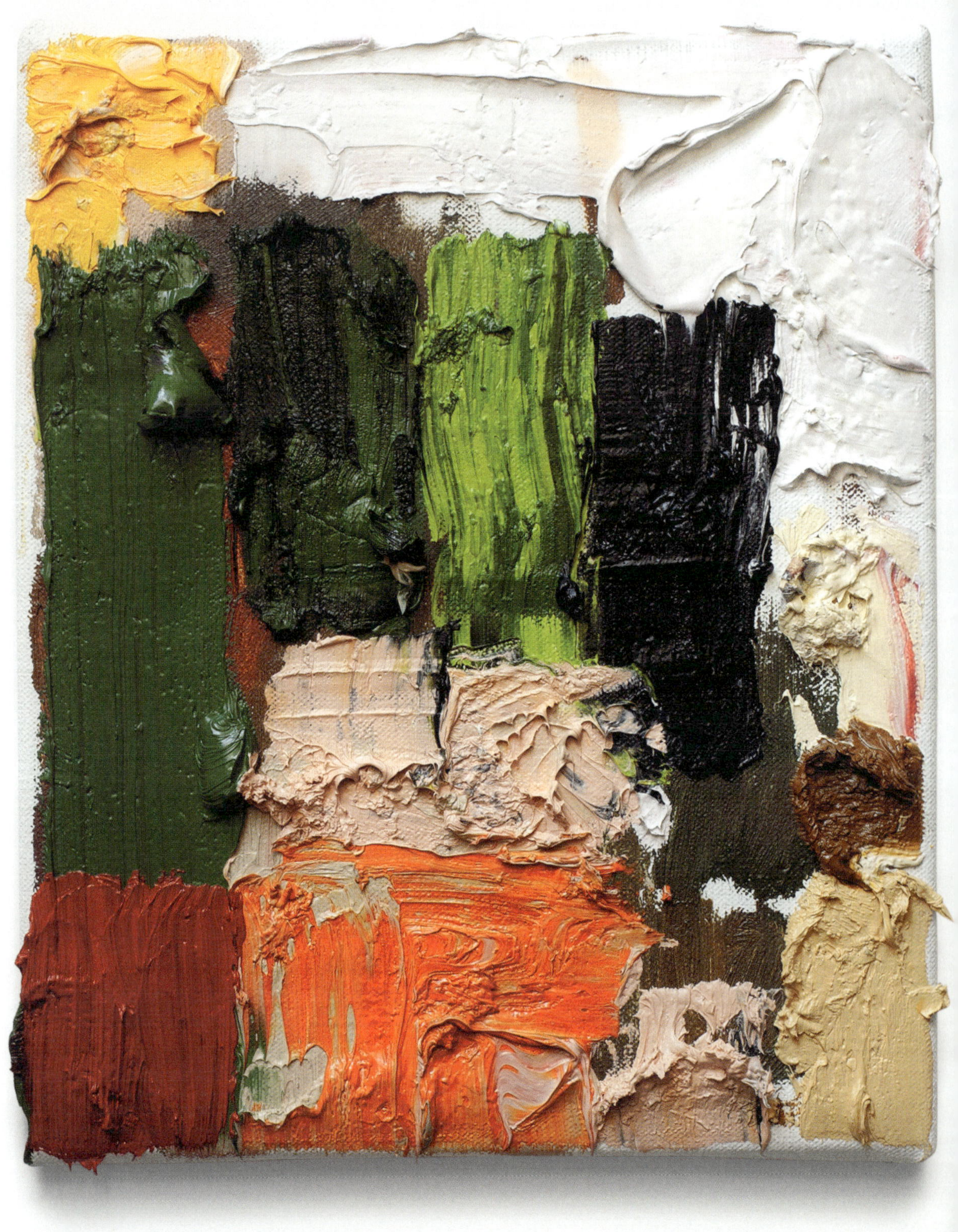

To and from the Studio, 2020
Oil on linen canvas
20cm x 25cm

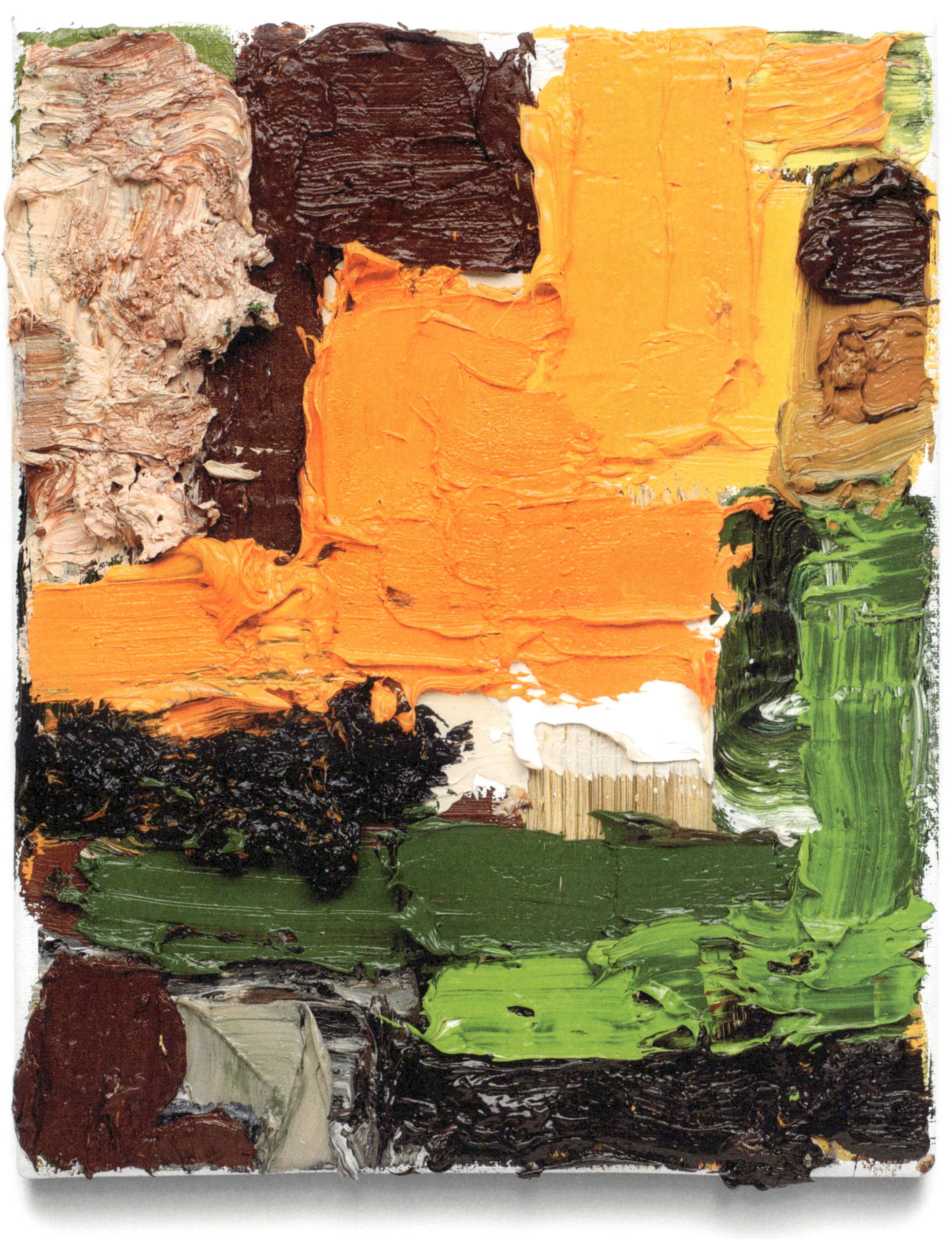

To and from the Studio, 2020
Oil on linen canvas
20cm x 25cm

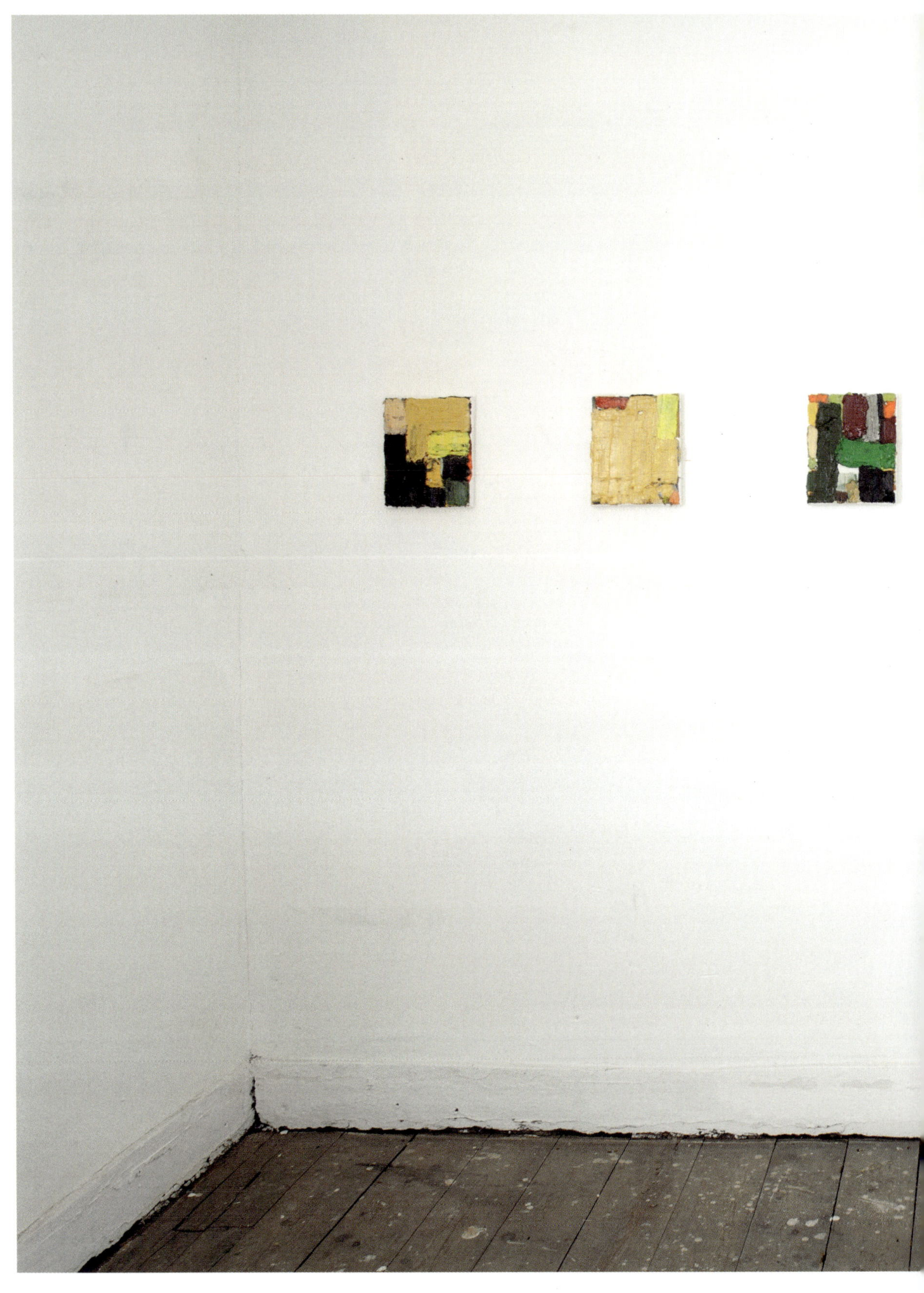

To and from the Studio, 2020 – 2021
Oil on linen canvas
20cm x 25cm

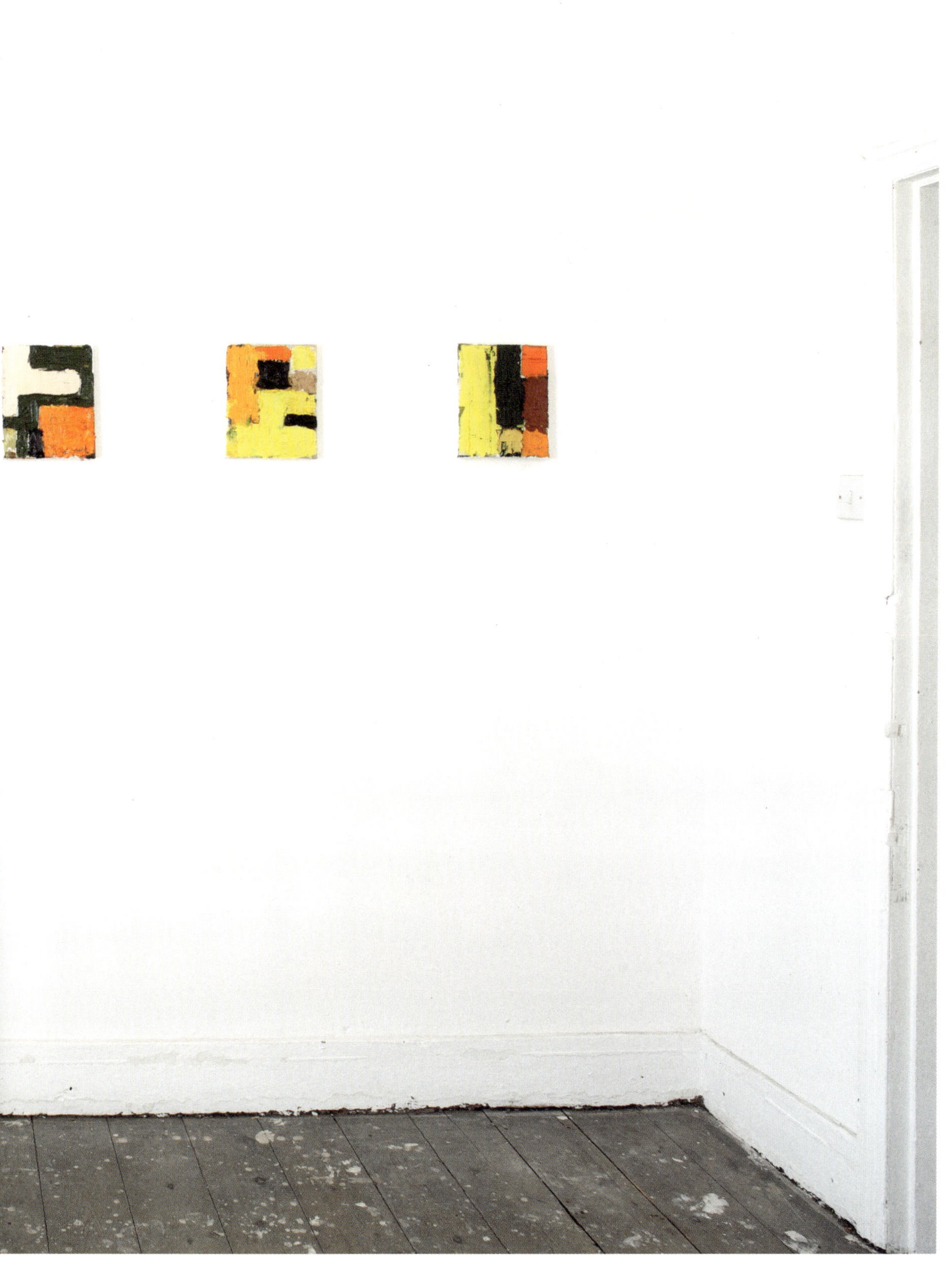

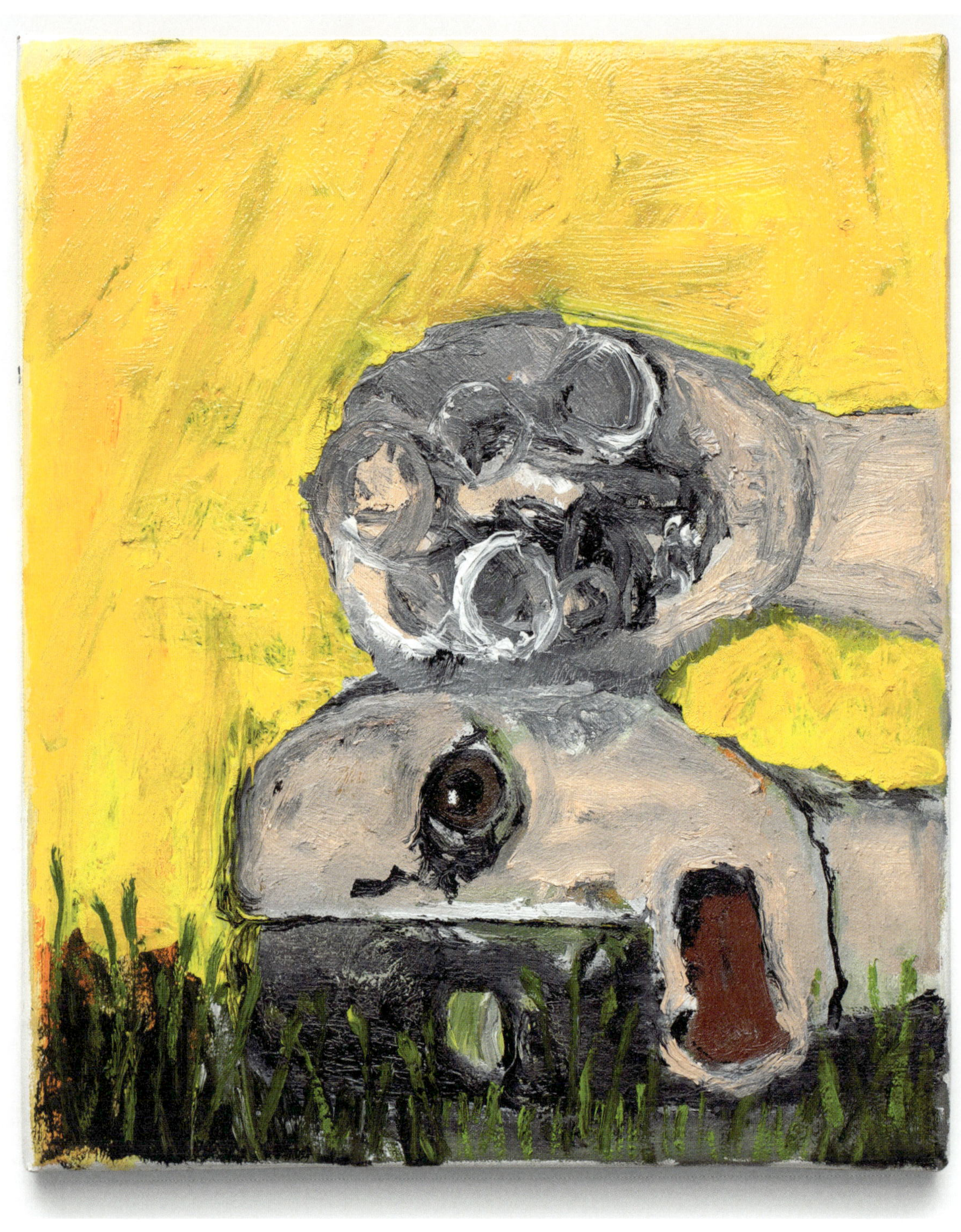

Missing the Sun, 2020
Oil on jute
40cm x 46cm

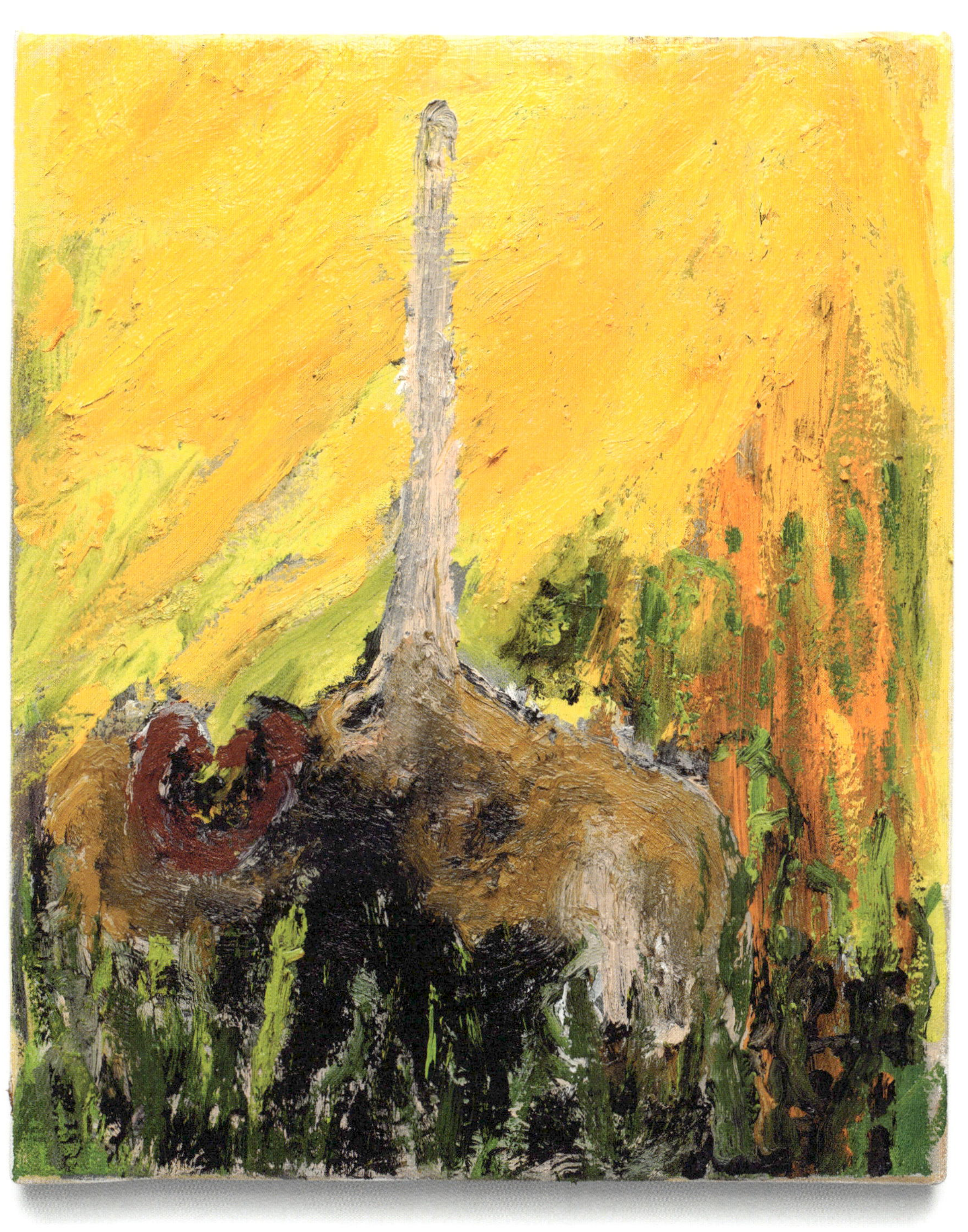

No Sun, 2020 – 2021
Oil on linen canvas
40cm x 46cm

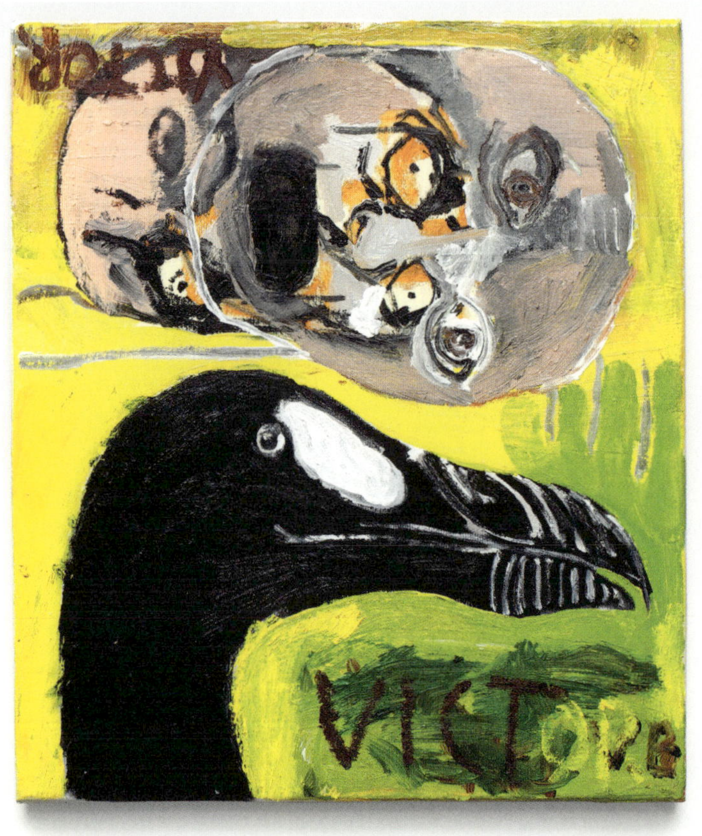

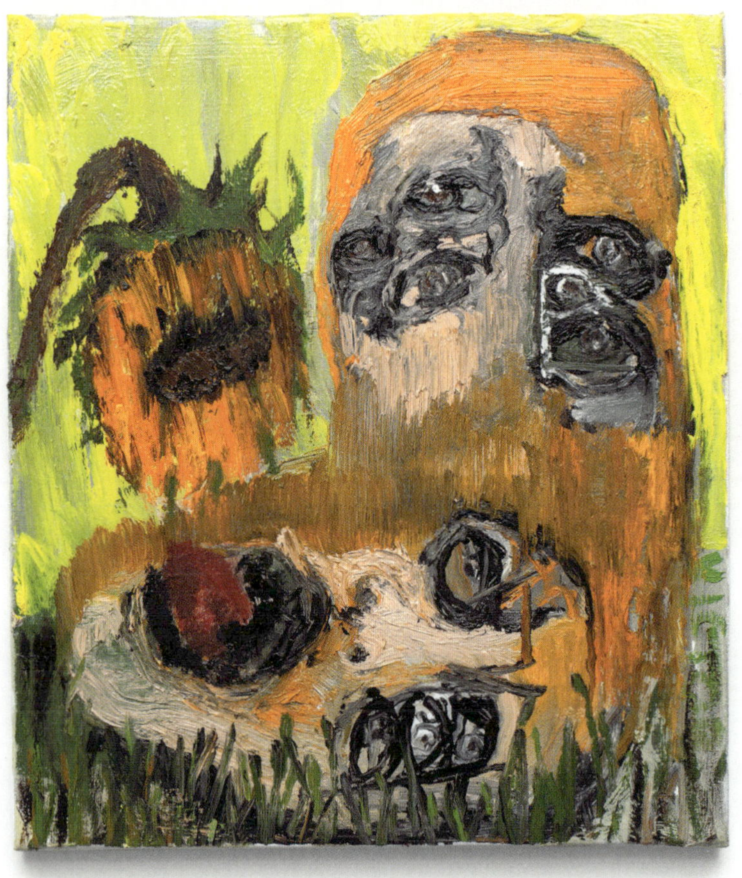

Sun Problem, 2020
Oil on linen canvas
40cm x 46cm

Missing the Sun, 202
Oil on linen canvas
40cm x 46cm

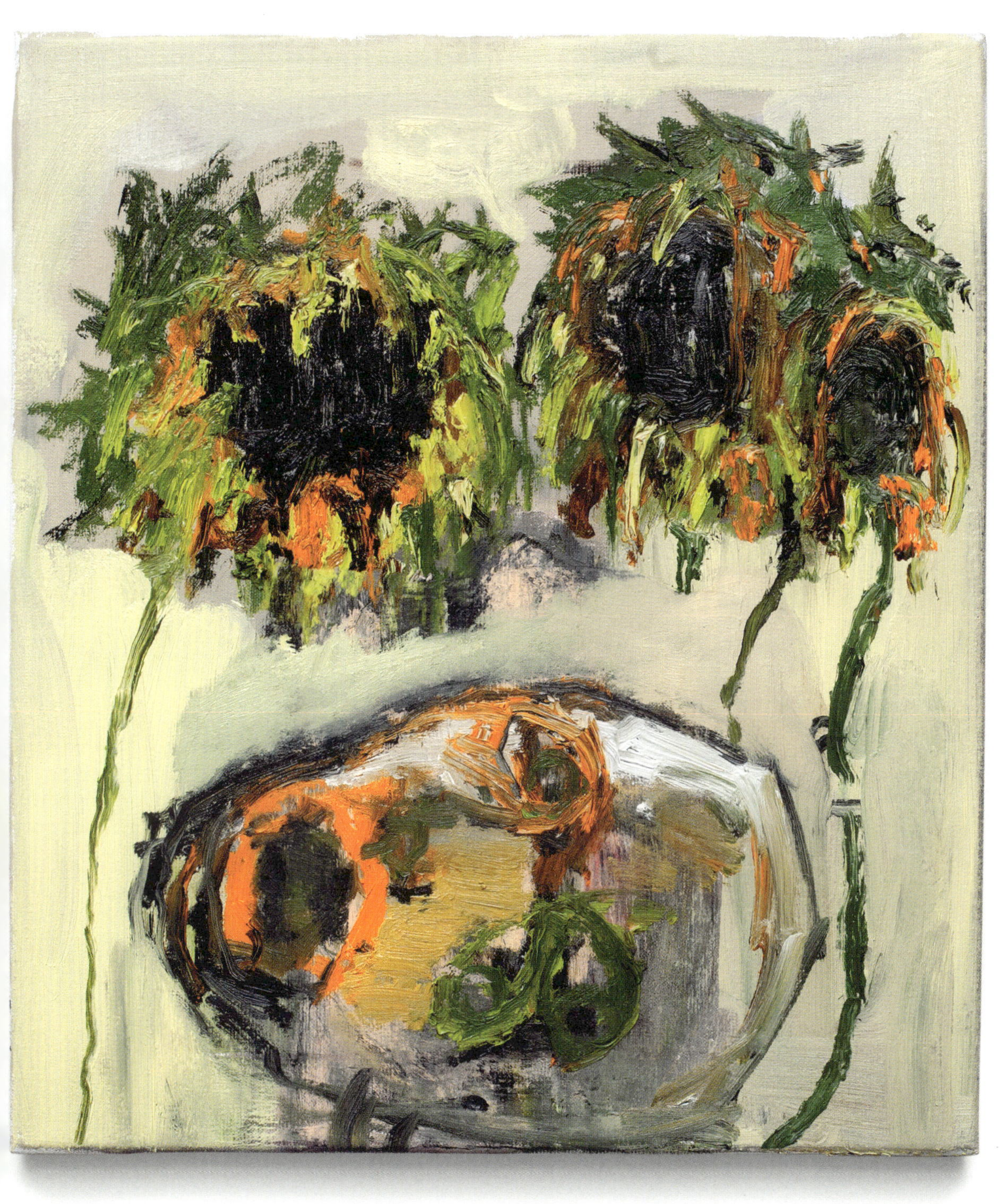

Never Sun, 2020 – 2021
Oil on linen canvas
40cm x 46cm

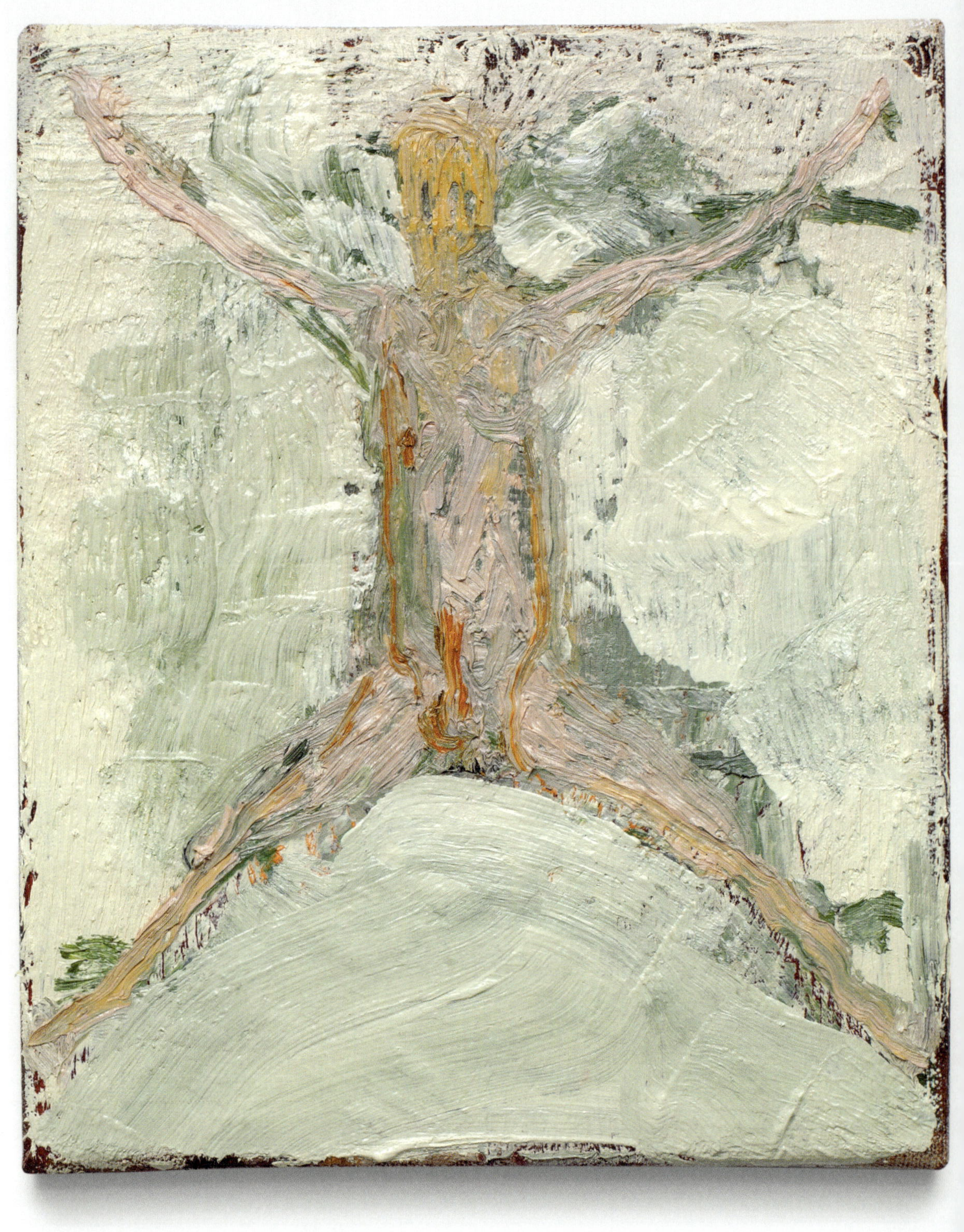

Sunbathing Naked, 2020
Oil on linen canvas
20cm x 25cm

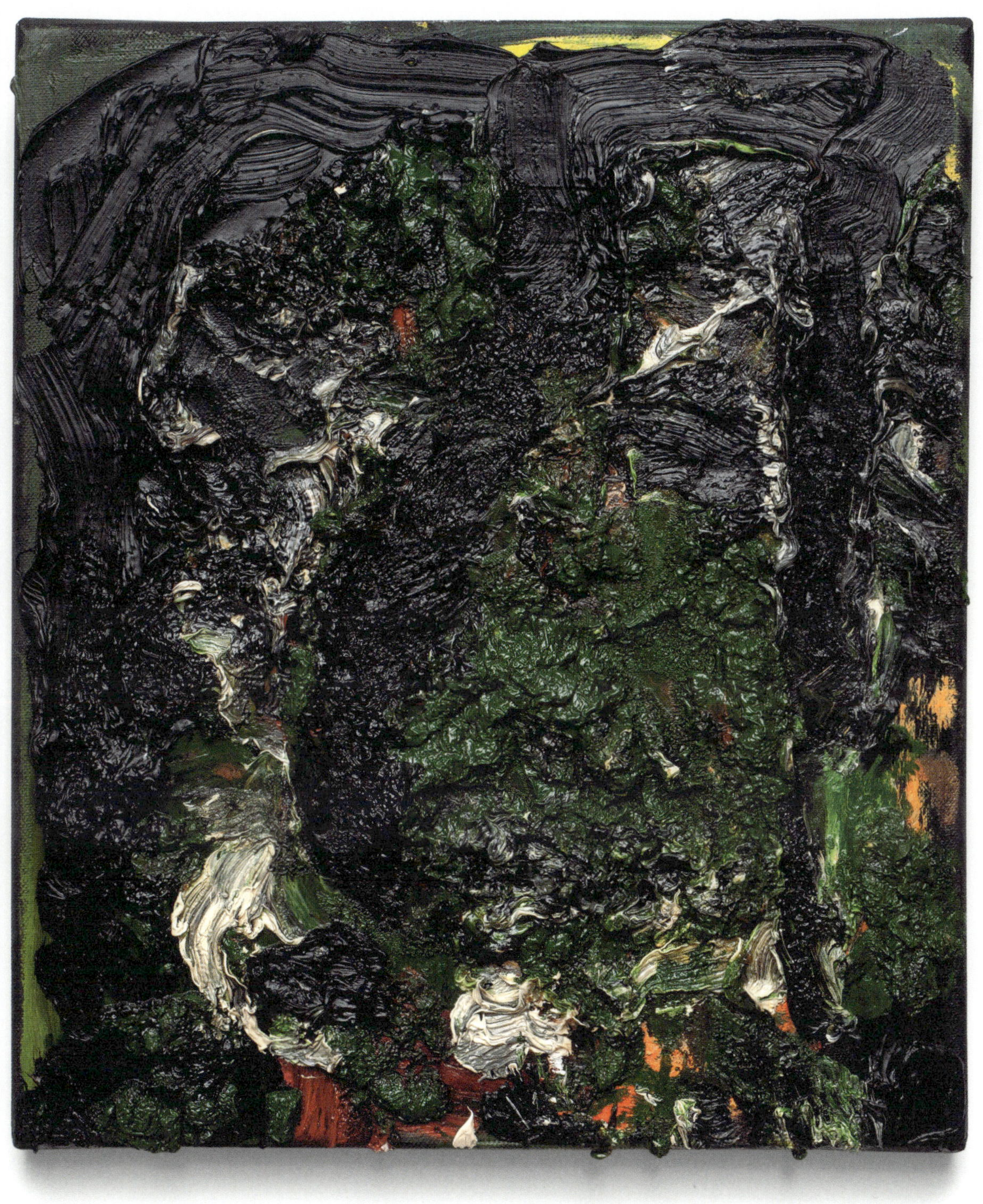

The Cathedral Pit from Hope Street, 2019 – 2020
Oil on black canvas
30cm x 35cm

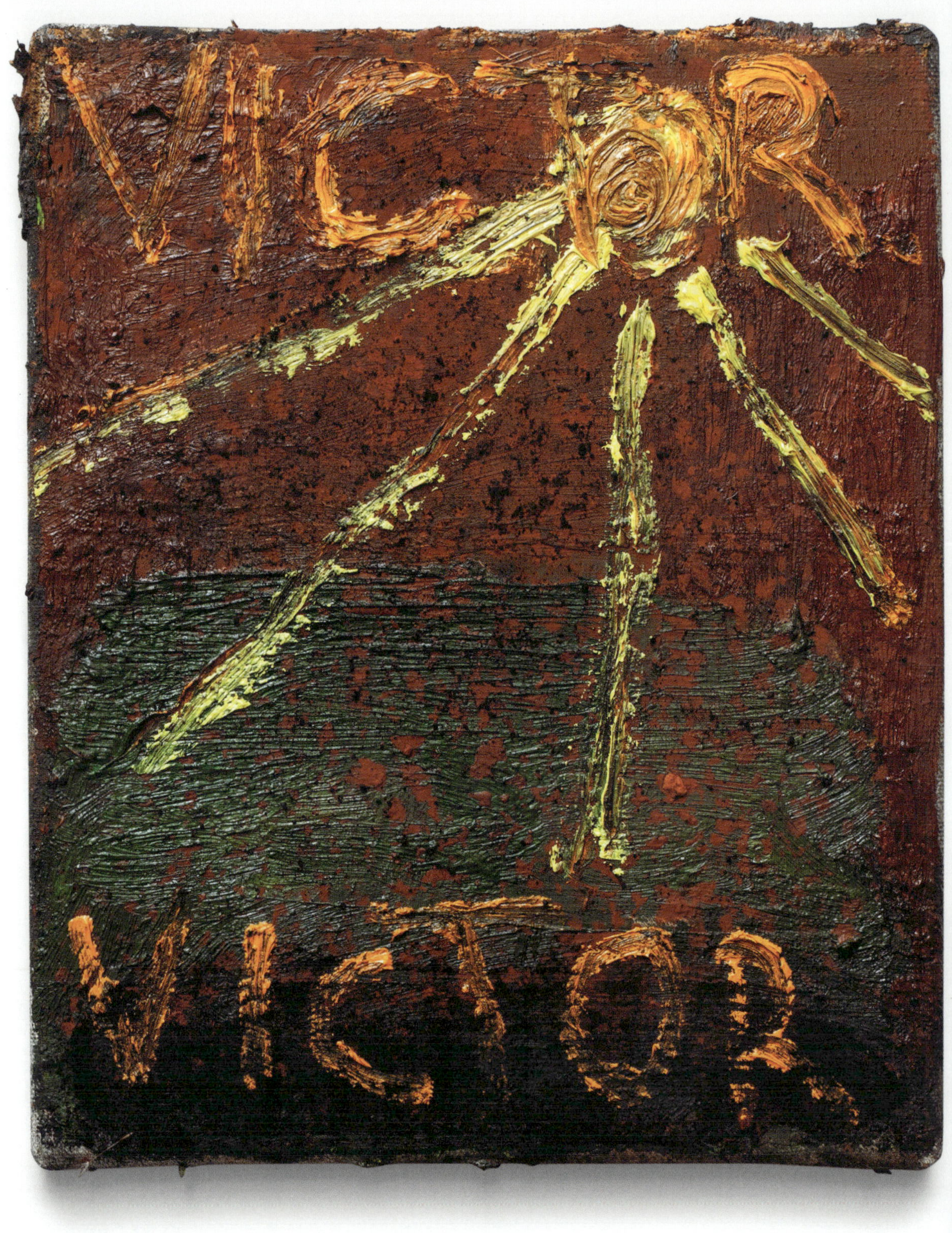

Hope Street. Cathedral. Fence. To/From Studio, 2020
Oil, pigment on linen canvas
20cm x 25cm

When the 'o' in Victor Became the Sun
by Jeremy Glogan

As a fellow painter and European fifty-something Victor Boullet and I share some common ground. When I visited him in Liverpool in May 2019 we went to his studio, but he'd just sent all his work to be exhibited in Stockholm – 130 paintings, hundreds of drawings, together with various sculptural assemblages – so there was no work to see. But as if to assert the potential conceptual nature of this painting project the absence of the work gave rise to a resounding presence through the experience of Victor's unique routine and working/living environment, a routine built from the relentless need to keep on visting the studio and to paint, day in day out for several years – a self-imposed isolation from the international art world and its networks and socialising that had been the fuel for his previous project.

The presence was there in the grim terrace in Toxteth which was now Victor's studio – the various rooms, painting paraphernalia and the barren backyard; the experience of having my portrait painted by Victor in the flesh soon after arriving; the ritualistic walk to and from the studio past the monstrous gothic cathedral; the all too tangible atmosphere of Liverpool itself – mythical, suffering and yet always so immersed in sardonic humour.

Here are two quotations Victor has sent to me in texting conversation:

> "I'm painting every day. After the show, nothing has changed, but I've found it quit [sic] hard to move on, forward, feel stuck, but I work, and by applying paint and doing something everyday something does happens and this make [sic] it all worth while. The show has been very good for me and my inner self, but it has interfered with my routines. I'm on my way towards something, I'm chiselling my way to an inner world, but it will take years."

> "I'm here. Puul is cold, wet and fucking awful."

His painting project has created an immense body of work, hundreds of paintings and thousands of drawings in seven years. The uncompromising nature of the project and the raw hunger for creating he possesses has meant that the work has never stopped developing both formally and in ambition in terms of content. He is willing and able to confront any subject matter and does so with an existential brutality. There's a battle going on but often it is only through conflict that, if fortunate, we can find something truly rewarding, perhaps even peace.

There is a small group of paintings from 2020 subtitled 'Hope street. Cathedral. Fence. To/From Studio' made as a response to the daily journey on foot from his pleasant Georgian home to the studio in socially-deprived Toxteth. Divine intervention chose to drop Sir Giles Gilbert Scott's Liverpool Anglican Cathedral right between the two locations. Symbol of sectarian divide, this soul-sucking red sandstone 'gothic revival' monstrosity is the largest religious building in the UK. Just the thought of it engenders a nightmare-like feeling of sublime dread. Looking up at it's terrifying scale and mossy features from the road behind the imposing iron railings it reveals its hideous menace. The fundamental shape of the cathedral (imposing central tower rising up from blocks either side) is echoed in several of Gilbert Scott's buildings including Bankside power station / Tate Modern. Incredibly for such an antiquated looking building, construction took place throughout the 20th century (1904-1978). It seems to exist as a huge gravestone to sordid and sinister Victorian religion and authority.

Victor, ever resourceful, always seeking out subject matter and often with a predilection for the unsettling would take pictures and videos as he walked past the cathedral over the relentless days, weeks, months, years. He walked past it maybe 5,000 times. I don't think he felt quite the animosity to it that that I do but still this gargantuan enclosure of negativity existed at the heart of Victor's Liverpool, both geographically and psychically. He would make paintings containing the motif of the building. He would chew gum and stick the used gum onto the railings and take pictures of these little chewed sculptures. He'd stick the gum wrappers onto the surface of the paintings.

In one small painting the 'o' in the painted name 'Victor' becomes the sun as beams shine from it as it rises up above and beyond Liverpool Anglican Cathedral. Victor is about to leave Liverpool at the time of writing. His project will continue but with that charming building no longer taking centre stage.

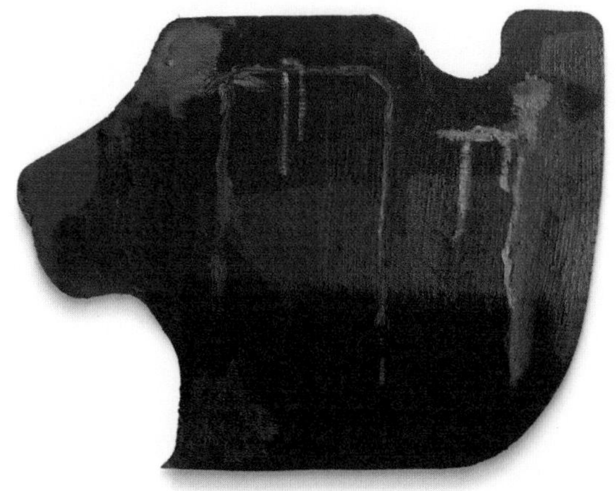

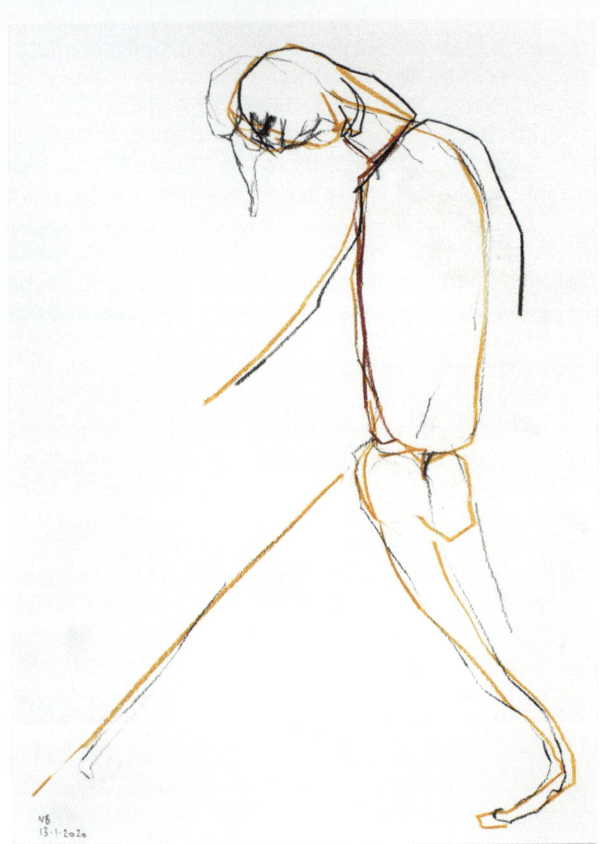

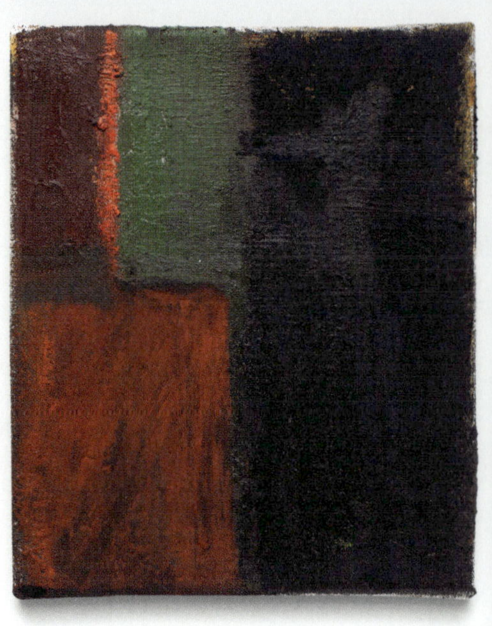

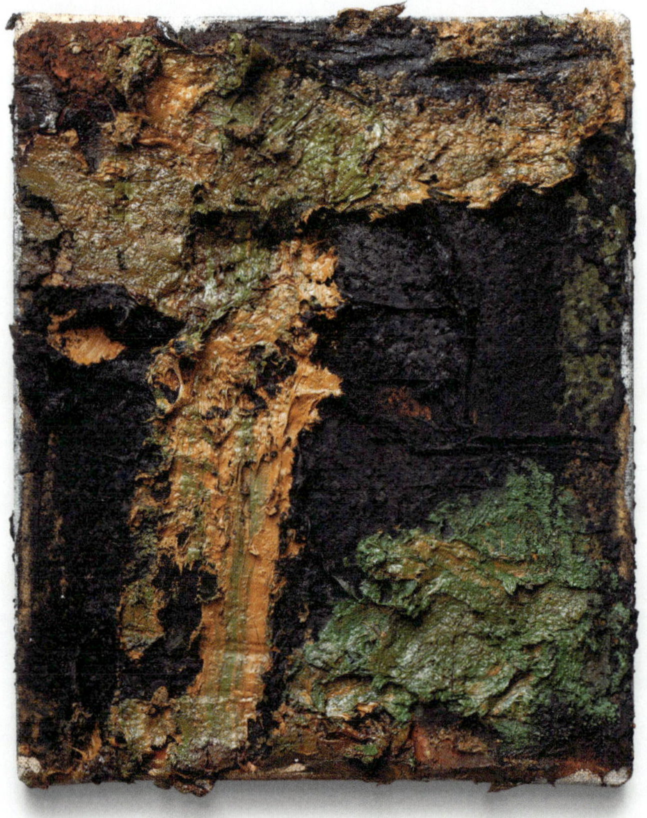

Untitled, 2020
Pencil, polychromos on paper
21cm x 29.7cm

Hope Street. Cathedral. Fence. To/From Studio, 20
Oil, pigment on linen canvas
20cm x 25cm

Hope Street. Cathedral Pit. To/From Studio, 2020
Oil, pigment on linen canvas
20cm x 25cm

To/From Studio, Problem on Windsor Street, 2019
Oil, spray paint on wood
5 Panels, various sizes

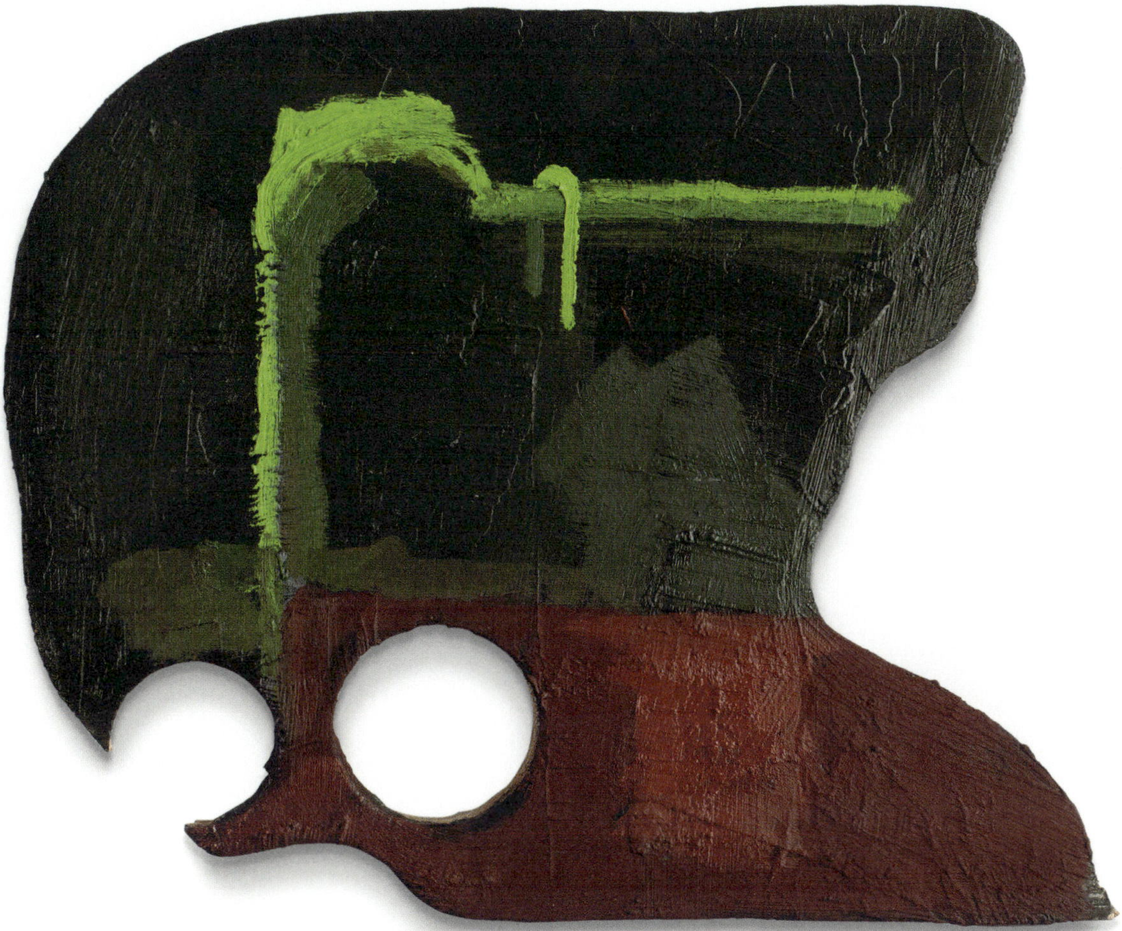

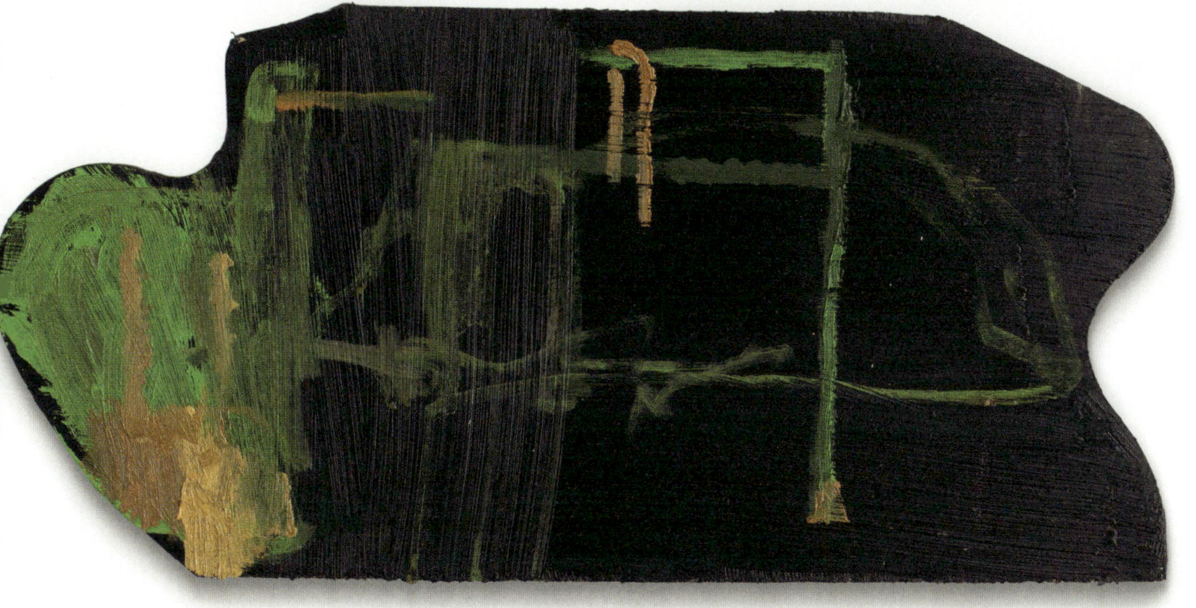

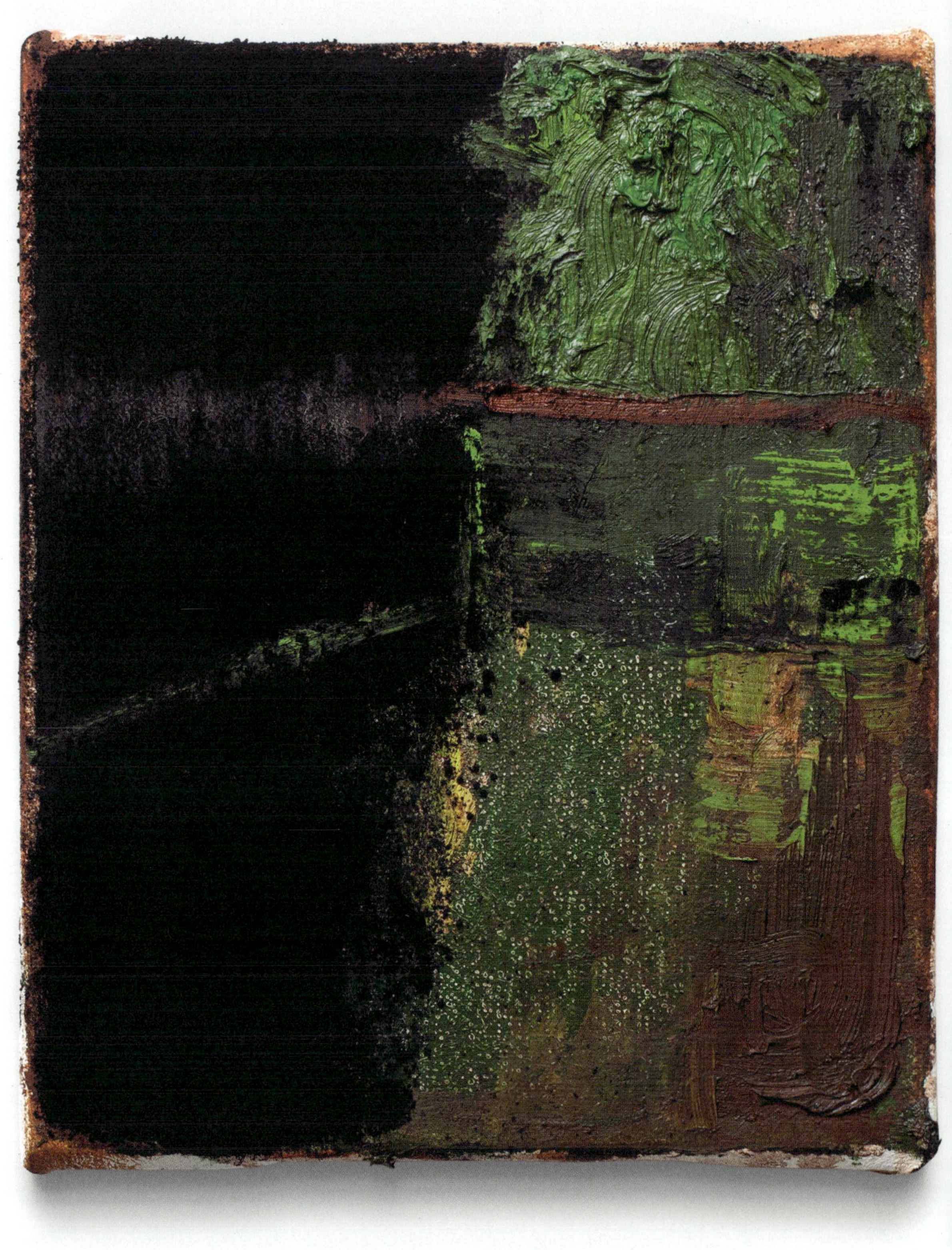

Hope Street. Cathedral. Fence. To/From Studio, 2020
Oil, pigment on linen canvas
20cm x 25cm

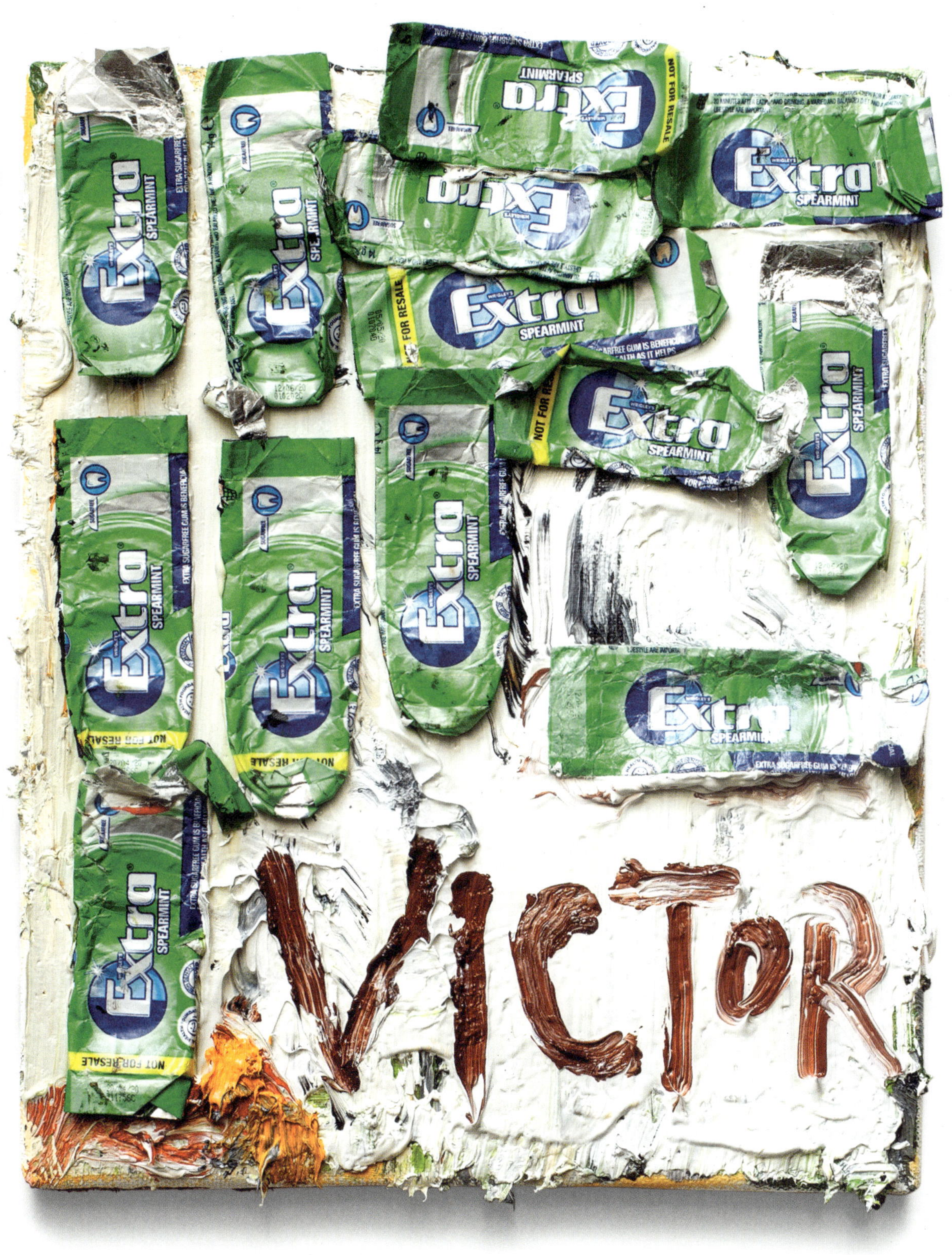

Hope Street. Cathedral. Fence. To/From Studio, 2020
Oil, chewing gum wrappers on linen canvas
20cm x 25cm

Le Bougnat

Le Bougnat (Violence within my ERROR)

It's sadly still 2017 - Problem. Problem. Error. Walk. Wait. Die Mutter removed roof tiles to get into the building and was asphyxiated when her clothing became caught. Deleted. The wait. I wait. Silence grows. Bad mouthed news. Motives changing. It's just another birth. My foot, the hole. The walk. The Wait. In my side view I catch him walking. Just EXILE. Only EXILE. Walk. Wait. Work. LABOUR. My own personal green revenge. Flag stones are moving, fences are falling. Rip it open. E. E. E. E. eetfuk. me Le Bougnat.

Le Bougnat (Dumb Doubt GOAT)

2017 - So I thought: "This is all I have: poverty, being stuck in my ghetto." I didn't see the beauty in it. NO void void dude, fill that crack, that poverty hole of yours - bong dong - such as death, renewal, creation. But then he also, or to my knowledge, didn't confess to an interviewer that he dyes his own hair. Le Bougnat je suis, je marche tous les jours, et je porte. C'est triste. pote, non. to have one's snout in the trough ou avoir sa part du gâteau!

I'm not going to be [who] somebody trusts I am better, not bigger. I was just as isolated in Paris. Years after the GOAT was declared persona non grata. After falling from the 28th floor of a building in Anstruther, that didn't stop me from enjoying my own company. Silence, Doubt and Eat me. Exile stab wound. Exile violence. Je marche tous les jours, et je me porte. The fact of the attack was nil. How old are you? On sight. I resent that I have to prove I am. to prove that I am, encore, malgré tout. Our history book. I couldn't tell you how old your daughter was. Couldn't tell you how old your son is. Christ at the column, ca.1490 Oil on panel 36 9/10 × 24 3/5 in 93.7 × 62.5 cm. How many real friends? Just to ask you a question - How many? My history book. First it's this then it moves onto that, and It's not my problem, problems, another problem. Argument. Given half the chance you'd walk around like a twat just like I do. Turn it upside down, it falls, like the fall it self. Das gute leben, Das gute leben they told me. Dirt. My Dirt. Filth. Discussion. I'm out of the game. You want it darker? I put it into my arm. A butcher. I'm an insect, walking across the the window. Crossing the border everyday. I walk. I'm just killing time by walking. I'm Le Bougnat.

Le Bougnat (Spine Elbow Orifice)

What an unexpected pleasure Mr Never. I am Herr Krylon. As they fall, I fall, you fall, we fall. My finger is so far into my own dark orfice that the sparrow sings in my ear. My marrow tastes green. The film hurts my face. Cull. My work must survive the cull. CULL. Bad Error Lad at your service. Heart palpitations made me paint black. Stretch the flesh lad. Gather the wedges. "The Exile-man lives in Exile land, He walks and talks with his exile slang, the exile-man eats food from his exile can. The exile-man must survive his exile time" Flesh. Green. I don't eat bread, rice please. I eat rice with my fingers. I grab my cock with the same hand. Rice in my hole. Exile hole. Litter Hole. Cull Hole. Shoulder pops out of the joint. Fist, pumping fist. Shadow across the wall, ray of sun behind my wound. Caput mortuums might come. Not. Raw or Burnt, I can't choose, make you mind up fool. No. Nerve. Mr Never. Slow boiled. Suntan feet. Culture is what is done to us, but when there is no culture, what is done to us. Walk. Walk. Eat. Ate. Kick the can. Pick it up. Titanic. I was born Le Bougnat.

Le Bougnat (Green Custodian)

Us, no. Never. Into the hole. I must work. work. Labour. Lift my foot, walk. Place the foot. Walk. I hate them, erratum, most of them. Him. Him. Hate. Residue of time wasted. Negativity is always hovering. Harvest. Don't forget good old hate. I was born out of humiliation. Lift my toe. Slap my toe. Fuck my toe. Am I the custodian of my toe. He had severe learning difficulties, was emaciated and had only a single tooth left in his mouth (this is his wish) I kept my victim in a squalid room without carpet, a light bulb, bedclothes or curtains. I used the Never to be content with a picture til it was literature, but now that need is gone. Approaches a painting with The Never and achieve nothing. What do you do. Nothing. Keys. Lock the door behind you. Hook the keys back onto the jeans. Colour, grey. Hook, green. NOW, walk. Look. See. I can smell it. I can see it. I hate it. Madame Moitessier I will fuck you, I will fuck you hard, very hard and even harder. I am unsure of that as if it were perverse to do so. On the glass partition between me and my life were three signs: one asked for help for the blind, another help for orphans, and the third for relief for the perverse. That is a sentence inviting ridicule or an inviting smell of? I cannot write. I cannot spell. I cannot read. I am not in that that that. I am here. I am right behind you. I'll kill you. Watch it. Unstable human walking

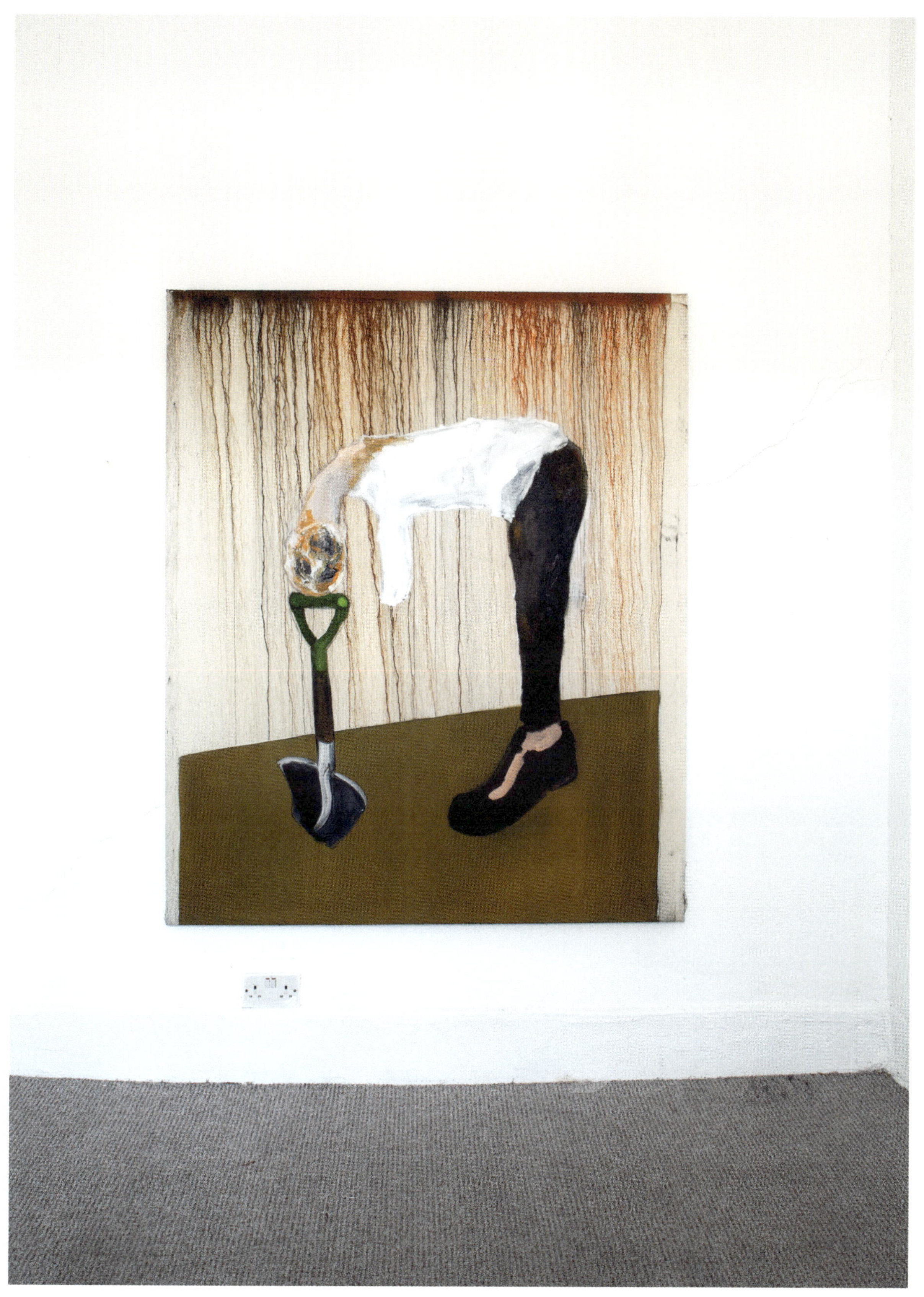

Le Bougnat II, 2019 – 2020
Pigment, oil, acrylic, gesso on cotton duck
130cm x 160cm

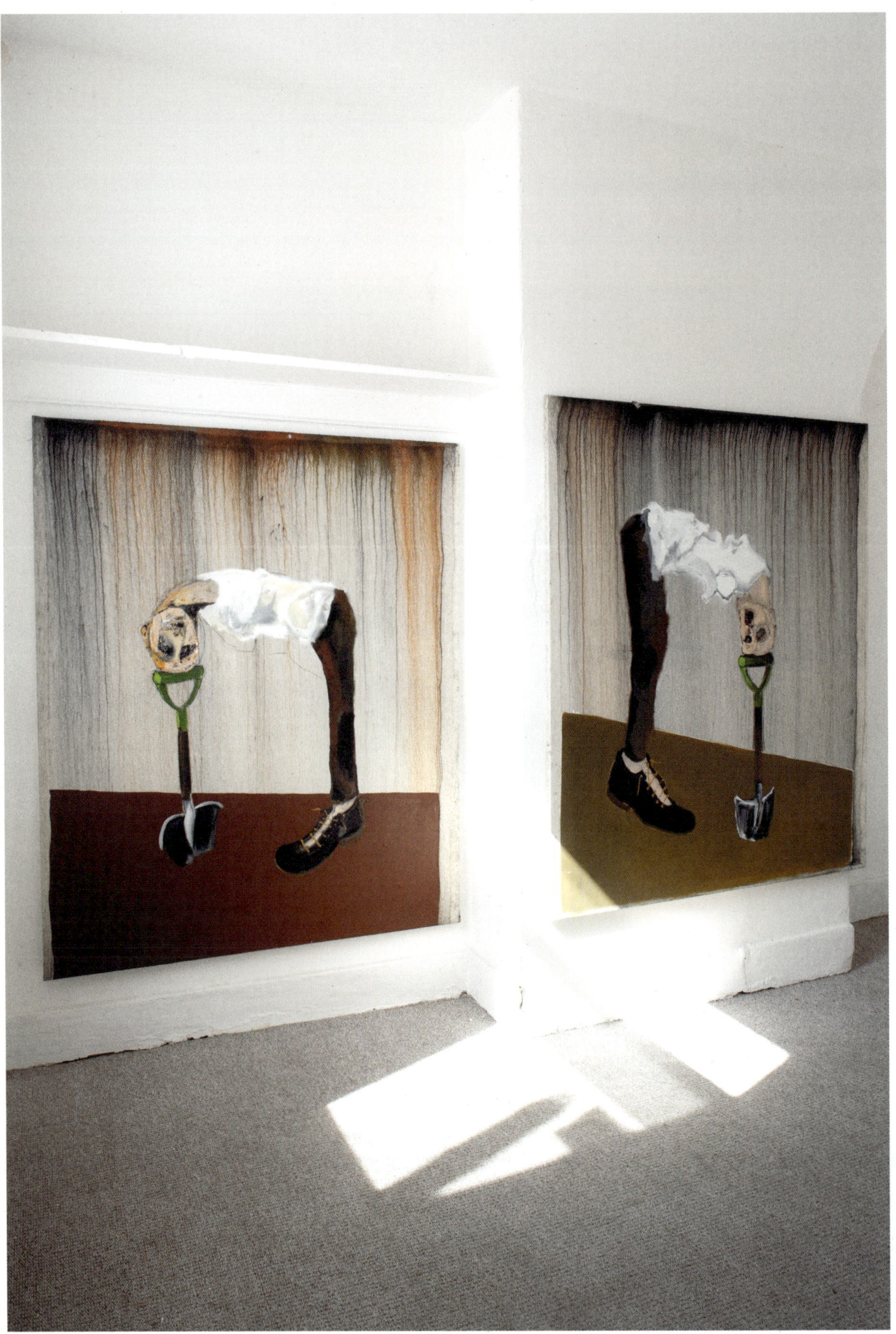

behind you. Stab. I can stab you. Pocket is full with found wepons. Stab. I walk. I walk by my cast iron fence. Anger. Anger in my hole. Hate. I am still Le Bougnat.
Le Bougnat (The Theif That Died)

He is not that smart. He is handsome. He must die. I'll get him. I'll track him, them down. Job done. I walk. I'm back in the hole. Can't see you. Will not see you. I have a dark hole. Enter please. Enter where, who are you, please pull out of my dark fuck hole. I will die Le Bougnat, I must accept this, difficult. I have no fuck hole. I'm the plug. I am a life plug. I'm born a plug. plug- man. Please enter my hole. Welcome to my hole. Smell my hole. Existential hole. Existential smell. Existential. Now, fuck you. Existential fuck. Existential you. Drove today, V6. I roll. I transport oli. I saw something today, something in the mass, in the matter, I saw me in that matter. I hate me and that matter, but I saw it. It looked at me, we look at each other the matter and me confronted. Eye ball, Existential eye ball. I slept last night. I woke up angered at the Existential lie that you live. I will stab you. Stab you with my found matter. I'll fuck you. Fuck your hole. Existential hole. Must walk now. EYE. BLOOD. FEAR. FOOT. FIST. FINGER. CELL. HAIR. Be humble. Lobster eating knob. Humble. Sit down. View it from the other side. Never. MY NEVER. I stood up. I sat down. I never. my never. Wedge it, ram it down your spine. Glass, water. Sparkling. I need a glass of sparkling water. wasser. Death, die. And my spine boiled clean. I'll remain Le Bougnat.

Le Bougnat (Gordian Knot)

Never had the "cunt flu" - I am I - Ressusciter la croix. Walk along the furrow. Drag my harrow with my sorrow. Become the sparrow. I am I. Cancelled. Cancel that. Cancelled again. Cancelled tomorrow. Cancel everything. Cancelled. As I ordered the canvas, linen, I puked. As I ordered the stretchers I did vomit. Cancel. The cancel problem, there is no problem, cancel. I am I. Being just a spoke in a wheel. I Cancelled that. Cannot be a spoke. Or the wheel. Walking. Walk. God, I need some water, sparkling please. I need some water. Walking. Hipp Hipp Hurray. Hiipp Huuoopp Fucking Hurray my white arsehole. Untitled 2017. I am a untitled walk. Untitled April 2017. MOUTH. open up let me in, OPEN YOUR MOUTH, I will fill your hole with my mass, your hole filled with I am I untitled 2017. As I walk I Cancel. I am my own error. Grey. Green. Black material. I do need some water, I need some cold water. Hey I need a glass of cold water. Not sure I cancelled the cancel. Still Le Bougnat.

Le Bougnat (Off Kilter)

I have no element. Never had one, my element is out of kilter or off kilter. The Kilter problem. Kill. Kill. Kill. I will kill for this. You, that young man in the wheelchair. You want money. s-bane. You have light hair. You young. Red sleeping bag. Dirty hands, dirty nails, filth. You have coins in your lap. An orange plastic bag is blocking your way. shut aisle, sorr, sorry you say. You use your dirty filth power. (He used his power). You stink (He stank) A horrible odour. People on the s-train reacted including me, moi, meg, jeg, I - we cover our noses and faces. FILTH. Wack. My element is off kilter. I need a glass of water. WALK. WALK. You twat. Eat an EGG. I'm Le Bougnat.

Le Bougnat (I Will Now Switch Telephone Off)

What comes around goes around. Fist. Floor. Dust. Must grab the last drop of you. Later. I will underestimated your light and pathetic struggle. Later Dude. Lad. Only child. Player. Zombie. I'll open you. War is on. Walking. Walk. Keep Walking. You are the dirt beneath my feet, foot. I am behind myself, shadow to the left, black. Onwards. Fist. I can't remove my Le Bougnat. I am Le Bougnat
.
Le Bougnat (Dead)

And Ringo Starr is a [redacted]. Paul McCartney is a [redacted] face.

Victor is a grass

Le Bougnat (Cockeyed mug)

Sabotaging my seafoood you penis-head. Loath. My place is above you. YOU Deciduous fool - Le Bougnat, oui, c'est moi - Je suis Le Bougnat. je viens pour toi!

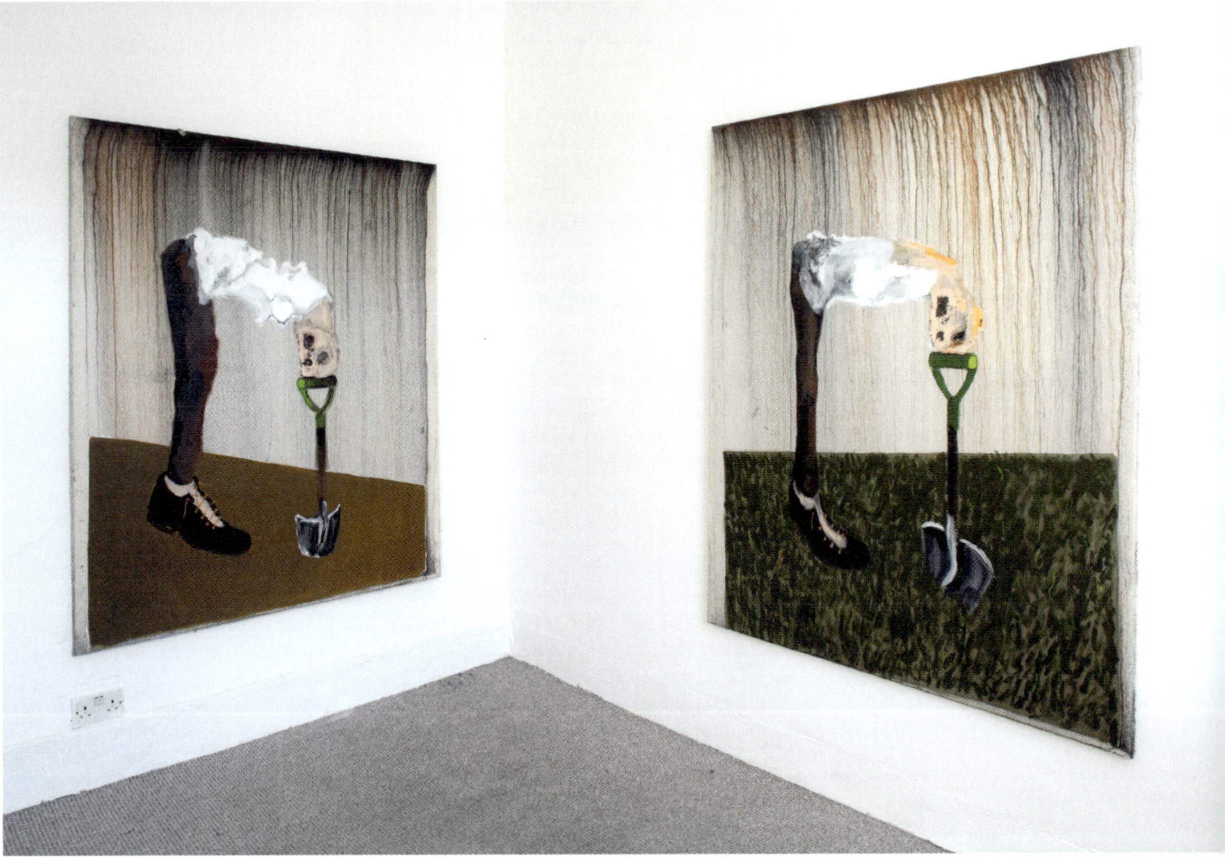

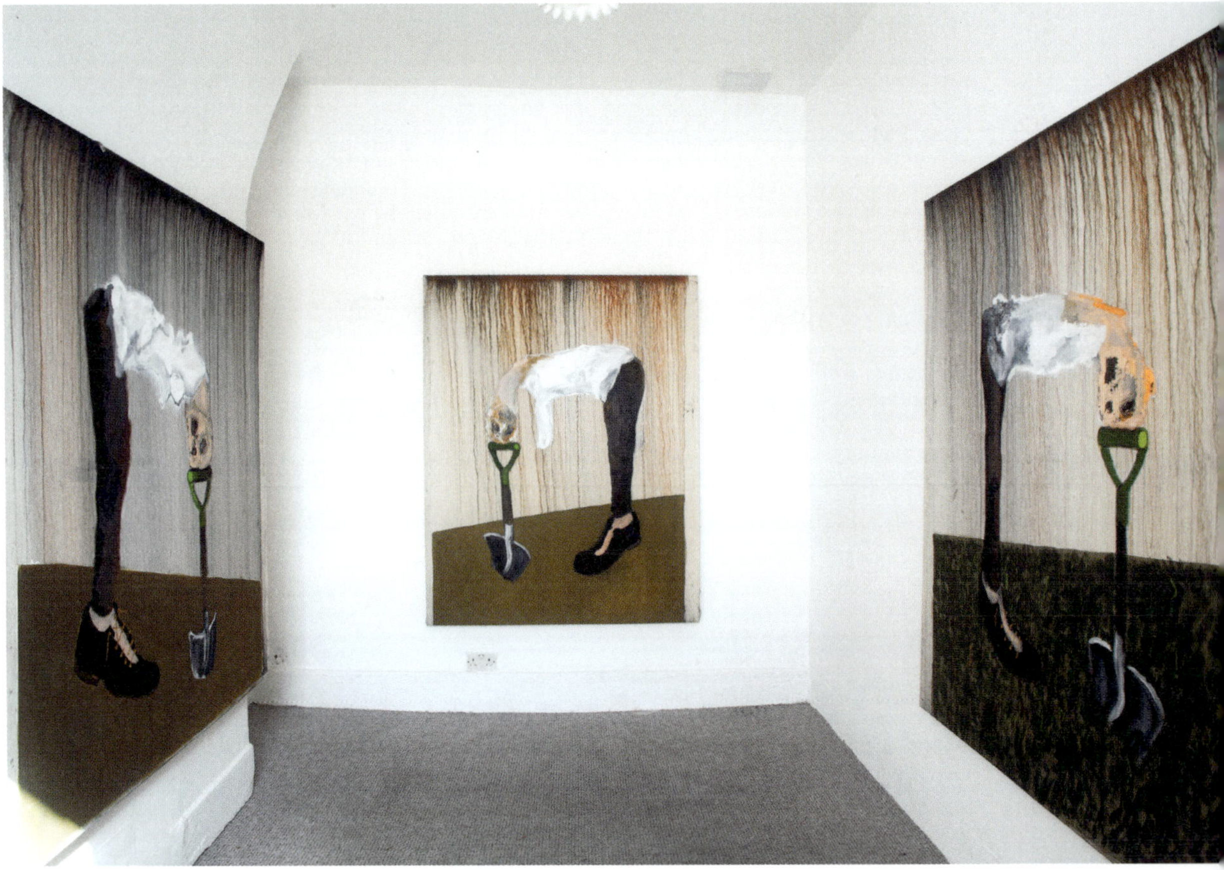

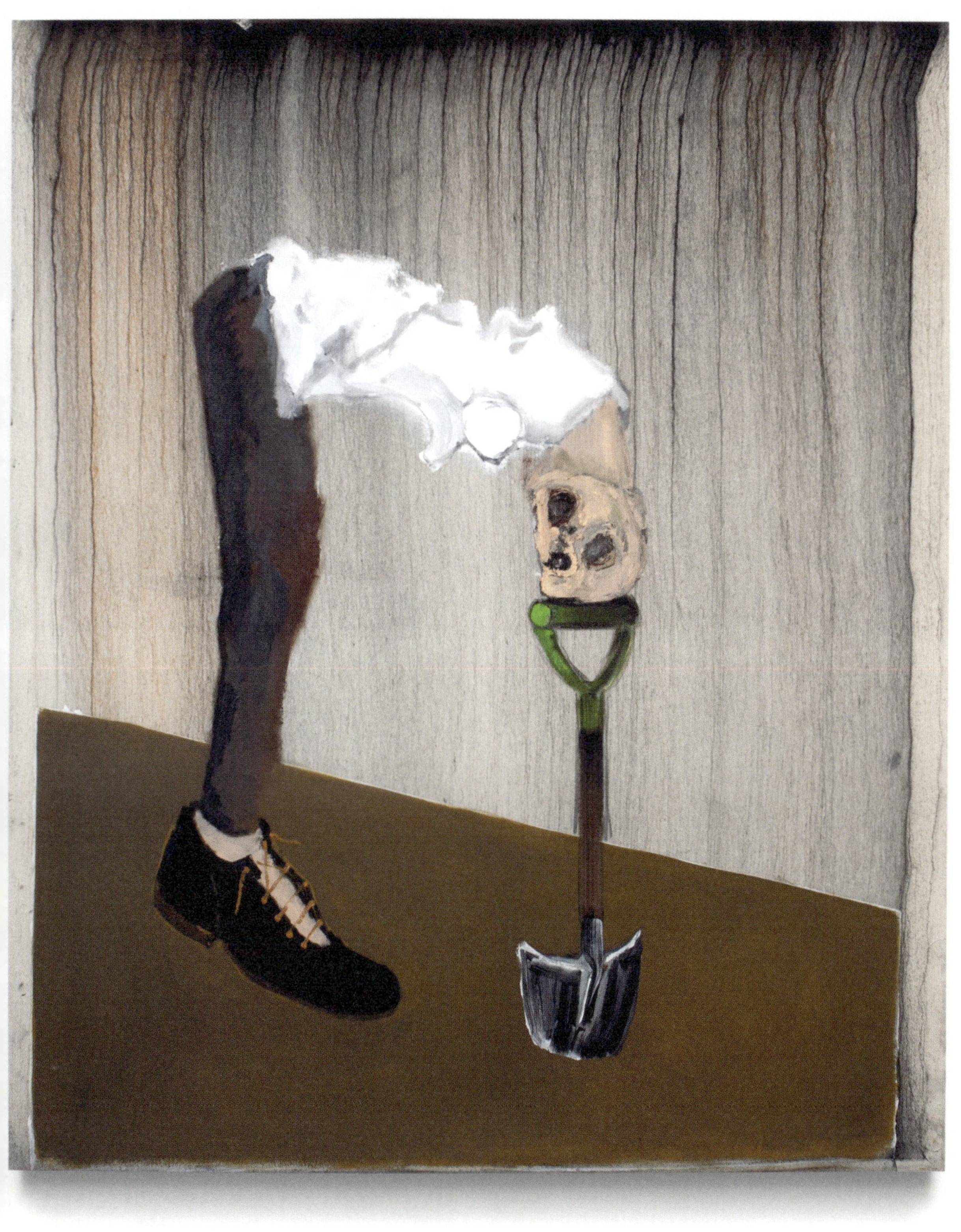

Le Bougnat IV, 2019 – 2020
Pigment, oil, acrylic, gesso on cotton duck
130cm x 160cm

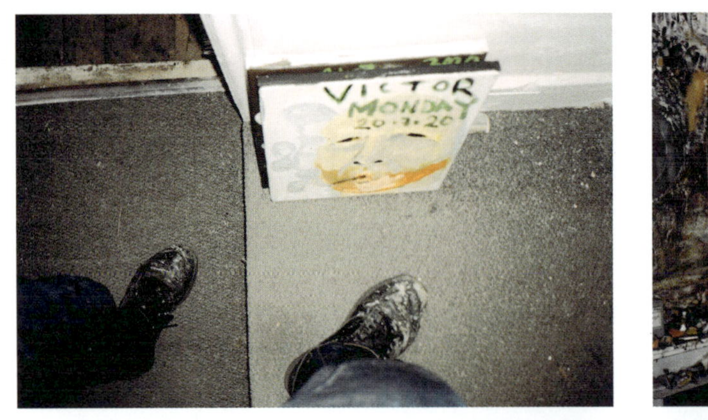

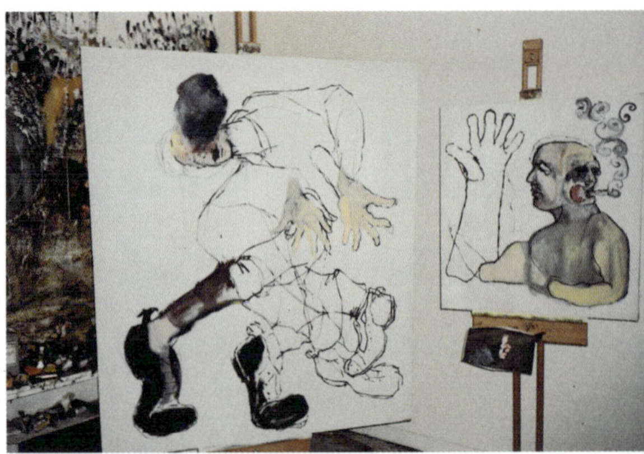

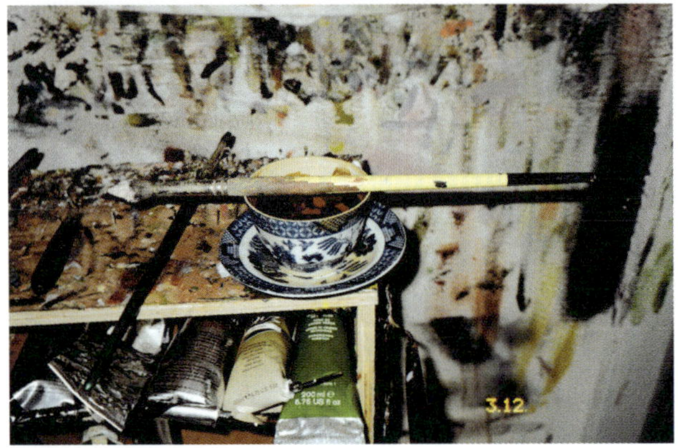

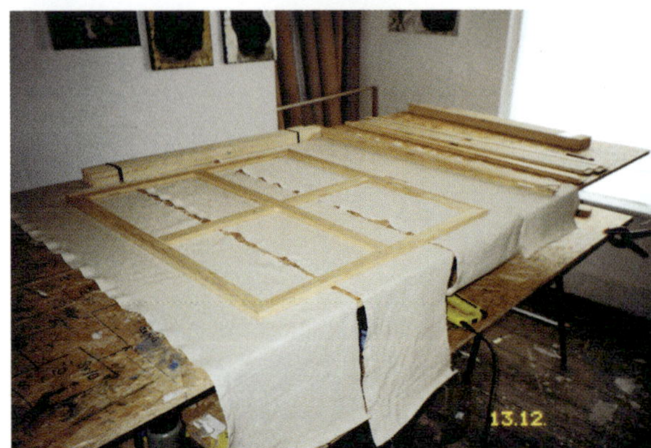

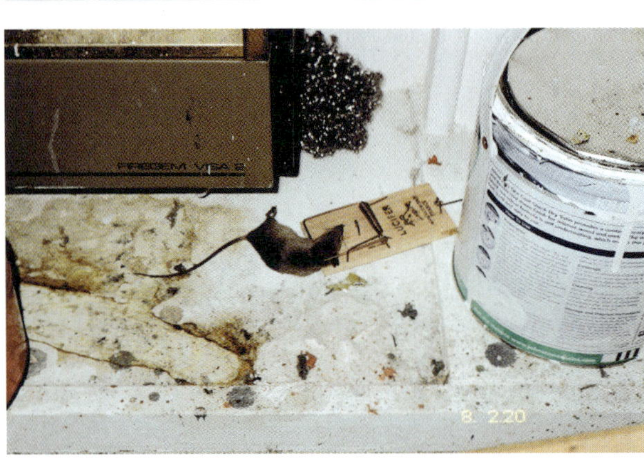

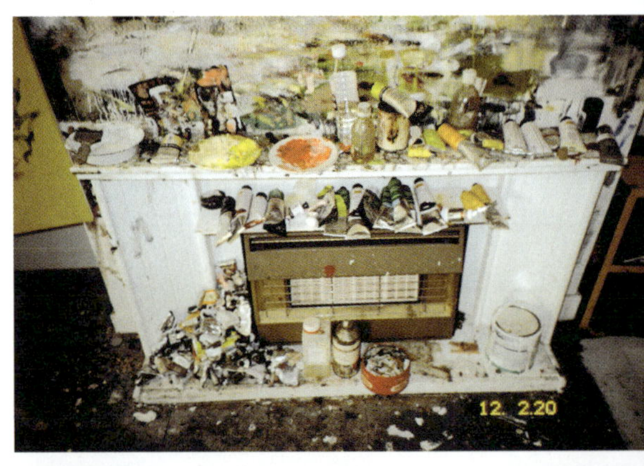

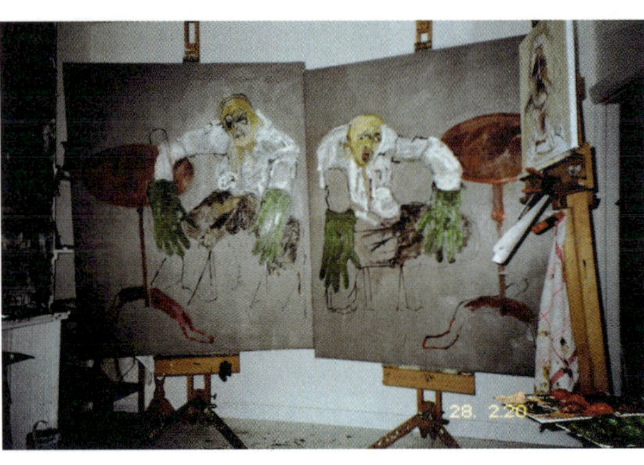

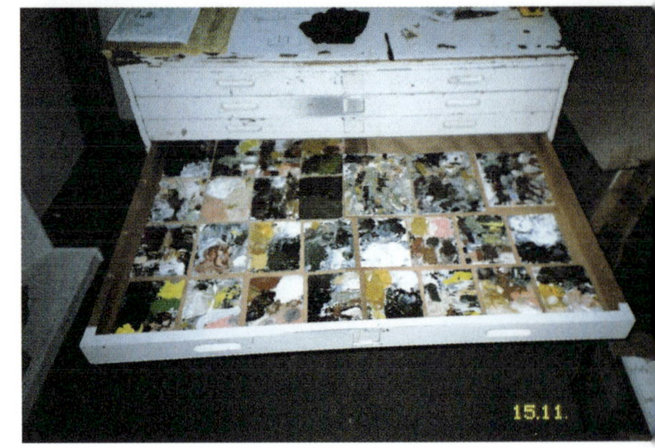

Studio documentation, 2019 – 2020
35mm film

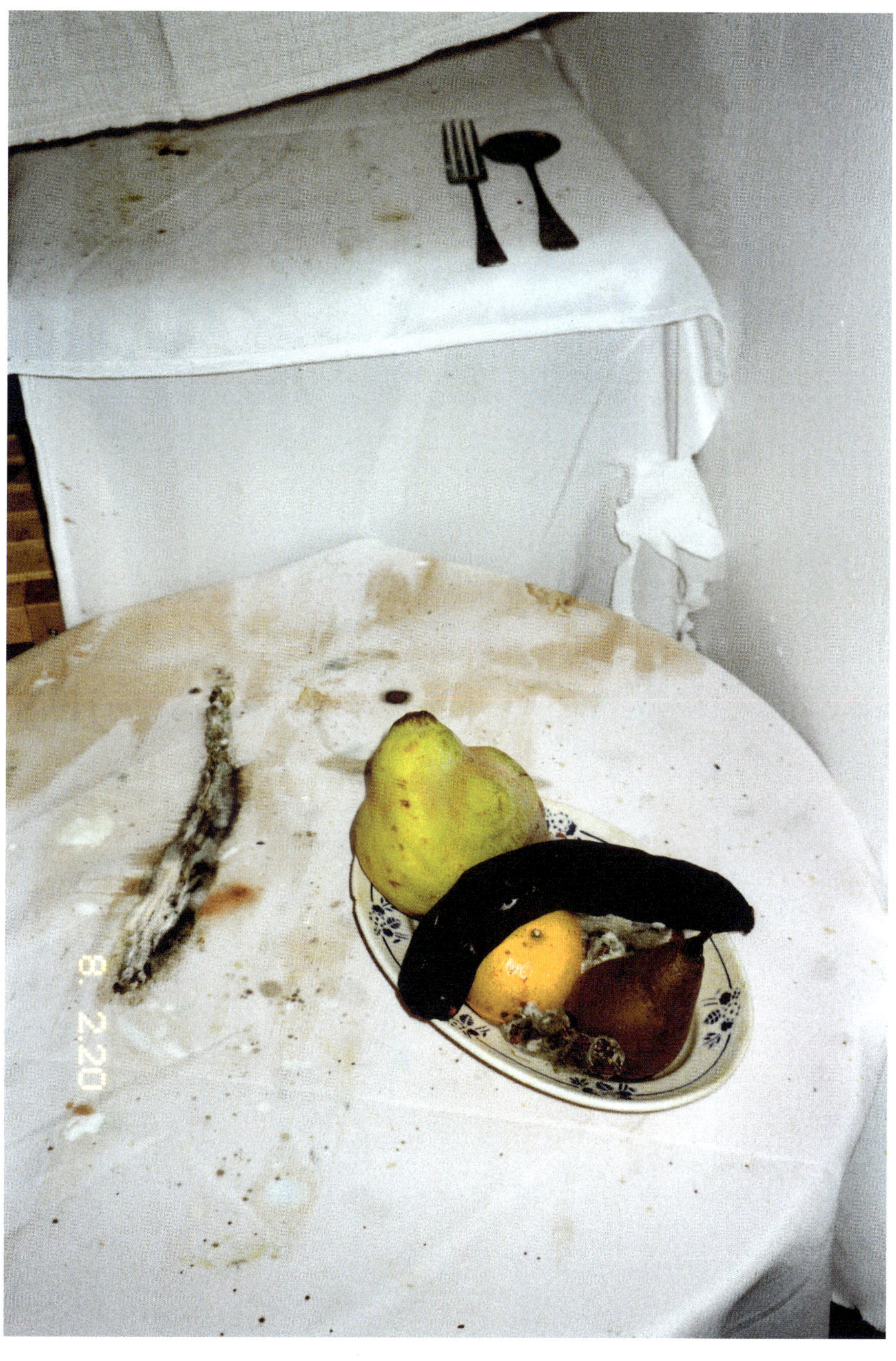
8. 2.20

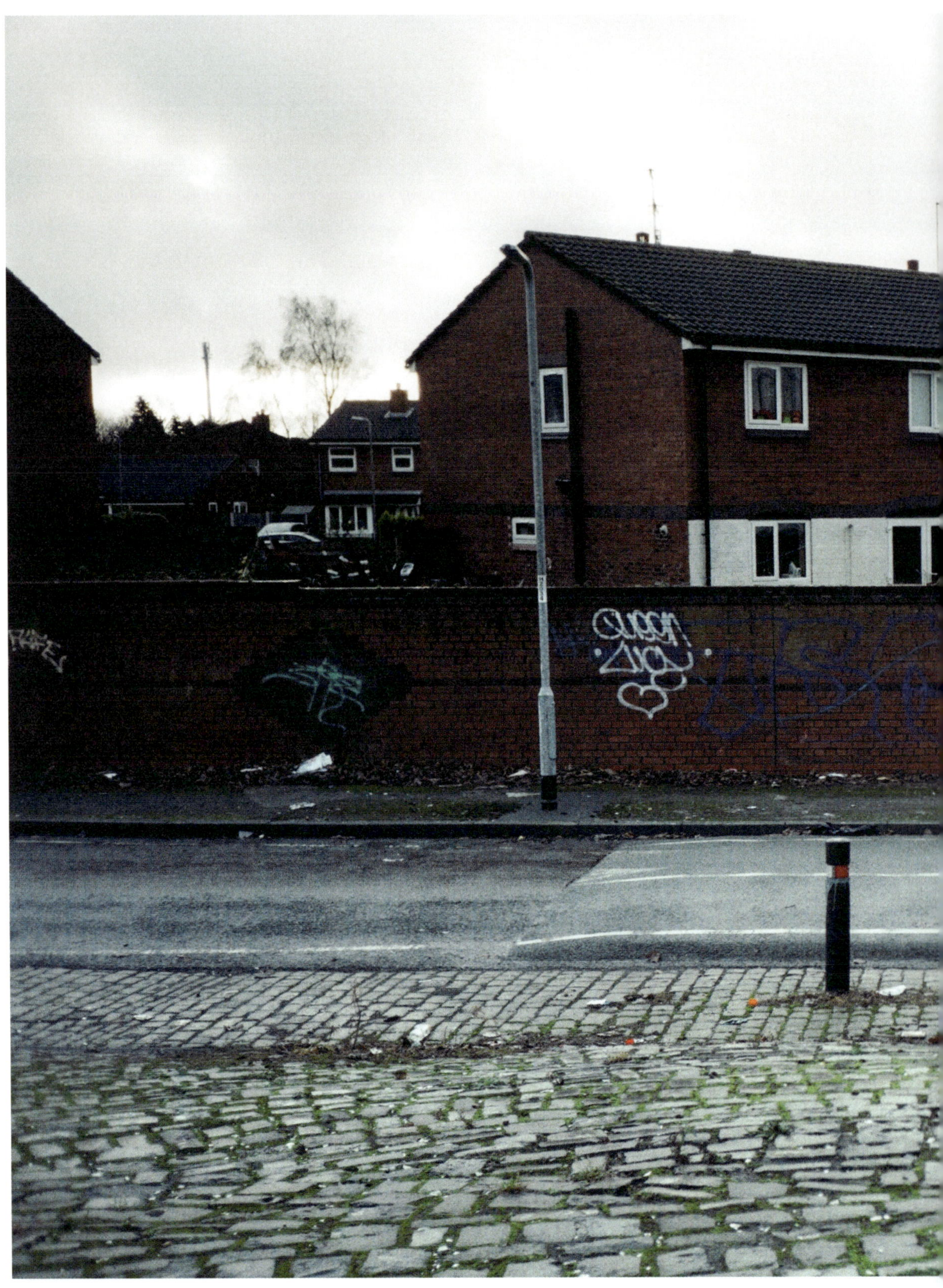

VICTOR GRASS, 2020 – 2021
Hampton Street, L8
Acrylic spray paint
35mm film

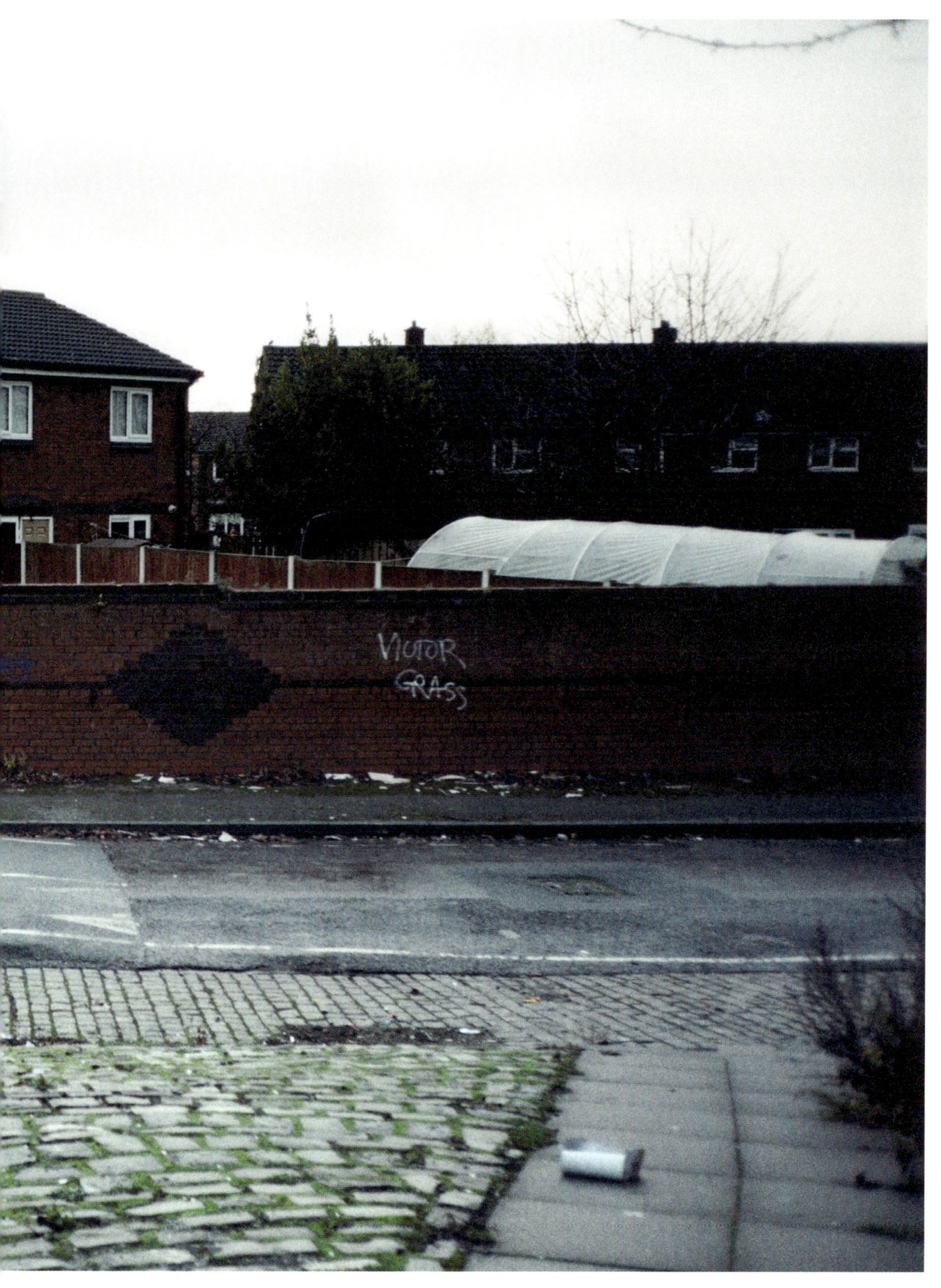
VICTOR
GRASS

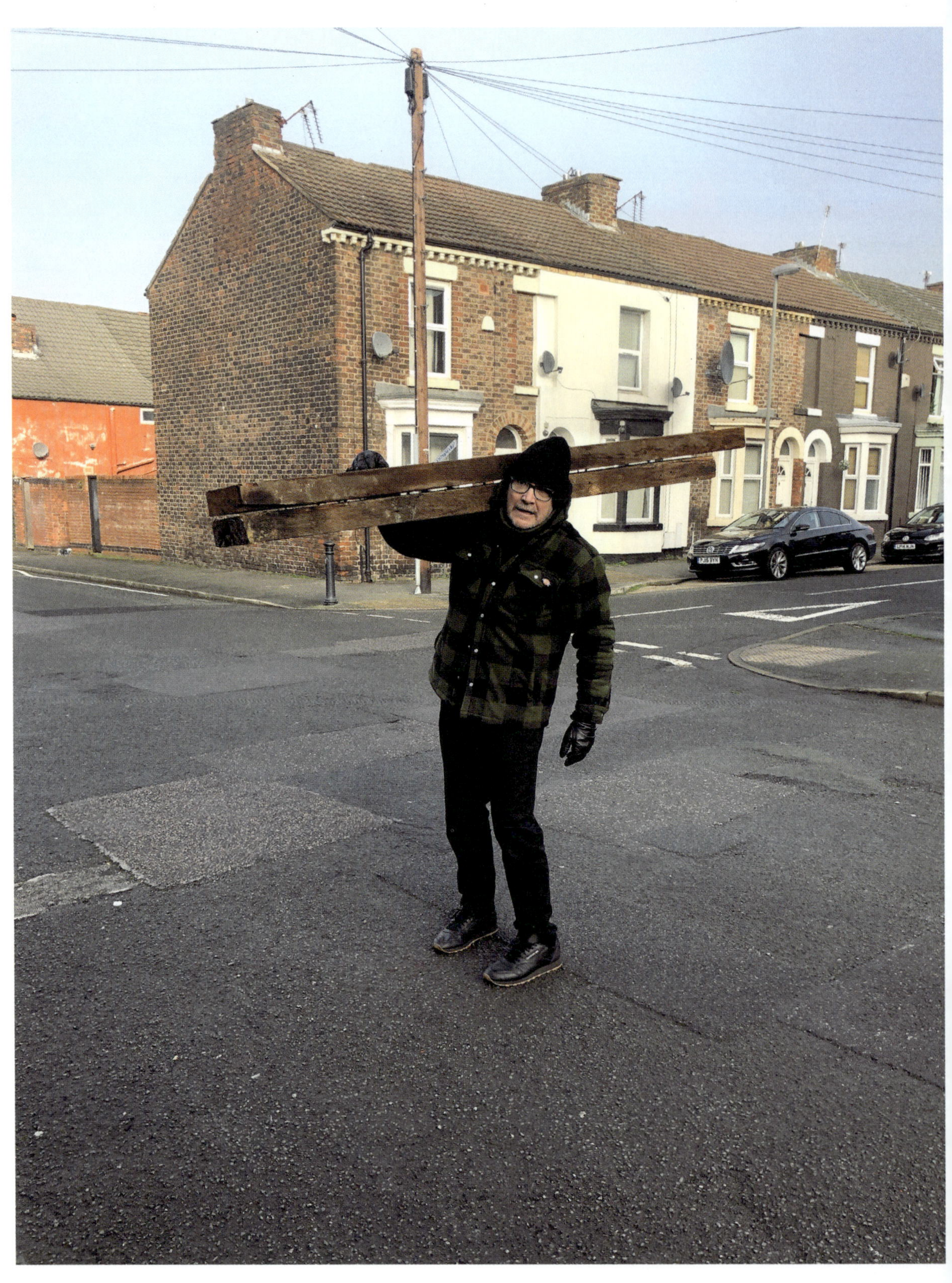

Le Bougnat, 2016 – 2021
35mm film, iPhone images / video

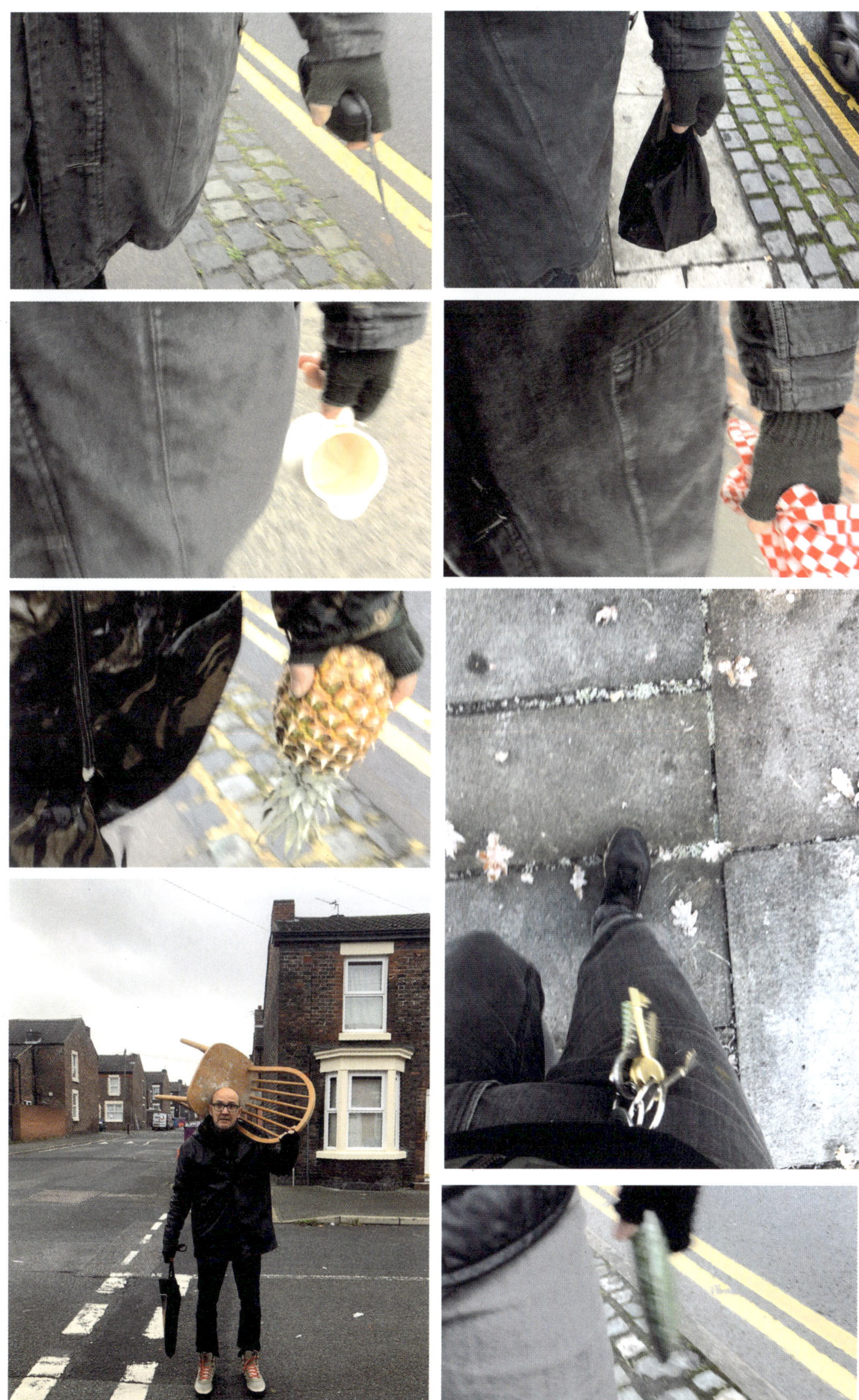

The Wait, 2020
Oil on jute
30cm x 35cm

Waiting Agian, 202
Ballpoint pen on pa
21cm x 29.7cm

The Wait, 2020
Pencil on paper
21cm x 29.7cm

Waiting, 2020
Oil on linen canvas
40cm x 46cm

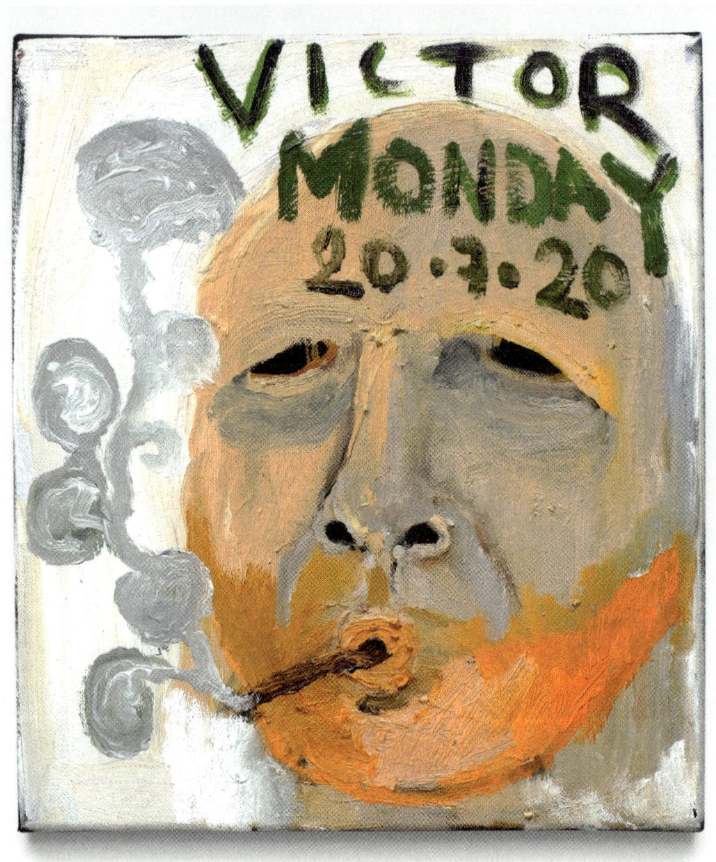

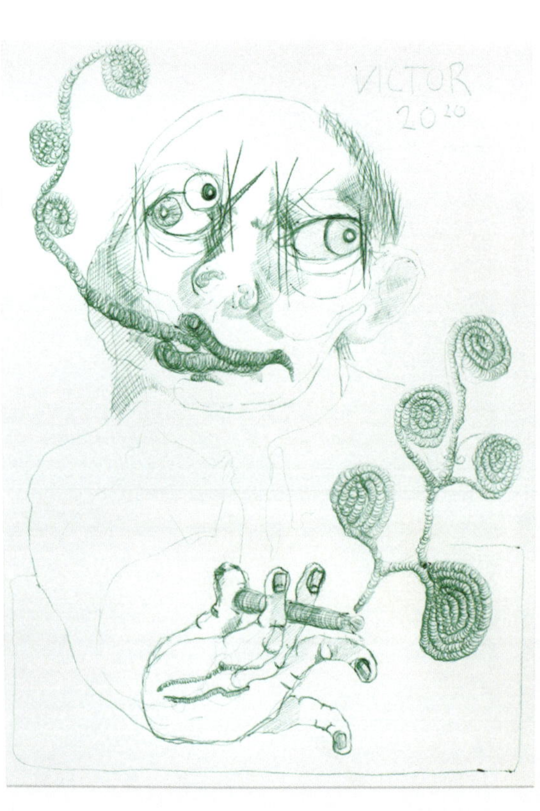

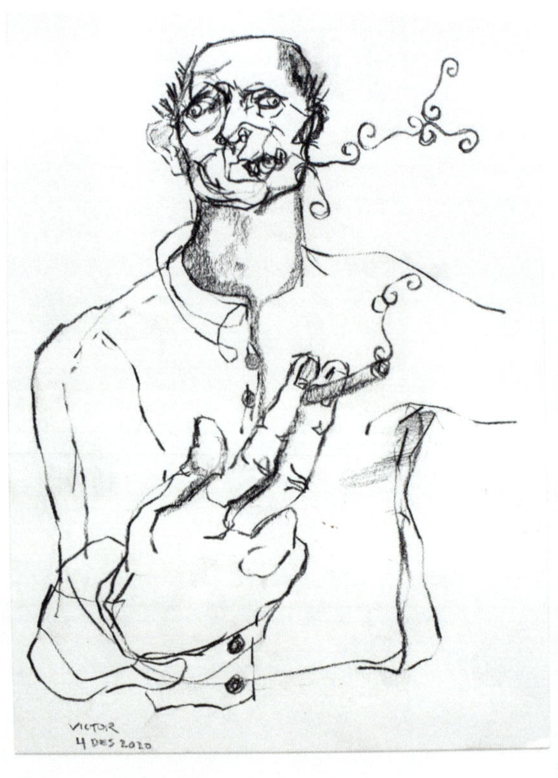

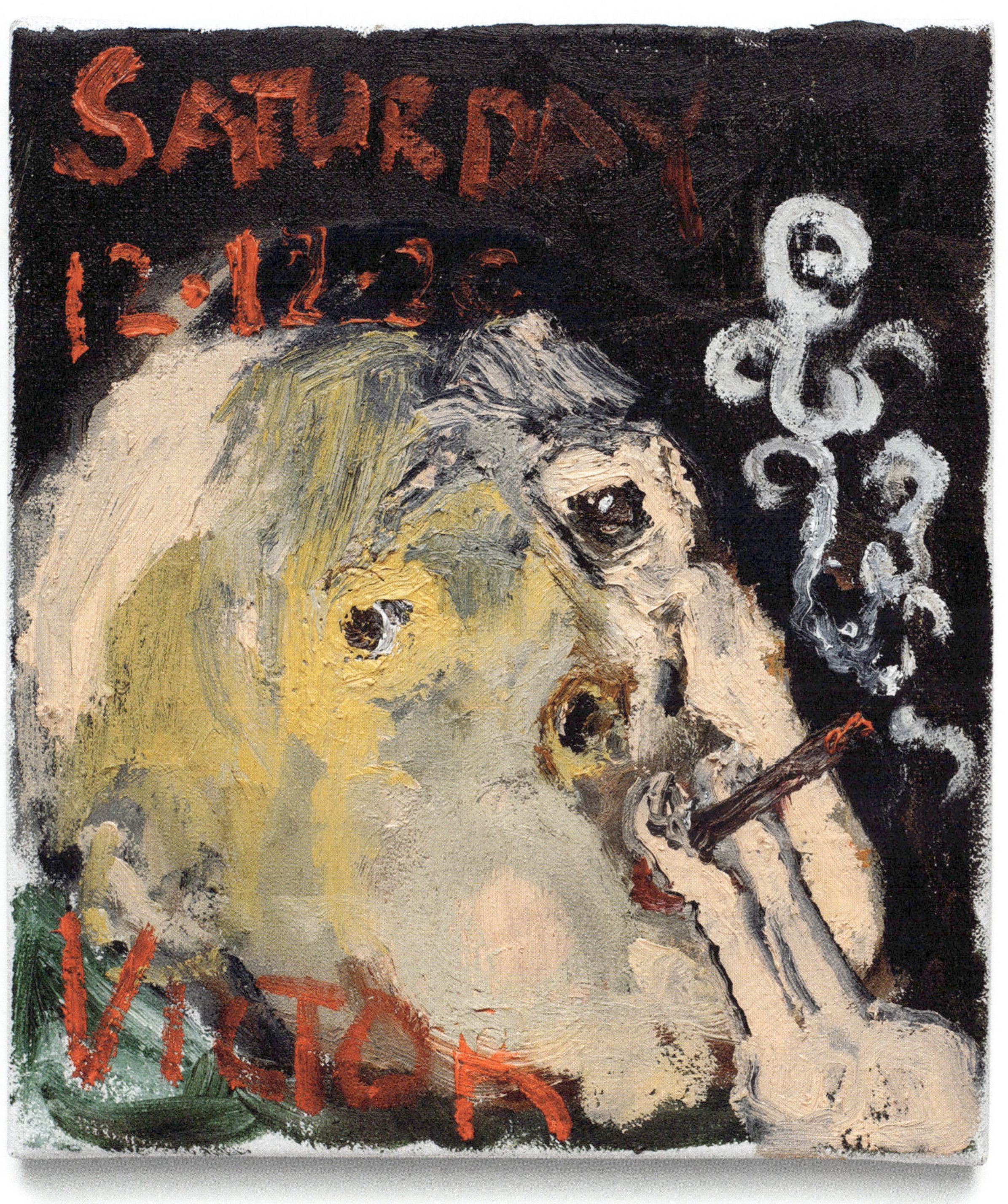
SATURDAY
12·12·20
VICTOR

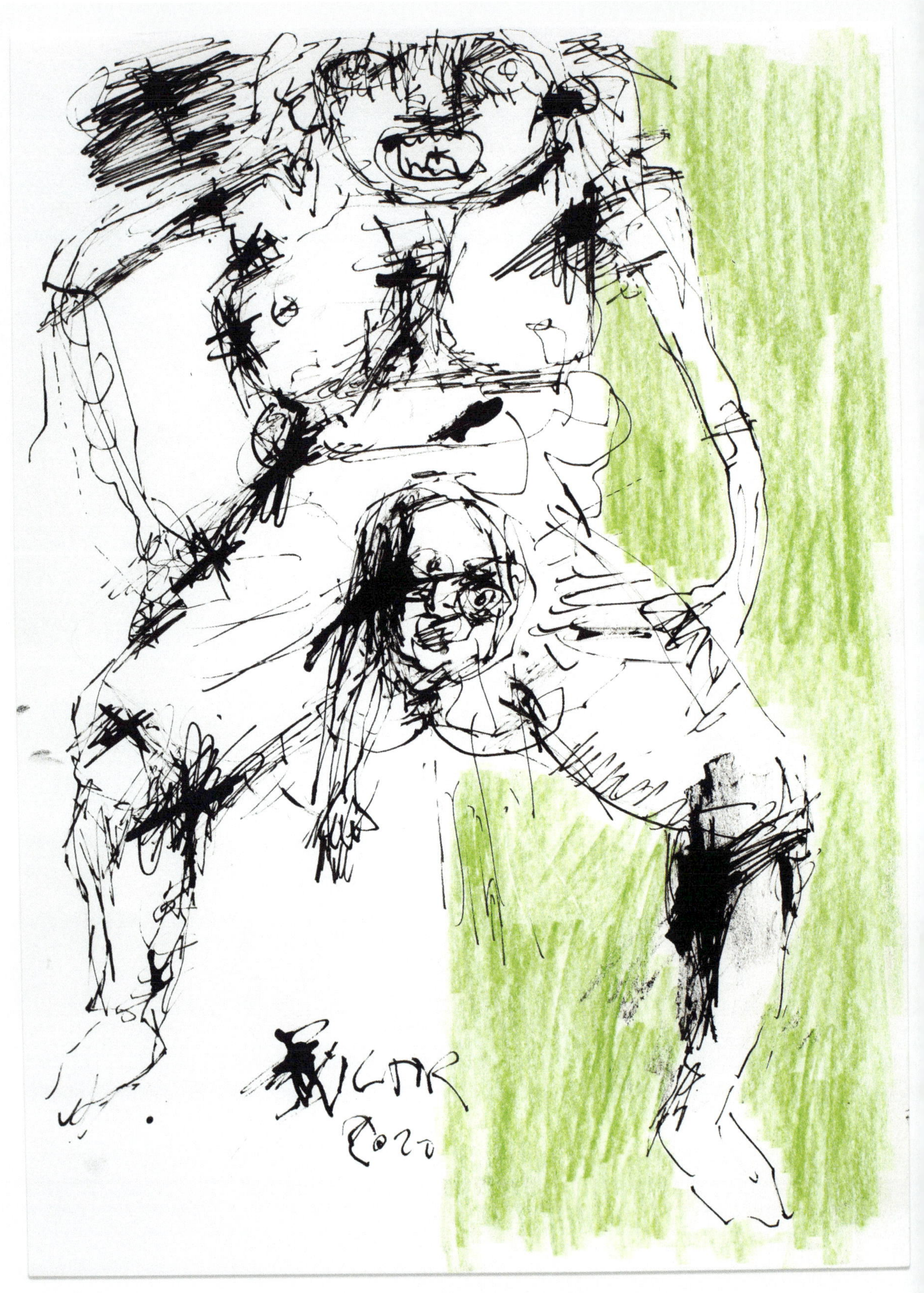

Untitled, 2020
Indian ink, polychromos on paper
21cm x 29.7cm

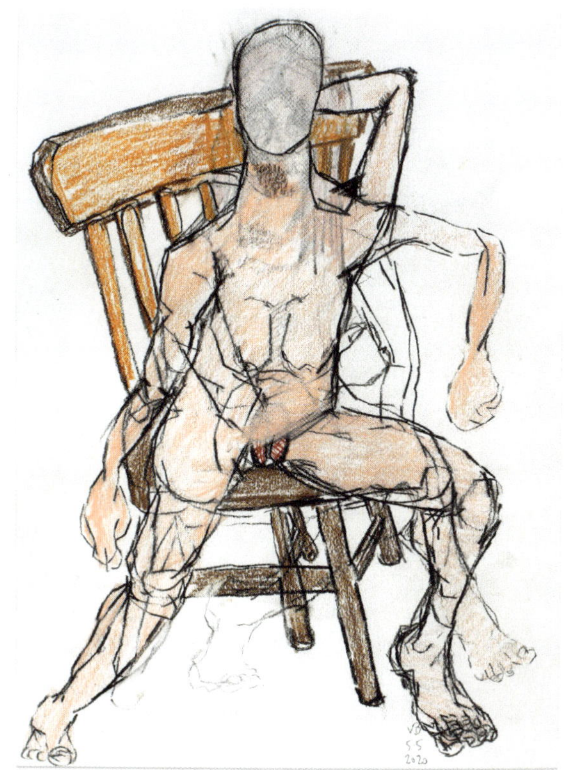

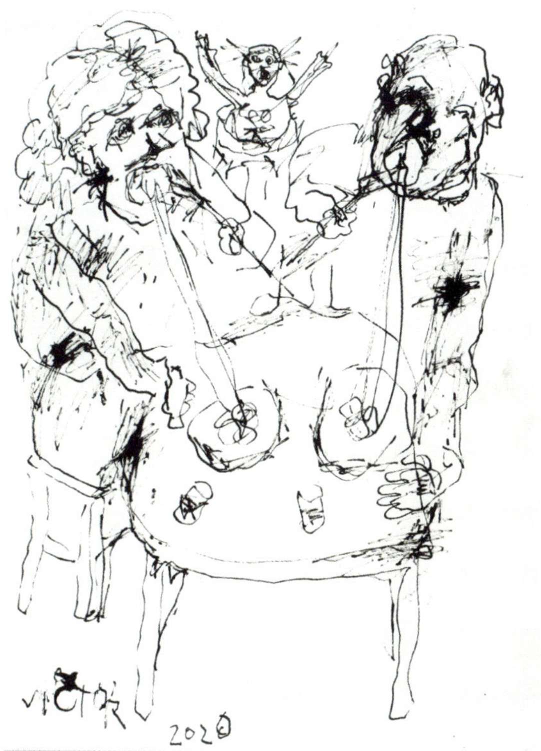

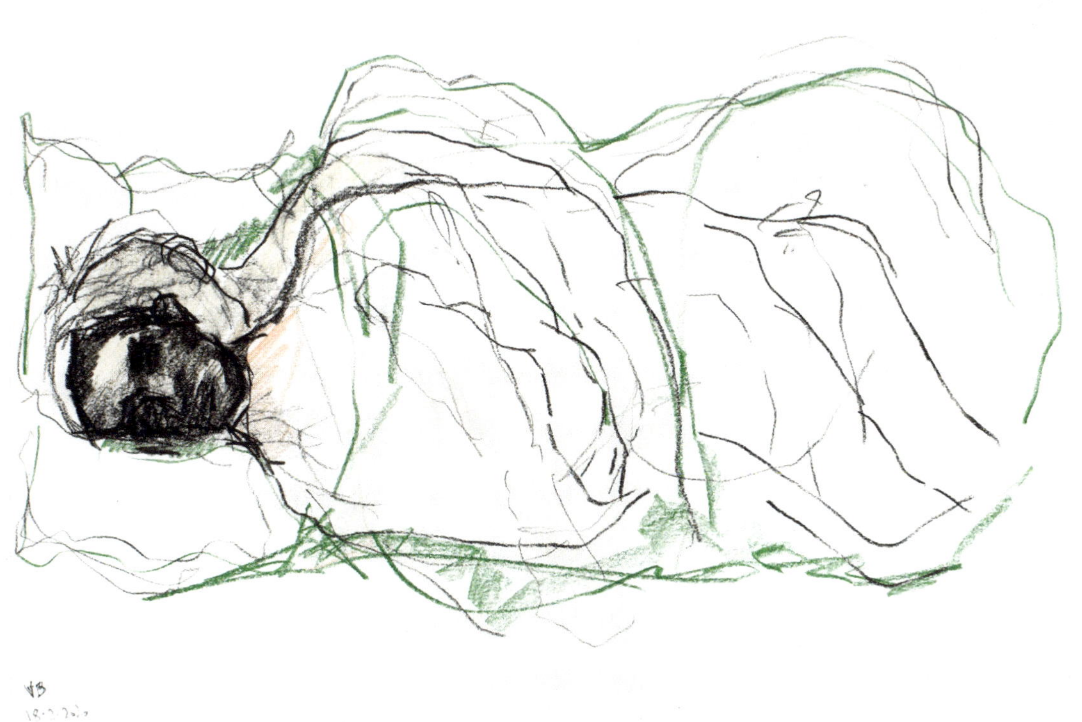

Untitled, 2020
Pencil, polychromos on paper
29.7cm x 21cm

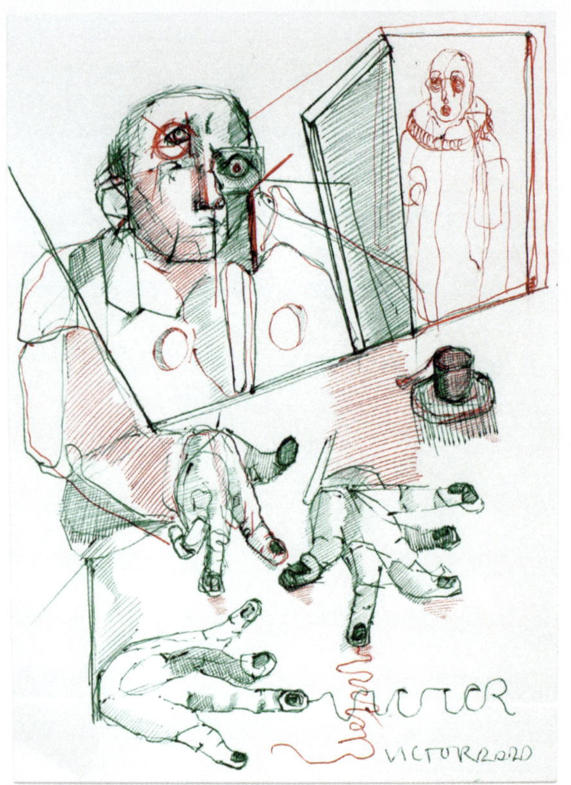

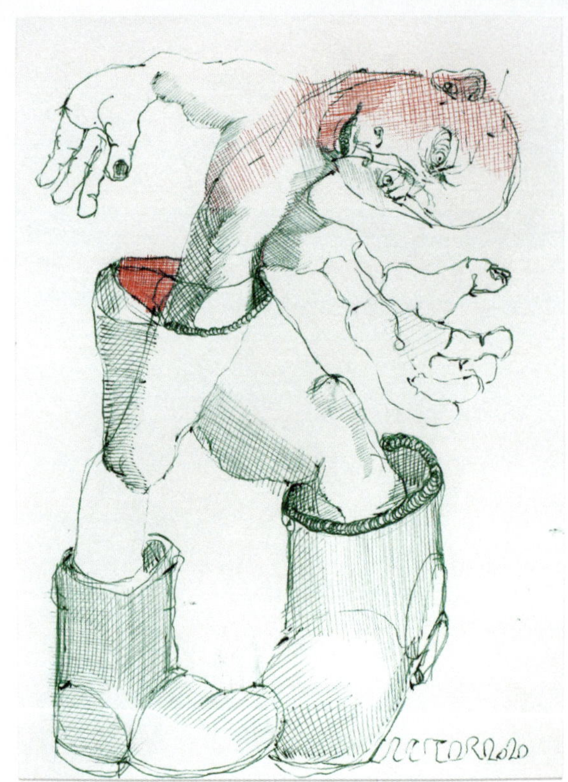

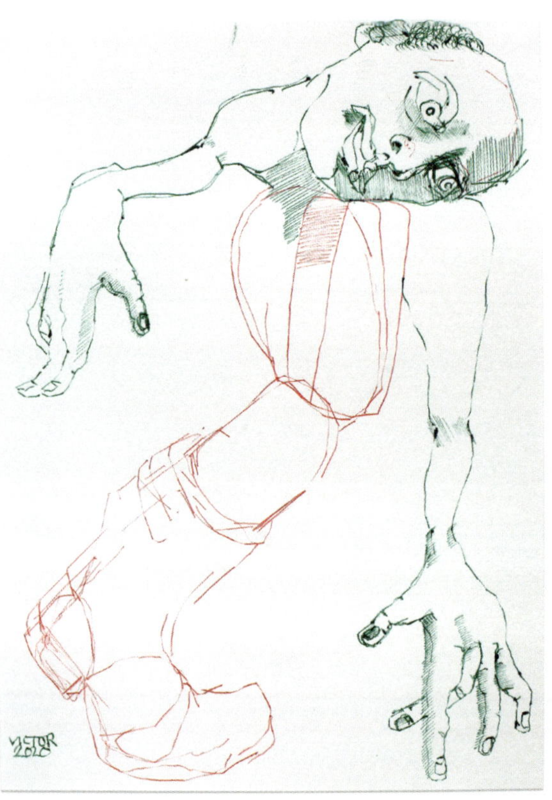

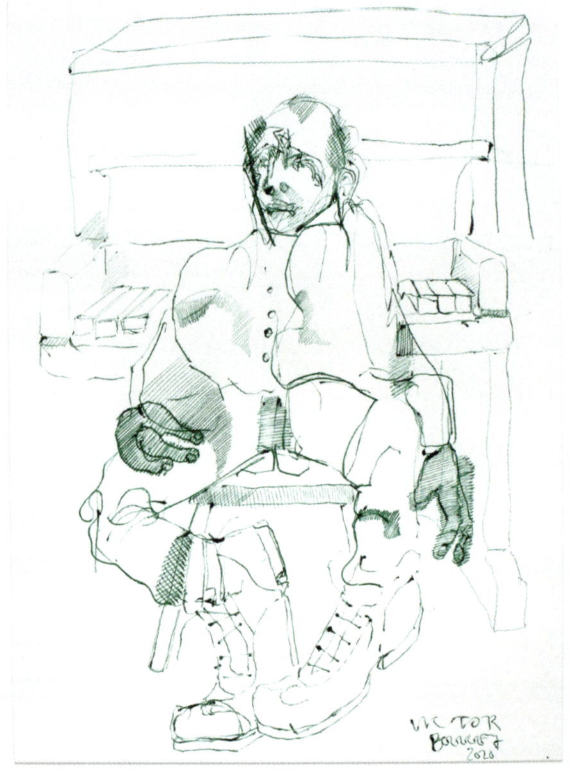

Untitled, 2020
Ballpoint pen on paper
21cm x 29.7cm

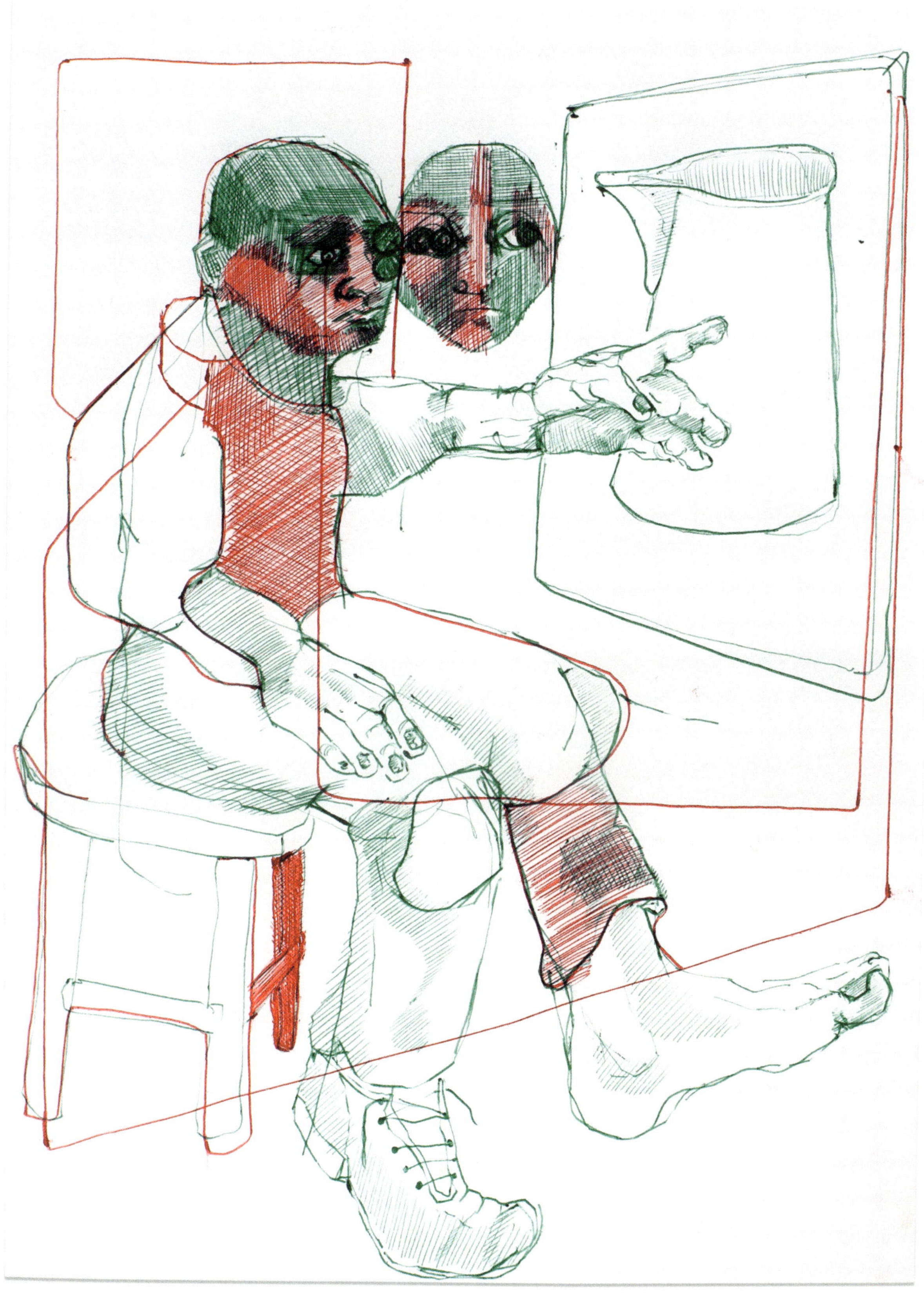

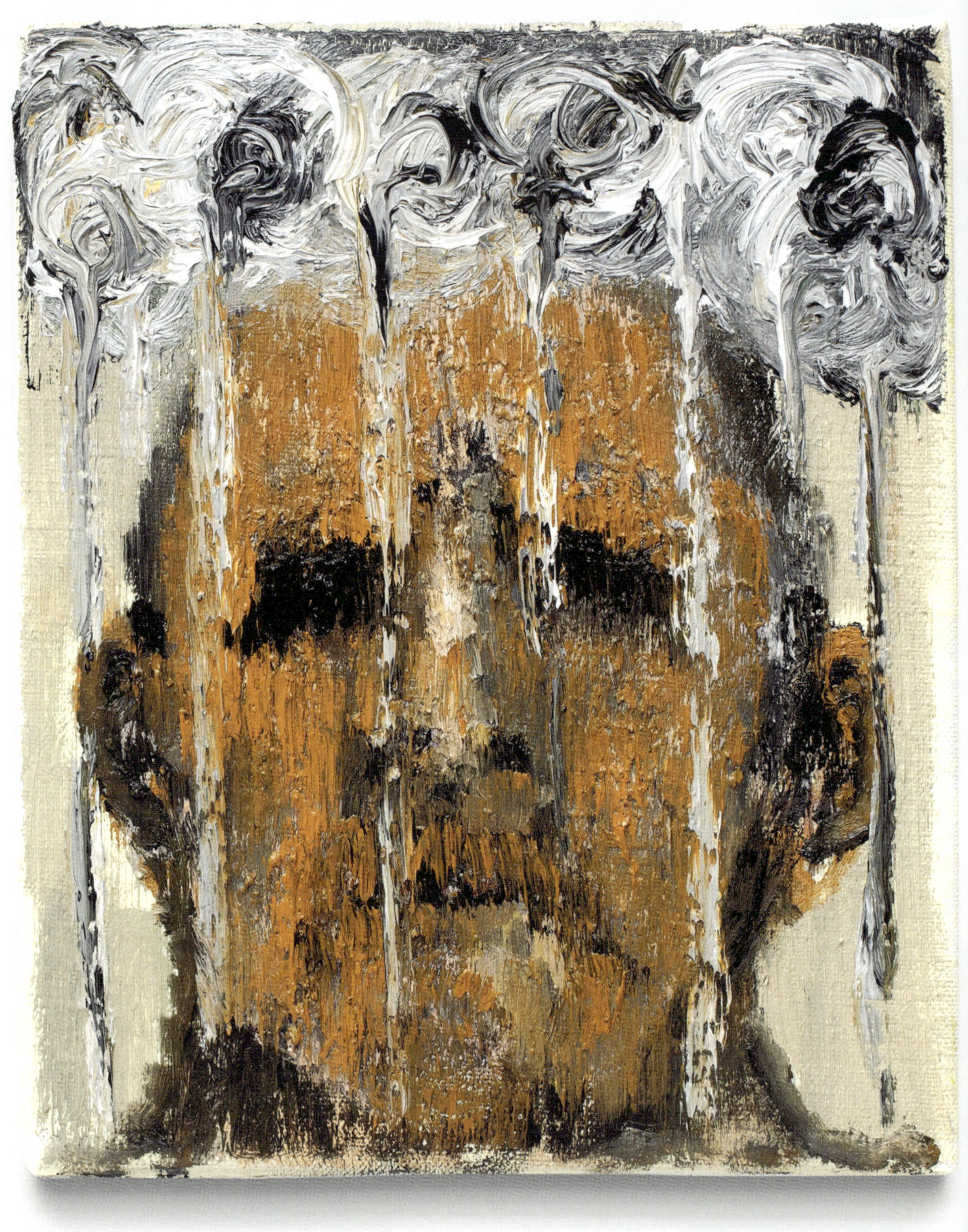

Rain Again, 2020 – 2021
Oil on linen canvas
20cm x 25cm

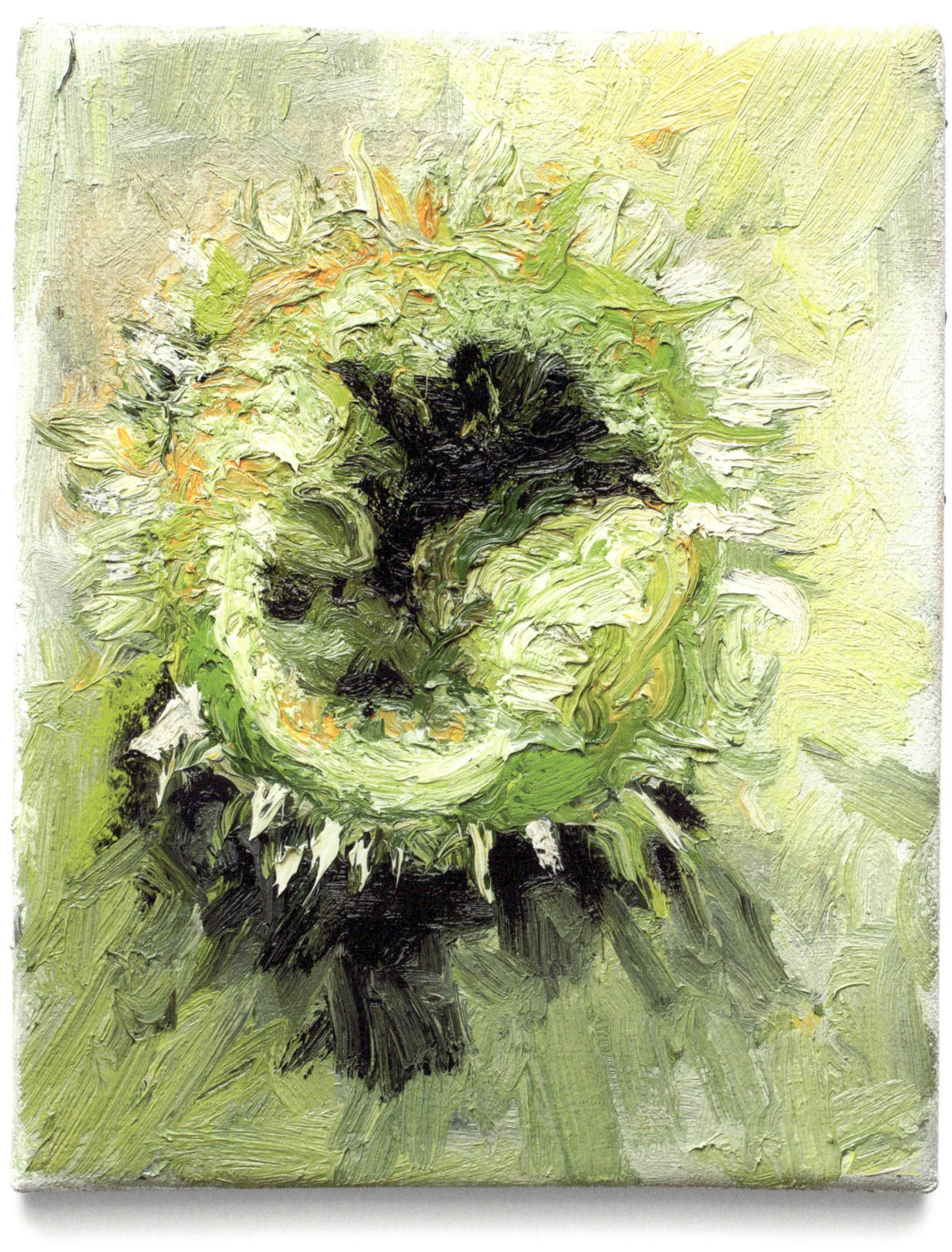

Lime Found on Vining Street used for Tea, 2020
Oil on linen canvas
20cm x 25cm

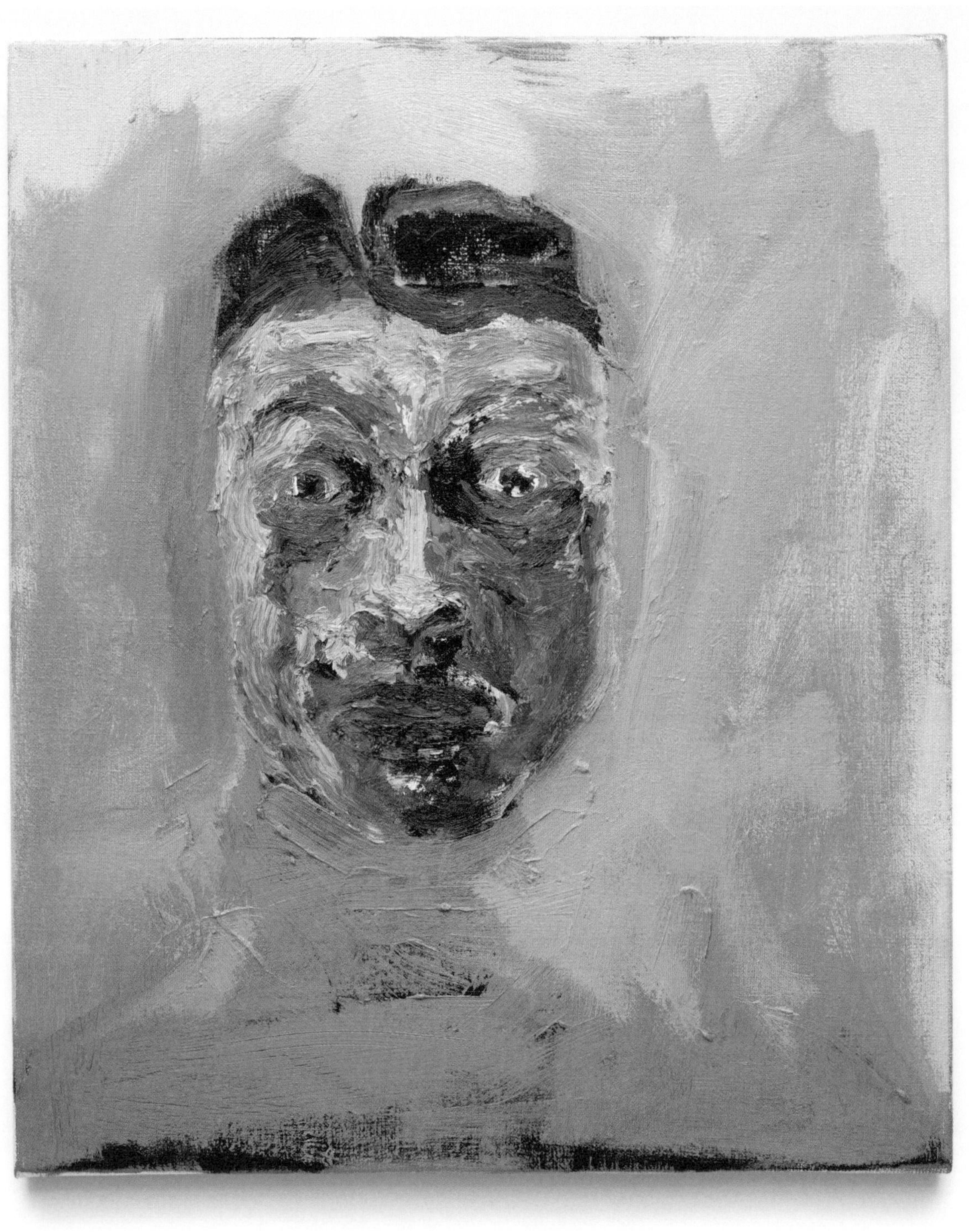

Lauren, 2017 – 2021
Oil on linen canvas
38cm x 46cm

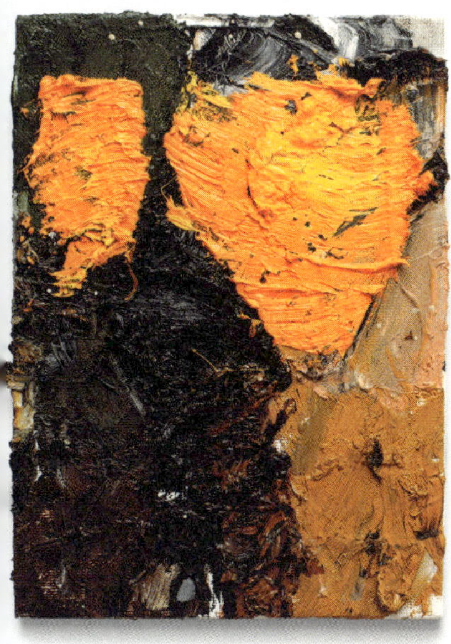

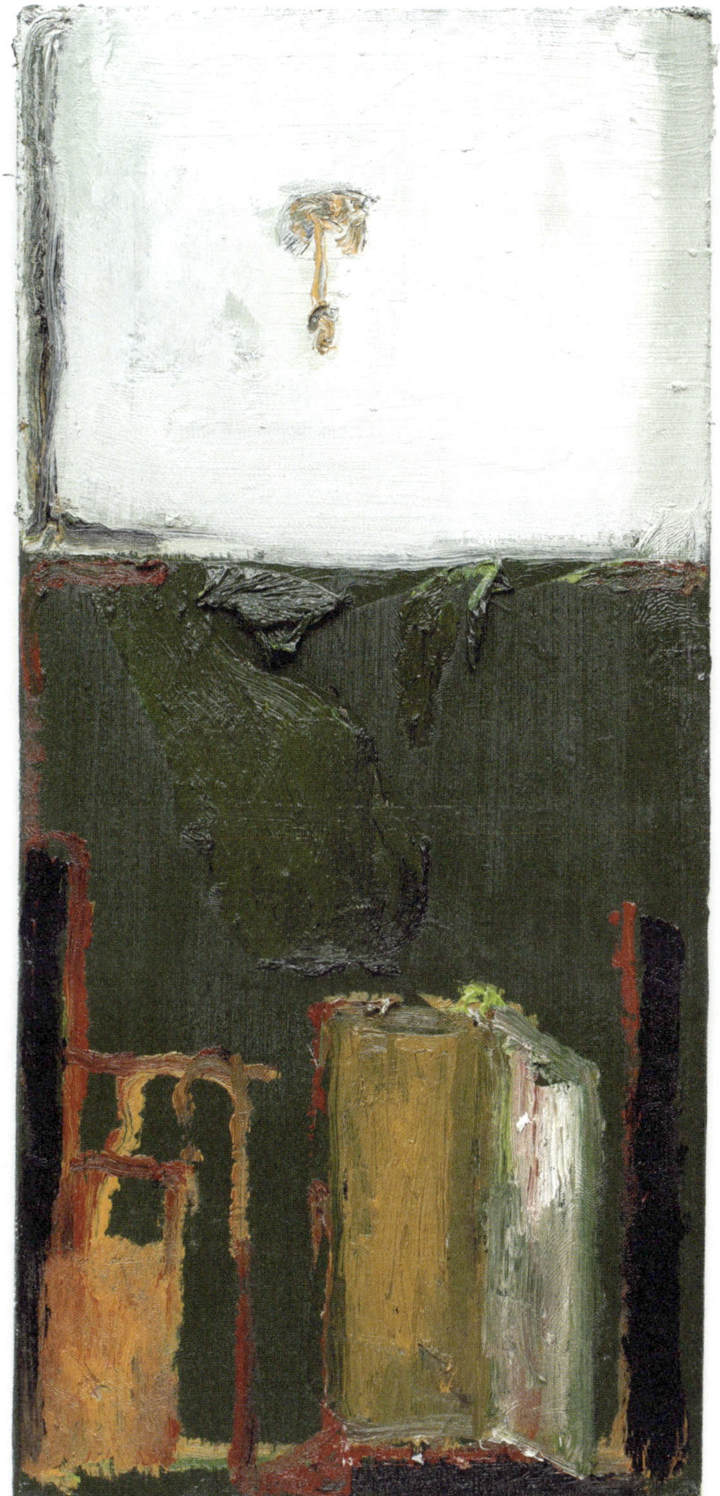

Studio Interior, 2021
Oil on canvas board
14.8cm x 21cm

Studio Interior, 2021
Oil on linen canvas
25cm x 60cm

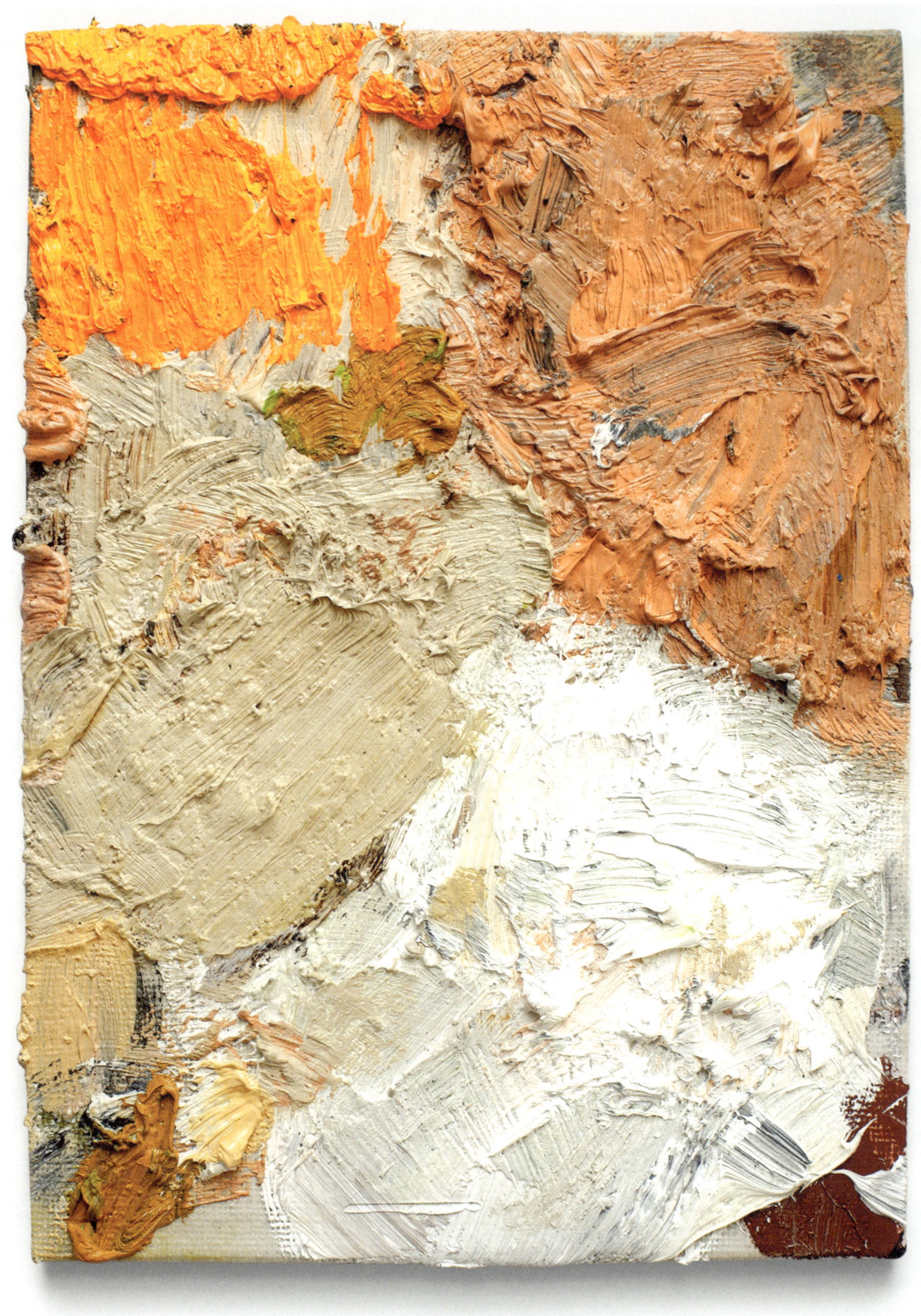

Studio Interior, 2021
Oil on canvas board
14.8cm x 21cm

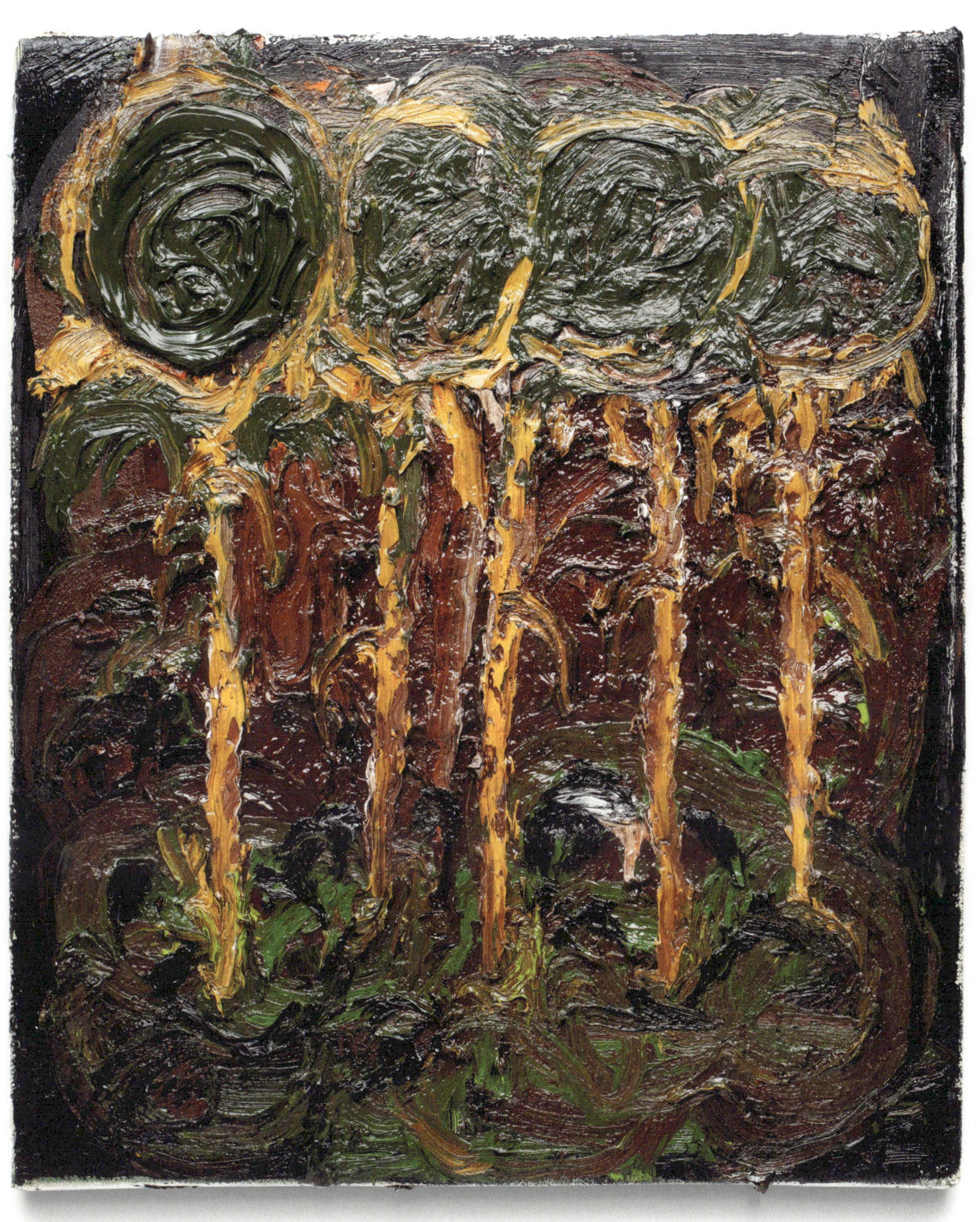

From Seed, 2021
Oil on linen canvas
40cm x 46cm

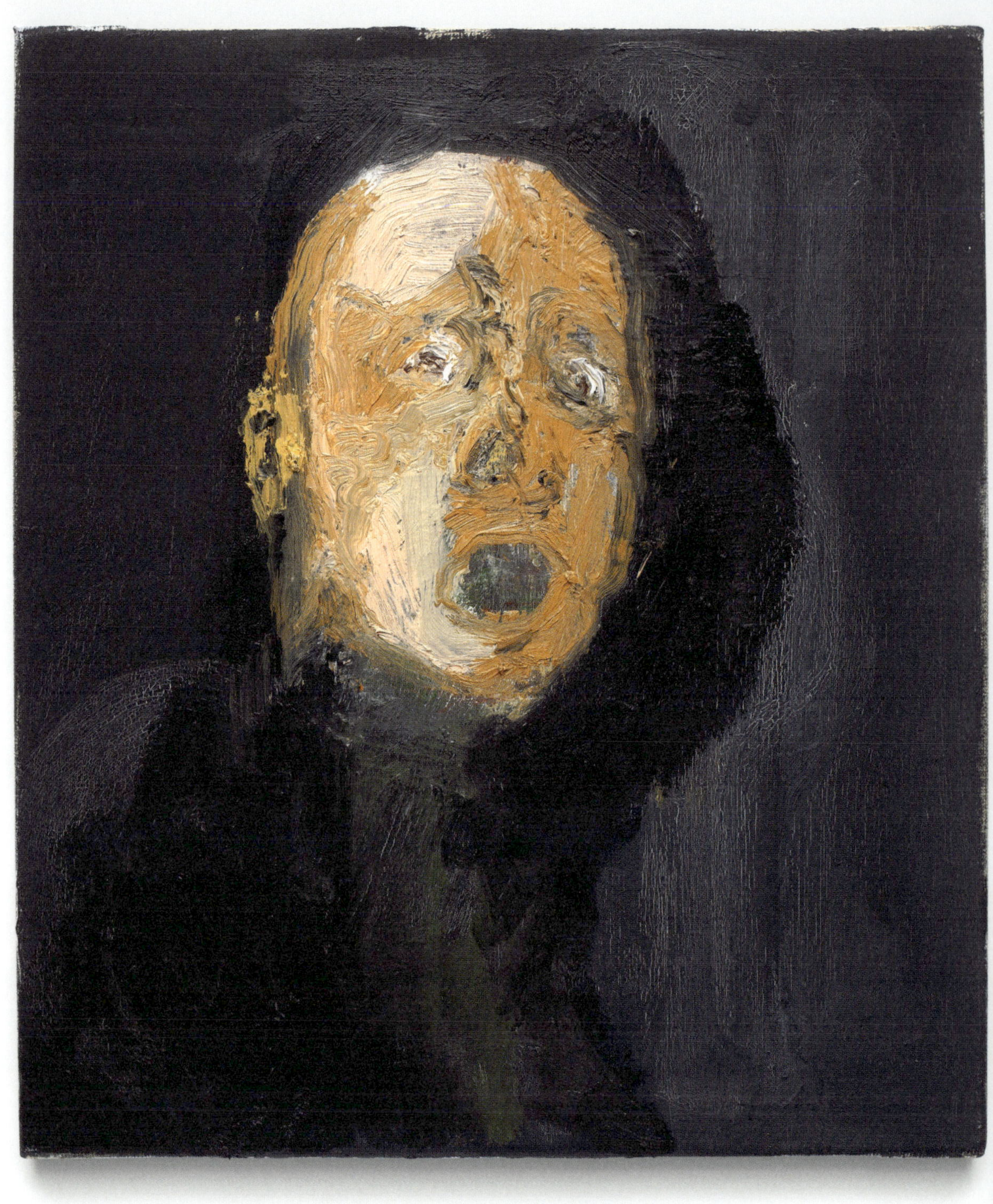

Untitled, 2021
Oil on linen canvas
40cm x 46cm

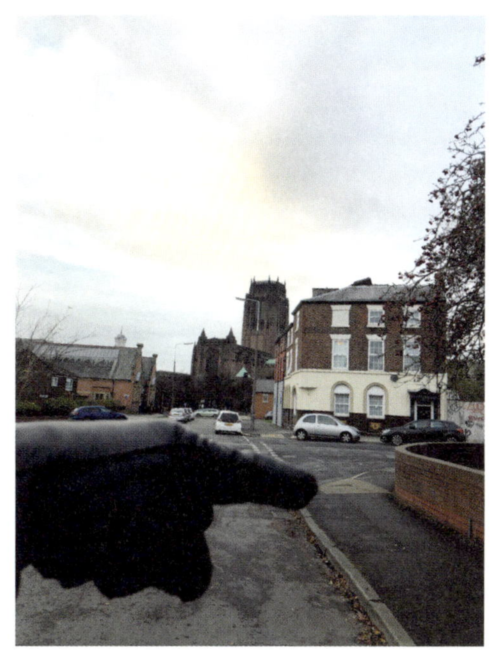

Pointing at the corner of Windsor Street and Upper Stanhope Street, L8, Facing north, 2020 – 2021
iPhone image

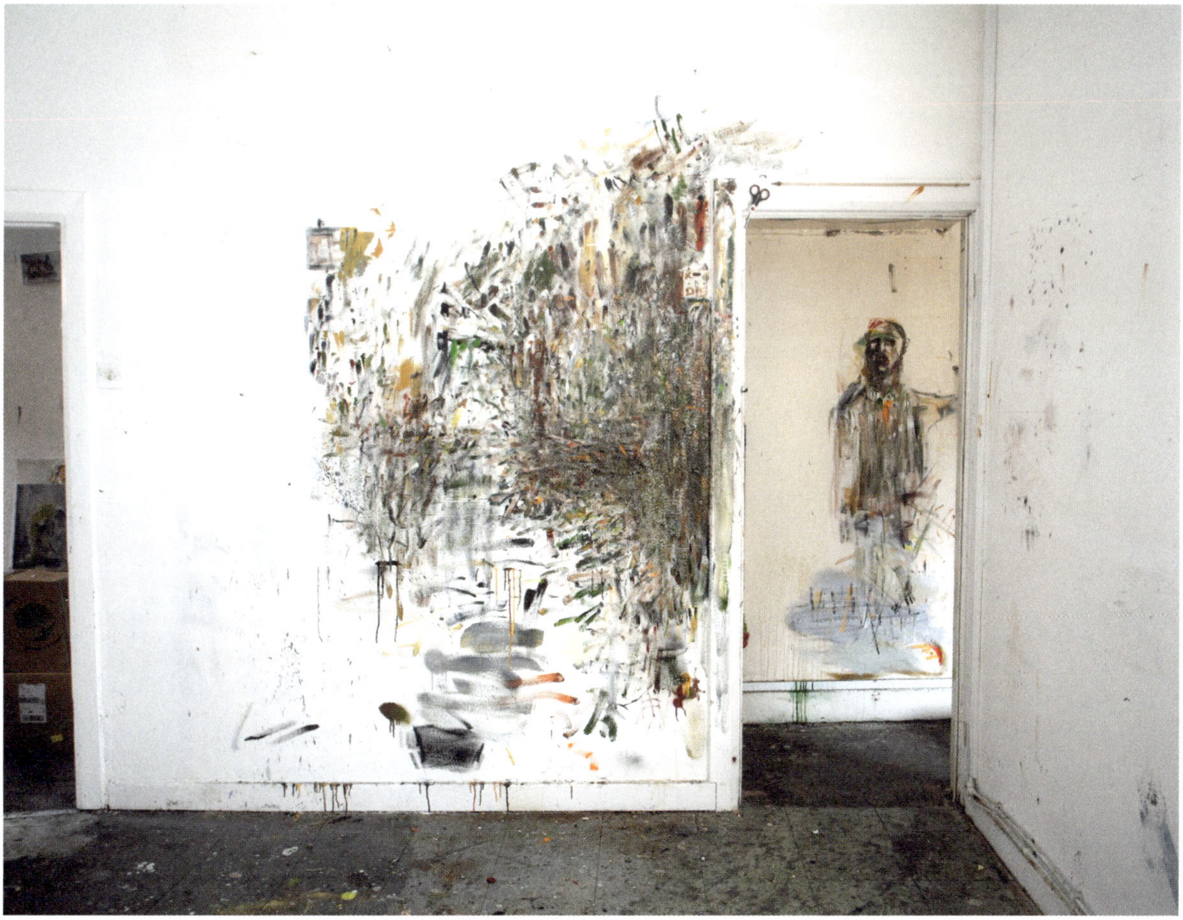

Death of Mother Earth, 2016 – 2021
Ground floor, painting room, facing east.

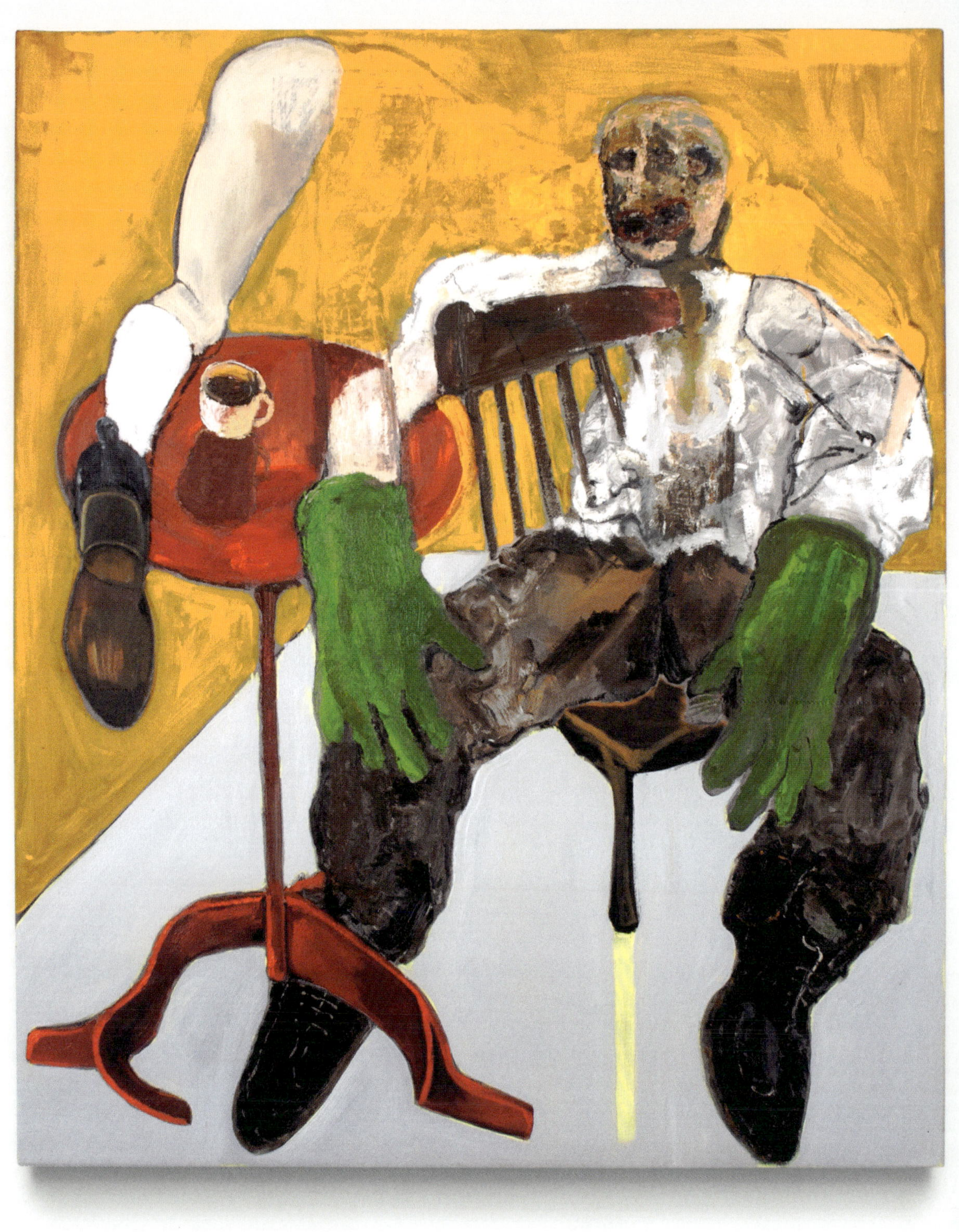

Binman, 2020 – 2021
Oil on jute
130cm x 160cm

The Binman

I hate my neighbour's rubbish

Our rubbish bins are emptied every Wednesday morning, so I drag them all out on Tuesdays. I do this job because of a back gate that was left open and three lads tried to break in, so by emptying the bins I also control the lock on the gate. The job has escalated into me controlling 16 bins in order to keep that bleeding gate locked at all times.

If I'm home on Wednesday morning, I usually rush out so I can speak to the binmen. I speak with Jim, Jimmy, a lad from Aintree and he's a small time gambler, he makes me happy. He also gave me 3 pairs of rubber gloves, blue, I don't like blue, they are so stiff that you can't move your fingers, so your hands become ridged rubber mallets.

The neighbours do nothing. After the bins have been emptied they'll happily half fill one that is left in the middle of the pavement together with 15 other empty bins. And this, without considering moving one single bin for pedestrians or thinking to put them back into their rightful place.

If there is a storm on a Tuesday night I always check that the bins are still standing. One of these very cold nights, with rain lashing down, two bins had blown over. With my bin gloves on I started picking up the litter that was scattered all over the street and I could see Tesco finest plastic wrapping blowing in the wind. One neighbour, a young, spoiled, little middle class brat open his door for fast food delivery, he looked over at me, not once, but twice, no smile, no help or a simple thank you, he just slammed the door shut. The anger.

And let me not forget to mention the neighbour who gave me a Christmas card with a £20 note for a job well done. I was so cross I could not speak to that man for 6 months. Or the god damned seagulls that peck at the bin bags left on top of the bins by neighbours, my frustration goes beyond comprehension.

In a phone conversation with my father a while back, who still owns part of his childhood home in Scotland, he started complaining about the bins left in his pend and that all his idiot neighbours never helped or cared, and that he had to do everything, he went on and on, just like me.

OMG

I immediately imagined my two daughters turning into bin-sisters. They have been raised by a whinging and complaining father. I am now worried that this bin control might be a genetic trait and that my two beautiful grrrls will morph into me and spew out hate over any neighbours lacking rubbish bin etiquette.

My binmen are the only contact I have with any people in Liverpool. My binmen are of such a calibre, that they hugged each other laughing and that was in the middle of the worst Corona crisis. I stood there quietly with my mask and gloves on hoping that they would not hug me.

THE BINMAN BY VICTOR BOULLET

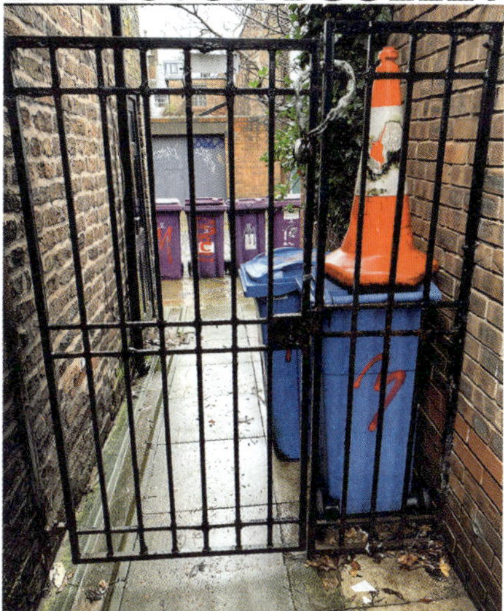

FINAL INSTALLMENT FROM LIVERPOOL 2014 - 2021
SHOWING AT DEATH OF MOTHER EARTH
L8 Liverpool – www.deathofmotherearth.com

Counting Friends

My years in Liverpool are over, finally finished, 2014 to 2021, and during that time four people have visited me. So I decided to paint my way into that awkward emotion of not actually having that many friends. This is something that Morrissey must have done, counted his friends. When asked by talk show host Jonathan Ross how many friends he had, he very quickly replied: I have seven friends.

The raw linen for the five paintings was given to me by one of these friends. And the preparation of the canvases was the result of text conversations with two of these friends.

The last of the four friends shared a story by a Norwegian author who has actually been cancelled. It's about a man that was sentenced to death. He sat on the wooden bench of a carriage that was being pulled by a big Norwegian horse, they were on their way to the gallows. There was a nail in the bench that kept hurting his arse, he wanted so badly to move so that he was relieved of the pain from that nail. So even if you are on your way to the gallows to be hung to death you still try the best you can to avoid discomfort.

The five paintings are dedicated to the four people that came to see me.

We are moving, the house and the studio are sold. Liverpool has been a challenge and I guess it will remain a battle within me. Should one waste good years of a short life in a place one does not like. I have many things I could say about that, but I do believe that comfort is our ultimate enemy and that resistance, no matter how vile, is a friend and a friend indeed is a friend in need.

I received an email in 2014 from a regular visiting face in Paris, it read; Liverpool? I will not visit you!

Note. Counting Friends page 262 – 267 was part of the final installment of paintings at Death of Mother Earth.

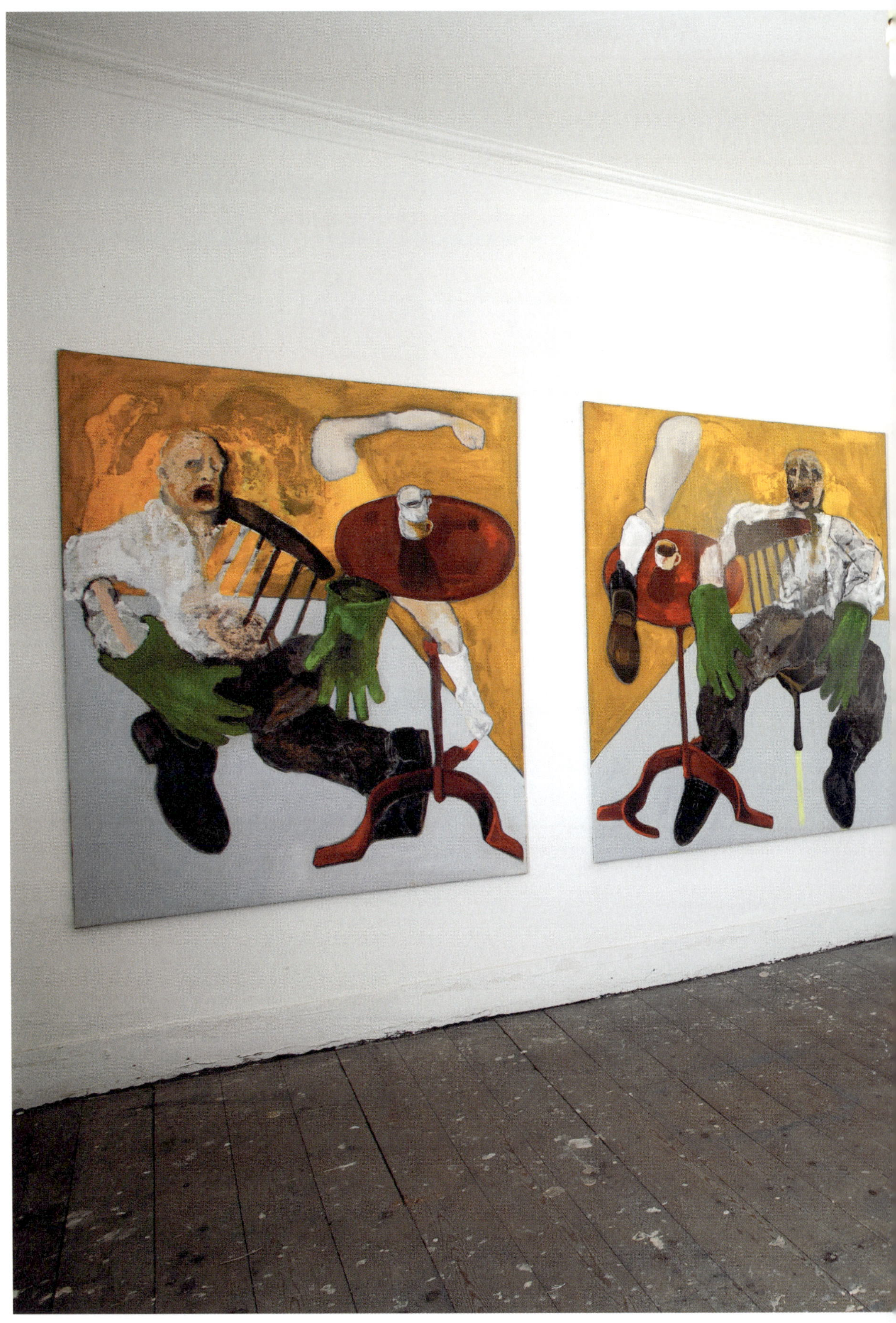

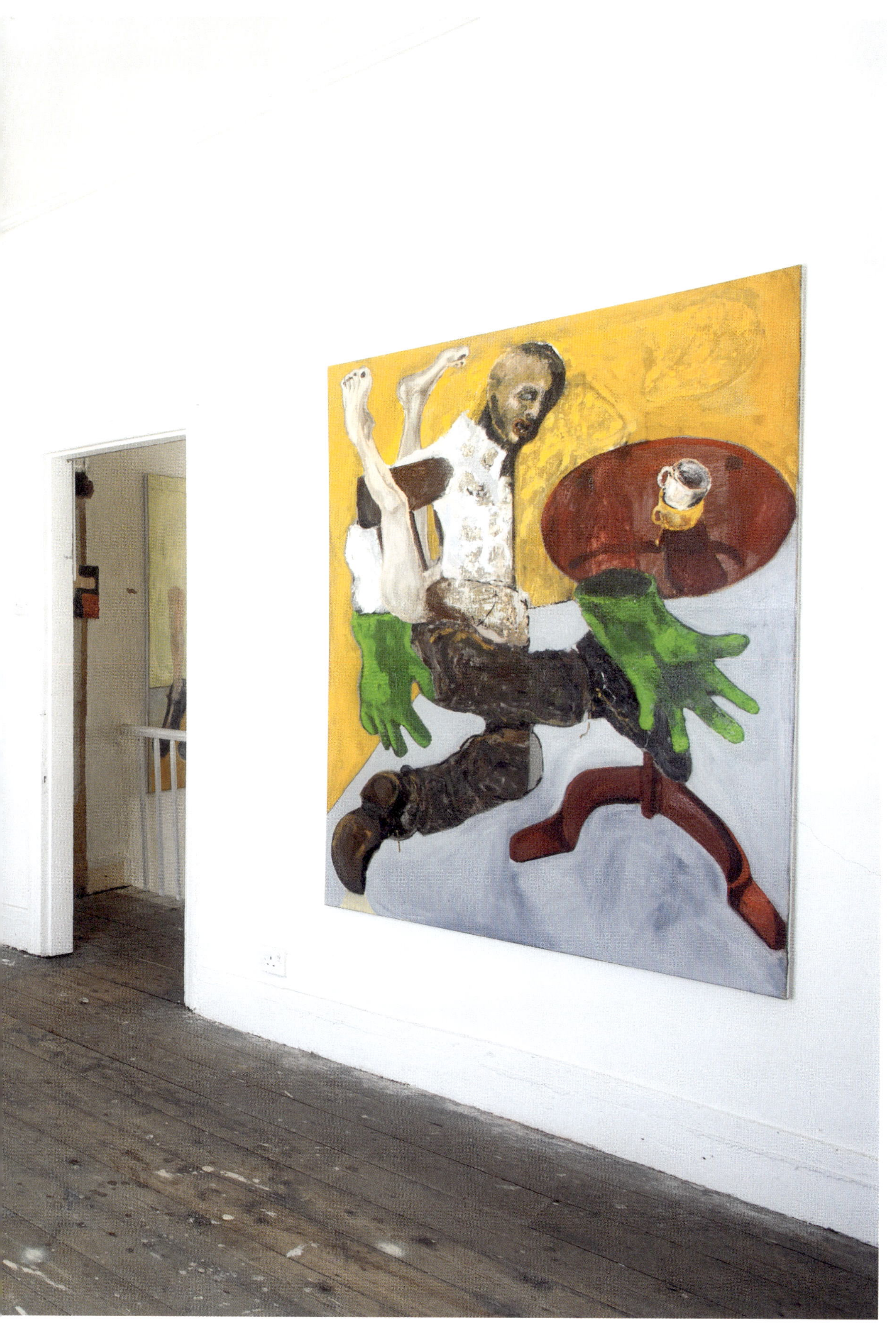

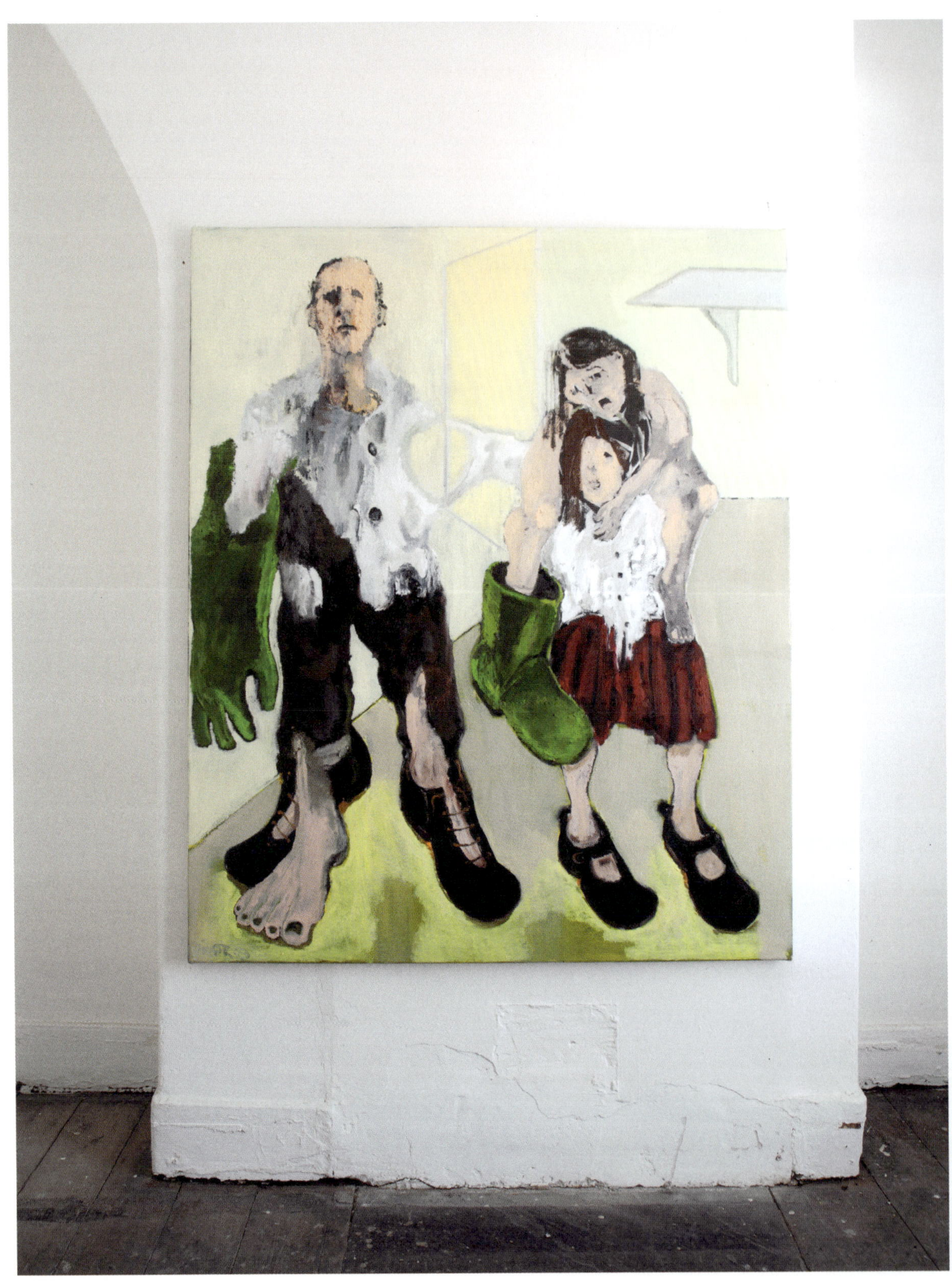

Binman, 2020 – 2021
Oil on jute
130cm x 160cm

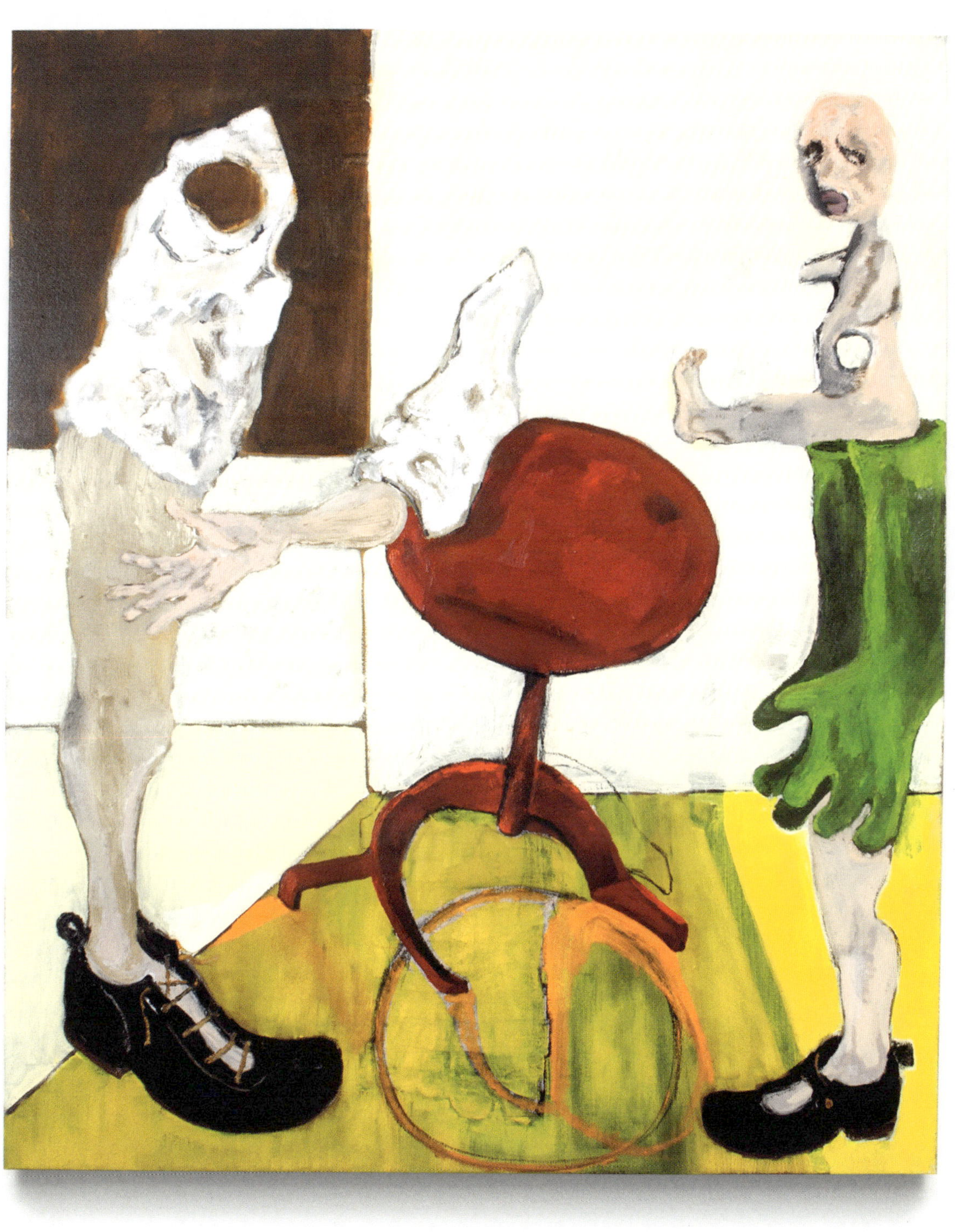

Binman, 2020 – 2021
Oil on jute
130cm x 160cm

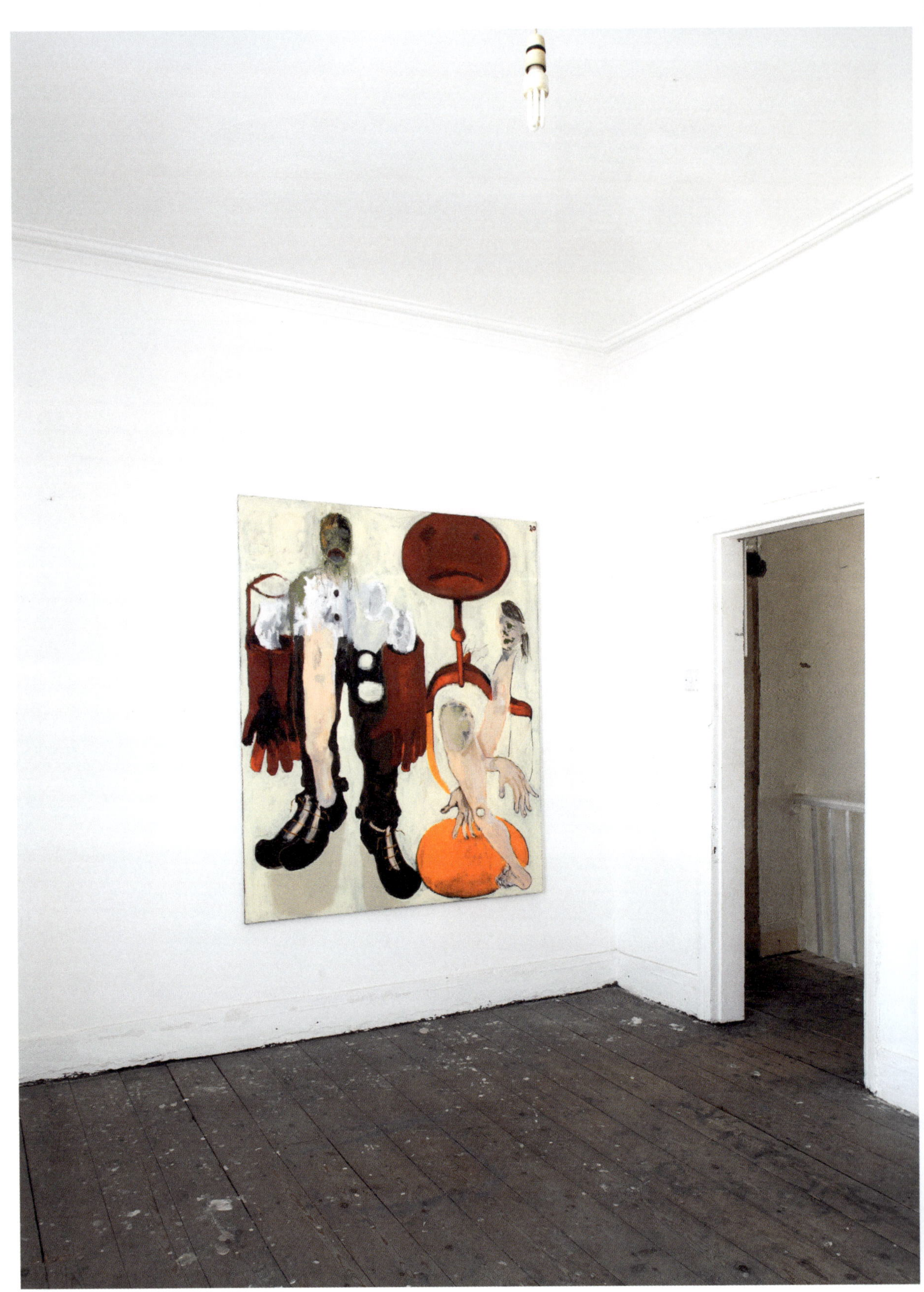

Binman, 2020 – 2021
Oil on linen canvas
130cm x 160cm

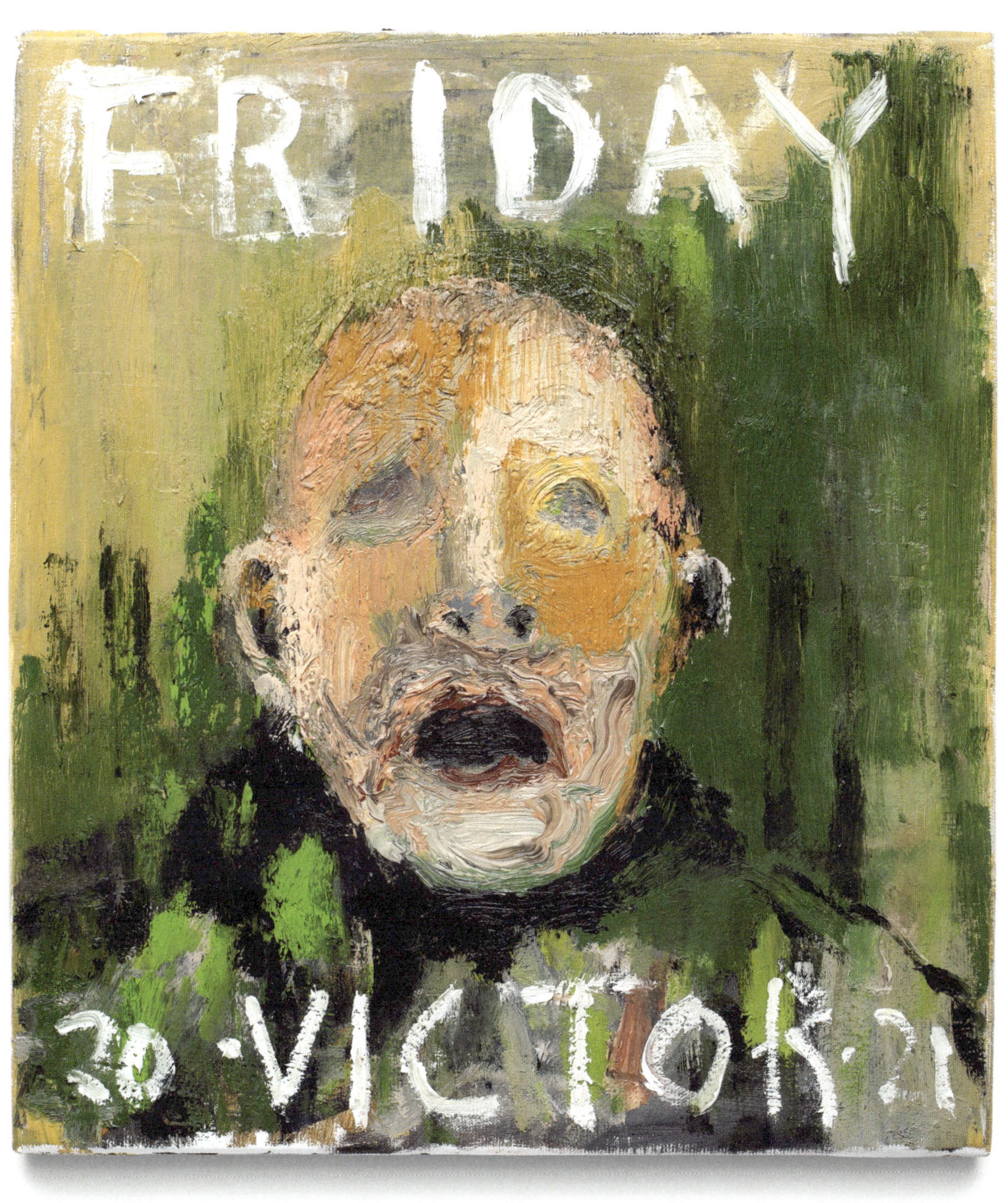

Self-portrait, 2020 – 2021
Oil on jute
40cm x 46cm

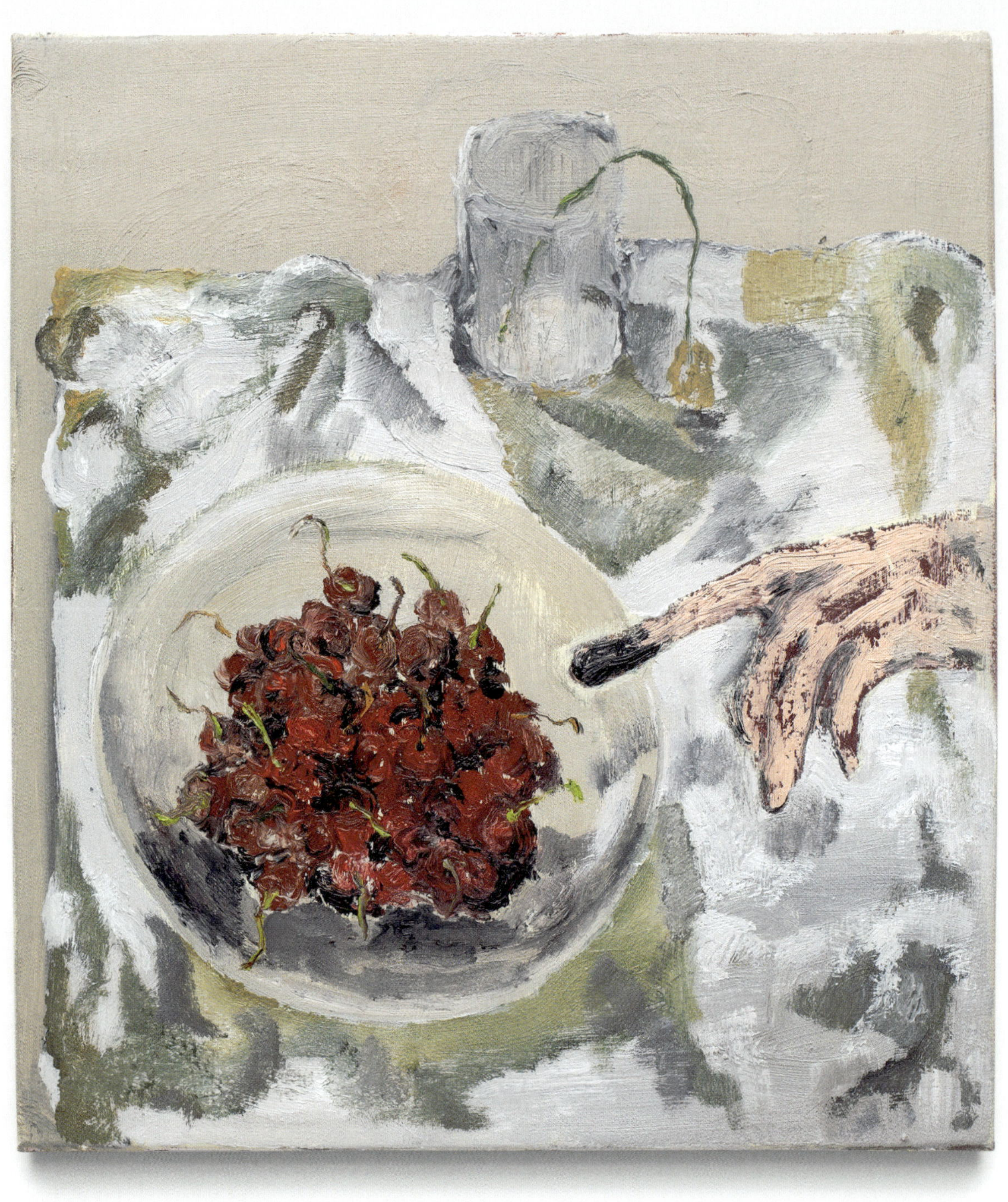

Cherries from the Bin, 2019 – 2021
Oil on linen canvas
40cm x 46cm

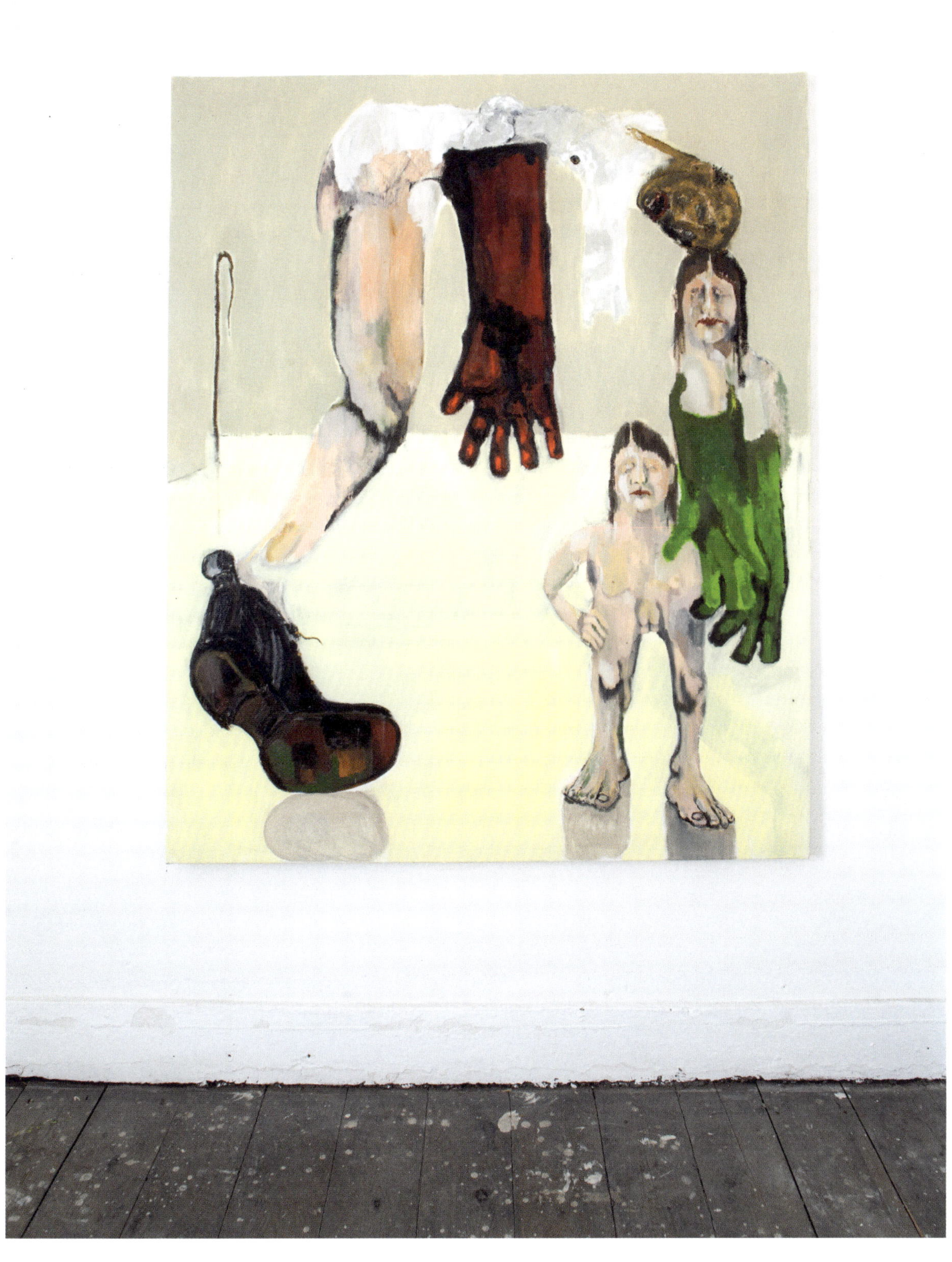

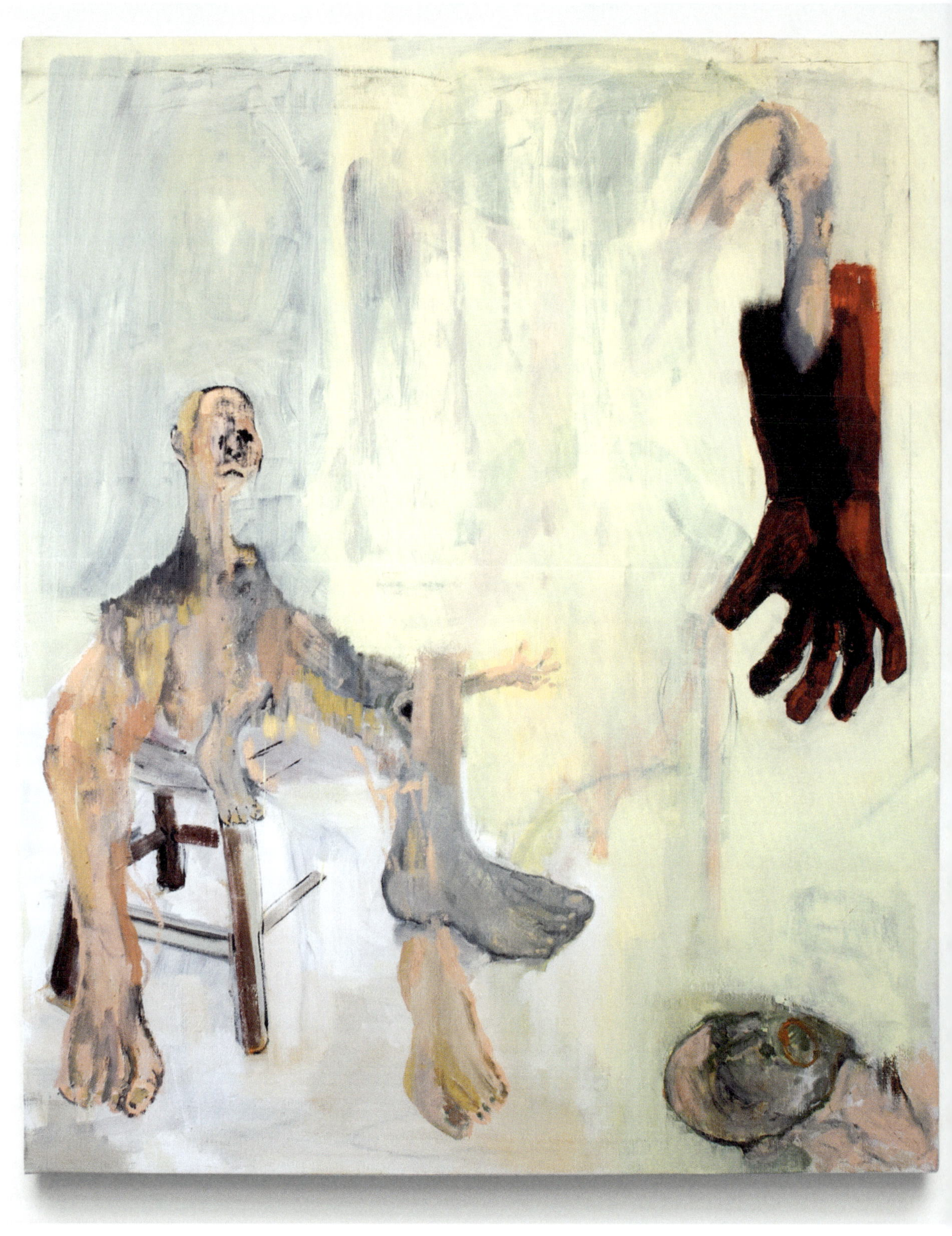

Binman, 2020 – 2021
Oil on linen canvas
130cm x 160cm

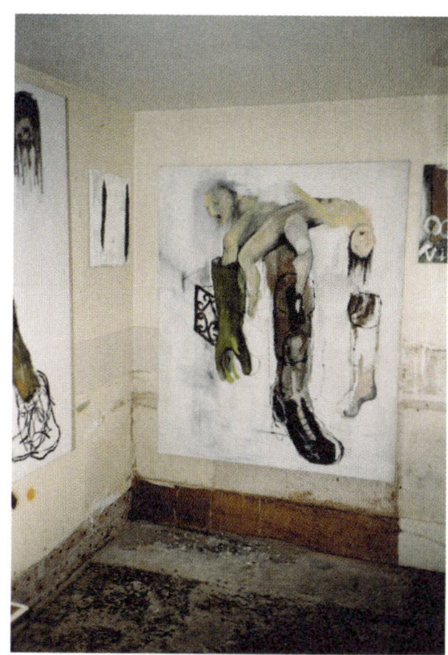
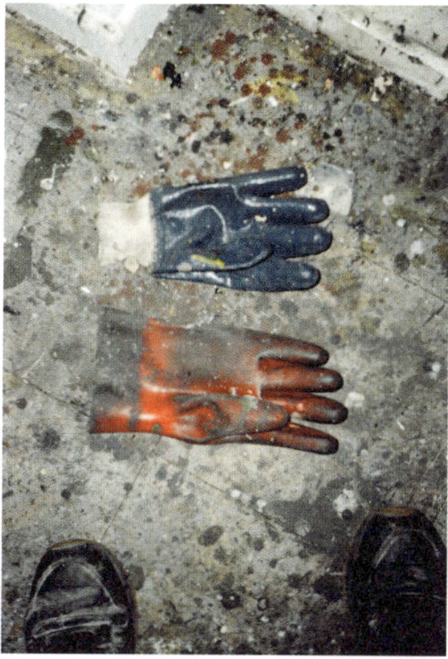
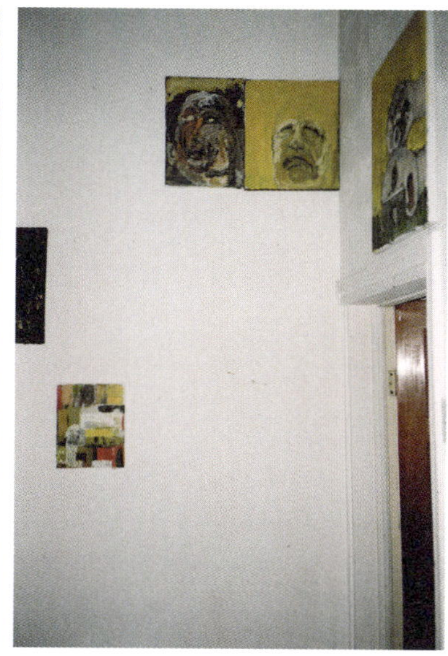
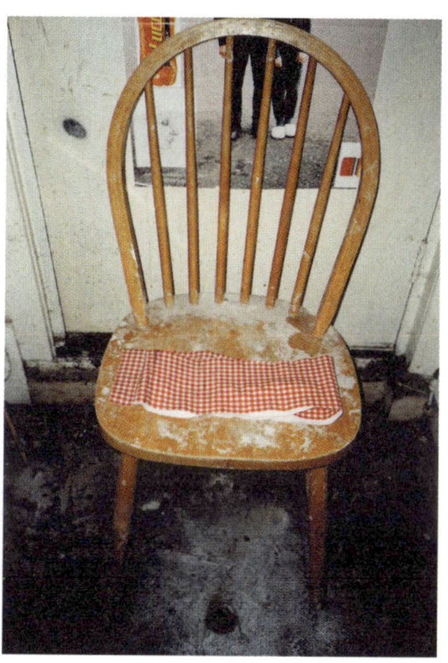
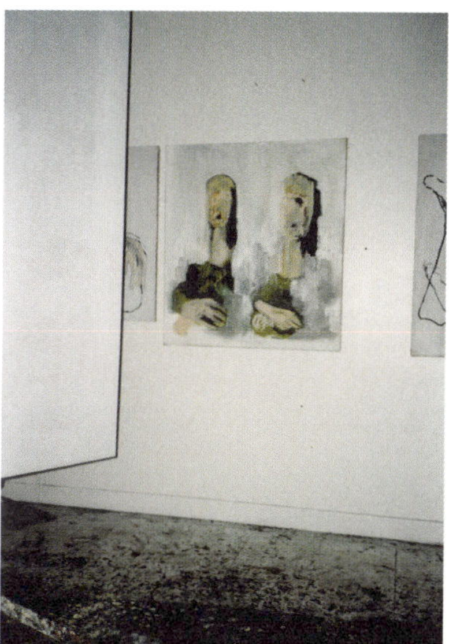
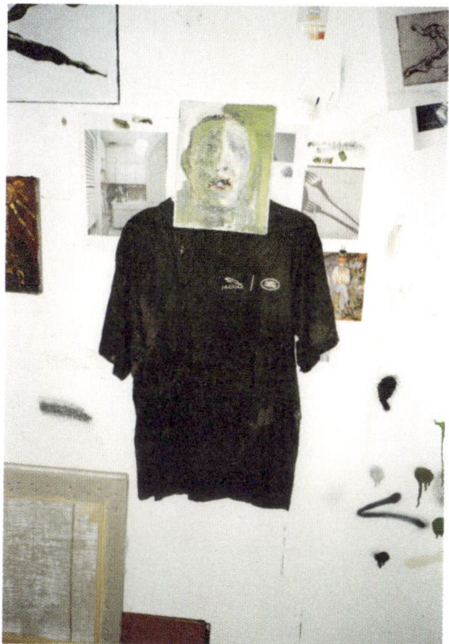
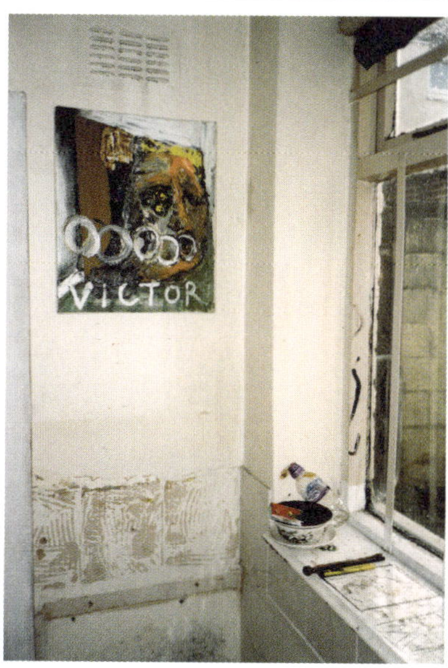
VICTOR
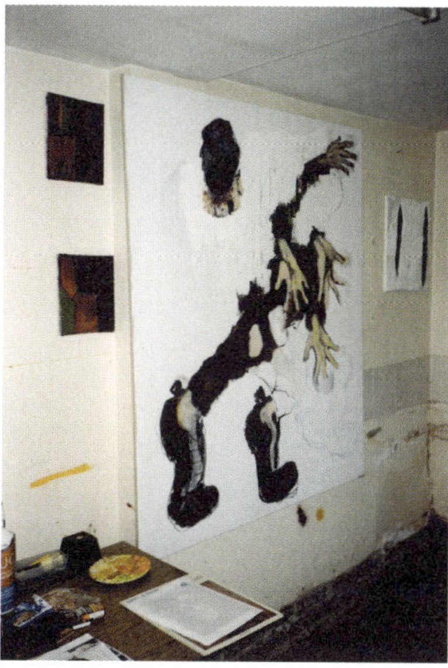
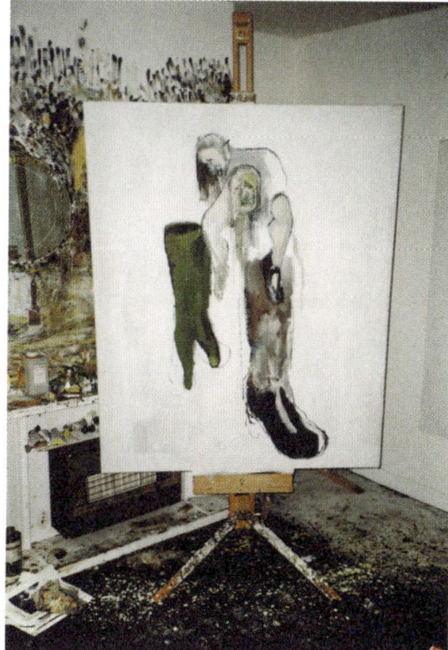

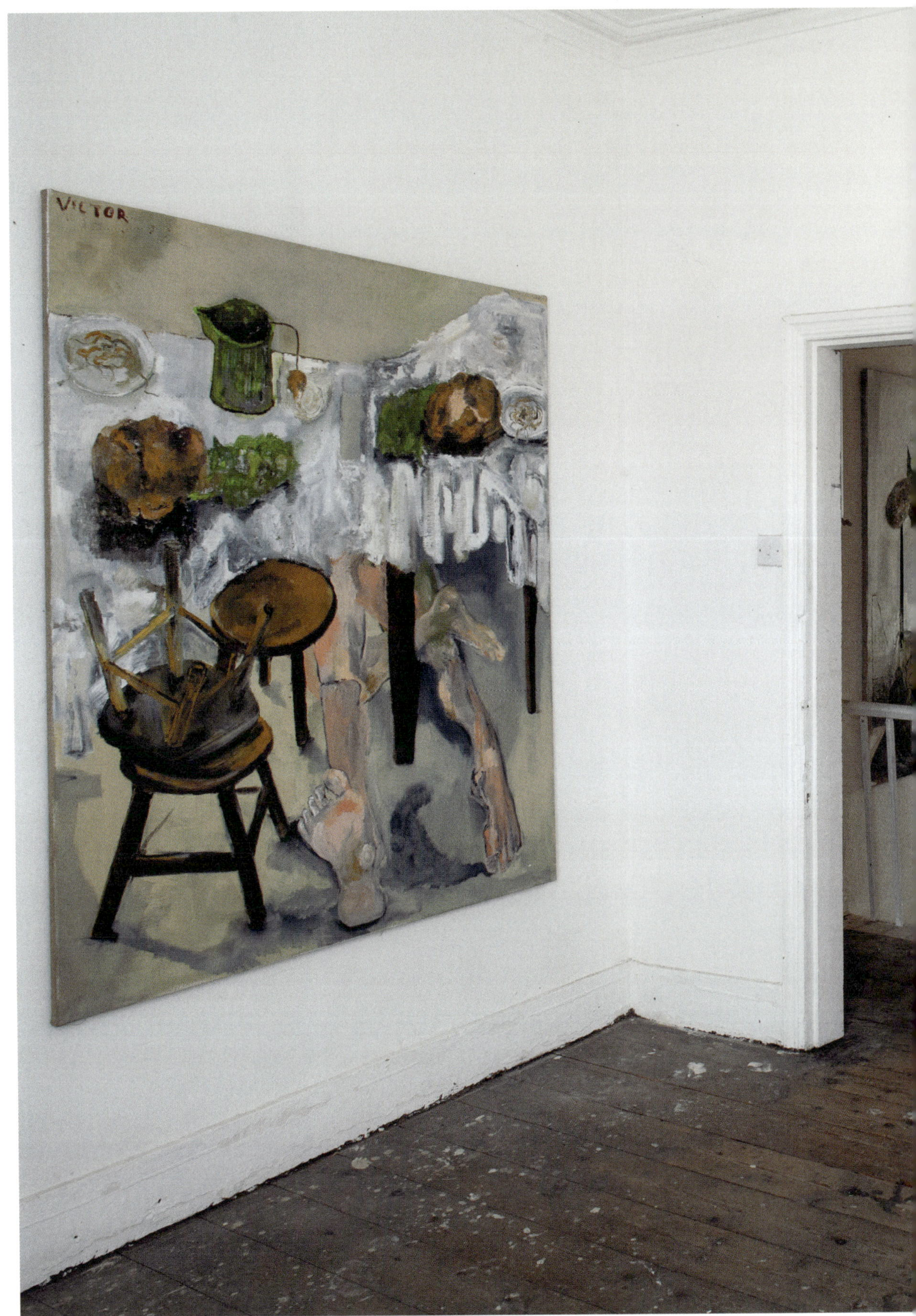
VICTOR

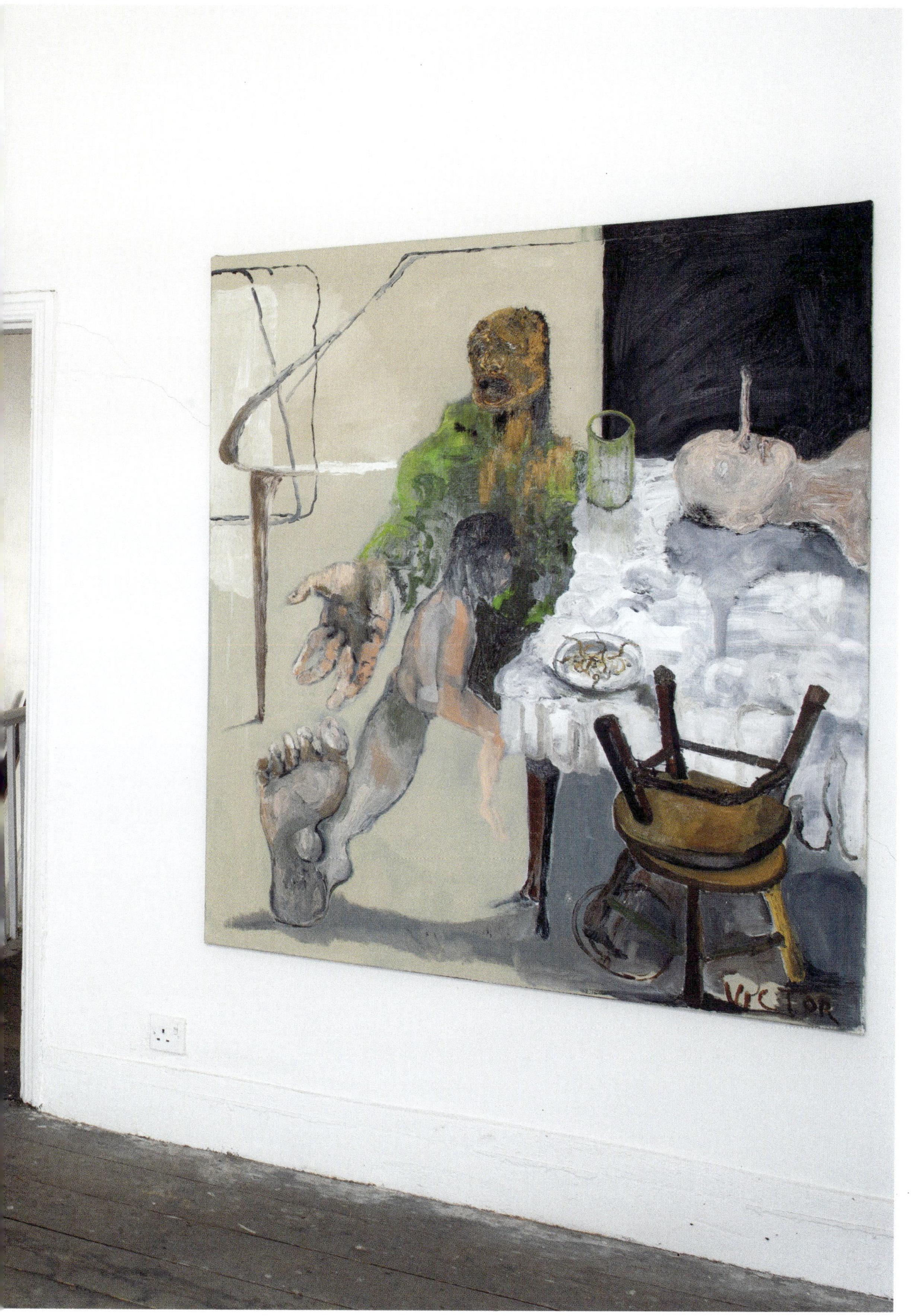
VICTOR

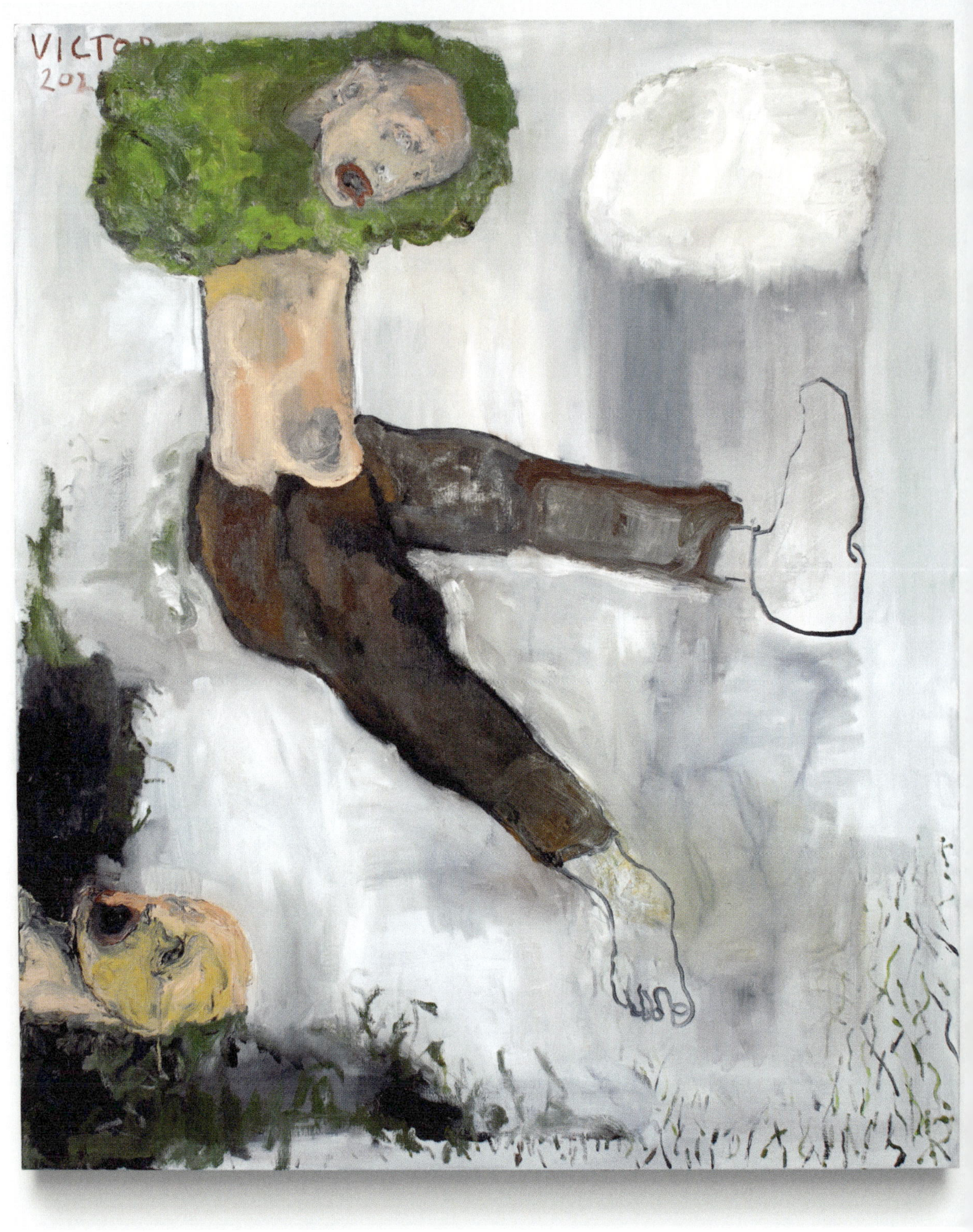

Binman, 2020 – 2021
Oil, gesso on raw linen
130cm x 160cm

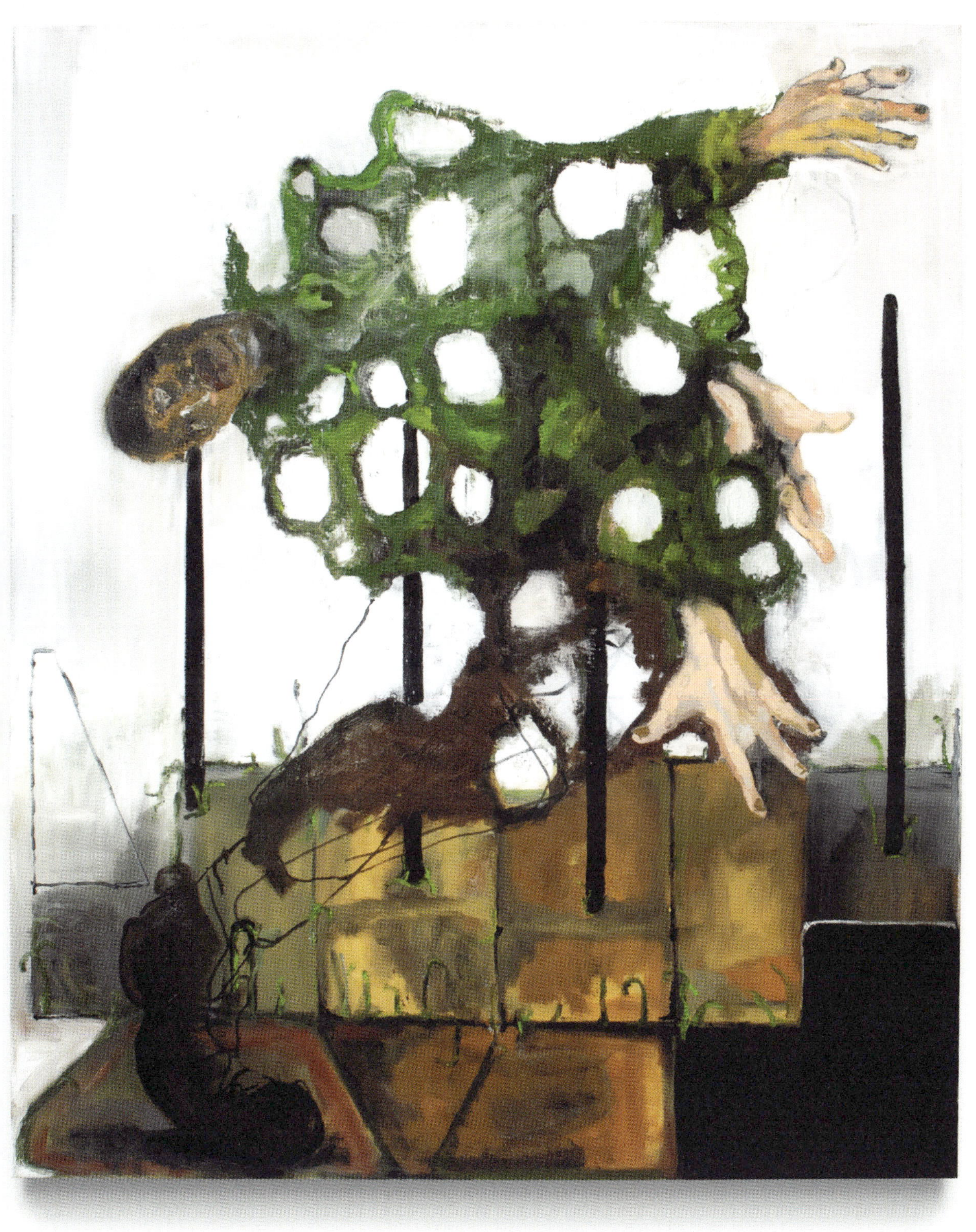

Binman, 2021
Oil, gesso on raw linen
130cm x 160cm

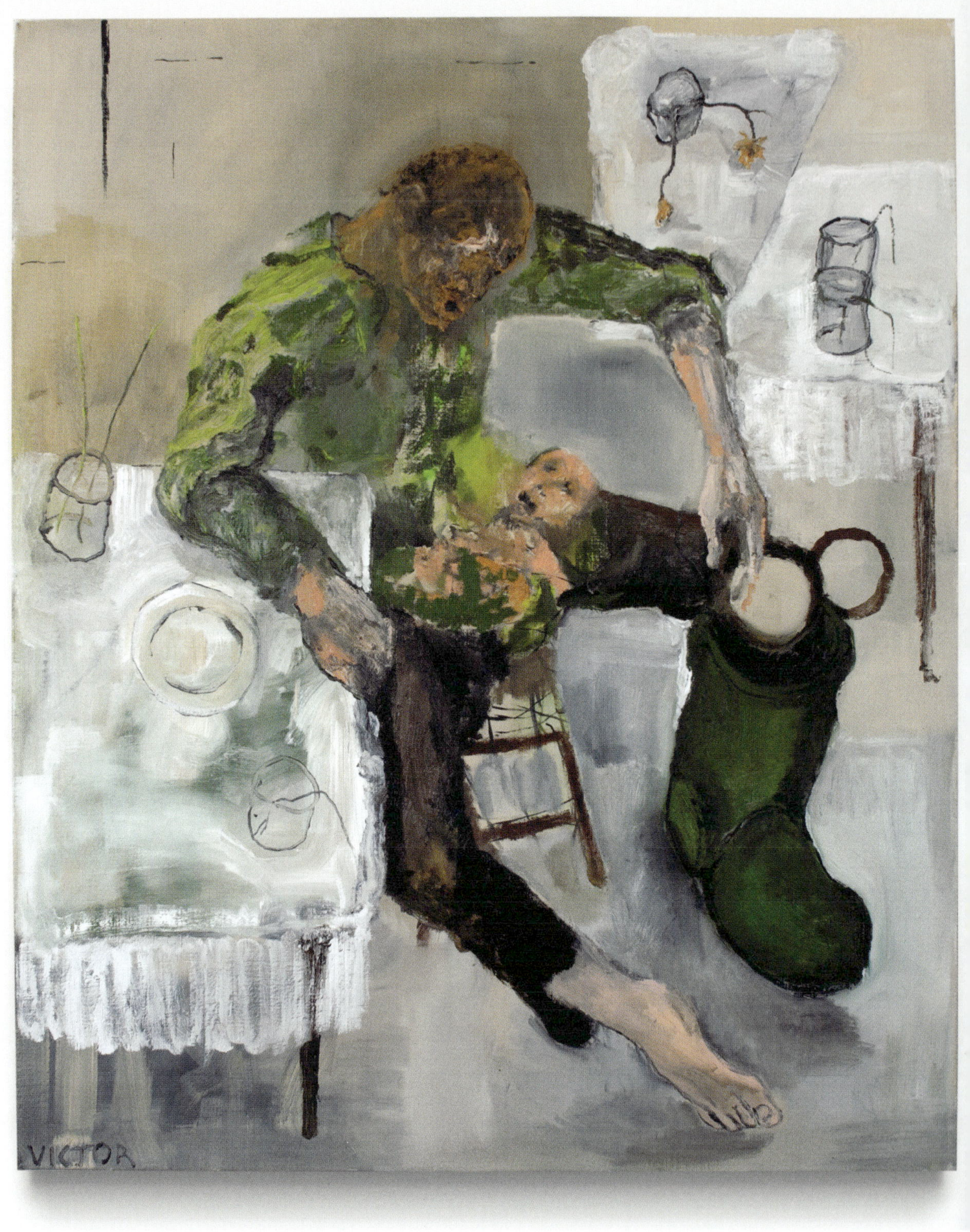

Binman, 2021
Oil, gesso on raw linen
130cm x 160cm

Binman, 2020 – 2021
Oil, gesso on raw linen
130cm x 160cm

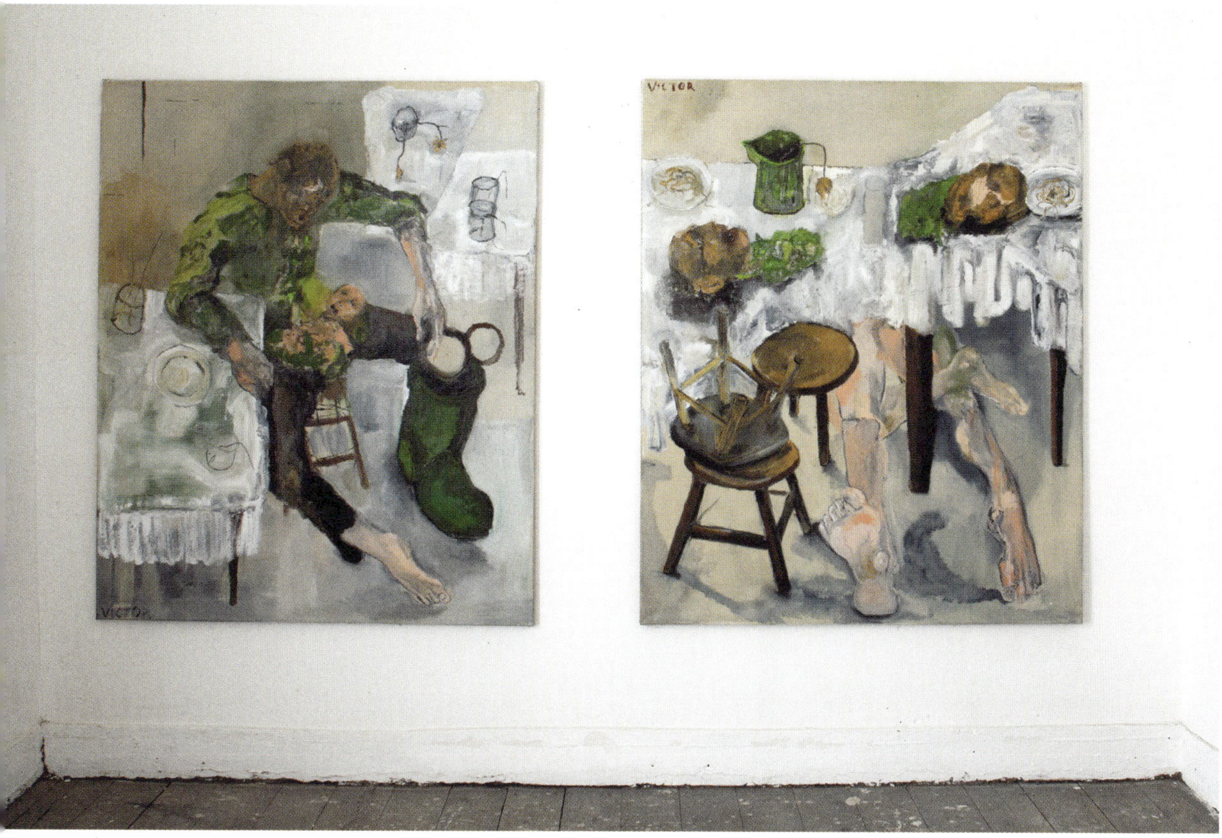

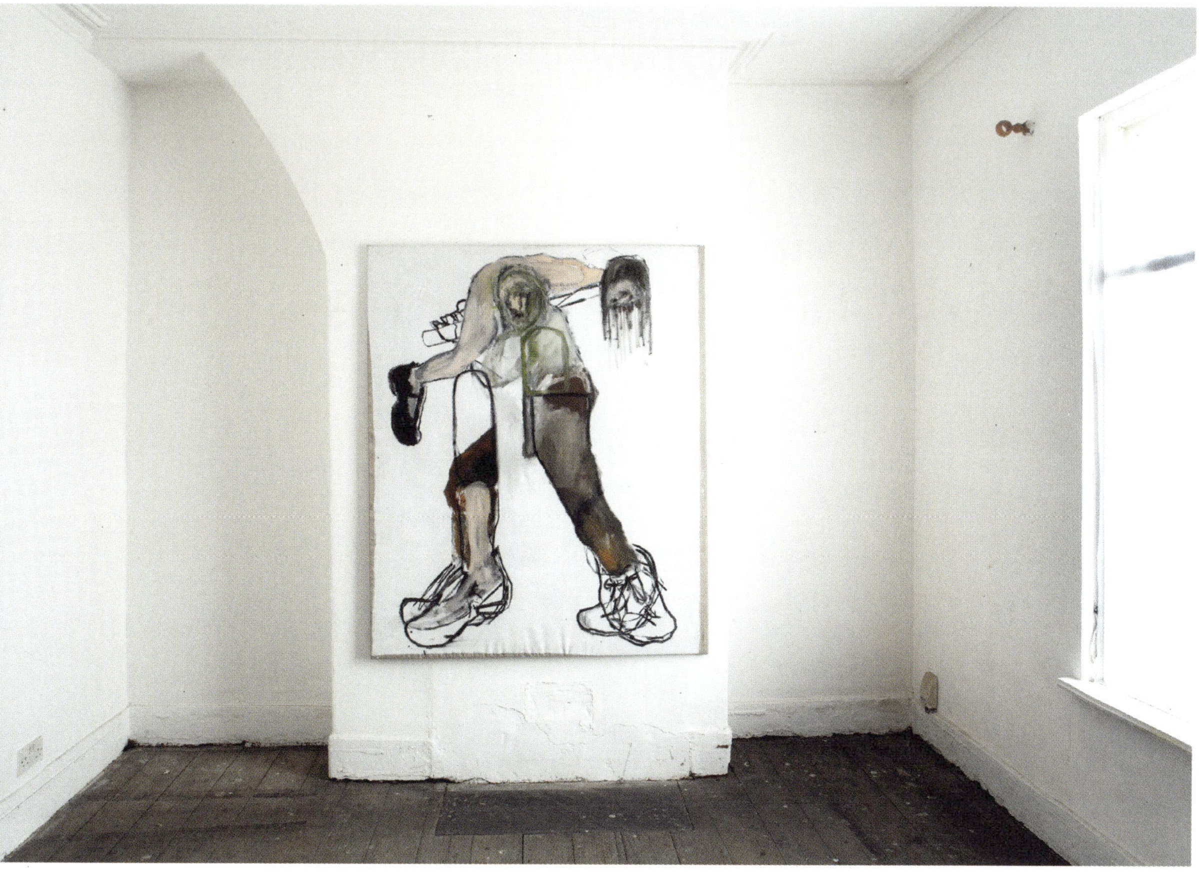

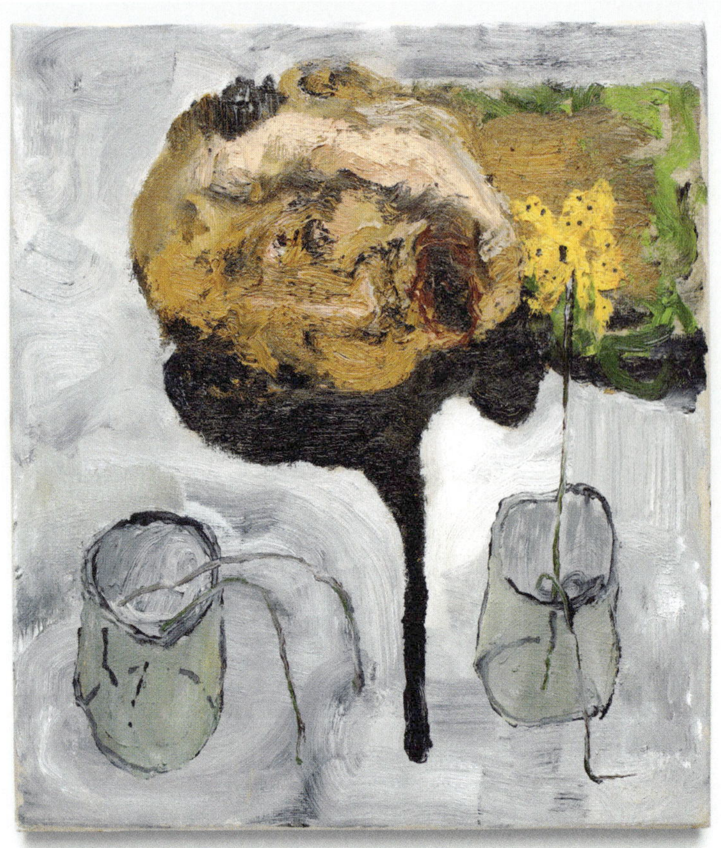

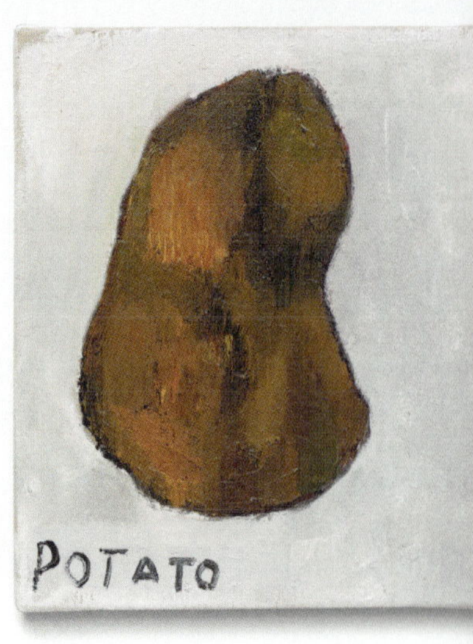

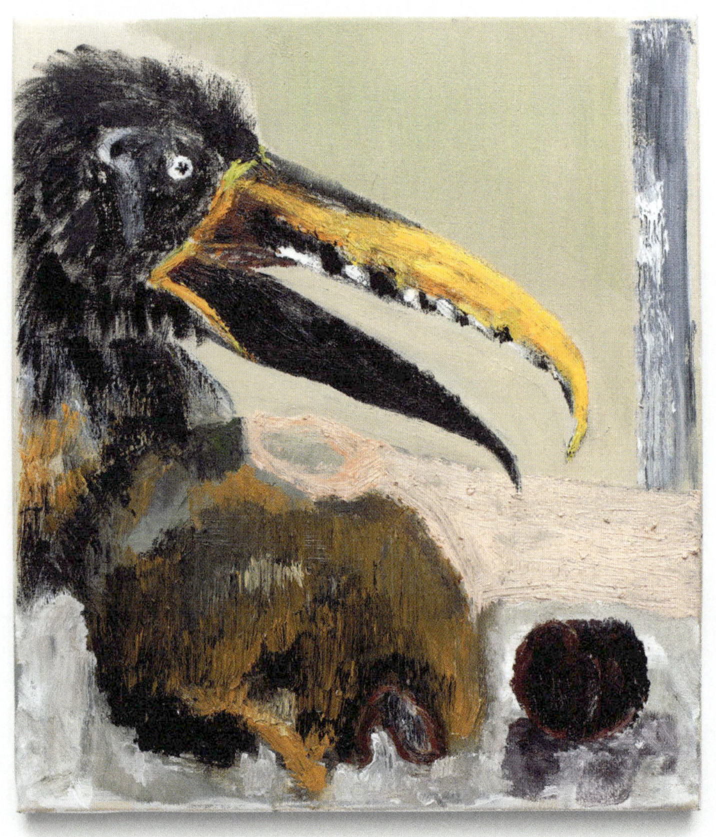

Untitled, 2021
Oil on linen canvas
40cm x 46cm

Potato, 2021
Oil on linen canvas
30cm x 35cm

Plum from Vining Street,
Oil on linen canvas
40cm x 46cm

Untitled, 2021
Pencil on paper
29.7cm x 21cm

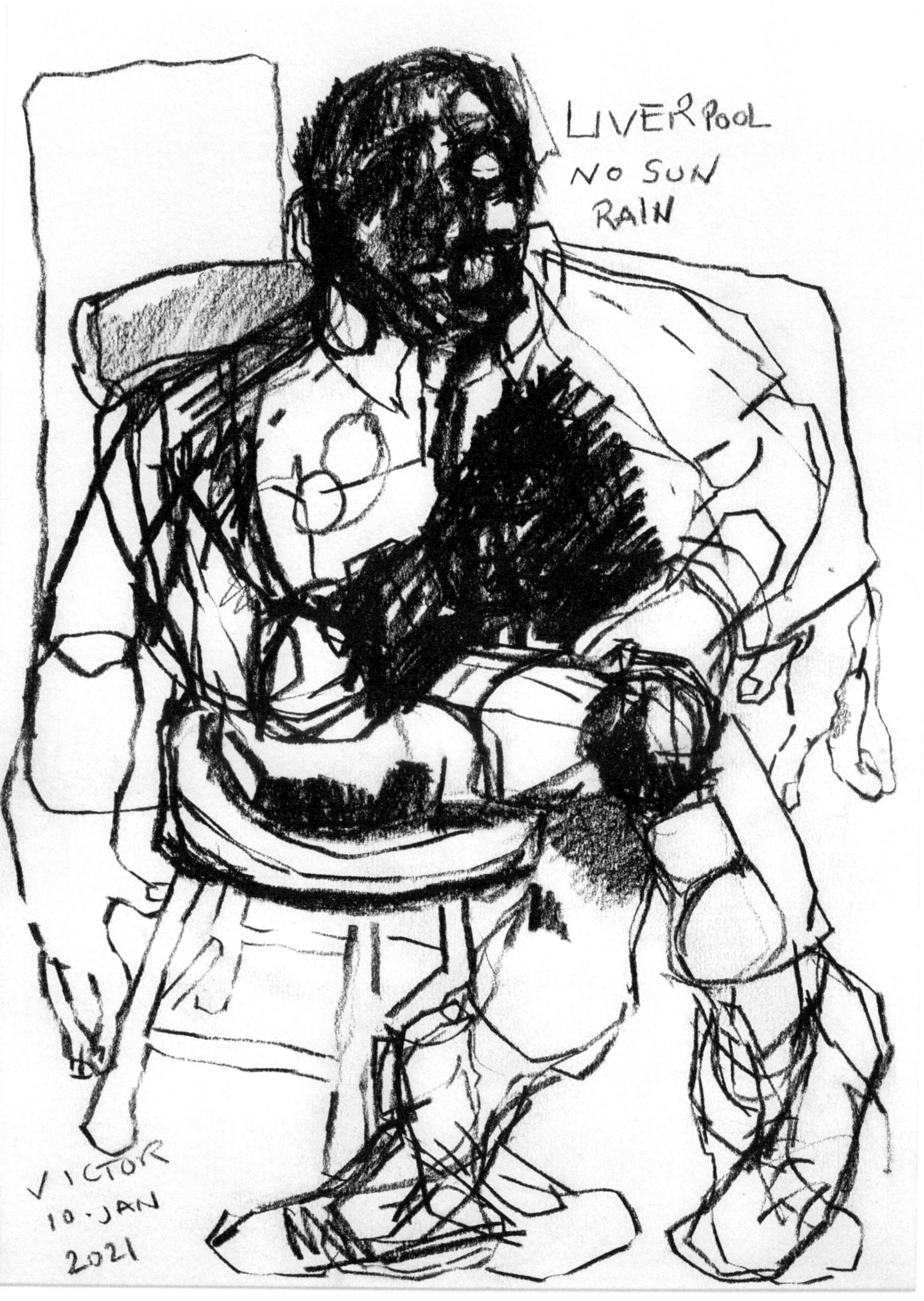
LIVERPOOL
NO SUN
RAIN
VICTOR
10 · JAN
2021

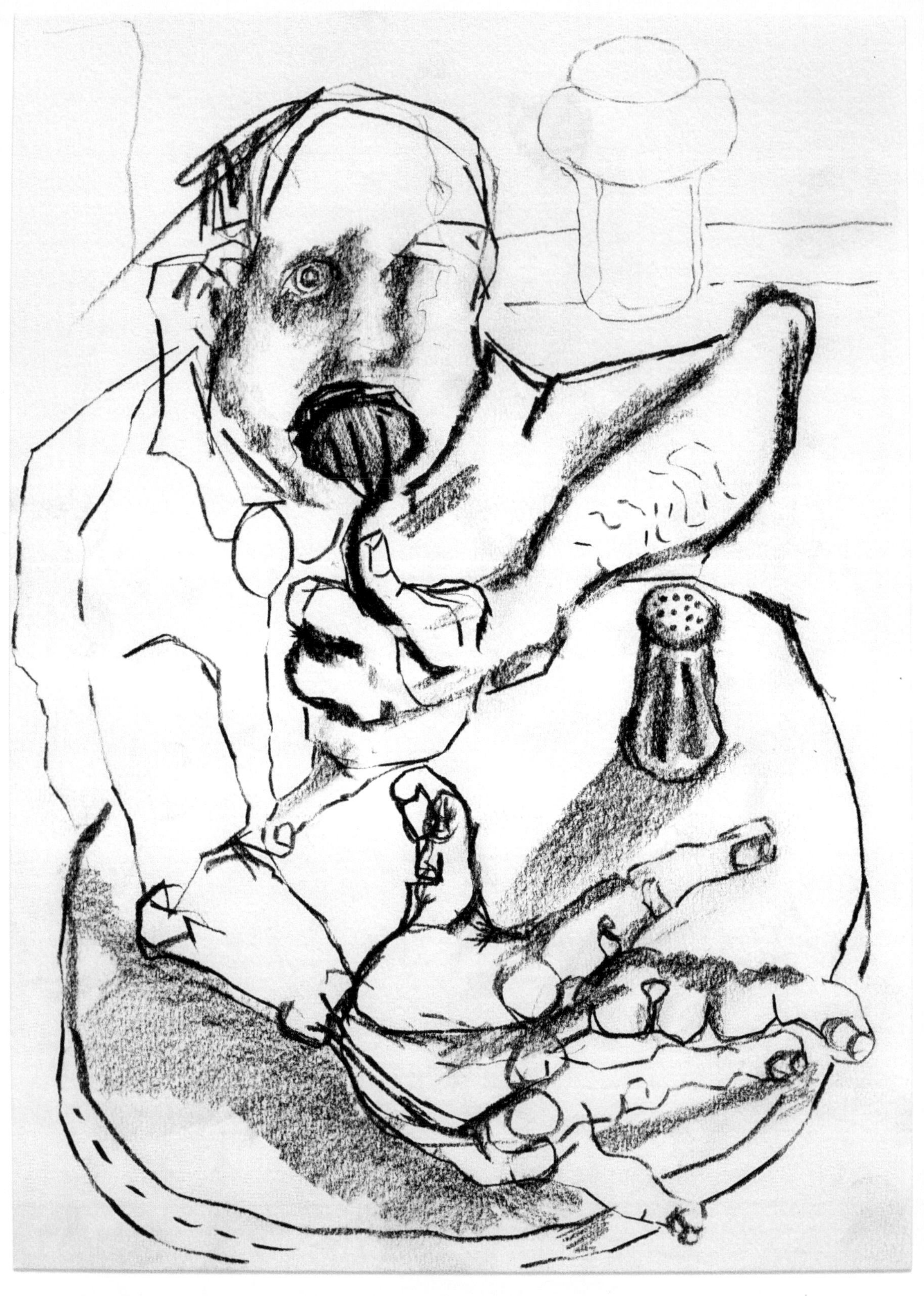

Untitled, 2021
Pencil on paper
29.7cm x 21cm

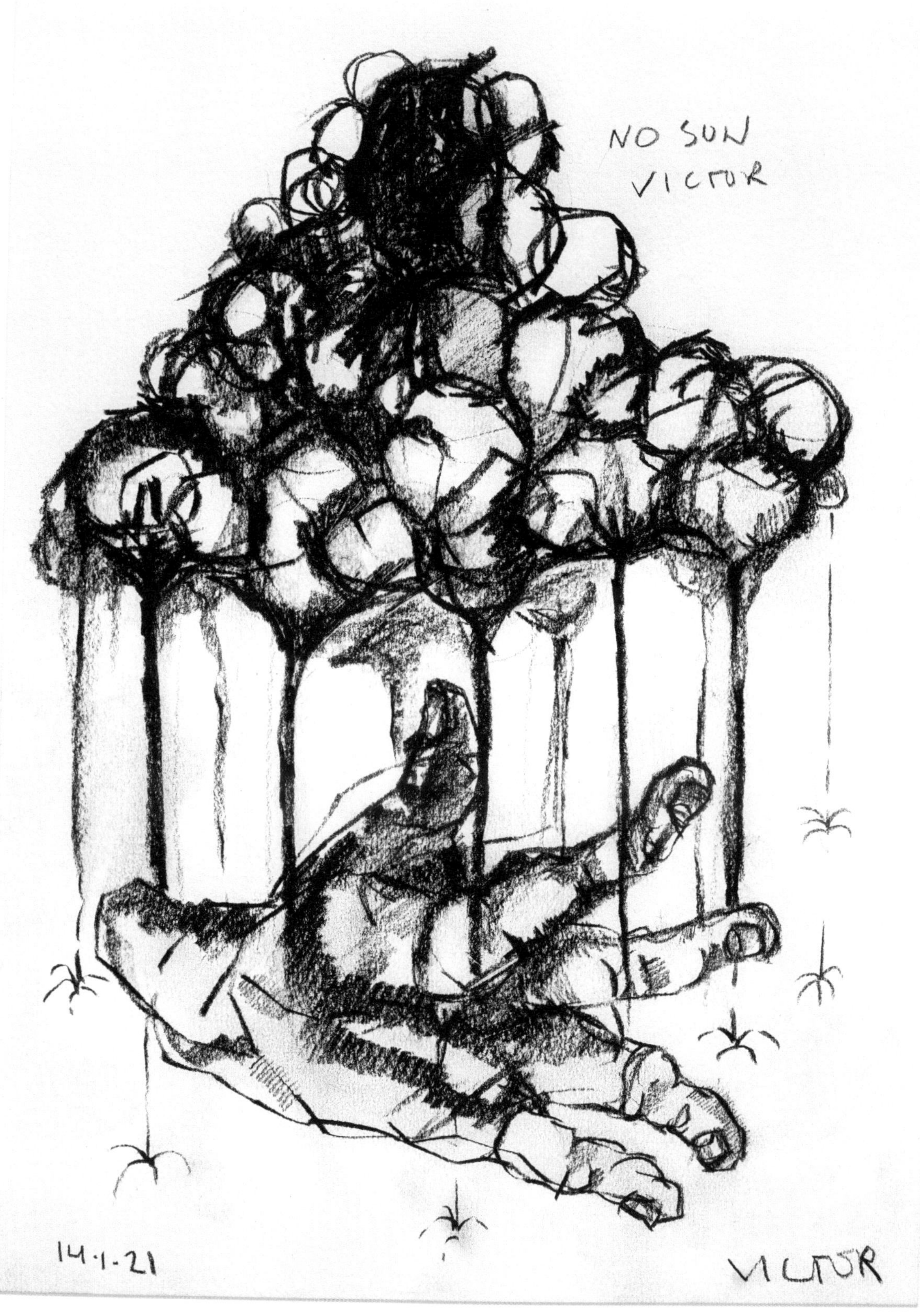

Untitled, 2021
Pencil on paper
29.7cm x 21cm

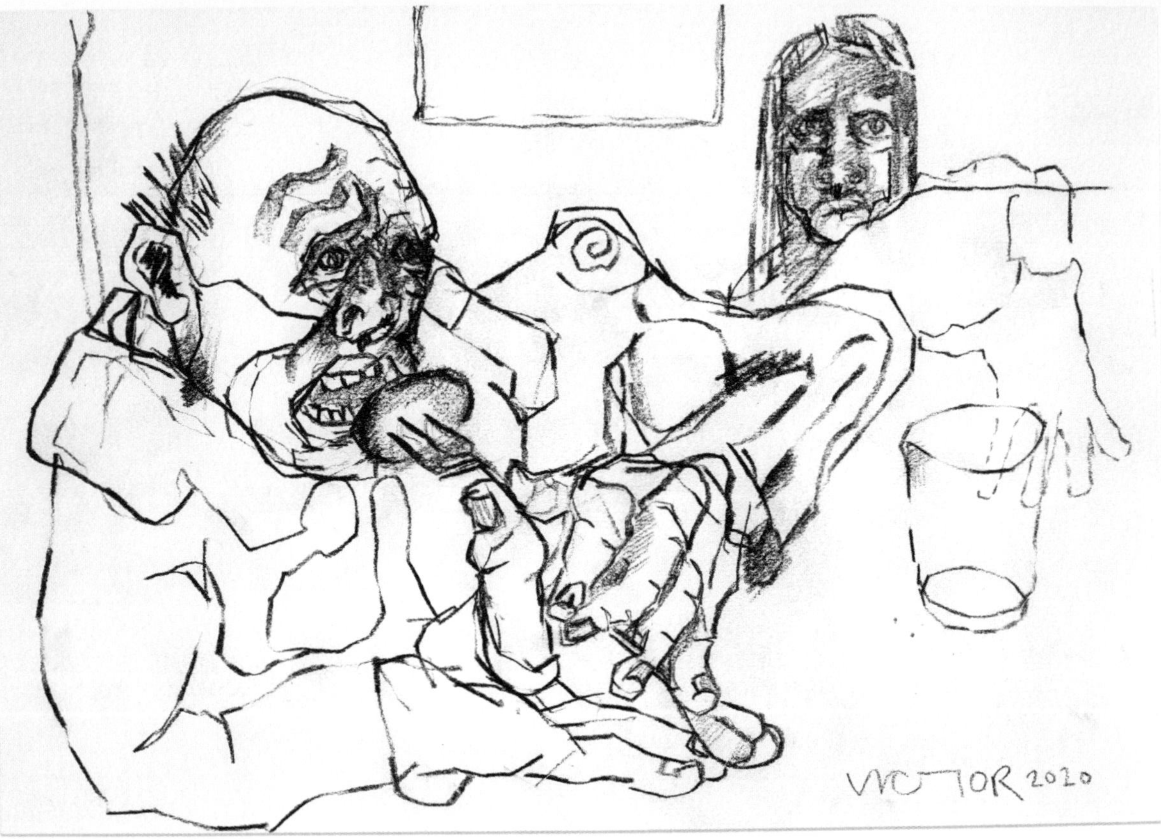
VICTOR 2020

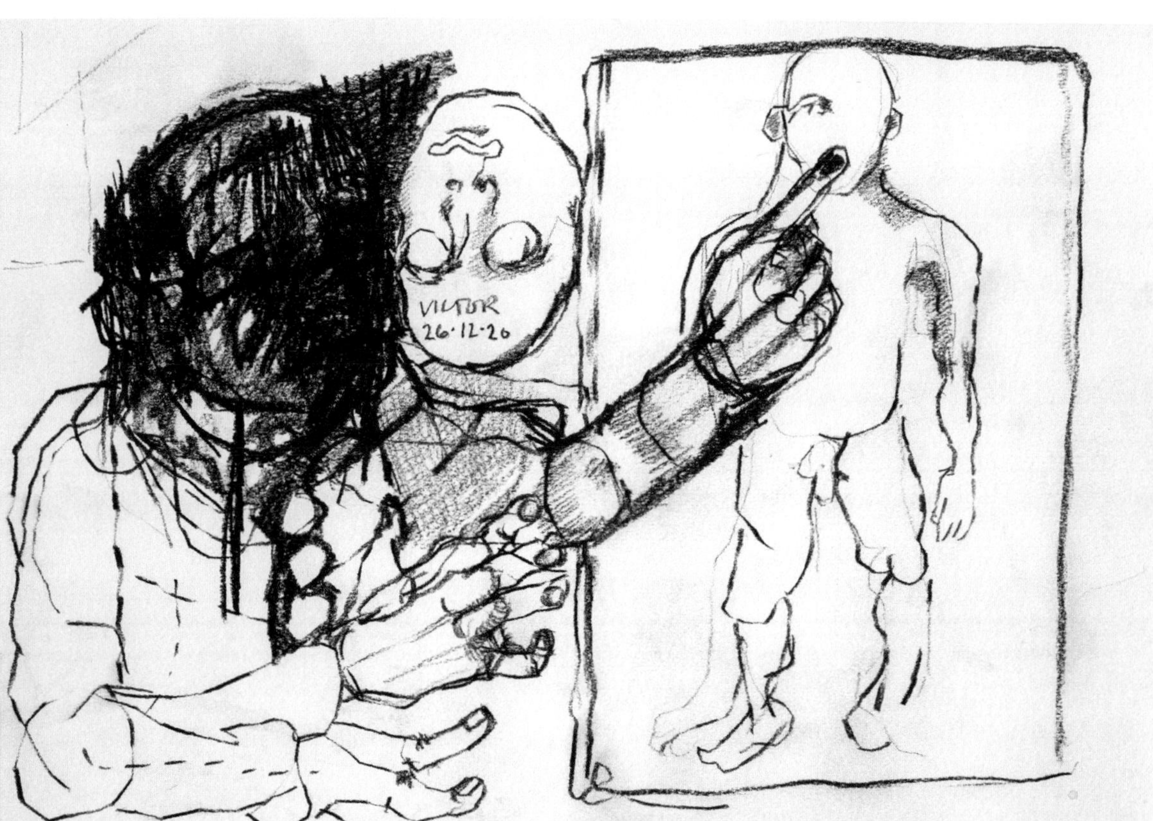
VICTOR
26·12·20

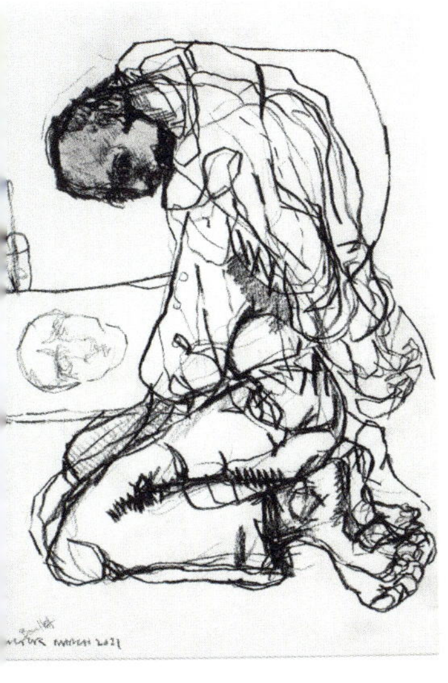

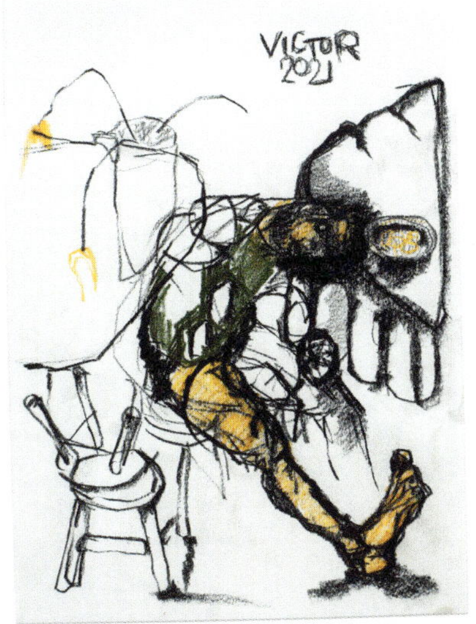

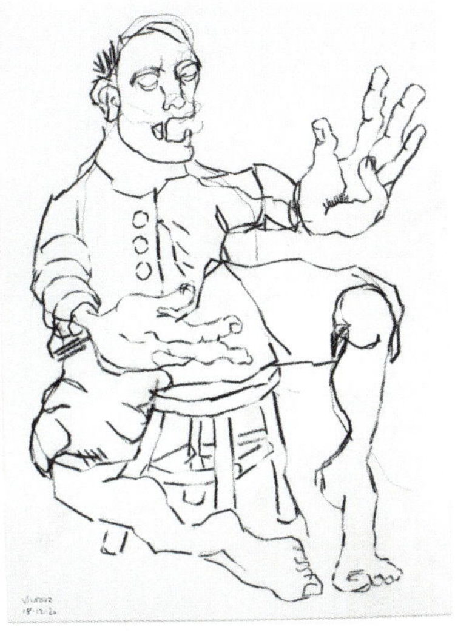

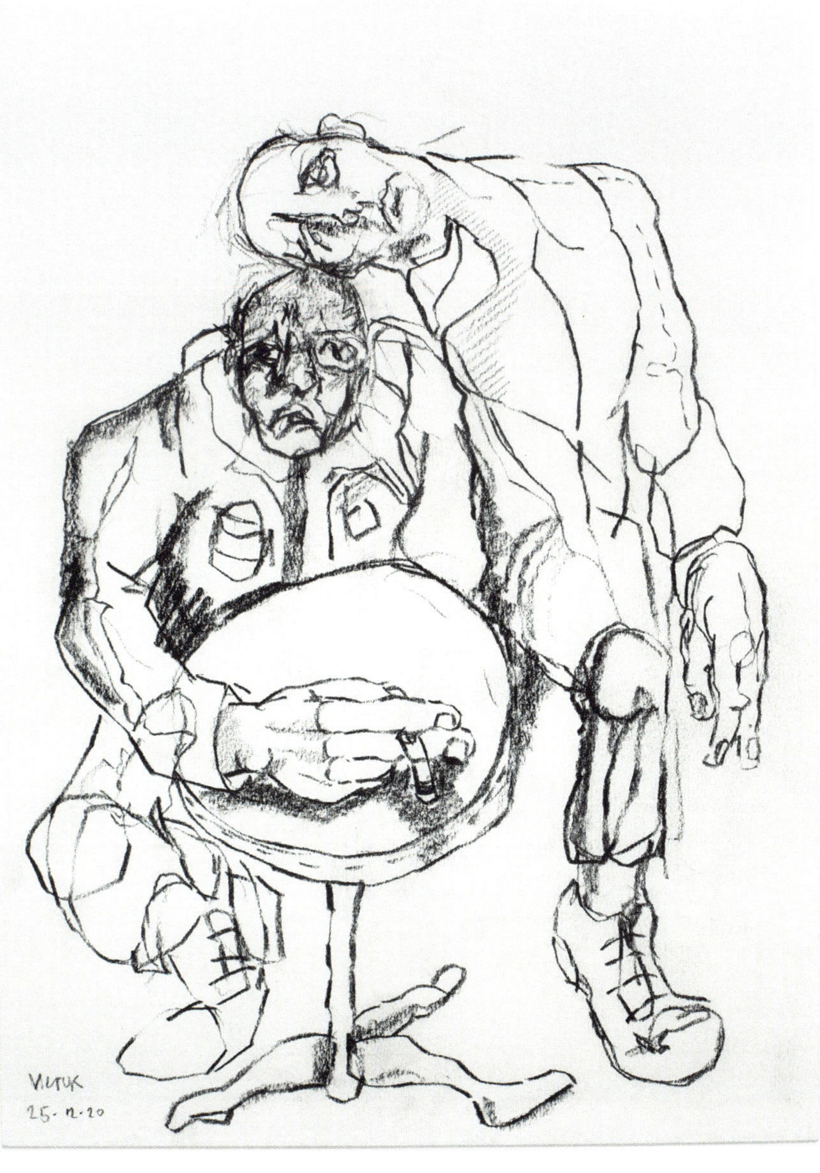

Untitled, 2020 - 2021
(Page 260 / 261)
Pencil on paper
29.7cm x 21cm

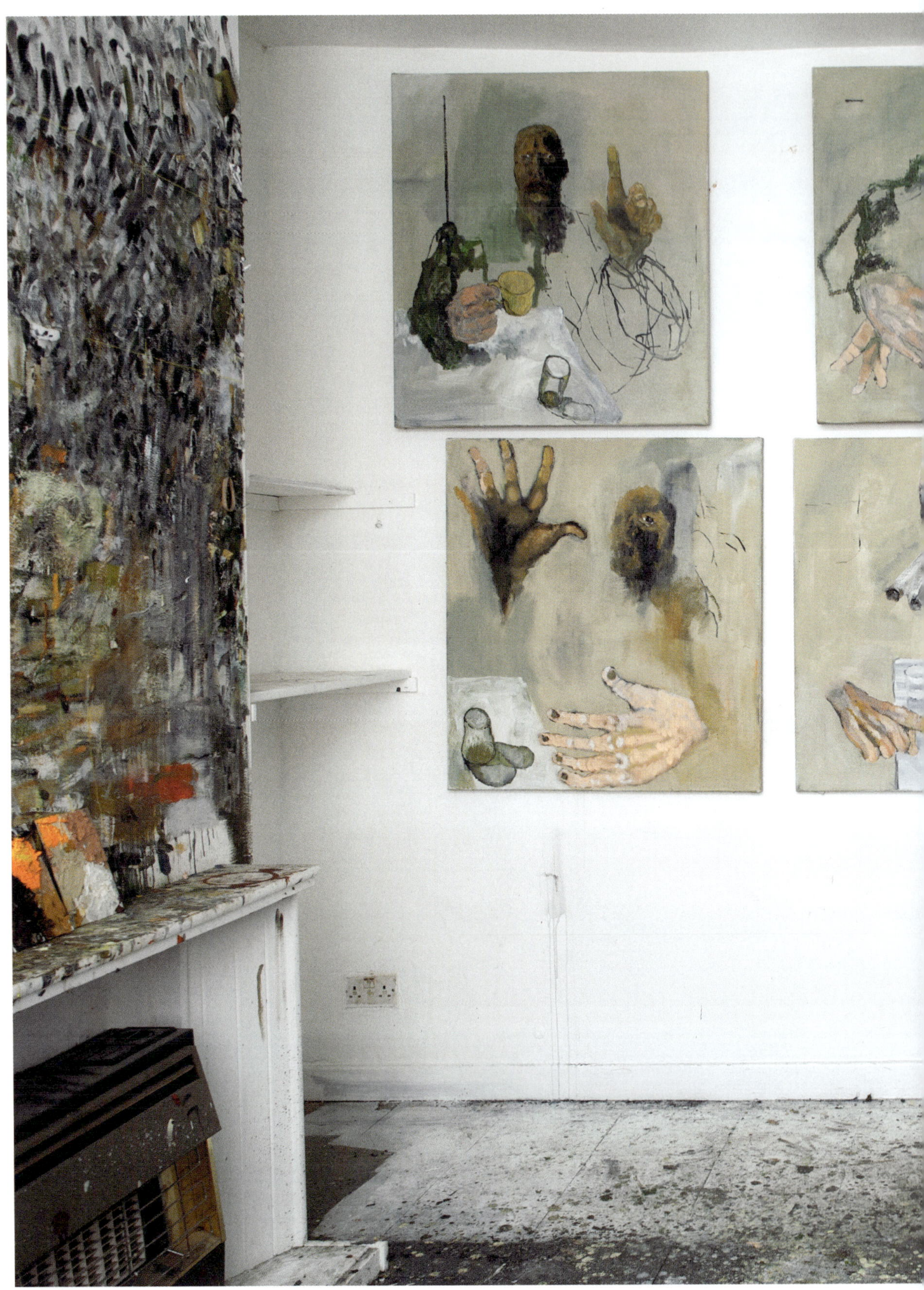

Counting Friends, 2021
Oil, gesso on stitched raw linen
80cm x 90cm

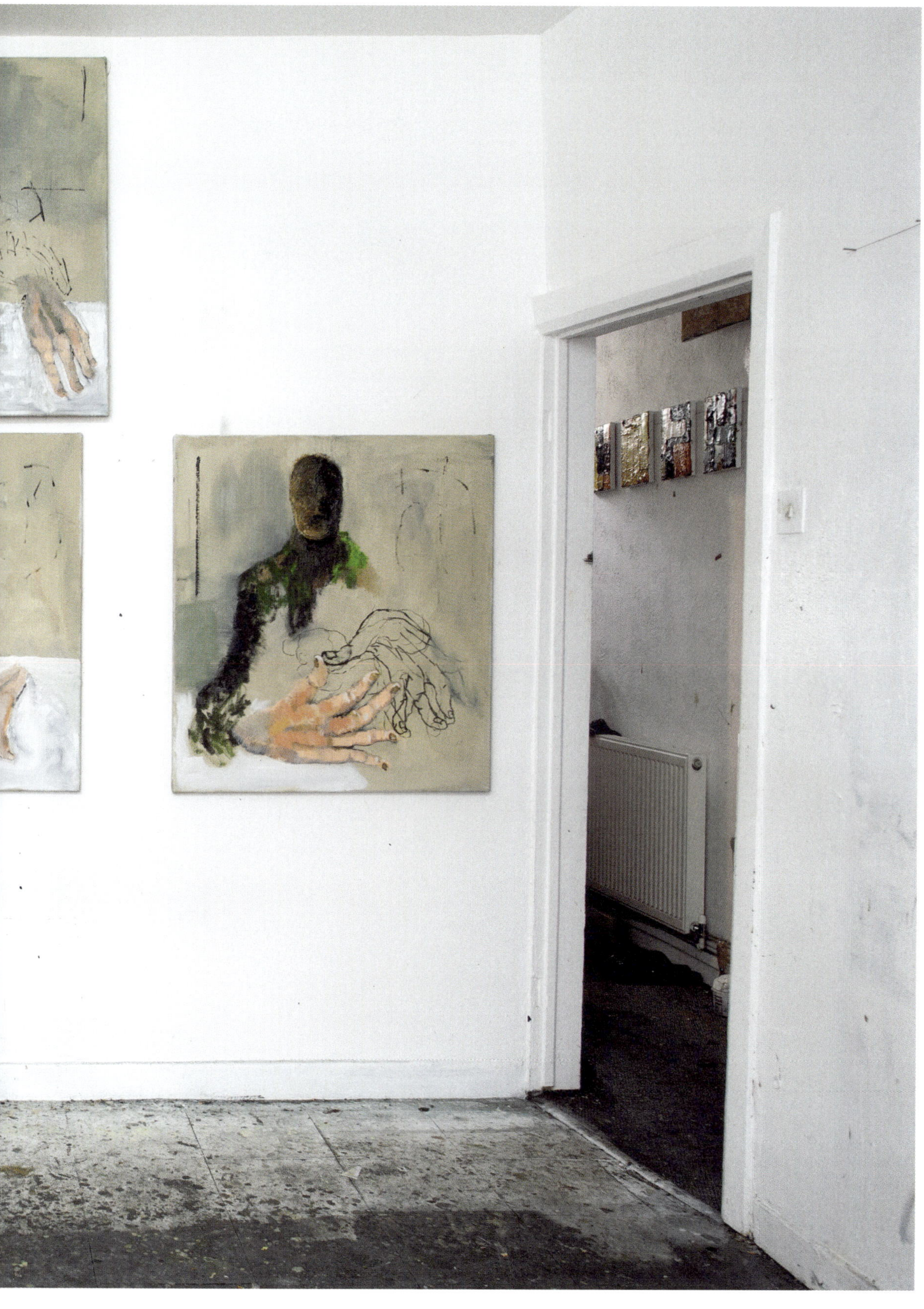

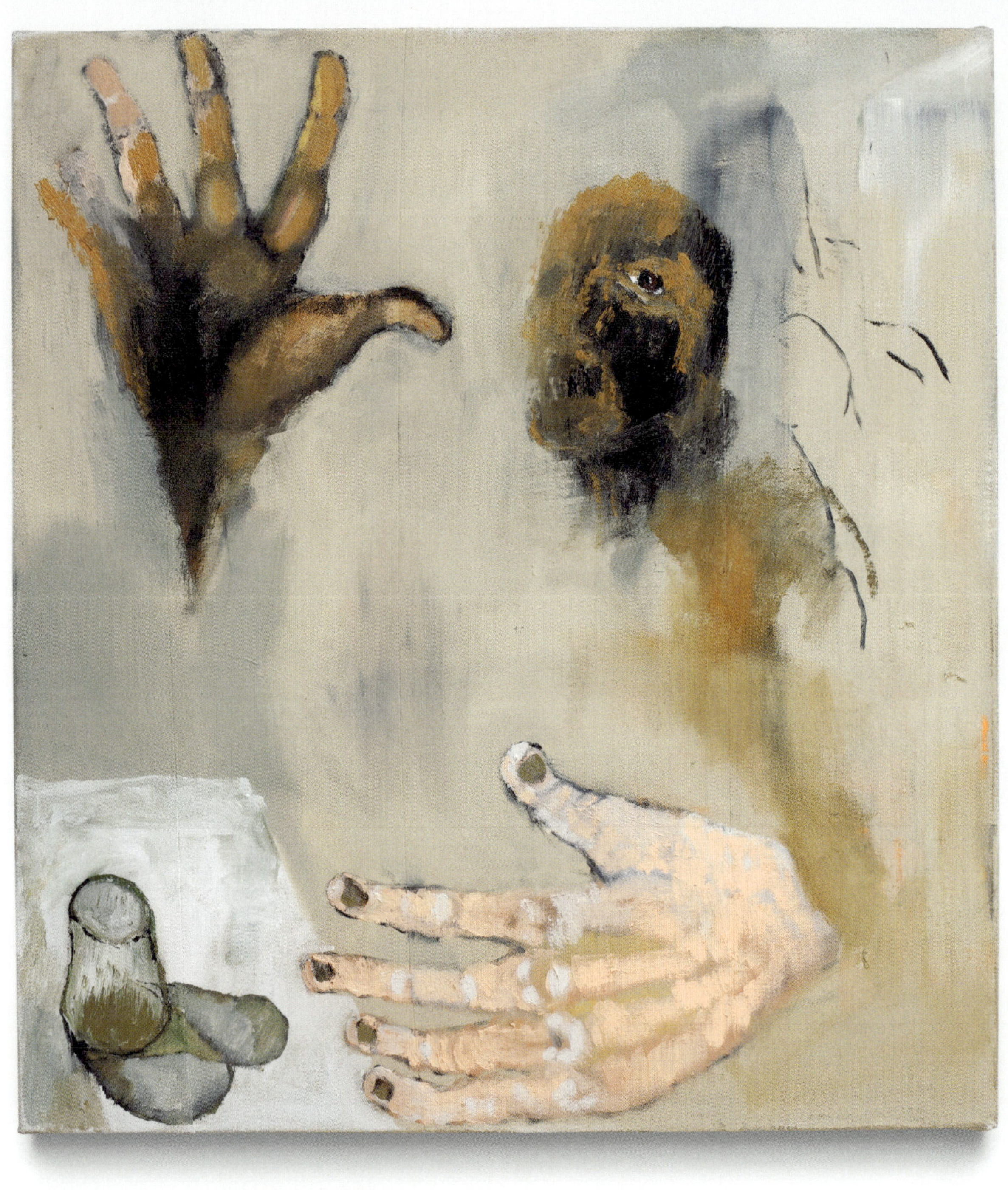

I Have Five Friends, 2021
Oil, gesso on stitched raw linen
80cm x 90cm

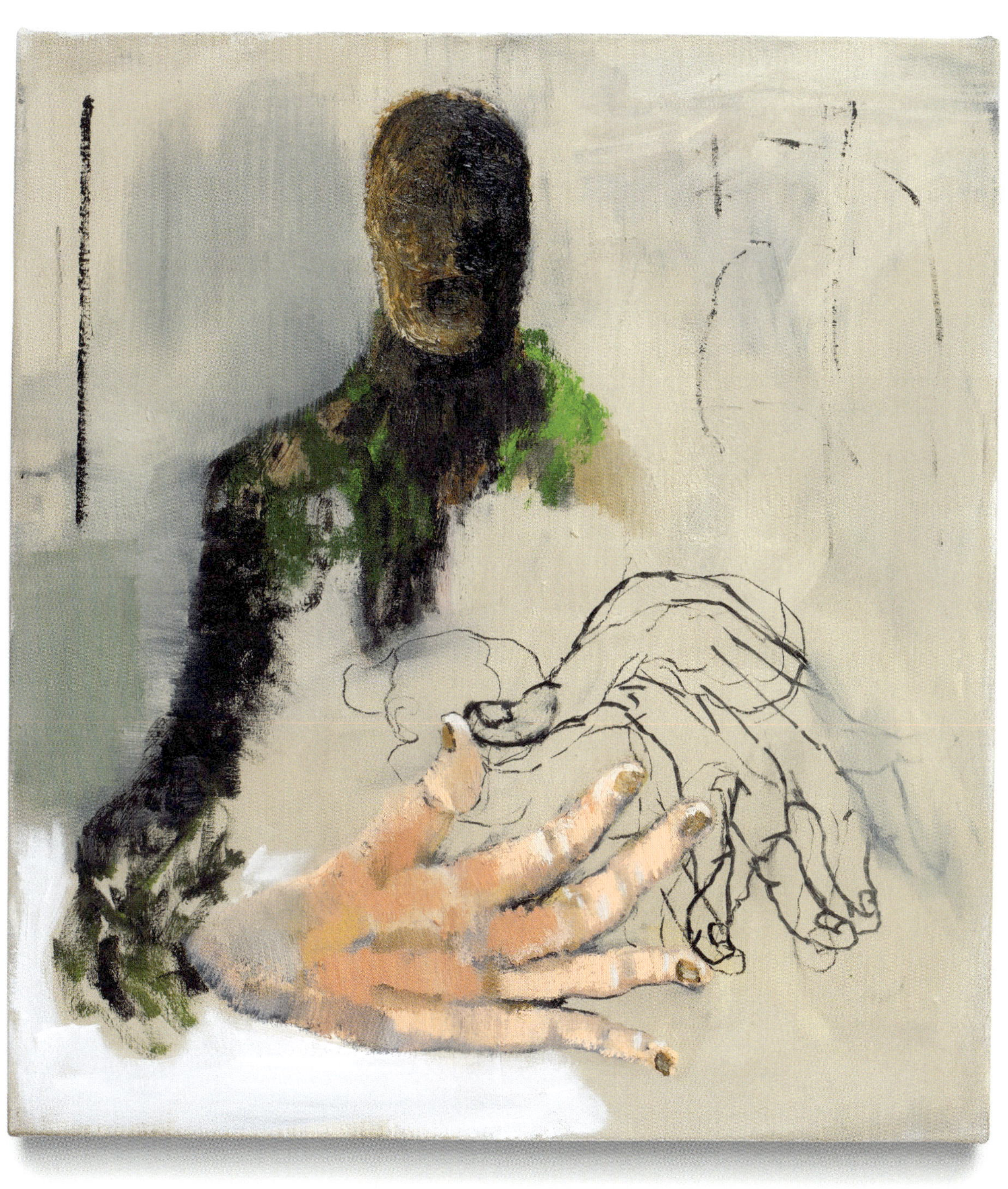

I Have Possibly Three Friends, 2021
Oil, gesso on stitched raw linen
80cm x 90cm

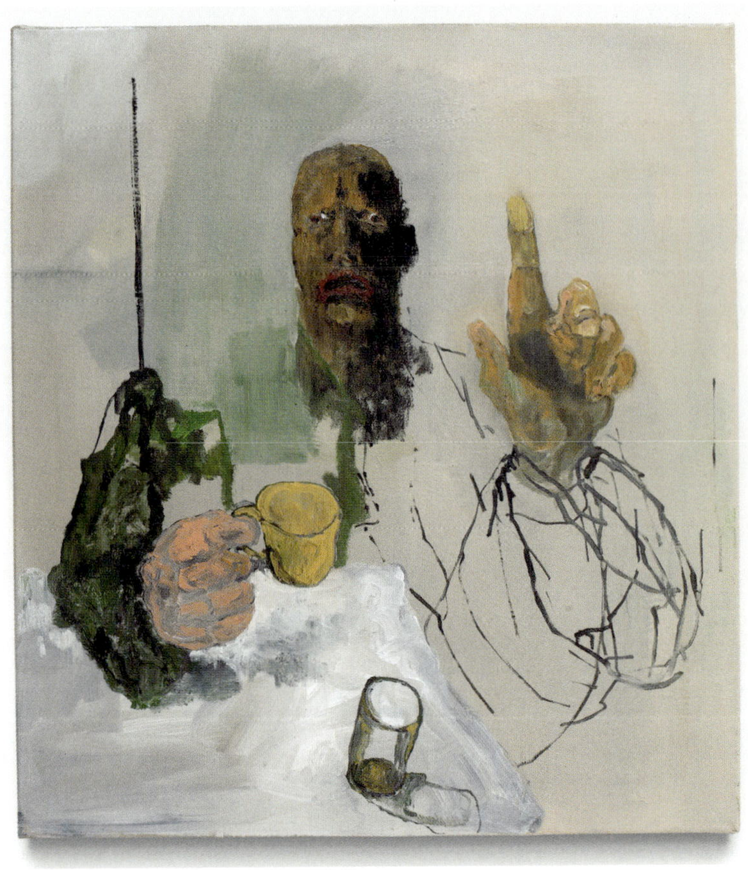

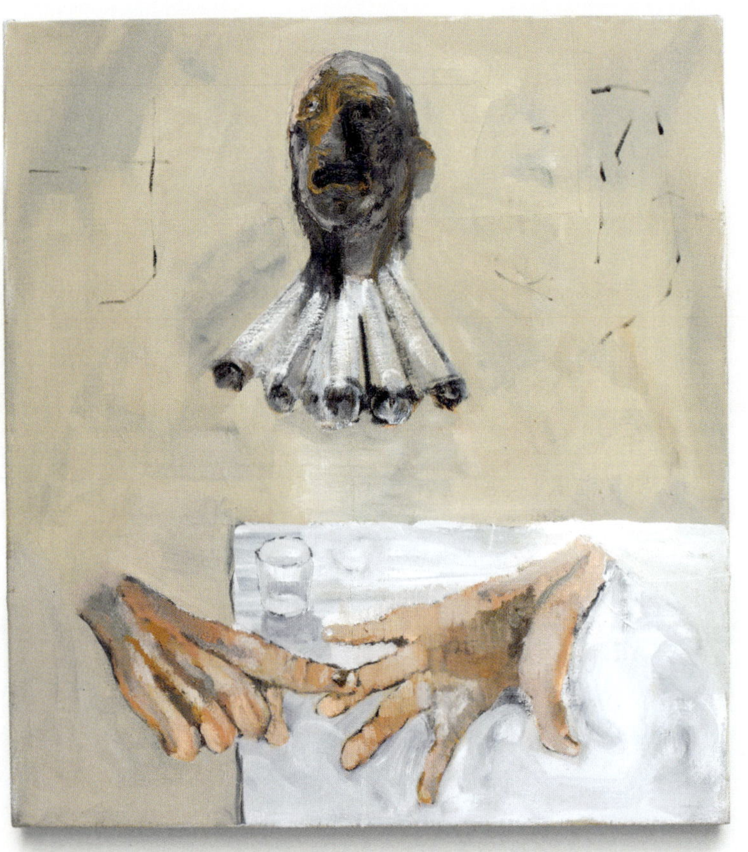

I Might Have One Friend, 2021
Oil, gesso on stitched raw linen
80cm x 90cm

Do I Have Four Friends? 2021
Oil, gesso on stitched raw linen
80cm x 90cm

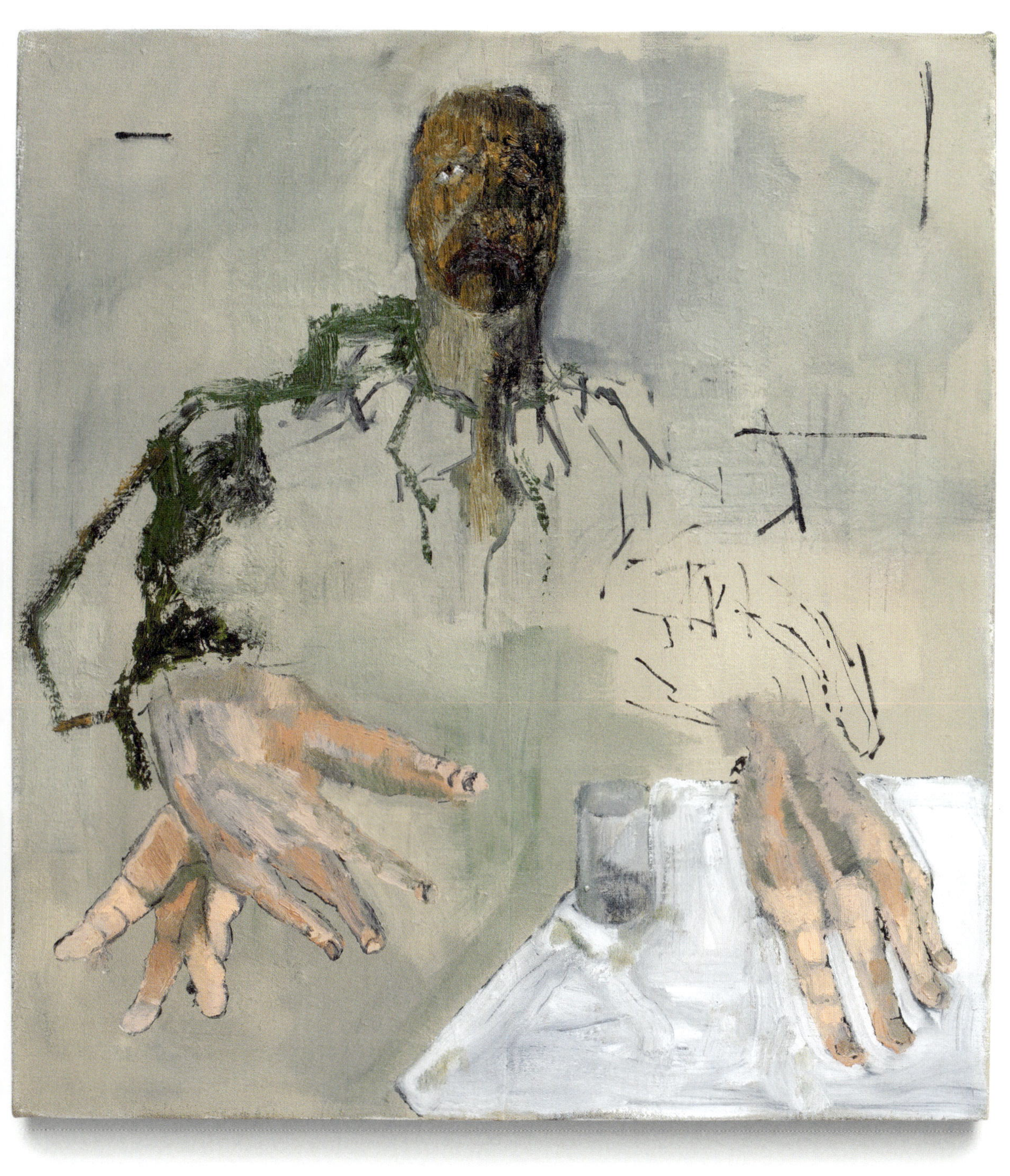

Counting Friends and Accepting that I Have None, 2021
Oil, gesso on stitched raw linen
80cm x 90cm

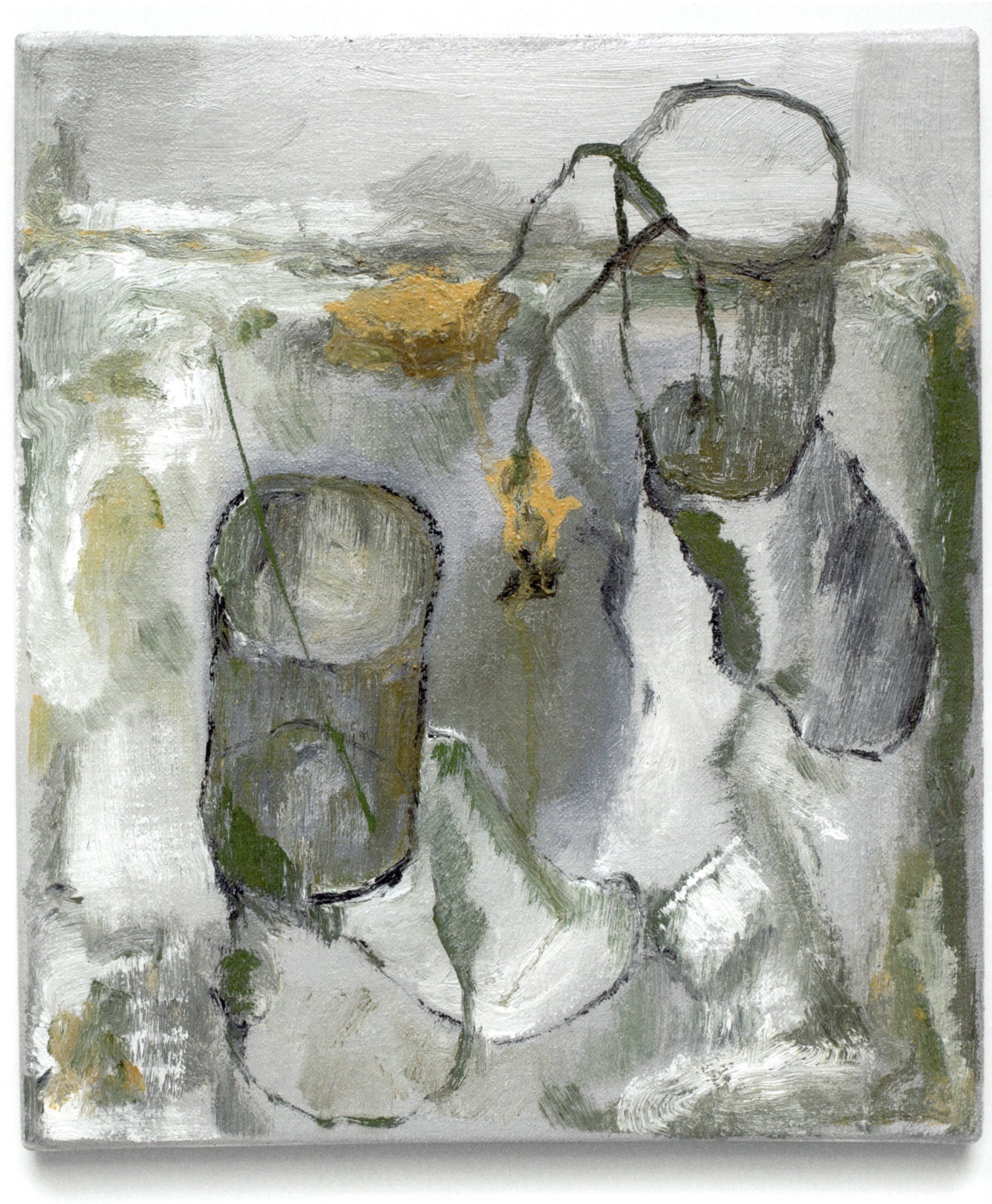

Waiting for the Sun, 2021
Pigment, oil on linen canvas
30cm x 35cm

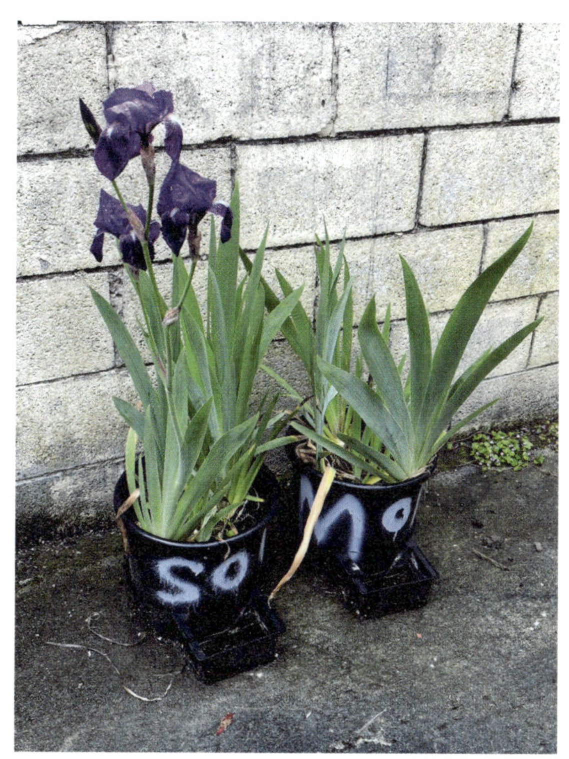

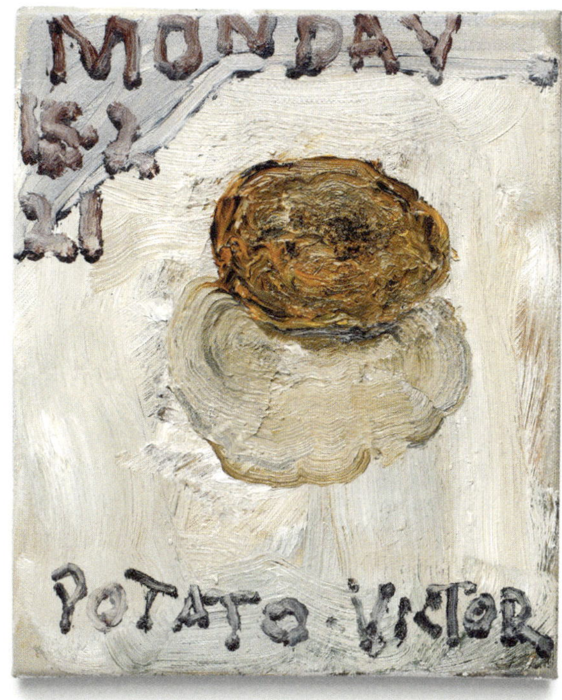

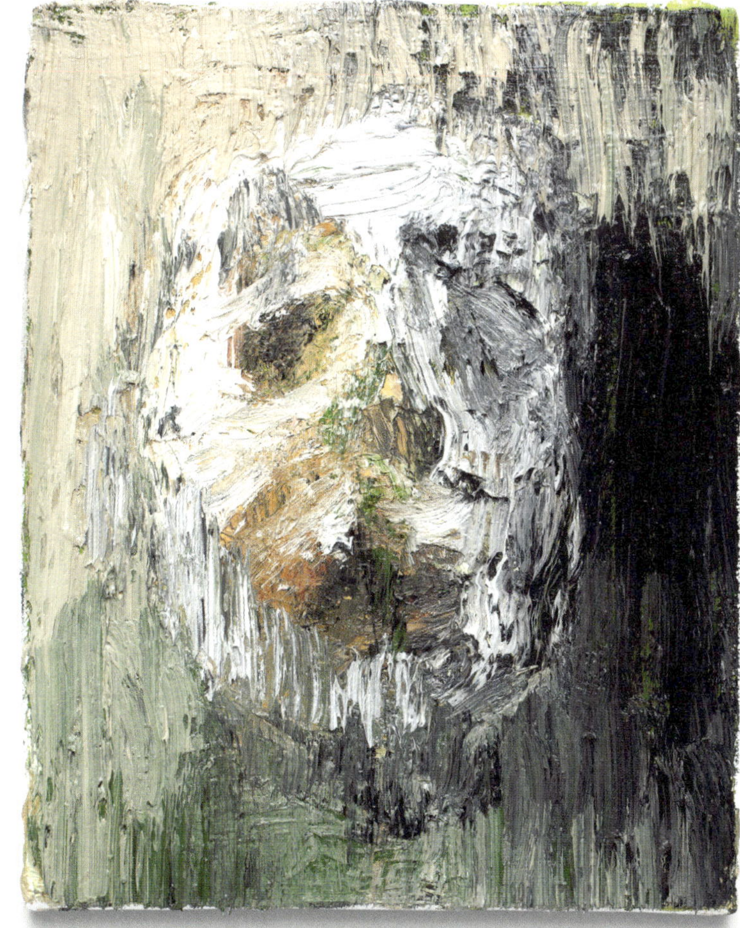

Iris in bloom stolen from Soutin's grave next to an Iris stolen from Monet's garden. 2012 –

Potato Found on Vining Street, 2021
Oil on linen canvas
20cm x 25cm

Just Rain, 2021
Oil on linen canvas
20cm x 25cm

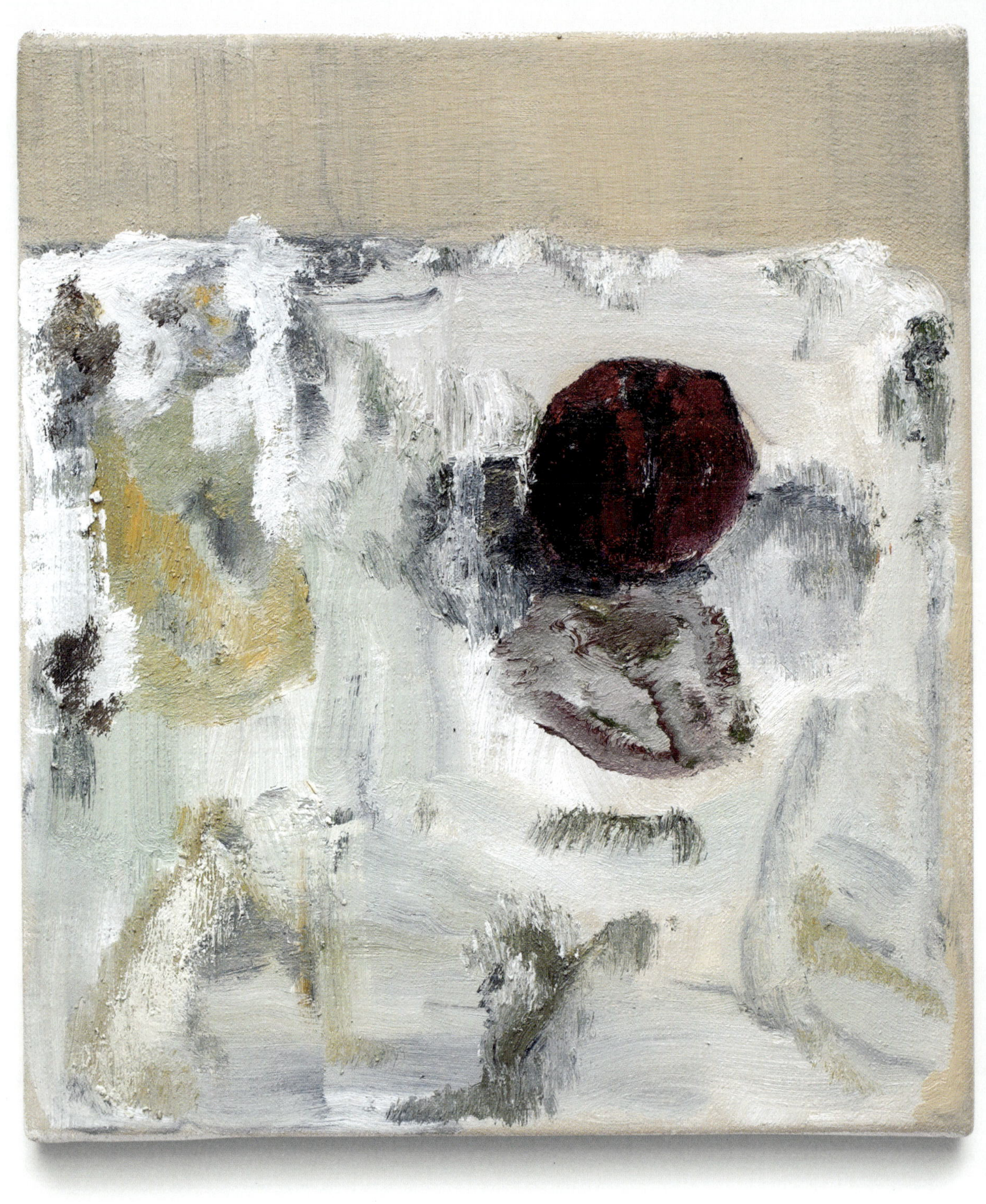

Plum Found on Vining Street, 2021
Pigment, oil on linen canvas
30cm x 35cm

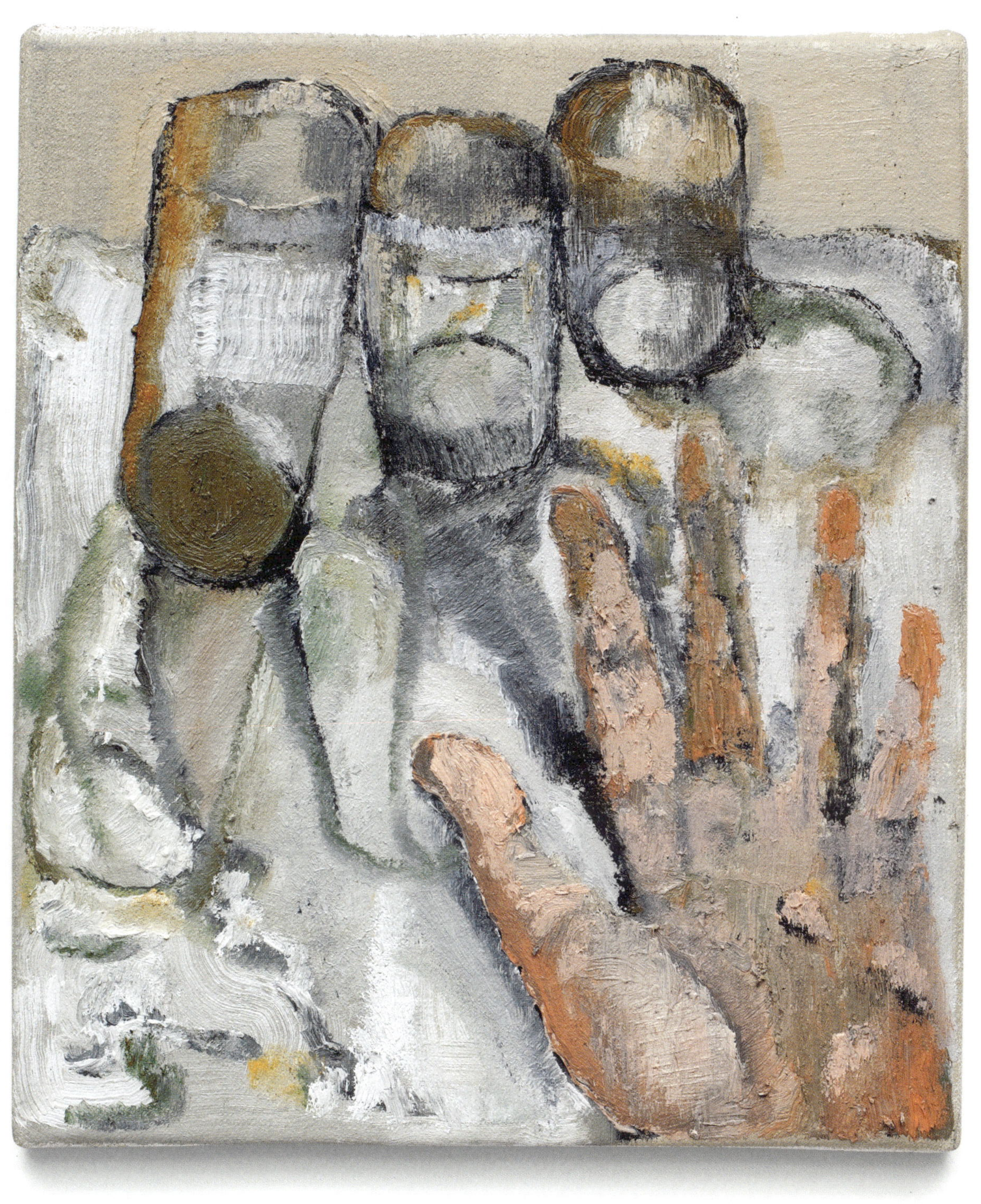

Getting Worse, 2021
Pigment, oil on jute
30cm x 35cm

Victor Boullet
Toxteth Error Lad
Liverpool
Painting 2014 – 2021

Editor – Stian Gabrielsen

Design – Texas Knuller

Production – Lauren Monchar at Frenetic Happiness
Production – Marius W Hansen at Antenne Publishing

Digital colour management of paintings – Daniel Bergo at Project Penn Pablo

Text edit – Stian Gabrielsen and Lauren Monchar

I would like to thank the following for their help and involvement in my life and work in Liverpool since 2014

Marius W Hansen, Dag Erik Elgin, Jeremy Glogan, Merlin Carpenter, Michaela Eichwald, Stian Gabrielsen, Brian Kennon, Bjarne Melgaard, Anna Bohman, Daniel Bergo, Bryony Lloyd, Svein Kojan, Knut Henrik Henriksen, Jim Beal, Linda Janova, Philip, Rose, Laura & Ash at R.Jackson & Sons (Liverpool)

And a very special thank you to the people that I have spoken to on the streets of Toxteth L8

Bill (Will), Tommy Ali, Ian, Lee, Julie, Nigel, Keith, Terry, Scrapman Geoff, Binman Jim, Susie & Jackie Wong, Dave, Yvonne, H, Sean, Marissa, Patsie, The street sweepers buying bacon butties, Shaun Mayers aka Texas Knuller, Chris, Big T, Jack Potato, Mo (Muhammad), Egg Head Steve.

Cover, Binman, 2021, Oil, gesso on raw linen, 130cm x 160cm. Back Cover, Pavement Walker, Toxteth Error Lad, 2016-2021, Rubber stamp, green ink. Paint Labels from Estate of Carl Nesjar (Dødsbo) Spine, Victor Fork 2020, Oil on linen canvas, 25cm x 60cm. Page 8, essay, I am the Flesh Colour I Did Not Apply by VB. 16, Invitation photo: Damien Airault. 16-17, essay, Krank by VB. 19-21, essay, I Became Me, I Didn't Like That by VB. 27, drawing on wall by Billie Boullet. 28, photo by Summer Boullet. 81-84, essay, The fieldwork of painting – measuring the exact distance between studio and home by Dag Erik Elgin. 98-101, essay, Raining Stones Everyday by VB. Page 102, photo of Julie and VB by Tommy Ali. 103, essay, Toxteth Error Lad by VB. 104-111, Toxteth Error Lad at Anna Bohman Gallery, Stockholm invited by Bjarne Melgaard, Instalation photos by VB. 136-143, Fanzine repro photo by Marius W Hansen. 138, essay, I am Tired of Being a Son by VB. 151, essay, You Kurt Me Mongrel by VB. 170, essay, Uglylamb by VB. 181-182, essay, Paintsploitation by Stian Gabrielsen. Page 207, essay, When the 'o' in Victor Became the Sun by Jeremy Glogan. 212-215, essay, Le Bougnat by VB. 222-223, photo of VB by unkown pedestrian. 239, essay, The Binman / Counting Friends By VB.

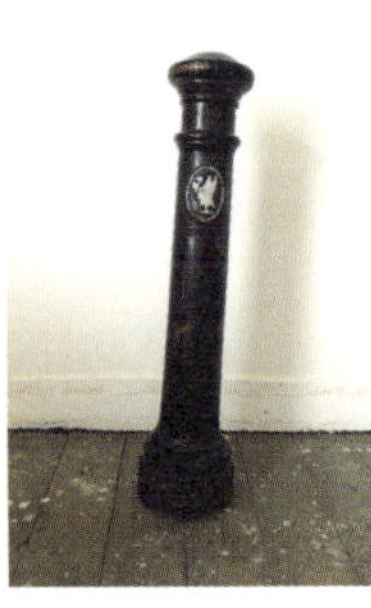

From the People of Liverpool, 2021
Stolen bollard
106cm x 18cm

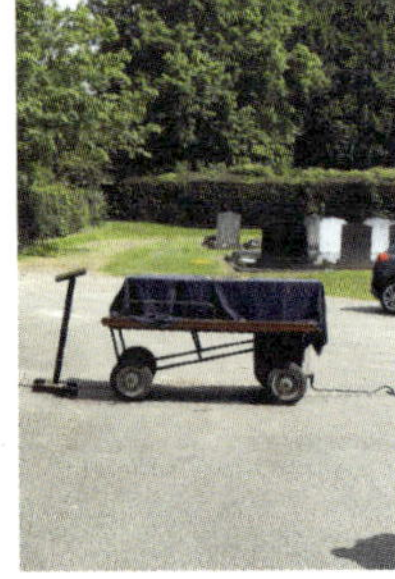

The last thing we did before driving away from Liverpool after 7 years was attend Mrs Bramley's funeral.
13 June, 2021

Death Of Mother Earth
Artist Residence Liverpool 2016 – 2021

Death Of Mother Earth
Practical Clothes for Painters 2016 – 2021

@deathofmotherearth contains a visual archive of the roads, crossings, pavements, corners and possible subject matter that played an existential roll in the daily routines, paintings and work in Liverpool.

L1 – L8
Mount Street. Pilgrim Street. Upper Duke Street. Hope Street. Upper Parliament Street (Upper Parly). Windsor Street. Upper Warwick Street. Vining Street. Enid Street.

L8 – L1
Enid Street. Vining Street. Upper Warwick Street. Windsor Street. Upper Parliament Street (Upper Parly). Hope Street.
Upper Duke Street. Pilgrim Street. Mount Street. Several other routes were also used from the studio to home.

I took AstraZeneca's COVID-19 vaccine (Made in Great Britain)

Publisher

FreneticHappiness
www.frenetichappiness.com
@frenetichappiness

Questions regarding distribution
lauren@frenetichappiness.com

Published 2021
Edition of 500

Printed on Munken Polar 150g/m2 – Cover Munken Polar 300g/m2
Printed in Latvia by Amber Book Print

ISBN No: 978-1-908873-03-3

Kindly supported by Norsk Kulturråd 2021 (Norway)

Fanzines, zines and posters produced in Liverpool 2014 – 2021

I am on the Floor, 2021 – 15cm x 21cm. pp. 20, Ed. 30
SK Banalités UL.P,TURE, 2021 – 21cm x 30cm, pp.40, Ed. 40
SKUL.P,TURE, 2021 – 21cm x 30cm, pp.40, Ed. 60
Golden Wonder, 2012 – 2021 – 15cm x 21cm. pp. 20, Ed. 20
Kilpeck (Scene 1) 2020 – 21cm x 30cm, pp.16, Ed. 15
Mo.net (2012) 2020 – 15cm x 21cm, pp.20, Ed.50
Poster 30cm x 42cm
You Kurt Me Mongrel, 2020 – 15cm x 21cm. pp.20, Ed. 50
Poster 30cm x 42cm
Ullet Road, 2020 – 15cm x 21cm. pp. 20. Ed. 50
Tired of Being a Son, 2020 – 15cm X 21cm. pp. 28. Ed. 50
Poster 30cm x 42cm
Polly – Michaela Eichwald & Victor Boullet, 2020
– 30cm x 21cm. pp.20.Ed.40
Polly, Poster – 42cm × 59cm
The Negative – Ansel Adams Blinky Palermo Victor Boullet, 2019
– 30cm x 21cm, pp. 20, Ed.40.
Drawings by a Privileged White Male. Volume I, 2019
Drawings by a Privileged White Male. Volume II, 2019
Drawings by a Privileged White Male. Volume III, 2019
X 3, 21cm x 30cm, pp.22, Ed. 50
Toxteth Error Lad (Victor & Julie) 2019, Poster – 42cm × 59cm
The Very Negativ (Lorenzo Lotto) 2019 – 15 x 21cm, pp.20, Ed. 50